An Integrated Approach to
BUSINESS STUDIES

BRUCE R. JEWELL

Longman

Edinburgh Gate
Harlow, Essex

Pearson Education Limited
Edinburgh Gate
Harlow
Essex
CM20 2JE
England and Associated Companies throughout the World

ISBN 0 582 40542 4

First edition published 1990
Second edition published 1993
Third edition published 1996
Fourth edition published 2000
Sixth impression 2004

Printed in China
GCC/06

The Publisher's policy is to use paper manufactured from
sustainable forests.

Acknowledgements

We are grateful to Kogan Page Ltd for permission to
reproduce an extract from HOW TO BE AN EVEN BETTER
MANAGER by M Armstrong.

Contents

Introduction   1

Part 1 Business organization   3

1   Business organizations   5
2   Introduction to management   19
3   Organizational structures   35
4   Business communications   46
5   The application of number in business   56
6   Applications of information and communications technology   82

Part 2 The external environment of business   93

7   Business and the external environment   95
8   Business and the law   106
9   Principles of microeconomics   119
10   Principles of macroeconomics   134
11   Business and economic policy   151
12   The international environment of business   164
13   Ethical and environmental issues   175

Part 3 Marketing   193

14   An introduction to marketing   195
15   Marketing research   202
16   Forecasting   214
17   Segmentation and consumer behaviour   225
18   Products and the product mix   233
19   Promotional strategies   241
20   Pricing policies   252
21   Channels of distribution   261
22   International marketing   267
23   The marketing plan   274

Part 4 Accounting and finance   287

24   The profit and loss account   289
25   The balance sheet   300
26   Working capital   311
27   Ratio analysis   321
28   Cash statements   330
29   Financing the business   342
30   Investment appraisal   359
31   Decision trees   372
32   Cost accounting   379

33	Break-even analysis	394
34	Budgets	403

Part 5 Production and operations 415

35 Production and operations management 417
36 Stock control 427
37 Quality management 434
38 Efficiency 442
39 Lean production 449
40 Critical path analysis 457

Part 6 People in organizations 473

41 An introduction to human resource management 475
42 Leadership and motivation 478

43 Teams 495
44 Human resource planning 502
45 Reward management 515
46 Industrial relations 523
47 Organizational culture and change 532

Part 7 Strategy 545

48 Strategic issues 547

Part 8 Study skills 561

49 Assessment in business studies – preparing for the examination 563
Appendix: Coursework diary 578

Index 581

Introduction

This, the fourth edition of *An Integrated Approach to Business Studies*, has been produced for the new-style A level introduced as part of Curriculum 2000. The focus and integrating feature of Business Studies remains decision making within business organizations, but the new A level has been drawn up in response to new criteria from the Qualifications and Curriculum Authority (QCA). Before embarking on our course of study it is worth while exploring the nature of the new-style A levels produced for the twenty-first century.

There are two stages to the A levels. Advanced subsidiary level (the new AS) is both a qualification in its own right and the first stage of advanced level. Unlike the advanced supplementary level (the old AS), the new AS is pitched at a level below full A level – in fact, at the general level of understanding of 17-year-old students after their first year of A level study. The second stage in the new A level is known as A2. This is marked at full A level standard, but, unlike advanced subisiary level, A2 is *not* a qualification in its own right, it is merely the second stage of a process that started with AS. The distinction between AS and A2 is not primarily in terms of subject content but in terms of depth of analysis and level of understanding. In general, we can say that A2 places a greater emphasis on the higher-order skills of analysis and evaluation and a lower emphasis on knowlege, understanding and application than is the case with the new AS.

Moreover, focus statements in the QCA criteria suggest that A2 requires a greater understanding of the interrelationships between topics and more emphasis on long-term strategy as distinct from short-term considerations.

A crucial feature of the new-style A levels is the emphasis placed on synoptic assessment in which examination candidates need to demonstrate an appreciation of how different topics within the subject relate to each other. Previously, synoptic assessment was only required for modular syllabuses, but it is now a universal requirement for the new-style A levels. As we will explore in the final chaper of the book, synoptic assessment does *not* mean an examination paper covering the subject with a series of questions on discrete topics. Instead, it means synoptic questions that explore the variours links between these topics.

Business and government concern about employees'/citizens' possession of the key skills of numeracy, communication and information technology has resulted in the addition of key skills to A level programmes. Along with other A level subjects, Business Studies is expected to play a part in the development of not only these key skills but also the wider key skills of problem solving, working with others and improving your own learning and performance. It is important that 'the tail does not wag the dog' (this subject is still about the study of business), but, nevertheless, all subjects are expected to make a contribution to improving competence in these areas, and clearly Business Studies is well placed to contribute in terms of report writing, presentations, application of numbers to solve problems, IT, problem solving and working with others (say, in joint research or a mini-business enterprise). Consequently, certain exercises included in this book are designed to combine a development of understanding of a subject with a development of key skills. Depending on the specifications for key skills assessment, it is possible that some of these tasks qualify for inclusion in the portfolio that is needed to complete the key skills qualification.

There are various other changes that are also worth stressing to teachers and students of Business Studies. 'Examination boards' are now known as 'awarding bodies', partly in recognition that assessment is not confined to time-constrained examinations. 'Syllabuses' are now known as 'subject specifications', thus placing greater emphasis on what students are required to do rather than just what they have to know. A modular or unit approach to A levels is now universal, although there is still an opportunity to take all modules at the same time. The limit on coursework has been raised to allow more to be done, but, at the same time, awarding bodies seem to allow candidates to take an extra examination in place of coursework. Finally, with mergers of awarding bodies and QCA-imposed rationalization, we have fewer specifications from which to choose. Fortunately, the awarding bodies still provide teachers and students with variety in terms of both content and forms of assessment.

This book is divided into eight sections. The first is an introduction to business and is designed to equip sudents with the terminology required to understand the more specialist areas. Part II explores the external environment in which businesses operate, whereas the next four parts cover the four functional areas of business. Part VII is on strategic management, which has been added to reflect the increased stress laid on strategic factors in the new specifications, especially in terms of synoptic assessment. The final part, Part VIII, offers invaluable advice on preparing for assessment.

Business
organization

Business organizations

One decision the new business owner needs to make is which legal form his or her business will take. This is an especially important decision because it has implications for finance and the control of business operations. In this chapter we will look at the legal aspect of starting and running a business.

Chapter objectives

1 To analyse the role of the entrepreneur and profit in private enterprise organizations.

2 To describe and analyse the different legal forms an organization can take in the UK's private sector.

3 To explain and analyse the governance of companies in the UK.

Business organizations in a mixed economy

Decision making in business organizations is the subject matter of advanced level Business Studies and of this textbook. The decisions relate to:

- the acquisition and use of human resources;
- the raising of finance;
- the acquisition of fixed assets, such as machines and buildings;
- the purchase of stock;
- the methods of making goods and providing services;
- the ways of making these goods and services attractive to potential customers;
- the setting of prices;
- strategies to secure a competitive advantage over rivals;
- strategies to achieve the objectives of the organization.

The term **business organizations** does require some clarification. It is tempting to confine the term to organization that sell goods and services for private profit. This would mean that our subject would be confined to **private sector** organization, whether they be sole traders, partnerships or companies. In many respects, confining the subject to the private sector would simplify the tasks for students as private enterprise firms have a clear aim of seeking profit for their owner. However, a large part of the UK economy exists outside the private sector. The term **public sector** is used to describe various types of State-run activities and enterprises. This sector takes the form of central government, local government, the remaining nationalized industries (such as The Post Office), trust hospitals, other parts of the NHS, incorporated colleges and grant-maintained schools. These organizations are owned by the State on behalf of the community and their objective is to provide a service rather than a profit for owners. Much of the public sector is classed by economists as the 'non-market sector' – that is, goods and services are provided free to consumers and are financed out of taxation. However, a small part of the public sector, such as The Post Office and local authority swimming pools, are in the market sector as consumers are required to pay for the service. Any profit (known as surplus) in the public sector is used to improve the quality of the service or to reduce the burden of taxation.

A third sector of the economy is the **voluntary or 'not-for-profit' sector**. The voluntary sector is owned by members of the various associations and raises its finance by appealing for donations. It exists to provide help for those in need or to promote a particular service. At first, it might appear that the voluntary sector is outside the scope of Business Studies, but it should be remembered that charities undertake marketing to maximize their income, they employ staff, keep financial records and have to make decisions about the best use of scarce resources. This sector does make 'business decision' and therefore can be included

within our subject. In fact, the differences between the three sectors lie not in the nature and quality of their decision making, but in their ownership and objectives, as can be seen in Table 1.1.

Types of business organization

Private enterprise firms in the UK conform to one of three legal forms:

● sole trader;
● partnership;
● limited liability (or joint stock) company.

The choice of legal form will be influenced by the financial needs of the business, considerations of the owner's liability and the degree of personal control sought by the founder of the business.

Sole trader businesses

In a **sole trader** business organization, one person provides the permanent finance and, in return, retains full control of the business and enjoys all the profits. It is possible and likely that the sole proprietor will eventually employ others, but the distinctive feature of this form of business is that there is a *single* owner. However, just as the sole proprietor enjoys all the profits, he or she is personally liable for all the debts and all the decisions made.

There are no legal formalities involved in setting up in business as a sole trader. However, under the Business Names Act 1985 a business (irrespective

Table 1.1 The three sectors in a mixed economy

	Private sector	Public sector	Voluntary sector
Ownership	Private owners (sole traders partners, shareholders)	The State on behalf of the community	Members
Objective	Private profit	A high quality, but cost-effective, service	Promote a cause, to provide help for those specified in the charity's objectives. To maximize income to carry out work
Market or non-market	Market	Mainly non-market	Non-market, but many charities have a 'trading arm'

of legal form) using a trade name other than that of the owner must conform to three basic requirements:

- the name of the owner must be displayed on all business documents;
- the owner must disclose information relating to ownership to anyone who has dealings with the business;
- a notice concerning ownership must be displayed in the business premises.

The Act replaced the previous obligation to register business names.

There are no other legal requirements when establishing a sole trader business except in a minority of trades that have the potential to cause a nuisance to others. The sale of alcohol requires a licence from local magistrates; other activities might require a licence from a local authority. However, these are exceptions rather than the rule.

Legally the business and its sole proprietor are inseparable. This means that the owner is responsible for all debts, is taxed in the same way as an individual (that is, by income tax) and must pay National Insurance contributions as a self-employed person. The trader is required to submit accounts to the Inland Revenue (income tax) and Customs and Excise (expenditure taxes). In relation to expenditure taxes, all businesses have to register for VAT purposes if their sales revenues exceed £46,000 per year. It is likely that the tax liability of a new and small sole trader will be lower (and he or she will have longer to pay) than if the trader established a company. Furthermore, as a simple form of organization, accountancy fees are likely to be lower than if the business was established as a company.

The sole trader enjoys distinct advantages:

- freedom and flexibility;
- personal satisfaction;
- secrecy – there is no need to disclose business affairs, except to the tax authorities and to creditors when seeking loans;
- personal control with no requirement to consult;
- personal contact with staff and customers;
- enjoyment of all profits;

- absence of legal formalities when establishing the business;
- financial advantages in terms of lower taxes, longer time to pay taxes and lower accountancy fees.

Against these advantages there are major drawbacks:

- limited sources of finance;
- restricted growth;
- limited scope for economies of scale;
- success depends on the owner's energy and continuing fitness;
- the constraints of the lack of time and specialization;
- full personal responsibility for decisions and for the debts of the business;
- no continuity of existence, with the business dying with the owner.

Partnerships

To overcome some of the problems inherent in the sole trader form of business a partnership might be formed. The law defines a **partnership** as 'the relationship that subsists between persons carrying on a business in common with a view to profit'. A partnership is an association of individuals and is not a legal entity in its own right. Consequently, it cannot sue or be sued in its own name but, instead, each of the partners has to be named. Each partner is responsible for the debts of the partnership. Moreover, every partner, when acting on behalf of the firm, acts as an agent of the partnership and can thus bind his or her fellow partners. In simple language, the individual partner can be personally sued and held liable for all decisions made, and all debts incurred, by other partners if these people were acting with the authority of the partnership. Therefore, one should choose business partners *very* carefully and draw up a legal agreement on the rights and responsibilities of each partner. The partnership agreement should deal with:

- the nature of the business and date of commencement;
- the amount of capital put into the business by each partner;

- the method by which profits (or losses) are to be shared;
- voting rights;
- the role of each partner;
- the duration of the partnership and methods of dissolving the partnership;
- arbitration procedure if partners cannot reach agreement;
- arrangements to cover absence, retirement and the admission of new partners;
- arrangements concerning finances, bookkeeping, banking and insurance;
- authority to sign contracts.

Where one of the partners contributes a disproportionate amount of the finance it is doubly important to draw up a written agreement. This is because the 1890 Partnership Act lays down that, except where there is a specific agreement to the contrary:

- all partners are entitled to an equal share of the profits;
- each partner is entitled to participate in the management of the firm;
- decisions are settled on a majority basis, *except* for any change in the nature of the business, which requires unanimous agreement.

As a business form, partnerships enjoy certain advantages over the sole trader:

- additional sources of finance;
- sharing of responsibilities;
- specialization;
- sharing of losses.

In addition, partnerships enjoy greater privacy and fewer legal formalities compared with the company form of organization.

However, the attractiveness of the partnership form of organization is reduced when it is remembered that each partner is fully responsible for decisions, and the ease with which companies can be formed has reduced the popularity of the partnership form. It is most commonly found in the professions, where the rules of the appropriate professional association (such as the Law Society) preclude the translation of the business to the company form. Outside the professions, there is a preference for the joint stock company form of organization. Table 1.2 illustrates some of the differences between partnerships and companies.

Limited liability (or joint stock) companies

Companies differ from partnerships in that the **act of incorporation** creates a new legal entity distinct from the shareholders who own the company. This has important implications in the separation of the affairs of the business from those of the people who own shares in it. Companies can make contracts, and they can sue and be sued. All actions taken by the company, including the contracting of debt, are actions of the *company* rather than actions of individual *owners*. Unlike the business forms described above, the legal position of a company is completely unaffected by the death (or retirement) of one of the shareholders.

Shareholders enjoy the privilege of **limited liability**, which means that they are liable to meet the debts of the business only to the extent that they have invested in the busines. Hence, if the shares they own are fully paid up, no further claim can be made on the shareholder. Limited liability (seen by early Victorians as an attempt to evade responsibility for the debts of a business) is regarded as essential in overcoming the reluctance of peope to purchase shares in a business.

There are two common misconceptions about limited liability. First, it is often stated (wrongly) that companies enjoy limited liability. The *company* is, in fact, fully liable for it debts; it is the *shareholders* who enjoy limited liability – they are liable only to a limited extent. Second, it is often stated (again wrongly) that limited liability reduces the risks of business. In fact, limited liability *transfers* the risk from the owners to creditors of the business. The greater risks now incurred by creditors provide the rationale for the greater scrutiny of companies and the requirement that the word 'Limited' should appear in the name, as a warning to potential creditors. Because of the limit to liability, creditors often insist that shareholders in a small private company (or directors

Table 1.2 Comparison of companies and partnerships

Company	Partnerships
● Owners are shareholders (members)	● Owners are partners
● 1 or more shareholders in a private company 2 or more shareholders in a public company Maximum determined by number of shares	● 2–20 partners (except in certain professions)
● Separate legal entity	● Not separate entity
● Limited liability	● Liability of partners is not limited (except in the case of limited partnerships)
● Amount of capital limited by authorized share capital stated in memorandum of association	● Capital determined in the partnership agreement
● Profits distributed in the form of dividends expressed in relation to shares	● Profits distributed in accordance with partnership agreement. Equal distribution if no agreement
● Shareholders are not entitled to take part in management — directors appointed for this purpose	● Normally all partners entitled to take part in running the firm
● Activity limited by objects clause	● A firm can do anything lawful
● Accounts generally open to public inspection	● Accounts are private
● Perpetual succession — company not affected by death of member	● Partnership ends wth death of a partner
● When a company is wound up no member is liable for its debts	● All partners are liable for its debts
● Shares are transferable in accordance with the articles	● No transfer possible
● Companies are liable to pay corporation tax on their profits	● No income tax on profits of partnerships but income tax is assessed upon the partners on their share of profits

in a larger one) accept some personal responsibility for the debt. This reduces the value of limited liability to people establishing a business.

Companies are established by registration under the Companies Acts (currently the 1985 Act). The founders or promoters are required to lodge a number of documents with the Registrar of Companies.

● **Memorandum of association** This establishes the company, states its name, registered office and authorized capital, and determines its objects. The latter is especially important because it means the company is established for a strictly limited purpose. If you buy shares in a company owning a chain of hairdressing salons you might not approve of a move into another market. It is possible to seek a court order to declare contracts outside these objects as **ultra vires** (beyond the powers of the directors) and therefore void.

● **Articles of association** The articles are the internal regulations governing the conduct of a company (such as the procedure for electing directors).

● A statement detailing the directors and secretary of the company and its registered office.

● A declaration that the requirements of the Companies Act have been complied with.

● A statement of nominal capital (that is, the face value of shares).

When these documents have been registered, the Registrar of Companies will issue a certificate of incorporation. This will enable a private company to commence trading. There are additional requirements in relation to a public limited company (PLC). At this point it would be useful to distinguish between these two types of company (see also Tables 1.3 and 1.4).

In late Victorian times many businesses were converted from partnerships to joint stock companies. This was partly to raise additional finance for expansion or for investing in new technology.

Table 1.3 Distinctions between public and private companies

	Public company	Private company
● Name	● Must end with public limited company (PLC)	● Must end with limited (Ltd)
● Memorandum of association	● Must state that it is a PLC	● –
● Minimum membership	● 2	● 1
● Minimum authorized capital	● £50,000	● None
● Share issue	● The public is invited to subscribe	● Cannot advertise to invite public to subscribe
● Accounts	● Strict requirements about the format of accounts	● Small companies may submit modified, simplified accounts
● Company secretary	● Must be qualified	● Does not have to be qualified
● Size	● Large	● Usually small

Table 1.4 From private company to public company and back again

	Going public	Going private
Reasons	To raise additional finance in order to: • develop new products • acquire new capital equipment • modernize • expand	To regain control of the business To eliminate threat of takeover To avoid administrative burden and costs associated with Stock Exchange listing To pursue independent long-term strategy without worrying about the short-termism of investors
Method	1 Special resolution at shareholders meeting 2 Change memorandum and articles of association 3 Submission and declaration to the Registrar of Companies 4 Re-registration 5 New certificate of incorporation and a certificate of trading issued	1 Special resolution at shareholders meeting 2 Change memorandum and articles of association 3 Submission to Registrar of Companies 4 Re-registration 5 New certificate of incorporation

However, it was also a way of acquiring the privilege of limited liability. Many family firms remained unchanged in ownership and control but took advantage of Victorian legislation which allowed the formation of companies by registration. The law was amended in 1907 to recognize the distinction between private and public companies. The fundamental distinction between the two types of company is that a **private company** cannot issue a prospectus and, therefore, cannot appeal to the public to subscribe to a share issue. It must sell its shares by private negotiations with interested individuals. A **public company**, on the other hand, is permitted to issue a prospectus inviting the public to subscribe to a share issue. Under the 1985 Companies Act a company is a private company unless it conforms to the additional requirements of **public limited company status**. For instance, even after incorporation a PLC can only commence trading when it has a certificate of trading from the Registrar. This confirms that the company has issued shares with a nominal (face) value of at least £50,000, which must be at least one quarter paid up.

The invitation to the public to subscribe to shares carries additional burdens and disadvantages.

First, public limited companies are under a greater obligation to disclose information. Second, they are subject to a greater degree of scrutiny, especially if they seek a quotation on the International Stock Exchange (ISE) or its junior partner, the Alternative Investment Market (AIM). The ISE and AIM are, in effect, markets for 'second-hand shares' and they play a crucial role in raising capital. Shareholders would be reluctant to buy shares if they were not assured that they could transfer their shares whenever they needed cash. The markets provide such a reassurance. However, the Stock Exchange Council has an obligation to protect investors against the kind of fraud that characterized the South Sea Bubble of 1719–20 and so it will scrutinize companies seeking a quotation to ensure they are properly constituted. This does not mean, however, that investors are given a guarantee against the normal risks inherent in any business venture.

One problem resulting from 'going public' is the danger of losing control of the company. When shares are freely transferable the company is vulnerable to takeover unless the founders (and supporters) retain more than 50 per cent of the shares. Directors have to satisfy shareholders (in terms of dividends and/or the prospect of capital gain) if they are to retain their position. Even though shareholders' control by means of voting at the annual shareholders' meeting is generally ineffective, shareholders can exert power by threatening to sell their shares, and thus make the company vulnerable to takeover.

The shareholders (or members) of a company are the owners and as such are entitled to the ultimate say in the business and to the distribution of the profits of the business. In a large company the running of the business is delegated to directors who are elected to the board by shareholders at the annual shareholders meeting. In a small, private company it is likely that shareholders and directors are one and the same people.

The governance of companies

In theory, ultimate control over a company lies with the members (shareholders) in general meeting. These meetings take the form of:

- **annual general meetings (AGMs)** at which dividends are declared, reports are issued and directors appointed;
- **extraordinary general meetings (EGMs)** called to discuss special business such as alterations to the articles and memorandum of association.

For most matters, a simple majority is required to pass a resolution (known as an ordinary resolution), but for certain issues an extraordinary or special resolution has to be passed. This requires a 75 per cent majority and is necessary when changes to the firm's constitution are proposed, such as:

- change of name;
- change in articles;
- change in memorandum;
- winding up;
- a change to the objects clause;
- re-registration of a private company as a public one;
- re-registration of a public company as a private one.

In most cases, however, a 50 per cent majority rules the day. This principle was established in the case of *Foss* v. *Harbottle* (1843) in which it was ruled that those who command 50 per cent of the votes at a general meeting are able to get the company to do what they want it to do, even if this does not suit the other (minority) members. The law does provide some protection for minority interests, however. The minority can seek legal protection if a proposed act is *ultra vires* (outside the objects clause) or where the majority abuse their voting control to commit an act of fraud.

Although ultimate control rests with shareholders, in practice considerable power resides in the board of directors, whose functions can be summarized as:

- setting objectives;
- determining strategy;
- approving plans;
- monitoring progress;
- determining policies;
- defining issues reserved for board decision;
- company financing;
- appointment of senior executives;
- approving the management structure.

Directors can be either executive directors or non-executive directors. **Executive directors** are employed as full-time salaried executives within the company. In addition to a managing director (chief executive), there might be executive directors covering functional areas such as sales, marketing, finance, personnel and production. In addition to contributing to board decisions, executive directors implement decisions. Their value is that of a specialist with detailed knowledge of the company.

Non-executive directors act in a part-time capacity. They attend board meetings but take no part in the day-to-day management of the company. Although there is a danger of non-executive directors being out of touch, they are seen as invaluable in terms of their independence and broader perspective. The Cadbury Report on Corporate Governance (1992) placed special emphasis on the role of non-executive directors in protecting the interests of shareholders. Table 1.5 sets out the main recommendations of the Cadbury Report.

Directors have the authority to act on behalf of members. Consequently, actions taken by directors are legally binding on the company provided they are acting within their authority. For instance, they can borrow money for the benefit of the company provided it is within the limits imposed on them. However, they may not borrow from the company. Moreover, they are liable for all the debts of the company if they allow the company to trade when they know it to be insolvent.

To balance the authority granted to directors, they have duties imposed on them by law.

- **Fiduciary duty:**
  - to use their powers for the benefit of the company and its members (although under the 1985 Companies Act they are required to have 'regard to employees' interests' as well);
  - not to allow a conflict of interest to arise;
  - not to take secret profit from the company.
- **Duty of care** not to act negligently. The duty of care required varies.
  - For a non-executive director without experience or qualifications, he or she is merely required to do his or her best.
  - In the case of a non-executive director with qualifications and/or experience, the law requires that he or she exercises such reasonable skill and care as may be expected from a person of his or her professional standing or experience.
  - In the case of an executive director, there is an implied term in his or her contract of service requiring that the degree of skill and care to be exercised is that which a person in his or her position ought to have.

Directors can be removed:

- by normal rotation (although they can seek re-election);
- at the retirement age of 70 (unless otherwise specified);
- by ordinary resolution of members in a general meeting – a simple majority is sufficient to remove a director, although if he or she is also an employee, he or she will have legal protection under employment legislation. This legislation might provide the director with financial compensation for the loss of a job but does not affect the

Table 1.5 The Cadbury Report on Corporate Governance, 1992

Purpose: Following a number of high-profile cases in which it was alleged that shareholders had been misled by executive directors, it was felt necessary to make directors more accountable

Recommendations

1 The roles of chairman and chief executive should not be combined
2 Independent non-executive directors should be appointed to monitor activities
3 All key matters should be decided at board level
4 Directors' remuneration should be clearly disclosed and reviewed by a committee of non-executive directors
5 Companies should appoint an audit committee composed of non-executive directors to appoint auditors and approve the accounts
6 Auditors should be legally empowered to report cases of fraud
7 Legislation to limit directors' contracts to three years

members' right to remove the individual from the board.

As well as being removed from office, directors can also be disqualified. The following disqualify a person from being a company director:

- persistent breaches of the Companies Acts;
- offences in relation to the Companies Acts;
- fraudulent trading;
- 'general unfitness'.

The duty of ensuring that the company operates within the law rests with the **company secretary**. The law requires companies to name a company secretary, and in the case of a public company it is a requirement that the person concerned has relevant qualifications. In addition to ensuring the the company operates within the law, the secretary:

- organizes shareholders' meetings;
- is the link between company and members;
- services the board;
- has various administrative duties.

Annual reports of companies

Disclosure of information to shareholders (and other interested parties) is a requirement of:

- the Companies Act 1985;
- professional accountancy standards (SSAPs and FRSs)
- where appropriate, stock exchange requirements.

The law permits small and medium-sized enterprises (SMEs) to submit accounts in a modified, abridged form. To qualify as a small or medium-sized company, two of the following three requirements must be met:

	Small Not greater than:	Medium Not greater than:
Turnover	£2 million	£8 million
Gross assets	£0.95 million	£3.90 million
Employess	50	250

If a company does not qualify as small or medium sized, full disclosure in the format laid down by statute and accounting standards is required.

The **annual report** of a company will consist of:

- financial statements;
  - profit and loss account;
  - balance sheet;
  - cash flow statement;
- reports from:
  - the chairman;
  - the directors;
  - the auditors.

The **chairman's report** will include the following items:

- a review of results, including information on divisional and product performance;
- a summary of financial results;
- a statement of paid and proposed dividends;
- an explanation of steps taken to improve efficiency;
- details of acquisitions;
- information about directors;
- comments about prospects.

The **directors' report**, separate from the chairman's report, will contain:

- a review of the business and its prospects;
- details of changes in fixed assets;
- an indication of likely future developments in the business;
- an indication of its research and development (R&D) activities;
- details of dividends and proposed transfers to reserves;
- details of directors and their shareholdings;
- disclosures relating to charitable and political donations;
- information on health and safety policy;
- a statement of the company's policy regarding the employment of disabled people (in the case of companies employing more than 250 people).

The **auditor's report** verifies that the accounts have been prepared in accordance with the

Companies Act and that they give a true and fair view of the company's affairs.

What is a franchise?

The word **franchise** is used in a variety of ways. For instance, it means the right to vote in an election. In the UK, franchises are granted to various companies that agree to provide a television service in return for the right to sell advertising space on the channel. A franchise, therefore, implies a right that, in the business context (although not, thankfully, in the parliamentary context), is purchased.

A dictionary might define a franchise as a business in which exclusive right are purchased for selling goods or services under a specified trade name and within a specified geographical area. It can take a number of different forms:

- the tied public house in which the licensee obtains his or her stock from a single brewer;
- a dealership or distributorship in which exclusive rights to sell certain products in a defined area are granted by the manufacturer (see Chapter 21, Channels of distribution);
- a licence to manufacture a product in a defined territory.

However, in this chapter we will focus on a specific form of franchise arrangement known as business format franchise. This is defined as a relationship in which 'the franchisor offers a business model which is designed to enable an inexperienced franchisee to set up business from scratch'.

The franchisor sells a business format in return for a fixed sum and/or a percentage royalty. The franchisee, who is likely to be locally based and possibly making an initial business venture, buys a format that has been tried and tested in other areas. The format includes a licence to trade under the franchisor's name and to use its trademark or logo. This right is limited to a specific area and for a specific time period. The franchisor provides a blueprint for the operation of the business and will provide training and back-up services. In return, the franchisee has to accept certain conditions relating to quality and the purchase of equipment and/or material.

The franchise contract

The British Franchise Association (a self-regulatory watchdog of the franchise industry) defines a franchise as 'a contractual licence granted by one person (the franchisor) to another (the franchisee)' that:

- permits or requires the franchisee to carry on during the period of the franchise a particular business under or using a specified name belonging to, or associated with the franchisor;
- entitles the franchisor to exercise continued control during the period of the franchise over the manner in which the franchisee carries on the business that is the subject of the franchise;
- obliges the franchisor to provide the franchisee with assistance in carrying on the business;
- requires the franchisee, periodically during the period of the franchise, to pay to the franchisor sums of money in consideration for the franchise or for goods and services provided;
- is *not* a transaction between a holding company and its subsidiary.

A typical franchise contract would cover the following.

- The nature and name of the activity.
- The geographical territory over which the franchise is being given exclusive rights. Delineation of territory, either by means of a map or by postal districts, is important for both sides. The franchisee will want a clear statement of exclusivity while the franchisor will be interested in minimizing the territory of an individual franchise to increase the number of franchises available to be sold.
- The duration of the agreement.
- What the franchisor agrees to do. Both parties will want a clear statement of what is being offered in terms of training,

advertising, supplies of materials, advice and assistance with matters such as layout.

- What the franchisee agrees to do. This would cover such issues as quality, use of equipment, pricing and purchase of inputs.
- The conditions under which the franchisee may sell the business. In most franchise contracts the franchisee has to give the franchisor first refusal. Where sale to a third party is arranged, it is usually subject to the approval of the franchisor.
- Termination of the franchise by either side. Franchise contracts usually allow the franchisor to terminate the contract if the franchisee:
  - fails to report sales;
  - fails to stay open for sufficient time;
  - trades in goods that are not part of the contract;
  - acts in a way that is prejudicial to the franchisor's good name,
- The franchise fee and royalty. This is a key element in the contract. A high lump sum imposes a burden, whereas a percentage royalty means that risks are shared.

Advantages and disadvantages of franchises

The continuing growth of franchising and the lower mortality rate of franchise businesses (in relation to non-franchise businesses) point to the benefits of franchise relationships. The benefits are share: the franchisor expands his or her business by sharing it with others, while the franchisee is able to purchase a successful business format. Obviously the benefits of a particular franchise arrangement will depend on the terms of the contract. A one-sided contract will result in unequal benefits from the franchise arrangement. A contract that balances the interests of each side will result in a mutually beneficial relationship. We should look at the advantages and disadvantages from the perspective of each side.

From the perspective of the franchisor
The main advantage of franchising out a business is that it facilitates rapid expansion without incurring the high capital cost of direct ownership of all businesses within the chain. A nationwide presence can be accomplished without heavy investment. In addition to saving on capital coasts, the franchisor will save on running costs, especially on pay, materials and administration. The franchisee will finance most of the expansion of the chain.

The franchisor will benefit from the efforts of committed enthusiastic franchisees. These people are self-employed and have a greater incentive to expand the business than if they were salaried managers. They will have local knowledge that will prove beneficial in the expansion of the franchise. It is likely that the self-employed franchisee will remain committed to the franchise whereas the turnover of a salaried managerial workforce would be higher.

If a new franchise outlet is in a 'marginal' locality there is a further benefit to the franchisor. A salaried manager would require at least basic pay, irrespective of sales revenue. Under the franchise arrangement, the personal income of the franchisee is dependent solely on his or her own business success. The franchisor does not pay the local representative of the franchisee.

There are, however, a few disadvantages that should be mentioned. First, as franchisees are self-employed there may be problems in ensuring that they all adhere to the operational methods that are designed to achieve uniformity. Failure by an individual franchisee will reflect badly on the whole franchise operation.

The franchisee will have different objectives from those of the frachisor. In the long run, they may begin to resent the control exercised by the franchisor. This could produce problems in terms of 'policing the franchisee'. For instance, the franchisee might under-declare sales (to reduce the franchise royalty payment) or engage in ancilliary activities that are not regarded as compatible with the franchise.

From the perspective of the franchisee
The advantages to the franchisee are derived from the fact that the franchise involves the purchase of a tried and tested business format. For many would-be entrepreneurs this is an excellent introduction to running their own business. The

franchise arrangement can be seen as an apprenticeship – independent yet with the support of the large and more experienced franchisor. We can detail the benefits as being:

- a ready-made product or format;
- a recognized name known to both potential customers and suppliers;
- public awareness;
- advice, assistance and training;
- a set of procedures;
- bulk purchasing on preferential terms;
- the benefit of the research and development undertaken by the franchisor;
- help with site selection and layout;
- access to the franchisor's legal and financial advisors;
- loan facilities;
- privileged rights to the franchise (and therefore the brand name) within a defined area;
- lower start-up costs.

There are, however, certain disadvantages to the franchisee. In particular, the franchisor will exert considerable control over the franchisee. The purpose behind the control is to achieve a degree of uniformity within the franchise group. However, it limits the franchisee's freedom of action in terms of product, price, terms of sales, place and on termination of the business. In the long run, resentment at external control will begin to outweigh the advantages of franchisor support.

Franchisees will suffer loss of trade if the performance of fellow franchisees causes dissatisfaction to the public. Moreover, an individual franchisee might feel that other operators within the chain obtain a disproportionate share of trade. For instance, although one franchisee in a printing business has exclusive rights in a defined territory, there is nothing to stop customers from that territory going to a shop in a neighbouring territory. In retail outlets (to which members of the public travel) territorial agreements are very difficult to enforce.

The final disadvantage relates to fees and payments to the franchisor – not only the initial fee and the annual royalty but also payments for inputs and services. An obligation to buy inputs from the franchisor places the latter in a mono-

poly position, which can be exploited (though this does not mean that franchisors always exploit their monopoly position to the disadvantage of the franchisee). Resentment at control and at the continuing payments may cause some franchisees to become completely independent once they can extricate themselves from the franchise arrangement. However, the franchise should not be seen in a negative light, even by the temporary franchisee. The franchise can be a valuable apprenticeship in entrepreneurship, which builds up sufficient business confidence to enable the franchisee to become completely independent.

Termination of business enterprises

As a business enterprise involves challenge and risk, it is necessary for entrepreneurs to be optimists. Business decision making is about devising strategies to overcome problems and achieve the objectives of the organization. In the same way, the subject of Business Studies should be approached from a positive angle: namely strategies to overcome problems rather than fatalistic acceptance of problems.

Despite the positive stance of Business Studies, we have to accept that large numbers of business enterprises suffer decline and many of these will be forced into closure. Symptoms of decline will be visible long before the eventual enforced closure:

- falling profit margins;
- increased debts;
- decreasing liquidity;
- longer time to pay debts;
- falling sales volume;
- falling sales revenue;
- late deliveries;
- problems in relation to quality and reliability of products;
- high labour turnover;
- poor labour relations;
- adverse budget variance;
- ageing products;
- falling market share.

These are symptoms of fundamental problems, such as **overtrading**. This is the name given to the attempt to expand too rapidly from an inadequate financial base. The owners seek increased turnover but ignore the importance of profit, or they seek increased profit but neglect the importance of cash inflow. The business that overtrades will be increasing its borrowing requirements and will take longer to repay its debts. It might be increasing its stocks without increasing its sales turnover. Overtrading is overambitious expansion of operations.

Other major causes of failure are:

● failure in the marketing process;
● competition;
● inability (or unwillingness) to respond to a change in the external environment;
● high gearing, resulting in a high commitment to interest payments;
● lack of managerial skills;
● lack of communication between management and employees;
● lack of financial dsicipline;
● inadequate planning;
● poor and inappropriate decisions.

Hopefully management will detect early symptoms of decline and take corrective action. In the event of action not being taken, it is possible that the business will become insolvent. An insolvent business will be unable to meet its financial liabilities when they fell due. At this point the law intervenes to protect creditors and perhaps bring the business to a close.

Bankruptcy

This does not apply to companies – only to individuals (sole traders, or partnerships). Where liabilities exceed assets, creditors can petition the courts to declare a debtor bankrupt. The court appoints a receiver to realize the bankrupt's assets for the benefit of creditors. The assets will be sold and the proceeds distributed among the creditors. It must be appreciated that the bankruptcy laws are designed to protect creditors rather than debtors. The latter will suffer the loss of assets as well as limitations on future action (a bankrupt is prohibited from seeking credit unless his or her status as an undischarged bankrupt is declared, for example).

The only advantage for the bankrupt is that he or she is freed from an overwhelming, impossible situation and is able to make a fresh start in life, albeit in reduced circumstances.

Insolvent companies

In the case of insolvent companies, creditors can apply to the courts for action to secure repayment of money owing to them. The action will take one of the following forms: liquidation, receivership or administration. Although the purpose of the action varies, all three have one thing in common: control of the business and its assets passes from the owners to a court-appointed official.

● **Liquidation** This involves the closing down of an insolvent company. Directors are dismissed and employees' contracts are terminated. The liquidator appointed by the court will attempt to realize the company's assets to pay outstanding debts. The proceeds will be shared among the creditors, although not necessarily equally. It is possible that there will be preferential creditors (such as the Inland Revenue) or secured creditors (on loans that are secured against specific assets) who will receive payment before the others. The liquidator makes no attempt to save the business.

● **Receivership** If there is a major creditor it is possible that the company will go into receivership. The receiver will dispose of assets while keeping parts of the business running.

● **Administration** Under the Insolvency Act, 1986, the UK has a third option known as administration. This has similarities with 'Chapter 11' provision in the USA. The administrator is appointed to rehabilitate the company rather than close it down. The rehabilitation may take the form of restructuring, or the sale of subsidiaries or the appointment of more competent management. The administration order issued by the court enables this to be done in an orderly and tranquil manner without further petitions from creditors. Administration preserves jobs (or most of them) and might be seen as the most humane of the solutions. Unfortunately, little use has been made of this provision.

In this section we have been concerned with the enforced closure of a business. There will also be voluntary termination caused by retirement, ill-health, declining interest or death of the founder. The sole trader can withdraw with little fuss (although settlement of taxes might delay final withdrawal). Partnerships can be dissolved and companies can go into voluntary liquidation (winding up).

Key concepts

Articles of association Rules setting out the relationship between members and directors in a company.

Franchise A business in which exclusive rights are purchased for selling goods or services under a specified trade name. In the case of a business format franchise, the franchisee buys the right to trade under a certain name using a particular format.

Limited liability The liability of shareholders to meet the debts of a company is limited to the nominal values of their share. The liability of the company is unlimited – it is the shareholders who enjoy the privilege of limited liability.

Liquidation (involuntary) The sale of assets following the enforced winding up of a company unable to meet its debts.

Memorandum of association A document that sets out the basic reasons for establishing a company and the amount and type of share capital involved.

Objectives Goals the business organization seeks to achieve.

Objects clause That part of the memorandum of association that states the purpose for which the company was established. Activities outside the objects clause are *ultra vires*.

Partnership A business based on formal agreement between two or more partners. It is not incorporated and therefore partners remain liable for actions of the partnership.

Private company A company in which there are restrictions on the sale of equity.

Public company A company that invites the public to subscribe to a share issue.

Shareholder A part-owner and member of a company. Shareholders have voting rights in a company and share in the profits of the company.

Sole trader Someone carrying out business on an individual basis.

Essay questions

1 Assess the advantages of:
   (a) a partnership over a sole trader business;
   (b) company status over a partnership.

2 (a) What are the advantages of converting to a public limited company?
   (b) In the light of these advantages, why did well-known entrepreneurs such as Andrew Lloyd Webber and Richard Branson opt 'to go private'?

3 (a) Describe the processes involved in privatization.
   (b) Analyse the consequences for an organization when it is privatized.

4 (a) Describe the contents of a memorandum and articles of association.
   (b) Assess the significance of the objects clause.

5 (a) Describe the roles of shareholders and directors in a large public company.
   (b) Evaluate the extent to which shareholders are able to control large companies.

Introduction to management

This chapter deals with the work of managers. It introduces the functional areas of management, which form the basis of Parts III, IV, V and VI of this book. It identifies the work that is common to all managers and outlines the process of decision making that is at the heart of management.

Chapter objectives

1 To explain the functional areas of management.

2 To identify and analyse the tasks that are common to all managers.

3 To analyse the process of decision making.

4 To provide a foundation for an understanding of subsequent chapters.

5 To explain and analyse the nature and purpose of objectives within business organizations.

6 To explain the process of evaluating the current situation in which a business finds itself.

7 To analyse the planning process.

8 To analyse the techniques of control.

9 To provide a foundation for subsequent analysis of the function plans of business organizations.

Management

Management is defined as the:

- art of getting things done by people;
- achievement of objectives via the effective utilization of resources;
- attainment of organizational goals in an efficient and effective manner by planning, organizing, leading and controlling organizational resources.

These definitions focus on the fact that management is concerned with the use of resources (equipment, finance, land, and people) to achieve the organization's objectives (such as a target level of profit). The management's job is to ensure that resources are used effectively so that objectives are achieved, but also that they are used efficiently, achieving the highest result for a given input. Derek Torrington and Jane Weightman (in *Effective Management*, Prentice Hall, 1994) put forward the mnemonic GROUP to reinforce the idea that managers:

- have **g**oals;
- are **r**esponsible for the achievement of results;
- work in **o**rganizations;
- must cope with **u**ncertainty;
- work in **p**artnership with people.

In our study of management we should realize that there are several broad functional areas of management (marketing, financial, production or operations and human resources management), but, whatever their specialism, managers undertake the same activities. Let us look first at the main areas of management.

Figure 2.1 shows an organizational chart for a traditional, function-based organization. In such a company, the managing director is at the apex of the structure and he or she has general, overall responsibility for the management of the business. Subordinate to him or her there are four specialist functional managers for production, personnel, marketing and finance. These people have responsibilities in relation to their specialist areas. Division into functional departments is common in many large organizations.

In small organizations, however, it is likely that all these roles will be combined in an individual manager. Nevertheless, the absence of a specialist department does not negate the importance of the functional areas.

It is appropriate at this stage to identify the main areas of work associated with each function.

The marketing function

This is seen by many people as the heart of the business organization as it is the department in direct contact with the customers the business seeks to serve. Marketing, which must not be equated with selling, is concerned with identifying and responding to the needs of customers. In a market-oriented organization (see Chapter 14), marketing provides the integrating force within the businesses as all decisions relating to the other functional areas are made with the market in mind.

Marketing managers are responsible for:

● researching the market by:
  – identifying market opportunities;
  – undertaking desk and field research;
  – analysing data for decision-making;
● new product development (in collaboration with the production function), which involves:
  – developing new products;
  – decisions relating to the continuation or aborting of products;
  – developing strategies for product launches;
● development of strategies in relation to:
  – products;
  – product mix;
  – markets;
  – market segments;
  – promotion of products;
  – pricing;
  – distribution;
  – sales.

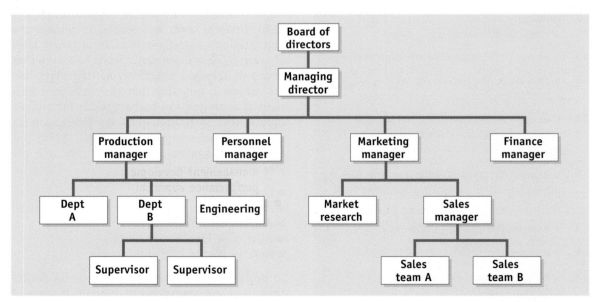

Figure 2.1 An organizational chart, showing organization by functional specialism

The accounting and finance function

This function deals with the 'money aspects' of the business. Accounting involves the collection, recording, presentation and analysis of financial data. The financial side concerns the raising of finance for business operations and making decisions about how the money should be spent. Thus:

- **financial accounting** is concerned with the preparation of final accounts for the benefit of shareholders and other stakeholders in the business;
- **cost accounting** is concerned with identifying the costs of producing output for the purposes of decision making on matters relating to price and output;
- **management accounting** involves accounting for decision-making purposes in relation to:
  - planning activities;
  - budgets;
  - capital investment.

The finance function involves making decisions about:

- methods of raising finance;
- cash flow;
- credit control;
- debt control;
- expenditure.

The production function

This area (called the operations function in a service firm) deals with the making of goods or provision of services. Production or operations involves the coordination of human and other resources to achieve the desired level of output at the lowest cost consistent with satisfying the needs of consumers.

Decisions relating to techniques of production, scheduling of production, stock levels, quality and maintenance all come under production and operations management (POM). Production and operations management involves:

- purchasing and inventories:
  - acquisition of materials;
  - stock control;
  - storage;
- research and development (R&D):
  - development of new products;
  - design;
  - development of new processes.
- production planning:
  - location;
  - layout;
  - capacity planning;
  - machine setting;
  - work and method studies;
  - control of operations;
- operations:
  - scheduling of activities;
  - maintenance;
- quality control;
- distribution:
  - movement of goods and services to customers.

The human resource (or personnel) function

The purpose of this function is to deal with the acquisition and deployment of the human resources of the organization. All management activities relating to employees' pay, welfare, conditions of employment and training are the responsibility of the personnel function. The work of a large personnel department can be grouped under the following headings:

- employee resourcing:
  - contracts of employment;
  - job analysis;
  - recruitment and selection;
  - termination of employment;
- training and development:
  - training;
  - work design;
  - management development;
  - performance appraisal.
- pay:
  - pay administration;
  - job evaluation;
  - pensions, sick pay;
  - incentives;
  - fringe benefits;
- employee relations:
  - negotiations;

– participation;
– grievances;
– discipline;
● welfare:
  – health and safety;
  – medical services;
  – disability;
  – social activities;
  – redundant and retired workers.

Irrespective of their functional specialism, all managers make decisions, deploy resources and seek to achieve goals. Henri Fayol, writing in the early twentieth century, **specified the five tasks common to all managers as:**

● planning;
● organizing;
● coordinating;
● commanding;
● controlling.

Planning

A plan is a predetermined course of action designed to give sense and purpose to an organization. Planning can be seen as the management function concerned with the defining of goals (or targets) for future performance, and deciding on the tasks and resources that are needed to attain the targets. Hence, planning starts with goals or targets (aims and objectives). It is necessary to decide where we are going before we decide on the means by which we will achieve the objective(s). The means of achieving objectives can be seen as strategies.

Organizing

This is the management function that is concerned with assigning tasks, grouping tasks together within subsections of the organization and allocating resources to these subsections. A formal structure is a means of establishing authority and responsibility, and of gaining the advantages of specialisation.

Coordinating

This means bringing the various parts together to ensure that they work in harmony and balance. For instance, the achievement of marketing objectives is dependent on coordination with other functional departments. Unless the production department acquires sufficient inputs it will not be able to produce the goods. Without the goods, the marketing department will not be able to satisfy customers.

Commanding

This takes the form of leading and directing. Both these activities are aimed at achieving the organization's goals, although the means by which the goals are achieved may differ. Directing suggests orders, instructions, supervision or, at the very least, guidance. Leading involves the use of influence to motivate employees to achieve the organization's goals. The techniques might be different, but the basic purpose is the same – getting employees to do the things the organization's managers want them to do.

Controlling

This is concerned with monitoring activities, keeping the organization on track so that it keeps moving towards its goals and taking appropriate corrective action as and when it is required. As we will see later, control involves the:

● establishment of standards of performance;
● comparison of actual performance with the standard set;
● implementation of corrective action.

In *The Nature of Managerial Work* (Harper & Row, 1973), Henry Mintzberg grouped ten roles of managers into three categories:

● **interpersonal** – the relationship a manager has with others;
● **informational** – the collecting and passing on of information;
● **decisional** – the making of different kinds of decisions.

These three categories are shown in Table 2.1.
    To carry out the essential tasks and roles, managers need three broad groups of skills:

● **technical skills** – the skills and techniques of their particular specialism;
● **human skills** – communication and interpersonal skills are essential in view of the particular importance of human resources;
● **conceptual skills** – the intellectual ability to

Table 2.1 Mintzberg's ten action roles of managers

	Characteristics
Interpersonal roles	
● Figurehead	● To attend ceremonies and represent the organization/work unit to external constituencies.
● Leader	● To motivate subordinates and integrate their needs with those of the organization.
● Liaison	● To develop and maintain contacts with outsiders to gain benefits for the organization.
Informational roles	
● Monitor	● To seek and receive information of relevance to the organization.
● Disseminator	● To transmit to insiders information relevant to the organization/work unit.
● Spokesperson	● To transmit to outsiders information relevant to the organization.
Decisional roles	
● Entrepreneur	● To seek problems and opportunities and take action in respect of them.
● Disturbance handler	● To resolve conflicts among persons within the organization/work unit or with outsiders.
● Resource allocator	● To make choices allocating resources to various uses within the organization.
● Negotiator	● To conduct formal negotiations with third parties, such as union officials or government regulators.

(Adapted from H. Mintzberg, *The Nature of Managerial Work*, Harper & Row, 1973)

see and understand a problem and devise solutions. Over the decades, the nature of management has changed (as shown in Table 2.2).

Decision making

As we have seen, decision making lies at the heart of management (and at the heart of our subject). Decisions have to be made about:

● what to produce or which services to offer;
● how much to produce;
● what price to charge;
● design specifications;
● the quality of products or services;
● the materials to be used;
● what level of stock should be held;
● the location of the business;
● the nature and extent of advertising that is necessary;
● where to obtain finance;
● the amount and nature of labour required;
● research and development into new products or services;
● the organization of the firm;
● the target market for the product or service;
● the proportion of profits to be paid out as dividends;
● how the product is to be transported to the market or service given to customers;
● the distribution channels to be used to sell the product;
● whether or not to engage in exporting;
● which of a number of candidates should be appointed to a particular post;
● whether or not to merge with another company;
● into which areas the firm should diversify.

Table 2.2 Changes in the nature of management

From	To
● Boss/superior/leader	● Team member/facilitator
● Stress on reward and punishment	● Stress on knowledge and relationship
● Individual	● Team
● Competition	● Cooperation
● Periodic learning	● Continuous learning
● Avoidance of threats	● New opportunities
● Resistance of change	● Acceptance of change

The different types of decisions

Some of these decisions are fundamental in nature, whereas others are more routine, everyday decisions. The former are said to be **strategic decisions**, whereas the latter are known as **tactical** and **operational decisions**.

Strategic decisions concern the objectives and overall plans of the organization, such as those relating to major capital investment, sources of finance, new products and markets and the future development of the organization. These decisions are made by senior management and directors. Strategic decisions affect the long-term future development of a business.

Tactical decisions are medium-term decisions concerning the use of resources to achieve the organization's goals. Examples include those to do with minor capital investment and changes to marketing activities.

Operational decisions are short-term in nature and are taken by departmental managers. Examples include those relating to ordering stock, detailed planning of production schedules and the control of credit.

Some of these decisions are routine, whereas others are unique. As we move up the hierarchy of decisions, the greater the probability that the decisions will be unique. These unique (one-off) decisions are said to be unprogrammed. They require a combination of problem-solving techniques, judgement, intuition and creativity. The programmed decisions made lower down the organization are routine, repetitive and are handled in the context of an established framework. This will take the form of a policy and a set of rules and procedures.

A **policy** is a framework (stated in general language) for organizational activity. It is a definition of what people in the organization may or may not do.

A **rule** is more specific than a policy. In a sense, it is a detailed interpretation of the policy.

A **procedure** is a statement of the standard method by which the work is to be performed.

The decision-making process

Figure 2.2 illustrates the steps involved in the decision-making process.

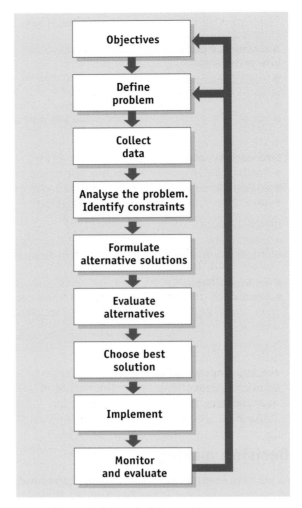

Figure 2.2 The decision-making process

1 The starting point for decision making is to **identify objectives**. Rational decisions are not possible unless there is a clear idea of what the decision makers want to achieve. For example, if the organization is a profit-seeking one, decisions should be made with reference to the profits likely to accrue from a course of action. Alternatively, in a not-for-profit organization (such as a public service) decisions will be made with reference to the extent and quality of service (subject to a financial constraint). This is a topic to which we will return, but for the moment, let us assume that maximum profit is the objective of the organization. The statement of objectives provides:

- a sense of purpose and direction;
- motivation;
- a sense of unity;
- a means of coordinating activities;
- a yardstick with which to measure performance;
- the criteria by which decisions are made.

2 **Define the problem or issue**. Before making a rational decision, it is necessary to define the issue to be decided on or problem to be solved. This means separating the symptoms of the problem (such as a high level of rejects in a manufacturing process) from the cause (a design or equipment failure).

3 **Collect data**. Techniques of investigation and data collection are used to gather both quantitative (numerical) and qualitative (non-numerical) data, on factors such as:

- growth in the market;
- consumer tastes;
- the cost of an investment project;
- manpower available;
- labour turnover.

4 **Analyse data and identify constraints.**

The data will form the raw material of the decision-making process. It is particularly important to investigate cause and effect and to identify the constraints on decision making.

Constraints are factors that limit the choice of action and/or prevent the organization from achieving its goals. Internal constraints include limitations on access to resources of finance, manpower, materials and machinery. There are also constraints of a qualitative nature, such as limitations in the ability or vision of management. Hence, a decision to expand may be constrained by financial and real resources at the disposal of the organization, as well as possible resistance from employees, which will reduce the room for manoeuvre.

Other possible internal constraints include:

- trade union opposition;
- the technology base of the firm;
- product portfolio;
- expertise;

- capacity;
- the skills of the workforce;
- location and room for expansion.

External constraints are outside factors that limit the ability of the firm to achieve its objectives or otherwise constrain decision making. They can include:

- the size of the market;
- competition;
- planning laws;
- consumer law;
- the state of the economy;
- government tax policy;
- pressure group activity;
- employment laws;
- availability of finance;
- interest rates;
- availability of labour.

5 **Identify alternative courses of action.** Once the data has been analysed, it is necessary to identify alternative courses of action. This requires some creativity to complement the rational, scientific approach of the other stages in the decision-making process.

6 **Evaluation.** Invariably making decisions involves choosing from a number of courses of action. Should the firm choose machine tools from one firm or more expensive, but superior, tools from another firm? Should a manufacturer of electrical goods buy in components or establish production facilities itself? Should the firm increase output by taking on more workers or by employing existing workers on overtime? The decision maker has to consider the costs and benefits of each alternative. This is done by means of a number of quantitative methods of analysis, such as:

- investment appraisal;
- decision trees;
- network analysis;
- time series analysis.

Quantitative analysis is an important aid to decision making, but it must complement rather than replace sound human judgement.

7 **Selection.** The final decisions will be made on the basis of the following criteria:

- financial cost and benefit;

- the human cost (such as the effect on the workforce);
- the opportunity cost (the cost in terms of alternatives that have been sacrificed).

  In addition, there might be some consideration of external costs (e.g. environmental impact).

8 **Implementation.** Once the choice has been made, the decision has to be implemented. This will require planning in order to ensure that resources are available to put the plan into operation.

9 **Monitoring and evaluation.** There must also be a control mechanism to ensure that the planned activity is guided towards its goal. Deviations from the standard set should be reported so that adjustments can be made. Then, the final stage in the process is to review progress to see if the objective has been reached. If it has not, the results of the monitoring process should highlight the reasons for any failure and these should be analysed. The evaluation process thus provides data for the next cycle of decision making.

Objectives

An objective is something that we seek to achieve. In planning (as well as in decision making generally) objectives are important in order to:

- determine strategy;
- provide a guide to action;
- provide a sense of direction and unity;
- provide a framework for decision making;
- coordinate activities;
- facilitate prioritization and resolve conflict between departments;
- measure and control performance;
- encourage a concentration on long-term factors;
- motivate employees;
- provide a basis for decision making;
- provide shareholders with a clear idea of the business in which they have invested.

Instead of a single objective, well-managed businesses have what is known as a hierarchy of objectives. At the top of the hierarchy is a **mission statement** identifying the organization's goals.

This is a rather general and visionary statement, such as 'It is our intention to have quality businesses, capable of maintaining leadership positions in long-term growth markets, capable of offering everyday low prices and superior value to the customer and capable of operating at simultaneously high levels of productivity and investment in people, customer service and the community at large.'

Notice that the mission statement is not specific and does not include performance measures. Instead, the mission statement should contain:

- a statement of the fundamental purpose of the organization so as to inspire those who work for it;
- a vision of what the organization wants to be;
- boundaries for the organization
- guidance for decision making;
- a statement of values to guide individual behaviour;
- a statement of the character of the organization and the customers it seeks to serve.

It is widely believed that an organization with a sense of mission will out-perform those that do not have one.

A well-produced mission statement:

- outlines clearly the way ahead for the organization;
- provides information and inspiration to their employees;
- identifies the business the organization will be in in the future;
- provides a definition of success;
- provides a living statement that can be translated into goals and objectives at each level of the organization.

Objectives can be seen as more specific and quantifiable. They are designed to assist in the achievement of goals set out in the mission statement. Sound objectives should conform to the **SMART** criteria, that is they should be:

S Specific, with regard to what is needed;

M measurable, and based on performance criteria that can be used to judge whether or not the objectives are being achieved;

A agreed, with people responsible for achievement of the goals;

R relevant (to the needs of the organization) and realistic (capable of being achieved within the time and resources available);

T timetabled, to give a signpost for fulfilment and a final date for completion.

If the overall corporate objectives are survival, profitability and growth in payments made to shareholders, the **strategic objectives** would relate to market share, sales revenue, cash flow and productivity. For instance, they might include 'to attain a 3 per cent market share within three years' or 'to increase sales revenue by 10 per cent next year.'

Tactical objectives can be seen as short-term departmental performance targets – for example, to raise output by 5 per cent within 6 months. The target has to be achieved if the organization is to satisfy its strategic objectives.

Operational objectives are statements addressed to small groups and individuals. They define outcomes to be achieved within a short time frame, such as sign up ten new dealers by the end of the month.

The objectives cascade downwards from the mission statement and overall corporate objectives. The relationship between these levels of objectives and how they are to be achieved can be remembered in another mnemonic – MOST (see Table 2.3).

Strategy

We can define strategy in a variety of ways. It is:

- a means to achieve an end;
- a long-term plan;
- an organization's planned response to the environment.

Corporate strategy concerns basic issues such as what business are we in? What are our products and markets? What should we do to achieve our objectives? In this sense, strategy unites the organization by ensuring that the more detailed functional plans are compatible with the overall strategy.

Strategic decisions go right to the very heart of the business. For instance, the decisions to develop a new product or seek export markets or withdraw from a declining market are all strategic decisions that will be made at the highest level within the organization. On the other hand, a decision to advertise in *The Times* rather than *The Sun* is not a strategic decision. It is a tactical decision relating to how to achieve the overall strategic objectives.

Corporate strategic objectives might take the following forms:

- to increase exports by 5 per cent per year in each of the next 5 years;
- to increase market share by 15 per cent in 5 years;
- to increase return on capital by 10 per cent in 5 years;
- to diversify into new products and/or markets.

To achieve these strategic objectives it is necessary to devise detailed plans for the main functional areas within the business (marketing, production, personnel, finance and so on) and these plans will be broken down further into detailed programmes. To show the relationship between objectives, strategies and functions, consider the following example.

Table 2.3 MOST		
What an organization is seeking to achieve	**M**ission	The organization's purpose and direction.
	Objectives	The organization's long-term goal
How an organization will achieve it	**S**trategy	Long-term plans designed to achieve the mission and objectives
	Tactics	Short-term plans for implementing strategies

The corporate objective is to increase profit by means of a strategy of increasing the firm's share of the market. For the marketing department, therefore, the objective that has been set is to increase market share. This is to be achieved by a strategy of further market penetration (selling more of the same in the existing market). The sales sub-department then has the objective of increasing sales by penetrating the market more deeply. Its chosen strategy is to target selected customers, which it will do by the tactic of sales presentations to retail store managers.

Notice that this process cascades downwards so that the objectives at one level in the hierarchy determine the strategy at the next level, which then sets the context in which the tactics (detailed working out of the plan) are formulated.

The strategy for functional areas will be expressed in the following terms:

● **marketing:**
  - market segments;
  - sales performance;
  - product range;
  - price–quality strategy;
  - distribution strategy;
● **finance:**
  - ratio of debt to equity finance;
  - dividend policy;
  - return on investment;
● **personnel:**
  - human resource requirements;
  - training and skills;
  - employee remuneration;
  - employee participation;
● **production:**
  - increases in productivity;
  - quality improvements;
  - stock levels;
  - production levels;
  - capacity;
  - production methods;
  - research and development.

Planning

Planning is the establishment of objectives and the formulation, evaluation and selection of policies, strategies, tactics and action required to achieve them. All planning requires forecasts, but let us understand the difference between the two.

A **forecast** is a prediction about the future course of events or future trends. We make forecasts about outside events over which we have little or no control. A **plan**, on the other hand, is a predetermined response to these external events. It details the actions we are going to take. This distinction can be illustrated by considering a weather forecast. A weather forecast attempts to predict the weather we are going to have in the immediate future, but we are unable to control whether it rains or not. If, after hearing the weather forecast, we take an umbrella with us (in case it rains), we have acted in response to the forecast and, at a very simple level, we have planned appropriate action.

Planning is an essential aspect of good management. Plans are drawn up for the business organization as a whole and in each of the various departments or divisions, thus making a hierarchy of plans. Although the nature of the plans might be different, they conform to a common format:

● a review of the current situation (known as a situational audit) and a forecast of likely changes in the environment (see below);
● a statement of aims, objectives and targets to be achieved;
● a statement of strategies and tactics to be undertaken so as to achieve the objectives;
● procedures for monitoring progress and, where necessary, taking corrective action (see below).

In essence, a plan outlines the current situation, forecasts the future, identifies the destination, describes how we are to get there and builds in mechanisms to check that we remain on the right course.

A plan is a document, whereas planning is the process of preparing a course of action (within constraints) to achieve certain objectives. The planning process is perhaps more important than the plan itself. In the words of US General Eisenhower, 'Planning is everything: the plan is nothing'. What is important is not the document that results, but the process of planning activities, ensuring that they are feasible within the inevitable constraints and that they are coordinated. Planning is important in terms of:

- forcing managers to look ahead, rather than being obsessed with day-to-day problems;
- forcing them to identify strengths, weaknesses, opportunities and threats (SWOT);
- providing a focus and sense of direction;
- coordinating activities;
- motivating;
- establishing priorities;
- establishing criteria by which performance is judged;
- facilitating delegation;
- reducing the gap between objectives and performance;
- encouraging teamwork;
- identifying inefficiencies and unnecessary duplication of effort;
- enabling people to respond more effectively to events than would be possible without planning;
- forcing managers to be realistic in terms of objectives set.

As we saw with decision making, planning takes place at three levels:

- **Strategic** deciding on the objectives of the organization, changes in these objectives, the resources used to attain them and policies that are to govern the acquisition, use and disposition of these resources;
- **tactical** ensuring that the resources are obtained and used effectively and efficiently in the accomplishment of the organization's objectives;
- **operational** ensuring that specific tasks are

carried out effectively and efficiently. (see Table 2.4).

Situational audit

It is necessary to analyse the current situation before deciding on a course of action to achieve objectives. The analysis involves an investigation of the external environment, competitors and internal strengths and weaknesses.

PEST analysis is the name given to an analysis of the external environment. 'PEST' itself stands for the **p**olitical–legal, **e**conomic, **s**ociocultural and **t**echnological environment. The factors to be taken into account for each of these aspects include:

- **political–legal** government stability, taxation, government spending, industrial policy, relations with other countries, employment and consumer law, competition policy, environmental protection and foreign trade regulations;
- **economic** inflation, unemployment, income, interest rates, cyclical fluctuations, economic growth, exchange rates, price of inputs;
- **sociocultural** demographic trends, income distribution, levels of education, lifestyles, attitudes to work and leisure, mobility of population;
- **technological** new discoveries, technological development, technology transfer, rates of obsolescence.

In **competitor analysis**, four key factors should be examined:

- entry of major competitors into the market;
- exit of major competitors;

Table 2.4 Planning spectrum

Aspects	Strategic, tactical and operational planning	
Time horizon	Long term —————	short term
Purpose	Ends oriented —————	Means oriented
Impact	Irreversible —————	Reversible
Focus	Whole organization —————	Parts of the organization
Degree of certainty	Low —————	Greater
Information requirements	Poorly defined —————	Well defined
Level of detail	Broad issues only —————	Very detailed

- the availability of substitute products;
- strategic policy changes of major competitors.

The data can be subjected to a **SWOT** (**s**trengths, **w**eaknesses, **o**pportunities, **t**hreats) **analysis**.

A SWOT checklist
- **Internal:** strengths and weaknesses:
  - people – skills, training, attitudes;
  - organization – structure and relationship;
  - products – quality, lifecycle, cost;
  - production – capacity, quality;
  - finance – cash flow, balance sheet, profit;
  - credentials – reputation, customer perception.
- **External:** opportunities and threats:
  - markets – trends;
  - technology – product development;
  - economy – income, employment, exchange rate, interest rates;
  - society – demography, social attitudes;
  - law – pollution, employment protection, consumer law, product liability;
  - natural resources – availability, cost.

We can adopt a matrix approach to analysis with the threat and opportunity grids (see Figure 2.3). In the SWOT grid the positive characteristics are either strengths or opportunities; weaknesses and threats are negative factors, detracting from the achievement of objectives. Strengths and weaknesses are internal to the organization, while opportunities and threats are external. The threat and opportunity grids take into account outcomes and probability of outcomes (in this respect, they bear a similarity to decision trees). Threats (or opportunities) that appear in the 'high/high' box demand immediate attention. Action is not required in the case of threats or opportunities in the 'low/low' box. Those that are placed in the 'high/low' boxes require monitoring rather than immediate action.

Business plans

At this stage, let us look at a particular type of plan known as a **business plan**. This type is particularly associated with new start-up businesses.

A business plan is not only a requisite for seeking finance from investors, but also an essential document for describing aims and objectives and

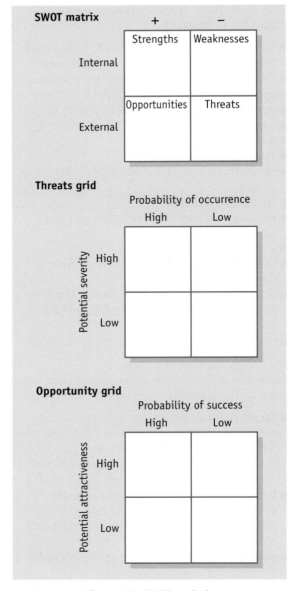

Figure 2.3 SWOT analysis

enabling measurement of progress towards achieving them. The business plan provides the means to:

- appraise the present and future of the business;
- work out short- and long-term objectives;
- establish a framework for action to achieve those objectives.

A business plan should be seen as a working document that helps the owner to monitor current operations, plan the future of the business and evaluate actions necessary for the success of the business. In essence, it is a statement of:

- the current situation – a situational audit;
- where the business is going – objectives;
- how it will get there – strategy;
- the financial implications of the proposed activities;
- the viability of the proposal.

Honesty is important when preparing a plan. Not only should strengths be highlighted, but constraints and expected difficulties should be taken into account as well.

The contents of a business plan

- **Summary** The introduction should clearly and concisely state the nature of the business, the amount of external finance it seeks and the purpose of the application.
- **A description of the business** Details should be given of:
  - the history of the business (if it is an existing business) or reasons for starting up the business (if it is a start-up business);
  - legal form or organization;
  - the capital structure;
  - the key personnel (qualifications, experience, responsibility, age).
- **The product or service** The product or service should be described and comparisons made with rival products. The 'position' in the market should be located and its **unique selling points (USPs)** should be emphasized. Reference should also be made to the ways in which the product is likely to be developed in the future.
- **The market** This section should be based on the market research data. The size of, and trends in, the market should be identified. The target customer (or target groups of customers) should be described. Market shares, the degree of competition and future threats should be included in the assessment.
- **Marketing plans** The previous section dealt with trends in the market and is in effect a forecast. As you will recall, the marketing plan details the marketing strategies that will

be followed. As you will recall, there is a fundamental difference between a forecast (a prediction about events beyond one's control) and a plan (a statement of action to be taken).

The marketing plan will detail strategies in relation to:

- pricing policy;
- advertising and other forms of promotion;
- selling and distribution;
- product launch and product development.
- **Manufacturing and operations plan** This section of the business plan deals with the production of goods (or means of providing services). Details of location, production facilities, techniques and capital equipment are given in this part of the business plan.
- **Financial information** The nature of the information included in this section of the plan will depend on whether the firm is an existing business or a start-up business. In the case of the former, it is essential to include actual balance sheets, profit and loss accounts and cash statements for the recent past. For both start-up and existing businesses it will be necessary to include the following financial information:
  - budgets for main functional areas;
  - cash flow forecasts;
  - costing and break-even analysis;
  - budgeted profit and loss account, with a clear statement of the assumptions on which it is based;
  - budgeted balance sheets;
  - total borrowing requirements;
  - working capital requirements;
  - security for the loan and proposals for repayment.

Gap analysis

Gap analysis (see Figure 2.4) is a forecasting technique used to help set future targets by comparing an organization's ultimate objective with what it is expected to achieve. The process of gap analysis involves establishing two figures:

- the organization's *targets for achievement* over the planning period – this will indicate the desired position or objective;

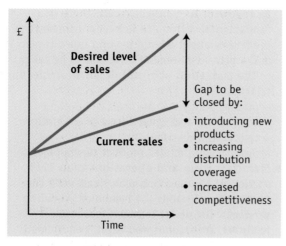

Figure 2.4 Gap analysis

- the organization's *expected achievements* if it did nothing to develop new strategies – this will indicate what will probably happen.

There will normally be a difference between the targets for achievement and the expected achievements. This difference is the 'gap'. After having identified the gap, a decision now has to be made about what strategies to develop to close the gap so that the organization can expect to achieve its targets over the planning period. The organization could continue its existing strategy, especially if the divergence was regarded as only minor. Alternatively, the organization's top management might decide to introduce new strategies to bridge the observed gap.

Control

Control can be defined as the process of evalu-
ating the organization's performance in relation to the objectives set and, where necessary, taking corrective action to keep the organization on track so it will achieve its objectives. An effective control system improves job performance and productivity by helping both employees and management correct problems. The control function is the final stage in the planning process and it provides the basis for corrective action in the next cycle of planning and operations.

Examples of controls that will be explored in greater detail in later chapters include:

- control of the financial function by means of:
  - budgetary control;
  - costing;
  - variance analysis;
  - ratio analysis;
  - final accounts;
- control of the marketing function by means of:
  - sales revenue analysis;
  - market share analysis;
  - budgeting;
- control of the production function by means of:
  - quality control;
  - stock control;
  - network analysis;
- control of the personnel function by means of:
  - evaluation of training;
  - labour turnover;
  - absenteeism.

The control process

All control processes involve a number of stages, as shown in Figure 2.5.

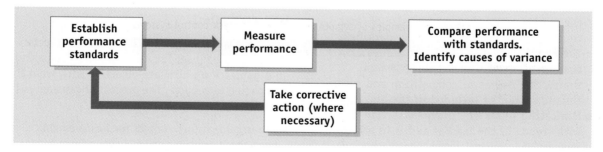

Figure 2.5 The control process

1 **Establish performance standards.** A standard is a unit of measurement that will serve as a reference point for evaluating results. These standards may be expressed in:
- physical units (output per unit of input);
- monetary units (sales budgets);
- units of time (as in critical path analysis).

Alternatively, the standard might be non-quantifiable.

2 **Measure performance.** Once a standard for performance is established, it is then necessary to record and measure results. Where output is standardized, this will be a relatively easy task, involving the same physical, monetary or time units as in the standard set. The process is more difficult where unique, custom-made goods are being produced or where the standard was not-quantified. For instance, it is difficult to measure the performance of a finance manager or an industrial relations manager.

We will see with reference to quality control that the timing of control can vary. In the case of quality control, the choice is between end-of-line (with the likelihood of destruction of defective goods) and placing the emphasis on an earlier stage in the production process (to get it right, first time). This distinction occurs in other aspects of the control process.

We can identify the following types of control.

● **Feedforward control** attempts to anticipate problems and deviations from the standard. This is a proactive approach that seeks to take corrective action in advance of the problem occurring.

● **Concurrent control** occurs while the activity is taking place. It involves ongoing monitoring of activities.

● **Feedback control** is historical in nature, thus preventing the use of corrective action during the existing cycle of operations.

The data in the control process may be collected by observation, by regular inspection or by spot inspection. Data is also contained in reports and may emerge from the process of performance evaluation or appraisal. Computers are now routinely used to collect data and this has led to the development of **management information systems (MIS)**, defined as systems in which specified data is collected, processed and communicated to assist those responsible for the management of resources. MIS are essential in providing information for control purposes as they facilitate the rapid collection and analysis of accurate, timely, concise and comprehensive data.

3 **Compare performance with standards and identify causes of variance.** Information generated by control systems can be categorized as either:
- positive feedback, which causes the system to repeat the condition being considered; or
- negative feedback, which reports deviations from standard and initiates the taking of corrective action – the purpose of corrective action is to bring performance into conformity with the standard.

For a control system to be successful it must:
- be accepted by those subject to its control;

Table 2.5 Examples of symptoms of tight and slack control systems

Tight control	Slack control
● Increased absenteeism and tardiness	● Increased accidents
● Increased turnover	● Disorder and dirt
● Declining morale	● Machine breakdowns
● Inaccurate reporting of control data	● Excessive costs and waste
● Sabotage and theft of products and equipment	● Customer complaints
	● Increased warranty claims
	● Poor quality and increased rework

– be appropriate and meaningful;
– provide diagnostic information;
– be timely;
– be cost-effective;
– not be contradictory;
– be sufficiently flexible to allow for random variations from the standard;
– be accurate and objective, and focus on key (rather than peripheral) performance areas.

Table 2.5 gives examples of extremes of control systems and the negative effects these have.

Key concepts

Coordination From the verb to coordinate, meaning to integrate harmoniously. The integration and synchronization of activities in order to work harmoniously towards the set objectives.

Constraint Anything that limits an organization's ability to achieve its objectives.

Control The process of comparing actual performance with planned performance and, where necessary, taking corrective action.

Directing Commanding.

Leadership The ability to influence the behaviour of others.

Objectives Goals or targets that the organization seeks to achieve.

Organize A verb meaning to coordinate and prepare for activity.

Plan Predetermined responses to anticipated events. A plan outlines the ways in which objectives are to be achieved.

Staffing Selecting appropriate people to occupy posts within the organization.

Essay questions

1 (a) Outline the main functional areas of management.
(b) Irrespective of function, there are activities that are common to all managers. Discuss.

2 (a) Outline the format of a functional plan in business.
(b) Planning is more important than a plan. Evaluate this statement.

3 (a) Explain the differences between strategic and operational management.
(b) How will the balance of managerial activities change as we move up the hierarchy towards top management.

4 Assess the value of a business plan, in the case of (a) a start-up business, seek external finance and, (b) an existing business, finance expansion from internal sources.

5 (a) Outline the principles of control.
(b) Describe the role and nature of budget control and quality control.

3

Organizational structures

The early writers on management were concerned with the formal structure of organizations.

This chapter will look in detail at the structural features identified by the classical writers. However, it must be appreciated throughout that modern thinking stresses not the single best type of organisational structure but emphasises instead that what is best is what is appropriate in the circumstances

Chapter objectives

1 To develop an understanding of organizational concepts.

2 To explain and analyse the main structural types.

3 To survey the arguments for and against decentralization.

4 To provide a foundation for subsequent chapters.

Classical management theory

Management theory is very much a product of the twentieth century. Although writers in earlier centuries had identified the benefits of division of labour and had realized the importance of leadership, there was no serious and systematic attempt to develop a body of theory and principles of management.

The owner-managers around the time of the Industrial Revolution took a simplistic view of the labouring classes – workers had to be forced to work by means of harsh rules, fines and the threat of instant dismissal. The nineteenth-century Poor Law was mobilized in an attempt to force the poor to work by presenting the unpleasant prospect of life in a workhouse as the alternative. By the end of the nineteenth century a more enlightened view emerged and the 'stick' of the earlier decades of the century was replaced by the 'carrot' of incentive payments. It was against the background of concern for order, efficiency, sober lives, hard work and productivity that classical management theory emerged. Classical theory has three strands:

● classical organization theory;
● a theory of bureaucracy;
● scientific management (see Chapter 42).

These should be seen as separate schools of thought linked by their emphasis on division of labour, the need to devise the 'best method' of working and their view of man as a 'rational economic animal'.

Classical organization theory

As stated above, classical organization theory is linked with, but should be seen as distinct from, scientific management. The difference is that scientific management seeks to improve work methods and measure work as a means of linking pay to performance. Classical organization theory (or administrative theory as it is sometimes called) is concerned with the formal structure of organizations. It focuses not on the work rates of individual workers but on the technical efficiency of the organization and is an attempt to formulate universally valid principles of sound and effective management of organizations.

Classical organization theory was developed by Henri Fayol (1841–1925), a French industrialist, whose book entitled *Administration Industrielle et Generale* was published in 1916. In it, Fayol identified the role of the manager as being one of:

- forecasting and planning;
- organizing;
- commanding;
- coordinating;
- controlling.

He then went on to establish the following principles for the sound and effective management of organizations.

- **Division of work** to increase efficiency and output.
- **Authority and responsibility** Authority means the *right* to act, whereas responsibility refers to the *duty* to act. Managers with responsibility for carrying out a task should be given the requisite authority to undertake the task. When authority and responsibility are delegated to a subordinate, he or she becomes accountable for ensuring the task is carried out.
- **Discipline** Fayol saw discipline 'as a respect for agreements which are directed at achieving obedience, application, energy and the outward marks of respect'. Discipline requires good supervision.
- **Unity of command** Each subordinate should have a single superior.

- **Unity of direction** is necessary to ensure that all people within the organization work towards the organizational goal.
- **Subordination of the individual** to the general interest.
- **The degree of centralization** (the extent to which authority is concentrated or dispersed) will vary with the circumstances of the organization.
- **Scalar chain** A hierarchy is necessary for unity of direction.
- **A fair system of remuneration** should be devised, affording satisfaction to both employer and employees.
- **Order** 'There is a place for everything and everything in its place.'
- **Equity.** Kindliness and justice are necessary to obtain loyalty and devotion from the workforce.
- **Stability of tenure** Fayol argued that a high turnover of staff was costly and was both the cause and effect of bad management.
- **Subordinates** should be allowed to exercise *initiative*.
- **Esprit de corps** Believing that there is strength in union, Fayol emphasized the need for teamwork and the importance of good communication.

The common element in classical organization theory is the concern for order, formal structures and discipline.

A theory of bureaucracy

A major contribution to classical theory came from Max Weber (1864–1924), a German sociologist. Weber believed that organizations could be instruments of efficiency if they were based on certain principles. In his book, *The Theory of Social and Economic Organizations* (translated by A. M. Henderson and Talcoff Parsons, Collier-Macmillan, 1964), Weber developed the idea of bureaucracy as the most appropriate administrative form for the rational and efficient pursuit of organizational goals. Whereas today we use the words 'bureaucracy' or 'bureaucratic' in a pejorative sense to mean 'inflexible and impersonal', Weber saw bureaucracy as the ideal organizational form. For Weber, bureaucracies had the following characteristics:

- a high degree of **specialization** based on functional specialisms;
- a **hierarchy** with well-defined levels of authority;
- duties carried out **impersonally**;
- employment and promotion based on **qualifications and merit**;
- a consistent system with **formal rules and procedures**;
- **written records** of decisions made;
- authority vested in **positions** rather than individuals;
- **separation of ownership from control**, resulting in decisions based on achieving overall long-term goals rather than any short-term advantage.

Organization and organizational concepts

Organization can be defined variously as:

- the means by which management coordinates the efforts of employees (and other resources) to achieve objectives;
- the formalized, intentional structure of roles or positions;
- the planned coordination of resources to achieve a goal via division of labour and a hierarchy of authority and responsibility.

From these definitions we learn that the process of 'organizing' involves:

- a structuring of activities;
- the allocation of roles;
- the assigning of responsibility and authority;

- the devising of rules and systems;
- the provision of means for coordinating the activities of various groupings of people and resources.

This chapter will focus on the formal or deliberately planned structure, although you need to be aware of the existence of informal organizational structures. Let us look at this distinction.

The term **formal organization** refers to the deliberately planned structure of roles within the organization. It is 'formal' in the sense that it is official and planned, but this does not mean that it is necessarily inflexible.

The **informal organization** is a network of personal and social relationships. It is not planned or official, but arises spontaneously as people associate with each other. The power of the group leader is personal (not related to position) and is given by the group. Behaviour is guided by norms (notions of what is acceptable) rather than by rules laid down. The group cannot control by means of financial rewards or penalties, but is able to impose sanctions (such as the threat of being 'sent to Coventry'). Some of the needs of the individual are satisfied by the informal organization and this is especially the case when the formal organization fails to give satisfaction.

The organizational chart

This is a pictorial representation of the formal organizational structure. It depicts the relationships between personnel (or more correctly, between 'positions') within the formal organization. The organizational chart shown in Figure 3.1

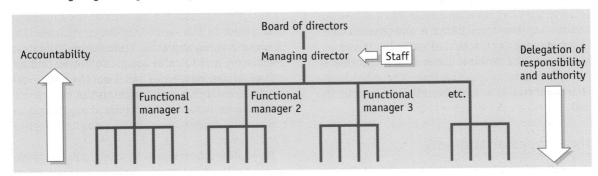

Figure 3.1 A chart of a formal organization

depicts a business enterprise departmentalized in terms of specialist functions.

Authority, responsibility and accountability

Authority is the legitimate exercising of power, which, in turn, is the ability to exercise influence over objects, people and situations. It is, therefore, possible to possess power without authority (and vice versa). Weber, the German sociologist whose ideas on bureaucracy we have already encountered, believed that authority was derived from tradition (for example, the choice of tribal chiefs), charisma (seen in the rise of dictators) or from a rational legal basis. In the case of the latter, authority is given to those appointed by the recognized, legitimate procedure. In this, the classical view, authority originates high up in the organization and is lawfully passed down. Under the capitalist system, risk-taking owners have the authority to make decisions that they may choose to delegate to paid professional managers.

The modern view of authority is the acceptance view. Acceptance of authority is necessary if a communication is to carry authority. The authority of the superior is more acceptable if he or she is respected. Combining the classical and modern views, we can state that authority is distinguished by three characteristics:

- it is vested in positions, not people;
- it is accepted by subordinates;
- it flows down the vertical hierarchy.

If authority means the 'right' to make a decision, responsibility is the duty to perform the task or activity that has been assigned. When a superior assigns a task to a subordinate, the latter is given the authority (or 'right') to carry out the task, but he or she is also given the responsibility (duty) of carrying out the task. The subordinate is accountable or answerable for carrying out the task.

Three types of authority

In large organizations, it is likely that there will be three distinct forms of authority, as follows.

- **Line authority** is direct authority as it involves the right to give orders and have decisions implemented. All superiors have line authority over the subordinates in their team or department. Line authority is a feature of the scalar chain of command, which runs from the top to the bottom of any organization. Authority is delegated from highest to lowest, and each superior within the hierarchy has authority and responsibility for all that occurs lower down the chain. Production managers are line managers responsible for the work of the production department.
- **Staff authority** can be seen as auxiliary authority in that it does not provide the right to command. Staff authority has come to mean advisory or supportive (as in the general staff that accompany a military leader).
- **Functional authority** can be defined as the right to give orders in a department other than your own. This relationship arises when a specialist is allowed to take over a limited, defined function. The line manager delegates authority to a specialist to carry out the task. Although this creates problems in terms of complicated relationships, coordination difficulties and confusion over authority, it does have the advantage of relieving line managers of certain tasks and making use of specialist expertise on specific projects.

Delegation

To enable top management to concentrate on major issues, it is necessary, especially as the organization grows in size and complexity, to delegate decision making and other tasks to subordinates. Delegation is the act of assigning duties to subordinates (see Figure 3.2) and it has the additional virtue of enlarging and enriching the experience of the subordinates and providing training opportunities to enable the subordinates to advance their careers.

To enable subordinates to carry out the delegated tasks, it is necessary to confer on them sufficient authority. It would be unfair to impose

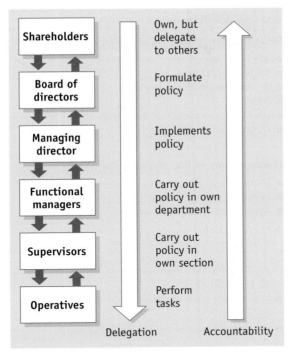

Figure 3.2 Chain of delegation

an obligation on subordinates unless they have the means to carry out the tasks. To this end, subordinates are given authority and made accountable to their superiors. Responsibility and authority should be equal in amount, but a major problem – which is why some managers are reluctant to delegate – is that the delegated responsibility does not negate the responsibility of the superior. The superior remains responsible for the work carried out under delegation.

There are additional reasons why supervisors are reluctant to, or feel unable to, delegate responsibility to subordinates. There might be a lack of confidence (justified or not) in the ability of subordinates. This problem is increased if the costs involved are substantial. Supervisors who feel insecure and threatened, or who are ineffective, might be reluctant to assign responsibilities to a junior. Alternatively, the reluctance might reflect the lack of delegation skills on the part of the superior.

Whatever the reason, the failure to delegate can have unfortunate results. As well as overloading

senior staff (who are, therefore, more prone to making mistakes), it can cause resentment. It leads subordinates to the conclusion that they are not trusted. Failure to delegate deprives subordinates of the experience necessary for them to progress in their careers. This undermines the morale of the staff and contributes to succession problems within the organization. Learning what and how to delegate is, therefore, an important management skill. Obviously, routine tasks should be delegated, but so should tasks in which the subordinate can be tested and can perform well. On the other hand, matters that are exceptions to routine or to standard policy should not be delegated. For delegation to be effective:

- the subordinate must possess sufficient skills and experience;
- the objective must be defined and understood;
- the subordinate should be given sufficient authority and responsibility, but both should be clearly defined;
- the procedure should be clearly understood;
- there should be a clear schedule for completion of the task;
- the subordinate should be given sufficient discretion to act;
- the authority and responsibility of the subordinate should be announced.

Line and staff conflict

A 'line and staff' organizational structure combines functionally based line managers with specialist support staff providing advice at the highest level. The line manager has direct authority and contributes to the production of goods and services. Staff personnel are supportive and advisory. Although the combination of line and staff has distinct advantages over the purely line organization (see Table 3.1), there is almost a clash between line managers and staff advisers.

Span of control

This is the number of people directly accountable to and reporting to a manager. Early management writers argued that any span in excess of six would result in ineffective supervision. Later, this was modified to a span of 4 to 8 at the upper

Table 3.1 Line organization and line and staff organization

Advantages of line organization	Disadvantages of line organization
● Rapid decisions and actions	● Overloads key people
● Unit of command	● Neglects specialism
● Clear responsibilities	● Depends on retaining key staff
● Clear line of communication	● Inflexible
● Clear chain of command	● Limits the experience of employees
● Simplicity	● Problems of coordination
● Widely understood	
Advantages of line and staff	**Disadvantages of line and staff**
● Specialist advice	● Friction
● 'Frees up' line managers	● Confusion over authority
	● Resentment and frustration

levels of an organization and 8 to 15 at the lower levels.

A narrow span has certain advantages:

● close supervision of subordinates;
● tight control;
● fast communication between superiors and subordinates.

However, it also results in:

● superiors being too closely involved in subordinates' work;
● many levels of management (in what becomes a 'tall' organization);
● high costs;
● excessive distance between the bottom and top of the organization.

In a wide span, superiors are forced to delegate more work to carefully selected subordinates. The latter will be given greater discretion over tasks and are less closely supervised. However, the wide span requires managers of high quality if problems of overload and loss of control are to be avoided.

We have seen that early management writers were concerned to discover the single best method to use whereas modern writers tend to argue in terms of contingency theory (what is appropriate in the circumstances). The 'ideal' span of control is therefore not fixed but is dependent on:

● the nature of the task, with repetitive work

permitting the supervision of larger numbers of subordinates;
● the ability and experience of the people concerned;
● the effectiveness of communications;
● the cohesiveness of the team;
● the degree of delegation exercised;
● physical conditions, such as the proximity of the people concerned.

Flat and tall organizations

The width of the span clearly has consequences for the 'height' of the organization. We can define a tall structure as one in which the span of control is narrow and, as a result, there is a large number of hierarchical levels. Conversely, a flat structure involves a broad span of control and relatively few hierarchical levels (see Figure 3.3)

In recent years there has been a shedding of management layers to create flatter organizations. It has been argued that this type of organizational structure is leaner and fitter, more flexible and better able to cope with a rapidly changing environment. However, it is also argued that the success of a flat organization does depend on staff:

● possessing a broader base of skills than is required in tall organizations;
● being adaptable;
● developing team skills.

Table 3.2 outlines the main characteristics of flat and tall organizations.

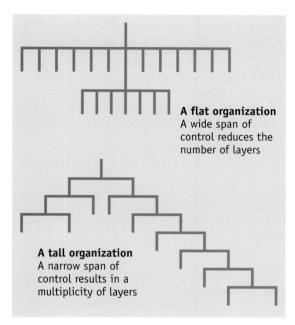

A flat organization
A wide span of control reduces the number of layers

A tall organization
A narrow span of control results in a multiplicity of layers

Figure 3.3 Flat and tall organizational structures

A classification of internal organizational structures

The internal organization of a business can be classified into the following types:

1 **entrepreneurial structure** organized around the owner-manager;
2 **functional structure** organized in terms of functional areas of management;
3 **product based** organized by product;
4 **geographically based** organized by regions;
5 **market segment based** organized by customer types;
6 **matrix organization.**

The advantages and disadvantages of each type are shown in Table 3.3. Each type is illustrated in Figure 3.4

Centralization v. decentralization

Earlier in this chapter we mentioned centralized and decentralized organizations. We will now explore these concepts in greater detail.

A **centralized organization** is one in which most decisions are taken at the centre or at the upper levels of the organization. This leaves little discretion and autonomy for the periphery or lower levels. A **decentralized organization**, on the other hand, is one in which there is considerable delegation and autonomy is the periphery or at the lower levels. It is important to realize that centralization is not necessarily related to the geographical spread of an organization. It is quite possible for a multi-plant firm (such as a retail chain) to be highly centralized, whereas a single-site organization can be highly decentralized. The centralization–decentralization spectrum has nothing to do with geography – it relates to the location of decision making within the organization.

We should think of this issue not in absolute terms, but as a spectrum running from highly centralized to highly decentralized. In fact, although it is possible for an organization to be totally centralized, complete decentralization is not possible.

Table 3.2 Tall and flat organizations

Tall	Flat
● Decentralized authority	● Centralized authority
● Many authority levels	● Few authority levels
● Narrow span of control	● Wide span of control
● High levels of delegation	● Low levels of delegation
● Long lines of communication	● Easier communication
● High degree of functional specialism	● Low degree of functional specialism
● Bureaucratic	● Easier coordination

(Adapted from P. W. Betts, *Supervisory Skills*, Pitman)

Table 3.3 Internal organizational structures

Types	Advantages	Disadvantages
Entrepreneurial organized around the owner-manager	• Flexible • Responsible	• Lack of specialization • Only suitable for small organizations
Functional organized in terms of the functional areas of management	• Efficient • Specialized • Simple lines of control	• Communication problems • Slow to respond • Over-specialization • Coordination problems • Decisions concentrated at the top
Product based organized by product	• Market oriented • Coordination across function • Flexible • Encourages entrepreneurial attitude	• Duplication of resources and functions • Less top management control • Poor coordination across division
Geographically based organized by regions	• Emphasis on local conditions • Better communications at the local level • Training ground for management	• Problems of control • High costs • Specialist sevices not economic except at national level
Market segment based organized by customer types	• Concentrates on customers' needs • Develop expertise in handling customers	• Coordination difficulties • Customer groups not always defined
Matrix organization	• Flexible • Interdisciplinary • Cooperation • Motivates and challenges • Develops managerial skills • Creativity encouraged • Frees up top managers for planning • Encourages decentralization	• Overlapping authority • Power struggles occur • Costly to implement • Split allegiances • Encourages discussions rather than action • Creates problems of control • Decision-making process can be slow

The centre must retain some control over the planning process. As we saw earlier, authority can be delegated downwards, but top management cannot abdicate all responsibility. Consequently, some decisions will always remain at the centre. The advantages and disadvantages of centralization and decentralization are set out in Table 3.4.

The degree of centralization within a particular organization will be influenced by the following factors.

• **Cost** As a general rule, the more costly the action to be decided on, the more probable it is that the decision will be made at the top levels of management. Thus, certain major decisions will always remain at the top level. Moreover, the greater the cost, the more top management is likely to centralize decision making.

• **Desire for uniform policy** Consistency and uniformity is associated with centralization.

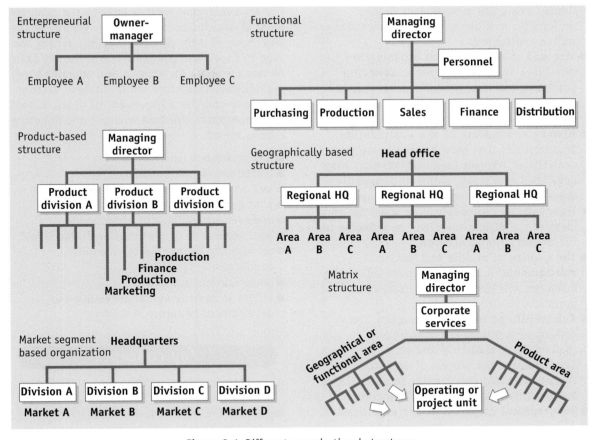

Figure 3.4 Different organizational structures

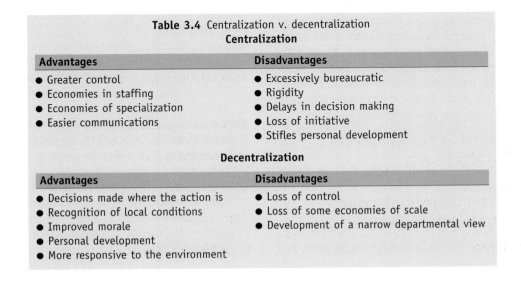

Table 3.4 Centralization v. decentralization

Centralization

Advantages	Disadvantages
● Greater control	● Excessively bureaucratic
● Economies in staffing	● Rigidity
● Economies of specialization	● Delays in decision making
● Easier communications	● Loss of initiative
	● Stifles personal development

Decentralization

Advantages	Disadvantages
● Decisions made where the action is	● Loss of control
● Recognition of local conditions	● Loss of some economies of scale
● Improved morale	● Development of a narrow departmental view
● Personal development	
● More responsive to the environment	

Hence, where top management desires uniformity, it is likely that decision making will be centralized.

- **Size and character of the organization** In very large organizations, especially those producing a diverse product range, it is not only possible but also highly desirable to decentralize decision making.
- **History and culture of the organization** Organizations that grow internally are often centralized, whereas organizations that have developed as a result of merger frequently show evidence of a decentralized structure.
- **Management philosophy** The character and ideas of top management will be reflected in the degree of centralization.
- **The quality of middle and junior management** A shortage of talented middle managers will limit the decentralization process.
- **Availability of control techniques** The development of computers and the availability of statistical and accounting data has facilitated the process of decentralization. Top management can practise decentralization and yet retain control over the operation.
- **Geographical dispersal of the organization.**

Before leaving this subject, mention should be made of the different forms of decentralization. **Functional decentralization** involves the delegation of decision-making authority to specialist functional departments (such as marketing, finance, personnel). **Federal decentralization** involves the grouping of activities on a product basis. Here departments or divisions are responsible for a range of products and operate autonomous business units. A large organization decentralized in such a manner is known as a divisionalized company. Finally, decentralization in terms of project teams combines functional specialism with responsibility for a group of products.

The consequences of poor organizational structure

Organizational structure should not be seen as a dry academic topic as it is vital to the achievement of organizational objectives. We saw at the beginning of this chapter that organizing was seen by Fayol (and others) as one of the key tasks of management. An appropriate, soundly based organizational structure will facilitate motivation, efficiency and the achievement of goals. A poor or inappropriate structure will have the following consequences:

- low motivation and morale;
- ineffective decision making;
- lack of coordination and control;
- poor communication;
- divisiveness and lack of cooperation;
- poor adherence to organizational objectives;
- an inability to respond to changing conditions;
- duplication of activities;
- failure to provide opportunities for the development of future managers.

Key concepts

Accountability Responsibility for results and an obligation to report.

Authority The right to make decisions. The legitimate exercise of power.

Centralization Decision making concentrated at the centre.

Decentralization Dispersal of decision making to lower and/or peripheral levels within the organization.

Delegate To assign responsibilities and authority to a subordinate.

Line relationships Relationship between a superior and a subordinate in a scalar chain.

Organizational chart A chart that records the formal relationships within an organization.

Responsibility The obligation or duty to carry out a task.

Span of control The number of subordinates directly controlled by a particular superior.

Staff relations Relations between a superior, staff and a specialist adviser acting in a supportive role.

Essay questions

1 (a) What do you understand by delayering?
(b) Assess its consequences.

2 Explain why in classical organizational theory six was considered the ideal span of control and yet today the notion of an ideal span is dismissed.

3 (a) What is meant by a hierarchical organization?
(b) Assess the adverse consequences of a rigid hierarchical structure.

4 (a) Why are managers often reluctant to delegate?
(b) Analyse the likely consequences of a failure to delegate.

5 Analyse the advantages of a product-based or divisionalized structure over a functional structure.

4

Business communications

Effective communication is an essential part of management. It is the process by which the management tasks of planning, organizing, leading, directing and controlling are accomplished. Managers devote a large proportion of the working day to communication of all types. On average, they spend 66 to 75 per cent of their time talking and listening to other people. At the highest levels of management, this is likely to rise to 90 per cent.

Thus, the study of business must include the study of communication. This chapter introduces the subject of communications within business and, at the same time, shows how it contributes to the development of key skills.

Chapter objectives

1 To develop an understanding of the role of communication in business.

2 To develop an understanding of the characteristics of different forms of communication.

3 To develop a model of the communication process as the basis for analysing the process of communication.

4 To analyse the causes of communication failure.

5 To develop an insight into methods of improving communications.

6 To develop key skills in communication.

The purpose of communication in business

Communication is defined as the exchange of information, ideas, opinions and feelings. Communication is said to be effective when it is received and understood in the manner intended by the sender. This means that communication can take a number of forms, including written, spoken, non-verbal (body language), graphical, pictorial or, increasingly, electronic forms using information technology (IT). Communication via data presentation and IT form the subject matter of the next two chapters, so here we will focus on written and oral communication. Before looking at particular communication skills, we need a theoretical understanding of communication and its role in business.

Communication is essential to the achievement of organizational objectives. This is because the basic purpose of any communication is to influence the actions of others. In an organizational context, the aim is to influence others to work towards the achievement of the goals of the organization. We can see the role of communications in terms of the well-known functions of management.

● Goals must be established for the organization and then communicated to employees.
● Communication is vital in the development of plans.
● Communication is also essential in the

organization of both human and non-human resources.

● Leading, directing and motivating inevitably require communication skills.
● The control function cannot be effective without the communication of accurate and up-to-date data.

In addition to these internal functions, communication is the means by which the business organization becomes an open system relating to the external environment. It links the organization with customers, suppliers, creditors, shareholders and the wider community.

Classification of communication

We can classify communication by:

● media;
● direction;
● degree of formality.

Media

This classification divides communication into verbal (spoken), non-verbal (expression, tone of voice, physical presentation, gestures), written and numerical forms. The spoken word lacks the permanence of the written word, but it is more rapid and flexible in terms of adjusting to circumstances. Moreover, the spoken word can be supported by non-verbal communication – body language, for instance, will reinforce the spoken message. However, one of the most difficult situations to handle in the workplace is where conflicting messages are received by the eyes and ears. For example, when the boss *sounds* easy-going, but this is the opposite of what is conveyed by the body language.

Another feature of the spoken word is that we convey meaning both in the words we use and in the way they are spoken. Hence, the same combinations of words can be a request or an order, a statement of fact or a question. This is both a strength and a weakness. It is a way of economizing on words and, therefore, time. However, it can cause confusion where the recipient is unable to pick up on the intonation. For workers whose first language is not English, this can cause particular problems.

The spoken word is important in some situations (for example, for conveying criticism of, or advice to, subordinates) where a bold written statement could cause resentment. It has to be appreciated that resentment is often caused not by criticism itself, but the manner of its delivery. Hence, unless a written statement is necessary as part of the disciplinary process, a quiet word might communicate the message without leaving a sense of grievance.

Non-verbal communication is limited to a supportive role, communicating very simple messages (pleasure, pain, criticism). Nevertheless, it is still very important in face-to-face communication. This is why a personal meeting might be preferable to a telephone conversation for some purposes.

Written communication has distinct advantages. The message can be precisely presented and is permanently on record. However, it is time-consuming to produce and may lack clarity. Its greatest defect as a form of communication is that is fails completely if it is not read.

Table 4.1 summarizes the advantages and disadvantages of different media.

Direction

Downward **communication** follows the authority and responsibility relationship in the organizational chart. It usually takes the form of giving instructions, directions, assigning duties or providing information to those delegated to perform a tasks.

Upward **communication** takes the form of reporting back results, making suggestions or perhaps airing grievances.

Horizontal communication refers to contacts (formal or informal) between people at the same level within the organization. It is coordinative in nature and usually involves sharing information, resolving conflicts and solving problems across and organization structure.

A further aspect of direction relates to whether communication is one way or two way. Where there is no facility for a reply (feedback) it is called **one-way communication**. An advertise-

Table 4.1 Advantages and disadvantages of different forms of communication

Verbal (spoken)	Written	Visual
Advantages	*Advantages*	*Advantages*
● Direct impact and feedback	● Same message to all and speed	● Of all information received, 75 per cent is visual
● Permits plain language	● Everyone can receive the message at the same time	● Possible to convey movement
● Permits presenter to check assimilation	● Can deal with a large audience quickly	● Graphical representation possible
● Allows presenter to gain audience commitment	● Simultaneous circulation by various means	● Participation possible (say, via flipchart)
	● A back-up to complicated verbal communication	● Vehicle for non-verbal information
Disadvantages	● Information exists in recorded form	
● Depends on presenter's communication skills		*Disadvantages* (when indirect)
● Uses only one of audience's senses	*Disadvantages*	● No guarantee of receipt or understanding
● Each presentation requires time to prepare	● No guarantee of receipt or understanding	● Impersonal, reduces participation
● Understanding uncertain	● Ambiguity of written language without feedback	
● Time-consuming and most effective for small groups	● Impersonal, inanimate, reduces participation	

ment or information posted on a noticeboard are both examples of one-way communication. One-way communication within an organization is associated with an authoritarian style of leadership, with the authority of the leader being preserved unchallenged. For simple communications, a one-way channel might prove satisfactory, but is carries with it the danger of being misunderstood (with no facility for checking) and/or causing resentment.

Feedback built into **two-way communication** is a feature of a democratic leadership style. The facility for feedback is important in ensuring that the message is fully understood and in enabling subordinates to contribute to the process of decision making. It is slower than one-way communication, but it helps to bind the two sides closer together. For complicated subjects or matters of a personal nature, two-way communication is vitally important. Table 4.2 summarizes which kinds of communication the different directions are best suited to.

Degree of formality

Communication can be classified as **formal**

Table 4.2 The direction and purposes different forms of communication are suited to

Direct	Purpose
Downward	● To give orders, instructions
	● To communicate objectives
	● To communicate goals
	● To assign work
	● To control
Upward	● To report back
	● To express views
	● To highlight problems
	● To offer ideas
	● To seek clarification
	● To request
Horizontal	● To coordinate
	● To solve problems
	● To offer advice

(meaning arranged, approved or official) and **informal**. The latter is unofficial, unplanned communication outside the organization's formal channels. It is a mistake to equate formal communication with the written form and informal with spoken and non-verbal forms. For example, when a superior reprimands a subordinate by means of the spoken word, it is a formal communication. However, a joke in written form passed around the office is informal communication. Small talk between a superior and subordinates can be informal, although it depends on the circumstances and the individuals involved. Informal communication channels:

● satisfy personal needs;
● counter monotony at work;
● provide a source of job-related information that is not provided by formal channels.

The last point is of particular concern as any deficiency in the formal channels of communication will lead to an increase in activity using informal channels. The grapevine, which is present in all organization, is efficient at disseminating information, although there is always a danger of its suffering distortion on the way. Managers should be aware of the disruptive effect of the grapevine and the surest way of reducing its activity is to be more open with employees in the formal communication channels. In some cases, senior managers will make use of the grapevine to selectively leak information, either to test reaction to it or to allow an idea to develop. Exploitation of the grapevine can be effective, but it is also a high-risk strategy in that it can contribute to conflict and/or grievances.

A model of communication

The model of communication shown in Figure 4.1 can be used to analyse the cause of communication breakdown and suggest remedies to improve the effectiveness of communication. First, it has to be appreciated that communication is the process by which an idea is transferred from one mind to another. The purpose is to make the receiver understand what is in the mind of the sender. To accomplish this task, it is necessary for the sender to encode a message in appropriate words, symbols or gestures.

We must not be distracted by the word 'code', which conjures up images of spies. Language is a 'code'. For instance, the word 'cat' suggests a four-legged feline animal only because we know what it means and have access to the code. To someone ignorant of the word's meaning, the word 'cat' is just a sound. Thus, a coded message has to convey the intended meaning and be intelligible to the recipient. However, a common failing is to encode the message in a way that is inappropriate. Effective communicators will adjust their style of language to different situations, but this must not result in talking down to people, which will cause resentment.

Technical jargon is common in most occupations and places of work. It serves as a shorthand form to speed the flow of communication. However, by its very nature, jargon is specialist voca-

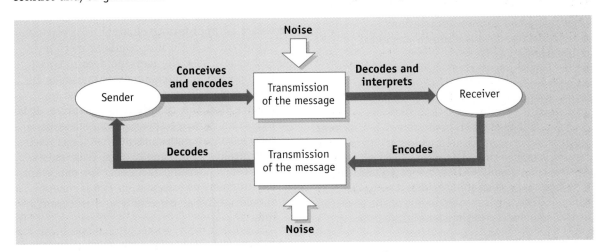

Figure 4.1 A model of communication

bulary that excludes outsiders. In its place, jargon is a valuable aid to communication, but if it excludes people from understanding the message there will be communications failure. The skilled, effective communicator will know when and when not to use the jargon of his or her group.

After the message is encoded, it is transmitted via a communication channel or medium. This can take various forms: sound, a sheet of paper, the telephone system, a television screen, film, a brochure or a VDU screen. To illustrate this point, consider a telephone conversation. The speaker's words are converted into electrical impulses (that is, they are encoded) and these are transmitted along the telephone line. At the other end, the impulses are converted back into speech, (that is, decoded) which is what is heard by the recipient. All communication involves this process of encoding, transmission and decoding.

Transmissions can be affected by **noise**. This word does not just mean sound, but refers to anything that distracts the recipient and causes either a failure to receive the message or a misinterpretation of the message.

Communication failure

Communication problems result in inefficiency, failure to achieve organizational goals and employment relations problems:

- bad decision making as a result of not receiving the correct information;
- misunderstanding leading to mistakes;
- low morale;
- poor-quality work;
- lack of coordination;
- inconsistent activities;
- conflict;
- lack of control;
- failure to implement plans.

Before it is possible to improve communications, it is necessary to diagnose what the problem is which is likely to be located in one of the elements in the communication model outlined above.

- **Encoding problems**
  - Lack of planning.
  - Unclarified, unstated assumptions behind the message.
  - Use of jargon.
  - Deficiencies in the use of language.
  - Use of obsolete words.
  - Verbosity.
  - Poorly expressed message.
  - Lack of empathy.
  - Inaccurate use of terminology.
- **Transmission problems**
  - Inappropriate channel used.
  - Failure to speak/write clearly.
  - Contradictory verbal and non-verbal message.
  - Noise.
  - Distortion.
- **Decoding problems**
  - Failure to take in the message.
  - Distractions.
  - Differing interpretations of words.
  - Lack of interest in the subject matter.
  - Emotional state of the recipient.
  - Stereotypical attitudes.
  - Information overload.

To improve the effectiveness of communication it is necessary to take the following steps.

- **Plan the message to improve encoding**. This might mean that the communicators need to undergo training and the message needs to be adapted to take account of the recipient's knowledge, education and interests.
- **Select an appropriate channel**. It is especially important to build in a feedback mechanism and ensure that the message does not pass through too many channels as messages are often distorted when they are passed on.
- **Ensure that the recipient is receptive**. It is important to make sure that the message is received in an environment that lends itself to concentration. Equally, that trust exists between sender and recipient. For important, urgent items of information the recipient should receive it personally and receive it in full.

It is also useful to analyse which communication net is at work within the group (see below).

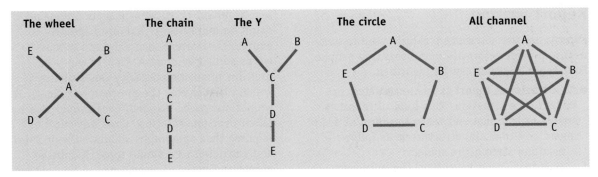

Figure 4.2 Communication nets

Communication nets

Figure 4.2 illustrates types of communication networks. The net diagrams illustrate the patterns of communications that can exist within a team. They can be used to identify deficiencies in communications and discover the most effective way of communicating to achieve organizational goals. Research shows that, for simple tasks, the wheel is more efficient and accurate than either the chain or the circle. However, the wheel, with its centralized pattern, retards adaptation of the group to changed circumstances. The chain emerges as being slow and the least effective pattern. The circle, on the other hand, is shown to be superior in terms of satisfying group members and adapting to changing circumstances.

Table 4.3 sets out the effects of the various patterns on communications within a team.

Table 4.3 Communication nets and consequences for communication

Types	Description	Consequences
The wheel	● Information flows to central person (E).	● Fast performance speed. ● Low creativity. ● Low interaction. ● Dominated by the leader.
The chain	● Information passes up and down.	● Hierarchical. ● Controlling. ● Moderate performance speed. ● Low creativity and interactivity.
The Y	● Combines the wheel and the chain.	● Led by C. ● Moderate performance speed. ● Fairly centralized.
The circle	● Members communicate freely.	● No necessary leader. ● Slower performance. ● Higher interactivity.
The all channel	● Information flows all around the network.	● No necessary leader. ● Slow performance. ● Decentralized. ● Democratic. ● Members communicate freely.

Report writing

Reports are the commonest vehicle used in business to provide information and persuade people. Four types or styles can be identified.

- An **occasional report** is written to alert or update on a situation. This kind of report is simple or informal and takes the form of a memo or e-mail. Its structure is as follows:
  - headline stating the subject;
  - an introduction to explain the purposes;
  - the essential information to be conveyed;
  - reaction, opinion, interpretation;
  - a close to summarize the essence of the report.
- An **activity report** is written to sum up a conference, meeting or other event. The structure needs to include information on the following:
  - the event, place, date;
  - its purpose;
  - contacts made – what arose from the event;
  - conclusion.

    An important focus must be to explain why the event matters to the reader.
- **Status or progress reports** are written to give a general review of activities in a department or progress on a particular projects. These reports generally consist of the following elements:
  - background, establishing the context for the report;
  - activities and results;
  - budgeted costs;
  - schedule;
  - conclusion.
- A **formal report** is designed to provide a comprehensive overview: 'The purpose of a report is to analyse and explain a situation, to propose and gain agreement to a plan. It should be logical, practical, persuasive and succinct.' (M. Armstrong, *How to be an even Better Manager*, Kogan Page, 1994, page 282). It should have a logical structure with a beginning (why the report has been written, what its terms of reference are), a middle (the facts collected and analysed) and an end (conclusions and recommendations). The

report should be written in plain language, using no more words than are necessary to express the writer's meaning, and precise words should be chosen. 'Fog' is the term used for linguistic obscurity (anything in writing that makes the message less clear). It should always be avoided. Care should also be taken over presentation. Good presentation requires that paragraphs should be kept short and restricted to a single topic. Numbered points and bulleted points should be used to highlight key pieces of information. Appropriate use should be made of graphs and tables of data. The format is as follows.

1 Title page(s)
This should include the following:
- title of the report;
- name of sponsor and/or customer for the report;
- title of researcher and organization;
- date of publication.

2 Table of contents
This should include page references for each heading contained within the report.

3 Executive summary or abstract
This is intended for casual readers who may have neither the time nor inclination to read the whole report. This often includes the person who makes the decisions! It should summarize the whole of the report, including the findings and recommendations. As a rough guide, this should not exceed an eighth of a page for each five pages of report.

4 Introduction or background
This should include the following:
- the purpose of the research (often this is referred to as the 'brief');
- supporting history and background information (other relevant studies);
- any assumptions made;
- specific aims of the research.

5 Methodology
This section should include the following:
- details of any material used (questionnaires, interview forms, special equipment);
- sample population (numbers and profile);

- design of study;
- procedure used (the sequence in which the study was conducted).

6 Results and analysis

The following information needs to be included here:

- details of analysis method(s) used;
- descriptive statistics for raw data;
- any advanced statistics;
- tabular and/or graphical presentation of data.

7 Discussion and conclusions

In this section, readers will expect to find the following:

- discussion of research findings;
- conclusions to be drawn from the findings;
- self-critique of study (unexpected problems that arose, why not enough people could be surveyed, flaws discovered in a questionnaire and so on);
- additional graphical presentation of summarized or combined data to support the discussion or conclusions.

8 Recommendations

For each recommendation, the following can be tabulated:

- *what* is recommended;
- *who* needs to act on the recommendation;
- *costs and benefits* of the recommendation, with figures if possible, and indicating the timescale involved;
- *cross-references* to the points in the report leading to the recommendation.

9 Appendices

To be included here are a listing of any references, any other appropriate bibliography, glossaries of technical terms used, and copies of any important supporting documentation. It may be necessary to include in an appendix any body of material that is too large or detailed for the findings section (for example computer analyses).

Delivering presentations

A career in business will require you to deliver a presentation to colleagues (senior and junior),
customers, suppliers, creditors or to the wider public at some stage or another. The purpose of a presentation is to persuade (in, for example, a sales pitch), instruct colleagues or inspire people (say, as part of a change programme).

In view of the importance of presentations in business it is appropriate that one part of communication key skills is delivering presentations to groups of people. It is likely that an A level Business Studies course will include delivering presentations both as part of the learning process and as a contribution to a key skills portfolio. The comments that follow are designed to offer guidance to students on how to deliver a presentation.

Most students are nervous about delivering a presentation, but the way to overcome the problem is to:

- practise speaking in public;
- know your subject;
- know your audience;
- define your objectives;
- prepare thoroughly;
- rehearse your presentation by trying it out on small groups of people.

In preparing for a presentation it is essential to be clear about your objectives. Facts and arguments need to be collected and arranged in a coherent way. The classic method of structuring a talk is to tell them what you are going to say, say it, then tell them what you have said. Never try to cram too much into a presentation – instead, develop a small number of key points. These can be written down on postcard-sized prompt cards. This makes for a better presentation (greater flow and emphasis on key points) than one read out as an essay. The cards should be arranged in the correct order prior to the presentation as nothing detracts more from a presentation than a desperate search for the next card halfway through the presentation.

A presentation will be strengthened by the use of visual aids, which can be classified as:

- **low complexity** handouts, whiteboard or flipchart;
- **medium complexity** slide projector, overhead projector or audio system;

Table 4.4 Some dos and don'ts of making presentations

Do	Don't
• Prepare	• Use inappropriate language
• Clarify objectives	• Fill your speech with irrelevant points
• Draft and redraft your presentation	• Read out a statement
• Practise	• Overwhelm the audience with too much detail
• Limit yourself to a small number of well-explained points	• Keep looking at your watch
• Be enthusiastic	• Mumble or hesitate
• Make eye contact with the audience	• Drop your voice at the end of each sentence
• Use simple, direct sentences	• Apologize for your lack of speaking experience
• Include examples and analogies	• Lose sight of the message that you are giving
• Use the pronouns 'you' and 'I'	
• Use visual aids	
• Be prepared for questions	
• Reach a clear conclusion	

• **high complexity** video, multimedia or computer graphics (such as Powerpoint).

For a major presentation – especially one linked to an IT course – it is useful to experiment with the methods that have a high complexity, but most student presentations will focus on handouts, an overhead projector (OHP), whiteboard and flipchart. The last two aids are useful in brain-storming sessions whereas handouts and materials for an OHP are recommended when you need to be prepared in advance.

OHP transparencies can be photocopied as handouts, thus serving a dual purpose of pro-viding impact during the presentation and notes that can be taken away. In both cases, the number of points included on each sheet should be strictly limited. Use a large font and bold letters for computer printouts from which the trans-parencies are made. It is no good putting lots of material on a single OHP transparency as it will not be seen and so cannot be absorbed – limit it to five points. Refer to the image projected on the screen during your presentation and, what-ever you do, do not obscure the audience's view of the projection. Test the equipment beforehand to avoid the embarrassment of its not working on the day.

Other device on presentations is contained in Table 4.4.

Key concepts

Communication The exchange of information, ideas, opinions and feelings. Communication is effective when it is received and understood in the manner intended by the sender.

Communication barriers Obstacles that prevent the flow of communication within the organization.

Communication, direction of The flow of communication up, down or laterally within an organization.

Communication nets (or networks) Diagrams depicting the structure of communications within an organization.

Communication overload The problem of excessive amounts of information.

Feedback A response to an initial piece of communication.

Formal communication Official and approved communication.

Informal communication Unofficial communication within the organization.

Noise Anything that interferes with the communication process.

One-way communication A one-way message in which there is no feedback.

Two-way communication Communication that encourages feedback.

Essay questions

1 Discuss the role of communication in relation to the major tasks of management.

2 New technology inevitably brings an improvement in communication. Discuss.

3 Communication is inevitably more difficult in large organizations. Evaluate what can be done to improve it.

4 Assess the causes and consequences of communication failure.

5 Analyse communication within groups in terms of communication nets.

Key skills development

Prepare and deliver a presentation on one of the following topics:

- the benefits to business organizations of employing part-time workers;
- job opportunities in your area;
- the changing structure of the national/local economy;
- developments in retailing.

This exercise is not designed to test subject knowledge, but, rather, to encourage the development of research skills and the key skill of delivering presentations. Your presentation must include at least *three* of the presentational aids referred to in this chapter. Your script should be in the form of notes, which must be photocopied and issued to the audience at the start of the presentation.

5

The application of number in business

As many business issues are numerical in character, it is necessary for students of business to have some understanding of quantitative methods. This chapter will concentrate on the descriptive aspects of statistics that all A level candidates are required to understand.

Chapter objectives

1 To enable the reader to become familiar with the terminology of statistics.

2 To develop an understanding of the techniques of data collection.

3 To develop an understanding of appropriate ways of presenting data.

4 To develop skills of interpretation and evaluation of data.

The use of numerical information

Business Studies is concerned with the process of decision making within the business context. Numerical information provides the raw material for much of that decision making. However, numerical information is only of value if it aids the process of decision making and is of relevance to the issue at hand. The raw, unprocessed figures obtained from research can be called **data**. After data has been processed into a form suitable for decision makers it can be called **information**.

Quantitative analysis transforms data into information. To accomplish this, a number of steps are involved.

1 The selection, collection and organizing of basic data.
2 The summarizing of essential features and relationships between variables.
3 The determination of patterns of behaviour, outcomes or future tendencies.

This places quantitative methods at the heart of business decision making, planning and control. External information of a quantified nature required by decision makers includes:

● size of the market;
● market shares;
● nature of customers;
● supply of raw materials and compounds.

Internal information relating to the following will prove invaluable to managers:

- orders in hand;
- future orders/contracts;
- credit levels;
- bad debts;
- complaints;
- suppliers' delivery periods;
- suppliers' prices;
- level of stock;
- usage of stock;
- value of stock;
- accidents;
- payroll costs;
- labour turnover;
- training completed;
- routine maintenance and cleaning of premises:
- short- and long-term forecasting;
- factory maintenance;
- machine breakdown:
- invoicing;
- targets;
- actual sales;
- projected sales;
- grievances;
- turnover.

In control situations, the information is required to highlight deviations from the norm. Hence, by analysing data, problems can be identified and referred to higher levels of management. This policy is known as **management by exception** – top management acts in exceptional circumstances when problems are identified.

Data collection

Data collected and used for its original purpose is known as **primary data**. It becomes **secondary data** when it is used for a purpose other than that for which it was collected. Secondary data costs less, but there are major problems. First, if the information has not been collected (or is not available), the researcher will be forced to obtain data from primary sources. Second, the fact that secondary data was collected for some other purpose reduces its usefulness. At least with primary data the decision maker has available information of known accuracy and known definitions.

Secondary data is often available in published form (such as government statistics, market research publications), but the reader should remember that our definition of secondary data as data collected originally for other purposes means that it also includes internal, non-published data (such as records of employee turnover, productivity, absenteeism).

Primary data is collected by means of surveys, observations, experiments and mechanical recording of facts. This is a subject we will return to in Chapter 15 when we discuss market research, but it must be emphasized that data is collected for a variety of reasons, of which market research is merely one.

For many purposes, data collected from the whole 'population' being examined would be prohibitively expensive and/or time-consuming. To reduce the cost of the data collection exercise, it is common to collect data from a sample of the total number of units under investigation. If a sample is used, answers to two related questions are required.

- How many units should be included in the sample?
- How is the sample to be chosen?

The sample should be representative of the population as a whole and of sufficient size to enable conclusions to be drawn about the whole population.

Presentation of data

After data has been collected, it needs to be presented in a form that communicates the information and enables conclusions to be drawn. As the purpose of the data is to aid decision making and to report back results (to facilitate control), it is necessary to choose a way of presenting the data that is clear, accurate and appropriate. The recipient should be able to interpret the material and, therefore, draw conclusions.

Tabulation

Tables are a non-graphical way of presenting a large quantity of data arranged in labelled rows and columns. To provide for rapid comprehension and assessment, it is essential that the material is dated, with sources and measurement units shown clearly. Tables convey a mass of information in an accurate way but they lack the visual impact of graphical representations.

Bar charts

Bar charts use bands of standard width (but varying lengths) to represent magnitudes. They can be used to illustrate comparisons over time or between items. A **compound bar chart** divides the bar into sections representing component parts. A **percentage component bar chart** consists of bars of the same height (representing 100 per cent) with components represented proportionately.

Bar charts facilitate comparison by virtue of their clear visual impact, but only relatively straightforward data can be shown in this way. In the case of the compound bar chart, only a few subsections can be shown and even then comparisons are difficult.

Bar charts are often confused with histograms but there is an essential distinction.

Histograms

The histogram is one of the most important of the various types of graphs used to depict business information and yet it is widely misunderstood. The histogram displays grouped data and the width of the bar is proportional to the class interval. The magnitude for a particular class is shown not by the *height* of the bar but by its *area*. Obviously, if class intervals are of equal length the histogram is similar to a bar chart, but where class intervals are not equal the histogram is very different.

This can be shown in the example below.

Income groups (£000)	No. of people (million)	Class interval length	Frequency density per £1000 (million)
10–10.99	1	£1000	1
11–11.99	2	£1000	2
12–14.99	6	£3000	2
15–20.00	5	£5000	1

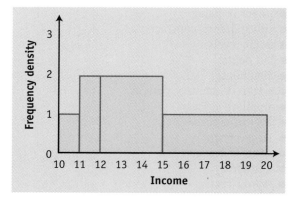

Figure 5.1 A histogram

When we produce a histogram to depict this information (see Figure 5.1), the 12–14.99 group has a bar the same height as that of the 11–11.99 group. The explanation is that although the size of one group is three times greater than that of the other, the class interval is also three times greater.

Another distinction between a histogram and a bar chart is that there are no gaps between the histogram bars. This explained by the fact that the data is continuous rather than discrete.

Frequency polygon

If we join up the mid-points of the top of each histogram bar we produce a many-sided figure which is known as a frequency polygon (see Figure 5.2). When the many sides are smoothed out, the

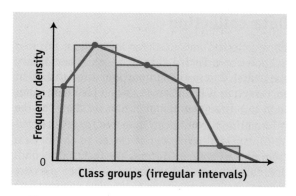

Figure 5.2 Frequency polygon – constructed by joining the mid-points of the histogram bars

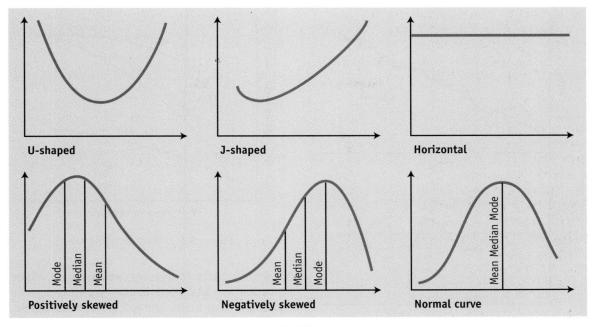

Figure 5.3 Typical frequency curves

result is known as a **frequency curve**. Frequency curves tend to conform to one of the following six types (see Figure 5.3):

● U-shaped;
● J-shaped;
● horizontal;
● positively skewed (to the left);
● negatively skewed (to the right);
● normal.

Pie charts

These are useful for depicting proportions, although, again, there is a limit to the number of items that can be included in an easily interpreted pie chart. Unless the proportions are written in each section it is difficult to use a pie chart other than to gain a general impression. To show change over time (as well as proportions) a second pie chart can be drawn.

It is important to remember that the total size is illustrated not by the radius or diameter of the pie but by its area. Hence, if a larger pie chart is drawn with a 4-cm radius, we should not infer from this that it represents twice the data of a 2-cm pie chart. (In fact, the larger pie represents data four times that of the smaller pie.)

Line graphs

Line graphs are a useful way of showing relationships such as growth over time. A line graph gives a sense of continuity that is lacking in a bar chart. The independent variable (say, time) is shown on the horizontal axis, while the dependent variable (such as output) is on the vertical axis. Line graphs combined with time series analysis can be used to separate out:

● the trend (long-term change);
● fluctuations around the trend (see Figure 5.4);
● random factors.

Strata charts

Strata charts combine a line graph with component sections depicting relative importance.

Semi-log graphs

Semi-log graphs show rates of change rather than

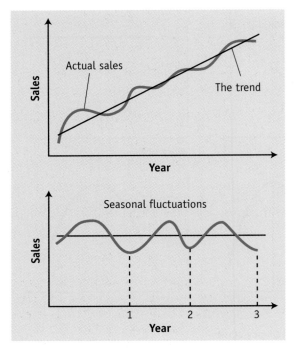

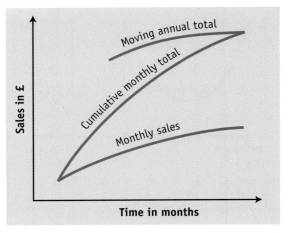

Figure 5.5 Z chart depicting sales

Figure 5.4 Analysis of time series to separate out the trend, fluctuations around the trend and seasonal fluctuations

magnitude. If the graph is a straight line, the data is changing at a constant percentage rate.

'Z' charts

A 'Z' chart is depicted in Figure 5.5. Notice that, plotted against time, we have:

- the original data showing current position (monthly sales);
- the cumulative total showing the position to date (cumulative monthly total);
- the moving annual total showing the trend. The moving annual total is obtained by adding a new month each time to replace a month from the previous year.

Pictograms and cartograms

Pictograms use pictures to represent data. Although the visual impact is strong, only simple and limited data can be shown.

Cartograms combine a map with graphs, symbols

and pie charts to present various data where location is considered important. It is a more pictorial than useful method of presenting data.

The Lorenz curve

This is useful for depicting the degree of equality/ inequality. Figure 5.6 illustrates a typical Lorenz curve. On the horizontal axis we have the cumulative percentage of people in a country; the vertical axis shows cumulative percentage of income earned.

In a situation of complete equality, 10 per cent of people would have 10 per cent of income, 50

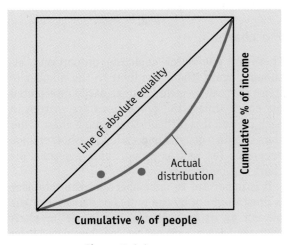

Figure 5.6 Lorenz curve

per cent of people would have 50 per cent of income and so on. In fact, inequality exists and, as the figure shows, the poorest 20 per cent have 10 per cent of income and the poorest 50 per cent have 30 per cent of income. The line of equal distribution (or absolute equality) is a benchmark. The further the Lorenz curve is from this line, the greater the inequality.

Lorenz curves can be used to illustrate inequality and the impact of taxes and benefits. A second Lorenz curve could be used to show the degree of equality after tax and benefits. If this is closer to the line of absolute equality, we can conclude that State intervention (in this hypothetical example) has reduced the inequality of income.

Making sense of data

The information that is collected has to be organized to enable us to make sense of it. This usually involves grouping data and measuring frequency. Frequency can be defined as the number of times an occurrence happens and to make sense of the data it is usual to identify three important characteristics of the frequency. These relate to:

● the measure of central tendency (that is, the average);
● the measure of dispersion (the spread of the data);
● the skewness (lopsidedness).

Central tendency

The central tendency (average) can be expressed in a number of ways:

● **mean** the sum of items divided by the number of them;
● **median** the value that divides the observations into two equal parts;
● **mode** the most frequently occurring observation.

In the example below, the mode is meaningless. However, in other situations the mean is of limited value as a measure of central tendency. For instance, if we added 200 to the series below,

---

Example

Calculate (a) the mean, (b) the median and (c) the mode of the following numbers:
12, 15, 8, 25, 12, 32, 31

Answer: The arithmetic mean from the above numbers is

12 + 15 + 8 + 25 + 12 + 32 + 31 = 135 ÷ 7 = 19.3

The **median** is 15 as, if the numbers are placed in rank order, there are three numbers below 15 and three above.

The **mode** is 12 as this is the only number that occurs more than once.

---

we would calculate the arithmetic mean as 335 ÷ 8 = 41.9. As only one number exceeds the mean average, this particular calculation tells us very little. The merits and otherwise of the measures of central tendency are shown in Table 5.1.

In the above example it is relatively easy to calculate the mean and to identify the mode and the median. The mean ($\bar{x}$ or x bar) is equal to

$$\frac{\text{the sum of values}}{\text{the number of values}} = \frac{\Sigma x}{n} \text{ where } \Sigma \text{ is 'the sum of'.}$$

The mode can be identified as the most frequently occurring value and to discover the median we simply rank the values and divide them into two equal parts (or take the mean of the two middle items in the case of an even number of values).

However, data used in business is likely to take the form of a frequency distribution. Moreover, the data is likely to be grouped. Let us consider measures of central tendency of a frequency distribution. The following example is of the number of items sold by sales staff on a particular day. Five salespeople sold 10 items, 6 sold 12 and so on.

Quantity sold (x)	No. of salespeople (f)	fx
10	5	50
12	6	72
13	4	52
	15	174

Table 5.1 Measures of central tendency (averages)

Type	Definition	Advantages	Disadvantages
Arithmetic mean	Sum of items divided by the number of them	Uses all the data Further statistical processing possible	Distorted by an extreme value The resulting figure may not be a typical value
Median	Middle value in order of size	Not distorted by extremes Can be computed from incomplete data	Further statistical processing impossible
Mode	The most frequently occurring value in a distribution	Represents a typical value Unaffected by extremes	Further processing not possible Does not use all values

The arithmetic mean is equal to

$$\frac{fx}{x} = \frac{174}{15} = 11.6$$

On average, then, each salesperson sold 11.6 items. The modal class is 12 items as this has the greatest frequency. The median value relates to the sales of the $\frac{n+1}{2}$ or eighth person.

This person sold 12 items.

Grouped frequency data adds a further complication. The example below is of the weekly pay of a firm's employees. Pay levels have been grouped into various bands, with the number of workers in each band shown in the second column. As we do not have any particular value and have no way of knowing the distribution within the bands, we base our calculations on the mid-point in each band.

Pay per week £	Number of workers f	Mid-point x	fx
140 to under 160	12	150	1800
160 to under 180	18	170	3060
180 to under 200	10	190	1900
	$\Sigma = 40$		$\Sigma = 6760$

$$x = \frac{\Sigma fx}{\Sigma f} = \frac{6760}{40} = 169$$

The modal class is £160 to £180 as this is the income band of the highest number of employees. The median value is the the weekly income of the $\frac{40+1}{2}$ or the 20.5th employee. This person earns between £160 and £180 per week but the problem is, where does this person figure within the band? The 20th person is 8th in the band of 18 people and the 21st is 9th. To calculate the median for the 20th person we multiply £20 (the width of the band) by $\frac{8}{18}$ to get £8.89. We do the same for the 21st person – £20 × $\frac{9}{18}$ – and get £10. The median value is therefore midway between the two, giving a value of £160 plus $\frac{£8.89 + £10}{2}$ or £169.45. If the frequency within the band had been an odd number, it would not have been necessary to split the difference between the two.

The exercises at the end of this chapter will help you develop competence in this kind of calculation.

Index numbers

Index numbers are designed to show changes in a value (such as a price or quantity) over time. The index number itself is a pure number, which is given the value of 100 at the starting point (known as the **base year**). Any percentage rise (or fall) over the value at base year is shown by an equivalent movement above (or below) the base figure. This is illustrated in Table 5.2.

In Table 5.2, 1980 was chosen as the base year for both indices. The base year should be carefully chosen because if an untypical or unrepresentative year (say, a slump year) is used it will produce a distorted picture.

Table 5.2 Index of output and manpower

	Output (tonnes)	Index of output	Labour	Index of labour
1980	500,000	100	1,000	100
1985	600,000	120	900	90
1990	750,000	150	1,280	128
1995	1,000,000	200	1,300	130
1998	1,100,000	220	1,500	150
2000	1,200,000	240	1,500	150

Table 5.3 Constructing an inflation index

Item	Price rise	Weighting	Price rise × Weighting
Food	4%	250	1,000
Housing	20%	400	8,000
Others	10%	350	3,500
		1,000	12,500 = 12.5
			1,000

The 20 per cent rise in output in 1985 is shown by the index moving from 100 to 120. In 1990 the index stood at 150, which is 50 per cent over base but 25 per cent over the 1985 figure. The 2000 index number will be:

$$\frac{1,200,000 \times 100}{500,000} = 240$$

We should not be puzzled by the labour index also having a value of 100 in 1980. This 100 refers to the number of workers employed in the base year. One of the advantages of an index is that it makes it possible to compare trends in factors measured in unlike units. In this case it shows trends in output against trends in the labour force.

We can see that, although output rose from 100 to 240 (140 per cent) it was achieved with a 50 per cent increase in labour employed. This represents a significant increase in the productivity of the workforce.

The most famous index in use in the UK is the **Retail Price Index (RPI)**, which measures the trends in the average level of prices. Often known as the cost of living index, it is widely quoted as the inflation rate experienced by the average family in the UK. To understand the RPI, it is first necessary to understand the concept of a weighted average – that is, an average that takes the relative importance of different variables into account.

The first step in constructing the RPI is to find out how the average family spends its income. This is done by means of the Family Expenditure Survey, which is a sample survey of the expenditure of 10,000 households. This enables statisticians to attach weights to various items of spending. The weights are designed to reflect the relative importance of the various items. For instance, a 10 per cent rise in the price of bread will have a greater impact on family finances than a 10 per cent (or even 100 per cent) rise in the price of matches. This fact must be taken into account when devising the index.

After attaching weights (out of 1000) to 11 categories of goods and services (food, alcohol, tobacco, housing, fuel and lighting, household durables, clothing, transport, services, meals out and miscellaneous goods), the statisticians take samples to calculate the average price change in each category. We are now in a position to calculate the weighted average price change. In Table 5.3 the average household buys three categories of goods: food, housing and others. The items absorb different proportions of household spending and their prices rise at different rates. What is its average price rise?

The crude average of price rises is:

4 + 20 + 10 ÷ 3 = 11.3%

but this has not taken relative importance into account. To calculate the weighted average, we multiply the price relative (price in the year relative to the price in a previous year) by the weighting. The resulting figures are added together and divided by the total weighting to give a weighted average inflation rate of 12.5 per cent, which is then expressed as an index number. The weighted average exceeds the crude average because of the high weighting given to the item that experienced the greatest price increase. Therefore, the 20 per cent rise in housing costs raised the average because of the higher weighting attached to this item.

The 12.5 per cent inflation during the time period is then expressed as an index number. If prior to this inflation the index stood at 150, it would now be:

$$150 \times \frac{112.5}{100} = 168.75$$

One major problem for statisticians is that the relative importance of the various items changes over time. For instance, the proportion of household spending going on food has fallen, while that going on housing has risen.

There are two approaches to this problem. The **Laspeyres** approach uses weights determined for the base year throughout the series. The **Paasche** approach uses weights based on current values. This means that the weighting is constantly updated to reflect the current situation. Clearly, the latter method is more time-consuming and costly to construct, but the updating provides a better reflection of the current situation. A compromise between the base-weighted Laspeyres index and the current-weighted Paasche index is to revise weights periodically rather than continually.

There are other problems associated with the RPI.

- It only tells us about inflation as experienced by the *average* household. Any household that does not conform to the average will experience inflation at different rates. Consequently, the RPI will not be a good indication of the inflation affecting pensioners or large families.
- International comparisons are difficult because of international differences in methods of construction. For instance the RPI in the UK includes mortgage interest whereas this is not the case in other countries. Consequently, a rise in mortgage rates pushes up the UK's official inflation rate, but this would not be the case in other countries.
- Changing patterns of spending and changing lifestyles mean that the value of the RPI for historical comparisons is limited to comparatively short periods.
- The RPI reflects changes in indirect taxation but not in direct taxation. Consequently, a shift from direct taxes (such as income tax) to indirect taxes (such as VAT) will push up

the RPI. As such shifts have been government policy since 1979, it is not surprising that the government has tried to express the inflation rate in different ways. The government and commentators now distinguish between the **headline rate** (of the RPI) and the **underlying rate** (which excludes changes in the RPI brought about by changes in mortgage rates and local taxation).

- The publicity given to the monthly RPI figures might aggravate inflation, contributing as it does to 'inflationary expectations'.

The RPI is not the only measure of inflation. The **Producer Price Index** measures changes in material and product prices. This shows inflation as it affects producers rather than consumers and, in many respects, it is more important for the business community. Moreover, it provides advance warning of retail price inflation trends. Finally, price indices can (and are) constructed for various groups for whom the RPI is of little value. For example, the Pensioners RPI indicates price changes in goods and services purchased by the retired.

Although we often associate indices with measures of inflation, we should also remember they are merely a way of expressing any change over time. Therefore, they can be used to present data on changes in values (such as sales revenue) and physical quantities (output, volume of sales, manpower). The great advantage of reducing a series to an index is that the reader is given data in a form from which it is easy to draw conclusions about percentage changes.

Measures of dispersion

Measures of central tendency provide an indication of location. To make sense of the data it is also useful to have an idea of the extent to which the data is spread from the central tendency. There are several measures of dispersion.

- **Range** the difference between the highest and lowest value in a set of data.
- The **interquartile range** the difference between the upper quartile and the lower quartile (that is, between the top 25 per cent and the bottom 25 per cent).

- The **mean deviation** the arithmetic mean of the absolute difference of each value from the mean.
- The **variance** and the **standard deviation**.

We will look at range, interquartile range and standard deviation in more detail.

The range

This is easy to calculate and easy to understand. We merely need to identify the highest and lowest values in a set of data and then take the latter from the former. Thus, if daily output varies from 250,000 to 220,000, the range is said to be 30,000. Although this gives some indication of the extent to which the data varies, it has only taken the two extremes into account. Both extremes might be very untypical, thus giving a distorted picture of the extent of variation.

The interquartile range

The **interquartile range** is the gap between the top of the bottom quarter and the bottom of the top quarter. In other words, the interquartile range covers the middle half of the set of values. It is easy to calculate in the case of discrete data – we merely line the data up in rank order and then separate out the bottom and top quarters.

However, as we saw in relation to the calculation of the mean, it is more complicated when we are dealing with grouped data. Consider the data below relating to employee absence.

No. of days absent	No. of employees	Cumulative frequency	
0	20	20	←
1	3	23	Lower
2	6	29	quartile
3	8	37	←
			upper quartile
4	6	43	
5	2	45	
6	3	48	
15	1	49	
	49		

The formula for the lower quartile pointer is:

$$\frac{n + 1}{4} \text{ where } n = \text{number of values.}$$

There are 49 employees and, therefore, the lower quartile pointer is:

$$\frac{49 + 1}{4} = \frac{50}{4} = 12.5$$

The lower quartile lies between the 12th and 13th values and from this we conclude that the people in the lower quartile had no absences. The upper quartile pointer is found by:

$$\frac{3(n + 1)}{4} = \frac{3 \times 50}{4} = \frac{150}{4} = 37.5$$

This lies halfway between the 37th and the 38th values – 3.5 days. We would conclude that the interquartile range for employee absence was 3.5 – 0 = 3.5 days. This is a more valid figure than 15, which would constitute the range of this data.

Standard deviation

This, the most important measure of dispersion, is the average deviation from the mean of a set of data. The greater the spread of the data, the higher the value of the standard deviation for the data.

The formula for calculating standard deviation is:

$$\sqrt{\frac{\sum (x - \bar{x})^2}{n}}$$

Where: Σ is the sum of
x is an observation
$\bar{x}$ is the mean
n is the number of observations.

Example
The weekly sales of a product over a 5-week period are 12, 18, 20, 25 and 30 units. This works out as a mean of:

$$\frac{105}{5} = 21 \text{ units per week}$$

Hence, $\bar{x}$ is equal to 21 and n is 5.

x	$x - \bar{x}$	$(x - \bar{x})^2$
12	−9	81
18	−3	9
20	−1	1
25	4	16
30	9	81

The sum of the five $(x - \bar{x})^2$ values is 188. Notice that by squaring the $x - \bar{x}$ value we eliminate the negative values. The sum of the squared deviations from the mean is then divided by n (5) to get 37.6. The standard deviation is the square root of this number, which is therefore 6.13.

The steps taken to arrive at this figure are as follows:

1 calculate the arithmetic mean ($\bar{x}$);
2 subtract the mean from each value to arrive at the deviation from the mean ($x - \bar{x}$);
3 square the deviations, thus eliminating the negative values $(x - \bar{x})^2$;
4 add up the squared deviations $\Sigma(x - \bar{x})^2$;
5 divide this total by the number of values $\dfrac{\Sigma(x - \bar{x})^2}{x}$. This is known as the variance;
6 finally, calculate the square root of the variance to obtain a value for the standard deviation.

We will see on page 70 that the standard deviation of a normal distribution opens up numerous possibilities for analysis and problem solving.

Skewness

In a normal distribution, the curve is symmetrical and the mean, mode and median all occur at the same point. However, many distributions are asymmetrical and pushed to one side. Figures 5.7 and 5.8 show two such asymmetrical distributions. Notice that one thing they have in common is a long tail pushed to one side. Unlike a symmetrical distribution, the mean, mode and median no longer coincide.

Figure 5.7 is positively skewed. Notice that the mean is dragged to the right by a small number

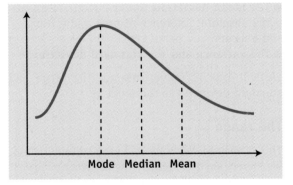

Figure 5.7 Positively skewed distribution

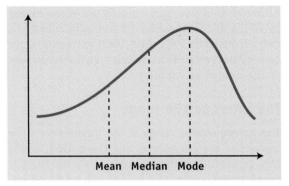

Figure 5.8 Negatively skewed distribution

of high values. The distribution in Figure 5.8 is negatively skewed, with the mean dragged to the left by a small number of low values.

What is correlation?

Correlation concerns the relationship between two variables, such as:

● advertising expenditure and sales revenue;
● pay rates and absenteeism;
● the age structure of the company's machinery and the level of output.

To assist in the formulation of policy, it is useful to know if there is an association between such variables, the strength of the association and the direction of the relationship. Intuitively we would expect a strong relationship between expenditure on advertising and the level of sales revenue. Moreover, we would expect it to be a direct relationship in which the two variables rose together. Conversely, there is likely to be an inverse relationship between pay rates and absenteeism in that a rise in one variable is likely to be coupled with a fall in the other variable.

To identify and measure the correlation between two variables it is first necessary to observe what is happening. A **hypothesis** (a much misunderstood word) is defined as a suggested explanation for a group of facts that is accepted as a basis for further verification or is accepted as likely to be true. In other words, it is a tentative theory put forward for further investigation. To verify the hypothesis, it is necessary to collect data in a systematic way – for example, annual expenditure on advertising and the corresponding level of sales revenue. This data can then be plotted on a scatter diagram.

Scatter diagrams

Scatter diagrams are used to illustrate the relationship between two variables. The independent variable (the assumed causal factor) is plotted on the horizontal axis, while the corresponding value of the dependent variable (the assumed consequence) is plotted on the vertical axis. For example, a scatter diagram to illustrate the impact of different levels of advertising on sales revenue would have advertising expenditure on the horizontal axis and sales revenue on the vertical axis. The various combinations of advertising spending and sales revenue are then plotted in order to detect a pattern.

Figure 5.9(a) shows a number of plot points through which is drawn a line of best fit. There is a mathematical technique for constructing the line but with good eye and a ruler we can draw it in its approximate position. Figure 5.9(b) illustrates a strong positive correlation in which the two variables move in the same direction. However, the scatter points are close to the line but not on it. This means that the correlation is strong but not perfect. In Figure 5.9(c) the plot points are in a straight line rising upwards to the right. Here correlation is positive and perfect.

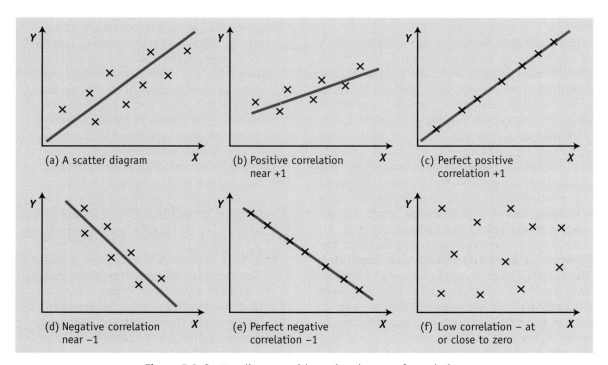

(a) A scatter diagram

(b) Positive correlation near +1

(c) Perfect positive correlation +1

(d) Negative correlation near −1

(e) Perfect negative correlation −1

(f) Low correlation – at or close to zero

Figure 5.9 Scatter diagrams with varying degrees of correlation

Figures 5.9(d) and (e) illustrate negative correlation. A rise in the value of the dependent variable is accompanied by a fall in the value of the independent one. For instance, a rise in price will, other things remaining equal, be followed by a fall in the quantity sold. In the case of (d) the correlation appears strong but not perfect whereas that in (e) is perfect.

The plot points in Figure 5.9(f) have no discernible pattern and, in consequence, we would conclude that there is low, or even no, correlation between the variables.

The scatter diagram enables us to identify the direction of correlation and provides a rough indication of the strength of correlation. However, it lacks the precision necessary for further analysis.

Risk and uncertainty

Risk is a basic feature of business life. The future is uncertain and business decisions are made in the absence of perfect knowledge of the future course of events. Although the words risk and uncertainty are often used interchangeably there is an important distinction to be made between the two.

Uncertainty is defined as the unpredictability of the future. It arises because it is difficult to predict changes and estimate accurately the likelihood of events occurring. **Risk**, on the other hand, describes situations where information about the extent of possible losses exists and, moreover, about the likelihood of such losses occurring. For instance, it is difficult to quantify the likelihood of success of a new product because of the uncertain external environment. However, it is relatively easy to calculate the likelihood of a building suffering fire damage based on data relating to the risk of fire damage.

We are concerned with situations in which the likelihood of an event occurring can be quantified. This is known as probability. If an event is impossible (such as a sub-three-minute mile in present circumstances) it has a probability of zero. If an event is certain to occur (for example, death, which is the only total certainty), it has probability of 1 (one). The closer to 1, the greater the probability of the event occurring.

Approaches to probability

There are three ways to assess probability, although the method used will depend upon the circumstances.

1 **Theoretical probability** This is based on an analysis of the situation. For instance, if a dice is known to be fair and not 'loaded', the probability of throwing a 6 is 0.1667. All six sides have an equal chance of appearing on the top of a dice and, therefore, each side has a one-sixth chance. This type of probability, which is based on a theoretical analysis of the particular circumstance, can be applied to situations where there is a finite number of possible outcomes that can be defined in advance.

2 **Statistical probability** This is based on repeated trials or past data. For instance, if we threw a dice 1000 times and discovered that 6 came up 167 times, we would conclude that the probability of 6 coming up is 0.167. It is the same answer as before, but the difference is the method by which we came up with the answer. In the theoretical approach, we analysed the situation to conclude that 6 would come up on one-sixth of all throws. In the statistical approach, we repeated the test 1000 times to conclude that it came up on one-sixth of all throws and, therefore, that there was a 1 in 6 chance of 6 coming up on the next throw. A more business-oriented application would be to conclude that if, during the last 100 weeks, a shop's sales exceeded £100,000 on 320 occasions, the probability of exceeding £100,000 sales next week would be 0.32.

3 **Subjective probability** This is a subjective assessment of probability based on a mixture of information, intuition and expertise. In fact, for a statement of subjective probability to be a reliable estimate, the person making the estimate must be an expert. Obviously, subjective probability lacks the precision and accuracy of the theoretical and statistical measures of probability. However, in most business situations probability tends to mean subjective probability.

The basic rules of probability

We can express the probability of certain events and certain combinations of events occurring by applying a series of rules.

Single events

There are six sides to a dice and each side has an equal chance of coming up. The probability of any one side coming up is therefore equal to one-sixth.

The probability of an event (A) occurring is:

$$P(A) = \frac{\text{Number of ways in which event can happen}}{\text{The total number of possible outcomes}}$$

If the probability of throwing a six is one-sixth, what is the probability of throwing any other number? Clearly, it is 5 times one-sixth (five-sixths). The probability of the non-occurrence of a six is equal to 1 – one-sixth, or five-sixths. This is the second rule to remember:

$$P(\bar{A}) = 1 - P(A)$$

where $P(\bar{A})$ is the probability of the non-occurrence of event A and $P(A)$ is the probability of its occurrence. As a six must either be thrown or not thrown, the sum of the probabilities must equal 1 (certainty).

$$P(A) + P(\bar{A}) = 1$$

Mutually exclusive events

Two (or more) events are said to be mutually exclusive if the occurrence of one of them excludes the occurrence of the other(s). In other words, only one of the events can happen. For instance, throwing a six and throwing a five on a single dice are mutually exclusive events. To calculate the probability of throwing either a six or a five we use the addition rule:

$$P(A \text{ or } B) = P(A) + P(B)$$

where A is six, B is five and P( ) is probability.

The probability of throwing either a six or five is one-sixth + one-sixth = one-third. The probability of throwing neither a six nor a five is 1 – one-third = two-thirds.

Independent events

Two (or more) events are said to be independent if the occurrence or non-occurrence of one of them in no way affects the occurrence or non-occurrence of the other(s). With two dice the probability of throwing a five with one is independent of any particular score with the other. But what is the probability of throwing both a five and a six with the two dice?

This is calculated by using the multiplication rule:

$$P(A \text{ and } B) = P(A) \times P(B)$$

The answer is the product of the individual probabilities so it is one-sixth × one-sixth = one thirty-sixth.

The probability of throwing three successive sixes is one-sixth × one-sixth × one-sixth = one two hundred and sixteenth.

Conditional events

Two (or more) events are said to be conditional when the probability of one event taking place is subject to the proviso that another event has already taken place. P(A/B) refers to the probability of A occurring given that B has occurred. To illustrate this situation consider removing coloured marbles from a bag containing eight marbles, of which two are red. The marbles are removed 'blind' by picking them out one at a time. The probability of taking one red marble at the first attempt is two-eighths, or one-quarter. If one red marble has been taken, the conditional probability of picking a second red marble is one-seventh (there are only seven marbles left, of which one is red). Hence, the probability of picking two red marbles is one-quarter × one-seventh = one twenty-eighth.

The multiplication rule for conditional probability is given by:

$$P(AB) = P(A) \times P(B/A)$$

where $P(AB)$ is the probability that both events occur, $P(A)$ is the probability that A occurs, and $P(B/A)$ is the probability that B will occur given that A has already occurred.

To calculate the probability that only one red marble is picked the addition rule is used:

P(A or B) = P(A) + P(B) – P(AB)

where P(A) is the probability of red at the first attempt and P(B) is the probability of red at the second attempt. In both cases this is one-quarter. However, we deduct the probability of picking two red marbles, which is one twenty-eighth. The probability of picking just one red marble is therefore one-quarter + one-quarter – one twenty-eighth = thirteen twenty-eighths.

Normal distribution

If we plotted on graph paper the height of everyone in the UK population, the resulting graph would be bell-shaped and it would possess distinct and useful properties. The graph would be of normal distribution, which is defined as a continuous probability distribution in which the horizontal axis represents all the possible values of a variable and the vertical axis represents the probability of these values occurring. The distinctive properties of normal distribution (see Figure 5.10) are that:

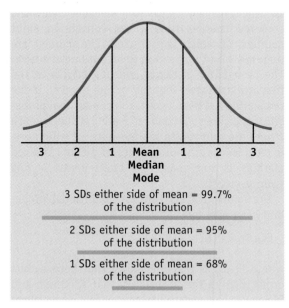

3 SDs either side of mean = 99.7% of the distribution

2 SDs either side of mean = 95% of the distribution

1 SDs either side of mean = 68% of the distribution

Figure 5.10 Normal distribution curve

- it is symmetrical and therefore has zero skewness;
- it is unimodal (one peak);
- the mean, median and mode all have the same value and therefore pass through the peak;
- 68 per cent of the values are within one standard deviation of the mean;
- 95 per cent of the values are within two standard deviations of the mean;
- 99 per cent of the values are within three standard deviations of the mean;
- although the base is equal to six standard deviations (approximately) the curve extends infinitely at each end.

If a lightbulb lasts on average for 2500 hours with a standard deviation of 300 hours, we can say that from a batch of 10,000, 68 per cent will last for some time between 2200 and 2800 hours (2500 plus or minus 300), 95 per cent will last for some time between 1900 and 3100 hours and 99 per cent will last for some time between 1600 and 3400 hours. These facts might be important when a firm makes claims about the life of its products. More importantly, knowledge of normal distribution is important when conclusions are attempted from sample data (statistical inference) or when hypotheses are tested.

To illustrate the use of normal distribution, let us return to the lightbulb example. The mean life is 2500 hours, but there is a standard deviation of 300 hours. What is the probability of a particular bulb lasting for more than 2900 hours? This is 400 hours above the mean. In terms of standard deviations, it is 400/300 or 1.33 standard deviations from the mean. This is known as a Z score, the formula for which is:

$$Z = \frac{\text{Original value} - \text{mean value}}{\text{Standard deviation}}$$

At this point we need to consult a table of Z scores (see Table 5.4 and Figure 5.11). The Z score table tells us the area under the curve at a particular Z value. For a Z value of 1.33 the score is 0.4082. Fifty per cent of light bulbs have a life of less than 2500 hours; 40.82 per cent have a life of between 2500 and 2900 hours. Therefore 90.82

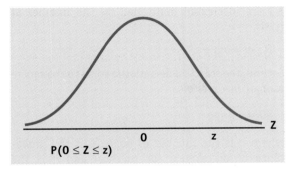

Figure 5.11 The Z value of a particular point can be read off the accompanying table, 5.4

Table 5.4 Area under a curve of normal distribution

z			z	
			1.5	0.4332
0.0	0.0000		1.6	0.4452
0.1	0.0398		1.7	0.4554
0.2	0.0793		1.8	0.4641
0.3	0.1179		1.9	0.4713
0.4	0.1554		2.0	0.4772
			2.1	0.4821
0.5	0.1915		2.2	0.4861
0.6	0.2258		2.3	0.4893
0.7	0.2580		2.4	0.4918
0.8	0.2881			
0.9	0.3159		2.5	0.4938
			2.6	0.4953
1.0	0.3413		2.7	0.4965
1.1	0.3643		2.8	0.4974
1.2	0.3849		2.9	0.4981
1.3	0.4032			
1.4	0.4192		3.0	0.4987
			3.1	0.4990
			3.2	0.4993
			3.3	0.4995
			3.4	0.4997

A Z score of 2.5 means that 49.38% of the area under the curve lies between the mean and Z

per cent of bulbs last for 2900 hours or less, leaving 9.18 per cent with a life of more than 2900 hours.

Binomial distribution

The **binomial distribution** is a discrete probability distribution that has a number of business applications, such as quality control or calculating the probability of use of a combination of telephone lines or petrol pumps. It applies where there are only two possible outcomes in a situation – heads or tails, success or failure, engaged or vacant.

Let us start with a very simple example. The probability of a coin landing heads up is 0.5. The probability of two coins landing heads up is 0.5 × 0.5 = 0.25. The probability of both coins landing tails up is also 0.25. However, the probability of the coins landing so that one is heads up and the other heads down is 2 × 0.25 or 0.5.

The reason for this being twice 0.25 is that the combined event can happen in two ways.

A more practical application concerns the use of telephone lines. Suppose there are two lines and the probability of a particular line being engaged at a moment in time is 0.1. Logically the probability of the line being free is 1 – 0.1 = 0.9. The tree diagram (Figure 5.12) shows that

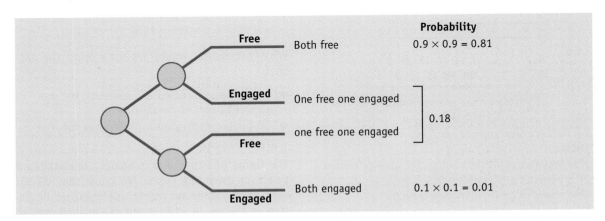

Figure 5.12 A probability tree

71

the probability of both lines being engaged is $0.1 \times 0.1 = 0.01$. The probability of neither line being engaged is $0.9 \times 0.9 = 0.81$. The probability of only one line being engaged is $1 - (0.81 + 0.01) = 0.18$ as, logically, there are only three outcomes to the test (both, neither and only one engaged).

The probabilities in the above example can be summarized as $p^2 + 2pq + q^2 = 1$, where p is the probability of the line being engaged and q is the probability of the line being free. This must equal one as all outcomes are covered. If there are three lines, the various outcomes can be summarized as $p^3 + 3p^2q + 3pq^2 + q^3 = 1$. If the number of lines is increased further, the equation becomes even more complicated, although in all cases it can be reduced to $(p + q)^n$ when p is the probability of the event occurring, q is the probability of it not occurring and n is the number of trials. We can expand the binomial for any value of n. Each successive term in the equation refers to different combinations of occurrence/non-occurrence of the event. The rules for expanding the binomial are summarized in Figure 5.13.

The binomial distribution has other properties that make it very useful in decision making. First, the mean of a binomial distribution is equal to np – that is, the probability of the event in which we are interested multiplied by the number of trials.

Mean = np

Second, the standard deviation is equal to the square root of $n \times p \times q$:

$$SD = \sqrt{npq}$$

where n is the number of trials, p is the probability of occurrence (or success) and q is the probability of failure.

The following example is designed to demonstrate the value of this property. Assume that a sample of 15 items is tested and that there is a 0.9 probability of an item being passed as satisfactory. What is the expected number of satisfactory items in a sample of 15 and what is the standard deviation?

The expected number of satisfactory items:

$$= np = 15 \times 0.9 = 13.5$$

Standard deviation $= \sqrt{npq} =$

$$\sqrt{15 \times 0.9 \times 0.1} = \sqrt{1.35} = 1.16$$

As the number of trials grows, the binomial distribution approaches the normal distribution. This opens up new areas of statistical analysis involving the drawing of conclusions from a sample.

Suppose a sample of 1000 people were asked a yes/no question such as expressing a preference for one product over another. The mean value is $1000 \times 0.5 = 500$. The standard deviation is equal to:

$$\sqrt{1000 \times 0.5 \times 0.5} = 15.8$$

What conclusion would we draw from the fact that:

- 516 people expressed a preference for one product?
- 550 people expressed a preference for one product?

The figure of 516 is approximately one standard deviation from the mean. We know that 68 per cent of all values are within one standard deviation of the mean. This is not really sufficient to be confident that the majority of the population

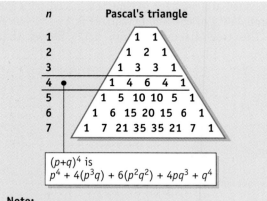

Note:
The sequence of numbers follows the appropriate line.
The power of p is in descending order.
The power of q is in ascending order.

Figure 5.13 The binomial expansion

will have a similar preference. The figure of 550, on the other hand, is more than three standard deviations from the mean. Three standard deviations either side of the mean cover over 99 per cent of values. Consequently we can be fairly sure that the view of the majority in the sample will reflect the view of the majority of the population.

Notice that the examples we have looked at are drawn from two important areas of business: quality control and market research based on a sample survey. In both cases, there is a margin of error – because the results are based on probability – but the application of statistical analysis enables decision makers to have a high degree of confidence in the data.

Key concepts

Binomial distribution A probability distribution for a dichotomous variable, such as success/failure, in/out, yes/no.

Binomial expansion The result of multiplying out the binomial formula for a particular value of n.

Class interval A subdivision within a frequency distribution.

Correlation The degree to which change in one variable is related to change in another.

Index numbers Numbers that measure the magnitude of change over time.

Mean A measure of central tendency. The average.

Measure of dispersion Measures of the spread or variation in the observations.

Median The middle value that divides the observations in two.

Mode The most frequently occurring observation in a frequency distribution.

Moving average The calculation of successive averages over time to identify the trend in a time series.

Normal distribution A standard, continuous probability distribution. It describes many situations where observations are spread symmetrically around the mean. Ninety-nine per cent of all values in a normal distribution are within three standard deviations of the mean.

Population The totality from which samples are drawn.

Primary data Information collected at first hand.

Range The difference between the highest and lowest value. The spread of the data.

Sample A number of observations from a subgroup of the population made up to be representative of the population.

Skewness Deviation from symmetry.

Exercises

1 Construct histograms to illustrate the data below.

(a)

Age groups of employees	Frequency No. of employees
16–under 21	30
21–under 26	18
26–under 31	18
31–under 41	20
41–under 51	25
51–under 65	24

(b) Life of electric bulbs

Hours	Frequency No. of bulbs
300–under 350	30
350–under 400	40
400–under 500	90
500–under 600	60
600–under 800	60

2 Monthly sales in two successive years are shown in the following table:

Month	Year 1	Year 2
January	50	60
February	90	100
March	100	100
April	120	140
May	150	150
June	180	190
July	190	200
August	200	200
September	150	180
October	120	140
November	70	100
December	40	50

Construct a Z chart to illustrate:
(a) monthly sales;
(b) the cumulative monthly sales;
(c) the moving annual total of sales for the period July year 1 to July year 2.

3 From a sample of his crop a farmer discovered the number of peas in each pod to be distributed as follows:

No. of peas	3	4	5	6	7	8
No. of pods	10	10	30	38	25	5

Calculate the mean number of peas per pod.

4 A long-distance bus company collected data on the arrival times of its buses on a particular day.

Minutes late/early	No. of buses
Early	10
On time	30
Up to 15 mins late	30
15 to under 30 mins late	45
30 to under 60 mins late	10

(a) What proportion of buses arrived late?
(b) Of the late buses, what is the mean number of minutes late?

5 Study the data below and calculate the percentage rise in output between:
(a) Year 1 and Year 2;
(b) Year 2 and Year 3;
(c) Year 2 and Year 4.

Index of output

Year 1	100
Year 2	120
Year 3	125
Year 4	135

6 Convert the output figures below into an index using Year 1 as the base year (= 100).

	Output in tonnes (000)
Year 1	160
Year 2	180
Year 3	220
Year 4	260
Year 5	290

7 Convert the output data below into an index using Year 2 as the base year (= 100).

Year	000 tonnes
Year 1	160
Year 2	180
Year 3	220
Year 4	260
Year 5	290

8 Convert the following data into two indices, using Year 1 as the base year (= 100) in each case. Comment on trends in productivity.

	Output (tonnes) (millions)	No. of employees
Year 1	2	1500
Year 2	2.1	1600
Year 3	2.1	1700
Year 4	2.4	1700
Year 5	2.8	1800

9 (a) Calculate the weighted average of:
(i)

Item	Weight	×	Price rise	
A	30	×	5%	=
B	20	×	20%	=
C	25	×	3%	=
D	25	×	2%	=
			Sum	=
	100			
				=

(ii)

Item	Weight	×	Price rise	
A	80	×	2%	=
B	20	×	6%	=
C	40	×	4%	=
D	30	×	3%	=
E	30	×	5%	=
			Sum	=
	200			
				=

10 Express the following data as a price index.

Year 1	Base year
Year 2	10% up on base
Year 3	20% up on base
Year 4	5% up on Year 3

11 Calculate the interquartile range for deliveries from the following data.

Delivery time (in days)	Frequency
5	10
6	12
7	20
8	30
9	20
10	8

12 The distribution of salaries paid to the 40 employees of a small company is shown in the table below.

Salary from £000	to below £000	Frequency (No. of employees)
6	8	5
8	10	6
10	12	6
12	14	7
14	16	8
16	18	3
18	20	4
20	30	1

Calculate:
(a) the mean, median and mode;
(b) the interquartile range.

13 Study the data below and calculate:

(a) the mean;
(b) the variance;
(c) the standard deviation.

Value (£)	Frequency
6	6
7	8
8	12
9	14
10	10
11	4

14 The duration of the telephone calls made by an employee were recorded for one month.

Duration (minutes) at least	less than	No. of calls
0	3	40
3	6	69
6	9	38
9	12	31
12	15	15
15	18	8

Calculate:
(a) the mean;
(b) the variance;
(c) the standard deviation of the duration of the calls.

15 A manufacturing firm is considering using one of two delivery firms. Their charges are broadly comparable but their delivery times over a three-month period are as follows.

Delivery time in days	Speedy Service Limited Frequency	High Speed Carriers Limited Frequency
2		6
3		8
4		5
5	10	19
6	30	45
7	55	40
8	20	29
9	12	12
10	2	10
11		5
12		5
14		2
15		2

For each carrier calculate:
(a) the cumulative frequency;
(b) the percentage cumulative frequency;
(c) the arithmetic mean;
(d) the range;
(e) the interquartile range of delivery times.

16 From the data below, calculate the range and the interquartile range of the weekly pay of 100 employees.

Pay (£)	No. of employees
90–99.99	20
100–109.99	25
110–119.99	20
120–129.99	10
130–139.99	10
140–149.99	10
150–159.99	5

17 A shop that holds 50 units of an item at the start of each week is concerned that this is too high a level of stock. Weekly sales of the item during the past two years have been as follows:

No. of items sold	No. of weeks
1–20	6
21–30	20
31–35	40
36–40	35
41–50	3
	104 weeks

(a) Identify the modal group and calculate the arithmetic mean and median value of the above distribution.
(b) Assess the appropriateness of the three measures of central tendency in the circumstances.
(c) Construct a histogram to illustrate the data.
(d) If each item makes a contribution (to fixed costs and profits) of £30, calculate the reduction in annual contribution that would result from maximum stock levels being set at 38 at the start of each week. State the assumptions you have made in arriving at your answer.

18 The table below shows the distribution of income for executives employed by a large public company in each of two years.

£	Year 2	Year 1
20,001–25,000	400	350
25,001–30,000	100	80
30,001–35,000	50	48
35,001–40,000	40	30
40,001–50,000	40	20
50,001–60,000	8	7
60,001–80,000	2	Nil
80,001–100,000	1	Nil

(a) Calculate:
(i) the arithmetic mean pay;
(ii) the median pay.

(b) Stating your assumptions, calculate the rise in the pay bill.

(c) Construct a histogram to illustrate pay distribution in Year 2.

(d) Convert your histogram into a frequency polygon.

19 (a) Four companies – A, B, C and D – have the same number of employees. From the information below, sketch the distribution curves, using the same axes for all four.

- The distributions of their pay have the same modes.
- The distributions for A and B are normal, but that for A has half the standard deviation of that for B.
- The distribution for C is negatively skewed.
- The distribution for D is positively skewed.

(b) The distribution of A's pay is shown below.

Pay scale (£)	No. of employees
8000–9999	40
10,000–11,999	260
12,000–12,999	500
13,000–14,999	100
15,000–20,000	100

(c) Estimate the median salary. Construct a histogram to depict the data.

(d) The mean salary is currently £12,300. If this produces a payroll bill 10 per cent higher than the previous year, calculate the mean salary in the earlier year.

20 The table below shows hourly earnings for labour and a price index for materials. It is known that labour constitutes 60 per cent of costs and materials represent 40 per cent of costs.

Year	Hourly pay costs	Price index for materials
1	£8.00	100
2	£8.50	110
3	£9.00	120
4	£10.99	125

(a) Calculate an earnings index (Year 1 = 100).

(b) Calculate a total cost index.

21 An importer buys five grades of a commodity. The price and relative quantities of his purchases are detailed below (bottom of page).

Using Year 1 as the base year:

(a) calculate the overall base-weighted price index for Year 2 and Year 3;

(b) calculate the overall current-weighted price index for Year 2 and Year 3.

Variety	Year 1 Price (£)	Quantity	Year 2 Price (£)	Quantity	Year 3 Price (£)	Quantity
A	100	100	110	120	130	130
B	110	50	130	60	140	50
C	120	20	130	20	145	20
D	130	20	135	20	150	20
E	140	10	145	20	150	10

22 The data below relates to advertising expenditure and sales revenue.

Year	Advertising expenditure £000	Sales revenue £million
1976	75	15
1977	80	17
1978	84	17
1979	105	20
1980	90	21
1981	100	23
1982	95	21
1983	90	20
1984	80	16
1985	90	17
1986	95	18
1987	102	18
1988	105	18
1989	90	21
1990	110	23
1991	105	24
1992	110	25
1993	120	28
1994	120	28
1995	120	26
1996	120	24
1997	115	23
1998	116	24
1999	120	27
2000	125	29

(a) Plot:
   (i) graphs to show advertising expenditure and sales revenue against time;
   (ii) a scatter diagram to show sales revenue against advertising revenue.
(b) Superimpose on your scatter diagram a line of best fit.

23 Calculate expected weekly sales, given the probability distributions below.

(a)

No. of units sold per week	50	60	55
Probability	0.3	0.5	0.2

(b)

No. of units sold per week	10	12	14	16
Probability	0.1	0.5	0.3	0.1

(c)

No. of units sold per week	24	26	28	30
Probability	0.2	0.2	0.4	0.2

(d)

No. of units sold per week	100	120	130
Probability	0.1	0.8	0.1

24 The probability that a new marketing strategy will succeed is assessed as 0.8. The probability that expenditure for the new strategy will be kept within its original budget is assessed as 0.7. What is the probability that:
(a) only one of the objectives is achieved;
(b) the marketing strategy will succeed given that expenditure is kept within budget?

25 A lightbulb lasts on average for 2500 hours with a standard deviation of 300 hours. What percentage of bulbs will have a life of:
(a) less than 2000 hours;
(b) between 2300 and 2500 hours?

Note: for (b) you will have to calculate two Z scores and combine them. It is always advisable to produce a sketch graph to help you decide which part of the graph you are concerned with.

26 The mean time taken by garage mechanics to change a tyre is 9 minutes with a standard deviation of 1.5 minutes. What proportion of tyres will be changed in:
(a) less than 7 minutes;
(b) more than 13 minutes?

27 The mean weight of a sample of packets is 30 grams with a standard deviation of 4 grams. What proportion of the packets will be:
(a) heavier than 32 grams;
(b) lighter than 25 grams;
(c) between 28 and 33 grams?

28 The probability that a salesperson will make a sale on a visit to a prospect is 0.25. What is the probability, in two visits, of:
(a) making no sales;
(b) making one sale;
(c) making two sales?

29 The probability of any one of four petrol pumps being in use at a particular moment is 0.3. What is the probability of:
(a) all four being in use at the same time;
(b) any three being in use at the same time;
(c) none being in use at the same time?

30 If the average demand for video recorders from a retailer is 50 per week, and the standard deviation is 10, what is the probability that the actual demand will be:
(a) below 30;
(b) greater than 60;
(c) between 40 and 60?
(Assume a normal distribution and use the table given below.)

Proportionate parts of the area under the normal curve

Distances from mean in terms of standard deviations in one direction	1	2	3	Over 3
Proportion of area in the above range	34%	14%	2%	Negligible

31 Over the past two years it has been found that the probability that an item will be returned because of a fault is 0.01. Write out expressions for the probability that, in a week when exactly five items have been sold:
(a) all items are faulty;
(b) three items are faulty;
(c) at least two items are not faulty.

32 A manufacturer produces electric lightbulbs with a life that is normally distributed, a mean life of 946 hours and a standard deviation of 57 hours.
(a) Find the percentage of lightbulbs that have a life between 900 and 1000 hours.
(b) The manufacturer guarantees a minimum life of 800 hours and will replace, free of charge, any bulbs that fail the guarantee. What percentage of bulbs can the manufacturer expect to replace?
(c) What percentage of bulbs will have a life in excess of 1100 hours?

33 A television repair company finds that the average time taken to repair a television set is 1.6 hours. Distribution is normal and the standard deviation is 0.4 hours.
(a) Find the percentage of repairs that take:
(i) in excess of 3 hours;
(ii) less than 0.5 hours.

(b) Labour costs for repairs amount to £20 per hour. Calculate:
  (i) the maximum cost of 75 per cent of the repairs;
  (ii) the maximum cost of 95 per cent of repairs.
(c) A minimum call-out charge of £30 is imposed on customers. This covers the first hour of labour with £20 for each further hour. What percentage of customers:
  (i) will pay only £30;
  (ii) will pay more than £60?

34 The attendance at rock concerts at a particular stadium has a normal distribution with a mean of 25,000 and a standard deviation of 3000. The promoters are able to break even with an attendance of 18,000.
What proportion of concerts will:
(a) break even;
(b) attract an audience in excess of 22,000;
(c) attract an audience in excess of 29,000?

35 A frequency distribution is normal with a mean of 500 and a standard deviation of 20. What proportion of total frequencies will be:
(a) above 510;
(b) above 485;
(c) below 475;
(d) below 535;
(e) between 490 and 520;
(f) between 470 and 505?

36 Invoices at a particular depot of a large company are for amounts that follow a normal distribution with a mean of £256 and a standard deviation of £18.
(a) What percentage of invoices will be for amounts above:
  (i) £280;
  (ii) £250?

(b) What percentage of invoices will be for amounts below:
  (i) £240;
  (ii) £220?
(c) What percentage of invoices will be for amounts between:
  (i) £245 and £260;
  (ii) £230 and £290?

37 Samples of 100 goods are tested. The average number of defective goods in each sample is 10 with a standard deviation of 3.
(a) How many defective goods can be expected in a batch of:
  (i) 2000 goods;
  (ii) 5000 goods?
(b) What proportion of batches of 100 will have:
  (i) more than 13 defective goods;
  (ii) more than 16 defective goods;
  (iii) more than 19 defective goods?

38 A product is made by an automatic machine and contains 1000 identical components. The average number of defective components per product is known to be 25. The products are inspected and faulty components are corrected manually.
What proportion of the product will be scrapped if:
(a) products requiring more than 30 corrections are scrapped;
(b) products requiring more than 35 corrections are scrapped?

39 A piece of equipment will only function if three components X, Y and Z are all working. The probability of X failing during the year is 0.2, that of Y failing is 0.1 and that of Z failing is 0.05.
(a) What is the probability that all three components will fail during the year?
(b) What is the probability that the equipment will fail before the end of the year?

40 A large batch of components is 2 per cent defective. If five components are tested, what is the probability that the test sample contains:

(a) no defective components;
(b) just one defective component;
(c) just two defective components;
(d) five defective components?

6

Applications of information and communications technology

As with the two previous chapters there are two aspects to IT as part of an A level course in Business Studies. First, IT is an essential part of business operations and, therefore, any student of business needs an understanding of IT and the uses to which it can be put. Second, IT is one of the key skills that should be developed on an A level Business Studies course and those for other subjects. This chapter does not aim to cover the details of IT skills, but, instead, it seeks to develop an appreciation of the applications of IT. Student activities at the end of this and subsequent chapters offer an opportunity to practise IT skills in a business context.

Chapter objectives

1 To develop an understanding of IT.

2 To develop an understanding of IT applications in business.

3 To develop an understanding of IT in manufacturing.

4 To explore business uses of the Internet.

5 To provide opportunities to develop IT skills.

What is information technology?

IT is the collective term for various technologies involved in the collection, storage, processing and communication of information by electronic means. With this definition in minds, it is clear that IT is broader than computing and includes telecommunications and microelectronics. Information is used in business organization for planning, organizing, monitoring and controlling. For most of human history, information was processed in manual ways, but, in the twentieth century, electronic technologies took over many of these functions. The process can only develop further in the new century because of the following advantages of IT:

- increased accuracy of information;
- increased speed of information processing;
- increase in the volume of information;
- easier access to information resulting in better decision making;
- increased productivity;
- it frees up the workforce to undertake work requiring skill and judgement;
- great consistency.

These far outweigh the disadvantages and problems of IT:

- the cost of installing and running the equipment;
- the cost of training staff;
- the problem of security, confidentiality and

compliance with the Data Protection Act 1984;

- the problems resulting from breakdown;
- possible staff resistance.

One problem that must feature high in management considerations is the health issue. Extensive use of visual display units (VDUs) can damage eyesight and be harmful to unborn children. Employers have an obligation to create a healthy working environment and, therefore must take the health implications of IT into account, both in planning and in using IT in the workplace.

What computer systems consist of

All computer systems have two main parts – **hardware**, the physical components, and **software**, the programming instructions that make the physical components work, (see Figure 6.1). The hardware consists of the following.

- **Input devices** which are used to get data into the computer. The major input devices for a personal computer are a keyboard, a mouse, a disk and a scanner.
- The **central processing unit (CPU)**, which is the computational and control unit (or brain) of the computer. The CPU has the ability to fetch, decode and execute instructions and transfer information over the databus (the nervous system).
- The **back-up data storage** (or disk drives)

store data when the power is turned off. The **hard drive** is used for permanent storage within the computer whereas the **disk drive** reads data from, and writes data to floppy disks, ZIP disks and CDs. These disks can be removed from the computer to increase space within its memory and are a vital back-up in case of power failure.

- **Output devices** make the processed data available to the user. The main output devices are the visual display unit (VDU) and printer.

Software consists of programs, procedures and instructions that make the hardware work. Below is a list of the main types of software.

- **Operating systems** the software that controls the allocation and usage of hardware such as memory, CPU time, disk space and peripheral devices. The operating system (such as Windows '98 and MAC OS) is the foundation on which applications are built.
- **Applications software** are programs designed to assist in the performance of specific tasks, such as word processing, spreadsheets and databases. The main applications are the following.
  - **Word processing applications** allow you to key in text and save it. Changes can be made to the text and it can be printed out.
  - **Database applications** allow you to store information in record format. The information can be saved, amended, sorted and searched.

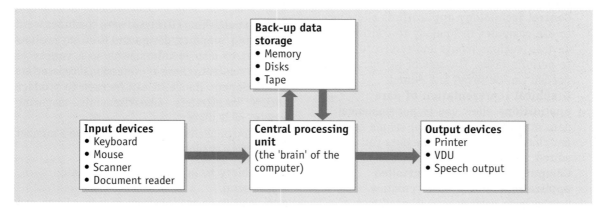

Figure 6.1 A simple computer system

- **Spreadsheet applications** allow you to enter data into a grid and save the information. You can perform numerical calculations.
- **Computer-art applications** allow you to draw shapes and use patterns. You can change and store the images and print out copies of your artwork.
- **Desktop publishing (DTP) applications** allow you to take prepared text and graphic images and display them in a variety of ways. The display can be edited and stored.
- **Computer-aided design (CAD) applications** allow you to create two- and three-dimensional designs on a computer screen. You can save the designs, change them and view them from different angles if necessary.
- **Stock control applications** allow you to set up stock control systems and enter information about stock held and save it. You can amend the information and print out stock lists and summary reports. The system will alert you to low stock levels.
- **Business accounting applications** allow you to set up ledger accounts that can be updated and amended. You can save the information and print out reports and accounts.
- **On-line communication facilities** allow you to use electronic communication systems. You can receive and send messages and use the system to retrieve information.
- **Control technology applications** allow you to use computer technology to control devices, such as robots and screen turtles, to perform tasks. The sets of instructions needed can be saved and edited.
- **Graphical representation of data applications** allow you to put numerical data into graphic forms such as pie charts, bar charts, line graphs. The data can be edited and saved.
- **Computer numerically controlled applications** allow you to program machines to perform complicated and exacting tasks using a series of numbered

instructions. The instructions can be stored, edited and recalled as required.

Word processing

For many people this is the most widely used application. Students use a word processor to write up their notes, produce essays and, especially, to write up a project (or research assignment), which is a feature of all A level specifications in Business Studies. Word processors have virtually taken over from typewriters for all forms of business documentation. Facilities offered by word processing packages include:

- creating documents;
- correcting;
- formatting documents – changing paragraphs, margins, fonts, font sizes, centring and so on;
- cutting and pasting;
- placing borders around a paragraphs;
- page numbering;
- creating headers and footers;
- linking to information in other documents;
- checking spelling and grammar;
- counting the numbers of words in documents;
- incorporating drawings, photos, graphs and so on;
- printing, all copies being of the same quality;
- saving for future reference or modification;
- merging documents;
- replacing words or names automatically throughout a document.

Desktop publishing

Desktop publishing (DTP) software combines word processing, graphics, design and printing to allow the user to display information in a variety of formats similar to those of professional typesetters and designers. Hence, it can be used to produce notices, newsletters, advertisements, magazine articles or leaflets.

Desktop publishing packages will have a number of facilities available, such as:

- the ability to import text from a word processor;
- the ability to produce text in many fonts and sizes;

- the ability to organize text in column form;
- the ability to import graphics from other packages;
- the ability to 'scan in' (digitally read) pictures and illustrations and convert them to an appropriate size and shape;
- the production of various geometric patterns;
- the merging of text, graphics and illustrations;
- the drawing of borders.

Spreadsheets

A spreadsheet program is an application used for budgets, forecasting and other finance-related tasks that organize data values using cells, where the relationship between cells are defined by formulae. In the example shown below, the vertical columns are labelled with a letter whereas the horizontal rows are numbered. Hence, a cell can be referred to individually. For example, C5 is column three, row five. By inserting a formula, the computer will undertake calculations on the numbers that have been entered.

A		B £000	C £000
1	Current assets	–	–
2	Stocks	100	120
3	Debtors	20	40
4	Cash	5	0
5		125	
6	Current liabilities	–	–
7	Overdraft	10	5
8	Creditors	70	60
9	Taxation	50	20
10		130	
11	Net current assets	(–5)	

Cell C5 is the sum of C2 + C3 + C4
Cell C10 is the sum of C7 + C8 + C9
Cell 11 is C5 minus C10

As well as addition and subtraction, it is possible to build in formulae for multiplication, division, averages and other statistical functions. If you change any of the data in your spreadsheet,

the program will automatically recalculate all the results in the sheet. This enables spreadsheets to answer 'What if?' questions – what will be the impact on the budget if the firm:

- raises its prices;
- is subject to higher interest rates;
- raises rates of pay;
- obtains materials at a lower cost?

A spreadsheet used to answer 'What if' questions becomes a model of the real world in which the user can learn about unfamiliar situations and experiment without danger or expense. It is an aid to problem solving and is a powerful tool in forecasting. Finally, spreadsheets generate graphs to illustrate the numerical data stored. These illustrations add visual impact to any report.

Databases

A database is a structured collection of data that may be manipulated to select and sort desired items of information. Sorting means placing the information in alphabetical or number order. Selecting involves searching records in the database to select all the people or subjects that satisfy the criteria chosen by the user of the database, for instance, to select all people in the database who live in a particular town.

Databases have widespread uses, especially in personnel and sales departments. In the case of sales departments, extensive records can be built up containing details of customers':

- names;
- addresses;
- age;
- purchases made;
- frequency of purchases;
- value of purchases;
- psychographic profile.

Obviously the same data could be stored in paper files in filing cabinets, but manual storage does not provide the user with as easy and rapid a way of finding and retrieving the information required as computer systems. The advantages and disadvantages of electronic filing are as follows.

Advantages	Disadvantages
● Speed of set-up.	● Costly to install.
● Speed of access.	● Possible staff
● Easy to distribute.	resistance.
● Low storage	● It is subject to
requirements.	breakdown – if the
● Cost-effective.	system crashes, it is
● Offers security	both costly and
and confidentiality	inconvenient.
with access	● Security can be a
controlled by	problem.
passwords.	● Computer databases
	come within the
	scope of the Data
	Protection Act 1984.

In a database, information is arranged as a file. The file is made up of records of related data (data relating to one person) and each record is made up of a number of 'fields' containing a specific item of information (a text field could be a name or an address whereas a numerical field might take the form of a date of birth or an account number).

When you sort information stored in a database, the records will be put in order – alphabetical order or in numerical order from highest to lowest or vice versa. You can then use a database to find a particular item of information. For instance, a database produced by an estate agent might enable the user to search the database to find all houses in a particular area or all houses of a certain price or even use both criteria to provide a shorter list of all houses in the specified area for a certain price.

Computers and manufacturing

Computers are used in:

● designing products;
● the manufacturing process;
● production planning;
● monitoring and control.

See Figure 6.2 for a summary of the various roles computers play in manufacturing.

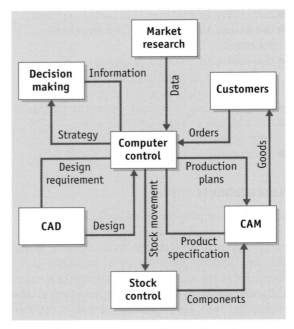

Figure 6.2 Computers in manufacturing

Computer-aided design (CAD)

This application allows the designer to produce two- and three-dimensional designs on a computer screen where they can be quickly and easily modified. It can be used to simulate performance to obviate the need to construct a prototype. The benefits are:

● it saves time in designing;
● it is easy to modify designs;
● drawings can be rotated to view the design from different perspectives;
● it is possible to calculate engineering stresses and financial costs as part of the design process;
● it will lead to enhanced quality and consistency of products.

Computer-aided manufacturing (CAM)

This involves the use of computers in a variety of manufacturing tasks beyond the use of robots on the production line. Computer-integrated manufacturing (CIM), takes it a stage further, with the use of computers to coordinate every aspect of production, from design through stock control to production scheduling and control. It involves:

- CAD;
- flexible manufacturing systems or highly automated manufacturing systems that are computer controlled and capable of producing a 'family' of products in a flexible manner;
- robots (artificial devices able to perform functions ordinarily carried out by human beings);
- numerically controlled (NC) machines that respond to programmed instructions;
- materials requirement planning (MRP) programs that calculate the materials required to complete an order;
- manufacturing resource planning (MRPII) – a computer-based planning system for the whole of a company's production process, including capacity planning, materials planning, monitoring and control.

The benefits of CIM are:

- increased productivity;
- reduction in waiting times;
- greater consistency;
- greater flexibility;
- improved coordination of all factory operations; including the flow of parts and materials;
- direct and flexible control of machine tools;
- economies in operation by virtue of continuous use of equipment and the avoidance of bottlenecks.

Against these significant advantages it should be appreciated that CIM involves a considerable investment in equipment and requires highly skilled staff. Therefore, it has important implications for both the finance and human resource functions.

Business and the Internet

The Internet is the worldwide computer network that carries the World Wide Web, electronic mail (e-mail) and other services. Note that the World Wide Web is only a part of the Internet. The Web is a large collection of information stored on a worldwide network of computers.

As part of key skills development, you should be making extensive use of the Internet as part of your programmes of study. You will find it especially useful for collecting secondary data for project work. To assist your exploration of Internet sources, useful Internet addresses are included at the end of some chapters.

In addition to using the Internet for study purposes, you should also develop an appreciation of the opportunities to use the technology in business. These include:

- information gathering, with the Internet rapidly replacing printed sources in desk research (see Chapter 15 Marketing research);
- advertising the firm's products;
- selling goods and services;
- delivery of services, such as distance-based training courses or electronic newspapers;
- recruitment of employees, by using it to advertise vacancies;
- information dissemination to customers, suppliers and the public;
- communication in the form of e-mail.

Benefits of using the Internet include that it:

- provides cheap and efficient long-distance communication;
- offers unlimited potential for personal networking;
- offers a platform for business transactions;
- has worldwide potential for marketing;
- opens up worldwide sources of information;
- is democratic and open.

However:

- it still mainly carries information that organizations give away free of charge;
- it includes incomplete, trivial and illegal information;
- it can be slow, both to connect to and use;
- it can produce information overload;
- employees can waste valuable time 'surfing the net';
- security and trust are necessary – these are there but will only increase further with time.

e-mail

e-mail is the main use made of the Internet. The advantages of e-mail over conventional letters (snail mail), telephone and fax are:

- delivery is faster than snail mail;
- it overcomes the problem of time zone differences as the recipient does not have to be available to receive it;
- like a fax, it is possible to send one message to many people with one original copy;
- e-mail addresses are portable;
- it enables users to exchange information with people previously unknown to them;
- the cost is not dependent on the distance travelled;
- it is cheaper than fax or telephone;
- although written, the style tends to be less formal than a letter;
- the message will remain in the recipient's e-mail account until they collect it.

But, there are some drawbacks:

- it is not always secure;
- it can be used inappropriately;
- the informality of the method can result in 'off-the-cuff' replies that are later regretted;
- printouts can look untidy compared with a word processed document sent by post or fax;
- the apparent immediacy of e-mail can panic recipients into thinking that they need to respond immediately;
- the promise of the paperless office is still some time off, especially as recipients are inclined to print off messages rather than merely reading and absorbing them.

Management information systems (MIS)

MISs can be defined as computer-based systems for processing and organizing information so as to provide various levels of management with accurate and timely information. Data collected in a routine manner (such as sales and production figures, staff turnover and so on) is then processed and made available to management to:

- aid decision making;
- track progress;
- isolate and solve problems.

An MIS is an efficient way of providing regular information, although it is less well equipped to deal with unpredictable, informal or unstructured information. For instance, whereas sales data can be analysed to provide information on profit margins for particular products and markets, it is less able to deal with a sudden change in the external environment (such as the emergence of a new rival in the market).

The quality of an MIS does depend on its design. It must provide managers with the information that they require, in the form they require and at the time they require it. This means that there needs to be close collaboration between the programmers (who produce the software) and the managers who need to access the information.

ICT and competitive advantage

For a business to be successul, it needs to have a competitive advantage – something that gives it an edge over rival businesses. ICT can be an important source of competitive advantage, whereas failure to invest in ICT creates a competitive disadvantage.

The competitive advantages resulting from ICT are as follows:

- closer links with customers and suppliers;
- improved information flow to increase the quality of decision making;
- improved quality control;
- increased responsiveness;
- improved integration of marketing (what to produce) with operations (how to produce it);
- increased management control;
- greater control over budgets;
- improved monitoring of the environment and performance indicators.

The Data Protection Act 1984

The Act was passed to prevent the misuse of

personal data (on employers, customers, potential customers and others) and to prevent it causing harm to individuals. The Act only applies to 'automatically processed information', not to information that is held and processed manually. Data users are organizations that keep data on computer files whereas 'computer bureau' is a broad term covering anyone processing personal data on someone else's behalf. Both have to register as data users, supplying information about the types of data held, their purpose, where they were obtained and to whom they will be disclosed.

The Data Protection Registrar maintains the register of data users, promotes compliance with data protection principles, considers complaints about breaches of the principles and, where necessary, prosecutes offenders. The principles of data protection are:

● information contained in personal data must be obtained, and the data processed, fairly and lawfully;
● the data must then be held only for one or more specified and lawful purposes;
● personal data must not be used or disclosed in any manner incompatible with the original purpose of its collection;
● personal data must be adequate, relevant and not excessive in relation to that purpose;
● personal data shall be accurate and, where necessary, kept up to date;
● it must not be kept for longer than is necessary;
● individuals must be informed by any data user that they hold information on them and must inform them at reasonable intervals and without overcharging for the service;
● individuals, where appropriate, must be allowed to correct or erase such data;
● appropriate security measures shall be taken against unauthorized access, alteration, disclosure or destruction of personal data and must also be taken against accidental loss or destruction of personal data.

Individuals on whom data is held are known as data subjects. The Act gives these individuals the right of access to the information, the right to challenge inaccurate information and the right to be compensated if they suffer harm. There are, however, some exceptions to the right to receive compensation:

● where data has been supplied by the individual;
● where data has been acquired with reasonable care;
● data held for statistical purposes, from which it is impossible to identify individuals.

Although the Act permits business organizations to make extensive use of personal data, it does impose some constraints. For instance, the sale of databases requires the consent of data subjects. Moreover, compliance with the Act imposes a cost on data users, especially in terms of:

● registration;
● ensuring that information is accurate;
● the appointment of a Data Protection Officer responsible for compliance within the legislation;
● ensuring that data is secure and that access is given only to authorized and registered users.

Key concepts

Cell the place for one item of information in a spreadsheet.

CD-ROM a disk on which information is stored digitally and 'read' optically by laser.

Computer a programmable, digital information processing device.

Computer-aided design (CAD) the use of computers to produce technical design drawings.

Computer-aided manufacturing computers to regulate production processes.

Database a structured collection of data that can be manipulated to select and sort items of information.

Desktop publishing (DTP) the use of microcomputers for small-scale typesetting and page make-up.

Disk drive a device that writes information to, and reads information from, a disk.

Electronic mail (e-mail) messages sent directly from one computer to another via the Internet.

Hard disk a high-capacity magnetic disk that is permanently kept in its drive.

Information and communication technology (ICT) the collective name for technologies involved in processing and transmitting information.

Internet global computer network carrying the World Wide Web, e-mail and other services.

Memory the set of chips that store information that the computer is working on at the time.

Modem the device which links a computer, via a telephone line, to the Internet.

Network a linking of several computers. A local area network (LAN) links computers in the same building, whereas a wide area network (WAN) links computers with others anywhere else in the world.

Processor a chip inside the computer that processes information.

Program a sequence of instructions that control the operations of a computer.

Spreadsheet a table of numbers, formulae and other information set out in rows and columns that calculates the figures for you.

Word processor a software tool to enable the user to manipulate text.

World Wide Web a collection of information stored on a network of computers.

Some useful Web sites

Major news media are always a useful starting point, not only for current and archive stories but also for Internet links. For instance, a current story on the BBC News web site will often carry a link to the web sites of the organizations mentioned in the story, and the political links section of the political page can route you into all government departments, political parties and EU institutions.

BBC News 24 http://www.news.bbc.co.uk/
CNN http://www.cnn.com/
Evening Standard http://www.thisislondon.co.uk/

The Guardian http://www.guardian.co.uk/
The Telegraph http://www.telegraph.co.uk/
The Times http://www.the-times.co.uk/
The Economist http://www.economist.com/
Financial Times http://www.ft.com/
Government Information Service http://www.open.gov.uk/
HM Treasury http://www.hm-treasury.gov.uk/.
Department of Trade and Industry http://www.dti.gov.uk/
(This is an especially usedful site for students of business.)
Foreign Office http://www.fco.gov.uk/
EU institutions these can be accessed via Europa http://europa.eu.int/
Institute of Management http://www.inst-mgt.org.uk/
Encarta Concise Enclyclopaedia http://www.encarta.msn.com/concise/find/find.aspa/
Biz/Ed- http://www.bized.ac.uk/
(This site is designed for teachers and students of Economics and Business Studies. Not only is it useful in its own right, it has excellent links with external web sites such as those of the FTSE 100 companies.

Essay questions

1 Assess the benefits and costs associated with computerization of the office.

2 Outline and assess the consequences of information technology on working practices in service-sector organizations.

3 Evaluate the use of:
(a) databases;
(b) spreadsheets.
(c) the Internet in business.

4 The paperless office: a real possibility or a theoretical ideal? Discuss.

5 Explain and evaluate the use of IT in manufacturing.

Keys skills development

1 Using a desktop publishing program, such as Microsoft Publisher, create the following brochures, written as information guides aimed at the owner-managers of small businesses. The brochures should each be confined to a single sheet of A4 paper, include at least one graphic/illustration and an eye-catching headline. You should use appropriate fonts and font sizes.
   (a) An information guide to the Data Protection Law.
   (b) An information guide to the working time directive.
   (c) A leaflet setting out the business arguments for OR against the UK adopting the euro.
   (d) An information guide to the Advertising Standards Authority's Code of Practice.
   (e) An information guide to venture capitalism.

2 Using an appropriate software package, design a school/college calendar for the next academic year. The calendar should distinguish between term and holiday dates in an appropiate way, record significant days (such as mock exam/unit exam dates, parents evenings, field trips and so on) and include an appropriate illustration for each month of the year.

3 Using an appropriate software package, create the following:
   (a) a business card for the owner of a new start-up business in a business field of your choice;
   (b) an advertising flyer for a horse-riding stable;
   (c) a letterhead to be used by a small plumbing firm.

Part
2

The external environment of business

7

Business and the external environment

This chapter introduces the reader to the external environment that faces a business organization and with which it interacts. A more detailed account of various aspects of the external environment will be developed in subsequent chapters but the concern here is to provide an overview of the environment and the process of interaction.

Chapter objectives

1 To introduce the components of the external environment of business organizations.

2 To develop an appreciation of the interaction between business organizations and the environment.

3 To develop an appreciation of the accelerating pace of change in the environment.

4 To develop an understanding of the need to respond to the environment in order to ensure long-term success.

5 To develop an appreciation of demographic analysis and demographic trends.

6 To explain recruitment strategies developed to overcome the perceived problem of the demographic time-bomb.

7 To develop an appreciation of sociocultural trends and how they impact on business organizations.

The changing world

We can define the external environment as those events, circumstances and factors that occur outside the organization and may influence what happens within it. Anything that impinges on the firm can be included in the environment. The role of the manager is to respond to the environment and devise strategies to take advantage of the opportunities that are presented or to cope with the challenges.

The environment is not stable – in fact, it is increasingly turbulent due to the era of change and uncertainty in which we live. Changes are happening faster and faster, requiring continual response on the part of businesses. Some of the changes take the form of dramatic shocks that become headline news, such as:

- a revolution abroad that threatens exports;
- a rise in interest rates that raises the cost of borrowing;
- a new law that requires firms to modify their existing practices;
- a technological breakthrough that leads to the development of new products and the elimination of existing products.

Other changes are not sudden or dramatic and will not make headline news – these can be seen as changing *trends*. Despite the absence of drama, they can have a pervasive impact on society, individuals and, most importantly for us, on business organizations. Examples include:

- a growing concern for the welfare of animals, leading to public distaste for certain practices;
- changes in family life, resulting in changes in the way we act, live and shop;
- a rise in living standards brought about by economic growth, resulting in changes in our spending habits;
- the spread of the motor car, which has revolutionized people's lives.

These shocks and trends provide a turbulent background against which business operates.

The elements of the external environment can be classified in two overlapping ways. First, we can classify them in terms of the extent and frequency with which particular forces impact a firm. This results in a two-way division between the immediate (or proximate) environment and the general environment. The alternative way of categorizing the elements of the environment is in terms of the nature of the forces. These are usually identified as.

- social;
- legal;
- economic;
- political;
- technological.

The immediate environment

Business organizations can be seen as resource conversion systems in which inputs are combined together to create outputs (see Figure 7.1). Hence, the immediate environment is concerned with the acquisition of the various resources (especially labour, capital, materials and land) and the distribution of output to customers. Consequently, the immediate environment is made up of customers, suppliers, the labour force, financial institutions, shareholders and competitors. These groups impact on the organization, both directly and frequently.

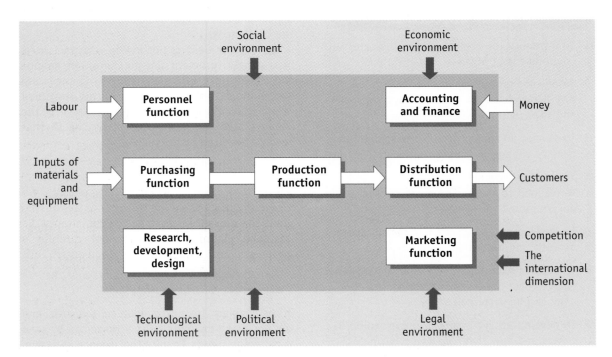

Figure 7.1 The organization in its environment

The general environment

The 'general environment' is those forces in the background that occasionally, irregularly and indirectly impact a firm. For instance, a change in the degree of adherence to religious beliefs might not have a direct and immediate impact on a business organization. However, if it results in a change in the patterns of consumer spending, then there will be an impact (either beneficial or harmful) on business organizations.

The nature of the elements comprising the external environment

As Figure 7.2 shows, both the immediate and general environment can be subdivided into the following elements:

- legal environment;
- economic environment;
- political environment;
- technological environment;
- social environment.

Figure 7.2 The general (outer) and immediate (inner) environment

The legal environment

Business organizations work within a legal framework that resolves disputes and regulates behaviour for the benefit of the community. Business relations usually involve a contract promising the delivery of goods or services or the payment of money some time in the future. It is, therefore, important for there to be a clear understanding of the rights and obligations of both parties to a contract. These rights and obligations are defined in **contract law**, which also provides remedies for failure to perform duties under the contract. It is difficult to see how the complicated system of exchange in a modern economy could function smoothly without this legal framework.

The contracts between business organizations and their consumers, and their employees are subject to special laws because it is felt that, in the absence of special protection, both consumers and employees would be in a vulnerable position. We should also be aware of laws affecting relationships between the business and its creditors, and the business and its owners. Company law, for instance, is designed to protect creditors and shareholders.

A further area of the law that is of concern to businesses deals with the relationship of the organization to the wider community. Where business activities cause an offence or nuisance, or could lead to disorder, they are subject to regulation and licensing (sale of alcohol, places of entertainment). Growing concern over the environment has lead to controls on certain industrial activities. Planning laws also act as a constraint on business. Whereas in the nineteenth century landowners could do whatever they wanted with property, today there are restrictions designed to limit the nuisance caused to the community. For instance, planning authorities look carefully at proposed new shopping developments. Large supermarkets and shopping centres affect traffic flows and, therefore, permission is sometimes only granted on the condition that the developer finances road improvement in the vicinity of the development. This practice – known as a planning gain – adds to the cost of development, but is seen as protection for the community.

The framework of law allows for the orderly conduct of business relations, providing a degree of certainty and stability. Nevertheless, legislation places a constraint on business, limiting what it can do or compelling firms to undertake actions they would not otherwise perform. Consequently, the legal environment adds to the cost of operation. The legal environment is explored more fully in Chapter 8.

The economic environment

As well as the impact of competitors on the business organization, we should be aware of the impact of economic variables on both the supply of resources and the demand from customers. These variables include the rate of growth of output and income, the level of employment (or unemployment), the rate of inflation, the exchange rate and the balance of payments. In addition to these changes, which occur naturally in the environment, we should also be aware of the impact of government policy on business organizations. Included in this are policies relating to interest rates, taxation, government expenditure and the exchange rate.

In an insular country (what economists call a closed economy) the only concern is about economic and social trends *within* the nation. However, as we live in an open economy, we should also be aware of the impact of events elsewhere in the world, especially in those countries providing the UK with imports and markets for its exports.

The economic environment is explored further in chapters 9–11.

The political environment

The political environment concerns the activities of the State and trends in politics. We should not confine ourselves to UK central government but should also be aware of the impact of local government an supra-national government (that is, the EU) on business organizations.

The State performs a number of roles within the economy. First, despite recent privatization, Britain still possesses what economists call a mixed economy. This is a mixture of privately and government-owned enterprises. Private enterprise sells goods and services in the marketplace and responds to the needs of customers because of the profit motive. The public sector is the government sector of the economy and consists of a number of component parts. Central government provide services such as defence and local authorities provide services such as education and council housing. Also included in the public sector is the National Health Service and the remaining nationalized industries. Parts of the pubic sector operate in the marketplace in that they sell their services and are required to be commercially efficient. Conversely, many government and local government services are provided free to consumers but are paid for out of taxation. Whatever the method of paying for and distributing services, the important point is that the State remains a major provider of goods and services.

Second, the State is also a buyer of goods and services. Many private-sector firms rely heavily on public-sector contracts. Manufacturers of military equipment, for instance, are very dependent on the government and, therefore, any cut in defence spending could have harmful consequences for these firms. There are many firms that supply materials to schools and colleges and a major problem that confronts them is the size and nature of the school and college budget. As the bulk of education expenditure is committed to teachers' pay, the easiest and quickest way to cut educational spending is to reduce the purchase of furniture, textbooks and stationery – directly affecting the business of educational suppliers.

Third, the State acts to regulate, encourage and guide the private sector of the economy. This may take the form of cash subsidies or tax concessions to encourage desirable trends, legislative controls to curb the excesses of the unregulated market, or changes in interest rates to correct macroeconomic problems. It is important to remember that much of what the State does acts as a constraint on, rather than giving assistance to, private enterprise. Government economic policy is explored further in chapters 10 and 11.

We should include in the political environment trends in political opinion. The impact of such trends is most evident in the run-up to a general election. The prospect of a change in government creates uncertainty, especially if the opposition parties are promising major changes that will have a direct impact (harmful or beneficial) on business organizations.

The technological environment

The technological environment in which the business operates is also subject to change, providing both opportunities and threats. As with the other aspects of the environment, the successful organization is the one that is willing and able to adapt to these environmental changes.

The most obvious way in which technological change affects a business is in terms of the changing demand for the firm's product. For instance, the development of the compact disc created market opportunities for some firms, but presented a threat to those that were committed to the other recording formats. Satellite television has presented opportunities for more businesses to supply television broadcasts and equipment to broadcasters, but it has also posed a problem for advertisers because the proliferation of television channels reduces the audiences for individual channels.

Changing technology also affects business organizations in other ways. It results in changes in the processes of production and in the size and type of the workforce required. In some instances (such as computerization of the office) new technology economizes on the number of staff, but places a greater emphasis on the skills and quality of staff. In other areas (such as automation in factories), new technology has *reduced* the skill element of work. Changes in technology have implications for the types of workers required and, therefore, the ways in which they should be managed.

Technological change is the most potent source of change in the environment of business organizations. It can be seen as a process of 'creative destruction' in which new products, processes and, therefore, working practices replace old ones.

We normally associate technological change with an invention or discovery (in particular a dramatic discovery of the 'Eureka' type). In prac-
tice it rarely happens like this. The invention is usually the culmination of a long period of research, usually undertaken by a team (or teams) of people. In fact, invention is less important than innovation. Invention can be seen as a technical process in which something is created that did not exist before; innovation is the application of the invention. The application is likely to occur some time (often some considerable time) after the invention and it is possible that the invention will remain dormant indefinitely.

Economists would argue that competitive forces are crucial in this process of technological innovation. There are numerous examples of ideas and inventions that were stifled by monopolistic or oligopolistic firms acting in collusion. Technology developments threaten their traditional product range or traditional methods of operation. However, the force of competition will stimulate the process of change. Each firm realizes that if it fails to engage in technological development it will lose out to rivals. Technological change has also been nurtured by the explosion of ideas and the 'knowledge industry'.

Although detailed knowledge of technology is not essential in A level Business Studies, it is necessary to appreciate the ways in which technology impacts business organizations. Philip Kotler, an American marketing expert, highlights five ways in which technology is affecting business:

- the accelerating pace of technological change is bringing about fundamental changes in working life and shorter product lifecycles;
- opportunities for innovation appear limitless, entailing new products, new processes and new ways of working;
- increasing expenditure on research and development is not optional, it is essential for modern business organization;
- there is a trend towards greater regulation of technology as its impact can be so profound and harmful (such as concerns about global warming, the ozone layer, nuclear power, toxic substances);
- continuous product improvement is essential, although there might be a preference for minor and less risky product changes than

major and risky ones as firms that pursue the former policy can be seen as being defensive whereas the latter policy can be seen as offensive (more profitable, but more risky).

The social environment

The most obvious component of the social environment is the size of the country's population. A growing population is beneficial to firms in increasing the size of the potential market and in terms of increasing the available supply of labour. Slow population growth will act as a constraint on the firm, both in terms of markets and available supplies of labour.

The UK has experienced slow population growth for a number of decades but, until recently, employers have benefited from plentiful supplies of young people joining the labour force. In the immediate future that supply of additional labour will decline in size. This is forcing firms to be more receptive to the employment of older workers, to value younger workers more and invest in training to maximize the benefit gained from scarce resources.

As well as the overall number of people, business organizations should study trends in the age composition of the population. Trends in the birth rate are crucially important for firms such as Mothercare or Early Learning Centre and they will investigate demographic trends before opening a new branch. At the other end of the age scale we have a growing number of retired people. Many of these people are fit and enjoy a comfortable lifestyle as a result of occupational pensions. Consequently, there are more and more firms that concentrate on this niche in the market (Saga Holidays, for example, specializes in off-peak holidays for older people).

Changes in society are not confined to changes in the size and age composition of the population. Lifestyles, values and beliefs, the ethnic or religious background of society and socio-economic classes are also subject to change. These changes are of significance to business organizations because of their impact on the pool of available labour and purchasing behaviour of people in society.

The twentieth century has seen a decline in the size of the traditional 'cloth cap' working class, but a rise in the size of the skilled manual and clerical classes. One consequence of these trends is the closing of some marketing opportunities and the opening up of new ones. Similarly, changes in the nation's lifestyle can bring about changes in the market. The modern concern for fitness and health has provided great opportunities for firms supplying sports equipment and leisurewear, but others have suffered (the decline in tobacco consumption has forced tobacco companies to diversify, for example).

There are also changes in family life that should be noted. The working wife, combined with widespread possession of a car and a freezer, has been a major factor in the rise of the large. out-of-town shopping centre. In our society there are also growing numbers of one-person households. This presents another challenge to businesses as these people seek small-sized packets rather than the common large family sizes. The customer-oriented firm will supply goods in packets of varying sizes to suit the needs of households.

Demographic trends

Demography (the study of population trends, see Table 7.1 for terminology used) is, or should be, of interest to directors and managers of business organizations. This is because the human population performs two essential functions in the economy. First, it provides the *labour force* for the economy in general and a firm in particular. Second, the population provides the *market* for goods and services. Changes in either the size or nature of the population will have an impact on the supply of labour and/or demand from consumers.

Before looking at specific trends it is worth considering what geographical area should form the basis of the study. Should we be concerned about the population of the immediate area (village, suburb or town), the UK, the EU or of the world? The answer to the question depends on the business organization, its size, objectives and the nature of the product or service. Providers of personal services (such as hairdressers) will be

Table 7.1 Demographic terms

Terms	What they mean
Age distribution	The number of people in particular age groups throughout the population.
Birth rate	
Crude rate	Number of live births in a given place over a given period per 1000 population.
Age-specific rate	Number of live births per 1000 population at each age level.
Death rate	
Crude rate	Number of deaths in a given place over a given period per 1000 population
Age-specific rate	Number of deaths per 1000 population at each age level.
Fertility rate	Number of births per 1000 females in the fertility age group (that is, 15–45 years)
Infant mortality rate	Number of deaths of infants below one year per 1000 live births.
Natural increase	Excess of deaths over births (excludes immigration and emigration).
Net migration	Excess of immigration over emigration (inward) or emigration over immigration (outward).
Reproductive rate	The extent to which females in the fertility age ranges are replaced by the next generation.
Structure of population	Analysis of a population in terms of age, sex and occupational distribution.

concerned only with the population of the area from which customers are drawn. Manufacturers will be concerned about both national and local demographic trends. The national trends are an important determinant of the size of the market and local trends are an important factor in location decisions. In this age of multinational production and the EU single market, very large organizations will be concerned about European and world demographic trends. Most of the analysis that follows will focus on Britain and Europe, but readers should appreciate the importance of adapting the analysis for both a micro- or a global survey of population trends.

The population of the UK and most other developing countries is growing only very slowly. The increase in population is a result of births and immigration exceeding the loss of population due to death and emigration by only a small margin. Ignoring migration across international frontiers, we can analyse this long-term slowing down of population growth in terms of the model of demographic transition (see Figure 7.3). Death controls

population growth in underdeveloped countries. As the economy develops, a gap opens up between the birth rate and the death rate and this results in a rapid natural increase in population (in the case of the UK this occurred between 1760 and 1914). With further development, the birth rate falls, closing the gap between the birth and death rates. Advanced, affluent countries have completed the process of transition and have moved into a new phase of slow growth caused *not* by death control but by birth control. Developing countries are at various points in the transitional phase and this explains why rapid population growth is to be expected in such countries until at least the second part of the twenty-first century. However, for the developed world (which constitutes the main market for most business organizations) slow growth is to be expected.

The slow expected population growth is shown in Table 7.2. These projections are based on known information on age structures (both today and in the future) and on assumptions about social habits (marriage, birth control, ideas on family

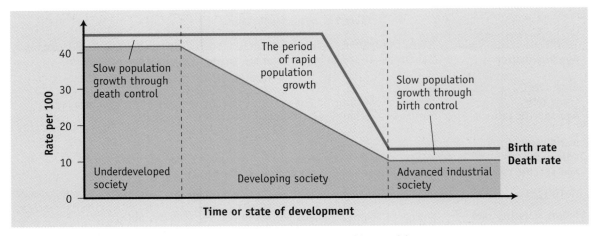

Figure 7.3 The model of demographic transition

Table 7.2 Some demographic statistics – projected population of the UK

Year	Millions
1989	57.2
1991	57.5
1996	58.4
2001	59.1
2006	59.7
2011	60.0
2016	60.4

Source: Office of Population and Surveys (OPS)

size). A simple example will illustrate this point. Statistics on the birth rate in the 1980s and 1990s can be used to predict the number of females in the child-bearing age group in the first decade or so of the twenty-first century. If we assume that social habits remain unchanged, demographers can predict the birth rate into the immediate future. In some situations it is possible to predict a population decline. The key concept for this conclusion is the reproductive rate. If females in the fertile age group are not being replaced by the next generation, there will be a fall in the number of women of child-bearing age and, if other factors remain unchanged, a cumulative fall in births and in the population as a whole will result.

The death rate can be projected into the future by collecting data on the age structure in the

future and by making assumptions about the impact of:

● disease;
● medical progress;
● social progress.

The long-term decline in the death rate has meant that people can expect to live longer (see Table 7.3) and that there is a rise in the number and proportion of people in the older age groups.

The population of a country is also affected by migration across national frontiers. For most of the last two centuries, the UK has experienced net outward migration, although, for short periods, Britain was a net gainer of migrants.

Immigration has the advantage of providing an immediate increase in the workforce. The only other causes of population growth are a rise in

Table 7.3 UK population over 75 years of age

Year	Millions
1989	3.9
1991	4.0
1996	4.2
2001	4.4
2006	4.5
2011	4.5
2016	4.9

Source: OPS

the number of births (which produces a rise in the labour force after a time lag) or a fall in the number of deaths (which is likely to increase, the size of the dependent, rather than the working, population). Immigration, on the other hand, will increase the workforce immediately, solving any problem of labour shortage. Immigration will also increase the demand for goods and services, although different patterns of consumption will mean that there will be some change in the structure of demand.

The demographic time-bomb?

Slow population growth caused by a low birth rate will result in an ageing population, although this term is often misunderstood. An ageing population simply means that there is a rise in the average age of people in society. It does not necessarily mean a rise in the number and proportion of retired people, although in practice this usually does occur. Any change in the age structure of a population will have consequences for the structure of demand in the economy and for the supply of labour. The ageing population in the UK has increased market opportunities for some firms and products but has led to setbacks for others. However, the most interesting and discussed aspects of the ageing population is the so-called 'demographic time-bomb'.

The low birth rate of the 1970s and 1980s meant that the 16–19-year-old population was one million lower in 1993 than it was in 1983 (with the bulk of the fall occurring in the period 1989 to 1993). The problem of the fall in the number of entrants to the labour market is made more acute by the long-term rise in the staying-on rate in full-time education and the early retirement of older workers.

In the expectation of the decline in the teenage population (which prompted the time-bomb notion) companies devised strategies to deal with the problem.

Women are usually seen as the solution to the problem of the time-bomb. We can identify the following main factors affecting the participation rate of women in the labour force:

- **fertility pattern** size and timing of families;

- **career-break patterns** usually breaks last eight years and are affected by household income, availability of childcare and supply of part-time jobs;
- **eldercare breaks** care of elderly relatives;
- **changing technology and working structures** 'some new technologies, and the shift towards knowledge-based jobs, offer the potential for greater flexibility over the timing and location' (*Skills and Enterprise Briefing* 14/19).

For many employers, the solution to the problem is to adopt new, more flexible working patterns:

- flexitime, including jobsharing;
- home-based work;
- career-break schemes as well as workplace nursery provision.

In addition to greater utilization of female workers, business organization are thinking about how they can retain and make best use of the skills and experience of older workers and using self-employed specialists rather than employing people directly.

Sociocultural factors

The social environment of an organization involves more than just demography. As well as the size and distribution of population, we should also consider aspects of lifestyle and culture that are relevant to the organization as a supplier of goods and demander of labour.

Our behaviour is affected by cultural influences and our membership of reference groups. **Culture** is a set of values, beliefs, attitudes and customs that are handed down through the generations. It is socially transmitted and learned behaviour but it does have a profound impact on what we buy and our attitude to work. For instance, cultural factors determine who does the buying and what is acceptable or unacceptable in a product (say, its colour). Those involved in marketing should be aware of the culture of a society and the many cultural groups within it, as a product that is acceptable in one culture might be unacceptable in another.

Reference groups are groups of people that influence our attitudes, opinions and behaviour. The group acts as a frame of reference both for members and those who aspire to be members. Those groups that we come into regular, direct contact with are the **primary groups** (such as family, friends and work colleagues). There are other groups (such as trade unions, religious groups and social clubs) with which we may come into contact less frequently. These can be termed **secondary groups**.

Lifestyles are the ways in which people live and spend their money, and are visible manifestations of the social environment. Broad categorizations (including suburban, two-career, single-parent, yuppies and the rest) can be developed, although they only give a very broad indication of spending patterns. Other classifications might be based on attitudes and values. We can classify people as survivors, sustainers, belongers, emulators, achievers, egoists (I am Me's), experientials, socially conscious and integrated. As we will see in Chapter 17, these classifications provide a basis for targeting different segments of the market.

Like all other aspects of the external environment, the sociocultural environment is subject to change. The so-called 'post-industrial society' will, it is said, continue the structural change from a goods-producing to a service economy. This is bringing, and will continue to bring, changes in the occupational distribution of the workforce and the role of information in our society. A similar fundamental change in society is encapsulated in the term 'post-materialistic society'. It is argued (for example, by Inglehart and Appel) that materialistic values emphasizing economic and physical security have given way to post-materialistic values that place greater emphasis on self-expression and belonging. Only the future will tell if these predictions will turn out to be true, although the evidence suggests that there is still some life left in the industrial and materialistic societies that characterized twentieth-century Western culture.

Leaving long-term futurology to one side, it is possible to identify a number of sociocultural changes that, both individually and collectively, have had a profound impact on business organizations. You should speculate on the impact for business organizations of the:

- increase in time available for leisure;
- changing roles of women in society and at work;
- concerns about healthy living;

Table 7.4 Examples of opportunities and constraints presented by the environment

Environment	Opportunity	Constraint
Economic	Growth in demand	Increased competition
	Rise in income	Rise in unemployment
	Fall in exchange rate	Higher interest rates
Political-legal	Tax concessions	Product laws necessitating product adaptation
	Deregulation	Reduction in public expenditure leading to fewer contracts
Technological	New product ideas	Rise in costs of capital
	New production processes	Higher entry costs to the market
Social-cultural	Rise in population	Decline in the number of new entrants to labour market
	Increased acceptance of the product Change in lifestyle favourable to the product	Change in fashion and taste unfavourable to the product
	Rise in educational and training standards	Reduction in the number of people in the relevant age group
		Growing distaste for certain activities (such as those relating to animals)

- emphasis on the quality of life;
- growth in owner occupation;
- increase in the proportion of people able to enjoy inherited wealth;
- increased life expectancy;
- limitation of family size;
- decline in formality within society;
- single-person households;
- the childless/child-free household;
- greater concern for the environment;
- greater concern about animal welfare;
- desire for greater convenience.

What is important to understand is that the slow but relentless pace of change produces over the years a profound change in how we live and what we buy. For instance, the increase in car ownership, which was made possible by changes in the economic environment, has profoundly affected life in our society. It has altered domestic architecture and the planning of residential areas. It has altered fashion – contributing to the decline of the hat and the mackintosh and aiding the growth of shorter, lighter and less formal clothing.

Examples of opportunities and constraints presented by changes in the environment are illustrated in Table 7.4.

Key concepts

A constraint A limiting factor to the attainment of objectives.

Culture The customs, beliefs, values and achievements of a society.

Demography The study of population trends.

Economic environment Factors in the economy that have an impact on the business organization, such as the state of the market, interest rates, changes in people's income.

External environment Factors external to the business organization that have an impact on the organization.

Legal environment Laws and regulations that have an impact on the business organization, such as planning, consumer, employment and health and safety laws.

An opportunity A favourable change in the environment that provides scope for achieving the organization's objectives.

Political environment Political and governmental factors that have an impact on the organization, such as a shift in policy to, or from, greater control or a change in policy on financial assistance for firms.

Social environment Social factors that have an impact on the business organization. These include demographic factors (such as an ageing population) and cultural and lifestyle factors (such as trends in divorce and people's aspirations).

Technological environment Technological factors that have an impact on business organizations. Changes in technology lead to the creation of new products (and the demise of others) and new processes of production.

Essay questions

1 (a) Identify the components of the external environment.
  (b) Analyse ways in which they impact business.

2 (a) Identify the major demographic trends in the UK.
  (b) Analyse their likely impact on business.

3 Analyse the role of SWOT and PEST analysis in business planning.

4 Using examples, analyse ways in which changes in the technological environment affect business.

5 (a) Identify trends in the social environment (other than demographic trends).
  (b) Analyse their likely impact on business.

Business and the law

This chapter deals in general terms with the impact of the law on business organizations. For the Business Studies student it is not necessary to know the law in detail, but it is necessary to understand the main thrust of the law as it affects business.

Chapter objectives

1 To develop an understanding of the nature of law.

2 To outline the law relating to contracts, employment, consumers and other areas with a direct impact on business.

3 To develop an understanding of the role of law, both in terms of providing a framework for relationships and acting as a constraint on business organizations.

The nature and sources of law

We should start by making a distinction between criminal law and civil law. **Criminal law** is concerned with the general wellbeing of society and defines actions that the State will punish. In criminal cases the accused, or **defendant**, is prosecuted and, if found guilty, punished. As is well known, there is no obligation on the part of the defendant to prove his or her innocence; instead the prosecution is required to prove the defendant guilty beyond all reasonable doubt.

Civil law provides rules for the conduct of relations between people or organizations. It includes laws concerning contracts, employment, consumer rights, property, succession and **tort** (negligence, nuisance, defamation and trespass). Civil proceedings are normally brought by private parties who are referred to as the **plaintiff** and the defendant. Unlike criminal proceedings, proof rests on the 'balance of probabilities', which means a lesser degree of proof is required to be shown. If the plaintiff is able to obtain a favourable judgment, then he or she will be awarded a 'remedy' to compensate for the civil wrong that has been shown to have been done. The remedy can take the form of an award of damages, a requirement that the defendant performs a contractual obligation (**decree of specific performance**) or a requirement that the defendant refrain from certain action (**injunction**).

In general, in business, our main interest is in

Table 8.1 Criminal v. civil law

Criminal law	Civil law
Defines actions that the State punishes ∴	Lays down rules for the conduct of relations between people and between organization
Deals with crimes against society	Deals with wrongs against individuals
The defendant is prosecuted	The defendant is sued
Punishes the guilty	Damages/compensation are awarded to successful claimants (the plaintiffs)
Proof of guilt beyond reasonable doubt is required	Proof on the balance of probability is required

civil law, although some business activity is constrained by criminal law (see Table 8.1). For instance, some aspects of consumer protection involve criminal law.

English law, which is distinct from the law in Scotland, is derived from a number of sources.

- **Common law** is a set of rules of behaviour and procedures established over centuries. The rules exist but require pronouncement by a judge. Hence, common law can be seen as judge-made law. Two key areas of the law relating to business are mostly common law: contracts and tort.
- **Statute law** is passed by Acts of Parliament. Acts tend to be written in general terms and have to be followed by judicial interpretation and/or delegated legislation. The laws relating to business organizations, employment and trade unions have all been created by statute law.
- **Delegated legislation** is the detailed regulations issued by government bodies as authorized under an Act of Parliament. Parliament delegates the authority to issue such statements, which have the force of law. By this means the details of legislation are filled in.
- **European Union law** Under the European Communities Act 1972, EU institutions have legislation power over the UK. At present, EU law tends to be limited to matters directly related to business, but as the scope of the EU widens, the impact of EU law will be felt in other areas. It takes the form of

regulations, directives and decisions. **Regulations** are binding on member states and become part of national law without any need for Parliamentary approval. **Directives** are, in effect, instructions to the governments and parliaments of member states to enact measures. **Decisions** are binding on those to whom they are addressed, which might be a member state or a particular company.
- **Statutory interpretation** As stated earlier, Acts of Parliament lay down general rules. The roles of judges is to interpret the law in particular circumstances.
- **Case law** has developed over the years, and continues to do so, as a result of interpretation by judges. If the facts of a case are similar to those of a previous case, then the rule of precedence applies and the judge will follow the decision of the judge in the earlier case.
- **Custom** Ancient custom that has acquired the force of law becomes binding provided it is reasonable, certain and not inconsistent with statute law. As 'ancient' means pre-AD 1189, this area of law is usually confined to matters concerning land use.
- **Equity** This allows justice and fairness to apply in situations where the law would otherwise lead to an injustice.

Contract law

A **contract** is an agreement (between two or more people) that is legally binding. Clearly, most business relationships are of a contractual nature and, consequently, contract law provides the basic framework of rights, obligations and remedies in this area.

For a contract to be legally enforceable, there must be:

- an **offer**, which is a statement without misrepresentation of the terms by which the party making the offer is prepared to be bound;
- **acceptance**, meaning the unconditional consent to all terms on offer;
- **consideration** or some element of mutual exchange that is measurable in money terms;
- the **intention** by both parties to be legally bound;
- **capacity**, or the ability and authority to make a contract.

Each of the above elements must be present if the contract is to be legally enforceable. The absence of any one of them would result in the contract being void, or destitute of all legal effect. In addition, there are certain types of contract that are only valid if they are written down, and in some cases witnessed and sealed. These contracts – known as **specialty contracts** – cover consumer credit, share transactions, sale of land, guarantees and leases on land.

Contracts are brought to an end (or **discharged**) in one of four ways.

- **Discharge by performance** means that both parties have done what they agreed to do.
- Contracts can be discharged by **mutual agreement**.
- Some event might **frustrate performance**. For instance, a change in the law might make performance of the contract illegal.
- A **breach of contract**.

A breach of contract qualifies the aggrieved and innocent party to recover **damages**. Damages are intended to restore injured parties to the position they would have been in had the contract not been breached. Alternatively, the plaintiff can sue for **specific performance**. This is a court order instructing performance of the contract. For work partially carried out, a plaintiff can sue

for **quantum meruit**. It goes without saying that the aggrieved party in a breach of contract is free of obligation for further performance of the contract.

Agency law

An **agent** is a representative of another legal party (a principal) who has powers to make contracts between his or her principal and third parties. In other words, the agent acts on behalf of the principal (such as an estate agent or an import–export agent would do). In view of the powers granted to make binding contracts between the principal and a third party, it is essential that the law establishes the rights and duties of all concerned.

No one can claim to be an agent of a principal unless the latter consents to them doing this. In most cases, agency is created by express contract, although there are other methods (including ratification after the event and by implication). An agent has a duty to:

- perform tasks with skill and diligence;
- avoid a conflict of interest with the principal;
- observe confidentiality;
- deal with the matter personally;
- not make a secret profit;
- act in good faith.

In return, the agent has a right to remuneration from the principal, indemnity for expenses incurred and exercise the right of **lien** (hold the principal's goods against payment of any debt outstanding).

In the event of contractual problems between the principal and a third party, it is essential that there are rules relating to who can sue and who can be sued.

- Where the existence of the principal is disclosed to the third party, any civil action will be between the principal and the third party.
- Where the agent does not disclose the existence of the principal, either the agent or principal can enforce the contract against the third party, who, in turn, can choose to

enforce the contract against either the agent or the principal.

- Where the agent acts outside his or her authority, the third party is entitled to sue the agent.
- Finally, if the principal generally pays the third party via the agent, then, in the event of non-payment by the agent, the principal remains liable for the settlement of the debt.

The law of tort

Tort is defined as a civil wrong and includes a variety of activities that cause harm. Assault, false imprisonment, defamation, trespass, negligence and nuisance are all examples of torts that can give rise to action in the courts. *Why* the defendant did what he or she did is irrelevant in tort; the key issue is *what* the defendant did and whether or not this caused injury to another.

Negligence

The most important of torts is **negligence** – failure to live up to the standard of care expected. To successfully sue for negligence, the plaintiff has to demonstrate that the defendant:

- has a duty of care;
- acted in breach of this duty;
- the plaintiff suffered as a result.

The burden of proof, therefore, is on the plaintiff. However, if he or she is able to demonstrate that the injury was of a kind that could not have occurred in the absence of negligence, then the burden of proof shifts to the defendant, who must demonstrate that he or she was not negligent. A plaintiff who is partly the cause of his or her own injury will share a percentage of the blame (and, therefore, suffer a corresponding reduction in damages). Carelessness in looking after one's own safety is known as **contributory negligence**.

Nuisance

Another tort that is relevant in a business setting is **nuisance** – the unjustifiable interference with the right to enjoy land and to live comfortably on it.

Public nuisance is suffered by a group of people and can be seen as a crime as well as a tort. **Private nuisance** involves a complaint by one person against the activities of another. The plaintiff can only successfully sue if he or she had an interest in the land when the nuisance was caused by the defendant or if the nuisance was the result of neglect of duty. The remedies are damages (compensation) and/or an injunction preventing further nuisance.

Vicarious liability

It is possible for individuals or business organizations to be liable for the crimes and torts committed by others. This is known as **vicarious liability** and, in a business setting, its most common form is the liability of employers for the actions of employees. For example, if negligence by an employees causes physical injury to a third party, the employer can be vicariously liable. This does not mean that the employee is excused liability – the vicarious liability of the employer is in addition to the liability of the employee.

The employer is only liable for torts committed by employees and not by independent contractors. Hence, distinction between the two is important in this aspect of law as well as in cases arising from the dismissal of workers. Evidence of a person being an employee include:

- deduction of tax and National Insurance by the employer;
- control of the worker by the employer;
- control of hours of work;
- provision of tools by the employer;
- whether or not the worker was an integral part of business;
- the labels applied by the individuals concerned.

Another common area of dispute is whether or not the employee was engaged in the normal course of work. Employers' vicarious liability obviously does not extend to work completed outside the workers' employment, but suppose injury is caused by an employee going against the express wishes of the employer. In Limpus v. London General Omnibus Co. (1862), the company was held to be vicariously liable for the actions of the driver who was racing his bus in contravention of company rules.

The rationale for vicarious liability (even when the employer was blameless) is that the employer:

- has control, or should have control, over employees;
- was negligent in selecting such employees;
- is better able to compensate the injured party than an employee;
- can provide an incentive for the employee to prevent a recurrence;
- benefits from the work of employees and must take the responsibility for the latter's actions.

Where employers are blameless, they can seek reimbursement from the employees concerned.

The law and employment

Until 1999, part-time employees enjoyed fewer legal rights than their full-time colleagues. For instance, they had to work continuously for an employer for five years to gain the same degree of employment protection that full-timers acquired after just two years. This made it attractive to employ part-time workers as it was easier to dismiss them, but it was clearly unfair and discriminatory (a disproportionately high number of part-timers are female and, therefore, female workers enjoyed fewer rights than male workers). The EU Part-time Workers Directive (issued under the Social Charter, which Britain belatedly accepted in 1998) gave part-time workers the same pro rata terms and conditions of employment as full-time workers. This removed legal discrimination against part-time workers so that they now enjoy the same employment protection rights as full-timers.

Contracts of employment

Employment contracts are substantially the same as any other contract. The two parties concerned voluntarily enter into a contract involving the exchange of labour for monetary reward. However, irrespective of the terms of the contract, there are rights and obligations derived from both common law and statute law. The **implied** (unwritten) terms of any contract of employment impose a duty on employers to pay staff, take reasonable care of them, treat them with courtesy, behave reasonably and, in the case of piece-rate workers, provide work. In return, employees have a duty to render service, obey reasonable and lawful instructions, act in good faith towards their employers and not impede employers' business. These are obligations stated in common law and failure to carry them out represents a breach of the implied terms of the employment contract.

In addition to common law, legislation passed by Parliament gives additional rights to employees. All employees have a right to:

- a written statement of the terms of employment;
- an itemized pay statement;
- notice of termination of employment;
- reasonable time off for public duties and trade union activities;
- redundancy compensation;
- statutory sick pay;
- a guarantee that they will be paid;
- maternity leave and the right to return to work after pregnancy;
- be treated without discrimination;
- a safe working environment.

The written statement of terms of employment must be issued within two months of taking up employment and include the:

- names of the employer and the employee;
- date when the employment (and, if different, the period of continuous employment) began;
- details of pay and the intervals at which it is to be paid;
- hours of work;
- holiday entitlement;
- entitlement to sick leave and sick pay;
- pension entitlement;
- entitlement of the employer and the employee to notice of termination;
- job title or brief job description;
- where it is not permanent, the period for which the employment is expected to

continue, or if it is for a fixed term, the date when it is to end;

- place of work;
- existence of any collective agreements that directly affect the employee's terms and conditions;

The statement must also include a note:

- giving details of the employer's disciplinary rules and grievance procedures, although employers with fewer than 20 employees need give only the contact name for raising a grievance; and
- stating whether or not a pensions contracting-out certificate is in force for the employment in question.

Sex Discrimination Act (SDA) 1975

The SDA applies to both males and females and makes sex discrimination unlawful in:

- employment;
- vocational training;
- education;
- the provision of goods, facilities and services;
- housing.

In employment, it is also unlawful to discriminate against someone on the grounds of being married.

There are two kinds of sex discrimination: direct and indirect. **Direct discrimination** is when a person is treated less favourably than another on the grounds of his or her sex. In determining whether or not direct discrimination has occurred, the following questions must be considered.

- Was treatment less favourable than the treatment that was (or would be) accorded to a person of the opposite sex?
  If so,
- was the treatment less favourable because of the gender of the person involved?

Indirect discrimination may occur even when a condition or requirement seems to affect men and women equally if, in practice, it disadvantages a far greater proportion of one sex than the other. However, such a condition will not be indirectly discriminatory unless all of the following are true:

- it is applied equally to both sexes;
- the proportion of one sex who can comply with it is considerably smaller than the proportion of the other sex who can comply;
- the individual suffers because he or she cannot comply;
- it cannot be shown to be an objectively justifiable condition or requirement by the employer.

There are two exemptions allowed under the Act. First, that the indirect discriminatory qualification was in fact a genuine occupational qualification and, second, that it is justified because it is a positive action to enable the disadvantaged sex to compete on equal terms.

Under the EU Burden of Proof in Sex Discrimination Cases Directive, the onus is placed on the defendant (the employer) to prove that sex discrimination has *not* occurred. The UK is obliged to implement this by 2001.

Parent Leave Directive (PLD)

This 'family friendly' measure gives workers the following rights:

- a minimum of three months' leave from work (unpaid) for each working parent to be taken up by a child's eighth birthday;
- family leave for working parents in the event of sickness or accident;
- parental leave for people who adopt children.

The attitude of employers to this Directive varies from hostility to a measure that creates staff problems to support for a measure that improves the employee retention rate and enables staff to concentrate productively on their work when they return.

Maternity Rights

Pregnancy entitles employees to:

- reasonable time off with pay for antenatal care;
- 14 weeks' maternity leave;
- the benefit of all their terms and conditions of employment, except for pay, during maternity leave;

● no dismissal or selection for redundancy for any reason connected with maternity.

Women with two years' continuous service at the eleventh week before the expected week of childbirth have the right to up to around 40 weeks' absence in total.

Racial discrimination

The Race Relations Act 1976 makes racial discrimination unlawful in employment, vocational training and related areas. The Act applies in Great Britain and there is similar legislation in Northern Ireland.

The Act defines **racial discrimination** as discrimination on the grounds of colour, race, nationality or ethnic or national origins.

There are two types of racial discrimination – generally referred to as direct and indirect. **Direct discrimination** arises where one person treats another less favourably, on racial grounds, than he or she treats (or would treat) someone else. In deciding whether or not a particular kind of treatment may constitute direct racial discrimination it is necessary to consider:

● whether or not the treatment was any less favourable compared to the treatment that was (or would be) accorded to another person;
● if so, whether or not the unfavourable treatment was due to the colour, race, nationality or ethnic or national origins of the person who was less favourably treated, or of someone else connected with that person (for example, their spouse).

It is not necessary to show that unfavourable treatment on racial grounds was **openly intended** – often it will be possible to infer that discrimination was intended from the circumstances in which the treatment occurred.

Indirect discrimination is treatment that may be equal in the sense that it applies to employees of different racial groups, but is discriminatory in its effect on one particular racial group. It occurs when one person applies, to another person, a condition or requirement with which he or she must comply to gain a benefit or to avoid a disadvantage. However, such a condition will not be

indirectly discriminatory unless all the following are true:

● it applies, or would apply, equally to other employees whatever their racial group;
● the proportion of people in the disadvantaged person's racial group who can comply with it is considerably smaller than the proportion of those not in that group who can comply;
● it is detrimental to the complainant because he or she cannot comply with it;
● the employer cannot show it to be a justifiable condition or requirement irrespective of the colour, race, nationality or ethnic or national origins of the person to whom it is applied.

If is also unlawful to segregate a person from others on racial grounds and treat someone less favourably than others because they have asserted their rights under race equality law.

As with sex discrimination, it is possible for membership of a particular racial group to be regarded as a genuine occupational qualification under the law. For instance:

● where a person of a particular racial group is required for a job involving participation in a dramatic performance or as a photographic model;
● where the jobholder provides to people of a particular racial group personal services promoting their welfare and those services can most effectively be provided by a person of the same racial group.

Other exception – known as **positive action** – can help members of under-represented racial groups compete on equal terms with others in the labour market. An employer or training body may, for example, encourage members of a particular racial group to apply for particular work or provide special training to equip such people better in particular work, where in either case people of that group are under-represented.

The law and pay

Two aspects of the law on pay are worth mentioning. According to the **Equal Pay Act 1970**, if a woman or man is doing work that is:

- the same;
- broadly similar;
- rated as equivalent under a job evaluation scheme; or
- or equivalent value;

to that done by a man or woman, then her or his conditions of service should be no less favourable than those of the man or woman. In deciding whether or not any term is less favourable, a comparison must be made with a man or woman employed by the same employer.

The **national minimum wage** came into force in 1999. The general adult rate for the national minimum is £3.60 per hour, with a lower rate for 18–21-year-olds. Workers aged 16 and 17 are not covered by the national minimum. The national minimum wage remains controversial – opponents argue that it leads to job losses and, therefore, a rise in unemployment.

The Working Time Directive (WTD) 1998

The WTD came into force in 1998 after much opposition from employers. The Institute of Directors argued that 'these regulations restrict labour flexibility and impose costly new obligations on firms'. Designed to protect employees from a requirement to work excessive hours, the WTD provides workers with the following statutory rights:

- four weeks' paid annual leave;
- a limit on average weekly working time to 48 hours (although this can be averaged out over 4 months and there are some exemptions);
- rest break after 6 consecutive hours of work;
- 11 hours' rest between working shifts;
- at least a day's rest per week;
- a limit on night workers' average daily working time to 8 hours;
- health assessment for night workers.

Dismissal and redundancy payments

An employer can dismiss an employee at any time, although a period of notice must normally be given. Employees in general have the right not to be unfairly dismissed, but a dismissal will be lawful provided that is for a fair reason and that the employer has acted reasonably in all the circumstances.

The length of notice an employer must give (normally) depends on the length of time the employee has been continuously employed:

- 1 month to 2 years' service equals 1 week's notice;
- 2 years to 12 years' service equals 1 week's notice for each complete year;
- more than 12 years' service equals 12 weeks' notice.

If a longer period of notice has been agreed in the employee's contract, then the longer period applies.

Instant dismissal is only allowed in cases of gross misconduct, such as theft or acts of violence at work.

Employers may seek to terminate the employment of workers for two basic reasons:

- redundancy, where workers are surplus to requirements;
- misconduct, incapacity or incompetence.

However, a major constraint on employers is the rights of employees under various Employment Protection Acts. When an individual considers that he or she has been unfairly dismissed, the former employee has recourse to an Employment Tribunal where the onus is on the employer to prove that the dismissal was fair. There are five reasons for dismissal that are statutorily fair:

- misconduct;
- incapacity to do the job;
- redundancy;
- continued employment would break the law, so the dismissal of a lorry driver who has lost his or her driving licence is fair;
- some other **substantial** reason, such as refusal to accept a change in duties or a personality clash.

It is automatically unfair to dismiss a worker for:

- being a trade union member;
- not being a trade union member;

- taking part in trade union activities;
- being pregnant or taking maternity leave;
- taking certain types of action on health and safety grounds – raising a concern with a health and safety representative, for example;
- refusing (in certain circumstances) to do shop work on a Sunday;
- reasons connected with the transfer of an undertaking from one employer to another, unless there are economic, technical or organizational reasons that make changes in the workforce necessary;
- acting as a representative for consultation about redundancy or business transfer or as a candidate to be a representative of this kind;
- performing, or proposing to perform, any duties relevant to an employee's role as an employee occupational pension scheme trustee;
- qualifying (or because she or he will or might qualify) for the national minimum wage*;
- reasons relating to the Working Time Regulations 1998.

Even when dismissal is fair and justified, it is still necessary to carry it out in accordance with procedures laid down.

Summary dismissal without notice is only lawful in cases of gross misconduct or gross negligence. Termination resulting from misconduct or unsatisfactory work should be preceded by a verbal warning, a second warning in the course of an interview, a third warning in writing and disciplinary action conducted in accordance with the rules of natural justice. To avoid the risk of an action for wrongful dismissal, the organization should clearly state the reasons for the action and allow the employee to be represented – by a trade union official, for example.

There is a distinction between wrongful dismissal and unfair dismissal. **Wrongful dismissal** is a breach of contract by the employer who terminates employment without giving the appropriate period of notice. **Unfair dismissal** is any dismissal that does not fall within the five definitions of fair causes of dismissal given above. In essence, unfair dismissal relates to *reasons* for termination whereas wrongful dismissal refers to the *procedure* used.

Redundancy is statutorily fair under the Employment Protection Act 1978. This Act identified three situations that give rise to redundancy:

- the employer has ceased the business for which the employee is employed;
- the employer has ceased business in the place where the employee is employed;
- the requirements of the business have diminished and labour is surplus to needs.

Redundancy will only be 'fair' if it is carried out in an approved manner. First, there is an obligation on the employer to consult with recognized unions and to give warning. Second, if the employee is unfairly selected for redundancy, he or she can claim unfair dismissal. What constitutes 'unfair selection' depends on the selection procedure agreed with the union. For instance, if a 'last in, first out' (LIFO) system is used, a redundant worker can claim unfair dismissal if he or she was made redundant in advance of employees who were taken on later than them.

Redundancy compensation is an entitlement for workers with two years' continuous service, working (16 or more hours per week).

- For each year of service beyond the age of 41, the redundant employee is entitled to compensation equal to one and a half week's pay.
- For each year of service between 22 and 40, the entitlement is one week's pay.
- For each year from 18 to 21, compensation is equal to half a week's pay.

It should be noted that redundancy compensation is not an entitlement for people under 18 or those over the State retirement age.

Employees' safety

Employers have various obligations in relation to the health and safety of their employees. Under common law, there is an obligation to take **reasonable care**. The Factories Act 1961 and the Offices, Shops and Railway Premises Act 1963 lay down minimum requirements relating to safety. Breaches of these Acts are breaches of criminal law and could result in prosecution. Moreover, many parts of the Acts impose strict liability on the 'occupier' of the premises. This means that liability does not rest on proof of negligence or recklessness – the occupier cannot plead that the breach was not his or her fault. In addition to criminal prosecution, the injured worker may bring a civil action in tort for breach of statutory duty.

The Health and Safety at Work, etc Act (HSWA) 1974 represented a new departure in respect of safety legislation. Under this legislation, employers must ensure, so far as is reasonably practicable, the health, safety and welfare of all employees. Among the duties imposed are:

● the provision and maintenance of plant and systems of work that are safe and without risks to health;
● arrangements for ensuring the safe use, handling, storage and transportation of articles and substances;
● the provision of the information, instruction, training and supervision necessary to ensure the health and safety of workers;
● the maintenance of any place of work under the employer's control in a condition that is safe and without risks to health;
● the provision and maintenance of a working environment that is safe, without risk to health, and adequate as regards facilities and arrangements for the welfare of workers.

The HSWA imposes a positive obligation to create a safe working environment and for employers to prepare a written safety statement. A breach of the employer's duties could make him or her liable to criminal prosecution as well as civil action for compensation.

In 1992, six EU Safety Directives (the Six Pack) came into force.

● **Management of Health and Safety at Work Regulations 1992** The main purpose is to improve health and safety management by introducing proper systems for coordinating, control and monitoring.
● **Provision and Use of Work Equipment Regulations 1992** The main purpose is to bring together and clarify the many regulations that deal with equipment.

● **Manual Handling Operations Regulations 1992** The main purpose is to lay down proper procedures for manual handling – for example, carrying heavy loads, which is a major cause of industrial accidents.
● **Workplace (Health, Safety and Welfare) Regulations 1992** The main purpose is to tidy up and clarify previous legislation covering working environment, safety, facilities and 'housekeeping'.
● **Personal Protective Equipment at Work (PPE) Regulations 1992** The main purpose is to tidy up and clarify previous legislation. It covers the use, type and storage of PPE.
● **Health and Safety (Display Screen Equipment) Regulations 1992** The main purpose is the laying down of rules and regulations for the health and safety of employees who continually use display screen equipment (DSE).

Enforcement of the law relating to health and safety is in the hands of the Health and Safety Executive (HSE) and the four groups of inspector under the HSE that cover:

● factories
● agriculture
● nuclear installations
● railways.

Inspectors have the right to enter and inspect premises and issue improvement notices instructing the employer to carry our improvements in the interest of health and safety.

Occupiers' liability

This is another area of law that impacts business organizations and can have a direct effect on the costs of a firm. Under the Occupiers' Liability Act 1957, the occupier (such as a shop owner) has a duty of care to ensure that all lawful visitors will be reasonably safe. A **lawful visitor** is someone who is invited on to the premises or who enters under contract, but clearly this does not extend to trespassers. A business sued under this Act can offer the following defences:

● warning notices were posted up;

- the person injured was a trespasser;
- the injury was caused not by the occupier, but by an independent contractor and, in the case of visitors under contract, liability was excluded – as in the case of a sports event.

To guard against being sued for injury, it is necessary for business organizations to ensure that premises are safe. Clearly, this has cost implications.

The Occupiers' Liability Act 1984 extends some protection to trespassers. An occupier has a duty to persons other than lawful visitors in respect of any risk or injury due to the state of the premises or by anything done or omitted to be done to them. An example would be injury to a trespasser who entered the premises through an existing hole in a fence. The erection of warning notices would provide some defence in such a case, but, once again, this has cost implications.

Consumer Law

When a customer buys goods in a shop, he or she is entering into a contract with the shopkeeper. In consequence, both sides have rights and duties under common law concerning contracts. However, in the light of the weak position of the consumer in comparison to that of the seller, it has been felt necessary to superimpose a body of consumer law on contract law. One effect of consumer law is to remove the principle of **caveat emptor** – let the buyer beware – from consumer contracts. The consumer is provided with additional protection that would not be available if the goods were sold by one firm to another.

Consumer law is part criminal law and part civil law. First, let us look at criminal consumer law.

Criminal consumer law

Under the Food and Drugs Act 1955, it is a criminal offence to sell food or drugs that are unfit for consumption. This Act also regulates hygiene conditions in connection with food and the labelling of food. Under the Consumer Protection Act 1961 it is a criminal offence to sell goods that do not meet safety standards. The Trades Description Act 1968 made it a criminal offence to give a false or misleading description of goods. This Act also

makes reference to price reductions. It is an offence to advertise a price as a reduction unless the initial price has been charged for 28 days in the previous 6 months. The Unsolicited Goods Act 1971 made it illegal to demand payment for goods or services that have not been ordered. In addition, the consumer is permitted to keep the goods without paying if the supplier fails to retrieve them within 30 days of being informed (or within 6 months if not informed). The Resale Price Acts 1964 and 1976 made it unlawful for suppliers (either individually or collectively) to fix minimum prices. This outlawed the previous practice of resale price maintenance (RPM) whereby manufacturers dictated prices to retailers. The Weights and Measures Act 1985 made it an offence to give short weights or a wrong indication of the amount being offered for sale.

Civil consumer law

Civil consumer law modifies the contractual relationship between buyer and seller. In effect, the terms of various Acts become the implied conditions in consumer contracts. The Sale of Goods Act 1979 states that goods must be:

- of merchantable quality;
- as described;
- fit for the purpose for which they were purchased.

These points are implied in all consumer contracts and the sellers may not exempt themselves from any of these conditions. Consequently, if the goods are *not* of merchantable quality, as described or fit for the purpose sold, the seller has failed to discharge his or her side of the contract, thus releasing the buyer from obligation.

The Consumer Credit Act 1974 is the key statute on credit trading. The Act requires anyone carrying on a credit or hire business to obtain a licence from the Director General of Fair Trading. The seller is also required to state the true rate of interest (known as the annual percentage rate of charge, or APR). The Act also makes it easier for consumers to extricate themselves from hastily signed agreements as it gives consumers a 'cooling off' period, during which they can withdraw if the agreement was signed anywhere other than the creditor's business premises. False and misleading advertisements relating to credit terms also constitute an offence under this Act.

The Consumer Protection Act 1987 consolidated a number of previous measures relating to product safety and trades descriptions. In addition, it implemented an EC directive relating to strict liability. This is defined as automatic liability, independent of fault on the part of the defendant. The purchaser no longer has to prove the negligence of the supplier.

Table 8.2 summarizes the legislation that has been passed to protect consumers.

Table 8.2 Consumer protection legislation

Date	Act	Main provision
1968	Trades Descriptions Act	Misleading descriptions banned. 'Price reductions' have to be genuine
1971	Unsolicited Goods Act	Illegal to demand payment for goods not ordered
1973	Fair Trading Act	Consolidated previous law Established the Office of Fair Trading
1973	Supply of Goods (Implied Terms) Act	Action against guarantees that took away customers' rights
1974	Prices Act	Display of price information
1974	Consumer Credit Act	Licensed firms involved in giving credit True rate of interest (APR) to be displayed Easier for consumers to extricate themselves from a hastily signed agreement
1977	Unfair Contract Terms Act	Dealt with unfair exclusion clauses
1978	Consumer Safety Act	Product safety
1979	Sale of Goods Act	Consolidated previous laws Goods to be of merchantable quality, as described and fit for the purpose sold
1987	Consumer Protection Act	Strict liability Anyone injured by defective products can sue the supplier
1994	Sales and Supply of Goods Act	Goods must be of satisfactory quality

Key concepts

Civil law Relates to disputes between individuals (including business entities). The object of civil law is to resolve disputes and provide a remedy for people who are wronged but not to punish wrongdoers.

Consumer protection law Law intended to protect the interests of consumers.

Contract A legally binding agreement.

Criminal law Concerned with conduct the State disapproves so strongly of that it will punish wrongdoers.

Employment law Law relating to contracts of employment and the rights and obligations of employees.

Negligence Failure to live up to the duty of care, skill and diligence expected of a person.

Nuisance Interference with another's use of, enjoyment of and rights over land.

Tort A civil wrong independent of contract, such as the tort of nuisance or defamation.

Vicarious liability Liability for the actions of others, such as an employer for the actions of their employees when action is undertaken in the normal course of employment.

Essay questions

1 (a) Analyse the distinctions between civil and criminal law.
(b) Explain three circumstances in which a firm selling a legal product might be subject to criminal prosecution.

2 (a) Describe the essential elements of a contract.
(b) Why are consumer contracts and contracts of employment the subject of statute law, which overrides the law of contract?

3 (a) Explain what is meant by vicarious liability.
(b) Vicarious liability only applies if the worker is an employee rather than an independent contractor.
(i) How would a court determine whether or not a worker was an employee?
(ii) In what other aspect of law is it essential to determine whether or not a person is an employee rather than an independent contractor.

4 (a) Explain the difference between unfair and wrongful dismissal.
(b) Analyse the circumstances in which dismissal is fair in law.

5 A threat to jobs or essential protection for the worker? Assess post 1997 measures relating to employment from the perspective of the employer and the employee.

6 (a) Outline the law relating to consumer goods considered to be of an unsatisfactory quality.
(b) What redress does a consumer have:
(i) if the goods are faulty; and
(ii) if the goods cause injury.

Principles of microeconomics

People involved in managing business organizations need to be sensitive to the economic environment, which, like the other elements in the environment, is continually changing. We live in a dynamic and changing economy. A knowledge of economics does not guarantee success in business but what it does provide is a way of interpreting and analysing trends in the economic environment. Economics is conventionally divided into microeconomics and macroeconomics. The former involves the study of a small part of the market (a single firm or product) while macroeconomics deals with the whole, interrelated economy.

Chapter objectives

1 To introduce the reader to the main concepts of microeconomics.

2 To develop an understanding of the theory of demand, supply and price.

3 To develop an understanding of elasticity.

4 To derive lessons from the theory of the firm.

Demand

In economics, **demand** is the desire to purchase a good or service, backed up by an ability and willingness to pay for the product. Mere desire is insufficient; only when both conditions (desire *and* ability to pay) are met is demand said to be effective. Ability to pay is clearly related to income and the other claims on our income. The desire to acquire a product or service is related to an assessment of the benefit or pleasure expected to be derived from it, compared with the sacrifice of money (and, therefore, other purchases) required in acquiring the good or service. Consumers are assumed to be rational. They make decisions that aim at maximizing the pleasure (known in economics as utility) gained from their purchases – the rational consumer will only purchase goods if the pleasure expected from consuming them is at least equal to the sacrifice of money in purchasing the goods. Although the theory is unprovable, it does have a common-sense appeal. It would be folly to buy something if you did not expect a commensurate amount of satisfaction.

If we consume up to the point where price and expected pleasure are equivalent, then any reduction in price will result in an increase in the quantity of the good that we purchase. This is the basis behind the downward-sloping **demand curve**. Table 9.1 shows a demand schedule. At a high price (say, £10), the quantity demanded is low (100,000 tonnes). As the price falls to £7,

Table 9.1 A demand schedule

Price	Quantity demanded (000 tonnes)
10	100
9	110
8	120
7	130
6	140
5	150

there is an increase in the quantity demanded to 130,000 tonnes. This principle is adopted intuitively by market traders or ticket touts outside a rock concert – when faced with a surplus, especially of a highly perishable product, they will reduce the price to 'clear' the market. The data in the demand schedule can now be plotted on a graph (see Figure 9.1). The downward-sloping demand curve informs us that the quantity demanded is inversely related to price.

Economists make a number of assumptions that, although somewhat divorced from reality, enable us to concentrate on the variable we wish to study. In this case, it is the impact of price on demand for the product. Hence, the demand curve is drawn on the assumption that other factors remain unchanged. This causes dismay to students new to economics, who rightly point out that other things

never remain unchanged in a dynamic economy. However, by holding other factors constant, we can focus on the impact of the single variable (price). In this respect, the economist is adopting an approach similar to that of a chemist conducting laboratory experiments.

When other factors do change, there is a change, in demand. For instance, a rise in income will lead to an increase in demand, with the demand curve shifting outwards to the right. At each price level, more is demanded than before (see Figure 9.2). A shift of the demand curve can also be caused by a change other than price, such as a change in taste or fashion, population, a successful advertising campaign, the price of complementary goods or substitute goods.

Complementary goods, such as petrol and cars or films and cameras, are jointly demanded. We derive little benefit from a car unless we can obtain petrol. Hence, a rise in the price of petrol may deter some people from purchasing a car and may encourage others to purchase a more economical car. Substitute goods, as the name suggests, are rival products such as butter and margarine or tea and coffee. They perform similar functions and, if we assume that some people are equally prepared to drink both tea and coffee, a rise in the price of coffee is likely to encourage some to switch to drinking tea.

We can now summarize demand theory by

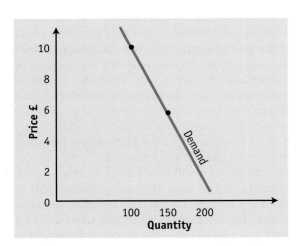

Figure 9.1 A demand curve

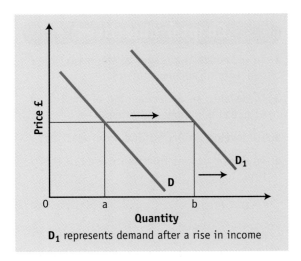

D_1 represents demand after a rise in income

Figure 9.2 A shift of the demand curve

stating that demand is a function of (related to) a number of factors:

Quantity demanded $= \int$ (price, income, price of complements, price of substitutes, taste, population)

If other things are held constant, then demand is a function of price. The relationship is inverse so that, as the price falls, the quantity demanded increases. A movement along the demand curve is caused by a change in the price of the good and, to avoid confusion, it is called an **extension** or **contraction of demand** (see Figures 9.3 and 9.4).

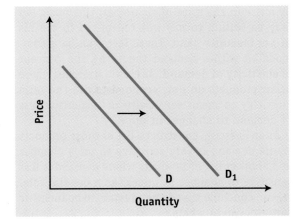

Figure 9.5 An increase in demand (caused by a rise in income; favourable change in taste; fall in the price of a complement; rise in the price of a substitute; rise in population)

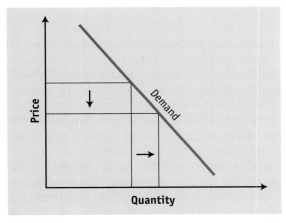

Figure 9.3 An extension of demand caused by a fall in price

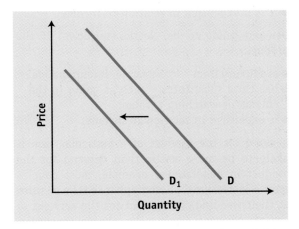

Figure 9.6 A decline in demand (caused by a fall in income; adverse change in taste; rise in the price of a complement; fall in the price of a substitute; fall in population

A shift of the demand curve is caused by something other than price and is called an **increase** or **decrease in demand** (see Figures 9.5 and 9.6).

Elasticity of demand

The enquiring mind will be thinking at this stage that there are some things we buy almost irrespective of price. The smoker is not discouraged

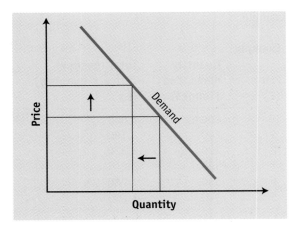

Figure 9.4 A contraction of demand caused by a rise in price

by a rise in the price of cigarettes; the music fan may be willing to pay inflated prices to see his or her favourite band. These facts can be accommodated within demand theory by the concept of **elasticity of demand**. As elastic stretches where other products do not, economists use the term elasticity to mean sensitivity or responsiveness of demand to changes in price.

As an exercise, construct a list of those products where demand is very sensitive to price changes and another list of products where demand is less sensitive to changes in prices. As a general rule, we can conclude that demand tends to be inelastic (unresponsive) where:

● the product is a necessity – such as bread;
● there are no close substitutes – as with electricity;
● the product is habit-forming – say tobacco; and/or
● it is inexpensive in relation to income.

Demand tends to be elastic (sensitive) if the product:

● is a luxury item – for example, foreign holidays;
● has close substitutes – such as going to the cinema or watching a video;
● is expensive in relation to income.

Demand for the product of a particular firm is likely to be more elastic than demand for the product in general. For example, most couples want a professional photographer to take pictures at their wedding, so demand for the services of a photographer is likely to be relatively inelastic. However, photographers are in competition with each other. If one photographer raises prices, he or she is likely to lose custom unless he or she has some distinctive advantage in another aspect of the marketing mix, such as a reputation for high-quality service. Firms with distinctive advantages may be able to retain custom even if they raise prices.

There is a simple formula for calculating price elasticity of demand:

$$\text{Price elasticity of demand} = \frac{\text{Percentage change in quantity demanded}}{\text{Percentage change in price}}$$

Example

Suppose a price rise from £1 to £1.25 was followed by a fall in quantity purchased from 100 tonnes to 80 tonnes. Assuming that the price rise caused the fall in quantity sold (an assumption that could be difficult to prove), calculate price elasticity of demand.

Quantity demanded falls by 20 tonnes or 20 per cent.

Price rose by 25p or 25 per cent.
Therefore, price elasticity of demand is:

$$\frac{20\%}{25\%} \text{ or } 0.8$$

Here, elasticity is less than one, which means it is relatively inelastic (price-insensitive). If elasticity exceeds one, demand is said to be relatively elastic (price-sensitive). If the resulting number is exactly one, we say that elasticity is unitary.

The calculation of elasticity is difficult in the real world, but some notion of price sensitivity is important to a firm considering altering its prices. A price reduction would produce little benefit for the firm if demand is insensitive to price. On the other hand, a firm considering a price rise may suffer a serious loss of trade if demand is sensitive to price. The relationship between elasticity and the firm's revenue after a price change can be illustrated in the following example.

Example

Price (£)	Quantity demanded (Tonnes)	Total revenue (Price × quantity) (£)
10	200	2,000
9	240	2,160
8	290	2,320
7	320	2,240
6	330	1,980
5	340	1,700

A price rise from £5 to £6 results in an increase in revenue (although, as we know nothing about costs, we cannot comment on profits). However, a rise from £9 to £10 causes a fall in the firm's revenue. A task for the reader is to calculate price elasticity of demand for both price changes. It will be discovered that demand is inelastic at the low prices but elastic at the high ones.

Income elasticity of demand

Income elasticity of demand is the responsiveness of demand to changes in income. For most goods, a rise in income is likely to be followed by an increase in demand (a rightward shift of the demand curve). This increase is likely to be greatest in the case of luxury goods, such as package holidays abroad. It is likely to be low in the case of a basic necessity, such as bread. It is possible for income elasticity to be negative. This applies to a situation in which a rise in income results in a fall in demand. Such products are known as **inferior goods** but this should not be taken to mean substandard or 'shoddy'. Public transport might be considered an inferior good if bus travellers switch to travelling to work by car following a rise in income.

The formula for calculating income elasticity of demand is:

$$\frac{\text{Percentage change in quantity demanded}}{\text{Percentage change in income}}$$

Cross-elasticity of demand

Cross-elasticity of demand is the least well-known elasticity of demand. It refers to the effect on demand for one product of a change in the price of another. The formula is:

$$\frac{\text{Percentage change in the demand for Product X}}{\text{Percentage change in the price of Product Y}}$$

Consider two very different examples. In the first, a 20 per cent rise in the price of coffee results in a 10 per cent rise in the demand for tea.

Cross-elasticity is $\dfrac{10\%}{20\%}$ or ½

As both percentages relate to rises, we should state that cross-elasticity here is positive (a plus divided by a plus).

In the second case, a 50 per cent rise in the price of video recorders results in a 20 per cent fall in the demand for video tapes.

Cross-elasticity is now $\dfrac{-20\%}{+50\%}$ or $\dfrac{-2}{5}$

The simple conclusion we can draw is that in the case of substitute products, cross-elasticity is *positive*, and that in the case of complementary products, cross-elasticity is *negative*.

Supply

The counterbalance to demand is supply. This is the quantity of a commodity (or service) that is offered to the market at a particular price. It should be appreciated that just as demand is not the quantity bought, so supply is not the quantity sold. Instead, these terms refer to the quantity that buyers seek to buy and the quantity that sellers seek to sell at a particular price.

As a general rule, the higher the price, the greater the quantity offered in the market. The higher price will encourage marginal producers to supply the market as well as tempting existing producers to supply more. The direct relationship between price and quantity supplied (that is, they move in the same direction) is reflected in the **supply curve**, which slopes upwards (see Figure 9.7). As with the demand curve, it is drawn on the assumption that other factors remain unchanged.

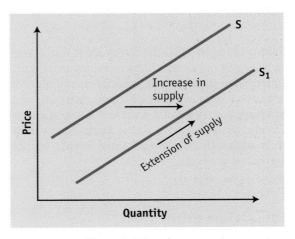

Figure 9.7 Supply curves

These 'other factors' mainly concern the cost of producing the goods. A rise in the price of inputs will raise the cost of production and reduce the profitability of supplying the market. In consequence, producers will reduce the amount supplied. This is illustrated by an inward shift of the supply curve. Economists distinguish between an **extension/contraction of supply** and an **increase/decrease of supply**. The former events are caused by a change in the price of the product; the latter by something other than price.

Price elasticity of supply is the responsiveness of supply to changes in price. The formula for calculating price elasticity of supply (PES) is similar to the previous elasticities that we have encountered.

$$PES = \frac{\text{Percentage change in quantity supplied}}{\text{Percentage change in price}}$$

Example

Price per tonne	Quantity supplied
£20	1500m tonnes
£22	1800m tonnes

As price rises from £20 to £22 (a 10 per cent rise), quantity extends from 1500m tonnes to 1800m tonnes (a 20 per cent rise). Hence, price elasticity of supply is 20 per cent divided by 10 per cent, which is 2. As the answer exceeds one, supply is said to be elastic. If elasticity was less than one it would be inelastic.

Supply tends to be elastic in the short run. A rise in price will encourage firms to supply more, but, unless they possess spare capacity or can quickly acquire additional inputs of labour, materials and machinery, they will not be able to respond immediately. Supply is more elastic in the long run as it is easier to obtain additional inputs of the factors of production.

Price

Equilibrium price

By combining supply and demand curves together

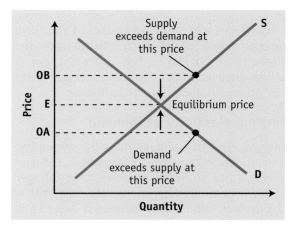

Figure 9.8 Equilibrium price

on the same graph we can determine the **equilibrium** (or **market**) **price** (see Figure 9.8). At the equilibrium price the amount that buyers wish to purchase is exactly equal to the amount that suppliers are willing to offer to the market. At all other prices, there is disequilibrium. For instance, at price OA, demand exceeds supply. Competition between buyers will force the price up to the equilibrium. At price OB supply exceeds demand. As a consequence, competition between sellers will force the price down to the equilibrium. The equilibrium price is, therefore, a natural market price. Market forces will push the price towards the equilibrium, which is the only sustainable price in the long run.

Price regulation

Interference with market prices will cause problems. Consider the impact of maximum price regulations. In Figure 9.9, the natural price is considered too high and the government seeks to impose a maximum price (OX). As a result, there is excess demand, leading to shortages. In a free (or unregulated market), the shortage disappears as a result of a rise in price, which chokes off some excess demand and encourages an extension of supply. In the regulated market, price is not permitted to rise and, as a result, the excess demand continues indefinitely. This is likely to lead to coupon rationing of supplies and the development of a black market.

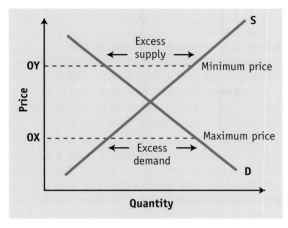

Figure 9.9 The impact of price regulation on supply

Minimum price regulation (such as minimum farm prices) is likely to produce equally undesirable consequences. At the minimum price (OY) there is excess supply or a surplus. In a free market, the surplus is eliminated by a fall in price. In a regulated market, the surplus continues indefinitely. The basic conclusion is that legislation to keep prices artificially high leads to surplus, while legislation to keep prices artificially low leads to shortage.

In a market economy, therefore, price plays an essential role in:

● signalling changes in customer wants;
● providing an incentive for entrepreneurs to respond to changing demand;
● rewarding the factors of production;
● rationing the supply of goods.

Economies of scale

As firms grow in size, they acquire certain advantages that are known as economies of large-scale production (economies of scale for short). This means that the average (or unit) cost of production falls as its scale rises. This is not to say that it costs less to produce 1000 motor vehicles than 990 vehicles, but that the cost of producing each vehicle is lower at the higher level of output. Although growth in size produces certain problems – known in economics as diseconomies of scale –

it is generally the case that growth in size produces cost advantages.

Some economies of scale accrue to the firm when the size of the plant (a factory) grows. These are known as plant-level economies. Other economies accrue to the firm as it experiences growth by acquiring more plants (rather than bigger plants). This distinction is shown in Figure 9.10, which summarizes the sources of economies of scale.

Plant-level economies

As the size of an individual plant grows, benefits are enjoyed in terms of labour, capital equipment and stocks of materials.

● **Labour economies** Large-scale plants benefit from a better use of specialist labour. The division of labour that is facilitated by increased scale will result in:
  – savings in time;
  – less waste;
  – reduction in training times;
  – workers employed on those tasks for which they are best suited.
● **Technical economies** In large-scale plants there are advantages in terms of the availability and use of specialist, indivisible equipment that are not available to a small-scale producer. Moreover, large-scale plants develop linked processes (for example, the integrated steel plant), which again produce cost advantages in terms of handling and energy.
● **Economies in stocks and storage** As the plant grows, it will operate on proportionately lower stock levels and storage space.

Firm-level economies

Firm-level economies are enjoyed by firms that have experienced growth either in the form of a growth in the size of plants or the acquisition of more plants. The major firm-level economies are as follows.

● **Purchasing economies** The bulk purchase of inputs will result in lower unit costs as a result of discounts.
● **Financial economies** Large firms have access

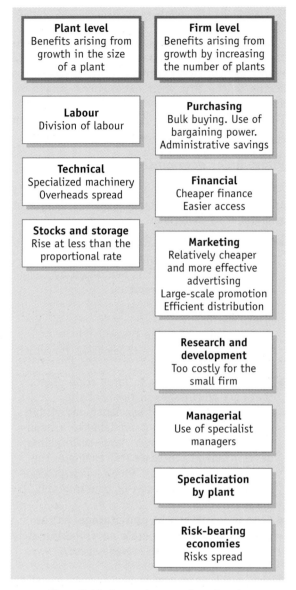

Figur 9.10 Internal economies of scale

to more varied forms of finance and often at lower cost. For instance, large firms seek finance from city institutions that is denied to small firms.

- **Marketing economies** The cost of advertising and distribution rises at a lower rate than rises in output and sales. In proportion to sales, large firms can advertise more cheaply and more effectively than their smaller rivals.

- **Research and development (R&D) economies** The costs associated with R&D fall disproportionately on small firms. In some industries, only the very largest of firms can finance new product development in order to stay competitive, and in the motor and aircraft industries even the largest of firms have to collaborate in joint ventures for R & D purposes (such as Rover and Honda before 1994 and the European Airbus).

- **Managerial economies** The larger firms benefit from the services of specialist functional managers, as distinct from the general managers that characterize the smaller firms. These specialists have expertise that benefits the firm.

- **Multiplant specialization** The large multiplant firm will benefit from specialization by plant. For instance, the large car manufacturers produce different models in each of their plants and transport finished goods (often across national borders) to satisfy demand in various locations. Specialization by plant produces savings in the cost of production as a result of the use of dedicated equipment and lower retooling costs.

- **Risk bearing economies** With a greater product range and diversity of premises large firms achieve economies in terms of risk bearing (e.g. insurance).

The economies referred to above are all internal economies of scale resulting from the growth of the individual plant and/or firm. There are also external economies that accrue as a result of an increase in the size of the industry irrespective of the size of the particular firm. External economies take the form of:

- improvements in infrastructure;
- development of service firms;
- availability of a pool of skilled labour;
- collaboration with other firms in trade associations, joint ventures and so on.

These external economies are available to all firms

and provide one explanation for the continued presence of small firms in mature markets.

The diseconomies of scale referred to earlier can be seen as the problems of growth. Beyond a certain size, the additional problems of growth exceed the benefits, leading to a rise in unit costs. These problems take the form of:

- loss of managerial control;
- overspecialization, leading to boredom;
- poor industrial relations;
- inflexibility.

The existence of these diseconomies points to the danger of excessive growth in the firm.

The theory of the firm

The theory of the firm is an important element of economic theory because it attempts to analyse and predict the behaviour of firms based on certain assumptions. Economists construct models of the market ranging, at one extreme, from the ideal of **perfect competition** through various forms of imperfection to pure **monopoly** (meaning a 100 per cent market share) at the other extreme. The basic purpose of the theory is to demonstrate the benefits of perfect competition and the loss of welfare resulting from monopolistic forces. Although the theory is not part of A Level Business Studies, it does provide students of business with an insight into the behaviour of firms.

The **traditional theory** of the firm assumes that the firm is a profit maximizer. This means that the firm seeks not just profit, but the highest level of profit. This is illustrated in Figure 9.11. Profits are maximized when marginal cost (MC) equals marginal revenue (MR). When output is below b, MR exceeds MC. In these circumstances it is worth expanding output as additional revenue exceeds additional cost. Above b, MC exceeds MR and, therefore, it is beneficial to the firm to reduce output. After all, there is little point in producing extra output if the additional cost exceeds the additional revenue. The firm that wants to maximize profit will produce at the level of output at which MC = MR.

In this model of perfect competition that economists have developed:

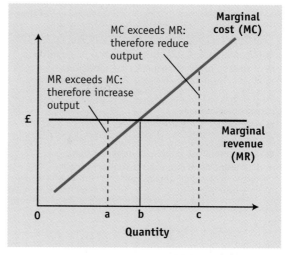

Figure 9.11 Profit maximizing in economic theory
MR is the extra revenue from one additional unit of output
MC is the extra cost of one additional unit of output

- there is a large number of buyers and sellers;
- no one is able to exert influence over price;
- the products of different suppliers are identical (there is homogeneity of product);
- there are no barriers to the entry of newcomers to the market;
- customers choose on price alone.

In these circumstances, the individual firm is a **price taker** – that is, it has to accept the market price. As it has no influence over price, it will seek the level of output at which MC = MR. This might provide a high level of profit, although in the long run this will be competed away as newcomers enter.

At the other extreme is pure monopoly, in which there is only one supplier who produces a product with no close substitute. The monopolist is able to fix prices and can, therefore, be called a **price maker**. Again, the monopolist will seek the profit maximizing output (that is, the output at which MC = MR), but this is likely to be a lower level of output than prevails under perfect competition. The monopolist will seek to withhold supplies to force up price in the interests of private profit. For these and other reasons (see Table 9.2)

Table 9.2 Monopoly

Criticisms	In defence
● The monopolist is able to fix price or quantity ● Output is lower than under competition ● Price is higher than under competition ● Absence of competition leads to complacency and inefficiency ● Less choice for the consumer ● Excessive profits distort the distribution of income ● The monopolist is able to practise price discrimination, charging a higher price to particular groups of people	● Only the largest monopolistic firms can enjoy full economies of scale (this defence is only valid if the benefits are passed on in the form of lower prices) ● Large firms can afford to undertake costly research and development ● It provides for greater price stability ● Elimination of wasteful competition ● Planning is easier in an orderly environment ● Even for a monopolist, the prospect of increased profit provides an incentive to be efficient

monopoly is regarded as less desirable than a competitive market.

Between the two extremes of perfect competition and pure monopoly are monopolistic competition and oligopoly. **Monopolistic competition** involves competition between the monopoly suppliers of branded or differentiated goods. The analysis is similar to perfect competition, except that by making the product distinctive the firm will seek to retain its high level of profits. **Oligopoly** is defined as competition between a handful of giant companies. A distinctive feature of this market structure is the interdependence of firms. Aware of the impact of its decisions on other firms, each firm will attempt to predict the likely reaction of rivals. This might incline oligopolists to a policy of caution. Rather than face a damaging price war, they might collude together or pursue a policy of price leadership in which rivals follow the pricing decisions of the market leader. Certainly one feature of oligopoly is 'price rigidity'. This does not mean that prices never change but that changes are infrequent. Between price changes, profit margins adjust to any change in production costs.

The traditional theory of the firm is subject to much criticism. It is argued that the theory adequately explains the unreal situation of perfect competition, but is less satisfactory in explaining the real world, which approximates more to oligopoly than either of the two extreme ends of the spectrum. A more fundamental criticism concerns the assumption on which the whole theory is based: profit maximization.

This assumption dates back to the nineteenth century, when management and ownership were in the same hands. The rise of the large modern corporation has brought about the divorce of ownership from control. Large companies are owned by the shareholders, but control lies with the directors (many of whom are full-time executive directors) and managers. Shareholder control by means of the annual shareholders' meeting is weak, leaving executives a free hand to run the company. Provided the latter deliver a satisfactory level of profits to keep shareholders content, they are free to pursue their own objectives. This is the starting point for what are known as the **managerial theories** of the firm. All these theories are based on the assumption that, subject to the constraint of delivering a satisfactory level of profit, firms seek to maximize:

● sales revenue
● market share
● growth
● security

or managerial utility (status, prestige, managers' pay). Central to the theories is the belief that managers (who derive no direct benefit from profits) are more interested in managing a large or a growing firm than a profitable one.

The other theory of the firm – known as the **behavioural theory** – starts with a different premise altogether. The firm is seen as a coalition of different stakeholders (owners, manager, employees, customers, society and so on). The stakeholders have different and, indeed, opposing interests. For instance, owners have an interest in profit, which might be seen as conflicting with the employees' interest in high pay and minimum effort. The outcome of the tension between the opposing forces is a compromise that is satisfactory to all concerned. Hence, whereas the traditional and managerial theories of the firm are based on the firm as maximizer, the behavioural theories are based on the firm as 'satisficer' where no stakeholders receive their ideal but where a satisficing compromise is reached.

Normal and supernormal profit

Economists make a distinction between normal and supernormal (or abnormal) profit. **Normal profit** is defined as the minimum return necessary to keep the entrepreneur in the market in the long run. It is the minimum level of profit regarded by the entrepreneur as satisfactory. **Supernormal profit** is profit in excess of the normal level. **Subnormal profits** are profits lower than the normal level.

Supernormal profits will tempt newcomers to the market. This will lead to an increase in supply of the product concerned, a fall in price and the elimination of supernormal profits. Unless existing firms can prevent the entry of newcomers, profits will be forced down to the normal level in the long run. By erecting barriers to entry (such as patents, exclusive access to inputs, high market entry costs) firms seek to maintain supernormal profit.

Subnormal profits are, by definition, regarded as unsatisfactory and will lead firms to leave the market in the long run. This reduction in supply will raise both prices and profits for firms that remain in the market. From this analysis we can draw an important conclusion. In competitive markets with no barriers to entry, supernormal profits are possible in the short run but will be competed away in the long run. In monopolistic markets with barriers to entry, supernormal profits are possible in both the short and the long run.

Economic theory does provide some insight into why a firm might remain in a market when suffering a loss (negative profit) or a subnormal level of profits: in the short run it is worth while remaining in the market provided revenue covers variable costs (or price covers average variable costs). Consider the following example. A firm sells its product for £1 when variable costs average out at 90p. At the existing level of output of one million, sales are inadequate to cover fixed costs of £200,000 per year. It the firm closes down it will still face a loss of £200,000 in the form of the inescapable fixed costs. By remaining in the market, the loss is £200,000 minus 10p × 1 million = £200,000 minus £100,000 = £100,000.

This example is designed to show that it is beneficial to stay in the market in the short run (although no firm will remain in the market in the long run when normal profits are not available). However, if the price fell below 90p it would not be worth while remaining in the market as every unit produced would increase the loss. Economists, therefore, conclude that firms will shut down:

- in the short run when the price falls below average variable costs;
- in the long run when the price falls below average total costs so that normal profits are no longer available.

Price discrimination

One feature of markets in which suppliers enjoy some degree of monopoly is the practice known in economics as **price discrimination**. This is the practice of selling the same product or service at two (or more) prices in different parts of the market. It should be distinguished from **differential pricing**, in which price differentials reflect differences in the costs of supplying various categories of customer. **Peak pricing**, designed to shift demand to 'off peak' and thereby make use of excess capacity, is a form of differential pricing, whereas price discrimination involves identical products being sold at different prices.

There are some questions that need to be asked about price discrimination.

- Why do firms seek to charge high prices to some customers but lower prices to others?
- How can they get away with it?

The conditions necessary for price discrimination are:

- the existence of some degree of monopoly power;
- a market split up into identifiable segments;
- different price elasticities of demand in different parts of the market;
- barriers to prevent 'seepage' from one segment to another.

Away from the jargon of economic theory, what this means is that there are two (or more) distinct types of customer. Their sensitivity to price changes varies: one group is deterred by price rises whereas others are less concerned. Provided the supplier can stop the 'high price customer' buying the product at the lower price, discriminatory pricing can be practised. A simple (and relatively effective) technique to separate the markets is to allow certain groups to buy at a lower price on presentation of a document (pension book, student union card and so on).

The supplier will seek to maximize profits in each segment of the market. Even in the lower price segment, therefore, marginal costs are covered and the price is set to extract as much profit as possible. In the higher price segment, customers are less sensitive to price rises and, therefore, the price is forced up higher. By this method, the supplier is able to tap both ends of the market. The method has the added advantage of encouraging the supply of a good service when a single, high price would result in a market that was insufficiently large to make supply worth while.

Key Concepts

Cross-elasticity of demand The responsiveness of demand for a product to changes in the price of another product.

Demand The quantity of a good or service desired at a particular price. In economics, desire has to be backed by ability to pay if demand is to be effective.

Economies of scale The reduction in average costs (per unit) as the scale of production is increased. The advantages of large-scale production.

Equilibrium price The price at which the quantity demanded equals the quantity supplied. It is the natural or market price that 'clears' the market.

Factors of production The essential ingredients of production – land, labour, capital, enterprise.

Income elasticity of demand The responsiveness of demand to changes in income.

Marginal cost The cost of producing one additional unit of output.

Marginal revenue The extra revenue obtained by increasing output and sales by one unit.

Microeconomics That part of economics concerned with the analysis of particular firms or products.

Mixed economy An economy in which there is both a public (government) sector and a private enterprise or market sector.

Monopoly In theory, monopoly means a single supplier of goods to the market. In everyday usage, we mean a firm with a large share of the market that is able to exert monopoly power over it.

Oligopoly Competition between a small number of large firms.

Perfect competition A theoretical market structure in which there is a large number of suppliers, none of which can determine price.

Price elasticity of demand The responsiveness of demand to changes in price.

Price elasticity of supply The responsiveness of supply to changes in price.

Price maker A firm able to determine price.

Price taker A firm unable to determine price and, therefore, having to accept the market price.

Supply The process of providing goods in response to and in accordance with customer demand. The amount that suppliers are willing to supply at each price.

Essay questions

1 The demand curve is drawn on the assumption that other things remain equal.
(a) Why do economists make this assumption?
(b) Analyse the consequences of:
  (i)   a rise in income;
  (ii) a fall in the price of a complementary good;
  (iii) a fall in the price of a substitute product.

2 (a) What is meant by price elasticity of demand and how is it measured?
(b) Assess the possible price elasticity of demand for:
  (i)   salt; and
  (ii) Ford cars.

3 (a) Explain the difference between an extension of and an increase in demand.
(b) Analyse the likely impact of a rise in income on the demand for each of the following:
  (i)   bread;
  (ii) bus rides;
  (iii) foreign holidays.

4 A manufacturer has been informed that the price elasticity of demand for its product is −1.25.
(a) Explain what this means and how it was measured.
(b) Analyse the significance of this information to the manufacturer.

5 (a) Using supply and demand graphs, analyse the consequences of:
  (i)   a rise in demand;
  (ii) a fall in supply.
(b) Analyse the consequences of imposing a maximum price below the equilibrium.

6 (a) A perfectly competitive firm has no discretion regarding price. Explain.
(b) Referring to both price and non-price factors, explain why monopoly is considered to be harmful to the consumer.

Exercises

1 Study the demand schedule below and answer the questions that follow.

Price (£)	Quantity demanded (tonnes)
15	8
14	9
13	10
12	11
11	12
10	13
9	14

(a) 'Demand is inversely related to price'. Explain the meaning of this statement.

(b) Calculate:
  (i)   the total revenue at each price, identifying the price at which revenue is maximized;
  (ii) the price elasticity of demand at each successive reduction in price.
(c) What can you conclude about price elasticity of demand at different points along a straight-line demand curve?

131

2 The demand schedule for commodity X is shown in the table below.

Price (£)	Quantity demanded (million units)
2.5	7.5
2.4	8.0
2.3	8.5
2.2	9.0
2.1	9.5
2.0	10.0
1.9	10.5
1.8	11.0
1.7	11.5
1.6	12.0
1.5	12.5

(a) Calculate price elasticity of demand as:
  (i) price rises from £1.50 to £1.60;
  (ii) price rises from £2.40 to £2.50.
(b) Calculate the total revenue at each price level.
  What conclusion can you draw about:
  (i) the consequences of raising the price?
  (ii) price elasticity of demand?
(c) It is known that income elasticity of demand is +2. Construct a new demand schedule following a 5 per cent rise in income.
(d) It is noticed that following a 10 per cent rise in the price of another commodity, there is a 2.5 per cent reduction in demand for commodity X.
  (i) Calculate cross-elasticity of demand.
  (ii) What conclusion can be drawn about the relationship between the two commodities?

3 The data below refers to different prices at which a product is sold and the resulting total revenue.

Price (£)	Total revenue (£000)
6	840
7	910
8	960
9	990
10	1000
11	990
12	960
13	910
14	840

(a) Calculate the quantity sold at each price.
(b) Over what price range is demand:
  (i) price elastic?
  (ii) price inelastic?
(c) Calculate marginal revenue (per unit) at the following quantities:
  (i) 120,000;
  (ii) 100,000;
  (iii) 80,000.
(d) Calculate marginal revenue at the point of highest total revenue.
(e) Is the point of revenue maximization necessarily the point of profit maximization? Give reasons for your answer.

4 (a) Calculate price elasticity of demand if price rises are as follows.

Price (£)	Quantity demanded (million units)
160	12
170	11

(b) Calculate price elasticity of supply if price rises are as follows.

Price (£)	Quantity supplied (million units)
21	8
23	11

(c) Calculate income elasticity of demand if income rises are as follows.

Average income (£)	Quantity demanded (million units)
13,000	21
14,000	22

(d) Calculate cross-elasticity of demand if the price of A rises as follows.

Price of A (p)	Quantity demanded of B (million units)
30	50
32	49

(e) Calculate cross-elasticity of demand if the price of X rises as follows.

Price of X (p)	Quantity demanded of Y (million units)
60	20
63	24

5 Read the data below and answer the questions that follow.

Price (£)	Quantity (sold)	Total cost (£)
20	10,000	200,000
19	11,000	201,000
18	12,000	203,000
17	13,000	204,000
16	14,000	210,000
15	15,000	220,000
14	16,000	240,000
13	17,000	270,000
12	18,000	300,000

Calculate:
(a) total revenue at each price level;
(b) marginal revenue at each output level;
(c) the revenue maximizing level of output;
(d) the profit maximizing level of output;
(e) profits at these two levels of output.

10

Principles of macroeconomics

Macroeconomics is concerned with the whole economy rather than one part of it. Trends in the macroeconomy clearly have a major impact on business organizations and so some understanding of macroeconomic variables is essential for Business Studies students.

Chapter objectives

1 To explain the nature and purpose of national income accounts.

2 To develop an understanding of the major economic variables.

3 To explain and analyse approaches to macroeconomic policy.

Macroeconomic variables

In the study of macroeconomics we are concerned with a number of key statistics. These are:

- national income, which is the sum of all incomes in the economy over a period of time (and is also equal to the value of output);
- the level and rate of unemployment (or its converse, employment);
- the rate of price rises (inflation);
- the balance of payments position and therefore the exchange rate (see Chapter 11);
- the rate of economic growth (at its simplest, the growth of output);
- cyclical fluctuations in the economy (booms and slumps in the economy).

By studying these variables, it is possible to analyse the situation in the market and, even more important, forecast future trends.

National income accounts

Basic information on the state of the economy is contained in the national income accounts produced by the UK government. These accounts are invaluable in the analysis of economic trends and economic policy making. It is for these reasons that students of business should be able to interpret the accounts, even though the mechanics of national income accounting do not feature in A level syllabuses.

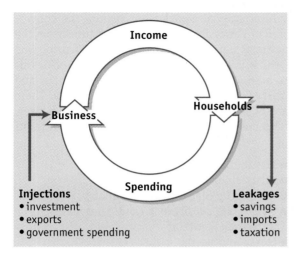

Figure 10.1 The circular flow model

National income can be defined as the flow of income earned by the economy's factors of production (land, labour, capital and enterprise – see Figure 10.1). Income should be seen as the reward for the output of goods and services produced during the time period under consideration (usually a year). As incomes are earned from contributing to production, national income is logically equal to national output (defined as the money value of goods and services produced during the time period concerned). As this output is purchased by various agents in the economy, it is also equal to the value of national expenditure (after allowance is made for complications such as unsold goods). Hence, in macroeconomics, national income = national output = national expenditure. Consequently, to calculate the level of national income we can use one of three methods:

- the **income method**, in which we add up the total amount earned;
- the **expenditure method**, in which we add up the total value of spending on UK goods and services;
- the **output method**, in which we add up the total value of output of goods and services.

The availability of three methods means that national income accountants are able to verify totals against each other and identify errors and omissions.

You will appreciate that, in compiling the accounts, adjustments have to be made for a series of complications that arise in the real world:

- transfer payments (such as pensions) for which no service is currently offered in return, are not included in the data;
- unpaid and do-it-yourself services are not included, even though they contribute to production;
- unsold goods are treated as though they were purchased by the company holding them;
- exports are treated as generating income for UK residents, while imports are treated as generating income for residents of foreign countries;
- net property income from abroad (rents, dividends, interest) is treated as adding to national income.

By making these and other adjustments, accountants produce the national income accounts that are published by the government.

Armed with national income accounts, we can investigate the:

- rate of economic growth (real national income per head);
- contribution to the economy of various industries or sectors of the economy;
- the distribution of income between various income groups or between the factors of production;
- changes in average standards of living (real national income per head);
- economic performance and living standards in a variety of countries.

For any historical comparison, adjustment must always be made for inflation and population changes.

Consider a rise in national income from £150 billion to £160 billion. This could have been the result of a rise in the physical quantity of goods and services produced (known as a rise in real output) or merely a rise in prices, which raised the value of output. Alternatively, it might have been a combination of the two factors. To separate out, or disaggregate, the two components we need to know the rate of inflation. Suppose that at the same time as national income rose from £150 billion to £160 billion prices rose by an average of 4 per cent. To calculate the rise in real output, we eliminate the inflation element of the rise in national income. This gives a figure for real national income – or national income at constant prices.

Year	National income (Y)	Price index
1	£150b	100
2	£160b	104

Y in year 2 at constant year 1 prices

$$= Y \text{ in year } 2 \times \frac{\text{Price index year 1}}{\text{Price index year 2}}$$

$$= £160b \times \frac{100}{104}$$

$$= £153.8b$$

This means that, in the absence of price rises, national income in year 2 would have been £153.8 billion or 2.5 per cent higher than in year 1.

If we then divided real national income by the population size, we would have a measure of the rate of real national income per head and, therefore, both economic growth and living standards. The reason economists analyse living standards in terms of real national income per head is that, ultimately, our living standards are determined by access to goods and services.

Even after making the adjustments for population and price changes, there remain other problems:

- national income per head figures might disguise great inequalities in income;
- national income data is artificially swollen when we pay people to perform tasks that previously we performed for ourselves;
- the data might fail to reveal a large hidden, or black, economy;
- an increase in quantitative output might have been achieved by a reduction in the quality of life.

Despite these deficiencies, national income data is essential for the understanding of trends in the economy and, as such, is an important first step in market research.

International comparisons require the conversion of national income per head figures from the national currency to a common measuring rod (which is always the US dollar). This enables us to assess living standards, growth potential and market opportunities in various countries. There are of course major problems in drawing international comparisons as countries differ in terms of:

- distribution of income;
- accuracy of statistics;
- size of the black, hidden economy;
- size of the subsistence (and, therefore, unrecorded) sector;
- tastes and needs;
- the proportion of national income used by the government for defence.

In addition, the usefulness of the comparison depends on the validity of the exchange rate used to convert national income into dollar terms. The problem associated with the exchange rate is most acute in relation to the former Eastern bloc and Third World countries. For advanced Western countries (including Japan) the exchange rate reasonably reflects differences in purchasing power, however.

International comparisons of national income provide useful indicators of economic performance and relative standards of living and, as such, represent the starting point for researching overseas market potential.

Personal disposable income

As its name suggests, personal disposable income (PDI) is a measure of income available to households to dispose of as they please. Essentially, it should be seen as the 'take-home pay' of people in the macroeconomy. It is a vital economic variable for those engaged in marketing because it is a measure of income available for spending.

To calculate PDI, we add transfer payments (pensions, welfare benefits, student grants) to national income, but at the same time we deduct a number of items:

> PDI = National income
> *plus* transfer payments

minus undistributed profit, direct taxation, National Insurance contributions, surpluses of public undertakings

Transfer payments are added in because they are not included in the national income figure, even though they are clearly available for expenditure by households. The deductions are made because, although they are included in the national income figures, these items are not available for households to spend as they choose.

The national income multiplier

One of the most important principles in macroeconomics is the **multiplier**, which enables us to analyse the impact of an injection of spending into the economy. At first, you would think that a £100 million injection of, say, government spending would raise the level of demand and aggregate spending by just £100 million. In fact, a chain reaction of additional income and, therefore, further spending means that the overall impact exceeds the initial injection.

To understand this process, we have to return to the circular flow model (Figure 10.1). The upper loop represents incomes paid to the factors of production (land, labour, capital and enterprise). The lower loop represents household expenditure on domestically produced goods and services. However, in addition to expenditure by households, there is also spending by three other economic agents:

● firms investing in equipment, buildings and stock;
● the UK public sector;
● residents of other countries purchasing UK exports.

These forms of expenditure are known as **injections** and they have the effect of raising the level of aggregate demand in the economy.

Let us consider the impact of a £100 million injection into the economy. The additional expenditure will flow around the upper loop as additional incomes paid to the four factors of production:

● additional pay to labour;
● additional rent to the owners of land;

● additional interest to the owners of capital;
● additional profit to entrepreneurs.

When additional income is received by householders, there will be additional household spending, as seen in the lower loop. However, not all the additional income will be spent on domestically produced goods and services. Some will leak out in the form of:

● savings;
● tax payments;
● purchases of imported goods and services.

The proportion of additional income that leaks out or is withdrawn from the circular flow is known as the marginal rate of withdrawal (MRW). Suppose the MRW is 0.5 – a half of each additional £1 of income leaks out and is not spent on domestically produced goods and services. We are now in a position to analyse the impact of the £100 million injection on an economy with a MRW of 0.5 (see Figure 10.2).

In the first round, national income (Y) rises by £100 million – that is, the initial injection. In the second round, expenditure (and therefore income in the upper loop) rises by one half of £100 million.

In the third round, it rises by one half of one half of £100 million and so the process continues:

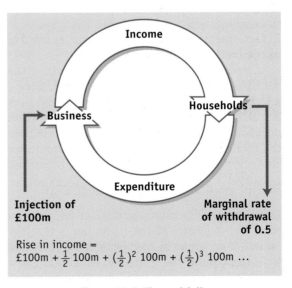

Income

Business

Households

Expenditure

Injection of £100m

Marginal rate of withdrawal of 0.5

Rise in income =
£100m + $\frac{1}{2}$ 100m + $(\frac{1}{2})^2$ 100m + $(\frac{1}{2})^3$ 100m ...

Figure 10.2 The multiplier

	Rise in Y £m	Rise in expenditure £m
1st	100	50
2nd	50	25
3rd	25	12.5
4th	12.5	6.25
5th	6.25	3.125, etc.

The successive rounds of the rise in income constitute a geometric series that, although becoming smaller at each round, will never reach zero. However, beyond a certain point, each round is so small that it can be ignored. What we now need is a way to sum up the series and, fortunately, mathematics has equipped us with an easy and quick way of summing the rise in income.

The rise in income (ΔY)

$$= \text{injection} \times \frac{1}{\text{MRW}}$$

In the example outlined above, the rise in income will be £100m multiplied by $\frac{1}{0.5}$. This becomes £100m multiplied by 2 and is therefore £200m. In this case, the rise in income was twice the injection.

If the MRW is 0.75, the rise in income would have been

$$\text{£100m} \times \frac{1}{[0.75]} = \text{£100m} \times 1.33 \text{ or £133m.}$$

In fact, the greater the MRW, the smaller the size of the multiplier.

As well as working in an upward direction, the multiplier works in a downward direction. Hence, a £1 billion cut in government spending will have a multiple impact on the economy, once again depending on the MRW. If the latter was 0.3 then the total reduction in national income would be:

$$\text{£1 billion} \times \frac{1}{0.3} = \text{£1 billion} \times \frac{10}{3} = \text{£3.33 billion.}$$

For students of business, as distinct from economics, the relevance of the multiplier is that the impact of a change in an injection is felt far and wide throughout the economy. In addition to a direct impact on supply firms and those employed in the public sector, a change in government expenditure affects many other people indirectly, via changes in the level of household spending. Consequently, even businesses that do not seek government contracts are affected by a change in government spending. Similarly, businesses that do not seek exports are affected by changes in the level of exports.

Investment

Chapter 30 looks in detail at the techniques by which business organizations appraise investment projects. Here we consider the way in which economists treat investment. It should be understood that economists define investment in terms of the accumulation of real capital (machinery, buildings and stocks of goods) to facilitate production and consumption in the future. Hence, the building of a factory, the acquisition of machinery and the accumulation of stocks constitute acts of investment. Financial transactions, such as depositing savings in a bank or the buying of shares, are not in themselves acts of investment.

Economists are interested in the overall level of investment for two basic reasons. First, investment is seen as the most volatile element in aggregate demand and, therefore, plays a crucially important role in cyclical fluctuations in the economy. To understand the functioning of the economy, it is necessary to understand the determinants of investment. Second, investment in capital equipment is seen as the prime factor in determining the rate of economic growth. Investment raises the productivity of labour and land, and is therefore essential if UK firms are to remain competitive. Hence for the short- and long-term health of the economy, investment is seen as being of crucial importance.

In the analysis of factors determining the level of investment, two theories predominate. First, the accelerator principle links investment to changes in the level of demand (see Figure 10.3). Notice that it is not the level of demand itself that is important, but changes in the level of demand. High investment is associated with rapid growth of demand, whereas a slowing down in the growth of demand will be accompanied by a cutback in new investment. It is because of this

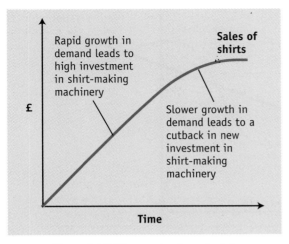

Figure 10.3 The accelerator principle

principle that the capital goods industries – industries that produce machinery – tend to fluctuate more wildly than consumer goods industries.

The alternative theory of investment links it with the rate of interest. At high rates of interest, only the most profitable project is worthwhile, but, as the rate falls so more projects are re-assessed as being profitable. The theory on which the principle is based is known as the **marginal efficiency of capital (MEC)** (see Figure 10.4). The

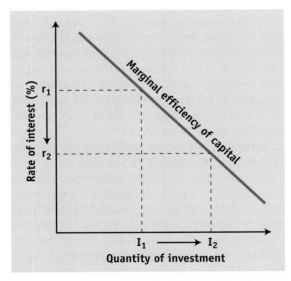

Figure 10.4 The marginal efficiency of capital

curve represents the boundary between profitable and unprofitable projects and, as shown in Figure 10.4 the boundary shifts as interest rates fall.

Although changes in the level of demand and the rate of interest are the prime factors affecting the level of investment, there are additional factors that inform the decision to invest:

- taxation of both consumers and of business profits;
- the level of public expenditure;
- the availability of credit;
- technological change;
- government and EU grants;
- entrepreneurial mood.

Growth and cyclical fluctuations in the economy

We have seen that, by studying changes in national income, it is possible to understand what is happening in the economy. Changes in real (inflation adjusted) national income are a reflection of either a long-term trend or a short-term fluctuation in the economy.

Growth in the economy is unlikely to be continuous over a long period. It is probable that there will be fluctuations around the long-term or secular trend (see Figure 10.5). The trade cycle of the nineteenth century led to boom and slump over a seven to ten-year period. The business cycle of the twentieth century has led to alternating phases of expansion and recession over a four to five-year cycle.

In the **boom phase** of a cycle, employment is high, unemployment is low, output is high and so is investment. On the other hand, there might be upward pressure on prices and a balance of payment deficit as imports are 'sucked in' by the high level of demand. In a **recession** (or **slump**), output is falling or at least not rising. There will be a rise in unemployment and investment is likely to be confined to replacing worn out machinery, with no increase in the stock of capital. Conversely, inflationary pressure will be reduced and the balance of payments is likely to be in surplus as the country reduces its imports.

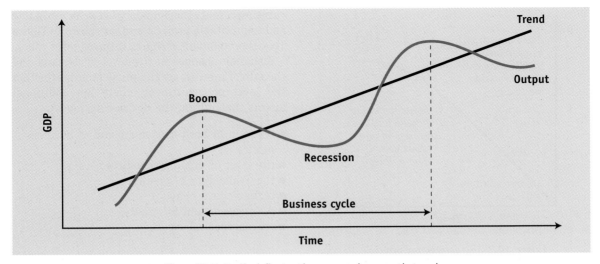

Figur 10.5 Cyclical fluctuations around a growth trend

Economic growth

Economic growth has been an objective of government economic policy since the Second World War, although policies to promote growth have frequently been sacrificed in order to combat inflation and/or correct a balance of payments deficit. Until recently, the desirability of growth was not questioned. Politicians and economists might argue about how to achieve growth and how the fruits of growth were to be distributed, but most people accepted the desirability of growth.

Economic growth is variously defined as an increase in the productive capacity of the economy or a rise in real national income per head. As it provides the means of achieving higher living standards for all, it opens up the prospect of reducing (and even eliminating) poverty without the necessity of income redistribution. Not only is income redistribution unpopular with large parts of the electorate, it might also undermine the incentives that are considered necessary to encourage hard work and enterprise.

Economic growth is obviously beneficial to private-sector firms. New market opportunities will be created in an expanding economy. This provides scope for the birth of new firms as well as the expansion of existing ones. Entrepreneurship is about identifying and responding to changing market opportunities. A growing economy will create these.

The main debate about growth has tended to focus on Britain's disappointingly slow rate of growth and how it is to be raised. The Labour Party traditionally favoured interventionist policies to raise the rate of growth. These involved direct government investment and government channelling of private-sector investment. This reflected a widespread belief on the Left that City institutions have consistently 'failed the nation'. The Conservative Party under Mrs Thatcher and John Major rejected the State involvement that was a feature of earlier Conservative governments and favoured a policy of freeing the private sector from regulation and opening up the market to competitive forces. Hence, alongside the policy of privatization, there has been a steady dismantling of controls. By unleashing the forces of private enterprise, it was hoped to raise the rate of economic growth in the UK.

The desirability of growth has been challenged by one group in the UK. People in the green movement believe that growth, which causes external costs (such as pollution) or threatens the precious natural resources of the planet, has to be controlled in the interests of future generations. Even though the Green Party is a minor party in British politics, many of the concerns of the ecology movement are shared by the wider public. Socially responsible private-sector firms will have to adjust to a public increasingly concerned about their activities.

Unemployment

The unemployed are defined in government statistics as those people seeking work who are unable to obtain a job. In the claimant count method only those registered for benefit are counted as unemployed. In the alternative labour force survey method statistics are collected by means of a sample survey. In theory, a high level of unemployment should increase the reserves of labour available to business. Firms seeking additional labour for expansion will benefit from the availability of labour. Moreover, excess supplies of labour will weaken the resolve of unions to seek high pay rises and/or improved conditions. In this way, unemployment might be seen as beneficial to business organizations. However, it is quite possible for high unemployment to coexist with shortages of particular types of labour or shortages in certain geographical areas.

In terms of demand for goods and services, unemployment is harmful to business. The higher the unemployment, the lower the demand for goods and services, and, consequently, the greater the problems involved in selling goods. These difficulties are likely to be most acute in the case of non-essentials, which are the first items we economize on as our income falls. Although the pain is experienced mainly by the minority without jobs (and their dependants), it must also be appreciated that there are additional indirect effects on business. Unemployment is likely to be accompanied by short-time working, so that even those in work suffer a decline in income. Moreover, the fear of unemployment will discourage some workers from forms of spending in which there is a long-term commitment (such as hire purchase, house purchase). Conversely, it is possible for rising unemployment to coincide with rising living standards for a large proportion of the community.

The solution to the problem depends on the analysis of its cause. Keynesian economists favour a combination of reflation to raise the level of demand and microeconomic measures to increase the mobility of labour and capital.

The monetarist and supply side schools of thought reject reflation as futile. They favour policies to make work and enterprise more rewarding and markets more competitive. Tax cuts to raise the income differentials between those in work and those on benefits are seen as a way of reducing what economists refer to as **voluntary unemployment**. Removal of market imperfections (such as restrictive trade union practices) will reduce the natural rate of unemployment. You will realize that a fundamental difference between the two schools of thought is that Keynesians believe that government action will solve the problem, whereas monetarists (and 'supply siders') believe that the solution lies in healthy and competitive private enterprise.

Table 10.1 illustrates ways in which unemployment can be classified, and its causes and cures.

Inflation

Inflation is defined as a rise in the general level of prices. In the UK, inflation is measured by a number of indices, of which the Retail Price Index (RPI) is most widely known and quoted. The RPI reflects a weighted average of price rises over the previous 12 months and, as such, it can be seen as the rate of inflation affecting the average household. The inflation rate affecting other households and, more importantly, business is reflected in other indices.

Economists attribute inflation to one of three causes:

- excess demand in conditions of full employment (known as demand pull inflation);
- an excess rise in the money supply (monetary inflation);
- a rise in the cost of production that is, in turn, passed on to customers by firms enjoying some degree of monopoly power (cost push inflation).

Although economists disagree about causes of inflation, there is widespread acceptance of the

Table 10.1 Unemployment: causes and cures

Type	Cause	Cure
Demand deficiency ● cyclical ● persistent	Indequate level of demand Temporary deficiency during recession Long-term deficiency	Raise the level of demand by fiscal and monetary measures
Technological	Labour-saving technology	Retraining to equip the unemployed to do new jobs
Structural	Change in the structure of demand leading to the decline of a major industry	Retraining – in the short term the industry could be supported
Regional	Decline in a major local industry	Regional policy
Frictional	Unemployment while job changing	Improve the flow of information about job opportunities
Search	Remaining in the market looking for ideal job	Improve information flow and reduce benefits
Classical	Too high a level of real pay	Reduce real pay to make it more attractive to employ labour. This usually means weakening trade unions
Voluntary	Unwilling to work at current rates of pay	Reduce benefits Reduce tax on the low paid to make it more worth while for them to work

role of inflationary expectations in sustaining inflation. If we expect inflation to occur we will act in ways that contribute to inflation, such as:

● demanding large pay rises in anticipation of inflation;
● buying ahead to 'beat inflation';
● taking anticipated price rises into account when setting prices.

In this way, inflation can become a self-fulfilling prophecy.

Consequences of inflation

All economists regard inflation as undesirable (although some might be prepared to tolerate mild inflation if it assists in achievement of some other macroeconomic aim). Because some groups in society gain (such as debtors) while others lose (savers, creditors, those on fixed incomes, those in non-union trades), inflation has the effect of redistributing purchasing power. Businesses might suffer if their customers experience a decline in their real incomes. Moreover, if the inflation is one of costs rather than prices, profit margins will be squeezed. Conversely, inflation caused by excess demand may lead to an increase in profit margins.

The most damaging aspect of inflation from the business point of view is that it makes planning for the future difficult. Assessing future investment projects is made more complicated by uncertainty about future prices. Budgeting of future spending is also more difficult. Making provision for the replacement of equipment as it wears out is more difficult when the replacement cost is higher than the initial (or historic) cost.

Inflation also raises the tax burden as some taxes (VAT, income tax, corporation tax) are directly related to income and the value of spending. Price rises are, in effect, VAT rises. Cost of living pay rises will, other things remaining equal, raise the amount of income tax paid by the individual (as well as the proportion of income paid in tax).

Solutions to the problem of inflation

Economists of all schools accept that it is within a government's power to control inflation, even though there might be disagreement between them about the most effective way of dealing with the problem. All techniques to remedy the condition will cause some pain and discomfort to the patient. To quote John Major, 'If it is not hurting, it is not working'.

The Keynesian solution to demand pull inflation is deflation by means of cuts in government spending, increases in taxation and a rise in interest rates. The process is painful to businesses, which experience decline in sales, and to workers, some of whom are made redundant.

The monetarist solution to inflation is to control the growth of the money supply. It has to be understood that when economists refer to the money supply, they mean coins, notes and bank deposits. Without going into the technicalities, control of the money supply means control of bank lending. In the 1970s and early 1980s, excessive government spending led to a large public-sector borrowing requirement (PSBR). Governments, in effect, 'printed money' to finance excess spending. The monetarist solution is to control the PSBR.

Private-sector borrowing can also increase the money supply. This is tackled by high interest rates to reduce the demand for credit. However, as with Keynesian deflation, the medicine can be painful. Investment is discouraged and, thus, the demand for capital goods and the demand for labour falls. Although householders might not be deterred from borrowing for the purposes of buying household goods, a high mortgage rate will result in a decline in discretionary income and, therefore, in spending. The pain of high interest rates will be even greater if it drives up the exchange rate.

The most common form of policy to tackle cost push inflation was incomes policy. This was a feature of pre-Thatcher Britain. Here the aim was to secure agreement with both sides of industry to moderate pay and price rises. The ideal was that pay should rise by no more than productivity, which meant pay increases were self-financing. Most incomes policies were successful in the short run, but disintegrated after three years. Even supporters of incomes policies accept that they only work with union cooperation. Critics argue that incomes policies fail to deal with the root causes of inflation. They hold down pay in an artificial manner and, consequently, distort market forces. To understand the latter point, it must be remembered that pay differences (which tend to be reduced by an incomes policy) are essential for shifting labour from declining and into expanding firms and industries.

Table 10.2 sets out some of the causes and cures of inflation. Table 10.3 illustrates the consequences of inflation.

Keynesianism v. monetarism

In the decades after the Second World War, governments in the UK (and elsewhere) sought

---

Table 10.2 Inflation: causes and cures

Causes	Cures
Excess demand	Reduce the level of demand by: ● rises in taxation; ● cuts in government spending; ● rises in interest rates.
Excessive growth in the money supply	Control the growth of the money supply by: ● controlling public-sector borrowing, which in turn means tax rises or spending cuts; ● controlling private-sector borrowing by interest rate rises.
Cost push	Control cost rises, usually in the form of an incomes policy.

Table 10.3 Consequences of inflation

- Redistribution of spending power from losers to gainers

Losers	Gainers
– Those on fixed incomes	– Those able to obtain pay rises above inflation
– Those unable to gain compensatory pay rises	
– Savers	– Borrowers
– Creditors	– Debtors
– Taxpayers who automatically pay more tax as prices and incomes rise	

- Profits rise in a period of excess demand inflation, but are squeezed by cost push inflation
- Exports are harmed and imports will increase
- A balance of payments deficit follows and this in turn puts downward pressure on the exchange rate
- Inflation makes planning difficult and increases business risks
- Some economists see mild inflation as the price for expansion and high employment. Others argue that its distorting impact undermines the market, harming both growth and employment

to manage the economy by regulating the level of aggregate demand. This approach to policy was based on the writings of John Maynard Keynes, the Cambridge economist who died in 1946. Keynes argued that the market is inherently unstable and, therefore, cannot guarantee full employment. Consequently, there is a need for State intervention to achieve full employment and/or other macroeconomic objectives. Intervention should take the form of managing the level of demand.

The objectives of economic policy during the Keynesian era (1940 to the late 1970s) were the following.

- **Full employment** This was usually regarded as a level of unemployment no greater than 2.5 per cent of the workforce. Alternatively, it might be regarded as a situation in which unemployment was equal to the number of vacancies. Any unemployment that existed was for reasons of friction and not a deficiency of demand.
- **Price stability** In the light of social and economic problems resulting from inflation, it is important that price rises are kept to a low level.
- **Balance of payments equilibrium** In an age of managed exchange rates (see Chapter 11), it was important to achieve a balance of international payments to protect the exchange rate.

- **Economic growth** In many respects, this is (or should be) the ultimate objective of economic policy as it provides the key to improvements in living standards and the provision of more and better social services (such as health care). Unfortunately, growth, a long-term goal, was frequently sacrificed to achieve short-term government objectives, such as full employment or balance of payments equilibrium.

According to Keynesian economists, these objectives can be achieved by regulating the level of aggregate demand – that is, the total of demand from:

- consumers (C);
- firms investing in new equipment (I);
- the public sector (G);
- people, firms and governments abroad buying UK exports (X);
- less UK demand for imported foreign goods and services (M).

Aggregate demand is therefore equal to $C + I + G + X - M$.

Demand can be managed by operating on any of the five variables, but, in view of the commitment to freeing trade from restrictions, governments sought to manipulate C, I and G. The latter is directly under the control of government as it is its own spending. C and I are not under government control as they represent spending by households and firms. However, by using the system of taxation and interest rates, governments sought to manipulate C and I. For instance, any increase in taxation will reduce disposable income and, therefore, reduce household spending. A rise in spending can be induced by tax reductions to raise disposable income. Investment spending can be regulated by changes in interest rates (high rates discourage investment whereas low rates encourage it). In addition, any change in the level of consumer spending will (via the accelerator principle) affect the level of investment.

The weapons of Keynesian demand management are:

● taxation;
● government spending;
● interest rates;
● to a lesser extent, controls on bank lending.

The first two weapons are referred to as fiscal policy, whereas the last two weapons are referred to as monetary policy. Reflation of the economy (raising the level of aggregate demand to combat unemployment) involves:

● cutting tax rates;
● increasing government spending;
● reducing interest rates;
● relaxing controls on bank lending.

To deflate the economy (to reduce inflationary pressure and improve the balance of payments), the policies are put into reverse. By careful management of demand, governments hoped to 'fine tune' the economy to achieve the four stated objectives. In fact, for many years, the policy worked reasonably well and there was a belief that high unemployment was a thing of the past. However, over the years it was appreciated that there were major defects in the theory of demand management.

● The first problem relates to the conflicting aims of government policy. Soon into the Keynesian era, the conflict between full employment and inflation was appreciated. The **Phillips Curve** (see Figure 10.6) shows that there is a trade-off between the two

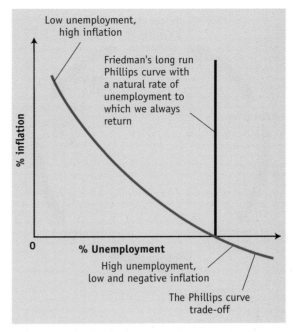

Figure 10.6 The Phillips curve

objectives, with the result that, as the economy approaches full employment, there is upward pressure on prices. It was further noticed that as inflation developed, there is a rise in imports, leading to balance of payment problems. To correct these, government sought to deflate the economy, thus bringing both a halt to economic growth and a rise in unemployment. The result was a cycle of 'boom and bust', known as the 'stop-go cycle' (see Figure 10.7).

● There are technical problems caused by time lags in the economy. There is a time lag involved in recognizing problems, deciding on appropriate policies and implementing them. Moreover, the medicine only starts to work after a time lag, so that, rather than stabilizing the economy, demand management can aggravate cyclical fluctuations.

● There are further technical problems relating to:
  – the accuracy of data in view of the existence of a black or hidden economy;

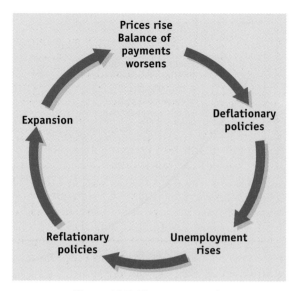

Figure 10.7 The stop-go cycle

- the problem of reducing government
  expenditure in the short run;
- the need to plan investment over a long
  period.
- Political commitment to public service,
  coupled with a desire not to raise taxation
  excessively, meant that, in the Keynesian
  era, there was a bias towards a reflationary
  budget deficit.
- It is alleged that the commitment to full
  employment and the Welfare State had long-
  term effects on the labour market, leading to
  abuse of trade union power, overmanning by
  firms hoarding workers and so-called
  voluntary unemployment.
- The fundamental criticism of Keynesian policy
  levelled by monetarists such as Milton
  Friedman is that reflationary policies do not
  reduce unemployment except in the short
  run. Instead, they merely lead to accelerating
  inflation, which damages the economy. It is
  control of inflation that should be the main
  focus of government policy.
- What undermined Keynesian economics more
  than any other thing was the 'stagflation' of
  the 1970s. Keynesians saw unemployment
  and inflation as opposing evils and found it
  difficult to explain the coincidence of the two.

With Keynesian economics dealt a severe blow, the stage was set for the revival of an ancient economic philosophy, namely monetarism.

Monetarism is a broad economic philosophy that predates John Maynard Keynes. In fact, in its simplest form, monetarism can be traced back to ancient times. It has long been known that an excessive rise in the money supply (such as that caused by an influx of bullion or the debasing of the coinage) is accompanied by inflation. The proposition that inflation is caused by a rise in the money supply was refined by Irvin Fisher in the first decades of the twentieth century, attacked by Keynes in the 1930s and revived by Milton Friedman in the 1960s and 1970s.

Friedman can be regarded as the founder of modern monetarism – a more refined version of the basic theory that relates inflation to a rise in the money supply. He argues that inflation is a monetary phenomenon caused solely by a rise in the money supply in excess of the output of the economy. This rise in the supply of money, which is attributed to excessive borrowing (especially by the public sector), is a 'necessary and sufficient condition' for inflation to occur. However, unlike earlier monetarists, Friedman believes that there is a time lag of 18 months between the rise in the supply of money and the subsequent rise in prices. During this time, it is possible that monetary expansion can lead to increased output and employment, but, eventually, it can only push up prices.

Although monetarism is primarily an explanation for inflation, there is an important conclusion that can be drawn about unemployment. Monetarists argue that there is a natural rate of unemployment to which the economy always returns. Although Keynesian-style reflation might reduce unemployment in the short run, in the long run it merely produces a higher rate of inflation with no long-term reduction in the level of unemployment. Governments cannot reduce unemployment below the natural rate, although by making the labour market more competitive it is possible to reduce the natural rate of unemployment (see Figure 10.6).

The lagged effect of government economic policy, coupled with the futility of attempting to reduce unemployment by Keynesian demand management, has encouraged monetarists to favour a radically different approach to economic policy. Whereas Keynesians favour short-term adjustments to economic policy to deal with immediate problems, monetarists favour a consistent policy over a long period with no deviations to deal with immediate problems. The Keynesian approach is a discretionary one, whereas the monetarist approach is known as an 'automatic rule' approach to policy. The rule that is advocated is controlled growth of the money supply by means of controlling public sector borrowing and by interest rate policy. (see Table 10.4).

Table 10.4 The impact of a rise in interest rates

On the macroeconomy
- A rise in the cost of borrowing.
- A fall in the level of investment.
- A rise in mortgage rates resulting in:
  - a fall in discretionary income;
  - a fall in consumer spending;
  - slow down in the housing market.
- A rise in exchange rates resulting in:
  - a fall in export competitiveness;
  - a rise in competitiveness of imports.
- The downturn in the economy is likely to be accompanied by job losses but a reduction in inflationary pressure.

On a particular business
- A fall in the volume of sales either because:
  - of the fall in discretionary income; and/or;
  - the interest rate on credit sales might discourage people buying on credit.
- A rise in the cost of borrowing (past and present borrowing).
- A cutback in the firm's investment plans (a higher internal rate of return is needed if investment is to occur).
- It raises the cost of working capital (investment in stocks).
- It increases the opportunity cost of converting liquid reserves into stock.
- Destocking might occur.
- Cash flow problems.
- Possible short-time working or staff lay-offs.
- Company shares are less attractive to shareholders.

Supply side policy

We have seen that Keynesian economics emphasizes the demand side of the macroeconomy. In Keynesian economics, problems of unemployment and inflation are analysed in terms of deficiency and excess of demand in the economy. The solution is to manage the level of demand to achieve full employment without permitting excess demand, which will merely lead to inflation.

The revival of monetarism (which, strictly speaking, relates to the relationship between the money supply and inflation) was accompanied by a switch in emphasis, both in theory and policy, from managing the level of demand to stimulating the supply side of the economy. Supply-side measures are designed to raise the productive capacity of the economy in order to:

- increase the rate of economic growth and thereby raise living standards;
- increase the supply of goods and services, thereby reducing inflationary pressure;
- reduce unemployment in the long run.

Supply-side economists favour a long-term approach rather than short-term measures (such as reflation), which merely store up problems for later. Supply siders also favour a non-interventionist, or free market, approach to policy. They argue that the market:

- is calm and orderly;
- solves problems;
- provides incentives;
- allocates resources in an optimum manner to provide consumers with the goods and services they require.

For these reasons, so-called supply-side measures usually take the form of freeing the market, thus making it more competitive and efficient. Consequently, these measures should be seen as microeconomic measures designed to impact macroeconomic variables (such as national income, the price level, unemployment).

Supply-side measures can be grouped as follows:

- **Industrial policy measures**
  - Privatization, or the sale of assets from the public to the private sector.

- Contracting out of public services to private enterprise firms (this process is now referred to as market testing).
- Deregulation, or the removal of barriers to entry and the elimination of unnecessary bureaucratic controls.
- The imposition of market discipline on public-sector bodies (such as the new NHS Trusts and opted-out schools and colleges).

● **Financial market measures**

- Deregulation of the financial markets to allow greater competition, increase the supply of funds and reduce the cost of borrowing (such as deregulation of building societies to allow them to compete with banks).
- Encouraging savings by granting tax concessions for tax exempt savings schemes (TESSAs) and personal equity plans (PEPs), now replaced by Individual Savings Accounts (ISAs).
- 'Popular capitalism', or measures to widen share ownership.

● **Taxation measures** The supply-side approach to taxation (the confiscation of funds to finance public-sector activities) is to:

- reduce the overall level of taxation;
- shift the balance of taxation from direct to indirect taxes in the belief that the latter do not have the disincentive effect of the former;
- minimise the distortion of the economy caused by taxing certain activities but not others.

    This preference for low taxation is designed to provide incentives, thus increasing national output and income. Paradoxically, this might result in a rise in the yield from taxation.

● **Labour market measures** These measures are perhaps the most controversial of the supply-side measures pursued by Conservative governments. The aim is to create a more flexible labour market in the interests of competitiveness and employment in the long run. The measures are designed to make it more worth while for employers to take on extra staff and at the same time provide greater incentives for the unemployed to accept the jobs that are available.

Labour market measures have taken the form of:

- reducing the power of trade unions (see Chapter 46);
- reducing taxation for the low paid;
- reducing employment protection;
- more flexible pension arrangements to encourage greater mobility of labour;
- measures to improve the training of workers, such as the creation of Learning and Skills Councils;
- abolition of wages councils, which previously fixed pay in specified industries;
- encouragement of local and regional, as opposed to national, pay bargaining;
- changes in the housing market to assist the geographical mobility of labour;
- reducing entitlement to State welfare benefits;
- encouraging the use of short-term contracts of employment.

    Supporters argue that the creation of a more flexible labour market will benefit the economy by making UK firms competitive. Given the belief of free market supporters in 'trickle down', they naturally argue that everyone will benefit in the long run – including the employees whose protection is being removed by the measures. Conversely, critics argue that supply-side measures in the labour market are designed to remove protection for workers in the interests of profits for entrepreneurs.

An overall evaluation of supply-side measures pursued by successive Governments should be based on achievements in relation to the:

● growth of productivity (output per head);
● level of investment (the major factor in economic growth);
● profitability of UK companies;
● international competitiveness;
● international trade performance, both in terms of expansion of exports and the level of import penetration;
● inflation rates;
● reduction of unemployment in the long run.

Key concepts

Aggregate demand Total demand for goods and services. In Keynesian theory, it determines the level of output and employment.

Balance of payments A set of accounts recording details of one nation's transactions with the rest of the world.

Deflation As a policy in macroeconomics, deflation is a reduction in aggregate demand designed to reduce inflationary pressure.

Economic growth An increase in the productive capacity of the economy. An increase in real output per head of population.

Exchange rate The price of one currency in terms of another.

Fiscal policy The use of taxation and government expenditure to regulate the level of economic activity.

Full employment Usually regarded as unemployment of 2.5 per cent or a situation in which the total number unemployed equals the number of vacancies.

Inflation A rise in the general level of prices. Inflation is caused by excess demand, cost push, or an excessive rise in the money supply.

Interventionist approach An approach to economic policy based on the belief that problems caused by the market can and should be cured by government intervention.

Investment The accumulation of capital assets.

Keynesian theory Macroeconomic theory developed by J. M. Keynes, who argued that the level of economic activity was determined by the level of aggregate demand and that the free market did not guarantee full employment.

Laissez-faire Non-intervention by the State in the economy.

Macroeconomics The study of the behaviour of the economy as a whole.

Monetarism A school of economic thought arguing that instability in the economy is caused by disturbances in the monetary sector. In particular, they argue that inflation is caused by an increase in the money supply.

Monetary policy A method of controlling the economy by means of controls over the price and/or quantity of money.

Money supply Economists define the money supply in terms of coins, notes and bank deposits.

Multiplier The extent to which an increase in spending on (for instance) investment produces a cumulative impact greater than the initial rise in spending.

Recession A contractionary phase in the trade cycle. A mild slump.

Reflation As an economic policy, reflation is an increase in aggregate demand to reduce unemployment.

Retail Price Index A measure of inflation.

Supply-side measures Measures designed to provide incentives to work and enterprise, and increase competitive forces within the economy.

Unemployment The stock of people who are seeking employment but are unable to obtain it.

Essay questions

1 (a) Explain what is meant by inflation and why it occurs.
  (b) Analyse the likely consequences of inflation for a firm in the manufacturing sector.

2 (a) What are the major features and symptoms of a recession.
  (b) Analyse the likely consequences of recession on a firm engaged in selling holidays abroad.

3 (a) What is meant by economic growth?
  (b) Critically assess the benefits of economic growth.

4 (a) Explain the difference between inflation and reflation.
  (b) Analyse the circumstances in which a government would pursue a reflationary policy.
  (c) What are the likely consequences of a reflationary policy that overheats the economy?

5 Analyse the consequences for business of a rise in interest rates.

6 (a) What are the objectives of governments' macroeconomic policies?
  (b) Analyse the weapons used to achieve these policy objectives.

Business and economic policy

Having gained an overview of microeconomic principles, we now move on to consider issues relating to the industrial policy of the UK government. Industrial policy should be understood in terms of its impact on the business community: the opportunities it offers and the constraints it imposes. Central to this chapter is the debate about intervention or non-intervention in economic matters.

Chapter objectives

1 To analyse the case for and against State intervention in the economy.

2 To analyse the free market policies of privatization.

3 To analyse competition policy.

4 To analyse regional policy.

5 To analyse small firms policy.

Government in the UK

The work of the UK government is undertaken by government departments (headed by a cabinet minister) supervised by the UK Parliament, based in Westminster. All government departments make decisions that impact private-sector business organizations. For instance, the spending departments (such as Health, Education, and Social Security) place contracts with private-sector firms. Consequently, the level of government spending has a major impact on the sales revenue of firms dependent on government contracts.

In addition to its role as a customer, the State fulfils both supervisory and sponsorship roles. The former role relates to regulation of the private sector. The sponsorship role involves more positive activity, including representing British business abroad and offering loans and grants to encourage desirable trends. The government departments that have the largest impact on business are:

- the Department of Trade and Industry (DTI);
- the Department of the Environment, Transport and the Regions (DETR);
- the Ministry of Agriculture, Fisheries and Food (MAFF);
- the Department for Education and Employment (DfEE);
- the Treasury (responsible for taxation, government spending and borrowing and macroeconomic policy).

In addition to these departments, reference should be made to the Department of Defence (which promotes and also controls arms sales abroad) and the Department of Culture, Media and Sport (which promotes the leisure industries).

The UK also has a system of local government with local councils being responsible for various services (such as street lighting, social services, education) and also for some aspects of the regulation of businesses. These include planning permission, which clearly has a major impact on business. Any proposal for new buildings or change of use of existing buildings requires planning permission. The denial of planning permission acts as a major constraint on business activity.

The system of government in the UK is changing fundamentally with devolution in the Celtic areas. The Scottish Parliament has been established to legislate for Scotland and to control a Scottish government headed by a First Minister. Westminster retains powers over trade, industry, foreign affairs and economic matters, but the new Scottish Parliament has powers over agriculture, fisheries, education, training, planning, financial assistance to industry, Scottish roads, the environment and tourism in Scotland. Businesses operating both sides of the border have to appreciate that devolution will result in what may be radically different policies and regulations on one side of the border from those on the other side.

The policy of the UK parties is devolution within a United Kingdom. The Scottish Nationalist Party (SNP) on the other hand, favours an independent Scotland within the European Union.

Devolution in Wales has resulted in the creation of a Welsh Assembly. This body does not have the same level of power and responsibility as that enjoyed by the Scottish Parliament. Westminster has retained control over primary legislative power in all areas and the assembly is taking over secondary legislative power in areas similar to those adopted by the Scottish Parliament. **Primary legislation** is law passed in Westminster laying down the scope of legislation. **Secondary legislation,** on the other hand, governs the way the law works in practice.

The position in Northern Ireland remains uncertain at the time of writing. The 1998 Good Friday Agreement commits all parties to the devolution of government functions to a Northern Ireland government headed by a First Minister.

The role of the State in economic affairs

The first 80 years of the twentieth century saw a substantial growth in State activity. The UK became a mixed economy with substantial public (government) and private enterprise sectors. Moreover, government bodies intervened in the private sector, encouraging certain desirable trends as well as curtailing trends that were considered undesirable. The arrival of the Thatcher Government in 1979 led to a reversal of the trend towards greater State involvement. Although the UK still has a mixed economy and substantial government involvement in the private sector, there has been a trend towards 'rolling back the frontiers of State'.

Conservative supporters see the so-called 'Thatcher revolution' as part of a worldwide trend towards free markets and private enterprise. To understand the different philosophical views on the role of the State, let us contrast the *laissez-faire* and the interventionist approaches.

The *laissez-faire* view

'And what is this building for?' This was the reported comment of a free market, Thatcherite Secretary of State for Trade and Industry as he entered the DTI for the first time as a minister. The comment does not reflect his ignorance of the role of the DTI, but his questioning of its value in a market economy.

The case for a minimalist role for government was first outlined by classical economists of the nineteenth century. According to them, it is the invisible hand of market forces (an idea developed by Adam Smith in *The Wealth of Nations,* published in 1776) that produces the optimum result:

● resources are allocated to produce the goods and services demanded by consumers;
● changing consumer wants are reflected in price movements;

- the profit motive ensures that supply responds to demand;
- competition provides a spur to efficiency;
- income from the provision of factor services (such as labour) enables people to purchase goods;
- the price mechanism provides a system for rationing the supply of goods and services to ensure that those with effective demand can obtain the goods they desire and are willing to pay for;
- competition in the factor markets (such as the market for labour) ensures that there is an equitable return on factor inputs.

In other words, non-interventionists believe that the market solves economic problems, whereas intervention is destabilizing and harmful to initiative. The removal of the profit motive from the public sector leads to inefficiency. In fact, the only correct role for the State is to provide a framework of law, order and stability in which competitive private enterprise can flourish.

The non-interventionist view lost ground in the first three-quarters of the twentieth century, but the election of the Thatcher Government in 1979 led to a return to *laissez-faire* thinking. More than their Conservative predecessors, the Thatcher and Major Governments pursued policies characterized by:

- **economic liberalism** a *laissez-faire* approach to policy;
- **monetarism** a determination to eradicate inflation by controlling the growth of the money supply;
- **anti-corporatism** opposition to powerful vested interests, especially trade unions
- **individualism** a concern for self-reliance based on an enterprise culture as distinct from the dependency culture of the Welfare State, which, the Thatcherites alleged, had played a major part in the economic decline of the UK.

The interventionist view

The interventionist view arises from criticisms of the free market or capitalist system. Left-wing radicals focus on the inequalities of income, wealth and power that are seen as inherent in the system. Marxists argue that the contradictions within capitalism will inevitably bring about its end.

Less extreme are those we can call reformists, who are found in all mainstream political parties. Such reformists accept the basic features of the private enterprise system, namely individual initiative, the profit motive and market forces. However, they also accept that the system produces some undesirable results, which are known in economics as market failures. If the market creates problems – or, at the very least, fails to solve problems – then there is a strong case for the State to intervene.

The undesirable features of the private enterprise or free market system are as follows (and are summarized in Table 11.1).

- The market fails to provide certain services, such as law and order. These are known as public goods and have to be provided collectively.
- The market fails to provide sufficient quantities of so-called merit goods, which, despite their beneficial properties, people often choose not to purchase. To overcome this problem, the state either subsidizes such goods or provides them free at the point of consumption (such as healthcare) and, in the case of education, makes it compulsory.
- However, the market does provide certain goods and services (such as alcohol, tobacco, pornography, drugs and guns) that, although harmful, are nevertheless still in demand. To deal with this problem, the State either regulates the sale of such goods (by means of licensing or taxation) or prohibits them altogether.
- The market system creates inequalities of wealth and income. Although some inequality is essential for the operation of the market, extreme inequalities and chronic poverty are unacceptable in a civilized society. This problem is tackled by a combination of progressive taxation (falling disproportionately on the well off) and welfare benefits. Most people accept the need for some

Table 11.1 Market failure and their solutions

The Market fails to ...	Solutions
Provide public goods	State provision
Provide sufficient quantities of merit goods	State provision Subsidies to encourage provision and/or consumption Compulsion
Control demerit goods	Prohibition Controlled access Licensing Age bans Taxation
Provide equality	Progressive taxation Welfare benefits
Prevent and control monopoly	Competition law
Take account of externalities: ● external costs	 Planning laws Pollution control Pollution (green) taxes
● external benefits	Subsidies
● Protect the consumer	Consumer protection law
● Solve macroeconomic problems, such as unemployment	Macroeconomic policy

redistribution in favour of the less well off, although there are considerable differences of opinion as to the extent to which redistribution should go.

● Domination of the market by a single firm (a monopoly) or a small number of firms (oligopoly) is another market failure. It should be noted that all the arguments in support of the market system assume the existence of competition. However, the cut and thrust of competition leads to business failure, takeovers and the emergence of large monopolistic firms. Some State regulations of monopoly are, therefore, necessary.

● Decision makers in the market are motivated by self-interest and, therefore, ignore what economists call externalities. These are the external costs inflicted on the community as well as the external benefits that are derived from the activities of others. To protect the community and the environment, planning controls, pollution controls and pollution taxes can be used. To encourage activities, in which there are spin-off benefits, subsidies can be given.

● The consumer is in a weak position in the market, given the complexity of many modern goods that we buy in a packaged form on trust (in the case of petrol we buy it without ever seeing it). A set of consumer protection laws is provided to redress the balance and to prevent the exploitation of consumers.

● The final market failure is that of failing to solve macroeconomic problems, such as unemployment. The market fails to guarantee full employment and, in consequence, there is a strong case for government intervention in the labour market.

Table 11.2 sets out the conflicting phisophies of the Conservative and Labour parties, in their past and present incarnations.

Table 11.2 Conflicting strands in the thinking of the two main parties

	Conservative			Labour	
	One Nation (paternalist)	New Right (libertarian)		Old Labour	New Labour
State	Interventionist	Limited	State	Interventionist	Supply-side economics
Economy	Mixed	Free market	Economy	Mixed	Free market
			Economic priority	Low unemployment	Low inflation
Welfare	As a universal right	As a safety net	Welfare	As a universal right	To reduce welfare dependency
Civil society	Pluralistic	Individualistic			
Change	Gradual	Rapid	Social goal	Egalitarian	Equality of opportunity
			Class	Pro-working class	Classless
Morality	Liberal	Conservative	Morality	Collectivist	Individualist
Trade unions	Legitimate/ constructive	Undemocratic/ destructive	Trade unions	Public good	No return to pre-1979 privileges
			Constitution	Keep status quo	Radical reform
			Europe	Right was pro-Europe; left anti-Europe in 1970s	Pro-Europe/ pool sovereignty
Nation state	European Integration/ pooling of sovereignty	Assert independence/ retain sovereignty	Nation state	Socialism in one country	Global economy

Business and taxation

Taxation can be defined as the levying by public authorities of compulsory contributions to defray the cost of their activities. Unlike a charge, it is compulsory and unrelated to the service that the individual taxpayer receives from the State. We can identify the functions of taxation as being to:

● raise revenues to finance government activity;
● regulate the economy;
● correct market failures identified earlier.

Clearly, supporters of a *laissez-faire* approach see raising revenue to finance the irreducible minimum of State activity as the only legitimate function of taxation. Reformists, on the other hand, believe that these other functions of taxation are legitimate, even though, on balance, taxation is likely to harm enterprise.

Economists classify taxes as **direct** and **indirect**. The former is levied on income and wealth; and the latter are levied on spending. There is a tendency to associate direct taxation with progressive taxation and indirect taxation with regressive taxation. **Progressive taxes** take a higher percentage of an individual's income as income rises.

Table 11.3 Direct taxation v. indirect taxation

Advantages of direct taxation	Disadvantages of direct taxation
<ul><li>Usually progressive</li><li>Redistribution in favour of low-income groups (whether this is beneficial is a matter of opinion)</li><li>Yield rises as income rises</li><li>Anti-inflationary</li><li>Incidence (burden) is easy to determine</li></ul>	<ul><li>Disincentive effect</li><li>Stifles initiative and enterprise</li><li>Evasion and avoidance encouraged</li><li>Discourages investment, including investment from abroad</li><li>Expensive to collect</li><li>Reduces savings</li></ul>
Advantages of indirect taxation	**Disadvantages of indirect taxation**
<ul><li>Convenient – payment is spread</li><li>'Voluntary'</li><li>Does not harm effort and initiative</li><li>Less chance of evasion</li><li>Flexible</li><li>Can be used for specific purposes</li></ul>	<ul><li>Regressive</li><li>Penalizes certain forms of consumption</li><li>Harms the industry concerned</li><li>Raises prices</li><li>Incidence (burden) is difficult to determine</li></ul>

Regressive taxes take a lower percentage of an individual's income (although not necessarily a lower amount of income) as income rises. Progressive taxes, when combined with welfare payments, can be used to redistribute income in favour of low-income groups.

Table 11.3 sets out the advantages and disadvantages of each type of taxation.

Business organizations are affected by taxation in a number of ways as it:

- reduces profits available for reinvestment and distribution to shareholders;
- reduces willingness, as well as ability, to expand;
- raises the prices of goods, thereby causing a contraction of demand;
- reduces disposable incomes and, therefore, consumer spending;
- alters income distribution – the impact on businesses will vary, but producers of luxury goods will suffer if income is redistributed to the less well off.

These consequences can be shown by reference to the main forms of taxation.

- **Income tax** is a progressive tax on the income of individuals. It directly impacts sole traders and partners and, in addition, has an indirect impact on all business via the reduction in disposable income of consumers.
- **Corporation tax** is a tax on company profits. It reduces profits available for distribution and might also reduce business incentives.
- **Capital gains tax** is levied on the increase in the value of capital when it is sold.
- **Inheritance tax** is levied on the estates of the deceased. This and the previous tax are not significant in terms of tax yield, although, potentially, they impose a disincentive effect on the business community.

Expenditure taxes are of two types. The specific taxes on petrol, tobacco and alcohol are related not to the value of goods, but to a physical measure such as weight or volume. Value-added tax (VAT) is a broad-based *ad valorem* tax as the rate is fixed as a percentage of the value of goods. All expenditure taxes, irrespective of how they are levied, will raise prices and reduce the volume of goods and services sold. However, the precise impact will depend on the price elasticity of demand for the product in question.

Local taxation has long been a matter of controversy and has undergone major changes. Domestic householders now pay local taxation related to capital values. This has an indirect impact on business via the ability to spend (consumers' disposable income). Businesses are currently subject to a nationally set **business rate** linked to capital values. The business rate, in effect, raises costs and, thereby, reduces profits for distribution. Moreover, as rateable values tend to be higher in the South than in the North, it does have a disproportionate effect on the South.

The other taxes worthy of mention are:

● National Insurance contributions – the employer's contribution is, in effect, a payroll tax;
● vehicle excise duty on vehicle ownership;
● North Sea taxes (petroleum revenue tax and oil royalties) that are levied in North Sea oil production.

Low taxation is favoured by the business community. The case for low tax rates is based on the belief that high taxes provide a disincentive to initiative and enterprise while low taxes will encourage enterprise, generating economic growth and employment. It is also argued that low tax rates will encourage growth to such an extent that the tax yield will actually rise, enabling the State to provide more of the social services that the electorate requires.

Public expenditure

Public (or government) expenditure takes two forms. First, government provides certain welfare benefits to various groups in society (pensioners, low-income families and the infirm). This form of government spending involves a transfer of income from taxpayers to benefit receivers. It might be thought that the overall impact of this transfer is neutral, but the purchases of those receiving benefit are likely to be different from those of the better off taxpayer. Consequently, even if income transfers have no impact on the total of spending (in practice they are likely to raise it), they will have an impact on the direction of that spending. Business organizations that provide goods and services for the better off may suffer a fall in the volume of trade, whereas businesses providing goods and services for the less well off might benefit.

The second type of government spending is direct spending on goods, services and labour.

Examples include defence procurement, motorway construction and school building. Although the business community in general favours low taxation and low government spending, there are many private-sector firms that rely heavily on government contracts. A reduction in government spending creates problems for such firms.

The business community also benefits from State spending on the **infrastructure**. This generic term covers roads, rail links, water supply, sewers, communications and power supplies. The infrastructure involves basic services that are essential in modern industrial society. Admittedly, many parts of the infrastructure are now provided by the private sector, but State expenditure remains vital for large parts of its development, especially transport links.

Privatization and related policies

The Conservative Government of Margaret Thatcher initiated a programme of rolling back the state. Within the framework of 'privatization' we can identify a number of distinct strands.

● **Denationalization** Before 1979, a large proportion of industry, especially transport and the utilities, was in government hands. The case for privatization is that:
  – the profit motive will increase efficiency;
  – greater competition will also increase efficiency;
  – privatized concerns will be more responsive to the needs of customers;
  – the discipline of the market will lead to improved decision making, especially in relation to investment;
  – management will be freed from political interference and make decisions purely on commercial grounds;
  – employee share schemes (promoted as part of privatization) will give workers a greater stake in the industry;
  – privatization raises finance for the government, enabling it to reduce public-sector borrowing.
● **The sale of government-owned shares** in existing public limited companies.

- **The sale of other assets** – for example, council houses.
- **Contractualization** The shifting of services, previously undertaken by the public sector, into the private sector. For instance, refuse collection remains a responsibility of local authorities, but many councils have contracted the work out to private-sector firms. Many State services are subject to tendering (or market testing) in which outside firms compete with in-house units for the contract to undertake the work.
- **Marketization** The shifting of services, previously undertaken in the non-market sector, into the market sector. Private education and healthcare have grown in recent decades, thus more of these services are available on a paying basis when in the past all but a very small percentage of them were financed out of taxation and free at the point of consumption. Even in the public sector, there has been an attempt to create an internal market with facilitators (such as Funding Councils) buying services from providers (incorporated colleges, for example).
- **Deregulation** The removal of government regulations that promoted monopoly and barriers to entry and thus prevented competition. Examples include deregulation of the buses, civil aviation, tele-communications, broadcasting and conveyancing. The advantages of deregulation, it is argued, stem from a freely operating price system and the virtues of economic liberalism:
  - the promotion of competition and enterprise;
  - greater efficiency;
  - lower prices and wider choice for consumers;
  - 'getting the State off the backs' of businesses by the removal of 'red tape' and bureaucracy.

Industrial policy

This is defined as government policies that explicitly seek either the achievement of production targets or a particular structure within an industry or to promote growth, investment or technical progress. As these policies involve government intervention in the market, they can only be justified if markets fail or do not work in a smooth, frictionless manner. Supporters of *laissez-faire* favour free market supply-side policies, but for the remainder of this chapter we shall focus on interventionist policies to:

- correct the abuse of monopoly power (competition policy);
- assist areas of high unemployment, declining industry (regional policy);
- assist small firms.

Competition policy

A large part of microeconomic theory is designed to demonstrate the advantages of a competitive market and the undesirability of monopoly. Unfortunately, economies of scale have produced a trend towards dominant firm situations and/or oligopoly, in which price competition has been replaced by tacit, or even formal, collusion between the small number of firms remaining in the market.

UK competition policy, which dates back to 1973, has always been pragmatic, trading off the gains from large firms against the undoubted losses from dominant firm situations. The gains for large dominant firms include:

- lower costs as a result of economies of scale;
- high profits to finance research and development;
- high profits to allow firms to survive in unstable trading conditions.

The losses to society resulting from dominant firm situations include:

- excessive profits at the expense of customers and employees;
- high prices;
- inefficiency as a result of the absence of the spur of competition;
- complacency.

Hence, UK policy seeks to deal with the welfare loss that results from monopoly power while permitting cases to be dealt with on a pragmatic or case-by-case basis.

Until 1999, dominant firms and proposed mergers could be referred by the Director-General of Fair Trading or the Secretary of State for Trade and Industry to the Monopolies and Mergers Commission (MMC) for an investigation. **Monopoly** was defined as a dominant firm with a market share in excess of 25 per cent. Similarly, a merger could be referred to the MMC if the combined market share exceeded 25 per cent. It must be stressed that the MMC was not a court of law and had no powers of enforcement. However, it could investigate and make recommendations to the Secretary of State, who in turn could issue orders to prevent mergers, break up monopolies or enforce compliance.

It was widely accepted that merger and monopoly policy was rather ineffective, especially when government often encouraged mergers or even created private monopolies in the process of privatization. State action to prevent **restrictive trade practices (RP)** was tougher. RP are agreements between firms to reduce the impact of competition – in other words, colluding at the expense of customers. The collusion took the form of:

● price-fixing cartels;
● market sharing;
● the rigging of tenders;
● full line forcing – forcing retailers to take the manufacturer's full range of goods;
● resale price maintenance – dictating prices at which retailers sell goods;
● aggregated rebates.

Under various statutes (most notably the Act 1973), all restrictive practices had to be registered with the Office of Fair Trading. The Restrictive Practices Court had power to decide whether or not a restrictive practice should be allowed to continue. The parties to the agreement had to prove that:

● the restrictive practice confers some benefit on the public in the form of one of the 'gateways';
● the benefits outweigh the disadvantages to the public.

The 'gateways' can be seen as the permitted defences of RP and they pass the first test if they:

● protect the public from injury;
● prevent local unemployment;
● maintain exports;
● give special benefits to customers;
● operate against existing restrictions on competition;
● support another acceptable RP;
● promote fair trading terms for buyers and suppliers;
● do not restrict competition.

The onus of proof in RP cases rests on the parties to the agreement. Unless they can demonstrate that the RP confer some positive benefits on the public that are not outweighed by disadvantages, they will be declared illegal.

The Restrictive Practices Court dealt with relatively few cases. Its supporters argue that its clear guidelines about what are and are not acceptable RP have meant that it has not had to try many cases. However, the unearthing of major cartel arrangements suggest that RP legislation is, like monopoly legislation, ineffective in the UK.

One RP was outlawed by specific legislation in 1964. The Resale Price Maintenance (RPM) Act of that year banned the practice of manufacturers dictating prices to retailers, except in circumstances where it could be demonstrated that RPM was in the public interest.

The existing structure of competition policy was radically changed by the Competition Act 1998, which is based on the EU approach to anti-competitive behaviour. Before looking at post-1998 UK competition policy, however, we need to understand EU competition law.

Article 85 of the Treaty of Rome 1957 (which established the original European Economic Community) prohibits all agreements and concerted practices that may affect trade between member states and have as their object or effect the prevention, restriction or distortion of competition within the EU. In other words, anti-competitive practices affecting two or more member states are prohibited.

Article 86 of the Treaty of Rome prohibits the abuse of monopoly and oligopoly power in so far as it may affect trade between member states. In addition, mergers with a 'community dimension'

– those cross-border mergers within the EU – are subject to EU law.

Notice the EU stress on prohibition: RP and abuse of monopoly power is prohibited although exemptions can be granted in special cases. The same emphasis on prohibition is contained in the UK Act 1998. The prohibition of anti-competition agreements and abuse by dominant firms is enforced by the Director-General of Fair Trading and by the Regulators in the privatized utilities (gas, electricity and so on). Companies breaching the prohibitions are liable to fines and parties harmed are entitled to seek compensation.

The Competition Commission (CC) has taken over from the MMC and continues its role of investigating and reporting on matters referred to it. These relate to monopolies, mergers, anti-competitive practices, regulation of privatized utilities, performance of public-sector bodies, restrictive labour practices, newspapers and broadcasting.

In addition, the CC has an appeals role. An appeal can be made to the CC concerning a decision on whether or not prohibition has been breached, the amount of penalty and whether or not an individual exemption should be granted or cancelled. In most cases, an appeal can be made not only by the party directly affected by the decision, but also by anyone with a sufficient interest, such as competitors and customers.

Regional policy

Regional policy is of relevance to us for two reasons:

- regional aid represents one form of government assistance to business;
- it provides an interesting illustration of the distinction between a free market and an interventionist approach to economic and social problems.

In the UK, there are regional differences in:

- unemployment
- wealth
- income
- economic growth
- industry
- population growth

- opportunities for the regions' inhabitants – perhaps the most important regional difference of all.

The market solution to this problem is for the government to do nothing and allow market forces to correct the imbalance. Labour will move to the more prosperous areas in search of work; capital (firms) will move to the less prosperous areas in search of low-cost labour and sites. This process will continue until all areas enjoy equality in terms of employment, average incomes and economic growth.

Regional policy, which has been pursued with varying degrees of vigour over half a century, is based on the proposition that the market fails to solve the problem. This is because of the relative immobility of labour, the powerful magnet of the South East (part of the 'golden triangle') and the existence of national rates of pay that reduce the incentive for firms to move to areas of high unemployment.

During the 60 or so years in which a regional policy has been pursued, a variety of measures have been used. In general, there has been a preference for encouraging expanding firms to move into less prosperous areas rather than helping the unemployed to move to more prosperous areas. In other words, 'taking work to the workers' has been preferred to 'taking the workers to the work'. At times, governments have used industrial development certificates to block expansion in the more prosperous regions. However, the 'stick' is an impotent weapon in a time of high unemployment. Instead, governments have preferred the 'carrot' of incentives to encourage expansion in the less prosperous areas – known as development areas.

The main forms of regional aid are the following.

- **Regional Selective Assistance** Financial assistance is given for investment projects in designated assisted areas. It is available to both manufacturing and service-sector firms that create or safeguard jobs.
- **Regional Innovation Grant** Funding available at 50 per cent of costs up to a maximum of £25 000 on projects leading to the development of new products or processes by firms with up to 50 employees.

- **Regional Investment Grant** For projects with up to 25 employees in areas affected by colliery closure. Funding is available at 15 per cent of expenditure on fixed assets up to a maximum grant of £15 000.
- **Single Regeneration Budget** This has replaced the Regional Innovation and Investment Grants.
- **Enterprise Zones (EZ)** These are designated for ten years and the benefits are:
  - 100 per cent capital allowances against tax;
  - exemption from the uniform business rate;
  - simplified planning regime;
  - preferential treatment in relation to customs;
  - exclusion from burdensome government statistical requirements.
- **Free Zone** Enclosed areas in which non-EU goods are treated for import duties as outside the customs territory of the EU. No customs duty, import VAT or other charges are due if the goods are not released for free circulation or entered under another customs procedure.

  All imported goods, including EU goods that are free of duty, may be stored or processed in a free zone without payment of import VAT. The supply of goods or services to or within the zone is subject to the normal domestic VAT rules. The supply of imported goods in a free zone may be zero rated for VAT on condition that the recipient clears the goods for removal from the zone to home use. Relief from excise duty is limited to the warehousing facilities available under existing legislation.

  Activities allowable in a free zone include:
  - loading, unloading and transhipment;
  - storage, including stockholding, pending the availability of quotas;
  - handling operations carried out to ensure preservation or improvement in the marketable quality of zone goods, preparation for distribution or resale;
  - processing of most third-country goods for export outside the EU and processing of EU goods;
  - destruction of unsaleable or surplus goods.

  Relief on customs duties relating to the transhipment, handling and processing of goods destined for re-export is widely available throughout the UK. However, Free Zones offer the following non-tariff advantages:
  - simplified customs procedures;
  - cash flow benefits resulting from the exemption from duty, unless and until goods are exported or released into free circulation;
  - security provided by a perimeter fence enclosing the zone;
  - economies of scale from the physical concentration of facilities;
  - greater potential for improved marketing and presentation;
  - greater flexibility in determining final destinations for goods subject to quota restrictions.

  Current examples include Birmingham and Southampton airports, together with the ports of Tilbury and Sheerness.
- **Urban Development Corporations** Established to regenerate areas of decline in or close to the inner cities.

  In addition to UK (or Scottish) government help, Assisted Areas also qualify for EU assistance from the European Regional Development Fund and from the European Investment Bank (EIB). The EIB provides loans for capital investment projects in industry or infrastructure within the EU. Typical sectors eligible for large EIB loans include:
  - regional development;
  - transport and telecommunications;
  - energy;
  - environmental protection;
  - competitiveness and integration of industry;
  - small- and medium-sized enterprises.

The Conservative Governments of Thatcher and Major pursued a minimalist regional policy in contrast to previous Labour governments. In part, this reflected the different economic philosophies of the two main parties in the UK. It can also be explained by the apparent failure of regional policy over the decades. Despite regional policy, differences between the various regions of the UK have persisted. The failure of regional policy can be attributed to the following:

- it does not 'create' jobs, it merely shifts them;
- capital grants encourage capital-intensive industry;
- most regional aid went to helping the declining manufacturing sectors;
- the performance of new firms in development areas was often disappointing and these factories were often the first to close in a period of downturn in trade;
- logically, regional policy is designed to encourage firms to move to a less than satisfactory location, one they would not ordinarily have chosen.

Defenders of regional policy would counter by arguing that if regional aid has not cured the problem, it might have prevented it getting worse.

Assistance for small firms

Small firms can be defined in four ways:

- the size of their labour force – 200 or fewer employees;
- their relatively small market share;
- they are managed by owners in a personalized way;
- they are independent of large groups.

Small- and medium-sized enterprises (SMEs) are seen as very important for a healthy economy as they:

- are seen as innovative;
- create jobs and help to reduce unemployment;
- occupy niches in the market;
- provide competition;
- could become the large firms of tomorrow.

Despite the benefits to the economy of SMEs, they suffer major disadvantages. Their small size results in the absence of full economies of scale and certain kinds of specialist expertise. With a limited product range and dependence on a single market, they suffer from greater risks than larger businesses. The greatest problem they face is lack of

access to finance. City institutions provide few facilities for small businesses, whereas the high street banks tend to offer only short-term loans and overdrafts. The rationale for government assistance for SMEs is based on the importance of the small-firm sector and the problems they face in a free market.

Government assistance has taken various forms, including the removal of 'red tape' (bureaucratic requirements) from small firms, advice and help with training, tax concessions and, most important of all, the Loan Guarantee Scheme.

The Scheme guarantees loans from banks and other financial institutions for small businesses with viable business proposals that have tried and failed to obtain a conventional loan because of lack of security.

Loans are available for periods between 2 and 10 years on sums from £5,000 to £100 000 (£250 000 in the case of businesses that have been trading for more than a couple of years). The DTI guarantees 70 per cent of the loan (85 per cent in the case of businesses trading for more than a couple of years). In return for the guarantee, the borrower pays the DTI a premium of 1.5 per cent per year on the outstanding amount of the loan. The premium is reduced to 0.5 per cent if the loan is taken at a fixed rate of interest.

The loan guarantee is available to new and existing companies with a turnover of £1.5 m (or £3 m in the case of manufacturers) or less. It is available for most business purposes, although there are various restrictions. It must be stressed that the State does not offer the loan, it merely underwrites a loan granted by a bank. The importance of the Scheme lies in the fact that it can overcome the reluctance of banks to lend to small businesses.

Key concepts

Competition policy Policy to increase the level of competition in the economy.
Deregulation The removal or relaxation of any regulation imposed by the government in its regulation of economic activity.
Direct taxes Taxes on income and wealth.
Indirect taxes Taxes on spending.

Intervention Any measure adopted by the government that affects the operation of market forces.

Laissez-faire The limitation of government intervention in economic activity to the minimum required to ensure the efficient running of a free market economy.

Market failure The failure of the market to allocate goods and services in the most efficient way. Problems created by the market.

Privatization The transfer of ownership from the public (government) sector to the private sector.

Regional policy Measures to influence location decisions of firms.

Essay questions

1 Interference in the operation of markets is unnecessary and harmful to enterprise. Discuss.

2 (a) Explain what is meant by market failure.
(b) Analyse the ways in which governments seek to correct market failures.

3 Governments should promote mergers, not prevent them. Critically discuss.

4 Analyse the consequences for business of:
(a) a cut in the standard rate of income tax;
(b) a cut in the higher rate of income tax;
(c) a cut in personal allowances against income tax;
(d) the abolition of zero rating for Value Added Tax.

5 (a) Assess the case for an interventionist regional policy.
(b) How would you evaluate the success of a regional policy measure?

6 Assess the benefits of:
(a) privatization; and
(b) deregulation.

The international environment of business

This chapter looks at the ways in which the international economy and membership of the European Union affects business enterprises in the UK.

Chapter objectives

1 To analyse ways in which the international environment affects UK firms.

2 To analyse government policies on trade and the balance of payment.

3 To survey the development of the EU.

4 To analyse the debate on the adoption of a single currency.

5 To identify other aspects of EU policy that affect UK businesses.

The impact of the international environment on UK firms

Business organizations are affected by the international environment. It:

● provides export opportunities;
● poses a threat in the home market;
● poses a threat in third-country markets;
● affects British firms that use imported materials and components;
● impacts firms other than those engaged in exporting or threatened by imports.

We will look at each of these factors in turn.

Export opportunities

Economic growth and rising living standards abroad will lead to higher demand for goods and services, including higher demand for UK goods and services. Exporting firms therefore benefit from increased prosperity in other countries, especially in those countries that are major trading partners. Conversely, recession abroad will reduce world demand and, therefore, reduce export opportunities for UK companies. The major macroeconomic variables – such as gross domestic product (GDP), GDP per head, unemployment rates, population size and growth – are all major factors that affect export opportunities.

Equally important is the ability of UK firms to enter overseas markets. This is affected by:

- the extent to which the foreign market is open to imports or closed by various forms of import control (see below);
- the competitiveness of UK firms.

Competitiveness is determined by relative UK performance (that is, relative to rivals) in terms of:

- quality;
- availability;
- reliability;
- cost of labour;
- cost of materials;
- cost of energy;
- cost of transport.

and by exchange rates. As we will see, a falling pound aids UK exports whereas a rising pound harms UK exports.

Import penetration

A major factor in the decline of many industries in Britain has been penetration into the UK market of manufactured goods from abroad. The openness of the UK economy has facilitated this rise in imports, generating a threat to existing UK firms. Given the commitment of the UK to EU membership and its support for the General Agreement on Tariffs and Trade (GATT), there is no question of import controls. UK firms can only repel foreign competition in the UK market by producing goods and services that UK customers want, in the right quantity and quality, and at the right price.

Threats in third-country markets

British firms compete with firms abroad. The nature of the international economy is such that the bulk of UK trade (exports and imports) is not with agricultural countries, but with similarly structured, industrial countries, such as EU partners, Japan and North America. British firms compete with German firms not only in their respective home markets, but also in third-country markets,

such as Italy or Turkey. British firms have to be competitive to stand a chance in the German, UK and these third-country markets. Any downturn in the German economy will lead to reduced sales to Germany and an increase in the desire of German firms to capture other markets. British firms will then find increased competition in these third-country markets.

Imported materials

Britain has traditionally relied on imported raw materials (timber, iron ore, non-ferrous metals) and foodstuffs (the raw material of the food processing industry). The internationalization of capitalism has now reached the stage where developed countries rely on other countries for components that go into complicated assembled goods (cars, electrical goods and so on). This means that UK producers are dependent on supplies from abroad. Any reduction in supplies as a result of:

- war and political tension abroad;
- natural disasters abroad;
- production or transport problems abroad;

will directly affect the UK firms that use such materials. Moreover, any rise in the cost of producing these imported materials will have a knock-on effect due to a rise in UK firms' costs and/or reduction in profit margins. A fall in the exchange rate (beneficial to our exporters) will raise the price of imported materials and components. This can set off an inflationary cycle in the UK.

The impact of the world economy

In Chapter 10, we considered the effect of the multiplier. An increase in one of the injections (such as exports) will produce a multiplier impact on the domestic economy, raising the level of national income and aggregate demand. Conversely, a reduction in one of the injections will produce a downward multiplier impact on the economy. This is the first linkage that needs to be explored in analysing the transmission of economic trends from one country to another.

Figure 12.1 The impacts of recession abroad

Imagine that there is a recession in one of our major customer countries. As a result, it will reduce its imports of goods and services from the UK. This reduction is the result of either a cutback in foreign demand (as a result of reduced income) or the imposition of import controls. Reduced exports from the UK will produce a downward multiplier impact in this country. This will not only harm exporting firms, but also those that concentrate on the home market (see Figure 12.1).

It is also possible that foreign producers, facing difficulties in their home markets, will attempt to market their products more aggressively abroad, thus penetrating further into UK and third-country markets.

The transmission process that has been described works in both directions and is particularly potent when being transmitted from major economic powers, such as the USA, Germany or Japan.

Another transmission mechanism is financial in nature. Since 1979, the UK has had no foreign exchange controls. This means that currencies can flow freely into and out of the UK without any restriction. One cause of outflow of currency is interest rate differences between London and other major financial centres. Higher rates in New York will see so-called 'hot money' flowing from London to New York. If the government is anxious to prevent an outflow of funds (say, to protect the pound against depreciation), it will be forced to raise interest rates in line with New York. As a result of this mechanism, high rates abroad (designed to reduce inflationary pressure) can force up rates in the UK, thus reducing borrowing and, therefore, spending in the UK. Once again, even firms that have no intention of exporting can be affected by this mechanism. This is because higher rates in the UK:

● raise the cost of borrowing to industry;
● reduce demand in the UK.

The balance of payments

The balance of payments is a set of accounts that summarizes one country's transactions with the rest of the world. The transactions concern:

● the sale and purchase of goods – so-called **visible trade**;
● the sale and purchase of services – **invisible trade**;
● capital movements, such as UK investment abroad and foreign investment in the UK.

The current account of the balance of payments relates only to the first two items above – that is, trade in goods and services. The balance is calculated by subtracting the total value of imports of goods and services from the total value of exports of goods and services. A **deficit** means that the total of imports is greater than the total of exports. A **surplus** means that the total of exports exceeds the total of imports.

A current account deficit is considered undesirable in that it has to be financed either by a run on the country's foreign currency reserves or by borrowing from abroad. Alternatively, if the currency is allowed to float freely, it will cause the exchange rate to fall.

Let us analyse the consequences of a fall in exchange rates (or depreciation). This makes UK exports cheaper to foreign buyers and will therefore boost sales of UK goods and services abroad. At the same time, depreciation will make foreign goods more expensive in the UK, thus reducing

Table 12.1 The impacts of exchange rate changes

	Depreciation or devaluation	Appreciation or revaluation
Direction of change	Fall in exchange rate	Rise in exchange rate
Exports		
Price	Cheaper	More expensive
Quantity	Likely to rise	Likely to fall
Imports		
Price	More expensive	Cheaper
Quantity	Likely to fall	Likely to rise
Balance of payments	Will improve if quantity changes sufficiently	Will worsen if quantity changes sufficiently
Consequences for UK firms	Helps exporters	Harms exporters
	Harms firms that rely on imports	Helps firms that rely on imports
	Boost to exports will provide stimulus to the economy	Reduction in exports will depress the economy
	Possible inflationary consequences of dearer imports	Possible disinflationary consequences of cheaper imports

the quantity bought. The twin impact on exports and imports will bring about an improvement in the balance of payments, provided the quantities bought and sold change sufficiently to counteract the fact that we pay more for imports and receive less for imports. In other words, the balance of payments will only improve if demand is sufficiently elastic. Unfortunately, a fall in the exchange rate has harmful consequences in the longer run. By making imports more expensive to UK buyers, depreciation will increase the inflation rate in the UK.

Table 12.1 shows the effects changes in exchange rates can have on business.

If the exchange rate is not allowed to fall, then alternative strategies are needed to correct the balance of payments. One strategy is to deflate the economy by raising interest rates and reducing government spending. This will reduce total spending in the economy, thus reducing spending on imports. Unfortunately, it harms the sale of domestically produced goods and leads to job losses. Deflation uses unemployment to correct a balance of payments deficit.

In previous decades, import controls were used to correct a deficit. The controls took a variety of forms, including tariffs (taxes on imported

goods). This policy weapon is no longer available to UK governments because of its commitments under the General Agreement on Tariffs and Trade (GATT). GATT seeks to reduce trade barriers between countries and agreements are now 'policed' by the World Trade Organization (WTO).

More important than commitments under GATT are the UK's commitments as a member of the European Union. EU members trade freely with each other and, in addition, operate a common commercial policy in trade with non-member countries. In other words, not only can the UK *not* impose barriers against goods from the rest of the EU, it has to impose common barriers against the rest of the world. Even if import controls could be imposed, it is unlikely that they would improve the balance of payments. By controlling *imports* from the rest of the world, we also limit *exports* to the rest of the world.

Let us look at the arguments for and against import controls in Table 12.2.

The European Union

An historical survey

After the experience of the two world wars, there emerged a growing desire for European cooperation,

Table 12.2 Free trade v. protectionism

The case against import controls	The case for import controls

● Prevent countries specializing in those forms of production in which they have a cost advantage
● Protect high-cost, inefficient production
● Protect monopolists
● Encourage resistance to structural change in the economy
● Reduce the volume of world trade
● Reduce world output
● Act as export controls
● Cause job losses in export industries
● Reduce living standards
● Are self-defeating attempt to 'beggar my neighbour'
	● Protect home producers against 'unfair' competition, which usually means:
	  – low-price imports from low-pay economies; or
	  – goods sold in the home market at a price less than the cost of production (this practice, known as 'dumping', is designed to eliminate a surplus by dumping it on others)
	● 'Cushion' the decline of traditional industries
	● Protect employment
	● Promote diversification by protecting infant industries
	● Can be used as a bargaining weapon to encourage mutual tariff reduction
	● Can be used to improve the balance of payments

The three policy weapons are summarized in Table 12.3.

Table 12.3 Correcting a balance of payments deficit

Weapon used	How it works	Problems
Devaluation/depreciation	Makes exports cheaper and imports dearer	Only works if volumes change sufficiently Rise in cost of imports is inflationary
Import controls, such as tariffs, quotas	Limits imports or makes them expensive	Contrary to the EU single market and GATT Will also reduce exports
Export promotion	Subsidies to exporters Advice and assistance to exporters	Illegal under GATT There is no substitute for being competitive
Deflation	Rise in taxation Cuts in government spending Rise in interest rates	A fall in demand depresses the economy, leading to unemployment

especially on economic and social policy. This led six Western European countries to sign the Treaty of Rome in 1957, which established the European Economic Community (EEC). At first, the UK remained aloof, clinging to an outdated view of itself as a world power with a large empire. However, post-war economic and military weakness led to a gradual (if somewhat belated, reluctant) acceptance of the UK's changed position in the world. No longer a world power, the UK's future lay in closer links with European neighbours.

In 1959, the UK, along with Austria, Switzerland, Portugal and three Scandinavian countries, became members of the European Free Trade Association (EFTA). EFTA shared some of the aims of the EEC – for instance, there was to be free trade in industrial products between members. However, the aims of EFTA were strictly limited. There was no common external tariff, no common policies in relation to agriculture, fishing, transport and social affairs and no ambition to move towards greater unity.

By the 1960s, it was clear that EFTA was no substitute for closer links with the major countries of Europe that joined the EEC. Moreover, the relative decline in Commonwealth trade placed greater urgency on admission to the EC. After two failed attempts, the UK eventually joined the EEC on 1 January 1973. At that time, the EEC was composed of the Federal Republic of Germany (West Germany), France, Italy and the UK (the Big Four), together with Belgium, Luxembourg, The Netherlands, Ireland and Denmark. Later on, these countries were joined by Greece, Portugal, Spain, Austria, Finland and Sweden. The reunification of Germany added the former East Germany to the territory covered by the EEC. The first decade of the twenty-first century is likely to see a number of Eastern European countries joining what we now call the European Union (EU). The first wave of Eastern European countries to join is likely to include Poland, Hungary, the Czech Republic and Estonia. By 2010 it is possible that the EU will consist of up to 30 countries.

Themes in the history of the EU

In addition to enlargement (the accession of new members), we can identify two other themes in the history of the EU. First, there was widening of the Union, taking it into new policy areas (such as policies on workers' rights). Second, there has been a deepening of the EU, involving closer relations in the existing policy areas. The last two can be seen in the following stages in the process of economic integration.

- **Stage 1: free trade area** This is a group of states that have abolished tariffs and quotas on trade between themselves, but retain independent controls on trade with the rest of the world.
- **Stage 2: customs union** This adds a common external tariff on imports from outside the area to the free trade that was a feature of stage 1.
- **Stage 3: common market** This combines a free trade area, a customs union with harmonization of key economic policies and the free movement of labour and capital across national boundaries. The Treaty of Rome of 1957 committed its signatories to the establishment of a common market, to promote the harmonious development of economic activities, a continuous and balanced expansion, an increase in stability,

accelerated raising of living standards and closer relations between states belonging to it (as stated in Article 2 of the treaty). Rapid progress was made in the first decade of the EU's history – there was free trade between member states, a common external tariff, the establishment of some common policies, especially in the field of agriculture. Nevertheless, the EU was far from being a common market in which trade between members (known as intra-Community trade) was conducted on the same basis as trade within member states (domestic trade). Intra-Community trade not only involved the complication of exchange rates, but there were still substantial differences in laws relating to the products and other aspects of economic life. These acted as obstacles to trade and could be exploited by member governments to frustrate the free trade ideal that was at the heart of the EU.

A desire to speed up progress towards the creation of a single market led to the Single European Act 1986. This involved an extension of qualified majority voting and the abolition of the remaining barriers to trade. These were identified as physical barriers (the paperwork associated with poor crossings), technical barriers (such as laws relating to product specifications, pollution and safety) and fiscal barriers (such as discriminatory tax arrangements). A single market requires that there is no discrimination in the awarding of government contracts. Hence, public procurement contracts should be open to firms from all member states. The Single European Act set 1 January 1993 as the target date for completing the single market measures.

- **Stage 4: economic and monetary union** For a market to be a genuinely common market, it is necessary to have a single currency or, at the very least, fixed exchange rates between member currencies. The Treaty on European Union 1992 committed members to the establishment of a single currency. In 1999, the euro was established as a trading currency, with a permanently fixed exchange rate

Table 12.4 Key dates in the development of the EU

Year	
1957	Treaty of Rome established pattern of the European Community
1968	Customs Union completed
1973	Accession of Denmark, Ireland and the UK
1981	Accession of Greece
1986	Accession of Spain and Portugal
1986	Single European Act
1992	Treaty on European Union
1993	Completion of the single market
1999	Introduction of the euro
2002	Replacement of national currencies with the euro

Economic and monetary union (EMU)

Under the Treaty on European Union of 1992, member states committed themselves to economic union by the end of the century. EMU involves:

● a fixed exchange rate between currencies for an interim period;
● the replacement of national currencies with a single currency known as the euro;
● the establishment of a European central bank to conduct monetary policy on behalf of member states.

In order to prepare for EMU, the economies of member states were required to converge in terms of inflation, interest and exchange rates, government borrowing and government debt. Convergence criteria acted as a test for membership of the single currency and, with the exception of Greece, the member states were deemed to have qualified. However, three states – the UK, Denmark and Sweden – chose not to join the single currency in the first wave.

In 1999, the euro was introduced as a trading currency and for banking purposes. Euro notes and coins will be introduced in 2002 and, by the middle of that year, the euro will have replaced national currencies in the 11 member states concerned. The UK has the option of, but is not committed to, joining the euro at a later stage. The issue of euro membership remains highly controversial.

between it and member currencies. This was the prelude to the introduction of euro notes and coins in 2002 and their replacing national currencies. The UK has the option of joining the euro, but has refused to commit itself to membership.

It is possible to envisage a stage 5 involving political union and the creation of a federal United States of Europe. This remains very controversial and would probably be opposed by most people in the UK. There is no immediate prospect of such a political union. (See Table 12.4 for the key steps in the development of the EU thus far and Table 12.5 for a summary of the types of economic integration and their main features.)

Table 12.5 The main features of types of economic integration

Types of economic integration	Removal of trade barriers between member states	Common external tariff	Harmonization of relevant laws plus free movement of capital and labour	Harmonization of economic policies	Single currency
Free trade area	✔				
Customs union	✔	✔			
Common/single market	✔	✔	✔		
Economic union	✔	✔	✔	✔	
Monetary union	✔	✔	✔	✔	✔

Supporters of membership argue that the euro will:

- produce great savings by eliminating transaction costs;
- reduce the risks involved in trading with EU partners;
- increase UK trade, thus boosting economic growth and job creation;
- be essential if the UK is to continue to receive inward investment by foreign multinational companies.

Opponents of membership argue that:

- as it removes control of monetary policy (such as interest rates) from national authorities, it represents a significant transfer of power to European institutions;
- the difficulty of setting interest rates appropriate for the *whole* of the EU will mean that some members will also have to suffer higher interest rates when a reduction is essential to enable them to recover from recession;
- the country will be surrendering an important policy weapon (alterations in exchange rate), so that never again will the UK be able to solve its economic problems by altering the exchange value of sterling.

The euro and UK business organizations

The introduction of the euro will have major implications for UK businesses. This applies whether the UK joins the single currency or remains outside. The arrival of the euro represents a large change in the external environment of business organizations and will necessitate both strategic and operational decisions.

If the UK remains aloof from the euro, there will be benefits to her European competitors in terms of the lower transaction costs, stable exchange rates and price transparency. Although the UK outside the euro will gain some of these advantages, the full gain will be reserved for the 11 euro states. UK businesses will definitely be at a disadvantage against competitors within the euro zone as the latter share the same currency as the importer. The elimination of transaction costs and exchange rate risks will increase the volume of the intra-euro zone trade, possibly at the expense of UK firms. It is also possible that there will be more cross-border mergers within the euro zone, again placing UK firms at a disadvantage. If there is a reduction in inward overseas investment, UK firms supplying multinationals will find a reduction or at least a slowing down in the growth of sales.

The existence of the euro zone with the UK on the outside does represent a threat to many UK firms. However, the creation of the euro zone, even without the UK, represents an opportunity in a growing market, provided UK firms are willing to adapt to the changed situation. The detailed issues to consider include implications for the following:

- **IT** the euro, with or without the UK, will require adaptations to be made to computer software, conversion of databases and a revision of electronic data interchange (EDI);
- **human resource management** the arrival of the euro has necessitated new staff training and the possible appointment of new staff, especially in the changeover period;
- **pricing** not only firms in the export trade, but others, such as retailers will be expected to quote prices in euros, which involves costs in terms of the printing of the invoices and promotional literature and will necessitate changes to accounting packages, and price transparency within the euro zone will require UK firms to charge the same (euro) prices to all euro zone customers;
- **accounting systems** the greater use of the euro will be reflected in changes in company accounting, especially in the case of multinational companies with a presence inside and outside the euro zone, and accounts will have to be prepared in terms of euros as well as sterling.

The Social Charter

The Social Charter was drawn up and adopted by 11 members of the EU in 1992. The exception was the UK as the then government argued that the provisions of some of the Social Charter were contrary to its economic policy and were harmful to job creation. The replacement of the Conservative Government with the Labour Government led by Tony Blair resulted in the UK's belated acceptance of the Charter in 1997.

The Charter sets out workers rights to:

● work in any EU country of their choice;
● a fair rate of pay;
● improved living and working conditions;
● social protection;
● freedom of association and collective bargaining;
● equal treatment for men and women;
● be informed and consulted;
● health and safety at work, protection for women and adolescents (with the minimum age of working being set at 15);
● guaranteed minimum living standards for the elderly;
● vocational training;
● integration into working life for the disabled.

There are many provisions in the Social Charter that few would object to and in many cases UK workers enjoy these rights as a result of national legislation. Why, then, has the Social Charter been a matter of such great controversy?

First, there was the political argument. Critics of the EU, especially in the Conservative Party, saw the Social Charter as EU intrusion into areas of economic and social policy for which it was not designed. Second, there was the economic argument. The Charter was seen as contrary to the then Government's supply-side policy of labour market flexibility. It was argued that some provisions of the Charter would raise the costs of employing people and would, therefore, lead to job losses. Multinational and even UK-owned firms would either leave the UK or at least not engage in further expansion in the UK if it was an area of high-cost labour. This argument is strengthened by the need to remain competitive with the Asian tiger economies.

The counters to these economic arguments are as follows. The Charter merely reinforces the protection given to workers by national legislation.

Second, there is what is known as the social dumping argument. In the single market of the EU, there is the danger that capital would leave those countries with high living and working standards and flow into the southern European states, where living standards are lower and worker protection less developed. The Germans in particular feared that, without the Social Charter, German jobs would be lost to Spain, Portugal and Greece. The Charter provides a vital element of protection in the new single market of Europe. In terms of the Asian tiger argument, supporters of the Charter argued that Europe is unlikely to be able to compete with the tigers on the basis of low rates of pay and so can only compete on the basis of quality and the skill of its highly trained workforce. Highly trained workers require reasonable pay and high standards of protection.

The Charter itself is a general declaration of workers' rights. Its importance is in terms of providing the European Union with competence in the area of employment legislation. Detailed legislation, in the form of directives, can be passed using qualified majority voting. In addition, national governments and parliaments passing legislation contrary to the Social Charter can be challenged in the law courts right up to the European Court of Justice. However, even without the Social Charter the EU was taking an interest in social and employment legislation. The Working Time Directive, which limits the hours of work to an average of 48 per week, was passed under the EU's commitment to health and safety. Other measures relating to pregnant workers and part-time workers were justified in terms of the EU's commitment to equal opportunities.

Other EU policies of significance to business

Other EU policies of significance to business organizations include the following.

● **The Common Agricultural Policy (CAP)** In essence, the CAP is a buffer stock scheme designed to regulate farm prices in the interests of the farming community and ensure adequate food supplies for the population of the EU. Excess supplies are purchased at intervention prices and stored for future release when supplies are less plentiful. Like many such schemes, the guarantee of purchase at a high intervention price results in overproduction by Europe's farmers. The continual growth of butter mountains, beef mountains, wine lakes and the rest was the main cause of the persistent budgetary problems of the EU. To overcome this problem, limits had to be imposed on production. Hence, individual farmers have a quota on the quantity of milk they are permitted to produce. Under the set-aside system, arable farmers are 'paid for not producing wheat'. On the positive side, guidance and assistance is offered to farmers.

● **The Common Fisheries Policy** This is concerned with access to the territorial waters of member states. The fleets of member states have preferential access to the waters of other states. However, to prevent overfishing and the depletion of fish stocks, limits are imposed on the size of fleets, nets and the number of days ships are permitted to fish.

● **Consumer protection** EU policy is to protect the interests of consumers by means of **directives** (EU laws that members are required to translate into national law) on matters such as product safety, doorstep selling, the selling of time-shares and labelling.

● **Regional policy** To reduce regional disparities within the EU, the European Regional Development Fund provides financial assistance for infrastructure development in areas of low income and high unemployment. The UK, Southern Italy, Ireland, Spain, Portugal and Greece are major beneficiaries of these funds.

● **The European Social Fund** The Fund provides financial support for vocational training and retraining of workers.

● **Competition policy** To create a level playing field, EU competition policy seeks to control:
- State aid (subsidies) to industry;
- cartels and abuse of dominant firm situations;
- mergers of large companies.

● **Environmental protection** This is an acknowledgement of the fact that pollution does not recognize national boundaries.

● **Support for small- and medium-sized enterprises**

● **Support for cooperative research and development**

● **Harmonization of company law** To safeguard the interests of shareholders and other stakeholders, directives have been passed relating to company accounts, auditing and the conduct of groups of companies. There are also directives (opposed by the UK government) relating to employees' participation in company decision making.

Key concepts

Appreciation/revaluation A rise in the exchange rate, such that the currency is worth more in terms of other currencies. Appreciation is the result of market forces, whereas revaluation is the result of policy decisions.

Balance of payments A set of accounts detailing transactions in goods, services and capital with other countries. If the country buys more than it sells, the account will be in deficit. If the reverse is the case, then it is said to be in surplus.

Customs union A group of states that trade freely among themselves and impose a common external tariff against goods from non-union countries.

Depreciation/devaluation A reduction in the exchange rate caused, respectively, by market forces and policy decisions.

Economic and monetary union (EMU) The harmonization of economic and monetary policies leading to a single currency for use throughout the EU.

European Economic Community (EEC)/ European Union (EU) A group of, currently, 15 European states that would seek to integrate economically. The European Community became the European Union after the treaty on European Union of 1992 in which cooperation was extended to foreign policy, defence and judicial matters.

Exchange rate The value of a currency in relation to a foreign currency or a group of foreign currencies.

Free Trade Area A group of states that trade freely among themselves, abolishing all import controls

General Agreement on Tariffs and Trade (GATT) A worldwide agreement leading to mutual reduction in tariffs and other restrictions on trade.

Import controls Restrictions on imports take the form of tariffs (taxes), quotas, embargoes, licences, exchange controls and administrative controls.

Import penetration The extent to which the home market is supplied by imports; the market share of importers.

Single currency The replacement of national currencies by a single EU-wide currency known as the euro.

Single market The elimination of all barriers to trade between members.

Social Charter The EU Charter on the rights of employees.

Essay questions

1 Assess the consequences of a fall in the sterling exchange rate.

2 A double blow to the economy. Assess the consequences of high interest rates pushing up the exchange rate.

3 Assess the benefits of the UK:
   (a) remaining outside the euro; and
   (b) adopting the euro.

4 Analyse the consequences for the UK of membership of the European Union.

5 (a) Distinguish between enlargement and deepening of the EU.
   (b) What are the likely consequences for the UK of EU enlargement?

6 (a) Explain what is meant by an emerging economy.
   (b) Assess the consequences for the UK of economic growth in the rest of the world.

Ethical and environmental issues

Business Studies has been defined as the study of organizational decision making set against the background of a changing external environment. For most of our study we are concerned with the impact of the environment of the organization. In this chapter, however, we are concerned more with the impact of the organization on the environment, and what constitutes ethical and socially acceptable behaviour by a firm.

Chapter objectives

1 To understand the concept of social responsibility.

2 To explore ethical principles in business.

3 To highlight areas of environmental concern.

4 To outline strategies for the socially and environmentally conscious firm.

Stakeholders

Stakeholders are people who are affected by and/or are able to influence the behaviour of business organizations. The 'original' stakeholders are the owners of the business – they have a financial stake in, and seek profit from, the organization. Traditional capitalist ideology stresses that businesses are run in the interest of the owners. Today, most people accept that there are other groups of people with a stake in the business and whose interests should not be ignored. These non-proprietorial stakeholders include employees who 'invest' their time and efforts in a business. From this new perspective, the employees have a right to be considered when decisions are made. However, it does not stop there – the term stakeholder extends to anyone who feels the impact of the organization. For convenience, we distinguish between **internal stakeholders** – who are directly involved with the firm – and **external stakeholders** – located outside the firm. The stakeholders and their interests are shown in Table 13.1.

Social responsibility

The term **social responsibility** means an organization's obligations to maximize its long-term positive impacts and minimize its negative impacts on society. It means the obligations of the firm to use its resources in ways that benefit

Table 13.1 Stakeholders and how they judge an organization

Stakeholders	Their requirements of an organization
Owners	Profitability, growth, dividends, stability/security, share value
Directors	Growth, market share, profitability, security
Managers	Growth, cash flow, security, promotion prospects, job satisfaction
Employees	Earnings, working conditions, job security, job satisfaction
Trade unions	An organization's willingness to negotiate
Suppliers	Size, variation and security of orders, payment period, prices
Customers	Price, quality, after-sales service, product variety, credit terms
Creditors	Promptness of payment, reliability
Competitors	Intensity and fairness of the competition
Society/the community	Job creation, impact on other firms, impact on the environment, ethical standards, contribution to society and its artistic and cultural life, assistance to the disadvantaged, equal opportunities
The government	Contribution to tax receipts, job creation, economic growth and balance of payments, trading practices, impact on the environment, compliance with the law

society. This term is sometimes used interchangeably with the concept of ethics, but there is an important distinction to make. Social responsibility is an organizational concern, whereas **ethics** are the concerns of individual managers or decision makers. Ethics can be defined as an individual's moral beliefs about what is right or wrong, good or bad, that guide his or her behaviour. We will look at ethics later in this chapter, but, for the moment, let us explore further the notion of social responsibility.

A socially responsible firm will honour its responsibilities to its internal stakeholders, but will also accept the need to act responsibly towards external stakeholders. This means acting in a fair way towards customers, financiers and suppliers – promptly paying bills, making quality products, dealing in an honest way and being reliable. Socially responsible behaviour clearly requires obedience to the law and payment of taxes, but it also means operating in an ethical way, having concern for the environment and undertaking philanthropic activities on behalf of the disadvantaged and to aid the cultural life of the community.

There are six areas in which corporate social objectives may be found.

● **The environment**
This covers pollution control, preventing or repairing damage to the environment resulting from processing of natural resources.

● **Energy**
This covers conservation of energy and increasing energy efficiency in business operations.

● **Fair business practice**
This concerns fairness in dealing with employees, suppliers and customers.

● **Human resources**
This means giving thought to the impact of organizational activities on the human resources of an organization.

● **Community involvement**
Business organizations are involved in community, education, art and health-related projects.

● **Products**
Socially responsible firms make products of quality in terms of user safety, serviceability

and durability. These products provide customer satisfaction and are honestly advertised.

Whether a business enterprise should accept social responsibility or not is a matter of debate. Let us consider four separate views on this issue.

● The far left in politics would argue that self-interest is the primary feature of the capitalist system. Private enterprise firms are run in the interest of private profit and it is naïve to believe that any part of that profit will be sacrificed in order to pursue socially responsible behaviour. When firms do undertake such activity they are merely pursuing self-interest by other means, such as charitable activities in order to boost public image and increase sales.
● Reformists would argue that business organizations should act in a socially responsible way. With economic power comes social responsibility towards the community (especially its disadvantaged members) and to the environment. Moreover, socially responsible behaviour is a form of enlightened self-interest as it enhances the corporate image and reduces the danger of legislative action to force business organizations to act in a socially responsible way.
● The paternalistic right wing would argue that business organizations should, and do, behave in a socially responsible way. Such behaviour is an acknowledgment of the benefits of a prosperous, secure and culturally rich community to all concerned.
● The new right favours an individualistic economic philosophy that rejects any notion of social responsibility. The eighteenth-century economist Adam Smith argued that the pursuit of self-interest in a competitive market would ensure the common good. In the twentieth century, American economist Milton Friedman has championed this view. He argues that the single social responsibility of business is to increase profit by legitimate means. All we should expect from business is efficient, profitable production that creates

jobs and provides goods and services at the price and quality customers desire. Expenditure by companies on social and/or environmental projects diverts money away from its proper purpose of financing production and generating profit. If directors and managers use funds for these purposes, they are reducing profits and/or raising prices to customers. They are, in effect, imposing a tax in order to finance activities that rightly belong with a democratically elected government. Curing the social and environmental problems of society is a matter for us as citizens and for governments, not for businesses. It should also be remembered that, under company law, directors and managers are required to serve the interests of shareholders, not those of employees, customers, or society at large.

The arguments for and against businesses accepting social responsibility are summarized in Table 13.2.

A comprehensive social responsibility policy involves acceptance of five principles:

● as society accords privileges to business organizations, they owe society a debt that is discharged by adopting socially responsible policies;
● the basic rule for firms is to do things with integrity, openness and honest cooperation;
● activities are to the evaluated on social responsibility criteria along with other criteria;
● social or external costs are to be seen as part of operating expenses;
● the firm needs to be prepared to use its resources for wider social purposes.

Ethical issues

Ethics, as we saw earlier, can be defined as a system of morals or rules of behaviour. To say that something is legal is not to say that it is ethical, and vice versa. For instance, the export of live animals for slaughter is legal (subject to laws concerning journey length and feeding), but many would argue that it is wrong, unacceptable and unethical. Advertising directed at children

Table 13.2 Arguments for and against social involvement of business

Arguments for	Arguments against
● Creation of a better social environment benefits both society and business ● Power should be used responsibly ● Social involvement creates a favourable image for the company ● Business has the resources to help solve social problems ● Business and society are interdependent ● Social involvement discourages additional government intervention	● The primary task of business is to maximize its profits by concentrating on commercial activities ● Social involvement results in higher prices to customers ● Social involvement reduces economic efficiency ● Social activities reduce the international competitiveness of British businesses ● Company directors have a duty to shareholders ● Businesspeople lack the social skills to deal with the problems of society

might be legal, but, again, many see it as unethical. In the past, the use of inside information in share dealing was considered unethical, but was nevertheless legal. The law has now caught up with ethics by criminalizing insider trading. The basic distinction to make is that the law states whether or not an action is allowed, whereas ethics is about whether an action is right or wrong, acceptable or unacceptable.

One approach to ethics is to say that certain actions are always wrong (such as murder) and can never be justified. This is known as a **deontological approach**.

Such absolute standards, usually religious in origin, define the rules of behaviour for individuals. A second approach, known as a **teleological approach**, looks at consequences. If the 'beneficial' consequences of an action exceed the 'harmful' ones, the action is acceptable. However, by using the words 'beneficial' and 'harmful' we are widening the debate to include outside stakeholders and are adopting the 'greatest happiness of the greatest number' principle associated with utilitarian philosophers. A third approach is known as **ethical relativism**. This means that action may be wrong in some circumstances and contexts but right in others.

To appreciate the distinction between these approaches, consider the payment of bribes to public officials who have the power to award public contracts. In the UK, this is seen as unethical, as well as being illegal. In other parts of the world, it is considered to be normal and necessary if you want to be awarded the contract.

Are bribes to public officials in other countries ever acceptable? The approach of the ethical relativists is that you consider the social and cultural context in which an action takes place. The teleological approach is to look at the consequences of the action. The deontological approach is that bribery is always wrong. It is not, as some would believe, a victimless crime. Bribes paid to corrupt officials in other countries mean that taxpayers in those countries are being forced to pay more for goods and services because a corrupt official took a bribe to accept a contract that was not the most favourable.

The major areas of ethical concern are:

● advertising that relies on sex, violence and stereotyping, or is directed at children;
● large payments to company executives;
● perks offered to top executives;
● corporate donations to political parties;
● political lobbying by companies;
● corporate hospitality;
● bullying in the workplace;
● treatment of employees who are HIV positive;
● asset stripping;
● the persecution of 'whistleblowers';
● the use of animals in, for example, circus entertainment;
● factory farming and the export of live animals;
● selling armaments to repressive regimes;
● testing on animals;

- misuse of proprietary information;
- misuse of company assets;
- 'kickbacks';
- misleading advertising;
- methods of gathering information on competitors.

Codes of ethics

Codes of ethics are guidelines to the moral principles or values used by organizations to steer conduct, both for the organization itself and its employees, in all business activities, internal and external. They are a likely to include reference to:

- use of insider information by employees for personal advantage;
- kickbacks;
- conflicts of interest between employer and employee;
- accuracy of records;
- use/misuse of company assets;
- deception;
- environmental issues;
- avoiding discrimination;
- duties to local communities;
- suppliers.

The benefits of such a code are as follows:

- it provides guidance to managers and employees so that they know what is expected of them in terms of ethical behaviour;
- it provides new employees with a framework within which to work;
- it enhances the organization's reputation;
- it signals to suppliers and customers the organization's expectations of them;
- it promotes a culture of excellence by emphasizing the commitment to ethical behaviour.

The impact businesses can have on the physical environment

Recent decades have seen a series of much-publicized disasters resulting from the discharge of harmful substances.

1976 Release of dioxin from a chemical plant in Seveso, Italy.
1984 Release of poisonous fumes at Bhopal, India.
1986 Explosion at a nuclear plant in Chernobyl.
1989 *Exxon Valdez* oil spillage off Alaska.
1992 *Aegean Sea* oil spillage off Spain.
1993 *Braer* oil spillage off the Shetland Islands.

These environmental disasters should be set against a number of interlocking environmental crises caused by the quickening pace of economic advance.

- **Acid rain** This is caused by industrial pollution and adversely affects human health, agriculture, fishing, forests and buildings.
- **Deforestation** The destruction of the rainforests reduces the Earth's capacity to absorb carbon dioxide in the process of photosynthesis.
- **Desertification** Climate change and poor management of the land has led to the expansion of deserts, thus reducing the ability of the peoples of the World to feed themselves.
- **Global warming** The release of gases such as carbon dioxide and methane is causing temperatures to rise, thus adversely affecting agriculture, fisheries and human health.
- **Ozone depletion** The release of chlorofluorocarbons is destroying the ozone layer, which protects the Earth from the Sun's harmful ultraviolet rays.

These trends are the result of economic activities designed to provide goods and services for consumers. Unlike dramatic disasters such as the *Exxon Valdez* oil spillage, they are not the result of individual mistakes or decisions. Instead, they are the result of decisions made by millions of producers and consumers. Unlike the pollution problems of earlier centuries, they are international in character (for example, pollution from Chernobyl affected hill farmers in Britain) and threaten the survival of the World and the human race.

179

The environmentally conscious firm

Although it is debatable whether or not firms ever act with no thought of self-interest and although, as we have seen, there is a strong case against businesses (as distinct from individuals) taking on social responsibility, it is possible that a business organization will act in an environmentally friendly manner for reasons of self-interest. There are several reasons for this.

UK and EU laws

Businesses would, and largely do, comply with UK and EU laws relating to the environment. First, the alternative to compliance is legal action, followed by fines and/or damages. Second, the system of planning laws (both for new buildings and change of use of an existing building) are designed to reduce the nuisance to the community. Third, State action might take the form of tax measures (green taxes) to discourage undesirable acts as well as subsidies to encourage desirable ones.

Pressure group activity

Pressure groups are so called because they seek to exert pressure, either on Parliament or business organizations themselves. Unlike political parties, they seek to influence rather than obtain political power. Pressure groups often focus on a single issue, or a group of related issues, and can be classified as either:

- **interest groups** established to further the interests of members (such as trade unions, consumer groups, local residents groups); or
- **cause groups** established to further a particular cause (such as animal welfare).

The cause groups that are most directly relevant to our purposes here are those associated with the **green movement**. The 'green' label actually includes more than concern about the environment. It extends to concern for:

- life on earth;
- future generations;

- people in other countries;
- sustainable development (as distinct from environmentally destructive development);
- the quality of human life;
- the creation of a fairer world by means of more equitable trade patterns and greater democracy;
- a shift from consumption and materialism towards conservation, sharing and self-reliance.

Pressure groups seek to exert influence on business organizations in a variety of ways. These include:

- consumer boycotts;
- adverse publicity;
- motions at shareholders' meetings;
- discouraging job applicants;
- opposing planning application;
- involving business in increased costs (such as public relations campaigns to counter adverse publicity);
- pressure on Parliament and government to take action.

If consumer boycotts are effective in reducing or threatening to reduce sales, they can bring about changes in business practices. For instance, in the summer of 1994, certain Channel ferry companies and British Airways responded to growing opposition from many of their customers to the live export of animals for slaughter. Because of customer pressure, they decided unilaterally to stop engaging in this trade. Similarly, other firms, aware of growing public concern about the environment, have developed ranges of green products. This is not altruism, it is good business sense.

Green finance

Another type of consumer action is financial in nature. Many savers make a conscious decision to place their savings with financial intermediaries that promise to use the money in an ethical and environmentally responsible way. The Co-operative Bank will not lend to countries governed by oppressive regimes or help finance companies that sell arms to such regimes. The Bank will not invest in businesses that test cosmetics

Table 13.3 Criteria for ethical investment

Positive criteria	Negative criteria
● Environmental awareness	● Poor environmental record
● Employee welfare	● Poor working conditions
● Equal opportunities	● Tobacco
● Community action	● Alcohol
● Good customer relations record	● Armaments
● Charitable donations	● Exploitation of animals
● Environmentally beneficial goods and services	● Furs
● Socially beneficial goods and services	● Animal experimentation
	● Nuclear industries
	● Drugs
	● Political donations
	● Sexually explicit or violent media
	● Relations with repressive regimes

on animals or cause suffering to animals by intensive factory farming methods. Similarly, the Bank will not invest in businesses connected to the fur trade, blood sports or tobacco.

There is also a growing number of ethical and environmental trusts (such as Merlin Jupiter Ecology Fund, Clerical Medical Evergreen, HFS Green Chip Fund) that guarantee investors that their funds will only be placed with business organizations that meet the positive criteria set out in Table 13.3. Such trusts refuse to invest in companies involved in the activities in the 'Negative criteria' list.

Insurance

The cost of remedial action following environmental damage can be enormous. This applies not just to oil and chemical companies, which can suffer disasters such as chemical explosions or oil spillages. It also applies to small businesses, such as farms, the activities of which can cause serious river pollution. It is essential to insure against such risks, but insurance companies and underwriters increasingly insist on environmentally responsible action from their corporate clients. This involves regular environmental audits (see below).

The sale of land

Land is a valuable asset that companies might

need or want to sell at some time in the future. In view of both the damage that can be done to land and watercourses by chemicals, and the compensation claims that can arise, any prospective purchaser will want an environmental assessment of the land before agreeing to purchase it. This means that there is a strong incentive for owners not to abuse the land, to do so might endanger future sale.

Reducing costs by reducing waste

Environmentally friendly behaviour does not necessarily add to costs. As Table 13.4 shows, there are advantages to companies in minimizing waste.

Green marketing

In Part III if this book, we will explore the Four Ps of marketing, but this is marketing according to orthodox ideas of profit seeking. **Green marketing** is concerned with the marketing of products in line with the Four Ss of:

Satisfaction of customers' needs;
Safety of products;
Social acceptability of products;
Sustainability of products.

Environmental audits

An **environmental audit** is a regular assessment of an organization's performance in relation to

Table 13.4 Why minimize waste?

To reduce:	And improve:
● production costs;	● income by virtue of the sale of reusable waste;
● on-site waste-monitoring and treatment costs;	● overall operating efficiency;
● handling, transport and off-site disposal costs;	● the safety of employees;
● raw material costs;	● the company's image in the eyes of shareholders, employees and the community.
● energy and water costs;	
● long-term environmental liability and insurance costs;	
● the risks of spills and accidents.	

Source: *Cutting Your Losses: A business guide to waste minimization*, DTI, 1990

the environment. The Confederation of British Industry (CBI) defines it as 'the systematic examination of the interaction between any business operation and its surrounding. This includes all emissions to air, land and water; legal constraints; the effects on the neighbouring community, landscape, and ecology; and the public's perception of the operating company in the local area' (*Narrowing the Gap: Environmental auditing guildelines for business*, CBI, 1990).

The aims of an environmental audit are to:

● verify compliance with environmental, health and safety legislation;
● verify compliance with the organization's own policy;
● minimize human exposure to risk and ensure that health and safety provisions are adequate;
● identify corporate risk from potential environmental failure;
● increase the workforce's awareness of the company's environmental policy;
● identify ways to further reduce waste and energy usage;
● satisfy external pressure from customers, insurers, ethical investment trusts and the community.

This last point does not mean that an environmental audit is merely a public relations exercise, but, obviously, there are public relations advantages in carrying one out.

The audit might take a number of forms, including an environmental SWOT analysis. This will highlight strengths and weaknesses in the organization's environmental performance and the environmental threats and opportunities that the organization faces. For example, a company might have strengths in terms of recycling, but weaknesses in terms of low energy efficiency or the toxicity of its waste. The audit might suggest opportunities in terms of further recycling and an enhancement of the company's role in developing new green products. However, new environmental legislation, the cost of future landfill and the cost of compensation following a chemical spillage might constitute threats.

A typical environmental audit will cover the following areas:

● compliance with current and proposed legislation and regulations (local, UK, EU);
● transport:
  - fuel efficiency;
  - precautions taken when transporting toxic substances;
  - vehicle emissions;
● energy use:
  - energy efficiency;
  - recycling waste energy;
● waste:
  - disposal methods;
  - waste management;
  - waste minimization;
  - recycling;
  - emissions;
  - procedures for dealing with accidental spillages;
● materials:
  - use of environmentally friendly materials;
  - extent to which materials are renewable;

- substitution of toxic materials with non-toxic ones;
● impact on landscape and habitats:
  - damage to habitats;
  - ways to reduce damage, preserve natural habitats and make sites as attractive as possible.

A large firm might possess the expertise to undertake the audit itself, although external consultants should be employed to verify the audit (in the same way that external auditors verify financial accounts). Smaller firms will need to bring in outside expertise to undertake the audit.

Two variations on the environmental audit are an **environmental review** and an **environmental impact review**. The former looks at current environmental performance before targets are set (strictly speaking, an audit is an attempt to measure the extent to which targets have been met). A review thus establishes a baseline to enable policy objectives to be set. Thereafter, performance is monitored by means of an audit. An environmental impact review looks at the environmental implications of a proposed development (such as a new chemical works).

organization has an obligation to a variety of interest groups, not just the owners of the business.

Waste management Policies and practices designed to minimize and recycle waste in the interests of the environment and cost reduction.

Essay questions

1 (a) What is meant by an external cost?
(b) Assess the benefits of taxing a polluter.

2 Analyse why it is in a manufacturer's own interest to control pollution and manage waste.

3 (a) What is meant by green marketing?
(b) Analyse the factors behind the rise of green marketing.

4 Evaluate the case for socially responsible behaviour by firms.

5 'Profits are everything'. Evalaute the role and importance of ethics in business.

Key concepts

Environmental audit A systematic review of the interaction between an organization and the physical environment. The audit looks at the organization's compliance with environmental regulations and its environmental policy, the environmental risks to which it is exposed, waste management and recycling.

Ethics A system of morals, rules of conduct.

Green business Environmentally friendly business practices.

Pressure group A group that seeks to exert influence on, and alter, the practices and policies of government and business organizations.

Social responsibility Concern for the community and the environment.

Stakeholder All those people and groups that affect, and are affected by, a business organization. In stakeholder theory, the

Further reading

Barnes, I. and Barnes, P. (1995) *The Enlarged European Union*, Longman.

Beardshaw, J., Brewster, D., Cormack, P., and Ross, A. (1998) *Economics: A Student's Guide*, 4th ed. Longman.

Campbell, D. (1997) *Organizations and the Business Environment*, Heinemann.

Campkin, P., Duncan, W., and Morgan, D (1999) *The Operating Environment*, Financial Times Pitman.

Cook, G. (published annually) *Economics Updates,* Sterling Books (available from 32 Shirley Road, Stoneygate, Leicester LE2 3LJ).

Griffiths, A. (ed.) (biannual publication) *British Economy Survey*, York Publishing Services.

Harris, N. (1999) *European Business,* 2nd ed., Macmillan.

Hornby, W., Gammie, B., and Wall, S. (1997) *Business Economics*, Longman.

Keenan, D., and Riches, S. (1998) *Business Law*, 5th ed., Financial Times Pitman.

Palmer, A., and Hartley, B. (1996) *The Business and Marketing Environment*, 2nd ed., McGraw-Hill.

Pettinger, R. (1998) *The European Social Charter: A manager's guide*, Kogan Page.

Roney, A., and Budd, S. (1998) *The European Union: A guide through the EC/EU maze*, Kogan Page.

Worthington, I., and Britton, C. (1997) *The Business Environment*, 2nd ed., Pitman.

Short answer questions

Critically explain each of the following terms using examples of their impacts on specified business organizations:

1 Demographic trend.
2 Lifestyle trend.
3 Pressure group.
4 Income elasticity of demand.
5 Minimum wage.
6 Cross-elasticity of demand.
7 Oligopoly.
8 Restrictive practice.
9 Economies of scale.
10 Merger.
11 Unfair dismissal.
12 Vicarious liability.
13 Health and Safety at Work, etc. Act 1974.
14 The law on product liability.
15 Contract law.
16 Free movement of labour within the EU.
17 EU directives relating to employment.
18 Equal opportunities legislation.
19 Minimum wage law.
20 Pollution.
21 Family-friendly employment law.
22 The Working Time Directive.
23 Part-time Workers' Directive.
24 The law relating to trades descriptions.
25 Agency law.

Exercises

1 The account that follows deals with a hypothetical industrial country. Read the account and answer the questions.

'The country is currently experiencing a boom in production. Order books in the manufacturing sector are fuller than they have been for a decade, with capacity utilization at 88 per cent, the highest since the boom of the late 1960s.

Domestic demand will receive a further stimulus as the tax reductions announced in the Budget feed through as increased disposable income. Household consumption will increase, adding to the problems of satisfying demand. Investment will also be at a high level given the present high-capacity utilization and the profitability of investment. The yields on real capital investment are expected to be greater than those on financial investment.'

(a) Define the following terms:
   boom; disposable income; real capital investment; monetary policy; real output.
(b) What evidence is there of upward pressure on prices?
(c) We are told that capacity utilization is 88 per cent, suggesting some spare capacity. Explain why delivery times are lengthening.
(d) Analyse the consequences of the tax reductions from a Keynesian perspective.
(e) In your own words, explain why investment is likely to be at a high level.
(f) Give two reasons for the possibility that exports may decline.

2 The data below refers to the highest marginal tax rates paid by individuals and companies in eight major Western industrial economies. In 1979, for instance, those on the highest incomes in the UK paid 83 pence in every additional £1 of income above a specified level of income.

Top tax rate	Personal %		Corporate %	
Country	1979	1989	1979	1989
UK	83	40	52	35
Italy	72	50	36	36
USA	70	28	46	34
France	60	57	50	39
Australia	60	50	46	39
Japan	75	50	40	42
West Germany	56	53	56	56
Canada	43	29	46	28

Source: OECD

(a) Using only the data above, can we conclude that the UK was the most highly taxed economy of the eight listed?

(b) Account for the widespread trend towards lower taxation.

(c) What are the benefits of lower taxation?

(d) Suggest three ways in which lower government spending (necessitated by lower taxation) harms business enterprise.

(e) Is there a correlation between tax rates and economic success?

(f) How will multinational companies react to the differences in corporate tax rates?

3 (a) Calculate the impact of a £600 million rise in income when the marginal rate of withdrawal is:
   (i)   0.4;
   (ii) 0.6;
   (iii) 0.7.

(b) Calculate the rise in national income when;
   (i)   the marginal rate of withdrawal is 0.6 and investment rises by £400 million;
   (ii) the marginal rate of withdrawal is 0.8 and exports rise by £300 million;
   (iii) the marginal rate of withdrawal is 0.75 and government spending rises by £1 billion.

(c) A £500 million cut in government spending is followed by a £750 million reduction in national income. Calculate the marginal rate of withdrawal and, therefore, the marginal rate of spending on domestically produced goods and services.

(d) The government wishes to expand the economy by £800 million. It is known that the marginal rate of withdrawal is 0.65. By how much should the government increase its own spending?

4 Some important facts about three non-European countries are given below.

	Country A	Country B	Country C
National income per head (US$)	17,000	430	2300
Population (million)	17	100	100
Population growth (%)	1.2	3	2
Economic growth (%)	1.8	6	1
Inflation rate (%)	7.5	13	600

Country A is politically stable. There is a deteriorating trade balance that will force the government to adopt firm monetary and fiscal policies. Interest rates are expected to rise. Concern about environmental issues has led to the rise of a Green Party.

Country B has suffered from recent political turbulence. Ethnic tensions as well as the conflict between modernization and traditional values are ever-present. IMF loans were conditional on severe budget measures.

Country C Stabilization measures to deal with chronic inflation and debt will restrict government and private spending. Foreign assistance was conditional on more market-oriented economic policies and the liberalization of trade and foreign exchange. Potentially very rich, this country has suffered from inequality of income, corruption and political turbulence.

Assess each of the three countries as:
(a) a market for high-tech goods from the UK;
(b) a market for engineering products;
(c) a market for UK consumer goods; and
(d) a place for UK investment overseas.

5 The late twentieth century has seen the internationalization of capital on a scale hitherto unknown. Foreign acquisition of prestige British firms of the likes of Westland and Jaguar hit the headlines; less well publicized is the British acquisition of substantial (and, in some cases, majority) holdings in overseas firms.

The 1992 *M and A Monthly* reported that, in July 1989, UK companies targeted for cross-border mergers and acquisitions constituted 40 per cent, by value, of all such targeted companies. This included Pepsi Cola's 100 per cent acquisition of Smiths and Walkers Crisps. At the same time, UK firms were second only to the Americans in acquisition of companies beyond their borders: for instance, Scottish and Newcastle Breweries acquired a 65 per cent share in a Dutch holiday village operator called Center Parcs.

This two-way flow of capital is confirmed in figures from the US Commerce Department reported in the October 1989 issue of *EuroBusiness* magazine. Europeans increased their investments in the USA by 60 per cent to $64 billion at the end of 1988. The UK was the largest investor in the USA, with Japan and the Netherlands following in second and third place. In terms of US investment in Europe, Britain was the preferred country; this is shown in the following statistics.

Country	European investments in the US ($ billion)	US investment in Europe ($ billion)	Net European investment ($ billion)
Belgium	4.0	7.2	−3.2
France	11.4	12.5	−1.1
Italy	0.7	9.1	−8.4
Netherlands	49.0	15.4	+33.6
Sweden	5.3	1.1	+4.2
Switzerland	15.9	18.7	−2.8
UK	101.9	48.0	+53.9
W Germany	23.8	21.7	+2.1
Other Europe	4.4	18.5	−14.1

(a) Should we be alarmed at foreign takeover of British industry?

(b) Is it 'unpatriotic' to invest overseas?

(c) Why is there a two-way cross-border flow of capital?

(d) The absence of exchange controls in the UK has contributed to this process of internationalization.
Explain how.

6 Read the extract below and answer the questions that follow.

'Simply stated, Barbados is an ideal location to reduce costs, increase profits, gain exemptions and conveniently serve the United States, European, South American and Caribbean markets.

Because of its abundant supply of highly literate, enthusiastic, easily trainable and dexterous English-speaking workers and its cooperative government, manufacturing operations in Bardados are smooth and problems are minimal.

The basic infrastructure is excellent. Electric power, roads, telephone, telex, airport and seaport facilities (including container-handling equipment) are, for all practical purposes, equivalent to those in the US and Europe.

Above all, Barbados provides economy of operation with savings of 30–50 per cent on US or European costs. Compared to Asian or African assembly, many products can be landed in the USA or Europe from Barbados at equal or lower total costs.

Under the Lomé Convention, a wide range of manufactured products can be imported into the EC from Barbados free of tariffs and quotas ... US imports from Barbados benefit from tariff concession.'

(Source: Barbados Industrial Development Corporation 1983)

(a) Why is the government of Barbados keen to attract multinational operations to the island?

(b) Explain what is meant by each of the following:
  (i) 'its cooperative government';
  (ii) 'the basic infrastructure';
  (ii) 'tariff concession'.

(c) Why are these important to firms contemplating establishing manufacturing facilities in Barbados?

(d) Does low pay always mean low production costs?

(e) Why are the stated attributes of the local workforce considered important when attracting multinational companies?

7 A business advertises for a technician and interviews nine applicants, including Jerome, a well-qualified black Briton. Jerome considers that, in rejecting him, the firm acted unfairly. Advise Jerome on:
(a) the legal position relating to his application and subsequent rejection;
(b) how he would have to proceed to seek legal redress;
(c) the likelihood of successful action.

8 A small building firm undertakes a variety of subcontracting work for larger firms and private work for householders. The firm was commissioned to resurface a domestic driveway and to lay flagstone to create a patio for Mr Shah. Work on the driveway was complete, but the urgent nature of new subcontracting work forced the builder to postpone the work on the patio. Mr Shah refuses to pay the builder for the driveway until the patio is completed. The builder argues that the two jobs should be treated separately and that he is entitled to payment for work completed to date. Advise both sides on their legal positions.

9 Describe and analyse how the law affects:
(a) product design;
(b) the keeping of records on computers;
(c) production processes;
(d) selection and recruitment practices.

10 A college lecturer is dismissed because of her involvement in a business enterprise. The college governors argue that their action was justified because of a clause in the contract of employment stating that 'Employees shall devote their whole time to duties assigned to them by the Principal and shall not engage in activities that interfere with the proper execution of those duties.' The lecturer considers that she has been dismissed unfairly and claims that these outside business activities are conducted in her own time. Advise the lecturer on how she should proceed and assess the likelihood of success of any legal action.

11 Explain what is meant by vicarious liability. Consider whether or not it applies in each of the following situations:
(a) damage to a car resulting from an accident caused by a lorry driver employed by Speedy Carriers Limited;
(b) injury to a member of the public caused by the negligence of Jim, a subcontractor with a large building firm.

12 Study the data below and answer the questions following the table.

UK demographic changes 1985–2025

Year	Working age population	Retired population	Age dependency ratio (retired population as % of working age population)
1985	61.2	18.0	29.4
1995	60.6	18.2	30.0
2005	60.5	18.3	30.2
2015	60.4	20.2	33.4
2025	57.9	22.3	38.5

Source: Government Actuary's Department

(a) How can statisticians predict the age structure of the population in the year 2025?

(b) What market opportunities and threats are presented by this changing age structure?

(c) What are the likely consequences for the NHS and government finances of these predicted trends?
What will be the knock-on effects for private-sector firms?

(d) The working age population is expected to stagnate in absolute terms but decline as proportion of the total population. Consider the consequences for labour recruitment and suggest strategies to enable firms to overcome labour supply problems.

13 Out-of-town shopping centres developed in the 1970s and 1980s as a result of changes in the social and economic environment. Expansion of demand for retail services coupled with problems in town-centre sites forced retailers to look to new and, in many cases, greenfield site.

An early example of a hypermarket outside the town centre was the Carrefour Hypermarket in Eastleigh, Hampshire. To allay fears that it would undermine the position of traditional retailer, Eastleigh Borough Council produced a report arguing that expansion of demand coupled with attraction of custom from outside the borough would enable existing retailers to prosper as Carrefour expanded.

These early out-of-town centres have been followed by the large regional centres such as Brent Cross in north-west London and, more important still, the Metro Centre in Gateshead (Tyneside). The Metro Centre is built on derelict land that was included in the Tyneside Enterprise Zone in 1981. Firms in enterprise zones are granted the following concessions:

- automatic planning permission for most activities;
- freedom from rate payments for ten years;
- capital costs set against tax.

The developers, Cameron Hall Developments Ltd, considered using the area for discount retail warehouses but decided that returns on investment would be greater in the case of a large, comprehensive shopping centre.

The success of large shopping developments in part hinges on the ability of developers to attract big-name stores. Consequently, the decision by Marks & Spencer to acquire premises was important to the success of the Metro Centre.

The Centre now contains a Carrefour Hypermarket, major chain stores (BHS, House of Fraser and so on), leisure facilities, a hotel, specialist attractions and space for 9000 cars. The weak pound and the high cost of living in the Scandinavian countries has contributed to the Metro Centre's attraction to people from outside the UK. The Metro Centre's supporters would, therefore, claim it has played a significant part in reviving an area usually associated with unemployment and despondency.

(a) Suggest changes in the social environment and the economic environment that encourage the development of out-of-town shopping.

(b) Why are local authorities keen to attract new firms into their area?

(c) Explain the phrase 'capital costs set against tax'.

(d) Why is it important to attract 'big-name stores'?

(e) Suggest concessions that developers might give to attract big names into retail centres.

(f) Explain the significance of the weak pound and the cost of living in Scandinavian countries to the Metro Centre's success.

14 Select a named business organization and write an environmental review of its operation. In your review you should make reference to:
(a) current and proposed legislation affecting its operations;
(b) activities that might be considered environmentally friendly;
(c) activities that are harmful to the environment;
(d) waste management and recycling activities.

15 Select a named organization and comment on its environmental performance in relation to:
(a) emissions into the atmosphere;
(b) waste disposal;
(c) use of sustainable resources;
(d) discharges into rivers;
(e) recycling;
(f) energy efficiency.

16 As the managing director of a large public company you face a number of ethical dilemmas. In each of the following situations, argue the case for and against the acceptance of a contract to:
(a) supply machine parts with a potential military use to a regime with a poor human rights record;
(b) buy materials from a company notorious for its treatment of workers in Third World countries;
(c) buy products made from animals that, although not yet on a list of endangered species, are expected to be so categorized within a year;
(d) buy materials from non-sustainable sources.

Key skills development

1 You are required to produce a report on demographic trends, both nationally and in your particular region. The report should cover the following:

- birth rate
- death rate
- infant mortality
- size of family
- size of household
- immigration and emigration
- internal migration
- urban/rural population balance
- age structure
- occupational structure
- ethnicity
- male/female balance.

You should collect the relevant data from both printed and electronic sources and present the data in appropriate forms using ICT. As part of the application of numbers, you should undertake relevant calculations, such as percentages, ratios, moving averages, mean, median, interquartile range and so on. Your report should draw conclusions about demographic trends and you should identify the business implications of your findings.

2 Using an appropriate desktop publishing package, produce an information leaflet (incorporating a headline, one graphical illustration, name and address of 'publisher') on one of the following:

(a) post-1999 competition policy;

(b) the taxation of business;

(c) the role of the regulator of a privatized utility;

(d) the EU budget;

(e) the rights of pregnant workers.

3 Produce a report on one of the emerging market economies of Eastern Europe. Your report must include appropriate economic statistics, such as national income, per capita income, unemployment, inflation, balance of payments, exchange rate movements, structure of the economy. In your report:

(a) assess the progress made towards a market economy and, where appropriate, EU membership;

(b) identify continuing problems in the transition process;

(c) identify export opportunities for UK-based firms.

Part 3

Marketing

An introduction to marketing

This introductory chapter to the marketing part of the book is concerned with the nature of marketing, and will introduce you to the basic ideas and concepts found in marketing. The chapters that follow explore these marketing ideas in greater detail.

Chapter objectives

1 To investigate the nature of marketing.

2 To introduce the basic concepts of marketing analysis.

3 To introduce the principles that underlie marketing strategy.

4 To provide a basic knowledge of the subject to aid understanding of the more detailed chapters that follow.

What is marketing?

A philosophy

Many students regard marketing as the most interesting and exciting part of the syllabus. It is often equated with the exciting world of advertising and the media, and these are business activities that we encounter on a daily basis. Moreover, despite the popularity of this part of the syllabus, it is frequently misunderstood by students, who also underestimate the degree of rigour needed to successfully answer questions on marketing.

We must establish what is meant by marketing. It is *not* a cynical attempt to persuade people to buy goods and services they neither want nor need. This view, that marketing is about manipulating people, is not only unfair to those people involved in marketing, it is also contemptuous of the intelligence of our fellow beings. It would be naïve to believe that people are never deceived by salespeople. However, deception rarely works twice, and successful, responsible business organizations seek to satisfy the public and thereby obtain repeat orders. Marketing is more positive than mere manipulation.

Marketing should be seen first as a business philosophy. It is the philosophy that business organizations exist and prosper by satisfying customer demand. In a dynamic economy this necessitates being responsive to continually changing demand. **Marketing** is defined as the management process responsible for identifying, anticipating and satisfying the requirements of customers profitably. This implies that the first task of marketing is to discover customers' current and future needs. Only by finding out the needs of customers can business organizations respond to those needs. The identified needs should then be satisfied by the production of goods and the provision of services in the quantity and of the quality required by customers.

To understand the marketing philosophy, consider some alternative approaches.

- The **production-oriented firm** concentrates on efficient, low-cost production in the expectation that the goods will find a market provided the price is low enough. Hence, this firm strives for productive efficiency rather than responding to customer needs.
- The **product-oriented firm** assumes that the supplier knows best. It will produce high-quality goods and expect customers to buy them.
- The **sales-oriented firm** focuses on the skills of selling rather than on the needs of the buyer.

This firm makes a product and then considers how customers can be persuaded to buy it. This distinction can be illustrated by two quotations:

'Selling tries to get the customer to want what the company has; marketing, on the other hand, tries to get the company to produce what the customer wants' (Levitt).

'Selling and marketing are antithetical rather than synonymous or even complementary. There will always, one can assume, be a need for some selling. But, the aim of marketing is to make selling superfluous. The aim of marketing is to know and understand the customer so well that the product or service fits him and sells itself. Ideally, marketing should result in a customer who is ready to buy' (Drucker).

The common feature of these alternative philosophies is that they place production and the product first and the customer last. Contrast these types of firms with the **marketing-oriented firm** (see Table 14.1)

The market-oriented firm starts with the

Table 14.1 Marketing orientation v. production orientation

Issues	Marketing orientation	Production orientation
Attitude to customers	Plans determined by customers' needs	'They should be glad we exist'
The product	Make what they can sell	Try to sell what they make
Role of marketing research	To determine customer needs	To determine customer reaction
Customer credit	Seen as a service	Seen as a necessary evil
Packaging	Designed for customer convenience and as a selling tool	Seen merely as protection for the product
Stocks	Set with customer in mind	Set with production requirements in mind
Innovation	To identify new opportunities	To cut costs
Profits	A critical objective	A residual after costs are covered
Transport and delivery	A customer service	Seen as part of production and storage with emphasis on cost-cutting
Advertising	Focus on the benefits that satisfy needs	Focus on product features and quality

customer and his or her needs. This firm will seek to produce what the customer wants rather than sell what the firm has produced. The market-oriented firm places the customer at the centre and devises an integrated strategy to satisfy the customer to the mutual advantage of buyer and seller. It is no part of market orientation that goods be sold (permanently) at a loss or with an unsatisfactory level of profits. The market orientation remains consistent with the profit objectives of the firm.

Marketing strategy

In addition to being a philosophical approach to business we can also see marketing in terms of a **strategy** (involving a coordinated plan of action) to identify, anticipate and satisfy customer demand and thereby achieve the organization's objectives. The components of the strategy can be identified as:

- **market research** identifying customer needs;
- **product planning and development** creating products to satisfy these needs;
- **pricing** determining the value placed on the product by customers;
- **distribution** the movement of the product to customers;
- **promotion** an exercise in communications that includes advertising and selling.

The framework within which marketing takes place is illustrated in Figure 14.1.

Marketing tactics

Tactics can be seen as the details within a broad strategy. Marketing tactics refer to the tools and techniques by which the marketing department will seek to achieve its objective. Hence, advertising, sales promotion, personal selling and publicity can be regarded as tactics or activities within the overall strategy.

Having established what marketing is, we now look at a basic concept in marketing: the product lifecycle.

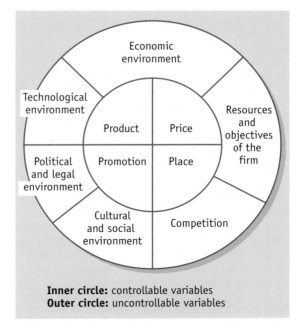

Inner circle: controllable variables
Outer circle: uncontrollable variables

Figure 14.1 The marketing management framework and the marketing mix

The product lifecycle

A basic fact of business life is that all products (including services) pass through a number of phases from introduction to eventual elimination (see Table 14.2). This is shown graphically in Figure 14.2. The sales revenue line shows growth

Table 14.2 Product and human lifecycles

Product	Human beings
Origination of an idea	Conception
Development	Gestation
Launch	Birth
Growth	Childhood and adolescence
Maturity	Mature adulthood
Saturation	Middle age
Decline	Old age
Elimination or product rationalization	Death

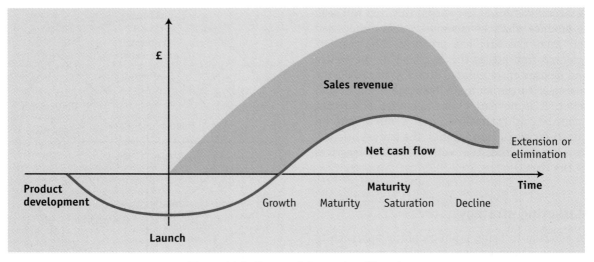

Figure 14.2 Phases of the product lifecycle

from launch to maturity but declines in 'old age'. The net cash flow line is initially negative but, after a time lag, rises to indicate a successful and profitable product. Again this will decline in the later stages.

The main features of each stage can be identified as follows.

- **Product development phase**
  - Research and development of the product.
  - High cost.
  - Preparation of marketing plan prior to launch.
- **Launch: the introduction phase**
  - Low volume of sales.
  - High costs.
  - Heavy promotional spending.
  - High risks.
  - The aim of the promotional strategy is to create awareness.
  - The product is purchased by innovators.
  - Growth in sales revenue, but high unit production costs (because of low volume), coupled with high promotion expenditure, mean the product is unlikely to be profitable at this stage.
- **The growth phase**
  - A higher volume of sales enables the firm to benefit from economies of scale.
  - Profits grow as sales rise and costs fall.

- The product penetrates the market.
- The product is bought by early adopters.
- The firm attempts to build up customer loyalty before the entry of competitors.
- **Maturity**
  - Sales continue to rise, but at a slower rate.
  - The product is now bought by the majority.
  - Brand preference is a crucial factor in continuing success.
  - Packaging, therefore, plays a significant part in the marketing effort.
  - The firm aims to retain its share of the market by capturing sales from weaker rivals.
- **Saturation**

  The saturation phase sees a continuation of the trends of the mature phase. The major difference, however, is that sales level off rather than rise at a slower rate. As the name suggests, most people who are likely to buy the product have purchased it (if it is a product we only buy one of) or are purchasing it at a rate that is unlikely to rise.
- **The decline phase**
  - Sales and profits decline.
  - Substitutes appear and the product becomes obsolete.
  - The firm seeks to cut its losses, either by cutting costs or by elimination of the product.

● Elimination

When faced with a decline in sales for a particular product, the firm has to decide whether the decline is:

- temporary;
- terminal and irreversible; or
- capable of being reversed by an adjustment in the marketing mix.

A product that is not making a contribution is, in effect, being propped up by others in the firm's product mix. This practice, known as **cross-subsidization**, involves profits from some products covering losses on others. Cross-subsidization is acceptable only if the firm is optimistic about an upturn in sales or where the availability of one product is necessary for the continuing success of another product in the firm's range. In other situations cross-subsidization is undesirable. Economists criticize it as arbitrary redistribution of income as customers of profitable products are being asked to pay more to support products for which demand is inadequate. Marketers criticize the harm done to a firm's reputation by carrying 'weak lines' that often take a disproportionate amount of marketing time and effort. Low-volume products also entail short production runs and, therefore, high costs.

Elimination (or product rationalization) is necessary if decline is irreversible. However, it is likely that both customers and employees will express their opposition to elimination, either on grounds of sentiment or vested interest.

● Extension

Extension strategies aim to rejuvenate the product to prolong its life (see Figure 14.3). Common strategies involve changes in:

- the product;
- its packaging;
- the way it is promoted;
- the channel of distribution used.

The patterns of sales over time vary, producing different lifecycle graphs (see Figure 14.4).

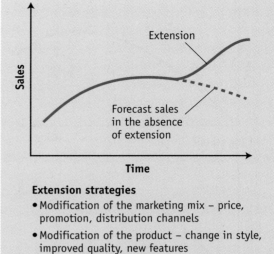

Extension strategies

- Modification of the marketing mix – price, promotion, distribution channels
- Modification of the product – change in style, improved quality, new features
- Encouragement of increased usage – new and more varied uses
- Expansion of the number of brand users – increase market share, convert non-users, enter new segments

Figure 14.3 Product lifecycle extension

Key concepts

Advertising A promotional activity involving one-way paid-for communication.

Brand A product with a set of characteristics that differentiate it from other products.

Channels of distribution The stages and organizations through which a product must pass between the point of production and the point of consumption.

Extension strategy A strategy to extend the life of a product.

'Four Ps' The four key elements in the marketing mix.

Marketing mix The factors that can be adjusted to increase the sales of a product.

Marketing orientation A business philosophy that places the satisfaction of customer wants at the centre of business activity.

Marketing planning Planning that focuses on a particular product or market and details the

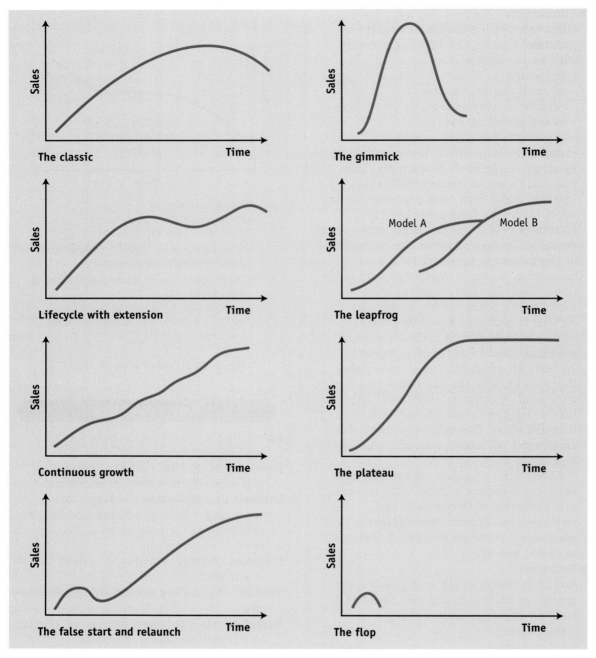

Figure 14.4 Varieties of lifecycle

resources, strategies and programmes for achieving the product's objectives in the market.

Market research A process concerned with discovering the needs and wants of customers.

Personal selling Two-way persuasive discussion designed to promote and sell a product or service.

Positioning Defining the location of a product relative to others and promoting it accordingly.

Product development Developing new products.

Product lifecycle The phases through which a product passes from introduction to decline.

Product mix The total assortment of products offered by a company.

Promotion A company's means of communicating with its public (including advertising, sales promotion, personal selling and publicity).

Promotional mix The blend of individual elements of promotion for a particular product.

Push/pull strategies Strategies designed to move the product through the channels of distribution.

Sales promotion Techniques to provide an incentive to purchase. They are used in support of advertising and/or personal selling.

Segmentation The process of dividing the market for a product into subgroups that can then be targeted through marketing activity.

Target The market segment at which activity is aimed. Targeting is a strategy for positioning goods to reach selected segments.

Essay questions

1 Marketing is designed to create demand and sell goods that few wish to buy. Discuss.

2 Are the principles of marketing appropriate for a public-sector organization? Justify your answer.

3 The marketing department is the focal point of a well-run business. Discuss.

4 With reference to a variety of examples, explain how and why the marketing mix will vary from product to product.

5 (a) What do you understand by a product or brand manager?
(b) Argue the case for the appointment of product managers in a large, multi-product organization.

Marketing research

In the previous chapter, the market-oriented firm was defined as one that seeks to identify and respond to changing demand. To accomplish this task, it is necessary to collect and analyse data about the market and its customers. This activity is known as marketing research, the subject of this chapter.

Chapter objectives

1 To explain and analyse the role of marketing research.

2 To develop an understanding of sampling.

3 To analyse the advantages and disadvantages of different methods of conducting marketing research.

4 To develop an understanding of sampling theory.

What is marketing research?

All definitions of **marketing research** emphasize that it involves the 'systematic and objective collection, analysis and evaluation of information relating to markets and marketing'. The adjectives 'systematic' and 'objective' mean that it is a social science process rather than a haphazard one. The references to analysis and evaluation mean that marketing research goes beyond mere collection of data. Data collection is followed by analysis and evaluation as a prelude to decision making within the firm. Marketing research is not undertaken for its own sake, but for the contribution that it makes to the quality of decision making within the organization.

You may have noticed that some books refer to *market* research while others refer to *marketing* research. Sometimes the terms are used interchangeably. The distinction between the two is that **market research** concerns the demands for the product (or service) in terms of both its extent and the nature of the demand (that is, what type of people buy the product). Marketing research is much broader as it also includes research into the effectiveness of the marketing strategy. For the purposes of A level Business Studies, this distinction is not vital, but it is useful to remember that marketing research is more than an investigation of 'how many and who' wish to purchase the product.

The scope of marketing research

Marketing research can be subdivided into the following elements.

- **Market research**
  - Size of the market.
  - Geography of the market.
  - Customer profile.
  - Future potential market.
  - Customer behaviour.
  - Market segments.
- **Product research**
  - Evaluation of strengths and weaknesses of existing products.
  - Investigation of new uses for existing products.
  - Product variations.
  - Packaging research.
  - Sales potential of new products.
  - Product development.
  - Research into pricing policies.
- **Sales research**
  - Examination of selling activities by outlet, territory, agencies.
  - Evaluation of sales methods.
  - Measurement of the effectiveness of salespeople.
  - Planning of sales calls.
  - Analysis of distribution systems.
  - Identification of suitable outlets.
- **Promotion research**
  - Analysis of the effectiveness of promotional activities.
  - Media research.
  - Copy research, formulation of advertising themes.
- **Business economics**
  - Research into the macro- and microeconomic environment.
- **Export marketing research**
  - Application of domestic marketing research to foreign markets.
- **Motivation research**
  - Analysis of motives that condition customer responses.
  - Customer perception of value.
- **Competitor research**
  - Research into the activities of competitors.

- Market shares.
- Trends.
- Identification of unique selling points.

The purpose of marketing research

Marketing research can be seen as a risk-reducing activity. Risks cannot be eliminated completely as they are inherent in a dynamic market. However, by 'intelligence gathering', analysis and evaluation, it is possible to devise strategies that increase the probability of success. Sound marketing research will aid the development of successful new products and the most effective way to market them. For instance, by building up a consumer profile, it is possible to identify distinct market segments, which can be targeted. Understanding what motivates the customer to purchase can play a major role in developing the product and devising the advertising campaign. The revelation that the decision to purchase particular goods is made at the point of sale, for example, will alter the promotional mix. Advertising will still be used to present the product to the customer, but resources will now be switched to selling and sales promotion at the point of sale.

In the closing decades of the twentieth century, the importance of marketing research increased. This can be explained by:

- the accelerating pace of technological change;
- the high cost of product development;
- shorter product lifecycles;
- increased uncertaintly;
- more intense competition within the UK and from outside;
- inflation.

Qualitative and quantitative research

The qualitative/quantitative distinction refers to the type of information collected, but it necessarily affects the research method used. **Qualitative research** is in-depth research into the motivations behind consumer behaviour or attitudes. Consequently, it provides information on consumers'

Table 15.1 The contrasts between qualitative and quantitative research

Aspects	Qualitative research	Quantitative research
Types of questions	Probing	Non-probing
Sample sizes	Small	Large
Information per respondent	Much	Varies
Administration	Requires interviewer with special skills	Fewer special skills required
Types of analysis	Subjective, interpretative	Statistical

tastes, preferences, attitudes and buying habits, and, although this is inevitably subjective, it provides insights into consumer behaviour to complement the quantitative data. Qualitative research is conducted by psychologists working with small groups of people within the target market for the product. These discussion groups are known as **focus groups**.

Quantitative research concentrates on factual information, such as market share, probable level of sales at a given price and ways in which the market can be segmented. In essence, quantitative research relates to who buys the product and how much will they buy, whereas qualitative research is concerned more with why people buy. Techniques of quantitative research include surveys (delivered face to face, by post and by telephone) and will be explored later. Meanwhile, Table 15.1 highlights the distinction between the two types of research.

The research process

This section will prove useful to students undertaking a written project as part of their course. The stages of a marketing research project described below should be replicated in your own projects (Figure 15.1 summaries the types of information you can use in your marketing research and Figure 15.2 shows the methods that can be used, which are described later in this chapter.).

1 Definition of the problem

Before launching a research project, it is necessary to clarify the type of information required,

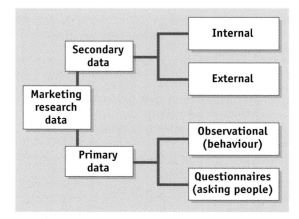

Figure 15.1 Types of marketing information

why it is required and what questions it is designed to answer. In essence, a research project should start with a statement of its objectives, such as a hypothesis, that is to be tested.

2 Investigation of secondary sources of data

It is a mistake to equate marketing research with questionnaires completed in the high street. In fact, before a business collects primary data by undertaking expensive field research, it should review secondary data collected by means of desk research.

Primary data is defined as data that originates as a result of that particular investigation. **Secondary** data involve the use and further analysis of data collected for another purpose and found by means of desk research. Some of the material will be available within the organization (sales

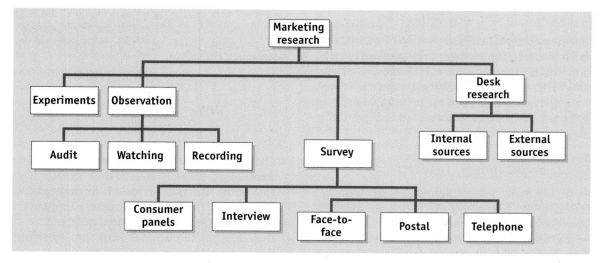

Figure 15.2 Marketing reseach methods

records, stock movements, accounts and earlier market research reports) while other material can be obtained from outside the organization. The main sources include government publications (such as the annual *Social Trends*), research organizations, market intelligence organizations (such as The Economist Intelligence Unit), and trade associations, the press and professional bodies.

Desk research is obviously cheaper than primary research, but the data may suffer from two serious defects: it could be dated and, it must be remembered that it was collected for a different purpose. Secondary data should, therefore, be handled with care.

3 Selection of primary data collection methods

There are three basic techniques of field research to collect primary data:

● surveys
● observation
● experiments.

Each technique can be conducted in a variety of ways, to which reference will be made later. The task for the researcher is to choose the most appropriate method. In making this choice, consideration should be given to relative costs, the time available, the type of information required, the type of people to be investigated and the degree of accuracy required. The last point might come as a surprise as, surely, the value of marketing research depends on its accuracy. However, primary research is both costly and time-consuming. The accuracy of the findings is likely to rise the greater the resources employed and the greater the time allowed. However, there is no point in undertaking research if the costs exceed the benefits to the firm. Moreover, it is shortsighted to delay a decision in order to obtain more data if it allows rival firms to take advantage of the situation.

4 Decide on details of research techniques

Included in this stage would be the formulation of questionnaires and deciding on sampling methods.

5 Analysis, interpretation and evaluation of the data

After collecting the data, it is necessary to draw conclusions from it that can be of value in designing marketing strategies. The analysis, interpretation and evaluation of results require an understanding of statistical theory.

Particular reference should be made to techniques that test the significance of the findings.

6 Recommendations for action

The final part of a research project consists of recommending the strategy to be pursued in relation to the product and the marketing effort. As explained above, marketing research is not pure research undertaken for its own sake – it is designed to provide answers to commercially important marketing questions.

Desk, or secondary, research

As we saw earlier, this is defined as the assembly, collation and analysis of marketing information that already exists. Some of the data is internal to the firm (such as sales records), whereas other data is external (such as government statistics or the reports of market research organizations, such as Mintel). Although this type of research has known disadvantages, it should not be dismissed too lightly (see Table 15.2). If nothing else, it provides a background for filed research by identifying and defining problems to be investigated.

Information collected from secondary sources should not be accepted unquestioned (this point should be appreciated by students when producing essays or projects). The following aspects should be investigated.

- **Character of the collecting organization** In some cases, data are collected to 'prove' something and may be biased, for example, information from political pressure groups.
- **The objectives of the original study** If these are not reconcilable with the objectives in hand, the data may not be suitably classified.
- **The methods employed** Inaccurate data will have been produced if sample selection or

Table 15.2 Desk research

Internal sources	External sources
• Customer sales records	• Trade information
• Client databases	– Trade press
• Sales representatives' reports	– Trade association reports
• Correspondence with customers	– Specialist publishers, such as Mintel and The Economist
• Unsuccessful bids and quotations	Intelligence Unit
• Customer payment records	• Company reports and accounts
• Customer guarantee documents	– Activities of rivals
• Internal assessment of markets	• Government and international statistics
and technological change	– National income
• Analysis of competitors	– Family Expenditure Survey
	– Trade figures
	– Social Trends
	– Demographic Trends
	• Retail audit data
	– Continuous sample audit of retail stock

Advantages	Disadvantages
• Inexpensive	• Often out of date
• Avoids repeating effort	• Might not be available
• Quick to obtain	• Little control over quality
• Enables cost-effective analysis of several data sources	• Coverage may be inappropriate
• Easier to establish trends	• Problems of interpretation
• Can preserve complete confidentiality	• Research methodology may be unknown
• Wide choice of data, useful for carrying out exploratory research	

data collection were badly done. Reputable organization appends a full description of their methods.

- **The definitions used** For example, of family, department store, employed, income – are these the same definitions as the ones used in the research?
- **Timeliness** The data may have become out of date.

Techniques of field research

Primary data can be collected by means of three techniques of field research: observations, experiments, focus groups and surveys (or questionnaires).

Observations

Rather than asking people about their behaviour or their views, market researchers can observe how people behave. The great advantage of this technique is that it avoids the subjective element that is present when people are questioned. Observations take the form of audits (such as a stock check), recording devices (such as those that record viewing figures for television channels) and watching. Observers can be employed to watch behaviour in shops and how people use the product once purchased.

Observation is an expensive technique of market research and provides only limited information.

For instance, it produces a description of events rather than an explanation and records what *has* happened rather than what *will* happen. Finally, results will be distorted if the person is aware of being observed.

Experiments

Experiments are used to test and assess the response of consumers to changes in the marketing mix. This might involve changes in the product or packaging, advertising, price and distribution arrangements.

Test marketing is, in essence, an experiment. It involves a limited launch of a product to test reaction, both to the product and the way in which it is marketed. It has the advantage of reducing marketing costs and targeting a particular area

before the firm is committed to a national launch. As ITV in the UK is regional, a test launch could be concentrated on, say, the North East region, which is served by Tyne Tees Television.

The main problems of experiments in market research relate to the choice of the participants and the difficulties in controlling random variables (such as weather conditions or the mood of participants).

Focus groups

This involves a group discussion in which people are encouraged to freely express views and opinions on a selected subject. The technique is used as a means of determining both overt and subconscious attitudes and motivations. The interaction between participants results in in-depth probing of topics and a wide range of views. Inevitably, it will be costly and time-consuming to organize and, in addition, requires high levels of interviewing skills from the market researcher.

Surveys

Most marketing investigations use some form of survey of customers' opinions. The advantage of a survey (over the two previous methods) is that it is flexible, yields a wide range of data and generates information on customers' opinions. This is also its main weakness (or at least the main problem to be aware of). As P. M. Chisnall points out (in *Marketing Research*, McGraw-Hill, 1997), 'Experienced researchers know well the inclination of respondents (to surveys) to protect their egos, to project favourable images of themselves, and even, on occasions, to distort their reputed beliefs and behaviour in order to shock those surveying them'.

Surveys can be delivered in a number of ways:

- personal interviewing;
- postal survey;
- telephone survey;
- panel survey, in which the opinions and behaviour of a representative group of people is obtained;
- group interviews to encourage free discussion and provide a psychological insight into consumer motivation.

Table 15.3 Advantages and disadvantages of survey techniques

Techniques	Advantages	Disadvantages
Postal	• Anonymity • Gives respondents time to check data • Reaches scattered populations • Eliminates interviewer bias	• Expensive in terms of post • Low response rate • No control over respondents • Limited to simple questions • Bias as a result of self-selection • As respondents can see all questions before, answering, it can lead to bias
Telephone	• Quick • Wide geographical spread • Less inhibited than face-to-face interviews • Better response rate than postal • Undemanding of respondents	• Costs necessitate short calls • Biased because it excludes those without phones or not in the directory • Not possible to control respondents • Limited to short, simple questions • No visual stimuli
Face to face interviews	• Flexible • Observation of reactions possible • Facilitates the asking of more complicated questions • Skilled interviewer can elicit information in greater depth • Visual material can be used	• Interviewer bias is possible • Time-consuming • Difficult to control interviewer • Difficult to sample a scattered population • Respondent bias – false answers can be given to impress interviewers, for example
Panels	• Members are cooperative • Panel members know procedures and time is saved • Trends over time can be revealed • Appointments avoid the expense of recalls • Control groups can be formed	• Panel members tend to be atypical • Panel sophistication develops

Table 15.3 identifies the major advantages and disadvantages of each of the survey techniques.

Questionnaire design

Questionnaires are likely to play a key role in most market research surveys. The types of questions posed vary from highly structured questions, designed to attract a limited range of responses (closed questions), to unstructured questions, to which respondents are invited to answer more freely (open questions). The use of open-ended questions allows for a free style of investigation, pursuing particular issues in greater detail. However, the wide range of responses makes classification of answers more difficult and requires greater skill in the interviewer.

As the design of the questionnaire is crucially important to the quality of the research (and the data obtained), it is advisable to undertake a pilot survey in order to assess the quality of the questions.

In designing a questionnaire, it is important to follow these principles:

● clarify the purpose of the enquiry;
● devise clear, unambiguous questions;
● use language intelligible to the respondent;
● avoid leading questions;
● follow a logical sequence in questions;
● avoid questions that tax the memory too much
● do not use multiple-choice questions where one of the offered answers appears to confer some status on respondents;
● avoid questions on topics that respondents will be reluctant to answer;

- confine questions to the personal experiences of respondents;
- introduce some control questions.

Question types

As mentioned above, we can make a broad distinction between **open questions** and **closed questions**. In the former, the respondent is given the opportunity to provide a reply in their own terms, uninfluenced by guidance within the questionnaire or by the interviewer. The main forms of open questions are:

- **completely unstructured** for examples, 'What is your opinion of Ford cars?';
- **word association** such as 'What is the first word that comes into your mind when you think of Ford cars?';
- **sentence completion** 'The main factor I take into account when buying a new car is…', for example;
- **story completion** an incomplete story is presented and respondents are asked to complete it;
- **picture completion** an example would be when respondents are presented with a picture containing two people, one complete and one with an empty speech bubble, and they are then asked to fill in the empty bubble;
- **Thematic Apperception Test (TAT)** a picture is presented, for example, and respondents are asked to make up a story about what they think is happening or may happen in the picture.

Open questions are useful for qualitative research and result in in-depth probing of customer attitudes and motives, but answers will be wide-ranging and so can be difficult to classify.

Closed questions, in which the respondent is asked to choose from a number of specific responses, facilitate precise quantification. The major types are as follow, with examples:

- **dichotomous** yes/no questions where there are only two possible answers;
- **multiple choice** questions with three or more possible answers, for which the chosen response is indicated by a ticked box;
- **Likert scale** a statement is written out and the respondent shows the degree of their agreement/disagreement on a five-category scale running from 'strongly agree' to 'strongly disagree';
- **semantic difference** here, a scale connects two opposing words (large/small, modern/old-fashioned) and the respondent selects the point that represents his/her opinion;
- **importance scale** a scale that rates the importance of something – from 'extremely important', through 'very important', 'somewhat important' and 'not very important' to 'not important at all' – follows each question;
- **rating scale** a scale is used on which respondents rate some attribute (quality of service) from 'excellent' too 'poor'.
- **intention to buy** a scale can be used that describes the respondent's intention from 'definitely buy' through 'probably by', 'not sure' and 'probably not buy' to 'definitely not buy'.

Having investigated **survey methods** (the techniques used to obtain data), let us now consider **sampling methods,** which are decisions relating to choice of respondents.

Sampling in marketing research

A survey of the whole population is known as a **census**. Clearly, it is impractical for a business organization to undertake a census survey on the market in, say, ice-cream. Consequently, rather than surveying the whole population in which it is interested, the organization conducts a **sample survey.** This is defined as a survey involving less than the whole population and it has advantages (over a full census) in that it:

- reduces costs;
- saves on time;
- requires fewer resources;
- is more reliable as there is a concentration on fewer units.

It is hoped and expected that a sample survey will provide information that is valid for the population as a whole, but this depends on the size of the sample and how it is selected. The law of the inertia of large numbers tells us that large groups of data show a higher degree of stability than smaller ones as variations in the data tend to be cancelled out by each other. This means that the larger the sample the more reliable it will be. Once the sample size has been decided, the next task is to decide on the method of selecting the sample.

We can divide sampling methods into two broad types: probability (or random) sampling and non-probability (or non-random sampling).

Probability sampling

Probability samples are so constructed that every member of the population has a known probability (or chance) of selection. As the name suggests, this method of sampling lends itself to statistical analysis involving the determination of sampling error expressed in mathematical terms. Moreover, the composition of the sample is not affected by interviewer likes and dislikes. However, it does require the use of a **sampling frame**. This is a complete list or complete identification of the population. From the sampling frame it will be possible to select individuals in a random fashion. Examples of sampling frames include subscribers to a certain magazine (if the population was limited to such people), the electoral register and the telephone directory (although the last two examples suffer from major limitations). Sample frames should be evaluated in terms of their completeness, accuracy, convenience and the extent to which items are duplicated in the list (for example, a household with two telephone lines will appear twice in a directory and has an increased change of being selected).

Here are the main techniques of probability sampling.

● **Simple random sample** This is a sample in which each person or unit has an equal chance of being selected. It can be done by pulling names out of a hat or using a computer to generate random numbers. This means that a genuine random sample requires an up-to-date and comprehensive sample frame.

● **Systematic sample** This involves choosing a starting point in a sample frame and then selecting every nth item thereafter. This is not fully random and will produce a bias if there is a regular, recurring pattern in the frame.

● **Stratified sample** With this method, the population is divided into subgroups and the sample reflects each subgroup in proportion to their representation in the population as a whole. The selection of people within each subgroup is made on a random basis. Hence, this method should be seen as quasi-random.

Non-probability sampling

In **non-probability sampling** methods individuals are selected on the basis of one or more criteria determined by the research. In other words, there is an element of human judgement in the methods. As a result, it is not possible to state a sampling error based on statistical theory. Nevertheless, a non-random sample can be as reliable as a random sample if it is based on up-to-date statistics relating to population structure and if the interviewer's selection of respondents is carefully controlled. The main techniques of non-probability sampling are as follows, and Table 15.4 shows which is best of the probability and non-probability methods for particular kinds of population being surveyed.

● **Cluster sample** This involves making a random selection from a frame listing not individuals, but groups of individuals. Everyone in the selected group is then interviewed or examined. This method is used when the population is widely dispersed and a full sample frame is not available.

● **Quota sample** Like a stratified sample, this method involves dividing the population into subsets with quotas attached that reflect accurately the known population characteristics in a variety of respects (age and sex distribution, income, occupation and so on). Unlike stratified sampling, the selection of individuals from each group is made on a non-random basis by the interviewer. The quota method is relatively

Table 15.4 Matching the sampling method to the population being surveyed

Populations	Sampling frame available	Sampling frame not available
Population resides in one place	Simple random sampling or systematic sampling	Systematic sampling
Population geographically scattered	Multi-stage sampling	Cluster sampling
Population is defined by categories	Stratified sampling	Quota sampling

quick and is used when a sample frame is not available. However, as a non-random method it is not possible to estimate sampling error and, therefore, there are problems of control and checking.

- **Multi-stage sample** This consists of a series of samples taken at successive stages, such as a region, then a town, then a suburb, then a street. It is used when groups selected in a cluster sample are too large, with the result that a subsample has to be selected from each group.

Sampling and non-sampling error

The value of marketing research is dependent on the results from a sample reflecting the population as a whole. For example, if a sample survey indicates that people buy a particular product ten times per year, then this statistic is valid both for the sample and for the population's as a whole. The total survey error is the difference between the overall population's true mean value of the characteristic of interest and its mean observed value obtained from a particular sample of respondents. The total survey error is made up of two elements:

- **non-sampling error** this is the extent to which the mean observed value for the respondent of a particular sample disagrees with the mean true value for the particular sample of respondents, and the size of the non-sampling error depends on:
  - **non-response error** differential response rates amongst various groups;
  - **response errors** such as giving an answer to please the researcher, giving a socially

acceptable answer or error caused by lack of knowledge of the subject matter;
- **sampling error** this is the difference between the estimate of a value obtained from a sample and the actual value, so, for example, if a sample shows that the average yearly purchase of a product is 30 per person, when in fact it is 32, then the sampling error is 2.

Sample size and confidence limits

Statistical theory enables market researchers to express statistically the confidence that they have in their findings. This is based on the properties of a normal distribution in which:

- 68 per cent of values lie within one standard deviation of the mean;
- 95 per cent of values lie within two standard deviations of the mean;
- 99 per cent of values lie within 3 standard deviations.

Consequently, we can be confident there is a 68 per cent probability that the mean of a population is equal to the sample mean plus or minus one standard deviation. There is a 95 per cent probability that the mean of the population will be equal to the sample mean plus or minus 1.96 per cent standard deviations. There is a 99 per cent probability that the mean lies within a range of the sample mean plus or minus 2.58 per cent standard deviations.

If we wanted results to a 95 per cent confidence level, we can manipulate the formula for calculating standard error. This is the standard deviation of the sampling distribution of the mean and is calculated by dividing the standard deviation of the sample by the square root of the sample size. Hence, a sample of 100 with a standard deviation of 5 will have a standard error of:

$$\frac{5}{100} = \frac{5}{10} = 0.5$$

$$\text{Standard error} = \sqrt{\frac{\text{Standard deviation of the sample}}{\text{Sample size}}}$$

Therefore, sample size is equal to:

$$\sqrt{\frac{(\text{Standard deviation of the sample})^2}{\text{Tolerance level}}}$$

Let us illustrate this with an example. The standard deviation of a sample is 25 and we have a tolerance level of 4 (a margin of error of 4 either side of the mean). To be 95 per cent confident of our results we need a sample size of:

$$\left(\frac{1.96 \times 25}{4}\right)^2 = 151$$

To increase confidence to 99 per cent, we need a sample size of:

$$\left(\frac{2.58 \times 25}{4}\right)^2 = 261$$

From this formula, we derive Table 15.5, which shows the sample sizes for given levels of statistical error. It can be interpreted as follows. To be 99.9 per cent certain that our result is within 1 per cent plus or minus that for the whole population, we need a sample size of 19,741. If we only seek a 95 per cent level of confidence, then the sample size could be as low as 9604. If we wanted results within plus or minus 4 per cent, then a sample size of 601 would entitle us to be 95 per cent confident of the results, whereas a sample of 1234 would give us 99.9 per cent confidence of the true result being within 4 per cent plus or minus the sample mean.

Key concepts

Desk research Research based on secondary sources.

Field research The collection of original data by means of surveys, experiments or observation.

Market research Research into the extent of the market.

Marketing research Research into all aspects of marketing a product. Marketing research is broader than market research, although there is a tendency to use the terms interchangeably.

Primary data Data collected for the purpose for which it is originally used.

Sample survey A survey based on a portion of the population. This contrasts with a census, which is a survey of the whole population.

Sampling method The method used to choose individuals for inclusion in the sample – random, quota, cluster and so on.

Secondary data Data collected for a purpose other than the original one.

Survey method The method used to collect data, such as questionnaire, interview, panel and others.

Table 15.5 Sample sizes required for given levels of statistical error

Margin of error	Level of confidence (%)				
(+ or − %)	75	90	95	99	99.9
1	3,307	6,766	9,604	16,590	19,741
2	827	1,692	2,401	4,148	4,936
3	358	752	1,068	1,844	2,194
4	207	423	601	1,037	1,234
5	133	271	385	664	790

Essay questions

1 (a) Identify the major sources of secondary data available to a small, local retailer.

(b) Assess the value of desk research to business organizations.

2 (a) Explain the differences between probability and a non-probability sampling.

(b) Analyse the causes of sampling error.

3 (a) Explain the differences between qualitative and quantitative research.

(b) Evaluate the benefits of qualitative research.

4 Explain the principles you would use to select a sample of people to question about the quality of service at a fast food restaurant. Justify your choice of sampling method.

5 Explain and evaluate each of the survey methods.

Forecasting

We live in a changing world and, therefore, there is uncertainty about the future. Despite this uncertainty (and perhaps because of it) it is important to try to forecast future trends and the course of events. This chapter seeks to introduce certain techniques of forecasting and, in particular, the statistical technique of times series analysis.

Chapter objectives

1 To introduce the major techniques of forecasting.

2 To develop understanding of, and skills in calculating, moving averages.

3 To explain techniques of extrapolation and adjusting for seasonal variations.

4 To assess the value of time series analysis for forecasting.

Forecasting

Forecasting, which is an attempt to predict the future behaviour of a variable, provides a basis for planning. Forecasting is used in:

- planning production schedules;
- manpower planning;
- investment appraisal;
- cost projections;
- stock (or inventory) control;
- distribution planning;
- market testing;
- corporate planning.

For decision making related to each of the above, it is important to have a forecast of future trends – only then can strategy be rationally planned.

Forecasting techniques can be broadly divided into two groups:

- qualitative or judgemental techniques;
- quantitative techniques.

Qualitative techniques

These techniques depend on human judgement and experience and are used when:

- data is scarce or unavailable (such as when a new product is introduced);
- the timeframe is so long that data is of limited use.

In the second case, human judgement, experience

and intuition are needed for interpretation of the data. By means of these techniques, qualitative information is turned into quantitative estimates. The main qualitative techniques are the following.

- **Personal insight** of an individual. Forecasts based on individual judgement are inexpensive, but the level of accuracy is low.
- **Panel consensus,** in which a panel of experts discuss issues to arrive at a consensus forecast. Although accuracy is likely to be higher than with individual personal insight, because it involves a pooling of knowledge and ideas, it is still inadequate for most business purposes.
- **Market surveys** Although these involve data collection and analysis, they are included in qualitative techniques as, in the absence of data, judgement is required. The accuracy of the resulting forecast is dependent on the:
  - representativeness of the sample;
  - quality of the questions asked;
  - reliability of replies;
  - quality of analysis and the resulting conclusions.
- **Historical analogy** In Chapter 14 we looked at the idea of the product lifecycle. This provides a model to help understand likely trends in the demand for a product. The performance of one product provides an analogy to predict trends in a similar product.
- The **Delphi method,** which involves a panel of experts responding to questionnaires. Unlike the consensus panel, experts are asked independently and the responses of each expert are presented anonymously to other panel members until a consensus emerges. In this way, the experts are not swayed by individuals who 'shout loudest' or have the greatest prestige. Consequently, the accuracy of the forecast increases.

Quantitative methods

These can be broadly divided into two types.

- **Causal methods,** which involve the use of mathematical models to link cause and effect (such as the relationship between price – or income – and demand). The aim is to identify the variable(s) that is (are) believed to cause changes in the variable we want to forecast. By establishing the statistical relationship between the dependent and independent variables (such as sales and advertising expenditure respectively), it is possible to forecast trends in one variable from movements in the other variable.
- **Time series analysis** A time series is a set of data recorded over uniform time periods, such as a year or a month. It shows how the variable has behaved over time. The analysis of a time series involves decomposing the data to establish a pattern. If a pattern is shown to exist, there is a basis for predicting trends into the future.

If the time series is plotted on a graph it is likely that the pattern will conform to one of the graphs illustrated in Figure 16.1. In all cases, you will notice that there is an underlying trend (upwards, constant or even downwards), but some fluctuation around the trend. In the case of the impulse and the step, an extraordinary event occurred to move the series to a higher level, although in the case of the former, it seems to have been a purely temporary phenomenon (a fad, say).

The long-term movement of a variable is known as **the trend,** but around the trend there are fluctuations, which are of the following types.

- **Seasonal fluctuations** These are regularly repeated fluctuations associated with seasons of the year, days of the week or even hours of the day. Although the seasons of the year provide the origin of the name, 'seasonal' has a wide meaning in time series analysis. If a fluctuation is regularly repeated, it is known as a seasonal fluctuation.
- **Cyclical fluctuations** These also occur in a repetitive cycle but over a medium-term period, such as five years. The business cycle of boom and slump results in cyclical variations in a time series.
- **Random variations** These occur as a result of a major disturbance such as war, a substantial rise in disposable income

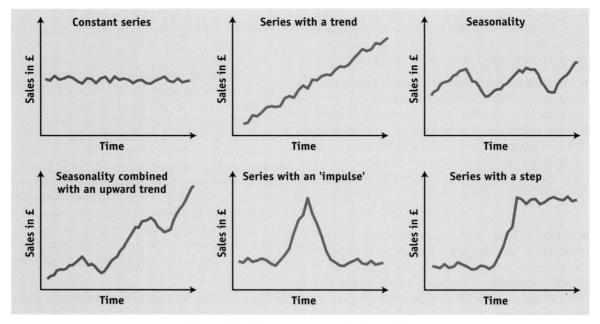

Figure 16.1 Common patterns in time series

following a tax cut, a change of government or a change in public taste. Random variations are, naturally, erratic rather than regular and can be seen as a residual factor after allowing for the other causes of variation.

As the data is made up of these four elements, we can express the time series as equal to $T + S + C + R$ where T is the trend, S is the seasonal variation, C is the cyclical variation and R is the random variation. Time series analysis attempts to separate out the various elements as the basis for forecasting.

Moving averages

A **moving average** (see Figures 16.2 and 16.3) is one that is updated as new information is received. For example, the inflation rate, which is published monthly, is an average of price rises in the previous 12 months. At each successive updating, one month drops out of the calculation, to be replaced by the latest month's data. By calculating a moving average, it is possible to 'smooth out' the data and isolate the trend from the fluctuations.

To illustrate the principle of the moving average, consider the example shown in Figure 16.4. This shows a 12-period moving cycle to eliminate the seasonal fluctuations associated with the seasons of the year. A basic principle of moving averages is that the period chosen must coincide with the cycle. Hence, within each average, we have the 12 months represented. We could have divided the year into quarters and produced a four-period moving average based on the same data. However, the greater the number of periods in the moving average, the greater will be the smoothing effect. The trend, therefore, will be better illustrated by dividing the year into 12 months rather than 4 quarters.

The first average covers the first 12 months, starting in January of Year 1. For the next average, January Year 1 drops out of the calculation to be replaced by January Year 2. This process is repeated for successive averages. Obviously, this involves a considerable amount of number crunching, but a shorthand method is merely to add on (or subtract) the difference in value of the month being deleted from the month being added.

One complication to mention at this point arises

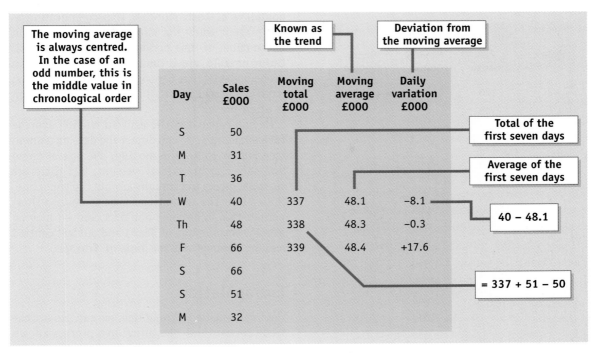

Figure 16.2 A seven-point moving average

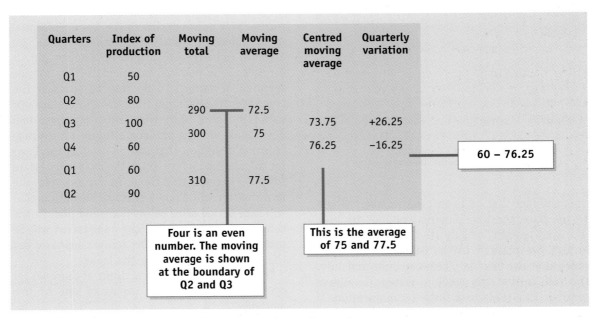

Figure 16.3 A four-point moving average

Sales in million units			
Month	Per month	Moving total	Moving average
J	100		
F	100		
M	120		
A	140		
M	160		
J	200		
		1,890	157.5
J	250		
		1,900	158.3
A	250		
		1,910	159.2
S	200		
		1,920	160.0
O	150		
		1,940	161.7
N	120		
		1,960	163.3
D	100		
		1,980	165.0
J	110		
		2,010	167.5
F	110		
		2,050	170.8
M	130		
		2,070	172.5
A	160		
		2,080	173.3
M	180		
		2,090	174.2
J	220		
		2,100	175.0
J	280		
A	290		
S	220		
O	160		
N	130		
D	110		

Figure 16.4 A 12-point moving average

from the fact that 12 is an even number. Where do we place the first moving average? In June (the sixth month) or July (the seventh month)? In fact, we place it in the centre of the year, which is at the boundary between June and July. The rule is that the moving average is always centred. This leads to a further complication. If we wish to compare the original data for the month with the identified trend, we have to calculate a centred average (to do this we merely average the two moving averages shown at the boundary of each month). This complication is not present when the moving average covers an odd number of time periods (five or seven days). Unfortunately, much time series analysis uses an even number of time periods (12 months, 4 quarters, 6 days) and, therefore, the centring complication is often present.

Having calculated the centred moving average for each month, we can depict the data on a graph (see Figure 16.5). The moving, average or trend line shows an upward movement, but there are seasonal peaks and troughs around the trend line. Notice that the trend line seems to cover a short period; this is because our first centred moving average was for July of Year 1 and our last centred moving average was for June of Year 2.

Extrapolation

Having identified a trend line, we can project the trend forward into the future in a process known as extrapolation. The validity of the technique is based on the assumption that the trend will continue.

However, having extrapolated the trend into the future, how do we deal with the known seasonal (and, indeed, cyclical) fluctuations? These are assumed to be regular in their occurrence and, as a result, it is possible to calculate the average seasonal deviation. To do this we subtract the trend (centred average) from the appropriate raw data (see Figure 16.6). With two or more seasonal deviations, we can produce a figure for average seasonal deviation that can be used as the basis for calculating by how much the data will deviate from the extrapolated trend. In our example, the first quarter will show a seasonal deviation that will take actual sales below the trend line. In the subsequent two quarters, the adjustment will be positive, so we should expect actual sales to exceed the quantity predicted by the trend.

The adjustment to take account of seasonal (or cyclical) variation is by means of one of two methods.

● **The additive method** This is the easier of the two methods and involves adding the appropriate average seasonal variations to the

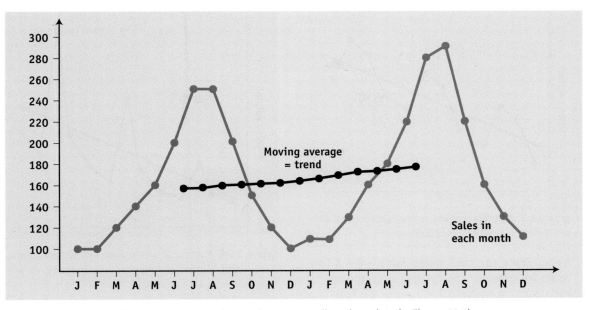

Figure 16.5 A 12-point moving average (based on data in Figure 16.4)

Quarter	Index of production	Moving total	Moving average	Centred moving average	Quarterly variation
Q1	50				
Q2	80				
		290	72.5		
Q3	100			73.75	+26.5
		300	75		
Q4	60			76.25	−16.25
		310	77.5		
Q1	60			78.75	−18.75
		320	80		
Q2	90			81.25	+8.75
		330	82.5		
Q3	110			85	+15
		350	87.5		
Q4	70			88.75	−18.75
		360	90		
Q1	80			92.5	−12.5
		380	95		
Q2	100			97.5	+2.5
		400	100		
Q3	130			102.5	+27.5
		420	105		
Q4	90			107.5	−17.5
		440	110		
Q1	100			111.25	−11.25
		450	112.5		
Q2	120			113.75	+6.25
		460	115		
Q3	140				
Q4	100				

Figure 16.6 A four-point moving average

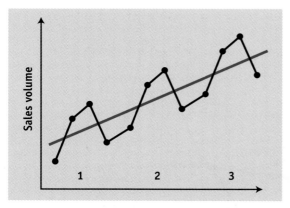

Figure 16.7 Additive method: extrapolated trend and regular fluctuation

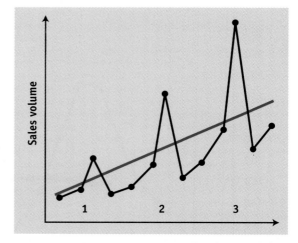

Figure 16.8 Multiplicative method: extrapolated trend and fluctuations that grow in intensity

trend. There the time series value = $T + S$ (or, when we consider the cyclical and random variations, is equal to $T + S + C + R$). For each period, the forecast will be the trend plus or minus the average seasonal variation. The graphical result of this is shown in Figure 16.7 where the fluctuations are identical in every respect. This simplistic view is only valid if the component factors (T, S, C and R) are independent of each other.

● **The multiplicative method** Where the components interact with each other, the complicated multiplicative method must be used. For instance, a higher trend value might lead to an increase in the seasonal variation. To reflect this we calculate not the seasonal variation in absolute terms but a seasonal index that depicts seasonal variation as a proportion of the trend. A seasonal index of 0.85 means that the actual figure should be 15 per cent below trend, whereas an index of 1.2 means that it should be 20 per cent above trend. For each successive time period, we merely multiply the trend by the seasonal index. The result is shown in Figure 16.8 where both the peaks and troughs grow larger as the trend shows an upward movement.

Evaluation of moving averages

We have seen that moving averages constitute a smoothing technique to isolate the trend from fluctuations around it. It is an invaluable technique in the construction of sales forecasts, although users should be aware of certain features and limitations of the method.

● The period of the moving average must coincide with the cycle so that each average captures both upturns and downturns.
● The greater the number of periods in the moving average, the greater the smoothing effect. A 12-month moving average is therefore preferable to a 4-quarter moving average.
● A greater number of periods should be chosen if the underlying trend is fairly constant but there is substantial randomness.
● Fewer periods should be included in the moving average if there is thought to be some change in the underlying state of the data.

The limitations of the method are as follows.

● Forecasting from the trend is an exercise in extrapolation of future data from the behaviour of data in the past. We have to question the extent to which we can forecast the future from the past.
● This problem is especially acute if the environment is unstable and if we are trying to project some way into the future. Moving

averages are best suited to short-term forecasting in relatively stable situations.

- In moving average calculations, equal weight is given to all values. It can be argued that the most recent data is more relevant and should be given a greater weighting.
- The moving average calculation takes no account of data outside the period of the average.
- Moving average calculations of thousands of items of stock (such as in a supermarket) require the storage of a considerable amount of data.

Key concepts

Extrapolation Inferring values by projecting trends beyond known evidence.

Fluctuation Movements around the trend. They can be classified as seasonal, cyclical or random.

Forecasting Predicting the size of a future quantity.

Trend The movement in the value of a variable over time with short-term fluctuations eliminated.

Time series analysis Analysis of changes in a variable over time.

Time series data Data arranged in chronological order.

Essay questions

1 Evaluate the role of sales forecasting to a well-run business.

2 (a) Explain four major techniques used in forecasting.
 (b) Assess the value of forecasts based on past experience.

3 (a) Explain the method of sales forecasting based on the extrapolition of moving averages
 (b) What is the basis for choosing a particular time period (say five or six years) for a moving average?

Exercises

1 (a) Calculate a four-quarter moving average from the data below.

	Quarter	Sales (£000)
2002	1	235
	2	202
	3	203
	4	192
2003	1	231
	2	199
	3	195
	4	180
2004	1	220
	2	193
	3	190
	4	170
2005	1	210
	2	190

(b) On graph paper, construct a graph for:
   (i) quarterly sales;
   (ii) the moving average.
(c) Extrapolate the trend to the four quarters of 2006.

2 The figures below represent cash sales of a store that opens on seven days per week.

Week	1	2	3	4
Day of the week	£	£	£	£
Sunday	300	310	330	350
Monday	400	400	410	410
Tuesday	400	400	420	410
Wednesday	400	410	400	420
Thursday	500	520	550	550
Friday	550	550	570	600
Saturday	600	600	620	630

From the data, calculate:
(a) the trend, using a seven-point moving average;
(b) the daily variation from the trend;
(c) likely sales on each day of Week 5.

3 The figures below represent the cash sales of a store over a four-week period.

Week number	1	2	3	4
Day of the week	£000	£000	£000	£000
Sunday	5.0	5.1	5.3	5.4
Monday	3.1	3.2	3.5	3.6
Tuesday	3.6	3.5	3.8	3.9
Wednesday	4.0	4.4	4.5	4.6
Thursday	4.8	4.9	5.1	5.2
Friday	6.6	6.8	6.9	7.0
Saturday	6.6	6.8	6.9	7.2

(a) Using a seven-point moving average, plot the trend on graph paper.
(b) For each of the seven days, calculate the average daily variation.
(c) Forecast the cash sales of the store for each day in the fifth week.
(d) Comment on the value of the moving average method of sales forecasting.

4 From the data below, calculate:

(a) the four-quarter moving average;
(b) the trend for as many quarters as possible;
(c) the average seasonal variation for each quarter.

Year	Quarter	Index
1	3	118
1	4	101
2	1	100
2	2	99
2	3	122
2	4	105
3	1	112
3	2	103
3	3	142
3	4	101
4	1	132
4	2	107

5 Arco Limited was established in 1972 to manufacture garden tools. Its sales revenue has fluctuated in line with the state of the domestic economy, although, over the long run, there has been an upward trend, as shown in the figures below.

Year	Sales revenue (£m)
1982	10
1983	12
1984	15
1985	13
1986	12
1987	16
1988	21
1989	24
1990	21
1991	19
1992	25
1993	28
1994	22
1995	24
1996	25
1997	26
1998	30
1999	26
2000	24
2001	23
2002	24
2003	31

You are the newly appointed sales manager of Arco and have been asked to produce a report forecasting sales revenue for 1994 and 1995.

(a) Using an appropriate time period, calculate moving averages of sales revenue over the life of the company.

(b) On graph paper, plot graphs for:
   (i) actual sales;
   (ii) the moving average.
(c) Extrapolate the trend for sales revenue figures for 2004 and 2005.
(d) In your report explain the limitations of the moving average and additive methods for forecasting purposes.

6 A seven-point moving average

Day	Sales £000	Moving total £000	Moving average £000	Daily variation £000
S	50			
M	31			
T	36			
W	40	337	48.1	−8.1
Th	48	338	48.3	−0.3
F	66	339	48.4	+17.6
S	66	338	48.3	+17.7
S	51	342	48.9	+2.1
M	32	343	49.0	−17.0
T	35	345	49.3	−14.3
W	44	347	49.6	−5.6
Th	49	349	49.9	−0.9
F	68	352	50.3	+17.7
S	68	355	50.7	+17.3
S	53	356	50.9	+2.1
M	35	358	51.1	−16.1
T	38	359	51.3	−13.3
W	45	360	51.4	−6.4
Th	51	361	51.6	−0.6
F	69	362	51.7	+17.3
S	69	363	51.8	+17.2
S	54	364	52.0	+2.0
M	36	365	52.1	−16.1
T	39	366	52.3	−13.3
W	46	369	52.7	−6.7
Th	52			
F	70			
S	72			

(a) Plot the moving average or trend line and extrapolate sales into the following week.
(b) For each day of the week, calculate the average daily variation in sales.
(c) Taking into account both the extrapolation of the trend and the daily variation in sales, suggest the likely level of sales on each day of Week 5.

Segmentation and consumer behaviour

(circle) **17**

To plan the marketing effort, it is first necessary to understand consumers and how they behave. This requires a scientific study of behaviour, with inputs from the major social or behavioural sciences. The behavioural sciences aim to describe and explain behaviour as the basis for predicting future behaviour.

Chapter objectives

1 To review the contribution of social science to the understanding of consumer behaviour.

2 To contrast consumers with industrial customers.

3 To describe and analyse segmentation policies.

4 To describe and analyse the process of diffusion of new products.

5 To relate behavioural theory to marketing practice.

Customers and consumers

The terms **customer** and **consumer** are often used interchangeably to mean the purchaser of a good or service. However, there is an important distinction between the two terms, relating to two distinct markets. Consumers can be seen as the end-users of goods and services. They are people (grouped into households) who buy goods and services for their own benefit and enjoyment (known in economics as the **utility** derived from goods). There is also a group of customers for goods and services, which are business organizations that purchase inputs from other firms. These are customers but not consumers.

Although this chapter is concerned with consumers, it would be useful to digress briefly to look at markets in which the customer is another firm. This comparison between the consumer market and the industrial market will provide an insight into buyer behaviour. Table 17.1 highlights the distinctions between the two markets. It should be realized that the numbers of customers will be relatively small in the industrial market (thousands rather than millions). This facilitates direct marketing techniques and there is a substantially greater role for personal selling than is the case in most consumer markets.

In the industrial market, the purchaser will be knowledgeable and take a rational approach to decision making. This means that the potential purchase will be evaluated in terms of price,

Table 17.1 Differences between consumer and industrial markets

Marketing activities	Consumer market	Industrial market
Numbers of customers	Very many	Relatively few
Relationship with customers	Remote	Often close
Importance of selling	Often low	Usually high
Importance of advertising	Very important	Less important
Media used	Mass media	Specialist media
Channels of distribution	Usually indirect	Direct
Terms of supply	Fixed	Negotiated
Motivation	Varied	Economically rational

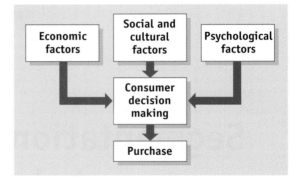

Figure 17.1 Influences on consumer behaviour

quality, performance and supply. The buyer will not be swayed by advertising and packaging. What advertising there is will tend to be informative and carried out through specialist media.

Finally, the buying power of the purchaser results in a greater amount of negotiation over terms than is the case when consumers buy goods. In essence, there is a substantial difference between the marketing mix used in industrial markets and that used in consumer markets. It is to consumer markets that we now turn.

The behavioural sciences

To devise appropriate marketing strategies, it is necessary to analyse the behaviour of consumers. At this point, we can call on the services of the major behavioural sciences (see Figure 17.1):

● economics
● sociology
● psychology.

Economics

As we saw in Chapter 9, economists are concerned only about **effective demand** and not about potential or latent demand. For demand to be effective, the *desire* to buy has to be combined with the *ability* and *willingness* to pay. The economist's analysis of consumer behaviour focuses mainly, but not exclusively, on the price of the product and the income of the potential buyer. In general, a fall in price or a rise in income will result in an increase in the quantity purchased. The size of the increase will depend, respectively, on the price elasticity of demand and the income elasticity of demand.

We need to qualify the word **income**. It is a flow of money over a period of time (unlike wealth, which is a stock of what we own at a moment in time). More important than the amount of money is its purchasing power. For real income (purchasing power) to rise, money income must increase faster than prices. **Disposable income** is left after compulsory deductions. It is this income that can be disposed of (or spent) as the earner chooses. Unfortunately, a large part of our income is committed to regular payments (mortgage, energy, travel to work, food). The residual amount is known as **discretionary income** and is crucially important for firms selling non-necessities.

There are additional factors we should consider. The demand for a product will also be affected by:

● the prices of substitutes;
● the prices of complements;
● the availability of credit (an important factor in the purchase of large, expensive items);

- the liquidity of the potential buyer (who might be reluctant to run down cash reserves);
- expectations about the future (future prices, future income, job prospects).

Economics provides a useful insight into buying behaviour, but does not provide a complete explanation. Hence, marketers turn to the other behavioural sciences to provide a different insight.

Sociology

The distinctive feature of **sociology** is that it involves a study of the impact of groups on the behaviour (in this case the buying behaviour) of individuals. The type of groups with which we are concerned are known as **reference groups**, defined as the group used by individuals as a point of reference for their own judgements, values and behaviour.

The reference group might take the form of a religious group, a club, a peer group or the family. The individual will identify with the values, beliefs and norms of the reference group, which in turn provides a model for behaviour. These norms of behaviour will either be **prescriptive** (laying down 'rules' of what group members must do) or **proscriptive** ('rules' about what they must not do). In addition, the reference group shapes the tastes and influences the expectations of the individual. In this respect, an understanding of reference groups provides a means of explaining and, more important for the marketer, predicting behaviour.

You should not conclude from this account of reference groups that everyone follows the group in a sheep-like manner. Clearly some people are individualists and are reluctant to follow the pattern of any group. Moreover, group members will vary in their commitment to the group. Group-oriented individuals, especially those who have recently joined, will be particularly anxious to fit into the group. This is shown by adherence to the behavioural patterns and beliefs of the group. As a general rule we can say that the level of conformity is related to:

- the degree of dependence on the group;
- the benefits of conformity;
- the sanctions arising from non-conformity;
- individual personality.

Two other sociological terms that should be considered are **culture** and **socialization**. The former can be defined as social characteristics, including behaviour, ideas and beliefs that are shared within a group. Socialization is the process by which this culture is transmitted to group members. For instance, the process by which a child learns to be a participating member of society is known as socialization. The education system, one's peers and, most important of all, the family control the process of socialization.

The predominant culture of a society (there will be a number of subcultures) is dynamic or changing. In a traditional culture, behaviour habits (including buying and consumption) are rooted in the past. Western culture can be better described as an achieving or affluent culture.

Psychology

Psychology is the science of behaviour and mental processes. Its relevance in marketing is that it provides an insight into motivation (why we buy certain goods) and the cognitive (or thought) processes involved in decision making.

First, let us consider motivation in relation to purchasing behaviour. Maslow's hierarchy of needs (see Chapter 42) is based on the proposition that we seek to satisfy a number of needs, arranged in an ascending order.

1 **Physiological** – basic biological needs.
2 **Safety** – concern for the future.
3 **Affection** – social needs.
4 **Self-esteem** – self-respect.
5 **Self-actualization** – creativity.

We purchase products in order to satisfy needs, but the hierarchy concept suggests that:

- we do not seek to satisfy higher-level needs until lower needs are satisfied;
- once a need is satisfied, we move on to the next level.

Maslow's theory now has to be translated into marketing practice. For instance, we can conclude that, in affluent societies, there will be a large market for products that satisfy the higher needs, but there will be little growth in the market for the type of product (say, food) that merely satisfies the lower-order needs. On the other hand, some products could be marketed in such a way as to satisfy a number of different needs. For example, food satisfies a physiological need, but could also satisfy the social and creative needs of people.

Psychology also provides an insight into the cognitive aspect of purchasing. An understanding of perception enables marketers to plan promotional strategy. Our perception of (or how we 'see') the product and the promotional message is a function of:

- the quality of our senses;
- the environment;
- our attitude;
- our experience;
- our expectations.

All these factors shape or distort our perceptions of the stimuli that confront us. Advertisers should devise an advertising message so that it is perceived in the manner intended.

The success of an advertising campaign is also dependent on people *remembering* the advertisement, its message and the product. Memory takes two forms: recall and recognition. The former activity occurs in the absence of any stimulus to prompt the memory. This is a more difficult task than recognition, which does involve some prompting. An understanding of how we remember is useful in the planning of the marketing effort. At its simplest level, we can see the advantage of integrating advertising with point-of-sale displays to aid the memory process.

A final input from psychology concerns models of the decision-making process. One such model combines the following:

- determinants of behaviour – personality, culture, reference groups;
- consumers' wants and needs;
- marketing activities of the firm;
- the perception of such marketing activities;
- inhibitors or constraints on our purchasing – price, availability, income;
- the decision whether to buy or not.

We have looked at aspects of three social sciences that provide different insights into buying behaviour. The theory has to be translated into practical marketing to be of interest to commercially-minded business organizations. The remainder of this chapter will provide examples of the translation of theory into practice.

Market segmentation

The population of any country is not uniform but consists of millions of individuals. These individuals can be grouped in a large number of ways, according to: gender, age, occupation, family status, size and so on. Each group (or segment) has a unity and distinctiveness that separates it from other segments. If the behaviour (especially the buying behaviour) of a particular group is distinctive, then it could have significance in marketing terms. Particular groups could be targeted in the promotional activities of the seller.

There are, however, some classifications that are of no significance in marketing terms. For instance, we could divide the population in terms of eye colour. If it could be demonstrated that brown-eyed people behaved differently from other groups, then eye colour could be used as the basis for segmentation. However, in the absence of such evidence, we can say that although classification by eye colour might be interesting, it does not form the basis of any marketing strategy.

The first task for those engaged in marketing is to segment the population in ways appropriate to marketing. The major methods of segmenting the market are shown in Tables 17.2 and 17.3.

There are some classifications that are worthy of more detailed examination. For instance, households can be categorized in terms of the family lifecycle, the phases of which are listed below.

- Single – young, no ties.
- Newly married – young, no children.
- Full nest (1) – youngest child under six.
- Full nest (2) – youngest child over six.
- Full nest (3) – children still at home, but working.
- Empty nest (1) – children left home, one partner still working.
- Empty nest (2) – both partners retired.
- Solitary survivor (1) – still at work.
- Solitary survivor (2) – retired.

Table 17.2 Segmentation in consumer and industrial markets

Consumer markets	Industrial market
Income	Type of business
Socio-economic group	Size of business
Occupation	Size of purchase
Benefit sought	Creditworthiness
Stage in family lifecycle	Service requirements
Loyalty status	Location
Geography, lifestyle	

Table 17.3 Socio-economic classifications

Social grade	Social status	Occupation
A	Upper middle class	Higher managerial or professional
B	Middle class	Middle managerial, administrative or professional
C1	Lower middle class	Supervisory, clerical, junior managerial, administrative or professional
C2	Skilled working class	Skilled manual worker
D	Working class	Semi-skilled and unskilled manual workers
E	Subsistence level	Casual or lowest grade workers

This classification is important for a number of reasons. First, the disposable income of the head of the household will change during the cycle. Although income in the single household is likely to be lower than that of the full nest (1), discretionary income could be much higher. Full nest households often have low discretionary income. Full nest (3) and empty nest households will benefit from a rise in discretionary income as children cease to be dependent and as mortgage commitments come to an end.

Second, the pattern of spending will change over the family lifecycle. For instance, consumer durable goods (such as furniture) will be sold to newly married households, and to full nest (3) and empty nest (1) households as replacement becomes essential.

Finally, the empty nest and solitary survivor households are likely to grow in importance because, with an ageing population, there will be more pensioner households. In addition, although many pensioners have low incomes and rely on the State pension, there is a growing number of people with an occupational pension and, moreover, a substantial asset (an owner-occupied house), which can be converted into cash. Business organizations are increasingly recognizing the importance of this market segment.

The **ACORN** classification (see Table 17.4) is segmentation based on neighbourhood types. The acronym stands for A Classification Of Residential Neighbourhoods, and it identifies 38 different types of neighbourhood according to housing and social characteristics. It is based on the proposition that most people in such neighbourhoods share common lifestyle features and patterns of behaviour, including purchasing behaviour.

ACORN is used by credit firms and those involved in mailshots. It might also be an important factor in the siting of a retail outlet.

Another interesting classification is based on attitudes and motivation. Three distinct types of people can be identified.

- **Subsistence types** These people choose on the basis of price and seek bargains.
- **Discriminators** These people choose on the basis of quality rather than price.
- **Hedonists** These people seek immediate gratification. This classification is independent of income so that the 'fun-loving' hedonist group includes both the very rich and people of limited income who spend their money on a hobby or going out.

This classification could be very useful in devising marketing strategies, especially in terms of the components of the marketing mix.

Table 17.4 ACORN classification of neighbourhoods

A1	Agricultural villages	F21	Council housing for the elderly
A2	Areas of farms and smallholdings	G22	New council estates in industrial towns
B3	Cheap modern private housing	G23	Overspill estates, high unemployment
B4	Recent private housing, young families	G24	Council estates with overcrowding
B5	Modern private housing, older families	G25	Council estates with worst poverty
B6	New detached houses, young families	H26	Multi-occupied terraces
B7	Military bases	H27	Owner-occupied terraces, Asians
C8	Mixed owner-occupied and council estates	H28	Multi-let housing with Afro-Caribbeans
C9	Small town centres and flats above shops	H29	Better-off multi-ethnic areas
C10	Villages with non-farm employment	I30	High-status areas, few children
C11	Older private housing, skilled workers	I31	Multi-let big old houses and flats
D12	Unimproved terraces, low-income families	I32	Furnished flats, mostly single people
D13	Pre-1914 terraces, low-income families	I33	Inter-war semis, white collar workers
D14	Tenement flats lacking amenities	I34	Spacious inter-war semi; big garden
E15	Council estates with well off workers	I35	Villages with wealthy older commuters
E16	Recent council estates	I36	Detached houses, exclusive suburbs
E17	Council estates, well off young workers	I37	Private houses, well off elderly
E18	Small council houses, often in Scotland	I38	Private flats with single pensioners
F19	Low-rise estates in industrial towns	I39	Unclassified
F20	Inter-war council estates		

A final classification divides consumers into four types based on their degree of brand loyalty:

- hard core loyal consumers;
- soft core loyal consumers;
- shifting consumers who shift for long periods but return;
- switching consumers with no brand loyalty.

One use of this classification is that it provides the basis for promotional activity as the last-mentioned group is very susceptible to brand switching induced by promotional gimmicks. More importantly, identification of these groups is an important prelude to understanding why brand switching occurs.

Targeting segments

When faced with the existence of a heterogeneous market, the firm has to decide on its strategy with respect to the various distinct segments. Should it target a particular segment or attempt to sell to all categories of customer? If it adopts the latter policy, should it offer the same mix of the Four Ps to all segments or adopt different mixes for each segment? Three segmentation strategies (see Figure 17.2) can be identified.

- **Undifferentiated marketing** can be compared to a shotgun. In effect, it ignores the existence of segments and offers a single mix to the heterogeneous market. This failure to target is likely to result in a disappointing level of sales.
- In **concentrated marketing**, a particular segment is targeted. The firm adopts a mix that it considers most effective and appropriate for that particular segment. If undifferentiated marketing can be compared to a shotgun, concentrated marketing is like a high-powered rifle. In some cases (such as retirement flats, certain holidays) the product is not available to people outside the target segment. In other cases, the product is available to all, even though the firm expects only its target group to purchase the goods. For reasons of economy, small firms are likely to adopt a strategy of concentrated marketing rather than disperse their efforts far and wide.
- In **differentiated marketing**, a separate mix is developed for each segment of the market. This strategy is very costly and is, therefore, only available to large firms. The major tour operators produce a general brochure for the

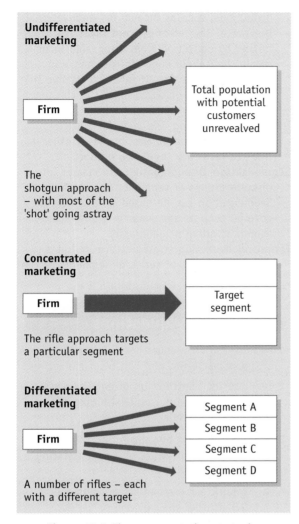

Figure 17.2 Three segmentation strategies

majority of potential customers who like a family holiday with sun, sea and sand. They all produce separate mixes for specialist segments, such as those who like lakes and mountains or 'city break' holidays; skiers; those interested in activity holidays such as pony-trekking; naturists; the young; and the old. Similarly, banks and building societies have developed different accounts to suit the needs of different types of customers.

The arguments for and against segmentation are summarized in Table 17.5.

The diffusion process

In Chapter 18 we investigate the development of a new product to the launch stage and beyond. An interesting phenomenon occurs in relation to the spread (or diffusion) of the product through the population. The early buyers of a successful product tend not to be typical people, but are what can be called **opinion leaders**. They are receptive to new ideas and enjoy higher than average income and status. Consequently, these trendsetters, who are prepared to behave in new ways, are important in terms of their influence on others.

A model of the diffusion process utilizes the curve of normal distribution to identify the following five groups of people in terms of their adoption of the product:

- **innovators** 2.5 per cent of the population, young, high status, high income;
- **early adopters** 13.5 per cent of the population, influential within a local area – together with the innovators, they are 'influentials';

Table 17.5 Market segmentation

Arguments in favour	Arguments against
● More efficient use of marketing resources	● Increased R&D costs to develop product variations
● Gain competitive advantage in part of the market	● Increased production costs for product variations (such as shorter production runs)
● Beneficial for small firms to concentrate their effort	● Higher stockholding costs
● Products tailored to match demand	● Higher advertising and administrative costs
● Marketing mix is targeted	
● Facilitates identification of market opportunities	

- **early majority** 34 per cent of the population, these people are deliberative, taking time to decide;
- **late majority** 34 per cent of the population, below average incomes;
- **laggards** 16 per cent of the population. Low income groups.

This model has more than academic interest. Marketers will conclude that the successful launch of a product should involve the targeting of the two groups of 'influentials'. There is little point in targeting the majority, who will delay the adoption of a new product until it has been accepted by the influentials.

The decision-making unit

Many goods are bought not by an individual acting alone, but by a group of people (such as a family). Marketers have found it useful to analyse decision making within the family in order to identify the key players in the process. Although it might be thought that 'Mum and Dad' make the decisions and the rest of the family is irrelevant, in fact even young members of the family can play one of the following roles:

- the **initiator** who suggests a purchase;
- the **influencer** who brings pressure to bear;
- the **gatekeeper** who is knowledgeable about the product and can filter information;
- the **decider** – the mother and/or father;
- the **purchaser** who actually makes the purchase;
- the **user** – often the whole family.

This analysis suggests that marketing should be aimed not just at the deciders but at each member of the family as they all contribute to the decision-making process.

Key concepts

Consumer The ultimate user of goods and services. Hence, the consumer market refers to the market in which households (as distinct from other firms) are the customers.
Disposable income and discretionary income The former is income after compulsory

deductions, such as income tax and National Insurance. The latter concept takes it a stage further by deducting from disposable income regular household commitments, such as payments to utilities. It refers to income that can be spent or disposed of as the consumer chooses.
Industrial marketing The marketing of industrial goods that are bought by other firms to facilitate their own production.
Segmentation Disaggregating the market into discrete groups or segments of customers. Segmentation can be based on a variety of criteria, such as age, income group, socio-economic group or geography.
Targeting Marketing strategies directed at a distinct segment or series of segments of the market.

Essay questions

1 Analyse the differences between business-to-business marketing and consumer marketing.

2 Evaluate the contribution of each of the social sciences to our understanding of consumer behaviour.

3 (a) What is meant by segmenting the market?
  (b) Analyse the benefits of a segmentation strategy.

4 (a) Explain four ways of segmenting the market other than by age or gender.
  (b) Justifying your answer, state appropriate ways to segment the market for the following products:
  • foreign holidays;
  • perfume;
  • cars;
  • computer software;
  • public transport;
  • mobile phones.

5 Explain why it is beneficial to analyse:
  (a) the process of decision making within households;
  (b) why people choose particular brands.

18

Products and the product mix

'Product planning is the process of developing and maintaining a portfolio of products which will satisfy defined customer needs and wants, maximize profitability and make the best use of the skills and resources of the company' (M. Armstrong, *A Handbook of Management Techniques*, Kogan Page, 1993).

Armstrong's definition of product planning identifies key elements in the process. First, 'developing and maintaining' means that it is a continuing process of planning. Second, in this context, 'portfolio' means a collection of products supplied by a firm. The analysis of the product lifecycle shows the folly of relying on a single (and ultimately doomed) product. Third, 'satisfying customers' needs and wants' is a reminder of the importance of marketing orientation.

The final part of the definition reminds us that the objective of private enterprise firms is to achieve at least a target level of profits, and this requires the effective and efficient use of resources.

Product planning is, therefore, a rational, market-oriented approach to decision making about both individual products and the mixture of products supplied by a business organization. This chapter surveys the various aspects of the process.

Chapter objectives

1 To analyse the process of new product development.

2 To analyse the technique of positioning products.

3 To survey the role of packaging and branding in the marketing process.

4 To provide an introduction to the strategic aspects of marketing, with particular reference to the analysis of the product mix.

New product development (NPD)

By a **new product** we mean one of the following:

- a new, innovative product distinct from anything else in existence;
- a significant adaptation of an existing product;
- an imitative or 'me too' product;
- a simulated adaptation in which the customer perceives a difference from an existing product.

Whatever category of new product we are talking about, it still requires a period of development prior to launch on the market (see Figure 18.1). The importance of NPD is easy to understand as

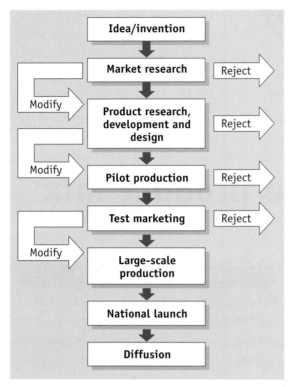

Figure 18.1 Product development

innovation is necessary for the continued success of the firm. No matter how successful its products are at present, they will eventually enter a period of decline. New products are essential to replace declining products and, given the long period needed to develop them (five years for a new car, ten years or more for some pharmaceutical products), it is important to have new products in the pipeline.

The process of NPD consists of:

● identifying and evaluating new product opportunities;
● developing products; and
● testing the marketability of the products.

The ideas for new products are generated from the firm's market research, technological forecasting (predicting the technology of the future) and from research and development (R&D) projects. It is usual to divide research into **pure research**, motivated by curiosity, and **applied research**.

Pure research sometimes results in commercial products (Teflon saucepans are a by-product of space research, for example) but this is not its main purpose. Business organizations are unlikely to put resources into pure research, preferring problem-oriented research with a view to commercial exploitation. Out of research come ideas and inventions, but they have to be translated into usable and commercially viable products.

Before an idea is developed into a product, it is necessary to evaluate the product in terms of marketability and profitability. The process of judging whether or not it is worth while proceeding with the product development is known as **screening**. The following questions should be answered.

● Does the product meet a defined customer need?
● In which segment or segments can it be sold?
● How well does it fit in with the existing range of products?
● What position will it occupy in the market?
● Does the firm possess the resources, skills and expertise to develop, produce and market the product?
● If not, how can they be obtained?
● What investment is required to develop the product?
● What is the expected return on investment?

After the screening process, new product ideas are developed into **product concepts** in which the market, the benefits of the product and its position in relation to rivals is tested by means of consumer research. It is only when the idea has passed the initial screening process that the firm will be prepared to commit large sums of money to the physical development of a product that can be marketed. The idea is converted into a prototype and is subjected to laboratory tests and other technical evaluation.

The **development process** converts the prototype into a saleable product. One aspect of this is design, which takes two forms. **Functional design** is concerned with the structure and operation of the product – does it work, is it suitable for its purpose? **Formal design** concerns the appearance of the product – is it appealing? The designer's problem is to reconcile the functional requirements with formal ones. Products that are attractive will not enjoy continuing success unless they serve the need for which they were intended. Similarly, a product that is functionally sound will fail if customers are repelled by its appearance.

Obviously, the relative importance of the two aspects of design will vary from product to product. At the fashion end of the clothing market, formal design is crucially important (although the product must also be functionally sound). However, when designing machinery for factory use, appearance is far less important than the performance of the product. Motor cars are purchased partly on performance (speed, fuel consumption, reliability) and partly on appearance.

Customer requirements will be uppermost in the minds of product developers and designers. A judgement has to be made as to what is an unnecessary 'extra' facility and what is crucial in gaining customer acceptance. For example, most motorists regard a car radio as an essential feature of a car, whereas more economically minded motorists might regard rear windscreen wipers or headlight wipers as an unimportant luxury with which they could dispense. An analytical technique to aid decision making in this respect is known as **value analysis**, which aims to optimize the value of the product to the customer. The vital question to ask is whether or not the same result can be achieved more effectively, or as effectively, at a lower cost. Consider a product assembled from a number of components. Suppose the finished product (say, a washing machine) has an expected life of 15 years, but that one of its components will last for 50 years. We might be tempted to see this as evidence of good design and craftsmanship, but it is not desirable commercially – the component is 'too good'. If a less costly component with a shorter life is available, it should be used as there is no point in producing components that outlive the overall product. Despite widespread criticisms of so-called 'built-in obsolescence', many consumers will *want* to replace furniture or kitchen equipment after ten or twenty years – they do not want goods that last forever. Consequently, the substitution of an expensive material with a cheaper (but less long-lasting) alternative is not cynical exploitation of the consumer, but sound marketing, responding to the needs of consumers.

As well as appearance and performance, there is a third criterion to satisfy. This concerns economy of manufacture and ease of storage and distribution. A product that is functionally sound and aesthetically pleasing but prohibitively expensive to manufacture will be of little use to a business organization. In processes that involve cutting out shapes (such as the clothing industry), design should take into account the production of scrap and waste materials. The greater the wastage and scrap element, the greater the cost.

The main factors influencing the design of a product can be summarised as:

- **performance** of the product, which can be subdivided into:
  - efficiency;
  - reliability;
  - ease of operation;
  - safety in operation;
  - ease of maintenance.
- **appearance** of the product;
- **economy** of manufacture, distribution and storage.
- **legal requirements** – for example, there are controls over the paint used in children's toys or the materials used in teddy bears;
- **environmental concerns** of the public – this is seen in the switch to unleaded petrol, to which car manufacturers have had to respond;
- **market requirements**;
- **company policy**;
- **competitor activity**.

After the design stage has been successfully completed, it is usual to engage in small-scale or pilot products to test whether or not the product can be manufactured economically. This will be followed by test marketing in which the product is launched on a limited scale in a representative part of the market. The objectives of this exercise are to gauge customers' reactions to the product and the way in which it is marketed, and to forecast future sales of the product. If, and only if, the product succeeds at this stage will the production department 'tool up' for, and schedule, the production of the new product ready for the national or international market.

Product failure

Most products fail at various stages of the NPD process. Given the escalating cost of NPD, it is always preferable for products to fail at the ideas stage rather than after a lengthy and costly process of development. Figure 18.2 shows the rising cost of NPD as it moves through the various stages. For this reason, business organizations will be prepared to abandon a new product, even at a late stage, rather than risk further losses, coupled with the morale-sagging effect of failure following a product launch.

Sometimes products do reach the market but fail to gain the acceptance of customers. This can be attributed either to failure in the marketing process or to an unanticipated change in the external environment. In particular, we can identify the following causes of new product failure:

- inadequate market research;
- misleading market research findings;
- defects in the product;
- activities of competitors;
- insufficient or inappropriate marketing efforts;
- distribution problems;
- unexpectedly high costs;
- inadequate salesforce.

Positioning a product

To 'position' a product, it is necessary to define the location of a product relative to others in the same marketplace and then promote it in such a way as to reinforce or change its position. Position is, therefore, relative to other products in the market.

To locate a product's **position**, it is first necessary to analyse the market to discover the key attributes that form the image of the product in the consumer's mind. This means the process is subjective and concerns the way in which the product is perceived by customers relative to other products. The key attribute will vary from product to product. In Figure 18.3 price and calorific value have been chosen. Alternative attributes for particular products might include strength (beer), fibre content (breakfast cereals) or quality. In the case of a business organization (such as a supermarket chain) the key attributes might include product range, quality, price range, size and location.

After identifying two key attributes, market research can be employed to gauge public perception of the product in terms of these attributes. Hence, a product might be high in price but low in calories. With information from market research, it is possible to map the position of the product and its rivals. The mapping exercise might reveal a cluster of products in one part of the map but a gap in another part of the market. For firms developing new products, and for firms trying to reposition an existing product (going upmarket, for instance), there is a choice of strategies. One strategy is to imitate an existing successful product. The different brands of cola provide an example of this 'me too' strategy (see Z in Figure 18.3). Alternatively, the firm might prefer to occupy a 'gap' in the market (see Y in Figure 18.3). The former strategy is often seen as less risky, but with lower prospects of substantial profits. Products that seek to occupy a gap in the market have a lower probability of success, although, if they are successful, profits will be substantial.

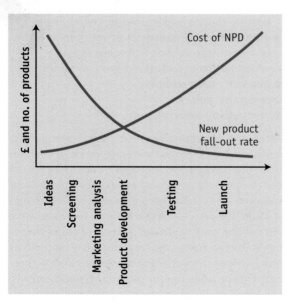

Figure 18.2 New product fall-out

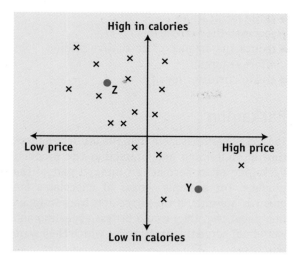

Figure 18.3 A positioning map

This suggests that decisions about positioning can usefully employ decision tree analysis.

Brands

In *Marketing Management* (Prentice Hall, 1996) Philip Kotler defines a **brand** as 'a name, term, symbol or design which is intended to signify the goods and services of one seller or group of sellers and to differentiate them from competitors'.

The brand becomes a force in the marketplace, adding to the appeal of the product. Its precise marketing functions are as follows.

- It provides the product with an identity and aids identification by the customer. 'The essence of any brand is that it is more than an undifferentiated commodity product. It is the perception of the buyers, it has a unique identity' (G. Randall, *Principles of Marketing*, Routledge, 1993).
- It is a shorthand summary of all the information customers hold about the product.
- It provides a sense of security, reassurance about the quality of goods inside the package. This arises out of our familiarity with the brand.
- It adds value to the product, making it more appealing.
- It is intended to help create and sustain the

loyalty of customers. Brand loyalty comes about as a result of customers' continuing satisfaction with the product and heavy promotion. Once brand loyalty is achieved, it reduces the impact of advertising by competitive brands and discourages brand switching.

To achieve these marketing benefits, the brand has to be built and maintained. To accomplish this it is essential to produce goods of the quality required by customers, differentiate them from rivals, ensure that the product is consistent, provide support (by promotional activity, for example) and ensure that the product evolves to match the needs and preoccupations of customers. Some brands relate to an individual product (such as Lenor, Branston Pickle, Brillo), whereas others cover a range of products (Heinz, Menu Master). Some are owned by manufacturers (Bird's Eye), while others are owned by retailers (St Michael). The main types of brand include the following.

- **Individual brands** for a particular product, such as Pampers.
- **Family brands** containing the name of the company making the product, such as Heinz Baked Beans, Heinz Tomato Ketchup. The great advantage of family brands is that customers loyal to one member of the family are more likely to try other products in that family than if there was no link with other products. These other products benefit from a 'halo' effect and, in the case of a new addition to the family, a 'piggy-back' effect.
- **Family brands** covering a range of products but not containing the name of the company concerned. For instance, Persil is a Unilever brand but the brand covers a range of different washing powers and liquids and now, by extension, washing-up liquid as well. In some companies, the family brand covers a range of products that are in competition with other products of the firm that are in a different family. The reason firms produce competing brands is to appeal to different market segments and reduce the chance of losing customers as a result of brand switching (a customer who abandons one

Proctor & Gamble product is likely to, unwittingly, switch to another Proctor & Gamble product).

- **Division brands** In some cases, the brand is attached to a division of a large organization. For example, McVitie is a division of United Biscuits and the firm's products are known as 'McVitie's Hob-Nobs' and so on.
- **Distributors' brands** The best examples of these are supermarket own brands made for, but rarely by, the major supermarket chains. For the retailer, the own brand is an attempt to create loyalty to the shop rather than the product. It enables them to assert greater control over the production function, with goods made to their specification. In most, but not all, cases they are cheaper versions of the famous name products. Manufacturers are usually willing to produce for supermarkets because of the regular and large orders this brings. Producing supermarkets' brands also provides a good example of marginal costing (see Chapter 32). It is also of interest that, under consumer law, supermarkets have liability as 'producers' of the goods. However, the policy of some manufacturers is not to produce supermarkets' own brands (Kellogg's famously proclaim that they do not produce for anyone else). In 1994, Coca-Cola strongly objected to Sainsbury's own brand Classic Cola, which was too similar in appearance to their own product. This was merely the most famous example in the UK of manufacturers resenting the attempt by supermarkets to capture a large market share by own brands that were too similar in appearance to the maker's brand.

To sum up, successful brand names:

- are remembered;
- convey the benefits and characteristics of the product;
- are short and easily pronounced;
- are distinctive;
- should be capable of being legally protected.

The main functions of branding are to:

- differentiate the product from those of rivals;
- aid identification;
- segment the market;
- reduce the amount of persuasive selling effort required;
- create customer loyalty.

Packaging

Packaging performs more than the utilitarian function of containing and protecting the product. Packaging often becomes an integral part of the product. For example, boxes of chocolates are given as presents; if the chocolates were wrapped in a paper bag, they would be less appealing and would not serve the function for which they were purchased.

Packaging helps to identify the product, especially when the colours, logos and designs on the packaging are used as themes in advertising. Packaging, therefore, offers a unique promotional opportunity to provide a constant reminder of the product. Firms will seek distinctive packaging so that the product is instantly recognizable (Toblerone and Biarritz chocolates, Mateus Rosé wine are examples). Distinctiveness is very important when goods are competing with rivals on the shelves of supermarkets. If advertising informs the customer, then packaging prompts the memory of the customer.

Packaging can be used to extend the life of the product, either by revitalizing interest in the product itself (such as a new cover design for a paperback novel) or by enabling the product to penetrate new markets. An example of packaging providing new market opportunities was the ring-pull can, which has enabled soft drink and lager makers to expand their markets, with the product being consumed by people 'on the move'. Similarly, the waxed carton has created new market opportunities for makers of wine and orange juice.

Product mix

A **product line** is a group of products that are closely related in that they have similar characteristics, similar uses or are sold to the same type of customer. Examples include different models of motor vehicles or different brands of detergent sold by the same business organization. Those in charge of marketing may wish to extend the length of the product line (greater differentiation of product) or, alternatively, to concentrate on a shorter line (reduce variations).

The **product mix** of a particular business organization is defined as a combination of all its product lines. In other words, it is the sum of all the different products, with model and size variations. The nature of the product lifecycle means that it is desirable, if not essential, for business organizations to possess a portfolio of products at various stages in their lifecycles. This portfolio has to be managed in response to changes in:

● population;
● buying habits;
● income;
● the activities of competitors;
● the technological environment;
● production costs.

The nature and direction of the changes in the mix will vary with circumstances. However, one interesting matrix provides a useful insight into changes in the marketing mix.

The Boston Matrix

Colourful terminology has made the Boston Matrix (see Figure 18.4) appealing to managers and students alike. The market share of a product is plotted on the horizontal axis with market growth on the vertical. Products within a firm's product mix can be classified in terms of four groups.

1 Products with small market share but high growth are known variously as **question mark**, **problem child** or **wildcat** products. All new products will start from this box but their future is uncertain. To increase market share, cash injection and a

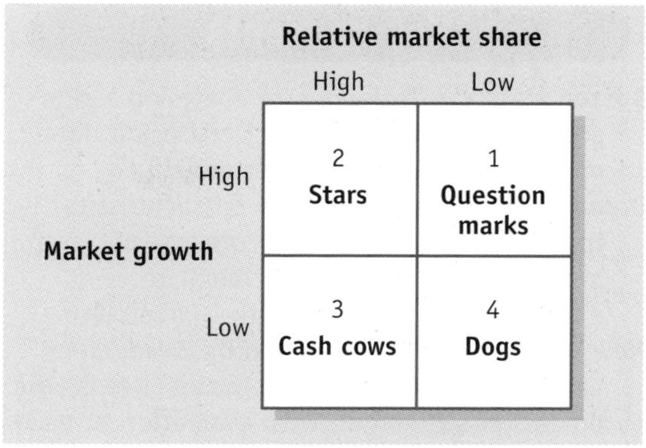

Figure 18.4 The Boston Matrix

planned, coordinated marketing effort is essential.

2 Successful products will eventually move into this box, where both market share and market growth are high. These **star** products are profitable and will continue to be so in the future.

3 **Cash cows** enjoy a high market share, although market growth is low. Cash cows, which are the net generators of funds, are 'milked' to supply finance for new product development.

4 This group of products are known as dogs. **Dogs** have both a low share of the market and there is little growth in the market. These products are, therefore, a 'lost cause'. There is little to be gained from any further investment in such products.

The Boston Matrix provides a valuable tool for analysing a firm's product range and helps to identify strengths and weaknesses. Not only does it provide a snapshot at a moment in time, it can be adapted to forecast the position of the firm's products at some point in the future. From such an analysis, strategies can be developed for each product.

Key concepts

Boston Matrix A technique of analysing a firm's product portfolio or product mix using data on market share and market growth.

Brand A product with a set of characteristics that makes it distinct from other rival products. Branding is an attempt to differentiate a product in the marketplace.

New product development (NPD) Developing new products to satisfy customers' needs. The process is sequential, with evaluation at each stage of development.

Niche marketing A strategy of concentrating on a particular segment or niche of the market.

Positioning Defining the location of a product relative to other products in the marketplace.

Product mix or product portfolio The complete range of products supplied by a firm. It comprises all the product lines (groups of products) of the firm.

Essay questions

1 (a) What is meant by a 'me too' product?
  (b) Evaluate the benefits of a 'me too' strategy for a firm seeking to enter an established market.

2 Identify and evaluate five strategies of extending the product lifecycle.

3 Evaluate the product lifecycle as a tool of analysis in marketing.

4 (a) Analyse the likely causes of product failure.
  (b) If a product fails soon after launch, there has been a failure in market research. Discuss.

5 Why do most product ideas never reach the market?

6 Evaluate:
  (a) the Boston Matrix; and
  (b) a positioning map;
  as tools of marketing analysis.

19

Promotional strategies

Business organizations have to devise appropriate ways of communicating with potential customers in order to sell their goods and services. The name given to the variety of communication techniques is promotion. It includes, but is not confined to, advertising. The different promotional forms are combined in a promotional mix that should be designed to be appropriate for the particular product. Our main concern with regard to promotion is the analysis and evaluation of the different promotional techniques available to business organizations.

Chapter objectives

1 To understand the role of promotion in achieving organizational objectives.

2 To survey and analyse different techniques of promotion.

3 To develop an understanding of methods of evaluating promotional techniques.

4 To develop an appreciation of the need to evolve a promotional mix appropriate to the particular product and organization.

Introduction to promotional activities

Organizations engage in promotional activities to communicate with customers or clients. Promotion should be seen as series of techniques for informing, influencing and persuading customers. It takes a number of different forms, of which advertising is merely one.

- **Advertising** is non-personal, one-way communication to promote the sale of goods or services via paid-for advertisements in the media.
- **Publicity** is promotion via press releases to the news media. Press releases are issued in the expectation that they will be given editorial mention at no charge.
- **Direct mailing** involves direct communication with customers, either in the form of a letter addressed to the recipient (in which case it is called a **mail shot**) or an unaddressed communication (known as a **mail drop**).
- **Packaging** is promotion by means of design and display. The intention is to create an impact at the point of sale.
- The term **sales promotion** covers a range of activities, such as competitions, gifts, point-of-sale displays, leaflets and sponsorship.
- **Personal selling** is a promotional presentation made on a person-to-person basis. The significant feature of this activity

Table 19.1 Promotional tools

Advertising	Sales promotion	Publicity	Personal selling
Print	Contests	Speeches	Sales presentations
Broadcasting	Games	Seminars	Sales meetings
Packaging inserts	Samples	Public relations	Telemarketing
Mailing	Trade shows	Sponsorship	Salespeople
Catalogues	Demonstrations		Samples
Brochures	Coupons		
Posters	Exhibitions		
Leaflets	Rebates		
Directories	Trade-in allowances		
Display signs	Trading samples		
Logos	Premiums		
Films			

is the two-way discussion between salesperson and potential buyer.

Table 19.1 sets out different promotional tools.

The promotional mix

The exact combination of promotional activities will vary with the product. Advertising and personal selling are the two main ways in which products are promoted. The remaining four techniques are employed in a supporting role to back up advertising or personal selling, which provide the main thrust to the promotional campaign.

The mix used for a particular product will be affected by a variety of factors.

● **The nature of the product** As a general rule, if products are inexpensive, simple and purchased by consumers, they are advertised but there is little personal selling involved. When you buy a Mars Bar, the sales assistant does not persuade you of its delicious taste or nutritional value. On the other hand, if you were purchasing complicated and expensive machinery for a factory, you would expect to engage in two-way conversation with the salesperson – advertising plays little or no part in that process. Between the two extremes, products such as cars or electrical goods (consumer durable products) are purchased after the customer has experienced a combination of advertising and personal

selling, supported by other promotional activities (see Figure 19.1.).

● **The nature of the market and its customers** Advertising plays a greater role in the consumer market than in the industrial market, in which the customers are other firms. Moreover, the nature of advertising will be substantially different (in style, content and delivery) in the industrial market.

● **The product lifecycle** The level of sales promotion employed will depend on which stage the product is at in its lifecycle. For

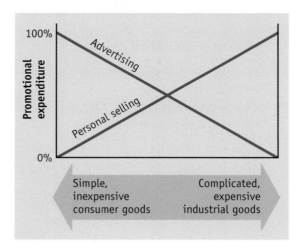

Figure 19.1 The relative importance of advertising and selling

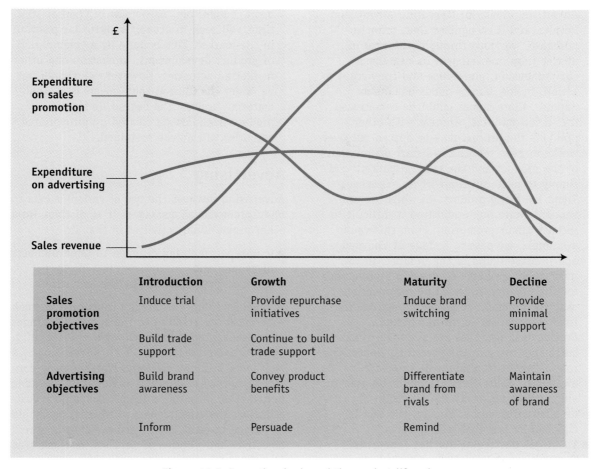

Figure 19.2 Promotional mix and the product lifecycle

example, sales promotion is widely used at the launch stage, or if the product lifecycle is being extended, but it is less likely to be used in the mature phase (see Figure 19.2).

● **Relative costs and the availability of funds**
Business organizations will seek the promotional mix that is most effective in terms of achieving the firm's objectives, subject to the usual financial constraints.

Promotional objectives

The ultimate objective of promotion is to increase sales and profits, but promotional activities might be designed to achieve particular tactical objectives.

● **To increase awareness of the product**
Figure 19.3 illustrates the Dagmar model of buying behaviour. Dagmar stands for Defining

Figure 19.3 Dagmar communication spectrum: defining advertising goals for measured advertising results

Advertising Goals for Measuring Advertising Results, and it recognizes that, prior to purchase, we move through a number of phases from unawareness to awareness, comprehension, preference and conviction to action. In the case of goods bought on impulse, these stages might be compressed into a few minutes, whereas with other products the process may be spaced out over weeks or even months. We start off unaware of the product and the task of marketing is simply to make us aware of its existence. There are many products of which we are vaguely aware but would find it difficult to recall without prompting. From this vague awareness, we pass to a stage of knowledge and understanding of the product. In the next stage, we begin to develop a preference for the product, followed by a conviction that the product should be purchased. The final stage is the act of purchasing. Promotional activities are designed to move customers through the spectrum. Hence, the role of advertising might be to create awareness. Sales literature might be used to aid comprehension by the provision of detailed information. Finally, the sale is clinched by personal selling.

- **To target particular market segments.**
- **To position the product** in relation to its

main competitors. As we saw in Chapter 18, firms will seek to occupy a particular position in the market. This is done by a combination of product development, promotion and other marketing activities. However, we should not be under the illusion that 'image' is all that matters – unless it is backed up by the product itself, image created by promotional activities will not be sustained.

Advertising

Advertising involves the use of various media to relay promotional messages. It is distinct from other promotional activities in that it:

- is non-personal and directed to large numbers of people; and
- involves media paid for by the advertiser.

In Business Studies we are not concerned so much with questions relating to the social advantages and disadvantages, or even with the morality, of advertising (see Table 19.2). Advertising is a legitimate business strategy. We should be concerned not with whether or not it is desirable but whether or not a particular campaign is cost-effective. The effectiveness of advertising should be judged in terms of the achievement of stated objectives and whether or not they were achieved in a profitable way.

Table 19.2 The cases for and against advertising

In defence of advertising	Criticisms of advertising
• Advertising informs • It is part of the competitive process • It allows consumers to make a more informed choice • It can act as a guarantee of quality • It allows a reduction of expenditure on other forms of sales promotion, such as personal selling • It acts as an aid to product identification • By helping to reduce sales fluctuations, it assists in planning production • An increase in the volume of sales leads to an increase in output and, therefore, economies of scale are passed on in lower prices	• Advertising raises costs and, therefore, prices • It is a waste of resources • It raises prices without adding to the value of products • It persuades people to consume unnecessary and unwanted goods and services (assuming that people are gullible) • It is often used as a way of maintaining monopoly power by preventing the entry of new rivals • It can be misleading (but advertising is controlled by bodies such as the Advertising Standards Authority) • Advertising stimulates wants that cannot be satisfied • The economies of scale are not passed on

A common fallacy is the belief that advertising guarantees success. Advertising will only be successful if the chosen message and media are appropriate, the product is able to satisfy a demand, the economic climate is favourable and other elements of the marketing mix are consistent. An inappropriate message will seriously harm the product. Today's big budget television advertisements are aesthetically pleasing and can be minor masterpieces of cinematography. However, this is not the same as success and effectiveness from the advertiser's point of view. In fact, sometimes an advertisement benefits rival products as the public remembers the jingle or visual image but may forget the name of the product.

The effectiveness of advertising is measured in terms of a change in sales revenue. Adapting the elasticity formulae encountered earlier, we can measure advertising elasticity as:

$$\frac{\text{Proportionate change in sales volume}}{\text{Proportionate change in advertising expenditure}}$$

If a 50 per cent rise in advertising expenditure on a product is followed by a 75 per cent rise in the volume of sales, advertising elasticity works out at 75/50, or 1.5. This suggests that the advertising was successful in generating additional sales greater than the rise in expenditure. However, we have assumed that there was a causal relationship between the two, that the increase in advertising expenditure was the *cause* of the rise in sales. It is possible that the extra sales would have occurred even without the advertising campaign.

Choice of media

One important factor in the success of an advertising campaign is the choice of media. The main media employed in advertising are newspapers, television, radio, magazines, cinema and outdoor posters. Although we frequently associate advertising with television, it should be remembered that, for the majority of firms in the UK, television advertising is not appropriate. The criteria by which the media should be judged are as follows.

- **The 'reach' of the media**, or the proportion of the target audience that can be contacted. In the case of the printed media, this is the readership of the publication (which, incidentally, is not the same as its circulation). In the case of television, the reach should be revealed by the ratings figures. However, the fact that a television set was switched on does not prove that people were either watching it or absorbing the advertising message.
- **The selectivity of the media** Specialist magazines may have a small readership but these readers may be the target audience. There is an old saying in advertising: '50 per cent of all advertising is wasted, unfortunately we don't know which 50 per cent'. Media that are highly selective will reduce the wastage in advertising.
- **The relative cost**, such as the cost per thousand of population. For firms that can afford television advertising rates, it is very cost-effective.
- **The impact of the media** This is the extent to which the message is effectively taken in. Outdoor advertising is inexpensive and reaches large numbers of people, but is its message absorbed?
- **The product itself** If it is necessary to demonstrate the product in action, then television is the most appropriate medium. If it is necessary to provide a vast quantity of information, then the medium of print is most appropriate.
- **The permanence of the advertisement** When advertising a service that people require infrequently, it is useful to advertise in a way that creates a permanent record. Firms that produce self-adhesive address labels (such as Able-Label) sold by mail order advertise weekly in the national newspapers to ensure that information is available to potential customers whenever they need it. The local plumber, similarly, finds it useful to run a regular advertisement in a weekly free newspaper to ensure permanence of record. Better still, is a block advertisement in Yellow Pages.

Table 19.3 indicates the advantages and dis-

Table 19.3 Evaluation of advertising media

Media	Advantages	Disadvantages
Newspapers	High coverage Flexible Relatively low cost Targeting via readership profile Local newspapers are selective geographically	Short life No movement or sound Problem of gaining and retaining attention
Television	High coverage – large reach Visual impact Targeting via audience for programme Sight, sound and motion all in one Demonstrations possible	High cost Short life Cannot refer back Conveys only limited information Low in terms of flexibility Proliferation of TV channels reduces audience for particular programmes Remote control channel tuners lose audiences
Radio	Geographically selective Low cost	Short life No visual stimuli Low attention
Cinema	Locally, high selectivity	Low cinema attendance Low attention level
Outdoor	High in coverage High readership Low cost Comparatively long life	Only conveys small amount of information Lost in clutter of information
Magazines	Targets selected audience Relatively long life High-quality reproduction	High cost Low in flexibility No sound or movement
Direct mail	Selective both geographically and qualitatively Flexible Conveys large amount of information	High cost Mailing lists become obsolete Low acceptance

advantages of the major media employed in the UK and Table 19.4 provides an advertising code of practice.

Advertising agencies

Instead of arranging their own advertising, many firms employ the services of an advertising agency, such as Saatchi & Saatchi or J. Walter Thompson. Advertising agencies are specialist firms employing experts to advise on the most effective ways of advertising the products and services of clients. Advertising agencies perform five main functions:

- Agencies carry out marketing research to discover information on which to base the advertising strategy.
- They select and book the appropriate advertising media.
- They create advertisements, devising appropriate themes and messages and writing advertising copy.
- They produce the advertisement.
- They look after the client's advertising budget and offer advice on future campaigns.

The agency will charge for its services and this will take the form of either a fee to the client (**below-the-line expenditure**) or commission from

Table 19.4 An advertising code of practice

- Advertisements should contain nothing that is in breach of the law
- No advertisement should contain any matter that is likely to cause offence
- No advertisement should seek to take improper advantage of any characteristic or circumstance that may make consumers vulnerable
- No advertisement, whether by inaccuracy, ambiguity, exaggeration, omission or otherwise, should mislead consumers
- No advertisement should play on fear or excite distress
- Advertisements should neither condone nor incite to violence or anti-social behaviour
- Advertisements should contain nothing that is likely to result in harm to children or exploit their credulity, lack of experience or sense of loyalty
- Advertisers should not seek to discredit the products of competitors
- No advertisement should so closely resemble another advertisement as to be likely to mislead or confuse

(Adapted from *The British Code of Advertising Practice*, Committee of Advertising Practice)

the media. The latter, known as **above-the-line expenditure**, is, in effect, a discount on the payment made by the advertiser via the agent to the media owner.

Firms considering using an agency should decide whether or not the benefits exceed the costs. The benefits of using an agency are:

- access to the specialist expertise of the agency staff;
- use of contacts (such as in the media) of the agency;
- expert advice;
- cost: it is likely to be less expensive than an internal advertising department.

There are also advantages to media owners of dealing with agencies. For instance, it is more efficient to deal with the small number of organizations that act as agencies than the thousands of separate producers of goods and services. The media might also prefer to deal with specialists who have expert knowledge of advertising (and its constraints).

Having decided to use an agency, the business organization has then to decide which agency to use. The criteria for choosing an agency include:

- its size;
- its specialisms;
- its client portfolio (for instance, an agency that acts on behalf of a rival might be considered inappropriate);

- its track record;
- the compatibility of working relationships;
- the range of services offered;
- its overall standing and reputation in the market.

Advertising and the product lifecycle

Both the extent and nature of advertising will change during the lifecycle of a product. Heavy advertising expenditure will accompany a product launch. In the case of an entirely new type of product, the advertising will concentrate more on the general product than any specific brand. After all, if it is quite unlike previous products, it is necessary to explain the product rather than point out why one brand is better than another.

As the product moves into the growth and mature stages, the emphasis will switch from providing information to persuading potential customers of the merits of a particular brand. The aim now is to increase market share as well as (or instead of) increasing the size of the market. Advertising to maintain market share is essential as the product reaches saturation stage. The emphasis now switches to reminding consumers of the product. This is especially important in the case of a product that faces significant competition from new, close-substitute products. Kellogg's Corn Flakes, for instance, is a mature product that consumers need to be reminded about.

We can conclude that advertising changes from

being informative, to being persuasive, to being 'reminder-oriented' as the product moves through its lifecycle. In the case of an extension of the lifecycle, it will be necessary to generate an increase in advertising activity to emphasize the new features of the product.

Sales promotion

As mentioned above, **sales promotion** is all forms of promotion other than either advertising or personal selling. Like advertising, sales promotion is a form of one-way communication, but, unlike advertising, it does not involve a paid medium.

Sales promotion is employed in a supportive role to the other techniques of communicating with customers. It is a method of:

- developing the product/brand image;
- enhancing the promotional activities undertaken by distributors;
- reinforcing advertising and selling messages;
- aiding recognition;
- attracting attention;
- encouraging consumers to try the product.

As Table 19.5 reveals, some promotional activities are aimed at 'the trade'. Contests for sales staff and special discounts are both designed to push the goods through the channel of distribution. Other promotional incentives are aimed directly at the consumer (such as coupons). This latter

Table 19.5 Sales promotions

Consumer promotions	Trade promotions
Functions	Functions
To draw attention to product	To gain shelf space
To encourage sales	To develop goodwill
To increase usage rate	To encourage the dealer to push the product
To assist other promotional activities	To assist the salesforce
To target a particular segment	To expand distribution
To expand off-season sales	To gain special featuring in stores
To activate slow-moving lines	To activate slow-moving lines

group can be subdivided into those incentives that produce an immediate result (free samples, trial packs, bonus packs) and those that produce a delayed benefit to the customer (coupons, mail-in refunds). An intensive promotional campaign will increase sales and, perhaps, market share. When the promotion is withdrawn, it is likely that sales will fall off but, it is hoped, not back to the pre-promotion level.

Table 19.6 sets out sales promotion techniques.

Personal selling

Personal selling is one element in the promotional mix. Operating at the point of sale, it pushes the product by emphasizing its uses and advantages. It involves two-way communication (unlike advertising, which is one-way).

Sales' staff engage in a number of different activities:

- obtaining orders;
- offering advice and guidance;
- demonstrating the product;
- showing samples;
- merchandizing;
- handling complaints;
- delivering;
- collecting payment;
- establishing creditworthiness;
- maintaining stock;
- training the sales staff of the firm's dealers;
- disseminating information;
- giving talks and presentations;
- staffing exhibitions.

However, not all salespeople perform all these roles. Depending on the product and other circumstances, salespeople will perform particular combinations of these roles. For instance, milkmen do not, in general, give presentations and sales staff in the engineering industry would not ordinarily deliver the product. We can identify the following types of selling positions:

- where the salesperson's job is primarily to deliver, with selling being secondary (such as a milkman);
- where the salesperson is mainly an inside order-taker (such as in a shop);
- where the salesperson is mainly an order-

Table 19.6 Sales promotion techniques

Technique	Example	Use in consumer markets	Use in industrial markets
Immediate customer incentive	Free samples Trial packs Bonus packs Price promotions BOGOF (buy one, get one free)	Common	Rare
Delayed customer incentive	Coupons Tokens Trading stamps Cash refund on mail order Self-liquidating offers Competitions	Common	Rare
Point-of-sale displays	Counter displays	Common	Occasional
Exhibitions	Ideal Home and so on Garden Festivals	Common	Common
Sponsorship	Sports, arts	Common	Occasional
Performance-related incentive	Bonuses Competitions Supply bonuses	Occasional	Common

taker employed by a wholesaler and whose customers are retailers;

- where the salesperson is expected not to take customer orders but, instead, to build goodwill or educate potential users of the product;
- where the emphasis is on technical knowledge and being a consultant to clients;
- where creativity is needed in the sale of tangible products (such as encyclopaedia salespeople);
- where creativity is needed in the sale of intangibles (such as insurance salesperson).

Selling, as distinct from order-taking, requires persuasiveness. The process involves a number of distinct stages.

- **Prospecting** is the search for potential customers, known as 'prospects'. Prospects emerge from responses to advertisements or are referred on by others or are identified from cold calling.
- The **pre-approach** stage involves the

gathering of information by the salesperson, followed by decisions about how to approach the prospects. The information will come from observations, other customers and other sales staff.

- In the **approach**, the aim is to gain the attention and interest of the prospect. This is an important stage in that first impressions are always critical.
- In the **presentation** stage, the salesperson attempts to convert a prospect into a customer by creating a desire for the product. Presentations range from the hard sell to the soft sell. Although the former might be successful, it might not lead to long-term customer satisfaction.
- The **close** is the stage at which the salesperson seeks a purchasing commitment from the prospect. It can take a variety of forms, including a movement to the till in a shop or allowing prospects to handle and become attached to goods (the so-called 'puppy dog close'). What these have in

common is that they attempt to bring the proceedings to a close and secure a sale. However, a premature, inappropriate or clumsy effort at closing the deal will put customers off.

- The **follow-up** is an important part of selling. Sales staff should ensure that the customer is satisfied with the product or service in order to assist repeat sales not just of this product but of other products in the firm's range.

Successful selling requires:

- interpersonal skills;
- intelligence;
- knowledge of, and faith in, the product;
- energy;
- determination;
- good appearance;
- an outgoing personality and empathy with customers.

The salesperson needs to be highly motivated, especially if working long, irregular hours alone and far from base. A financial incentive in the form of commission on sales is, therefore, essential to secure commitment, although there is a strong argument against straight commission (with no basic salary), which might lead to a neglect of the business' long-term interests. Other methods of motivating staff involved in selling include:

- regular sales meetings;
- contests;
- performance evaluation schemes;
- equipment to assist the salesperson;
- promotion opportunities;
- targets for sales.

The salesforce will be led by a sales manager (not to be confused with a marketing manager). The sales manager will:

- plan the size, nature and extent of the personal selling operation;
- recruit and train staff;
- select administrative methods to be employed in support of the salesforce;
- devise schemes to monitor performance of individual salespeople;
- organize salespeople into teams with particular responsibilities.

The 'area' to be covered by a particular team or salesperson will be defined in terms of geography, product or size and nature of product. In some cases, the division will be made on a regional basis, whereas in others it may be made in terms of different types of retail outlet. The sales targets will be broken down by area and market to provide each member of the salesforce with sufficient motivation. However, each area will have unique features that should be taken into consideration when planning the selling operation. For instance, a large but geographically dispersed market will require greater effort than a more compact one.

Key concepts

Advertising A form of promotion that involves one-way communication (an advertisement) being placed in recognized media.

Media Plural of medium. Advertising media refers to newspapers, magazines, television and other channels that are paid to carry advertisements.

Personal selling Oral presentation to potential purchasers undertaken for the purpose of making a sale.

Promotion Any device designed to increase purchases by consumers. It includes advertising, personal selling, sales promotion, sponsorship, publicity and public relations.

Promotional mix The combination of promotional techniques employed to increase sales of a product. It will vary from product to product.

Sales promotion All techniques of promotion other than advertising, personal selling, public relations and publicity. Sales promotion techniques such as competitions, coupons and sales literature are used as a supplement to the major forms of promotion.

Essay questions

1 Evaluate the main advertising media for:
   (a) a national supermarket chain;
   (b) a car manufacturer;
   (c) an electrical products retailer.

2 Explain how you would evaluate the success of a promotional campaign.

3 (a) What do understand by the term promotional mix?
   (b) Analyse how it varies from product to product.

4 (a) Explain the terms promotional mix and product lifecycle.
   (b) Analyse the ways in which promotion changes over the product lifecycle.

5 The sole aim of advertising is to increase sales. Discuss.

6 Evaluate the role of personal selling in the promotional mix for:
   (a) car; and
   (b) soft drinks.

Pricing policies

Pricing decisions are crucial to the success of the firm and its products. This chapter will therefore focus on the pricing strategies adopted by business organizations and the methods used to set prices.

Chapter objectives

1 To understand the objectives for pricing policies.

2 To understand the constraints on firms when setting prices.

3 To analyse pricing policies available to firms and the circumstances in which each is appropriate.

The objectives of pricing policies

Before setting prices, decision makers should clarify the firm's objectives in relation to the marketing of the product (see Figure 20.1). Private enterprise firms will set prices to achieve one of the following objectives.

- **Profit maximization** For private enterprise firms, profit remains the overriding objective. Economists assume that firms are profit maximizers and, in the theory of the firm, it is demonstrated that profits are maximized when marginal cost equals marginal revenue – that is, when the cost of *producing* an additional unit of output is equal to the revenue derived from *selling* an additional unit of output. This is very attractive theoretically, but does not explain how prices are set. Moreover, there are likely to be other objectives influencing the pricing behaviour of firms.

- **A target level of profits** This is different from profit maximization in that the firm seeks a certain level of profits rather than the maximum possible level of profits. The target is set either in monetary terms or as a percentage of capital employed.

- **An increase in market share** Firms may seek to increase their market share even to the extent of sacrificing short-term profits. Penetration pricing is particularly successful when demand is elastic. By building up sales

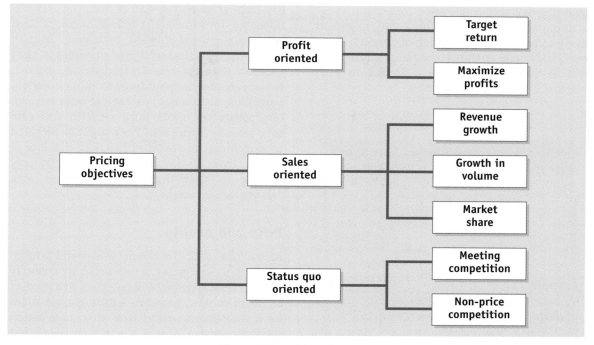

Figure 20.1 Pricing objectives

and, therefore, market share, the firm will benefit from greater discretion over price in the long run. Hence, the market share objective involves a sacrifice of profits in the short run to enjoy higher profits in the long run.

- **Sales revenue maximization** Firms may choose to set prices to maximize current sales revenue, especially if they seek an early recovery of cash.
- **Profit margin** This is pricing to maximize profit margin on each unit sold (rather than overall profits). This objective, which is seen in skimming, is based on the assumption that buyers are still prepared to purchase the goods despite the high price (that is, demand is inelastic) and the firm has a sufficient lead over rivals for there to be little danger of high prices attracting competitors in the immediate future.
- **Risk minimization** Economics is based on an assumption of rational behaviour, which in traditional economics meant maximization of profits (or income). However, action to minimize risk is also rational. Firms may, in

the short run at least, set prices to minimize risk and maximize survival. Prices might be set to meet competition or abandon competition in favour of non-price competition.

Constraints

Price setters need to appreciate the constraints under which they operate. Their discretion over price is limited by:

- the cost of production;
- demand from customers;
- competitor behaviour;
- the need to be consistent in terms of other elements of the marketing mix.

At this stage it would be useful to review relevant aspects of economic theory.

Economic theory relevant to price setting

The theory of demand in economics informs us that there is an inverse relationship between quantity demanded and price (other things remaining equal). Consequently, a rise in price is likely to result in a contraction of demand. Moreover, if demand is elastic the fall-off in demand will be sufficient to cause a decline in sales revenue as shown in Table 20.1.

Table 20.1 Demand and revenue

Price (£)	Quantity demanded (000)	Sales revenue (£000)
9	11	99
10	10	100
11	9	99
12	8	96
13	7	91

Example

To prove the relationship between elasticity of demand and sales revenue, calculate the price elasticity of demand when the price rises:

(a) from £9 to £10;
(b) from £11 to £12;
(c) from £12 to £13.

Answer

(a) $\dfrac{-1/11}{+1/9} = -0.8$ (inelastic)

(b) $\dfrac{-1/9}{+1/11} = -1.2$ (elastic)

(c) $\dfrac{-1/8}{1/12} = -1.5$ (elastic)

The conclusion is that when demand is elastic, a price rise leads to a fall in sales revenue.

The theory of the firm provides an analysis of the discretion that firms have when setting prices. In the theoretical ideal of perfect competition, firms are merely price takers – that is, they are forced to accept the ruling market price. The more monopolistic the market, the greater the firm's discretion about price. Typical market structures are somewhere between the two extremes of monopoly and perfect competition. Oligopoly, for instance, is defined as competition between a handful of 'giant' companies. As each oligopolist fears the reaction of competitors, they choose not to compete over price, but, instead, to compete in other ways (product differentiation, promotion, distribution, packaging, extra service). Oligopolists will avoid price reductions in case they provoke a price war. They might be prepared to absorb cost increases rather than risk loss of sales to rivals. Therefore, the theory of oligopoly informs us that firms will set prices with competitors in mind.

Price and quality

As we have said, the theory of demand informs us that price and quantity demanded are inversely related. Hence, people will buy more of a product as the price falls. However, a price change might have the opposite effect from that predicted in economic theory. The reason for this perverse effect relates to the difficulties we have in assessing quality.

In economic theory, the customer is assumed to possess perfect knowledge of the market and the product. The customer is able to evaluate the product and its quality and decide, on the evidence, whether or not it is worth committing money to the purchase of the product. However, this is not the case in real life. Many of the products we purchase are too complicated for us to evaluate fully before we commit our hard-earned money. Many products are wrapped in a way that prevents us inspecting the goods fully until we get home. When we make our choices, we have imperfect information and, therefore, we rely on the reputation of the supplier, the claims made for the product, recommendations, general appearance and instinct. Because we lack perfect knowledge, we frequently judge quality in terms of price, and end up assuming that high price means high quality and low price means low quality.

The lesson for people involved in marketing is twofold. First, the price must 'fit' the other aspects of the marketing mix. Hence, it must be consistent with the product, promotion and the

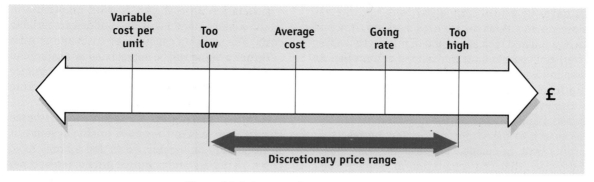

Figure 20.2 Customers' perceptions of value

channels of distribution employed in marketing. Second, customers have a perception of what the price should be. Hence, when we say that firms have discretion regarding price, the discretion is within a limited range, as shown in Figure 20.2. The closer price is to the limit of the discretionary range, the greater the marketing effort required to sell the product (Figure 20.3). Figure 20.4 illustrates Kotler's price – quality strategy matrix.

We are now in a position to identify three broad approaches to pricing:

- cost-based pricing;
- customer-oriented pricing;
- competitor-oriented pricing.

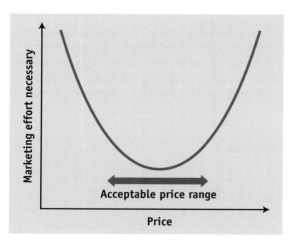

Figure 20.3 The acceptance of price range
Note: The marketing effort has to be increased if price is too low or too high

		Price		
		High	**Medium**	**Low**
Product quality	**High**	Premium	Penetration	Superbargain
	Medium	Overpricing	Average price, average quality	Bargain
	Low	Hit and run	Shoddy goods	Cheap goods

The choice of strategy will depend on:

- the market segment being targeted;
- stage in the product lifecycle;
- the likelihood of repeat purchase behaviour;
- competitive circumstances.

Figure 20.4 Kotler's price–quality strategy matrix (Adapted from, Kotler, *Marketing Management*, Prentice Hall, 1996)

Cost-based pricing

There are variations on the theme of cost-based pricing, but, in essence, it involves the addition of a profit element to the costs of production. For instance, **cost plus pricing** involves the calculation of the full cost of producing or providing each unit of output. Both direct and indirect costs are included in the calculation, to which is added a fixed percentage mark-up for profit. High turnover items will carry a low mark-up, whereas slow-moving items carry a high mark-up. It is said to be a fair and logical method of pricing to recover overhead costs and maximize long-run profits. As demand is uncertain, there is much to be said for a pricing strategy based on known costs.

However, cost plus pricing ignores customer demand and is based on the mistaken belief that, because it is based on costs, it guarantees that profits will be made. Decision makers should appreciate that the calculation of average costs (especially the apportionment of overheads to each unit) is dependent on the level of output. If cost plus pricing raises the price to a high level that is unacceptable to customers, then sales will fall – thus raising average costs above the set price. Moreover, the difficulty is increased when the firm produces a multitude of products – there are major problems in allocating overheads to the different products. Although there are conventions to be followed in relation to the allocation of overheads, the inescapable fact is that all methods are arbitrary (see Chapter 32).

Full-cost pricing can be criticized on the grounds that it:

- ignores demand and the price elasticity of demand;
- ignores the competitive situation;
- does not take advantage of market potential;
- is inflexible in the face of demand changes;
- exaggerates the precision with which costs can be allocated;
- does not distinguish between out-of-pocket and 'sunk' costs (those which are spent regardless of the level of production);
- ignores capital requirements and the return on investment;
- does not take account of the fact that many costs vary with volume of output and volume of output depends on price charged;
- can result in underpricing or overpricing.

For a new product, price could be based on a mark-up above standard costs (see Chapter 32). **Standard costs** are the expected costs of production based on certain standards. Hence, we are dealing not with what it did cost, but what it is expected to cost to produce.

A variation on cost plus is mark-up pricing in which a percentage mark-up is added to variable costs. The mark-up covers fixed costs and profits.

Target pricing will be appreciated after studying break-even analysis (Chapter 33), but the essence of the technique can be understood by working through Example 1.

Marginal pricing can be seen as a cost-based system, but, unlike the above pricing systems, it is based only on variable costs and ignores fixed costs. To understand marginal pricing (sometimes known as contribution price), consider Example 2. Marginal pricing is widely employed in service industries (such as public transport, hotel and holiday firms), which suffer from daily or seasonal fluctuations in demand. **Peak pricing**, with off-peak prices reflecting variable rather than full costs, has, as one of its aims, a reduction in demand fluctuations. Clearly, this is moving away from purely cost-based pricing to a consideration of demand factors.

Example 1

A company produces a product for which:

- allocated overhead costs are £1m;
- target profit is £2m;
- variable costs amount to £5 per unit;
- planned output is 600,000 units.

What price should it charge?

To calculate the answer, we should appreciate that the price should be sufficiently above £5 to generate a total of £1m plus £2m from the 600,000. This equals £5, which must then be added to the variable costs. Answer: £10.

Example 2

A firm that produces aerosol products is currently operating at 90 per cent of its capacity. It has fixed costs of £1 million per year. A large supermarket chain wishes to place an order for 200,000 cans of 'own brand' air freshener, for which it is prepared to pay 40 pence per can. The aerosol company calculates that this special order will add

£40,000 to labour costs, £20,000 to the cost of materials, with additional overhead costs of £10,000. By taking on this special order, the aerosol company can now operate at full capacity. Should it accept the order? The answer is yes, but with certain qualifications.

The special order generates additional revenue of £80,000 whereas costs rise by £70,000. Hence, the special order provides a contribution of £10,000 towards fixed costs and profit. In evaluating this deal, the £1 million of fixed costs is irrelevant. These are costs that will be incurred whether or not the special order is accepted and be covered by the firm's regular production. Provided additional (or marginal) revenue covers additional (marginal) cost, the special deal is worth while. The additional cost of the own brand air fresheners works out at £70,000, or 35 pence per can. Therefore, any revenue above 35 pence per can will make a contribution to fixed costs and profit.

Marginal cost pricing is only suitable where the firm:

- has spare capacity and can take advantage of increased sales;
- cannot put its resources to more profitable use;
- is able to segment its market to avoid a diversion of its regular customers to the low-priced alternative.

Customer-oriented pricing

This is pricing based on demand for the product and customers' perceptions of value rather than the costs of production. **Perceived value pricing** is used in markets where demand is known to be price inelastic. The price will be chosen to position the product in the market. As quality is informally assessed by the price charged, it is important to choose a price that is consistent with the image of the product and the other elements of the marketing mix.

If the market is segmented, it is possible to charge different prices to different segments of the market. This practice is called **price discrimination** if different prices are charged for goods (or services) that are identical in every respect. Where there are slight differences in the products sold to different segments (brand names, slight differences in quality or the timing of a service, say) the practice is known as **differential pricing**.

The **price discriminator** will charge a higher price in a segment where demand is inelastic, but reduce the price for the segment where demand is elastic. The principle can be illustrated by train fares. The commuter and business traveller will make the journey irrespective of price. Hence, full fares are charged when these people travel in the early morning or late afternoon. The social traveller is more sensitive to price, however, and will be unable, or unwilling, to pay the full fare, but will be attracted by reduced fares. To prevent commuters taking advantage of the lower fares, they are only available after 9.30 a.m. The time restriction separates the two segments of the market. This practice is useful in shifting some trade to off-peak times in an attempt to even out the flow of travellers.

There are special problems associated with the pricing of a new product, especially one that is very different from any previous product. The absence of data on costs, customer demand or competitors' prices, makes **pioneer pricing** difficult. Firms will adopt one of two basic strategies – skimming or penetration.

Skim pricing involves entry to the market at a high price that is later reduced (in real, if not in money, terms) as the product becomes more acceptable and the volume of sales increases. With an increase in sales volume, the firm will enjoy economies of scale and can, therefore, afford to reduce prices.

The opposite strategy is known as **penetration pricing**. By introducing the product at a low price, the firm can penetrate deep into the market. As volume increases, price is raised. These strategies are shown in Figure 20.5.

Skimming is the preferred strategy for many radically new products (such as colour televisions in the early 1970s and video recorders later in the same decade). It allows for the early recovery

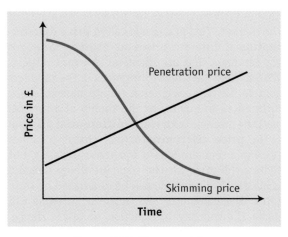

Figure 20.5 Pioneer pricing

of research and development costs. A high profit margin on each unit sold reduces the need to sell a large volume. The strategy will succeed if:

- by means of patent rights or technological lead, there is little danger of rivals entering the market in the short term;
- unit production and distribution costs are not substantially greater for small quantities than for large quantities;
- there are sufficient buyers prepared to pay the high skimming price.

One additional argument for skim pricing is that the early buyers of an innovative product will not be deterred by the high price. In fact, the high price might add to its appeal. Hence, the top of the market is 'skimmed off' in the early stages of the product lifecycle. As the price is reduced, other segments of the market purchase the product.

Penetration pricing is, superficially, an attractive way to obtain a large volume of sales and a major market share. However, it is a high-risk strategy. It is only suitable when the firm possesses the capacity for high sales volume and when a low price generates sufficient sales to compensate for low profit margins. If the product is expected to have a short lifecycle, penetration does not provide sufficient time to recover R&D costs. It is not surprising that many firms choose skimming as their pioneer pricing strategy.

Competitor-oriented pricing

These prices are related neither to costs of production nor to customer demand, but to the prices charged by competitor firms. In some cases this will mean keeping in step with competitors. As a rule, we can say that the more competitive the industry and the more homogeneous the product, the greater the pressure to keep in line with competitors. In the economists' model of perfect competition, all firms charge the same price as they are all price takers.

Oligopolists also carefully study rivals when setting prices. A price truce, with recognized price leaders, is common in oligopolistic markets. It is less disruptive to follow the lead set by competitors than engage in mutually harmful price warfare. Occasionally, the truce breaks down and price warfare breaks out. Competitive price cutting is designed to weaken and destroy smaller and less efficient rivals. Price wars are used as a way of forcing rivals out of the market or weakening them prior to a takeover. **Destroyer pricing** is the name given to a policy of aggressive price cutting to eliminate rivals.

Penetration pricing can also be mentioned in the context of competitor-oriented pricing. Firms that seek a rapid increase in market share at the expense of rivals might choose to pursue a policy of penetration pricing.

Table 20.2 summarizes the pricing strategies discussed.

Price variations

Firms will adopt one or other of the above broad strategies to determine the general price level. Once this has been fixed, prices can be adjusted in particular circumstances.

It is common to offer discounts for:

- bulk purchases;
- prompt payment;
- purchases that are off-peak;
- favoured customers.

Firms that offer a 'family brand' of products will want to ensure that goods are priced in relation

Table 20.2 Summary of pricing strategies

Cost-based pricing
- Standard cost pricing – based on cost standards in management accounting
- Cost plus profit pricing – add standard mark-up to total cost
- Target profit pricing – based on break-even analysis
- Marginal pricing – selling price of additional units fixed by reference to the marginal or additional costs of producing each unit
- Mark-up pricing – percentage mark-up added to variable costs

Market-oriented pricing
- Perceived value pricing – based on assumptions of customers' beliefs about the value of the product to them
- Psychological pricing – for example, prestige pricing, value-for-money pricing, setting the price at £9.99 rather than £10.
- Promotional pricing – to clear excess stocks by discounts
- Skimming – a high price for a new and unique product to skim the cream off the market

Competitor-oriented pricing
- Competitive pricing – tackling the price leader by setting the price slightly higher but demonstrating a discernible product difference
- Discount pricing – to increase market share at the expense of rivals
- Penetration pricing – introducing a new product at a low price to secure a place in the market

to each other. At the same time, the psychological importance of price might dictate that certain goods are sold at a limited number of prices. This practice, known as **price lining**, is seen in standardized fares on public transport and the practice of selling clothes at prices ending in 95 or 99 pence.

Many retailers adopt **loss leader prices** for a small range of their products. These goods are sold at a loss to tempt customers into the shop, knowing that profits will be recovered on other items in the shopping basket.

Conclusion

This chapter has provided an introduction to the pricing strategies of business organizations.

Its inclusion in the marketing part of the book reflects the importance of pricing strategy within the marketing mix for the product. As with so many other aspects of the subject, there is no pricing strategy that is suitable for *all* circumstances. Firms must choose the strategy that is most appropriate in view of their objectives, the situation in the market and their capacity utilization. For example, marginal pricing or penetration pricing is only appropriate where the firm has the capacity to increase output to satisfy the demand that emerges with low prices. Skimming is only appropriate where the firm enjoys a lead over its rivals and is able to enjoy a temporary monopoly position in the market. Full-cost pricing is only appropriate when the resulting price is within the customer's perceived range of value.

Key concepts

Competition-based pricing A pricing strategy in which prices are set with reference to competitors (such as in oligopolistic markets, where price leaders and price followers are frequently found).

Cost-based pricing A pricing strategy that focuses on the cost of production to which is added a mark-up for profit.

Customer-oriented pricing A pricing strategy that sets prices in terms of what the market will bear.

Penetration Prices set low to achieve a high volume of sales.

Price discrimination Charging a separate price to different, discrete segments of the market. To succeed in this strategy it is necessary for the market to be divided into distinct segments with differing elasticities of demand and some means of keeping the segments distinct.

Skimming The price of a new product set at a high level in order to 'skim' the top segment of the market. A high profit margin is achieved, but at the expense of sales volumes. Once established, the price will be reduced.

Essay questions

1 (a) What do you understand by price discrimination?
  (b) In what circumstances is it an appropriate strategy?

2 (a) What is meant by cost-based pricing?
  (b) Analyse the weakness of pursuing such a pricing policy.

3 (a) What is meant by destroyer pricing?
  (b) To what extent is it in the consumers' interest?

4 Evaluate marginal cost pricing for a manufacturer currently operating at 80 per cent capacity.

5 Assess the value of an understanding of price elasticity of demand when setting prices.

6 (a) Distinguish between skimming and penetration as pricing strategies.
  (b) Analyse the circumstances in which each is appropriate.

7 (a) To what extent do firms have discretion over pricing?
  (b) Analyse the linkages between price and other aspects of the marketing mix.

Channels of distribution

The channels of distribution are the paths that goods and services follow in moving from producer to customer. We are not so much concerned with the physical route taken, but with the institutions in the route of exchange. In some cases, there is a direct relationship between manufacturer and end-user. However, more typical (especially in consumer markets) is the involvement of one or more intermediaries. This chapter will investigate strategy in relation to channels of distribution.

Chapter objectives

1 To develop an understanding of the different channels of distribution available to business organizations.

2 To provide a framework for understanding the principles of channel choice.

3 To analyse strategies for moving goods through the channels.

4 To develop an appreciation of the changing nature of channels.

Institutions in the channels of distribution

Manufacturers produce goods that are sold to customers. As we saw in Chapter 17, customers can be divided into industrial customers (other firms) and household consumers. Between the two ends of the channel it is likely that there will be intermediary firms involved in selling on the product to the next institution in the channel. These intermediaries are of three kinds:

- agents
- wholesalers
- retailers.

Agents

An **agent** acts on behalf of another firm to perform certain specified services. Agents are widely used in importing and exporting but are by no means uncommon in domestic trade. We can make a distinction between a commission agent and a stocklist agent.

A **commission agent** secures orders from customers but does not take 'title' to the goods. This type of agent does not become the 'owner' of the goods and might not even take physical possession of them. The **stocklist agent** carries a stock of the manufacturer's products, either purchasing them or holding them on consignment. This second type of agent clearly has greater

261

independence, but this should not obscure the fact that agents act on behalf of other firms.

Wholesalers

A **wholesaler** buys goods for resale to someone other than the eventual consumer. Wholesalers supply goods to retailers (who will then sell the goods to the public) or to manufacturing firms, who will use the goods in a production process.

The traditional and primary function of the wholesaler is to break down bulk consignments into smaller quantities suitable for individual retailers. The advantages of having intermediaries to break bulk can be seen in Figure 21.1. The existence of intermediaries simplifies and reduces the lines of communication and transportation, producing considerable economies of distribution.

Apart from breaking bulk, wholesalers perform a number of other functions:

- they provide storage facilities, thus reducing the need for both manufacturer and retailer to hold such large stocks;
- they even out irregular flows of goods;
- by taking goods off their hands, wholesalers improve the manufacturer's cash flow;
- wholesalers also shoulder some of the marketing risks of the producer;
- wholesalers (other than the cash and carry kind) provide credit facilities and other services for retailers as well as assisting with the promotional effort.

Retailers

The retailer buys goods from the wholesaler (or, in some cases, direct from the manufacturer) for sale to the public in shops and other retail outlets. From the personal contact with the end-user we can identify a number of functions performed by the retailer.

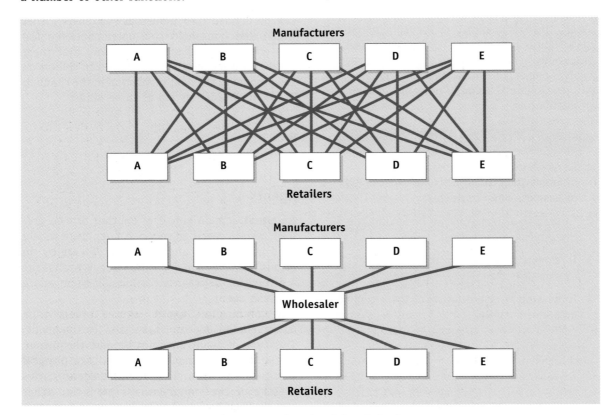

Figure 21.1 The role of the wholesaler

Table 21.1 Trends in retailing

- Growth in the market share enjoyed by the multiples
- Continuing trend towards self-service
- New methods, new technology:
  – computerization of stock
  – EPOS (electronic point of sale)
  – credit cards
- Out-of-town retailing
  Customer demand for car parking
- Changing time patterns
- Emergence of shopping as a leisure activity
- New marketing techniques:
  – lifestyle retailing
  – 'focused' retailing (such as Tie Rack)
- High investment in store design

The retailer provides:

- a variety of goods from which choice can be made;
- a convenient service;
- information and advice to consumers;
- delivery of goods, where appropriate;
- credit, where appropriate;
- packing;
- market information for manufacturers.

(See also Table 21.1 on trends in retailing).

Channel routes

The five players in the distribution system – manufacturer, agent, wholesaler, retailer and customer – are combined in a variety of ways (see Figure 21.2).

- **Route 1: Direct marketing from producer to customer** Apart from industrial markets, where it is very common, this route is usually employed by specialist mail-order manufacturers and factory (or farm) shops.
- **Route 2: Manufacturer–retailer–consumer** The rise of the large supermarket chain has reduced the importance of the independent wholesaler. The retail chains are able to deal directly with the manufacturers and undertake their own wholesale functions (like breaking bulk).

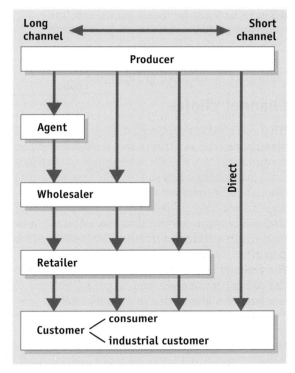

Figure 21.2 Channels of distribution

- **Route 3: Manufacturer–wholesaler–retailer–consumer** This is the traditional channel in consumer goods markets. Small retailers depend on wholesalers for supplies and manufacturers are also keen to avail themselves of the services of wholesalers.
- **Route 4: Manufacturer–agent–wholesaler–retailer–consumer** As mentioned above, agents are especially common in the import–export business. Hence, a foreign producer might use the services of a UK import agent to assist in the movement of goods through the channel.
- **Route 5: Manufacturer–agent–customer (industrial or household)** On this route, the manufacturer uses the services of an agent to sell the goods direct to the public. The agent acts on behalf of the manufacturer, who in turn exercises considerable control over the agent's activities. This route is used by car makers and in the financial services industry.

● **Route 6: Manufacturer–agent–retailer–consumer** This is similar to Route 4 but eliminates the wholesaler. A large supermarket chain buying imported goods provides an example of this route.

Channel choice

What combination of intermediaries, if any, should manufacturers use? This is an important decision for producers as 'place' (or channels of distribution) is one of the key elements of the marketing mix. Channel decisions usually involve a long-term commitment. Given the dynamic nature of the environment, no manufacturer will want to be locked into a declining channel. Channel decisions also affect other aspects of the firm's marketing. The channel that is used must be consistent with the pricing, promotion and targeting policies of the firm and also with the product itself.

There is no universal formula for deciding on which channels to use. However, we can identify the factors that tend to result in shorter (or more direct) channels and longer (or less direct) channels.

● As a general rule, industrial products sold to other firms use shorter channels, while consumer products sold to households use longer channels.
● Where there are relatively few customers and/or they are geographically concentrated, the greater is the likelihood of shorter channels being used. On the other hand, the existence of a large number of dispersed customers would incline the producer towards longer, less direct channels.
● Where the producer wishes to exert control (such as over quality of service) it will have a preference for short channels. Hence, firms selling complicated and expensive consumer goods will use a network of dealers. Where control is unimportant (as in the selling of simple, inexpensive goods) longer and less direct channels will prove satisfactory.
● Short, direct channels will be used where customers buy goods in large amounts but infrequently. Where customers buy in small amounts but frequently, it is more likely that indirect channels will be used.

● Products that are:
  – bulky;
  – expensive to handle;
  – custom built;
  – of high unit value; or
  – perishable
  are likely to be moved through short channels. On the other hand, products that have the opposite characteristics are more likely to be moved through indirect channels.
● Services are usually sold direct (although the package holiday trade is an exception) whereas goods are more likely to be sold through indirect channels.

Although these points should not be treated as universal rules, they do provide a framework for understanding some aspects of channel choice. However, the producer will always take into consideration its own resources (financial and human) and the availability of suitable intermediaries.

The more direct the channel, the greater the producer's investment in the marketing effort. However, if middlemen are either not available or are considered to be unsatisfactory the producer might be forced to engage in direct marketing.

This analysis of channel choice has been based on the assumption that a producer will choose one particular channel of distribution. In many cases, however, producers will seek to increase market exposure by using a variety of channels (a **multiple channel strategy**) for the same product. Part of the output might be sold direct to consumers, while the remainder might be sold through a variety of intermediaries. By this strategy the producer will seek to increase sales to different segments of the market.

Intensive and selective distribution

A further aspect of market exposure relates to the number of shops permitted to stock the product. A producer that wishes to secure the maximum possible number of stockists for its goods is said to be pursuing an **intensive system** of marketing. If the producer deliberately restricts the number of stockists it is said to be pursuing a **selective distribution strategy** (or even exclusive if the policy is to restrict sales to a single retailer in each area).

Intensive distribution to increase market exposure, and thereby sales revenue, does not require explanation as we have to assume that the producer has objectives in terms of sales, sales revenue, market share and profit. What does require explanation is why a producer would deliberately restrict the exposure of its product.

Selective distribution is used when:

● the customer expects and/or requires advice or after-sales service;
● selectivity (and exclusivity) confers status on the product;
● the producer wishes to exert control over the intermediary;
● the market is insufficient to warrant more intensive distribution;
● intensive distribution would result in conflict between intermediaries.

In general, we can say that selective distribution is most common where goods are of high value, have high margins and are complicated.

Channel support strategies

The use of intermediaries reduces the marketing risk and the marketing effort for the manufacturer, so they can, instead, concentrate on production and product development. However, manufacturers that use intermediaries face the problem of having only indirect contact with their customers. They rely on intermediaries to be active and enthusiastic in selling their products. When we remember that the intermediary is likely to be performing the same function for rival manufacturers, we can appreciate the need to develop strategies to support and enthuse the intermediaries.

To force the goods through the channel, one of two strategies (or a combination of both) will be employed. **Push strategies** are aimed at intermediaries. They take the form of:

● discounts;
● increased dealer margins;
● dealer competitions;

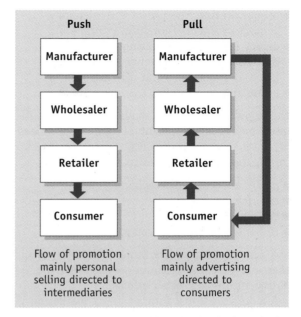

Figure 21.3 Pushing v. pulling the goods through the channel

● point-of-sale displays;
● incentives for sales staff;
● trade advertising;
● trade exhibitions.

The aim is to increase the intermediaries' interest and motivation to stock the product.

Pull strategies are focused on the final customer. The aim is to appeal to customers over the heads of intermediaries. By developing customer interest, the manufacturer's goods will be pulled through the channel of distribution. By advertising they hope to encourage customers to ask for the goods in the shop, thus encouraging the retailer to place orders (see Figure 21.3).

Direct marketing

Direct marketing is a generic term for selling methods in which business organizations approach customers directly rather than using intermediaries. It takes a number of forms:

● **direct mail** personalized letters and promotional material sent to named individuals;

- **telemarketing** the use of the telephone to contact prospects (potential customers);
- **direct response marketing** any approach that asks a target audience to take action (such as complete a tear-off coupon);
- **e-mailing** of potential customers.

The activities described above have been facilitated by the development of the computerized database to store information about customers. Information stored relates to such things as:

- name, address and telephone number;
- age, marital status;
- customer needs;
- responses to previous campaigns.

Not only do computers store the information, they also play a key role in devising and coordinating future marketing efforts.

A more traditional form of direct marketing is mail order. This takes two forms: first, the use of part-time agents to sell goods shown in a large, glossy catalogue (such as Freemans, Kays and Littlewoods); second, specialist manufacturers advertising a single (or limited range of) product in small advertisements in newspapers.

Direct marketing has the advantage of being selective and well targeted. It fits in with other promotional activity, is easy to monitor and cheaper than conventional advertising. It also eliminates the intermediaries. However, databases become obsolete as people's circumstances change, there is resentment at 'junk mail' and the invasion of privacy, and some forms of direct marketing have a distinct downmarket image. Nevertheless, it represents a growth area in marketing, especially as the proliferation of television channels has reduced the effectiveness of television advertising.

Key concepts

Channel of distribution All the stages and organizations through which a product must pass between producer and user. The length of the channel refers to the number of intermediaries involved.

Channel strategy The strategy used by the producer to move its goods to the customer. The strategy might be direct or indirect or take the form of a variety of routes (a multichannel strategy).

Direct marketing Sales direct to the customer without the use of intermediaries.

Pull strategy This involves appealing to consumers, who pull the product through the channel by placing orders.

Push strategy Forcing the product through the channel by persuading intermediaries to carry it.

Retailer An establishment that sells goods for personal and household consumption. The retailer is typically the intermediary with whom the public deals.

Wholesaler An establishment the business of which is to buy for resale to retailers.

Essay questions

1 Evaluate the case for direct marketing of products cutting out all intermediaries.

2 Analyse strategies employed by manufacturers to move goods through the channels of distribution.

3 (a) Analyse the role of the wholesaler in consumer markets.
  (b) Why has the position of the independent wholesaler been under threat for a number of decades?

4 (a) What are the main types of retailer in the UK?
  (b) Describe the changes in the market share of each type of retailer and account for the trends that you have identified.

5 Analyse the case for employing a variety of different distribution channels.

International marketing

International marketing can be defined as the management process of identifying, analysing and satisfying the needs of overseas customers. The principles of marketing that we have explored in earlier chapters of this part of the book are equally relevant when businesses market their goods overseas. However, what makes international marketing different is that we are concerned with distinct market segments for which appropriate policies should be formulated and pursued.

Chapter objectives

1 To investigate the distinctive problems of engaging in international marketing.

2 To analyse why firms seek to market goods and services overseas.

3 To identify factors relating to the choice of overseas markets to enter.

4 To analyse the different methods of entry into overseas markets.

5 To analyse the arguments for and against adaptation of components of the marketing mix to suit the requirements of overseas markets.

Five questions to be answered

Business organizations considering venturing abroad should address the following questions.

1 Should the organization seek markets overseas?
2 To which country (or countries) should it direct its marketing effort?
3 How should it seek to enter foreign markets?
4 What products should it seek to sell abroad and to what extent should they be adapted to suit the requirements of different countries?
5 How, and to what extent, should other aspects of the marketing mix be adapted to suit the needs of overseas markets?

Should the organization seek to market overseas?

Overseas trade carries certain problems and risks that are either not present in the domestic market or not present to the same extent. The additional complications of international marketing are:

- foreign barriers to imported goods (such as tariffs);
- political risks (such as consequences of political instability abroad);
- legal differences (such as contract law, product safety);
- increased transport and distribution costs;

- longer supply chain and, therefore, remoteness from the customer;
- longer delay in receiving payment;
- cultural differences concerning:
  - acceptability of the product;
  - promotional mix;
  - choice of name;
  - ways in which business is conducted;
  - units of measurement;
  - packaging;
  - colours used in the product and packaging;
- economic instability abroad (such as firms dependent on export markets are affected by the state of the local economy);
- exchange rate movements.

Lack of expertise in overseas markets coupled with the expense and extra risks deters many firms from seeking overseas sales. However, despite all these problems, many firms do choose to enter overseas markets. They do so in the belief that it will prove profitable. A fuller analysis of why firms seek overseas markets would identify the following reasons:

- to achieve growth in sales, especially when the domestic market is static, declining or characterized by increased competition;
- to utilize excess production capacity;
- to achieve economies of scale by virtue of increased output and sales;
- to spread R&D costs over a larger market (the so-called technological imperative);
- to develop new markets for existing products as distinct from new products for existing markets;
- to reduce dependence on the domestic market.

Which countries should be targeted?

Once a business organization has chosen to enter the overseas market, it has to decide which country or countries to target, given the fact that only the very largest of companies can hope to sell on a worldwide basis. The choice of target markets requires market research data (both primary and secondary) on the potential overseas markets. The data will include the following:

- consumer behaviour;
- culture;
- demographic trends;
- distance and transport costs;
- economic trends;
- market prospects;
- market size;
- social influences;
- availability of trading relationships (such as agents);
- competition in the market;
- infrastructure;
- geographical factors (such as size and distance);
- the skill and technological base of the country.

This process should be conducted on a systematic basis as shown in Figure 22.1. As we saw in relation to new product development, there is a series of screening exercises to identify not just the target country or countries but specific segments in the chosen countries.

One way to analyse the data is by means of the **Business Environment Risk Index (BERI)**, which assesses countries on a scale of 0 (unacceptable conditions) to 4 (superior conditions) on 15 economic, political and financial factors, namely:

- political stability;
- attitude to foreign investment and profits;
- attitude to nationalization;
- degree of inflation;
- balance of payments;
- bureaucratic delays;
- economic growth;
- currency convertibility;
- enforcement of contracts;
- labour costs and productivity;
- professional services;
- state of communications infrastructure;
- local management;
- short-term credit arrangements;
- loan facilities.

By aggregating scores for each of the variables, the suitability of the country can be assessed. In this way, management can screen various countries as potential export markets.

Once it has been decided which countries to

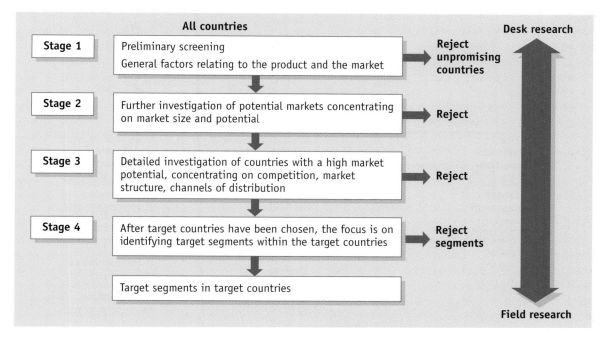

Figure 22.1 The screening of target markets

target, the next question is how to take advantage of the overseas market.

How to enter overseas markets

As we have seen, 'place' (or channel of distribution) is one of the four 'Ps' of the marketing mix. In international marketing, this element of the marketing mix takes on a unique form and significance in the formulation of marketing strategy. Exporting, the production of goods in one country and their subsequent transfer abroad, might be the most well known of the ways of selling abroad, but it is just one way of entering the overseas market. Moreover, exporting itself takes a number of forms. It is to these different methods of entering overseas markets that we now turn (see Figure 22.2).

Exporting

The distinctive feature of exporting is that goods are transferred from one country to another. However, exporting takes a number of distinct forms, defined primarily in terms of the extent to which

the producer is actively involved in the process. There is a broad distinction between direct exporting and indirect exporting. In direct exporting, the producer is actively involved in seeking distribution channels, although the distribution itself might be undertaken by an overseas agent, a foreign distributor or a wholly owned marketing subsidiary. Indirect exporting, a more passive method of entering overseas markets, involves the selling of goods to an export or trading company, which then undertakes the marketing of the goods abroad. Because of the involvement of other principals (a company buying and selling on its own behalf), the producer has to accept a lower price for the goods but is spared the expense and risks associated with overseas markets. A company venturing into overseas markets for the first time and lacking experience and expertise will probably use indirect channels.

Production abroad

Production abroad is not exporting in the usual sense, but it is nevertheless a way in which companies can seek to profit from selling goods

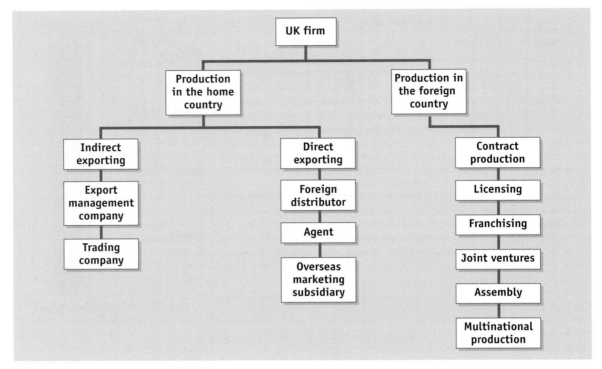

Figure 22.2 Methods of entering overseas markets

abroad. Production abroad has obvious economies in terms of transport costs and is a way of entering overseas markets that are otherwise blocked by import and exchange controls.

Production abroad takes the following forms.

- **Contract production** goods are manufactured abroad on behalf of a UK company seeking to sell goods in the country of production.
- **Production under licence** allowing foreign firms to produce and market the product in specified areas in return for financial compensation.
- **Franchising** selling the right to produce a branded product in specified areas together with technical knowledge and management services.
- **Joint ventures** joining with locally based companies to establish a company abroad to produce and market a product in specified areas.
- **Assembly abroad** the establishment of

'screwdriver' plants abroad to assemble goods that originate in the home country.
- **Multinational production** the establishment of production facilities abroad with products being transported to other countries, including the country in which the parent company is resident.

In choosing their entry strategies, companies will take account of the following internal and external factors (see also Figure 22.3).

- **Internal factors:**
  - financial resources;
  - level of expertise;
  - ability to cope with risk;
  - need for control;
  - corporate objectives and strategy;
  - costs and profitability.
- **External factors:**
  - market conditions;
  - market potential;
  - political factors (such as political stability);

Figure 22.3 Considerations relating to entry to overseas markets

– competition in the market;
– availability of distribution outlets.

The product: standardization or adaptation?

Some businesses prosper by selling the same product in overseas markets as they do in the domestic market (and in the same way). Prime examples of the global approach include Coca-Cola, Pepsi Cola and Kellogg's breakfast cereals. Other companies produce different products for different markets, as in the motor industry (for example, the products of Ford in Europe are different from those of Ford in America). A strategy of producing the same product for the whole European market is known as a pan-European strategy. Alternatively, a firm might produce an individual product variation for each separate market.

There are obvious economies in producing a standardized product in terms of:

● product development;
● scale in production;
● marketing.

The development of mass communications has reduced national differences, creating more of a global market. However, there are continuing differences in:

● consumer needs and behaviour;
● government regulation (such as on product safety);
● national culture;

● market opportunities;
● competition in the market;
● conditions under which the product is used;
● opportunities for after-sales service, for example.

These differences suggest a need for adaptation of the product to suit local requirements. After all, responding to the needs of the market is what marketing is all about.

The exporter has to weigh up the cost of adaptation (including the lost opportunities for economies of scale) against the marketing benefits of changing the product to suit the market. If the cost of adaptation exceeds the benefits in terms of increased sales revenue, the business will either try to sell the standardized product or forgo that particular market.

Brands

It is not just the product that can be varied to suit overseas requirements. Other aspects of the marketing strategy can be organized on either a global, Continental (pan-European) or national level. Coca-Cola and Mars Bar are global names. The Mars company famously changed the name of a number of its products (Marathon became Snickers) as part of its move towards a global strategy. On the other hand, some large companies prefer to use local brand names (such as soap powders).

The advantages of a worldwide brand are:

● reduction in advertising costs;
● economies in packaging;

- easy identification;
- uniform image;
- increased marketing efficiency;
- increased prestige;
- easier penetration of new markets.

Despite such advantages, there are problems with global branding. Language, and cultural and legal factors, might make the domestic brand name inappropriate. The imposition of a Western brand name might cause resentment in certain countries in the Third World.

If the brand owner uses contract or licensed production to penetrate overseas markets, there are problems associated with guaranteeing quality. If the quality of a globally branded product is inconsistent, it could harm sales elsewhere in the world.

It is because of these problems that there is sometimes a need for branding on a local level. Despite the higher costs and loss of economies of scale, the local brand can be devised to suit local requirements and aid identification locally. This also allows variation of quality across different markets without the danger of adversely affecting sales back home.

Promotion

As in domestic marketing, decisions relating to promotional activities in the overseas market will be conditioned by considerations of the cost-effectiveness of method, media and message. Where a company is producing substantially the same product to be sold under the same brand name in a number of different countries, it will be tempted to adopt a standardized approach to promotion. However, this assumes a certain homogeneity across the countries concerned. It is true that the countries of western Europe have great similarities in terms of living standards, outlook on life and media availability. However, there are also substantial differences that result from religion, language and other aspects of national culture. Consequently, it might be necessary to adapt the promotional strategy to suit local requirements. This might entail the use of different promotional methods, including different advertising media, and the formulation of a different promotional message. Most readers will have enjoyed television programmes in which fun is made of the different styles of television commercials in Europe, the Americas, Japan and Australia. What we should remember is that some advertisements on UK television might seem equally eccentric and bizarre in other countries.

Pricing

In setting the price of the product for overseas markets, a company will take into account the following factors:

- those internal to the firm (such as objectives and costs);
- those specific to the product (such as the stage in the lifecycle, quality, delivery costs);
- those specific to the market (such as consumer demand);
- environmental (such as competition, government policy, state of the economy).

After these factors have been considered, pricing strategies can be devised. It is likely that the eventual strategy will involve either market penetration or market skimming. Alternatively, the strategy may be market- (competitor-) based. However, the significant point is that a different pricing policy can be adopted because it relates to a different segment of the total market for the product.

From the theory of price discrimination in economics it is possible to identify the prerequisites of a discriminatory pricing policy. First, the market has to be divided into segments (and this is certainly the case when national boundaries effectively separate out different groups of customers). Second, price elasticity of demand varies from segment to segment (and this is likely to be the case as different nationalities have differing degrees of sensitivity to price changes). Third, the supplier has to be able to prevent buyers reselling goods bought at a low price in one market at a higher price in another (reselling across national boundaries can be reduced and even prohibited by clauses in the contract of sale). The international market provides near perfect conditions for discriminatory pricing with the result that the pricing strategy can be adapted to meet local circumstances.

Conclusion

The central point that emerges from this overview of international marketing is the question of standardization or adaptation. The decision facing a company embarking on marketing overseas is: 'Should we seek to sell the same goods abroad as we do in the domestic market, and in the same way, or should we adapt the marketing mix to suit local conditions?' The policy of standardization involves less expense, but will not succeed if it ignores local needs. The marketing philosophy suggests that each market should be separately investigated and, where necessary, a policy of adaptation should be applied to the various elements of the marketing mix.

Key concepts

Adaptation Adapting one or more elements of the marketing mix to suit local requirements.

Entry methods The different methods by which business organizations can profit from supplying goods to overseas markets. The methods include exporting, franchising, contract production, licensing, joint ventures and multinational production.

Exporting A method of entering overseas markets by means of the physical transfer of goods across national borders. Exporting can be direct or indirect depending on the extent of involvement of the producer in the marketing operation.

Global product A product with a brand name which is universally recognized.

Global strategy International marketing using the same marketing mix in every country and region.

Multinational corporation A company with production facilities in two or more countries.

Pan-European strategy International marketing using the same marketing mix throughout Europe.

Essay questions

1 Analyse the ways in which international marketing differs from domestic marketing.

2 Analyse the different market entry strategies available to manufacturing companies.

3 Analyse the particular risks and problems associated with international marketing.

4 Standardization or local variation? Analyse the case for each in relation to:
(a) the product;
(b) promotional strategy.

5 (a) Explain the role of agents in international marketing.
(b) Analyse the reasons for long, indirect channels of distribution being especially common in international marketing.

6 (a) Analyse the long-term impact of the EU single market on UK marketing to the rest of the EU.
(b) Analyse the likely impact of possible UK adoption of the euro on the marketing strategies of UK firms.

The marketing plan

Having investigated the basic principles of marketing and the different strategies to be pursued, we can now draw all the elements together in the plan for the marketing of a product.

Chapter objectives

1 To identify the role, advantages and limitations of marketing plans.

2 To describe and analyse the contents of a marketing plan.

3 To provide a sense of unity and integration to the reader's understanding of the marketing process.

Marketing – the integrative function

Let us return to the marketing philosophy with which we started Part III of the book. Marketing is the all-embracing function that links the company with customers' needs to get the product to the right place at the right time. Marketing is not just one of the functions of management, it is the central function, with the customer at the heart of the process. This was illustrated by Philip Kotler, the leading American marketing expert (see Figure 23.1).

The customer is at the centre because satisfying customers' needs is the means by which the organization can achieve its objectives. Marketing is at the interface between the customers' and the other management functions. Therefore, it has an integrative role within the organization, ensuring that resources are used to produce the goods to satisfy customers' needs.

A variation on this approach to marketing is **asset-led marketing**. These strategies are based on the organization's strengths (products, brands, technology, human resources and finance) rather than just customers' needs. Hence, instead of posing the question 'What do customers want and how can we satisfy them profitably?', asset-led marketing poses the question 'How can we use our assets more effectively?' Business organizations should 'play to their strengths' and not just follow every change in customers' needs.

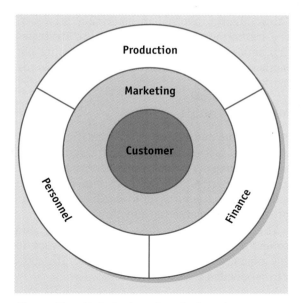

Figure 23.1 Kotler's view of marketing: the customer as the controlling function and marketing as the integrative function

POISE

This is the basis of the approach to marketing strategy developed by Hugh Davidson in *Even More Offensive Marketing* (Gower, 1998) – offensive, meaning being proactive rather than giving offence: 'Offensive Marketing involves every employee in building superior customer value, very efficiently, for above-average profits.' This definition stresses that marketing is everyone's business and not just the preserve of the marketing department. The definition stresses adding value for the benefit of customers, but undertaking this activity in an efficient and, therefore, profitable manner. POISE stands for:

Profitable the skill of marketing is to achieve a proper balance between the organization's need for profit and the customers' need for value;
Offensive offensive marketing involves taking risks, devising long-term strategies and investing heavily;
Integrated the philosophy must permeate the whole organization;
Strategic the well-conceived marketing plan

must be developed after probing analysis and an evaluation of alternative strategies;
Effectively executed the plan must be effectively executed and this obviously requires cooperation and commitment from all concerned.

After this further and deeper look at marketing philosophy, let us seek to bring together the elements of the marketing mix into a marketing strategy and the marketing plan.

What is a marketing plan?

McDonald defines it as follows: '**Marketing planning** is simply a logical sequence and series of activities leading to the setting of marketing objectives and the formulation of plans for achieving them.' A marketing plan is 'a plan which focuses on a particular product and/or market and details the resources, strategies and programmes for achieving the products' objectives in that market' (Baker).

Like all plans, marketing plans are concerned with:

● where we are at present;
● where we want to go;
● how we are going to get there;
● mechanisms for evaluating whether or not the organization has succeeded.

The first component involves a diagnosis of the present situation in relation to the product, company and market. This is achieved by a marketing audit. The second component is a statement of the marketing objectives together with the overall corporate objectives. The third component is the heart of the plan as it details strategies and tactics for getting there. **Strategies** are the broad outlines of the methods to achieve the aims. **Tactics** are the specific programmes of action to be taken to make the plan work. The final part of the plan builds in a mechanism for evaluating progress towards the achievement of the marketing goals. Figure 23.2 sets out the elements of a marketing plan.

It must always be remembered that the process of drawing up the plan is considered to be as important as the plan itself. The planning process imposes a discipline on those involved in manage-

Figure 23.2 Format of a marketing plan

ment. It forces them to clarify objectives, appreciate constraints and devise appropriate strategies. The formalized process of planning encourages a rational approach to decision making, it provides an integrating element to the management of business functions (thus avoiding conflict). By developing a strategy, senior management is able to delegate tactical decision making and implementation to middle and junior management.

Corporate objectives

Returning to the notion of a hierarchy of objectives, the **corporate objectives** are at the apex of the hierarchy. As we saw in Chapter 2, the qualitative mission statement is followed by a quantitative statement of objectives expressed in SMART terms – that is, Specific, Measurable, Agreed, Realistic and Time-specific. Corporate objectives relate to the level and/or growth of profit (either expressed in money terms or as a percentage of sales revenue or capital employed). Corporate objectives are set by top management rather than those directly involved in marketing. However, the marketing planner must draw up strategies and action plans in line with the corporate objectives, which, in turn, are incorporated into the marketing plan.

Marketing audit

A **marketing audit** involves a systematic appraisal of all the factors (external and internal) that affect a company's commercial performance over a defined period. The purpose is to reveal and analyse the strengths and weaknesses of the organization's marketing function.

The first task, therefore, is to identify and collect data and subjective opinions relevant to the assessment of the marketing effort. The audit can be divided into four sections:

- the general business environment;
- the market environment for the particular product (or products);
- the competitive environment – that is, the firm in relation to major competitors;
- an internal audit of the company and its marketing policies.

Each section can be subdivided as shown in Table 23.1 – which can be regarded as a checklist of factors to be considered in the marketing audit. It should be stressed that the audit will cover past, present and future variables. As such, it will reveal not just strengths and weaknesses, but also threats and opportunities. A **threat** is a challenge posed by an unfavourable trend or event that would lead to product stagnation or decline unless countered by purposeful marketing action. A marketing **opportunity** is an attractive arena for marketing action in which the organization could enjoy competitive advantage.

The **internal audit** concentrates on the planner's own company, its operational efficiency and service effectiveness, its key skills, competences and resources, its products and the core business it is in.

Analysis

The previous stage was concerned with collecting information. It is now necessary to use analytical

Table 23.1 The marketing audit – a checklist

External audit	Internal audit
Business environment	**Own company**
Economic	Sales (total, by location, customer, product)
Political	Market shares
Fiscal	Profit margins
Social	
Business	**Marketing mix variables**
Legal	Market research
International	Product development
Intracompany	Range
	Quality
The market environment	Distribution
Total market size	Stock levels
Segments	Price
Channels of distribution	Packaging
Products	Promotional activities
Geography	
Needs, tastes	**Customer classification**
Habits	Customers' buying power
Prices, profits	Customers' problems and requirements
Communication	Customers' methods of supplier selection
Competitive environment	
Major competitors	
Size	
Market shares	
Market standing	
Marketing skills	
Production capabilities	
Marketing methods	
Personnel	
Key strengths and weaknesses	

techniques such as PEST and SWOT to identify **trends** (or **market drivers**), which create good marketing opportunities. These should be evaluated in terms of the following.

- **Market size** especially if the organization needs a large market share to provide a satisfactory return on investment.
- **Market growth** an 'expanding pond means room for new fish' to develop without preventing the growth of existing fish. Rapid growth provides opportunities for all whereas in a static or declining market, competition is fierce. Growing markets tend to tilt the supply and demand equation in favour of the supplier because there is usually a time lag before the supply side catches up with increases in demand.
- **The competition** Analysis of the competition will either suggest segments to target or it will discourage entry or continuation in the market. The planners should:
  - identify the competitors;
  - assess their performance;
  - check with customers what they look for in a supplier.

  Michael Porter, a leading authority on strategic management based at Harvard

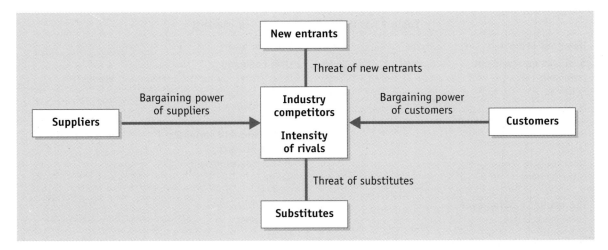

Figure 23.3 Porter's model of competition

University, developed an approach to analysis of an industry (or market) based on five factors that influence profitability within the industry (or market). The five factors are (see Figure 23.3):
- the intensity of competition among existing firms;
- the threat of potential competitors who will be drawn to the market if profits are high (so-called supernormal profits in economic theory);
- the threat of substitute products that will attract customers, again if prices are high;
- the bargaining power of suppliers (monopoly suppliers of inputs can force up prices and reduce profit margins);
- the bargaining power of customers (large monopsonistic customers can bargain to buy at a low price).

These five factors affect the general level of profits within the industry. The profits of the individual firm will reflect its efficiency.

● **The cost of entry** There are three factors to consider before answering the question 'Can we realistically enter the market?' The factors are as follows.
  - The **learning curve** How deep is the organization's knowledge of the technology, product area and the way the market works? The cost of learning

can be high – even fatal – if mistakes are made.
  - **Accessibility**, in terms of distribution and ability to deliver a competitive customer service.
  - **Promotion** How easy will it be to get the message across to potential customers? In markets dominated by large companies, it will be difficult for a small company to make its voice heard against the large-scale advertising of the industry giants.

Assumptions

The audit provides data about the past, present and likely future trends. One difficulty in predicting future trends is the uncertainty about the future. The validity of predictions depends on a series of assumptions made about interrelated events and trends. The assumptions built into a marketing plan might include the following:

● the economy will grow by 2 per cent in the next year;
● there will be no significant change in the structure of taxation;
● our competitors will not introduce a new product next year;
● the birth rate will rise next year;
● world capacity in the industry will rise by 20 per cent over the next two years.

The objectives contained in the marketing plan will depend on these assumptions, as will the choice of strategy. In effect, the planners are identifying the opportunities and the constraints under which they will operate. The value of the whole plan will depend on the accuracy of the assumptions made. They should be clearly stated and be realistic.

Marketing objectives

The setting of achievable and realistic objectives is based on the analysis of the marketing audit and are derived from the corporate objectives. **Marketing objectives** are concerned with which products are to be sold in which markets. It is important not to confuse *objectives* (what you want to achieve) with *strategies* (how you are going to achieve them).

A marketing plan is likely to include objectives concerning:

● market share (share of the total market in the hands of the firm);
● sales revenue;
● market penetration (increase in sales to existing customers);
● contribution or profit.

In all cases, the target can be set either in terms of a level or percentage growth rate.

In addition to *quantitative* objectives, the firm is likely to formulate *qualitative* statements on matters such as market position, product quality and product development. These are *policies* rather than objectives as they are guidelines on the approach to the marketing of the company's products.

Continuing the idea of a hierarchy, there will be sub-marketing objectives for each of the elements of the marketing mix. These might be:

● a promotional objective of securing an *x* per cent recognition rate;
● a place objective of securing a *y* per cent increase in outlets stocking the product;
● a product objective of securing a particular market share for each individual product in the range;

● a price objective, such as remaining competitive with rivals.

Marketing strategies

Strategies are broad statements of the action to be taken to achieve the objectives identified in the plan. Marketing strategies are all the methods used by an organization to achieve its long-term marketing objectives. They will specify:

● a **target market** the group of customers to whom a company wishes to appeal;
● a **marketing mix** the controllable variables the company puts together to satisfy this target group.

Marketing *tactics*, on the other hand, are the methods used by the organization to achieve its short-term marketing objectives. Note that the distinction between strategy and tactics is in terms of broad statement/detailed statement and long-term/short-term plans. Both are expressed in terms of the elements of the marketing mix – the four Ps (see Figure 23.4).

● **Product:**
 – range;

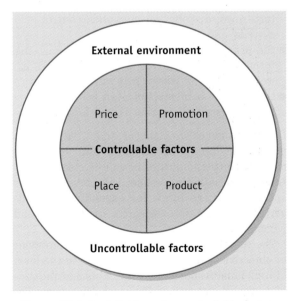

Figure 23.4 Contollable and uncontrollable factors and the marketing mix of the four Ps

- quality;
- degree of standardization;
- market position;
- branding;
- packaging.
● **Price:**
  - skimming;
  - penetration;
  - differentiation;
  - terms and conditions.
● **Promotion:**
  - advertising;
  - selling;
  - sales promotion.
● **Place:**
  - channels of distribution;
  - delivery;
  - direct or indirect methods.

Programmes or plans of action (tactics)

Programmes specify what has to be done, who is to do it and by when. Programmes are developed for major functional areas within marketing. For example:

● the **sales plan** will include details of territories, distribution networks, control systems and sales teams;
● the **promotion plan** will specify, in detail, the forms of promotion that will be employed, as well as how and when they will be used;
● the **market information plan** will specify the details of the market research effort.

The programmes or plans of action will be expressed in terms of budgets, and individual responsibility and authority will be clearly identified. The marketing budget will include targets and will allocate funds for expenditure on advertising, promotion, research, distribution and personal selling.

The marketing plan started with a statement of objectives. We have now got down to the level of individual responsibility for implementing programmes in support of the marketing plan. The final section of the plan specifies the control mechanism.

Evaluation and control

The plan lays down procedures to monitor progress towards achievement of the objectives. The aim of these is to assess performance and, where necessary, take corrective action – either by changing strategy and/or tactics, or by revising the marketing objectives in the next planning cycle.

A system of evaluation and control will highlight weaknesses in the marketing effort, whether they be in terms of human failing or of inappropriate strategies and tactics.

Common causes of failure in marketing planning

Although the benefits of marketing planning are substantial, there are some common mistakes and pitfalls in the process:

● confusing tactics with strategy, resulting in 'short termism';
● lack of integration with other functional areas of management;
● organizational barriers, such as bureaucracy;
● lack of in-depth analysis;
● lack of knowledge and skills;
● a hostile corporate culture;
● lack of systematic approach;
● confusion about the marketing function – marketing viewed as sales, advertising and product management or customer service rather than satisfying the customer for profit;
● competing on price rather than developing a competitive advantage (or unique selling point);
● expanding sales of the least profitable products;
● expanding sales with insufficient working capital;
● staying too long in declining or unprofitable markets;
● launching new products with inadequate prior research.

These problems can be avoided only by analysis and detailed planning bringing together all the components that make for successful marketing.

Key concepts

Assumption A statement or proposition that is taken as true and on which various courses of action will be based.

Marketing audit A set of techniques designed to reveal and analyse strengths and weaknesses in the marketing function.

Marketing objectives Statements of what is to be achieved in terms of product sales in the market.

Marketing plan A plan focusing on a product and/or market that states details of resources, strategies and programmes for achieving the objectives for the product in particular markets.

Marketing strategy The establishment of marketing objectives and the means by which they are to be achieved.

Tactics or programmes of action The methods to be employed in implementing the strategic plan.

Essay questions

1 (a) With the use of examples, explain what is meant by marketing objectives. Clearly distinguish a marketing objective from a corporate objective.
(b) Analyse the role of marketing objectives in the development of a marketing strategy.

2 (a) Describe the likely contents of a marketing plan.
(b) Assess the benefits of drawing up marketing plans.

3 Suggest and evaluate marketing strategies available to:
(a) a market leader: and
(b) a market follower.

Further reading

Adcock, D., Bradfield, R., Halborg, A., and Ross, C. (1998) *Marketing: Principles and Practice*, 3rd ed.,

Financial Times Pitman.

Blythe, J. (1998) *Essentials of Marketing*, Financial Times Pitman.

Hill, E., and O'Sullivan, T., (1999) *Marketing*, 2nd ed., Pearson Education.

Kotler, P., Armstrong, G., Saunders, J., and Wong, V. (1996) *Principles of Marketing*, Prentice Hall.

Lancaster, G., and Massingham, L. (1998) *Essentials of Marketing,* McGraw-Hill.

Lancaster, G., and Reynold, P. (1998) *Marketing*, Macmillan.

Proctor, T. (1997) *Essentials of Marketing Research*, Pitman.

West, C. (1999) *Marketing Research*, Macmillan.

Short answer questions

Critically explain each of the following using examples from specific business organizations:

1 Boston Matrix.
2 Below-the-line promotion.
3 Above-the-line promotion.
4 Penetration pricing.
5 Desk research.
6 Non-price competition.
7 Product differentiation.
8 Mark-up pricing.
9 Product positioning.
10 Product range.
11 Extension strategy.
12 Marginal cost pricing.
13 Direct marketing.
14 Personal selling.
15 Closed and open questions in questionnaires.
16 Segmenting by lifestyle.
17 The ACORN classification.
18 The product lifecycle.
19 Undifferentiated marketing.
20 Sample frame.
21 Random sampling.
22 Selling via the Internet.
23 Agents.
24 Informative advertising.
25 The print media for advertising.
26 Price discrimination.
27 Target market.
28 Globalization of markets.
29 Quota sampling.
30 Either exclusive or selective channels of distribution.

Exercises

1 As the marketing manager of a clothing manufacturer, you have been asked to prepare a report to cover:
  (a) the current state of the market;
  (b) marketing strategies available to the firm;
  (c) recommendations for strategies in relation to:
      (i) pricing
      (ii) promotion
      (iii) channels of distribution.

  The following information provides some background to the present situation.

  ● The firm and its products are positioned at the popular end of the market.
  ● The bulk of its products are sold to people aged 15–30.
  ● The firm has a 2 per cent market share.
  ● The promotional budget is £1 million.
  ● The economy is slowly recovering from a prolonged recession.
  ● The firm sells the bulk of its products through indirect channels, using retailers other than the big name chains.
  ● Product lifecycles are short, but the firm does benefit from the services of a talented design team.
  ● The firm is currently taking its first tentative steps into export markets.

2 The owner of a grocery shop in your town has commissioned you to undertake some marketing research. She is interested in extending the range of products sold in the shop to include one or more of the following:

  ● greetings cards;
  ● newspapers and magazines;
  ● selected records and tapes;
  ● rented videos.

  In addition to deciding which, if any, of the above to stock, the owner also requires information to enable her to make decisions on pricing and promotion of the new range of stock. Produce a report in which you should:

  (a) outline the main sources of secondary data you will use in your research;
  (b) specify, with reasons, the survey techniques you plan to use to collect primary data;
  (c) specify, with reasons, the sampling method you plan to use to collect primary data;
  (d) devise an appropriate questionnaire;
  (e) collect and present primary data appropriate to the task;
  (f) state the conclusions you draw from your research;
  (g) make your recommendations to the shop owner.

3 The following table of contents is taken from a marketing plan.

Section

1 Introduction
2 Summary
3 Situation analysis
   ● assumptions
   ● sales
   ● key products
   ● key markets
4 Marketing objectives

5 Marketing strategies
6 Schedules
7 Sales promotion
8 Budgets
9 Profit and loss account
10 Controls
11 Update procedures
   Appendix

(a) Explain the significance of assumptions within a marketing plan. Suggest appropriate assumptions in relation to the marketing of a new car.
(b) Explain the difference between marketing objectives and the overall objectives of the company.
(c) Suggest appropriate marketing objectives in relation to a new premium ice-cream.
(d) Explain the relationship between objectives, strategies and tactics.
(e) What is meant by a budget in this marketing plan?
(f) Why is certain material placed in an appendix rather than in the body of the plan itself? Suggest the kind of material that might be inserted in the appendix to a plan for the marketing of trainer shoes.

4 As marketing manager, you have a £5 million budget to launch one of the following:

(a) a fashion magazine;
(b) a brand of ice-cream;
(c) a range of furniture.

Produce a marketing plan for the chosen product to include the following:

(i)   a review of the current situation in the market;
(ii) assumptions on which forecasts are based;
(iii) marketing objectives;
(iv) strategies and tactics;
(v)   budget for promotional activities.

5 As brand manager, produce a marketing plan (including situational audit, assumptions, forecasts, objectives and strategies) for either:

(a) a car model entering the mature phase of its lifecycle; or
(b) a family brand of cosmetic products.

In both cases, your products enjoys a 5 per cent share of the UK market and the export potential is limited.

6 The graph below depicts the pattern of sales and the cash flow generated in the first decade of a product's lifecycle.

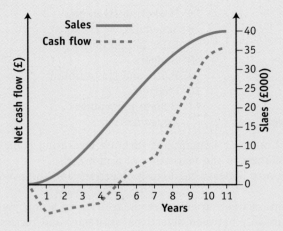

(a) Describe and explain the relationship between product sales and cash flow as shown in the graph.
(b) Suggest:
  (i) marketing objectives
  (ii) promotional strategies
  for each of the years 1 and 6.
(c) Describe the situation that arises in years 10 and 11 and suggest strategies to cope with the situation.

7 The graph below illustrates sales revenue and profit for a product over its lifecycle.

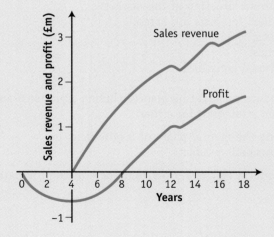

(a) Comment on the relationship between sales revenue and profits over the 18 years.
(b) In year 10, a design change was introduced to extend the life of the product. What was

the impact on profits? A second extension strategy was pursued in year 14, but did not involve a design change. Suggest what it might have been.

(c) What evidence is there that the product changed from being a star to a cash cow by year 16?

(d) (i) What was the pre-launch R&D time for the product?

(ii) Suggest, with explanations, three products for which R&D time is likely to be longer.

(iii) Suggest four reasons for abandoning products before launch.

Accounting and finance

The profit and loss account

This first chapter in the accounting and finance part of the book introduces the reader to financial accounting. This is the aspect of accounting in which the controllers of the organization (that is, managers) report back to stakeholders on the performance in the previous time period. After a brief look at the principles underlying financial accounting, we then explore the first major account – the profit and loss account.

Chapter objectives

1 To develop an understanding of the principles of financial accounting.

2 To understand the role and purpose of a profit and loss account.

3 To develop skills in interpreting a profit and loss account.

4 To explain methods of stock valuation.

Financial accounting

Financial accounting is that part of accounting that is concerned with external reporting – to shareholders, government and other interested parties. Managers act as stewards of the financial and physical resources that are entrusted to them by the owners of the enterprises. Accounting provides the data on performance that enables owners of the enterprise to assess performance and hold managers accountable. However, it is not just shareholders who are interested in the financial performance of a business enterprise. The following groups of people and organizations also take a keen interest in the accounts of business enterprises:

● employees and their trade unions;
● creditors;
● suppliers, especially where materials are supplied on credit;
● customers;
● government;
● tax authorities;
● regulatory agencies;
● competitors;
● potential investors;
● rival companies;
● those considering a merger or takeover;
● interest groups concerned with the environment and local economy.

The criteria by which these groups evaluate

company performance will vary. For example, employees are interested in profitability, for the purpose of securing pay rises and/or guarantees of job security; creditors are interested in the liquidity position of the firm for evidence that it will be able to settle its debts as they fall due.

A financial accountant has the responsibility of compiling a series of accounts, of which the most important are the balance sheet, profit and loss account, and cash flow statement. Because financial accounts are prepared for stakeholders it is essential that they are produced under a standard set of rules. The Companies Act 1985 requires companies to prepare accounts to a prescribed format. The Accounting Standards Board issues accounting standards on the method of dealing with particular items in the accounts. These took the form of Statements of Standard Accounting Practice (SSAPs) and are now known as the Financial Reporting Standards (FRSs). Where companies are given a discretion over the treatment of particular items, they are required to reveal their accounting policy. This provides the informed reader with the opportunity of assessing accounts in the light of this information. The fundamental framework of accounting ideas is expressed as accounting concepts. These can be seen as the basic principles governing the way accounting data is prepared. The main concepts are as follows:

- **Going concern** It is assumed that the business is a going concern and will continue to trade.
- **Double entry** All transactions are looked at from two angles (such as expenditure of money and the acquisition of assets) and are recorded in two ways. As a result, the accounts will always balance.
- **Prudence** Final accounts always record the least favourable position (for example, sums due for payment are treated as provisions). The consequence of this principle is that losses are, if anything, overstated while profits might be understated.
- **Verification** In final accounts, all statements must be capable being verified by independent people.
- **Matching** This is concerned with matching the revenue earned in an accounting period

with the expenditure incurred earning that revenue.

- **Realization** Sales revenue is based on figures produced when the goods have been invoiced, even though cash might not have been received. Similarly, purchases are included when the goods are taken into stock whether or not they have been paid for. As a result of this principle, there is an important distinction between the profit and loss account and the cash flow statements (see Chapter 28).
- **Consistency of method** Accounts have to be based on consistent methods if they are to be useful in comparing performances over time or between different business enterprises.

The format of the profit and loss account

The **profit and loss account** (see Figures 24.1 and 24.2) is a financial statement that shows the

Profit and loss account for the year ending 31 March 20XX		
	£000	£000
Sales revenue		1000
Less Cost of goods sold		
Direct materials	300	
Direct Labour	200	
Production overheads	100	600
Gross profit		400
Less Selling expenses	100	
Administrative expenses	100	200
Trading profit		200
Other operating income		10
Profit before interest		210
Less Interest		50
Net profit before tax		160
Less Tax		60
Profit after tax		100
Less Dividend		20
Retained profit		80

Figure 24.1 A profit and loss account

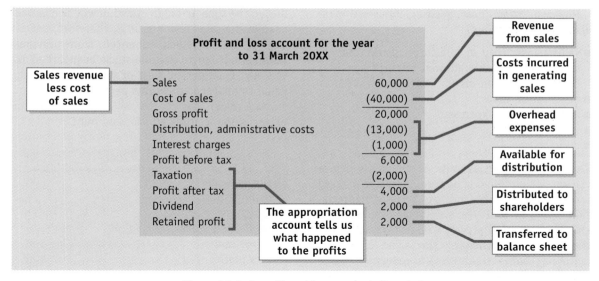

Figure 24.2 A profit and loss account dissected

profit (loss) made by a business during a defined period of time (normally one year). The account also shows the uses to which the profit has been put (or how the losses were financed). Unlike the balance sheet, this statement covers a period of time rather than being a snapshot at a particular moment in time.

The profit and loss account is divided into three sections as shown in Table 24.1.

Table 24.1 The sections found in a profit and loss account

Section	Format	Purpose
Trading account	Sales revenue less cost of sales	To calculate gross profit
Profit and loss account	Gross profit plus other income less expenses = Net profit	To calculate net profit
Appropriation account	Net profit less tax and dividend = Retained profit	To show what happens to net profit or how a loss is financed

Trading account

The **trading account** reveals the **gross profit** of the business. This is defined as the difference between sales revenue (turnover) and the direct costs of the goods sold. The latter is the cost of purchasing the goods from suppliers (in the case of a retail business) or the cost of producing the goods that are sold (in the case of a manufacturing business). The production cost of goods sold is equal to the cost of raw materials in the finished goods plus the cost of labour required to make the goods and an amount for production overhead costs. Because of the important matching principle, only the cost of producing the goods sold in the period concerned is charged against that period's sales revenue.

The profit and loss account

This section of the account shows the **net profit** of the business, defined as the difference between gross profit (plus income from sources other than the sale of goods) and various expenses. The other income might be the profits from selling an item of machinery. It can, therefore, be regarded as other operating income.

However, from these positive items we must deduct the following:

- selling costs (pay of salesforce, marketing expenses, discounts allowed to customers, bad debts written off);
- distribution costs;
- administrative expenses;
- interest paid;
- depreciation.

The balance sheet records accumulated depreciation, which is deducted from the value of fixed assets. In the profit and loss account depreciation refers to that year's depreciation, which is charged against that year's sales revenue under the matching principle. The same choice of methods (that is straight line or reducing balance method) is available to calculate depreciation. (See Chapter 25.)

The appropriation account

This account reveals what happened to net profit. It is likely that the government will claim a proportion of these profits as corporation tax and, if the company operates abroad, it is possible that it will have had to pay equivalent taxes to foreign governments. However, the appropriation account does not include payments of value added tax as sales revenue (the opening line of the account) is net of VAT.

Profits after tax are available for distribution (to owners of the business) or for retention.

The size of the dividend is determined by the board of directors, who are of course answerable to shareholders. Total dividend is often considerably less than the total of post-tax profits. The difference is retained profit available for reinvestment in the business. This retained profit will then be transferred to the balance sheet as one of the reserves.

Cost of sales

Cost of sales is the direct costs associated with the generation of sales revenue over the trading period concerned. It is important to appreciate the application of the matching principle in the calculation of cost of sales. Only the stock used

during the time period in question will be charged against the sales revenue. It is, therefore, necessary to include stock 'inherited' from previous time periods but to exclude stock 'bequeathed' to the next time period. Cost of sales is, therefore, equal to opening stock plus purchases but minus closing stock. This can be seen in the following extract from a profit and loss account.

	£000	£000
Sales revenue		200
Opening stock	50	–
+ purchases	150	–
Less Closing stock	(100)	–
Cost of sales		100
Gross profit		100

The closing stock figure will be included in the balance sheet at the end of the time period. This treatment of stock makes the choice of stock valuation method important.

Stock valuation

Valuation of stock is necessary for the pricing of materials issued from stores and for the final accounts of a business. The value of stock at the end of the year appears in the balance sheet and the value of opening and closing stock affects the cost of sales shown in the trading account. Consequently, the value placed on stocks affects the profit figure and, therefore, the tax to be paid by the business organization.

The **principle of prudence** dictates that the value attached to stock must be the lower of purchase price and net realizeable value. In an inflationary period, it is likely that the current net realizeable value will be greater than the purchase price. This means that the purchase price should be chosen as the basis for valuation. The problem is that stock is likely to be received at various times over the year, perhaps from different sources and probably at different prices. Which price paid should be used for valuation? One of three methods will be chosen.

- **First in, first out (FIFO)** This method is

based on the presumption that materials are used in the order in which they were acquired. Thus, the oldest stock is issued first and the price paid for the first batch of materials is used for all issues until that particular batch is used up. Thereafter, the issue price paid for the next batch is used until that, in turn, is depleted. The closing stock is valued in terms of the more recent purchases.

FIFO is a complicated method requiring considerable record keeping. The effect of FIFO (compared with the alternatives) is to produce a higher value for closing stock and, therefore, a lower value for cost of sales. This in turn produces a higher figure for trading profits. In other words, it results in a lower charge to the profit and loss account but a higher valuation for stock in the balance sheet than is the case with other methods. It is acceptable to the Inland Revenue for tax purposes as costs are related to those actually incurred and the value of closing stock is close to current market value. However, when FIFO is used for costing purposes, it has the disadvantage that the issue price lags behind current prices. There will be a delay before the prices paid for materials are passed on to production.

Table 24.2 shows that FIFO method of stock valuation.

- **Last in, first out (LIFO)** Under this method there is a presumption that issues are drawn from the latest batch. When that has been used up, the price of the previous batch is used. The result is that production is charged with costs that are close to current market prices but closing stock is valued at a price (or prices) paid for the oldest existing stocks. LIFO thus understates the value of closing stock and thereby reduces both the cost of goods sold and the figure for profits. Because LIFO understates the profitability of the firm, it is not acceptable to the Inland Revenue for tax purposes. This does not prevent the firm from using LIFO for its own internal purposes. The great advantage is that the price of the latest item is passed on to production.

  Table 24.3 shows the LIFO method of stock valuation.

- **Weighted average cost (AVCO)** This is a comparatively simple method and is acceptable to the Inland Revenue. All stock is valued at a single representative average cost, calculated by dividing the total value of stock purchases by the number of items. With this method, all issues (and the closing stock) are valued at a single price, which will be between that produced by FIFO or LIFO. This method has the advantage of smoothing out price fluctuations, but, on the other hand, issues do not reflect the actual prices paid for stock.

Table 24.2 The FIFO method of stock valuation

Date	Purchases	Issues	Value of issues	Balance
1	6,000 × £12			6,000
2		4,000	4,000 × £12	2,000
3	8,000 × £13			10,000
4		6,000	2,000 × £12	4,000
			4,000 × £13	
5	8,000 × £14			12,000
6		10,000	4,000 × £13	
			6,000 × £14	2,000
7	10,000 × £15			12,000
8		6,000	2,000 × £14	
			4,000 × £15	6,000
Cost of sales				£348,000
Closing stock			6,000 × £15	£90,000

Table 24.3 The LIFO method of stock valuation

Date	Purchases	Issues	Value of issues	Balance
1	6,000 × £12			6,000
2		4,000	4,000 × £12	2,000
3	8,000 × £13			10,000
4		6,000	6,000 × £13	4,000
5	8,000 × £14			12,000
6		10,000	2,000 × £13	
			8,000 × £14	2,000
7	10,000 × £15			12,000
8		6,000	6,000 × £15	6,000
Cost of sales				£354,000
Closing stock			2,000 × £12	
			4,000 × £15	£84,000

Table 24.4 Advantages and disadvantages of different methods of stock valuation

FIFO
Advantages
- Realistic – based on the assumption that issues are made in order of goods received
- Based on prices paid
- Closing stock based on most recent prices
- Acceptable under Companies Act 1985 and SSAP 9, and for tax purposes

Disadvantages
- Identical items will be priced differently because they are deemed to be from different batches
- FIFO values stock at the latest price, which, in a period of rising prices, means the highest price. This is contrary to the principle of prudence as it gives a lower cost of sales figure, thereby increasing profit

LIFO
Advantages
- Value of closing stock is easy to calculate
- Based on prices paid
- Issued at the most recent prices

Disadvantages
- Unrealistic because it assumes that recent stock is used/sold first
- Closing stock is not valued at most recent prices
- Not acceptable for tax purposes or under SSAP 9, but is acceptable under the Companies Act 1985
- Identical items issued at different prices because they are deemed to be made from different batches

AVCO
Advantages
- Prices averaged out, thus recognizing that all items should be included in the calculation
- Variations in prices minimized
- Has the effect of smoothing out the costs of production and cost of sales
- Profits of different periods can be realistically compared
- Acceptable under SSAP 9 and the Companies Act

Disadvantages
- The average does not represent prices actually paid
- A new average must be calculated with every purchase of stock

Table 24.4 summarizes the advantages and disadvantages of the different methods of stock valuation.

Window dressing the profit and loss account

Window dressing is the practice of presenting accounts in a way that flatters the financial position of the firm. One window dressing technique is to include in the current years' sales invoices relating to the early part of next year. This has the effect of concentrating two months' sales revenue into the last month of the financial year. The artificial boost to revenue will result in a higher than justified profit figure. Another technique is to delay the writing off of bad debts so as not to reveal losses in the current account. These practices could be seen as equivalent to tidying up before the arrival of visitors. Alternatively, it could be seen as, at best, sharp practice and, at worst, fraud as it offends against the true and fair principle that is at the heart of financial accounting.

Key concepts

Appropriation account The account that records the profits available for distribution and retention.
Cost of sales The costs directly associated with the generation of sales revenue – that is, direct costs.
Expenses/overheads Indirect costs not directly associated with the sales revenue.

FIFO A method of stock valuation based on the principle that quantities in hand are those most recently acquired.
LIFO A method of stock valuation based on the principle that quantities in hand represent the earliest units acquired.
Profit gross The excess of sales revenue over the cost of goods sold.
Profit net The excess of sales revenue over all costs.
Profit and loss account A financial statement of an enterprise's revenue, expenses and profits.
Window dressing The practice of bringing forward or delaying transactions with the intention of presenting a more favourable position in a set of accounts

Essay questions

1 (a) Explain the role of financial accounting in business management.
 (b) Analyse what each of the major stakeholders look for in a set of accounts.

2 Profit figures are not objective but can be manipulated. Discuss.

3 Analyse the possible explanations for a satisfactory gross profit figure being converted into an unsatisfactory net profit figure.

4 Analyse the factors taken into account in relation to the appropriation account.

Exercises

1 The following information relates to a company's accounts for the year ending 30 April.

	£000
Sales	500
Purchases	400
Opening stock	50

The value of closing stock under three different methods of stock valuation is as follows:

	£000
FIFO	70
LIFO	55
Weighted average	57

Calculate:

(a) gross profits, using each of the three methods of stock valuation:
(b) gross profits ratios in each case – the gross profit ratio is gross profit as a percentage of sale revenue.

2 The following information relates to stock purchases and issues at a garage.

Date	Purchases (units)	Sales (units)	Balance (units)
January	100 at £20		100
February		70	30
March	100 at £21	50	80
April		60	20
May	300 at £22	200	120
June		50	70

Calculate the value of closing stock using:

(a) the FIFO method;
(b) the LIFO method;
(c) the weighted average method.

3 The following are details of the movements in the stock level of a product that is purchased for resale.

Date	(Units) Purchases	(Price per unit)(£) Purchases	(Units) Issues	(Units) Balance
Year 1				
1 June B/forward	–	–	–	300
8 August	200	8.00	–	500
15 September	–	–	500	–
17 September	500	8.25	–	500
Year 2				
5 January	–	–	100	400
8 January	–	–	200	200
16 March	200	8.75	–	400
31 May	–	–	200	200

(a) Explain the meaning of the following terms:
  (i) FIFO;
  (ii) LIFO.
(b) Using the available information, calculate the value of the closing stock:
  (i) if the method of valuation is FIFO;
  (ii) if the method of valuation is LIFO.

4 Complete the profit and loss account below.

	£	£
Sales revenue (50,000 @ £6)		
Less Cost of sales		
Labour (£2 per unit)		
Material (£1.50 per unit)		
Gross profit		
Less Overhead expenses	20,000	
Trading profit		
Less Interest (£600,000 @ 10%)		
Profit before tax		
Less Tax (@ 33%)		
Profit after tax		
Less Dividend (75% of post-tax profit)		
Retained profit		

5 Construct a profit and loss account from the information given below.
Sales revenue was £6m.
Interest payments of £0.2m were made.
To the stock, valued at £0.2m, left over from the previous year was added £2.5m of purchases.
Closing stock was valued at £0.3m.
Overheads amounted to £1.5m.
£1m of staff pay was paid.
Tax is 30 per cent of profits after all expenses.
50 per cent of post-tax profits were retained.

6 Construct a profit and loss account from the information below.
Output: 60,000 units.
Price: £7 per unit.
Labour costs: £3 per unit.
Materials: £2 per unit.
Overheads: £30,000.
Interest payments: £200,000 loan at 10 per cent.
Tax payments: 33 per cent of profits before tax.
Dividend: 75 per cent of post-tax profit.

7 Prepare a trading and a profit and loss account from the information below.
Barry stated trading as a van-based mobile ice-cream salesman on 1 May. The account will cover the first three months of trading.

He rented the van at a cost of £700 per month.

Running expenses for the van averaged £200 per month.

Part-time labour cost £200 per month.

Total sales for the three months were £15,000.

Barry purchased ice-cream from a local manufacturer at a total cost of £7500.

All his stock had been sold by the end of the three-month period, although Barry still owed £800 for stock purchased on credit.

He used his own home for office work. Telephone and postal costs associated with the business came to £250 for the 3 months.

Each month, Barry paid himself £600.

8 Complete the profit and loss account below and calculate profit before interest and tax as a percentage of sales revenue.

	Company				
	A	B	C	D	E
	£000	£000	£000	£000	£000
Sales revenue	500	800	900	2,000	5,000
Cost of sales	400	400		1,000	3,000
Gross profit			200		
Overheads	80				1,000
Operating profit		200	−100	300	
Non-operating profit	100	0	500		1,000
Profit before interest and tax				300	
Interest	50	100	100	150	500
Profit before tax					
Tax	30	30	200		500
Profit after tax				100	
Dividend	30		40		500
Retained profit		20		50	

9 An abridged version of the profit and loss account of a public company is reproduced below.

	£000	£000
Turnover		4,562
Less Cost of sales		3,309
Gross profit		1,253
Less		
Distribution costs	872	
Administrative costs	624	(1,496)
Profit (Loss) for the year		(243)

Prepare a new profit and loss account to take account of the following changes:

(a) a 10 per cent rise in turnover;
(b) a rise in gross profit margin to 35 per cent;
(c) a 10 per cent reduction in the fixed element of distribution costs, but with the variable element remaining constant as a proportion of sales. The fixed element is currently 40 per cent of distribution costs;
(d) a 10 per cent reduction in administrative costs.

10 The profit and loss account shown below refers to the year ending 30 April.

	£000	£000
Sales		2,000
Less Cost of sales		1,300
Gross profits		700
Less		
Administrative costs	300	
Selling costs	200	500
Profit before taxation		200
Less Corporation tax		50
Profit after taxation		150
Less Dividends paid		50
Retained profit		100

Prepare a profit and loss account for the subsequent year based on the following assumptions:

(a) sales and cost of sales both rise by 10 per cent;
(b) administrative and selling costs rise by 5 per cent;
(c) corporation tax is levied at a rate of 25 per cent on profit before taxation;
(d) 50 per cent of post-tax profits are retained.

The balance sheet

The **balance sheet** is the second type of account that Business Studies students need to understand and interpret. Unlike the profit and loss account, it does not show changes over the year but, instead, is a snapshot of the position of the firm at the end of the year. In essence, it records what the firm owns, what it owes, what it is owed and how it was financed. To further develop an understanding of the balance sheet this chapter should be studied in conjunction with Chapter 27, Ratio analysis, and 29 Financing a business.

Chapter objectives

1 To explain the purpose and structure of a balance sheet.

2 To develop skills in interpreting a balance sheet.

3 To develop an understanding of the limitations of the balance sheet.

4 To develop an understanding of depreciation of fixed assets.

The balance sheet

The double entry system of bookkeeping is based on the simple fact that there are two sides to any transaction. When an organization makes a cash sale, the increase in cash is matched by a reduction in the total value of stock. Similarly, the purchase of machinery is matched by a reduction in cash, a rise in borrowing or the raising of funds by shares issued.

From the double entry system of bookkeeping, we can derive a basic equation that must always hold true:

Assets = Capital + Liabilities

Assets are resources (premises, stock, equipment, cash) that are acquired by the organization and put to use to achieve the organization's objectives. **Capital** represents the owners' financial interest in the organization. In the case of a company, it will take the form of share capital plus reserves. **Liabilities** are amounts of money owed to others (such as from banks, bills not yet paid). If the assets of the organization increase, there will be an equivalent increase in capital or liabilities or both. If the assets are reduced, there will be a reduction in capital or liabilities or both.

The balance sheet: horizontal and vertical formats

The balance sheet is a statement of the firm's assets, liabilities and owners' capital at a specific

Assets	Capital + liabilities
(Resources of the firm)	(How the resources are financed)
Fixed assets	Capital and reserves
Investments	Loans
Current assets	Long-term liabilities
	Current liabilities

Figure 25.1 Horizontal format balance sheet

Fixed assets
Less Depreciation
= Net fixed assets

Current assets
Less Current liabilities
= Working capital (or net current assets)

Total assets less current liabilities
Less Long-term liabilities
= Owners' capital (or owners' equity)

Figure 25.2 Vertical format balance sheet

date. Whereas the profit and loss account covers a period of time (usually a year), the balance sheet gives a snapshot at a particular moment in time. It summarizes the financial state of the business at that date, although, for reasons that will be made clear below, it is a fallacy to believe that the balance sheet shows what a business is worth.

The traditional format for the balance sheet is horizontal, with assets on one side and capital plus liabilities on the other (see Figure 25.1).

The balance sheet equation

The format above is based on the basic balance sheet equation:

$$A = C + L$$

where A is assets, C is owners' capital and L is liabilities. By manipulating the equation, we can highlight important aggregates in the balance sheet. Liabilities can be divided into long-term and current liabilities, the latter being defined as liabilities due for payment some time during the next 12 months. Similarly, assets take the form of machinery (a long-term feature of the business) and stock (which is sold off). Hence the equation can be rewritten as:

Fixed assets (F) + Current assets (CA) = Capital (C) + Long-term liabilities (L) + Current liabilities (CL)

This becomes:

$$F + (CA - CL) = C + L$$

The item in brackets (current assets minus current liabilities) is known as net current assets or **working capital**. Therefore, the sum of fixed

assets and net current assets is equal to owners' capital and long-term liabilities.

A further manipulation enables us to highlight the owners' capital still further: $F + (CA - CL) - L = C$. This tells us that the owners' stake in the business is equal to the total value of assets less the total value of liabilities. This is the basis of the modern format of the balance sheet known as the vertical, or narrative, format (see Figure 25.2).

Balance sheet items

The first part of the balance sheet (see Figures 25.3 and 25.4) gives details of fixed assets, which take a number of forms. **Intangible assets** include goodwill, licences, trademarks, brand names and development costs. By definition they do not have a physical form, yet they add to the value of the business. For instance, the value of a newspaper company is far in excess of the value of its capital equipment. The real value should include human resources on contract and the value of a famous name, such as *The Times* or *The Observer*.

Tangible fixed assets take the form of premises, plant and machinery used in the production process. These assets are acquired for use by the firm rather than for sale (although they might be sold off when no longer required).

There is, however, an important difference between premises and the other tangible fixed assets. Premises are likely to rise in value whereas the other fixed assets are likely to fall in value.

Balance sheet at 31 March 20XX			
	(£000)	(£000)	(£000)
Fixed assets			500
Premises			
Plant/equipment	200		
Less Accumulated	100		
depreciation		100	
Total fixed assets			600
Current assets			
Stock	70		
Debtors	50		
Cash in bank	50		
		170	
Less Current liabilities			
Creditors	50		
Provision for tax	20		
Overdraft	30		
		100	
Working capital			70
Assets *less* Current liabilities			670
Less Long-term liabilities			170
			500
Shareholder's funds			
Shares issued	400		
Share premium	50		
Reserves	50		
			500

Figure 25.3 A balance sheet

If the balance sheet records the value of premises in terms of historic cost price, it will understate the current value of business assets. In the case of a public limited company, this could make the business a target for takeover, especially by people more interested in acquiring assets (such as a prime site) than acquiring the business as a going concern. When a business is about to be sold, it is especially important to record the current value of premises. From our understanding of the double entry process, we know that the change in value recorded on the assets side must be accompanied by an equivalent change in the owners' capital.

Machinery, plant and vehicles used in the business are likely to lose value over time and, eventually, they will need to be replaced. This decline in value is reflected in the depreciation figure. **Depreciation** is the decline in value of fixed assets as a result of wear and tear and over time. You will notice that the value of fixed assets is shown net of accumulated depreciation – that is, the depreciation over the life of the capital item. The methods of calculating depreciation will be explored later in this chapter.

The second part of the balance sheet concerns the working capital of the business. **Current assets** covers three items. **Stock** is the goods that the firm possesses and expects to sell in the normal course of business. It is usual to distinguish three forms of stock: raw materials, work-in-progress and finished goods. The importance of each category varies with the nature of the business. Bespoke tailors, for example, are unlikely to hold large quantities of finished goods, whereas retailers are unlikely to hold stocks of raw materials. There are problems about how such stock should be valued, as we saw in Chapter 25.

The **debtors** item in the current assets is goods and services sold but not yet paid for. A small proportion of this money may become 'bad debt' – where there is little likelihood of receiving payment – but, for most of the money categorized as debtors, it is only a matter of time before it is received. **Cash in bank** is self-explanatory. All firms should hold some money in reserve to meet forthcoming payments. As payments and receipts are not synchronized, some reserve is essential. However, excessive holdings of cash are undesirable as businesses profit by putting money to good use.

Listed after the assets are the liabilities of the business, starting with **current liabilities**. These are defined as obligations or debts of the business with settlement due within one year. **Creditors** refers to money owed to, say, supply firms. Expected **tax payments** are also treated as a current liability. Here the business is making provision to discharge its tax obligations. Similarly, **dividends** to shareholders that have been declared (but not yet paid) are treated as a current liability for which provision is being made. Finally, **over-**

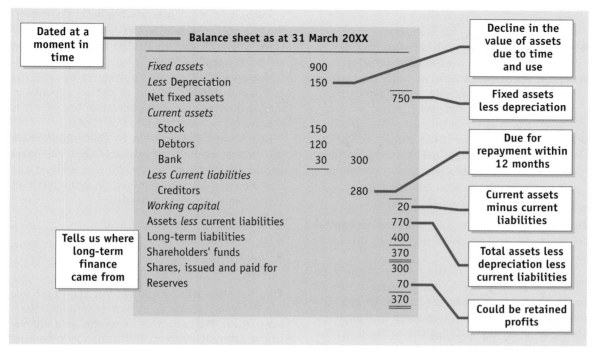

Figure 25.4 A balance sheet dissected

drafts are regarded as a current liability as banks can demand repayment without notice.

Working capital is the sum of current assets minus the current liabilities of the business. It can be seen as the investment in stocks of goods (both being processed and those sold) less the short-term borrowings of the business. The management of a firm's working capital is crucial to the health of any business – we will look at this in Chapter 26.

The final sections of the balance sheet concern **sources of finance**. Long-term loans (or debt finance) provide one such source. Creditors are not the owners of the business and, therefore, do not have a right to participate in decision making or to share in profit. However, they do have a right to repayment of capital with interest and to sue if payment is not forthcoming.

By subtracting liabilities (long-term and current) from total assets, we get a figure for owners' equity or owners' capital. In the case of a company, this could also be called **shareholders' funds**. This is the finance that owners have put into the

business, either in the form of the purchase of a share issue or profits that were withheld from them.

The balance sheets records:

- the amount of authorized share capital;
- the amount of called-up capital that has been paid;
- the number and aggregate value of each class of allotted shares;
- the redemption date of any redeemable shares;
- details of allotment of shares since the previous balance sheet;
- details of any holdings of the company's securities by subsidiaries.

The difference between, first, the value of total assets less all liabilities and, second, share capital subscribed and paid for is entered as **reserves**. These take the following forms.

- **Revenue resources** These are profits that have been retained in the business and, therefore, withheld from shareholders. This is recorded in the balance sheet as transferred from the profit and loss account.

- **Revaluation reserves** These arise from the revaluation of assets, especially property.
- **Capital redemption reserve** Such a reserve is required when redeemable shares are issued. As these shares are redeemed out of profits, a reserve is created to finance redemption.
- **Share premium** This is the surplus of the issue price of the share over its nominal (or face) value. By issuing shares at a premium, the company raises more finance than is shown in the (nominal) share capital.

The last three reserves, jointly known as **capital reserves,** cannot be called on to pay dividends to shareholders.

A common fallacy relating to reserves is to believe that they are a ready source of funds to finance investment in the future. In fact, the reserve has already been translated into an asset. The reserve merely matches the existing asset.

Depreciation

As noted earlier, the value of fixed assets (other than buildings) is shown on the balance sheet net of depreciation. Let us now explore what is meant by depreciation.

A motor car purchased for £9000 in one year might have a trade-in value of £5000 three years later. Over the three years, the car has depreciated, or declined in value, by £4000. Not only has the possession fallen in value, but when the owner comes to replace it he or she will need a further £4000, and this assumes that prices have not risen in the meantime.

Depreciation in accounting is a recognition of this decline in value. SSAP 12 defines it as 'a measure of the wearing out, consumption or other reduction in the useful economic life of a fixed asset whether arising from use, effluxion of time or obsolescence through technological or market changes'. In terms of the balance sheet, the purpose of recording depreciation is to account for loss in value. The net value of fixed assets (the so-called **net book value**) is historical cost less accumulated depreciation. In terms of the profit

and loss account, depreciation reflects the matching principle of allocating the cost of an asset over time. Depreciation can also be seen as providing a fund for replacement.

However, although it is a negative item on the profit and loss account, it is not an expense as money does not leave the business. Instead, it is a provision – a setting aside of funds.

How should depreciation be calculated? There are several techniques available, but the most important ones are the straight line method and the reducing balance method. In both methods three items of data are needed:

- the historical cost of the asset;
- its expected life;
- its residual value when sold off (either as scrap or as a working asset).

The first item will be known, but the other two can only be forecast from past experience. However, these forecasts can be wrong as a change in the external environment (a change in demand or in technology, say) could affect either the commercial life of the asset or its residual value (or both). Hence, the net book value is not necessarily equal to the current market value of the asset.

Straight line method

In the **straight line method** of calculating depreciation, a fixed sum is deducted per year from the value of the asset. The sum is calculated by dividing historical cost less expected residual value by the time in years that the business expects to own the asset.

$$\text{Annual depreciation} = \frac{\text{Historical cost} - \text{Expected residual value}}{\text{Expected life}}$$

> **Example**
>
> | | |
> |---|---|
> | Historical cost | £800,000 |
> | Expected residual value | £200,000 |
> | Expected life: | 6 years |
>
> $$\text{Annual depreciation} = \frac{£800,000 - £200,000}{6}$$
>
> $$= \frac{£600,000}{6} = £100,000$$

After the first year, the net book value of the asset will be £700,000; after the second year it will be £600,000 and so on. The advantage of this method is that it is easy to calculate, but it is unrealistic to assume that an asset would deteriorate by an even amount each year. Motorists are aware that the decline in value of a car tends to be greatests in the early months of its life.

Reducing balance method

The **reducing balance method** takes into account the fact that decline is greatest in the early months but slows down later. Thus, rather than deducting a fixed amount from the value of the asset, this method takes a fixed percentage of the balance of value. In the example below, the depreciation rate is 50 per cent, but the 50 per cent is removed from the declining balance. Thus, it is 50 per cent of £100,000, then 50 per cent of £50,000, then 50 per cent of £25,000.

Example

	[£]
Original price	100,000
Depreciation year 1 (50%)	50,000
Balance at start of year 2	50,000
Depreciation year 2 (50%)	25,000
Balance at start of year 3	25,000
Depreciation year 3 (50%)	12,500
Balance at start of year 4	12,500
Depreciation year 4 (50%)	6,250

This method is seen as more realistic than the straight line method but one problem is calculating the appropriate percentage to apply. Figure 25.5 shows the contrasting impacts of the two methods.

As stated above, the net book value is not necessarily equal to the current market value of the asset as the former is based on a forecast. Where an asset is sold for more than its net book value, the firm has, in a sense, 'overdepreciated'. To balance the books, it is necessary to record a surplus on owners' equity.

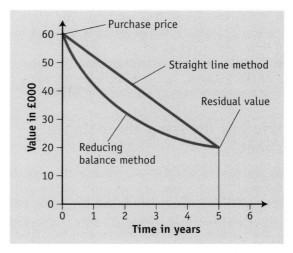

Figure 25.5 Depreciation of fixed assets

Example

	[£]
Market value after 3 years	14,000
Net book value after 3 years	12,500
Surplus	1,500

Limitations of the balance sheet

Although the balance sheet is a fundamental statement about the business, readers of balance sheets should be aware of their limitations.

● A balance sheet is prepared as at a certain date and it is, in a sense, a snapshot of the position at that date. It is possible that the position will change fundamentally within a short space of time.
● The balance sheet only includes items that can be expressed in monetary terms and ignores assets the monetary value of which cannot be expressed.
● There is considerable discretion over the valuation of assets. We have seen that the net book value of fixed assets varies with the method of depreciation used, and in Chapter 24 we saw that the stated value of stock depends on the method used for valuing stock.

- The balance sheet does not reveal the current value of assets unless property is revalued to show its current value.
- The balance sheet does not record the value of the business, unless it includes the value of intangible assets, especially goodwill.

Window dressing the balance sheet

As we saw in Chapter 24, window dressing is the practice of presenting accounts in the most favourable manner. It is not just the profit and loss account that is subject to window dressing – the balance sheet can also receive this treatment. One such technique is sale and leaseback of fixed assets. We will see in Chapter 29 that this is a legitimate way of financing expansion, but it can also be exploited in order to 'dress up' the balance sheet. The sale of assets will result in an inflow of funds that, in turn, either increases the cash figure in the current asset section or is used to pay back or reduce current liabilities. Whatever happens, the fact is that an improvement in liquidity is revealed in the balance sheet. As for the fixed assets that were disposed of, they can be leased back in a way that is not revealed in the balance sheet. In the longer term, it will prove more expensive, but it gives a short-term boost to the balance sheet. Delaying the writing off of bad debts will improve the debtor figure and show an unjustified improvement in liquidity. Liquidity can also be improved by converting current liabilies (such as an overdraft or trade credit) into long-term debt. The conversion might be justified in some circumstance, but it also provides an opportunity to 'massage' the figures.

Goodwill

A window cleaner who retires will want to sell his or her business for thousands of pounds. However, the fixed assets of a simple window-cleaning business might be limited to a ladder and bucket and the use of the family car. Assuming the car is not sold, the value of the fixed assets is likely to be less than £100. So, what is the justification

for placing a value on the business in excess of £1000? The answer lies in the customer base built up over the years. The purchaser is buying the goodwill associated with the business.

Goodwill is defined as the value of a business less the value of assets net of liabilities. As an example, consider a business that has a net asset value of £12 million recorded in its balance sheet but which is purchased for £15 million. The purchaser has paid £3 million for goodwill because of the advantage of the business as a going concern. These advantages include:

- existing customer base;
- reputation for quality;
- marketing skills;
- technical know-how;
- business connections;
- management ability;
- workforce.

It is possible for goodwill to be negative, meaning that the current market value of the business as a going concern is less than the net book value of the business.

One method of calculating goodwill is to value it at, say, three years' past profits or average weekly sales multiplied by a given number. After calculating goodwill, it is easy to calculate the value of a business. The value of a business = net asset value + goodwill.

Alternatively, the earnings basis of valuation can be used. For instance, if a return of 10 per cent per year is expected, a business that records a profit of £50,000 is worth £500,000. Once the value of the business is known, it is easy to deduct the value of net assets to produce a figure for goodwill:

Purchase price – value of net assets = goodwill

Purchased goodwill (arising from the acquisition of a business) is included as an intangible fixed asset in the balance sheet. Non-purchased goodwill is not shown. Under accounting standards, purchased goodwill is amortized over a period of up to 20 years. This means that it is written off over the years in a way similar to the depreciation of fixed assets.

Key concepts

Accounting concepts The framework of ideas underlying the discipline of accounting.

Accounting standards The prescribed methods of accounting for a particular type of transaction or situation.

Balance sheet A statement of the assets, liabilities and capital of an organization at a particular date.

Capital employed The funds used by a company to acquire assets.

Creditor A person or organization to whom money is owed.

Current assets An asset that is not intended for use on a continuing basis by a firm. Consists of stock, cash and debtors.

Current liabilities A debt to be paid within one year

Debtors In the balance sheet, the figure for debtors represents money owed to the business.

Depreciation A measure of the gradual wearing out, consumption or other loss of value of a fixed asset.

Double entry bookkeeping A system of recording financial events that recognizes that each financial event has a dual aspect: a debit and a credit.

Equity The owners' stake in a business.

Fixed assets Assets intended for use on a continuing basis in an enterprise's activities.

Reserves Items of owners' equity arising from share premiums, retention of profits and upward revaluation of assets.

Stock Goods and other assets acquired for resale. Consists of raw materials, work-in-progress and finished goods.

Work-in-progress Goods in the intermediate stages of production.

Working capital Current assets less current liabilities.

Essay questions

1 Analyse the role and nature of the balance sheet.

2 Is the true value of a company revealed in a balance sheet? Justify your answer.

3 Analyse the impact of the balance sheet items of each of the following:
  (a) the purchase of stock on trade credit;
  (b) the purchase of fixed assets with a long-term loan;
  (c) revaluation of property to reflect current values.

4 (a) Analyse the reasons for subjecting fixed assets to depreciation in financial accounts.
  (b) Analyse the consequences for the balance sheet and the profit and loss account of using the reducing balance methods rather than the straight line method of depreciation.

5 Tidying up the house before the arrival of visitors' or 'cooking the books'. Evaluate the ethics of window dressing.

Exercises

1 The table below records the annual depreciation provision for two assets.

	Asset 1	Asset 2
Cost	20,000	10,000
Year 1	6,315	1,295
Year 2	4,321	1,127
Year 3	2,957	982
Year 4	2,023	854

For each asset calculate:

(a) the annual percentage depreciation;
(b) the depreciation in year 5;
(c) the net book value at the end of year 5.

2 Jones and Khan Limited purchased machinery for £2 million. For accounting purposes, they plan to use the reducing balance method of depreciation at the annual rate of 40 per cent.
(a) Calculate the:
   (i) annual depreciation of the asset for each of the first three years;
   (ii) net book value of the asset at the end of each year.
(b) If Jones and Khan used the straight line method of depreciation, what is the annual depreciation required to reach the same net book value after three years as you identified in (a) (ii)?
(c) Annual profits in each year were £10 million before allowing for depreciation. Analyse the consequences of the two methods of depreciation for the profit and loss account in each of the three years.

3 (a) If the purchase price of an asset is £1.5 million and its residual value after five years is £300 000, calculate:
   (i) annual depreciation using the straight-line method;
   (ii) the net book value at the end of each year up to five years.
(b) The purchase price of an asset is £20 million. Using 25 per cent per annum reducing balance method. calculate:
   (i) annual depreciation over five years;
   (ii) net book value at the end of each year.
(c) The purchase price of an asset is £600,000 and annual depreciation, using the straight line method, is £80,000.
Calculate:
   (i) the net book value after four years;
   (ii) the expected life of the asset assuming a residual value of £200,000;
   (iii) the expected life, assuming a residual value of zero

4 An engineering company purchases equipment of £40 million that will be depreciated over a five-year period using the reducing balance method at the rate of 50 per cent per year.
  (a) Calculate:
      (i) depreciation in each year;
      (ii) the net value of the asset at the end of each year.
  (b) If, instead of the reducing balance method, the company used the alternative straight-line method, calculate the annual depreciation necessary to produce the same net value after five years.
  (c) On the same graph paper, plot two curves to illustrate the depreciation of this asset.

5 From the data given below, construct balance sheets in both the horizontal and vertical formats.

	£000
Machinery	180
Stock	62
Cash at bank	11
Freehold land and buildings	210
Fixtures and fittings	53
Debtors	19
Creditors	34

It is known that 75 per cent of long-term capital takes the form of owners' equity.

6 Arrange the following data in a vertical balance sheet format, filling in the missing information.

	£000
Creditors: bank loan	5,000
Fixed assets at historic cost	60,000
Stock	11,000
Debtors	8,000
Capital ordinary shares fully paid	35,000
Reserves	?
Current liabilities	?
Working capital	8,000
Balance at bank	3,000
Current assets	?
Depreciation	20,000

7 Study the information below and construct a balance sheet for the company as a 31 March 2005.

Balance sheet as at 31 March 2004

	£000	
Fixed assets	1,500	
Less Depreciation	300	1,200
Current assets		
Stock	200	
Debtors	100	
Cash	20	
Current liabilities		
Creditors	200	
Tax payable	50	
Working capital		70
Net assets		1,270
Long-term liabilities		570
Shareholders' equity		700
Share capital		400
Reserves		300

During the year 2004–5, the following occurred:
Stock rose by £100,000
Debtors rose by £30,000
Creditors fell by £50,000
Long-term liabilities rose by £30,000
£100,000 worth of shares were issued
£200,000 of buildings were acquired
Annual depreciation was £100,000
£70,000 tax bill was payable on 5 May 2004
Working capital was £130,000

8 During a company's first year of operations, the transactions listed below occurred. Study the information and construct a balance sheet for the company's first year of operation.

£20,000 of shares were issued.
£10,000 borrowed on a long-term basis.
£28,000 of fixed assets were purchased.
£8000 of stock purchased with cash.
£20,000 of stock bought on credit.
£7000 of stock sold for £14,000 cash.
£18,000 of stock sold for £36,000 on credit.
£20,000 of cash collected from debtors.
£10,000 paid to creditors.
£3000 depreciation provision.
Expected tax liability of £2000.
Expected electricity bill of £100.
£8000 of costs incurred and paid for.
£1000 of interest paid on the loan.

Working capital

This chapter focuses on the constituent elements of working capital and introduces the idea of managing working capital to improve the performance of the firm.

Chapter objectives

1 To develop an understanding of the elements of working capital.

2 To develop an understanding of ratio analysis in relation to working capital.

3 To introduce elements of the management of working capital.

4 To develop an understanding of cash statements.

The importance of working capital

From the previous chapter you will be aware that working capital represents the firm's holding of cash and its investment in goods that are unfinished, unsold and/or unpaid for minus its debt with less than a year to run. In terms of the balance sheet it is equal to:

Current assets – Current liabilities
or
Stock + Debtors + Cash – Creditors + Provisions for payment within one year

The working capital of a business organization can be illustrated by comparing the assets of the business with its permanent capital and liabilities (see Figure 26.1).

Working capital management

Working capital management involves monitoring the cash flow of a business to ensure that it has access to cash to finance normal operations. This, in turn, means monitoring three **pressure points** in the working capital cycle:

● creditors
● stock
● debtors.

Creditors

It must be remembered that the **creditor figure** in a balance sheet relates to money owed by

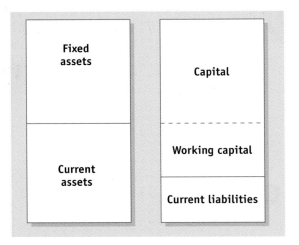

Figure 26.1 The derivation of working capital

the firm to others (such as trade creditors). The credit is used to buy stock that will eventually be sold. Although some credit is both necessary and desirable for any business, it is important to monitor the level of indebtedness by the firm to outsiders. This is especially true when the firm has credit from a number of different sources. This might lead to a neglect of the overall creditor situation.

A high creditor figure will lead to problems in payment. One way to check the position is by calculating the length of time taken by the firm to pay its creditors. This is expressed as a ratio.

$$\text{Average payment period} = \frac{\text{Average trade creditors}}{\text{Purchases of stock on credit}} \times 365$$

A single figure is of little value, but a comparison over time (or with comparable firms) can be very informative. A lengthening of the 'creditor days ratio' is desirable in one respect but could presage disaster in another. First, extension of credit means that the firm has access to means of payment for long periods. But, second, if the delay in payment is the result of inability to pay, it suggests a fundamental problem for the firm.

Another technique for monitoring the creditor figure is to rank creditors in terms of length of credit. In this way, those that have been owed money for the longest period can be identified to ensure that they are dealt with as soon as possible.

Stock

Stock control is an issue within the production function as well as the accounting function. It is given lengthy treatment in Chapter 36, but a few comments applicable to the accounting function can usefully be made at this stage.

Obviously, it is necessary to maintain sufficient stock levels to continue production and satisfy demand. However, excessive levels of stock represent a substantial financial burden. The purchase of stock will have either depleted cash reserves or increased the firm's indebtedness to outsiders. If nothing else, it will involve an opportunity cost in terms of an alternative forgone. **Stock control** is concerned with achieving an optimum balance between excessive investment in stock and insufficient investment leading to **stockout** (running out of stock).

Ratios can be employed to evaluate stock levels but, as always, they should be used with caution. Interfirm comparisons are only valid for broadly comparable firms; historical comparisons are only valid if there is no substantial change in the nature of the firm.

The working capital of a business can be seen as its life-blood and, like blood within a body, there is a circular flow. From its holdings of cash, together with short-term loans and overdrafts, the firm is able to purchase stocks of raw materials. These stocks are processed and transformed first into work-in-progress and then into finished goods. The sale of goods will result in either an immediate cash inflow or the creation of debtors who will pay for their purchases after a time lag (see Figure 26.2).

The inflow of cash over the period should be in excess of the cash outflow. This is because of the need to pay:

- interest
- dividends
- taxes
- to acquire additional (or replacement) capital assets.

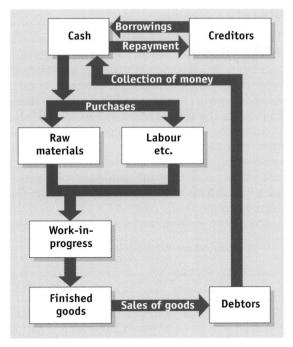

Figure 26.2 Working capital cycle

Liquidity ratios

Before dealing with the management of the constituent elements of working capital, it is necessary to refer to the two liquidity ratios. The **current asset ratio** expresses the balance between current assets and current liabilities in ratio form:

$$\frac{\text{Current assets}}{\text{Current liabilities}}$$

A rule of thumb to bear in mind is that if the resulting number is less than 1.5, the firm might have difficulty in raising the means to settle debts. On the other hand, a ratio in excess of 2 might mean that there is an excessive amount of cash or stock, or money outstanding from debtors. This is generally seen as being excessively cautious, with a consequent failure to take advantage of profitable opportunities elsewhere.

The **liquid**, **quick** or **acid test ratio** expresses the liquid capital of a firm (that is, current assets less stock) as a ratio of current liabilities:

$$\frac{\text{Current assets less stock}}{\text{Current liabilities}}$$

The significance of the elimination of stock from the calculation is that a firm anxious to raise cash to settle immediate debts may be reluctant to dispose of stock at a discount. Liquid capital combines accessible cash with money that is promised to the firm. The rule of thumb here is that 1 represents an ideal – a ratio of less than 1 is often seen as dangerous, whereas more than 1 is seen as unnecessarily cautious.

Despite the reference to these ideals, we should interpret these ratios with caution. You will discover that the ratios of retail businesses, especially those trading in fast-moving goods, will be much lower than these textbook ideals. Moreover, the ratio will vary according to the time of year, so that, for example, there will be a high investment in stock in December and a high cash and debtor figure in January. The conclusion to draw is that, despite these textbook ideals, the ratios will reflect the circumstances of the firm and the date of the balance sheet concerned. You should not jump to the conclusion that a supermarket

If the inflow is less than the outflow it will be necessary to seek further credit. Continuing the life-blood analogy, this can be seen as haemorrhageing – the outflow of blood is endangering the continued life of the body. Drastic action is necessary to keep the blood flowing – a transfusion of new blood, coupled with a tourniquet to stop the dramatic blood loss. In the case of a firm, the remedial action will be a transfusion of new credit and/or a cutting back of stock levels to improve the cash inflow.

You should now be able to appreciate the vital importance of managing the working capital of a firm. It is a sobering fact that the failure of firms is often not the result of unprofitability but of problems with cash flow and liquidity. In other words, a business that is fundamentally sound might have difficulties in raising sufficient means to repay its debts as they fall due. This will certainly be true in the case of a firm involved in **overtrading**. This is a situation of excessively rapid growth with insufficient working capital.

chain with a low liquidity ratio is on the verge of insolvency.

● **Stock turnover**

$$= \frac{\text{Cost of goods sold in a year}}{\text{Average stock}}$$

Broadly, this tells us how many times the average stock level is sold during a 12-month cycle (however, valuation problems mean that this is only broadly true). A rise in the turnover ratio suggests an increase in efficiency or a rise in the level of activity.

● **The quantity of finished goods that are being held in stock** can be assessed by the following ratio:

$$\frac{\text{Stock of finished goods recorded in the balance sheet}}{\text{Cost of sales for the year}} \times 365$$

Hence, if stock at the end of the period was £10 million and cost of sales for the year was £100 million, then we could conclude that, on the date of the balance sheet, the firm had

$$\frac{10m}{100m} \times 365 = \begin{array}{l}\text{36.5 days of finished goods} \\ \text{in stock}\end{array}$$

Though this does not inform us of how much should be held in stock, it does provide some means of drawing a conclusion about stock levels over time.

Debtors

Except in parts of the retail trade (such as fast-moving goods like sweets) credit sales are unavoidable. To gain custom it will be necessary to offer credit terms, especially if competitors offer goods on credit. Generous credit terms are likely to increase the volume of trade, but they will also increase the expense for the seller. It is, therefore, necessary to strive for a balance between good terms to attract customers and a strict collection policy that will minimize cash outlay but also alienate customers. Table 26.1 shows the costs associated with credit.

The debtor position can be monitored by ratios.

Debtor collection time (debtor days) =

$$\frac{\text{Average debtors}}{\text{Total credit sales}} \times 365$$

An isolated figure is meaningless, but a lengthening of a debtor's payment times over a period of time means a growing delay in the receipt of cash. Moreover, if it is accompanied by pressure for prompt settlement of the firm's *own* debts, the firm could be exposed to difficulties. Hence, the debtor and creditor days figures should be studied together.

Another technique of monitoring debtors is to rank them in terms of age of debt. Again, the aim is to identify long outstanding debts in order to concentrate efforts on recovering this money.

The control of debtors will involve the encouragement of prompt payment and the minimizing of bad debt. **Prompt payment** is facilitated

Table 26.1 The costs associated with credit

The costs of granting credit	The costs of denying credit
● Lost interest. The opportunity cost involved in an interest-free loan	● Loss of customer goodwill
● Loss of purchasing power as prices rise reduces the real value of repayments	● Loss of sales
● Cost of assessing customer's creditworthiness	● Inconvenience and cost of collecting cash
● Administrative costs	
● Bad debt	
● Discounts for prompt payment	

by efficient administrative systems to invoice customers and identify outstanding money owed to the firm, coupled with action to collect money. Prompt payment can be encouraged by a discount or some other incentive. However, as a discount involves a cost to the firm, there is an inevitable trade-off between prompt receipt of money with a discount and delayed receipt without subtracting a discount.

Debtors should be seen as money that is promised to the business. It will be received but after some delay. **Bad debts** represent amounts that are almost certainly irrecoverable. In terms of the balance sheet, they are shown as a deduction from debtors and, in terms of the profit and loss account, they are shown as an expense. There is an intermediate category of **doubtful debts** – in other words, there is some possibility of recovery, but the chances are considered low.

By their very nature, bad debts cannot be managed after the event. The only action the firm can take is to tighten up its system of credit references to minimize the risk of such bad debts in the future. The dilemma faced by firms is that there is always some risk involved in giving credit – the only *sure* way to eliminate all risk of bad debt is not to offer credit, but this will be at the expense of sales volume. 'Doubtful debt' should, however, be monitored by means of an ageing schedule where debtors are analysed according to the length of time that their debt has been outstanding.

Cash

Cash (and its negative, an overdraft) represents the residual element in our analysis of working capital. A period of cash outflow (such as heavy investment in stocks without a corresponding increase in credit) will deplete the cash reserves and possibly result in the emergence of an overdraft. A period of inflow (say, payments by customers without a corresponding increase in stocks) will increase cash reserves, or reduce or eliminate an overdraft.

By monitoring the cash position it is possible to make better use of resources available to the firm and ensure that cash shortage does not act as a constraint on the firm's activities. A shortage of cash should be tackled by:

- a reduction in debtors;
- a reduction in stocks; and/or
- an increase in creditors.

A surplus of cash represents an opportunity cost, especially if it is held in a bank account paying zero or low interest rates. Any surplus should be:

- used to make early payments to creditors in order to claim discounts;
- deposited in interest-bearing accounts;
- used to buy marketable securities (such as shares);
- lent profitably to others;
- used to make forward purchases of raw materials in situations of expected price rises.

In Chapter 28 we will encounter the cash flow forecast. This is a projection of the inflow and outflow of cash over a period of time. It should be remembered that not only is this a *forecast* rather than a statement of past transactions, but it is also concerned solely with the movement of cash in to and out of the firm.

Cash flow statements, which are drawn up after the event, are distinct from profit and loss accounts. There are several features present in the profit and loss account for which there is no corresponding flow of cash in to and out of the business.

- **Provisions** This refers to sums set aside for depreciation, immediate debts and tax payments. By definition, these deductions from final accounts do not involve a cash outflow. Consequently, to calculate the cash position, it is necessary to add these sums back in.
- **Sales revenue** is based on invoice data. In accounting, income is usually recognized as having been earned when the goods are despatched and the invoices sent out. Hence, the sales revenue figure for the year is not the same as cash inflow.

Because there is a difference between the cash position of a firm and its underlying profitability, it is necessary to produce cash flow statements.

This is similar to what a prudent current account holder will do when he or she receives a bank statement. The statement drawn up for a particular day shows the 'cash position' of the account. However, the account holder knows that cheques have been signed that have not yet been debited from his or her account. In addition, he or she knows that, before the next pay day, there will be certain standing order or direct debit charges he or she is committed to paying. Conversely, there may be a high expectation of an irregular payment into the account. In thinking along these lines, the account holder is acting in a manner equivalent to an accountant in separating out the cash position *today* from the position once committed money has flowed in and, more importantly out.

Key concepts

Acid test ratio $\dfrac{\text{Current assets} - \text{Stock}}{\text{Current liabilities}}$

Current assets A current asset is one that is not intended for use on a continuing basis in an enterprise's activities. Consists of stock, cash, debtors.

Current asset ratio $\dfrac{\text{Current assets}}{\text{Current liabilities}}$

Current liabilities A liability that is expected to have been paid within one year from the date of the balance sheet.

Debtors In the balance sheet, the figure represents money owed to the business.

Liquid assets Assets that can easily and quickly be converted into money.

Stock Goods and other assets acquired for resale. Consists of raw materials, work-in-progress and finished goods.

Work-in-progress Goods in the intermediate stage of production.

Working capital Current assets less current liabilities. The capital that is available for day-to-day operation of the business.

Essay questions

1 (a) Define working capital.
   (b) Analyse its importance in the successful running of business.

2 (a) Evaluate the usefulness of the textbook ideals for the major liquidity ratios.
   (b) Comment on the relative merits of the current asset ratio and the acid test ratio.

3 Analyse the consequences for working capital, the current asset ratio and the acid test ratio of each of the following:
   (a) the purchase of stock using cash;
   (b) the sale of surplus stock;
   (c) the use of cash to purchase a fixed asset;
   (d) the use of cash to reduce an overdraft.

4 Analyse the consequences of different ways of financing the purchase of stock.

5 Analyse the consequences of:
   (a) creditors demanding payment more promptly;
   (b) debtors paying up more slowly.

Exercises

1 The following data is taken from the balance sheet of a public limited company that has as its financial year end the 30 September.

	Year 1		Year 2	
	£m	£m	£m	£m
Current assets				
Stocks	24	–	35	–
Debtors	20	–	24	–
Prepayments	2	–	2	–
Bank	5	51	0	61
Creditors due in less than one year				
Trade creditors	25	–	35	–
Dividend proposed	4	–	6	–
Corporation tax	6	–	7	–
Bank	0	35	20	68

(a) For each year calculate the:
   (i)   working capital;
   (ii) current asset ratio;
   (iii) acid test ratio.
(b) From the information given, explain the possible causes of the change in the liquidity position.
(c) Advise the company on how the liquidity position could be improved.

2 The data below has been extracted from the balance sheet of a private company:

● At the end of year 1, current assets were valued at £1.5 million. By the end of the year 2 they had risen to £2 million.
● The corresponding figures for current liabilities are £0.5 million and £1.0 million.
● In each of the two years the acid test ratio was 1.
● In each year the stated figure for debtors is the same as that for cash.

(a) For each year, calculate the:
   (i)   current asset ratio;
   (ii) working capital;
   (iii) level of stocks;
   (iv) level of cash recorded in the balance sheet.
(b) Compare the current asset ratio with the acid test ratio and offer an explanation for the divergence between the two.

3 The following data has been extracted from the balance sheets of six firms.

			£000			
	(A)	(B)	(C)	(D)	(E)	(F)
Current assets						
Stock	100	10	200	50	20	20
Cash	20	40	10	50	50	100
Debtors	50	80	10	50	50	20
Current liabilities						
Creditors	40	80	200	120	10	50
Overdraft	40	0	20	0	50	0

(a) For each firm, calculate:
  (i) its working capital;
  (ii) the current asset ratio;
  (iii) the acid test ratio.
(b) Comment on the liquidity position of each firm, suggesting circumstances in which the resulting ratio would be considered:
  (i) satisfactory;
  (ii) unsatisfactory.

4 The data recorded below relates to debtors and creditors of two separate firms in each of two years.

	Year 1 £m	Year 2 £m
Firm A		
Credit sales	2,500	2,800
Debtors	500	700
Firm B		
Credit sales	950	920
Debtors	25	20
Firm A		
Credit purchases	280	290
Creditors	40	50
Firm B		
Credit purchases	300	340
Creditors	30	50

Assuming in all cases that the debtor and creditor figures represent the average throughout the year:
(a) for each firm calculate the debtor collection time (or debtor days ratio) in each of the two years;
(b) comment on the trends that you observe;
(c) for each firm calculate the creditors' payment time (or creditor days ratio) in each of the two years;
(d) comment on the trends that you observe;

(e) For each firm compare the trends in the two ratios;
(f) comment on the value of these two ratios in assessing the performance of a business.

5 Dudley Limited supplies materials to the building trade. Fifty per cent of sales are paid for at the time of purchase and the remainder are credit sales. The average debtor collection period is 40 days, but 10 per cent of credit sales are eventually classified as bad debts. The company plans to introduce a new product to its range of goods. It expects to sell 10,000 units per year at £10 per unit. The variable costs of the new product amount to £8 per unit.
(a) Explain the difference between debtors and bad debt.
(b) If we assume that the purchases of the new product are cash customers, calculate the total contribution to Dudley Limited from the new product.
(c) If we assume that the new product attracts the same proportion of credit sales and bad debts as existing products, calculate the rise in bad debts.
(d) If the current rate of borrowing is 15 per cent, calculate the cost to the company of financing the credit sales of the new product.

6 The following data has been extracted from the profit and loss accounts of six companies.

£000

	A	B	C	D	E	F
Opening stock	1,000	2,500	6,000	6,000	10,000	1,200
Closing stock	1,400	2,700	5,000	6,000	12,000	1,400
Cost of sales	12,400	20,000	72,000	42,000	198,000	42,000

(a) Calculate the stock turnover for each company.
(b) Comment on each ratio indicating circumstances in which it would be considered:
    (i) normal;
    (ii) unusual.

7 (a) Complete the balance sheets below.

Company

	A £000	B £000	C £000
Fixed assets	1,000		100
Depreciation		10	20
Net fixed assets	800	50	
Stock	100	20	50
Debtors	100	20	50
Cash	10	20	10
Creditors	120	50	
Overdraft	0	0	10
Net current assets			50
Financed by:			
Share capital	500	20	
Reserves	60		10
Long-term loans		20	100

319

(b) For each company, calculate the:
  (i) working capital;
  (ii) current asset ratio;
  (iii) acid test ratio.
(c) For each company, calculate the proportion of long-term finance in the form of loans.

8 The following data has been extracted from the balance sheet of a retail shop.

	£000
Stock	500
Debtors	200
Balance at bank	50
Current liabilities	600

(a) Calculate the:
  (i)   current asset ratio;
  (ii) acid test ratio;
  (iii) working capital.
(b) Recalculate the values to take into account each of the following separate actions:
  (i)   the purchase of £40,000 of stock with cash;
  (ii) the purchase of £40,000 of stock on credit;
  (iii) the sale of £100,000 of fixed assets;
  (iv) payment by debtors of £100,000.
  For each of questions (i) to (iv), go back to the original data, ignoring previous questions.

Ratio analysis

We have now seen how the final accounts of business organizations are prepared. Let us move on now to consider how these accounts may be analysed. We will see in this chapter that accounting ratios provide us with the means by which accounting information can be analysed and evaluated.

Chapter objectives

1 To introduce the major accounting ratios.

2 To develop an understanding of their value in assessing the performance of a business organization.

3 To develop an understanding of their limitations.

4 To develop skills in handling accounting data in order to assess performance by the use of ratios.

Ratio analysis

A statistic has little value in isolation. Hence, a profit figure of £100 million is meaningless unless it is related to either the firm's turnover (sales revenue) or the value of its assets. Accounting ratios attempt to highlight relationships between significant items in the accounts of a firm. By calculating ratios, we can assess the profitability, efficiency and solvency of the firm. Areas of concern can be highlighted and decision making can be improved.

The accounting ratios can be grouped into five categories (see Table 27.1 for a quick reference list of the equations for these):

● **profitability ratios** relate profits to sales and assets;
● **liquidity ratios** show the extent to which the firm can meet its financial obligations;
● **efficiency ratios** indicate how active the firm has been;
● **gearing ratios** show the balance between equity and loan finance;
● **shareholders' (or investment) ratios** are a measure of the return on investment.

Profitability ratios

Gross profit margin

$$= \frac{\text{Gross profit}}{\text{Sales revenue}} \times 100$$

Table 27.1 Summary of major ratios

Profitability ratios

Return on capital employed =

$$\frac{\text{Net profit before interest and tax}}{\text{Capital employed}} \times 100$$

Gross profit ratio =

$$\frac{\text{Gross profit}}{\text{Total sales revenue}} \times 100$$

Mark-up =

$$\frac{\text{Gross profit}}{\text{Cost of goods sold}} \times 100$$

Net profit ratio =

$$\frac{\text{Net profit before interest and tax}}{\text{Total sales revenue}} \times 100$$

Liquidity ratios

$$\text{Current assets ratio} = \frac{\text{Current assets}}{\text{Current liabilities}}$$

$$\text{Acid test ratio} = \frac{\text{Current assets} - \text{Stock}}{\text{Current liabilities}}$$

Efficiency ratios

$$\text{Stock turnover ratio} = \frac{\text{Cost of goods sold}}{\text{Average stock}}$$

Fixed asset turnover =

$$\frac{\text{Total sales revenue}}{\text{Fixed assets at net book value}}$$

Trade debtor collection period =

$$\frac{\text{Average trade debtors}}{\text{Total credit sales}} \times 365 \text{ days}$$

Trade creditor payment period =

$$\frac{\text{Average trade creditor}}{\text{Total credit purchases}} \times 365 \text{ days}$$

Investment gearing and shareholders' ratios

Dividend yield =

$$\frac{\text{Nominal value per share}}{\text{Market price per share}} \times \frac{\text{Declared dividend}}{\text{rate}}$$

Dividend cover =

$$\frac{\text{Net profit after tax and preference dividend}}{\text{Paid and proposed ordinary dividend}}$$

Earnings per share =

$$\frac{\text{Net profit after tax and preference dividend but before extraordinary items}}{\text{No. of ordinary shares issued}}$$

Price–earnings ratio =

$$\frac{\text{Market price per share}}{\text{Earnings per share}}$$

Gearing ratio =

$$\frac{\text{Preference shares} + \text{Long-term loans}}{\text{Shareholders' funds} + \text{Long-term loans}} \times 100$$

This shows the percentage profit from sales that is available to pay for overheads. Most businesses require a gross profit of at least 20 per cent if overheads are to be covered. If the ratio is falling over time, it could be because of failure or inability to pass on cost increases to customers, stock losses, fraud, a change in the mix of sales in favour of lower margin goods or an attempt to increase market share by keeping prices down.

Gross profit mark-up

$$= \frac{\text{Gross profit}}{\text{Cost of sales}} \times 100$$

Mark-up is the amount of profit added to the cost of goods sold. A low mark-up might reflect an attempt to increase gross profit by gaining a larger volume of sales.

Net profit ratio

$$= \frac{\text{Net profit (or earnings before interest and tax)}}{\text{Sales revenue}} \times 100$$

This indicates the percentage of operating profit generated from the sales effort. As interest is excluded, it shows the operational efficiency of the business without reference to the method used to finance it.

Return on capital employed (ROCE)

$$= \frac{\text{Profit before interest and tax}}{\text{Capital employed}} \times 100$$

Once again, this is a measure of the operational efficiency of the business. Capital employed is equal to owners' equity plus long-term debt and is equal to the net asset figure in the balance sheet. If ROCE is lower than interest rates in the market, it is very unsatisfactory as it indicates that the business would have prospered better by depositing the money in a bank.

Liquidity ratios

To understand liquidity ratios, it is necessary to look at working capital. As we have seen, this is the life-blood of any business as, without it, the business will not survive. When the business starts up, it is necessary to invest in stocks of materials. These may be held for a long period before they are sold to the customer. Moreover, receipt of money from the customer may be delayed and the business then has the problem of financing the purchase of further stocks. As we saw earlier, working capital is equal to current assets (stocks, cash and debtors) minus current liabilities (debts due for repayment within a year). If current liabilities exceed current assets, the business will be unable to meet its immediate debts without selling some of its fixed assets. It is, therefore, important to control working capital to ensure that cash flows in insufficient amounts and at appropriate times to meet the liabilities of the company.

The two liquidity ratios, which we first encountered in Chapter 26, measure the extent to which the business can meet its immediate obligations.

Current asset ratio

$$= \frac{\text{Current assets}}{\text{Current liabilities}}$$

As a general rule, the current asset ratio should be between 1.5 and 2. If the ratio is too low, the business may face difficulties in repaying debts. If the ratio is greater than 2, it suggests that money is tied up unprofitably in excess current assets. This could be either money remaining idle in bank accounts or excessive stock levels. Although 1.5 to 2 is generally regarded as an ideal ratio, it should be seen as merely a rough guide.

If a high proportion of current assets take the form of stock, the business might be faced with a difficult dilemma. To meet current liabilities it might be necessary to sell off stock quickly and, therefore, at a discount. The acid test ratio has been devised to give a better indication of liquidity.

Acid test (or quick) ratio

$$= \frac{\text{Cash + debtors}}{\text{Current liabilities}}$$

$$\text{or} \quad \frac{\text{Current assets less stock}}{\text{Current liabilities}}$$

As a general rule, the ratio should be 1. If a combination of cash held by the business and cash it expects to receive when customers eventually pay is equal to current liabilities, the business should have little difficulty in meeting its obligations. Furthermore, it can do this without selling off stock at a discount. However, we should be flexible in the interpretation of a business' quick asset ratio. For instance, a toy shop in early December may have invested heavily in stock and have a high expectation of a substantial cash inflow before the end of the year. A low quick asset ratio should not necessarily be interpreted as a sign of imminent business failure.

Efficiency ratios

Stock turnover

$$= \frac{\text{Cost of sales for a period}}{\text{Average stockholding}}$$

In general, a high stock turnover suggests that the business is active and efficient in selling goods quickly to customers. A stock turnover of 10 suggests that stock is turned over every 36 days. It will vary from business to business but, in general, firms supplying high-value goods will turn over stock slowly, whereas suppliers of low-value goods will turn over stock more rapidly.

If we invert the formula and multiply by the number of days per year, we can find the time taken to turn over stock:

$$= \frac{\text{Stock}}{\text{Cost of sales}} \times 365$$

Fixed asset turnover ratio

$$= \frac{\text{Total sales revenue}}{\text{Fixed assets at net book value}}$$

This is a measure of the productivity of assets. An investment in fixed assets should pay off in terms of an increase in sales.

Average trade debtor collection period ratio (or debtor days)

$$= \frac{\text{Average trade debtors}}{\text{Total credit sales} \div 365}$$

$$= \frac{\text{Average trade debtors}}{\text{Total credit sales}} \times 365$$

This shows the average time taken to collect trade debts. If debtors are taking a long time to pay, the business could experience trouble in paying its own debts. There is no typical figure to use as a yardstick as it will vary according to the type of business.

Average trade creditor payment period (creditor days)

$$= \frac{\text{Average trade creditors}}{\text{Total credit purchases}} \times 365$$

This shows the average length of time taken by the business to pay its own debts. If this is rising, it could indicate difficulties in finding sufficient cash to meet its obligations.

Other efficiency ratios

$$\frac{\text{Sales revenue}}{\text{No. of employees}}$$

This shows the sales revenue per employee.

$$\frac{\text{Selling expenses}}{\text{Sales revenue}} \times 100$$

This shows the percentage of sales revenue absorbed by the cost of selling the goods.

$$\frac{\text{Administration expenses}}{\text{Sales revenue}} \times 100$$

This shows how much sales revenue is absorbed by administration costs.

Gearing ratios

Gearing ratios concern the balance between fixed interest finance and equity finance or the balance between loan and share capital. If we are interested in the ability of the company to meet its interest payments, then the ratio is:

$$\frac{\text{Loan finance}}{\text{Loan and share finance}} \times 100$$

In a highly geared company, a high proportion of finance is loan finance and, as a result, there may be a question mark over its ability to meet its interest payments.

If, instead, we are interested in dividend fluctuations, we would calculate the gearing ratio as:

$$\frac{\text{Fixed interest capital}}{\text{Fixed interest capital} + \text{Equity}} \times 100$$

The higher the gearing, the greater the dividend fluctuations.

Shareholders' ratios

These ratios enable the investor to make an assessment of the return on his or her investment.

Dividend yield

The dividend on a share is expressed as a percentage of its nominal value. This is not very useful to shareholders who have paid more than the nominal price of the share. Hence, dividend yield is useful in that it expresses the dividend as a percentage of the market value of the share.

$$\frac{\text{Declared dividend per share}}{\text{Market price of the share}} \times 100$$

or

$$\frac{\text{Nominal value per share}}{\text{Market price per share}} \times \text{Declared dividend rate}$$

Earnings per share

By dividing the profits that are (potentially) available for distribution by the number of shares, we get a figure for earnings per share. This is likely to be lower than dividend per share as some of the money available for distribution as dividend is, in fact, retained.

$$\text{Earnings per share} = \frac{\text{Net profit available to pay shareholders}}{\text{No. of ordinary shares}}$$

Dividend cover

This is calculated by dividing the profit available for distribution by the dividend to be paid. This shows how many times over the dividend could have been paid.

$$\text{Dividend cover} = \frac{\text{Profit available for distribution}}{\text{Paid and proposed dividend}}$$

Price–earnings ratio

This ratio, usually referred to as the P/E ratio, is calculated as:

$$\frac{\text{Market price per share}}{\text{Earnings per share}}$$

The P/E ratio provides a measure of the profitability of the share in terms of both capital value and earnings.

The value of ratio analysis

Accounting ratios facilitate the evaluation of business performance. By making comparisons over time or with other similar firms (interfirm comparisons) ratios can be used:

● in forecasting and planning;
● to summarize data;
● to identify problems before they become acute;
● to assess performance.

However, ratios should be used with caution. First, we should always remember the accounting conventions and procedures by which various values were arrived at – accounting information often lacks the precision that we would like. Interfirm comparisons are only valid if the firms adopt the same practices in relation to depreciation and stock valuation.

Second, published accounts are, by nature, *historic*, in that they relate to a previous time period. Hence, ratios based on published accounts may not be valid today.

Third, when ratios are used for interfirm comparisons, we must bear in mind differences in the product mixes of various firms. Even if they appear to be in the same industry, it is possible that the figures of one of the firms are distorted by its interests in activities that are not common to its rivals.

Fourth, comparisons over time are made more difficult by changes in the value of money (inflation) and changes in the environment. Hence, a rise in profit ratios might result from windfall gains of inflation rather than improved performance and efficiency. Changes in foreign exchange rates, interest rates, taxation or industrial policy might be reflected in apparently improved performance. However, this is not the result of greater efficiency but of events beyond the control of management.

Fifth, ratios are distorted by short-term fluctuations and by their timing. For instance, the liquidity ratios are greatly affected by seasonality in sales. Finally, ratios highlight problems but do not tell the whole story. The current health of a firm might not be accurately reflected in its ratios. We should also consider non-quantitative information, such as quality of the workforce, goodwill, labour relations and the R&D programme.

Key concepts

Efficiency ratios Efficiency concerns the relationship between inputs and outputs. Hence, efficiency ratios show output or sales per unit of input.

Gearing The ratio of debt finance to equity finance.

Historical comparison Comparison of a particular ratio in one year and the same ratio in previous years.

Interfirm comparison Comparison of the performance of one firm with that of other, similar firms.

Liquidity ratios Measures of the availability of cash and other liquid assets to meet the current liabilities of the firm.

Profitability ratios Measures of profit in relation to sales, capital employed or similar factors.

Shareholder ratios A series of ratios of particular interest to shareholders because they focus on dividends.

Essay questions

1 Analyse the problems associated with:
   (a) interfirm comparisons of accounting ratios;
   (b) historical comparisons of accounting ratios

2 (a) Explain how you would evaluate the profitability of the company.
   (b) Analyse why it is important to treat all profits figures with caution?

3 (a) Identify the major categories of accounting ratio.
   (b) Justifying your answer, identify the ratios

that are likely to be of greatest interest to each of five named stakeholders in a large public company.

4 Comment on and analyse possible explanations for a company recording the following results:
   (i)   2 per cent return on capital employed;
   (ii) 50 per cent gross profit;
   (iii) 10 per cent net profit.

5 Analyse the reasons why it is essential to understand the nature of a company before commenting on its accounting ratios.

Exercises

1 The following data relates to a large public company:

	Year X
Sales revenue (£m)	700
Operating profits (£m)	80
Price–earnings ratio	14
Earnings per share	35p
Interest cover	3.8
Dividend cover	10
Dividend per share	11p

From the information, calculate the:
(a) market price of a share;
(b) dividend yield;
(c) profit margin;
(d) interest payable by the firm.

2 After studying the following two sets of accounts, undertake a full ratio analysis of this firm.

Profit and loss account for year ended 31 March 20XX

	£m	£m
Sales revenue		800
Less cost of goods sold		
Materials	200	
Direct labour	200	
Production overheads	50	450
Gross profit		350
Less Selling expenses	50	
Administrative expenses	50	100
Trading (operating) profit		250
Add: Non-operating income		50
Profit before interest and tax		300
Less Interest expense		100
Profit before tax		200
Less Taxation		50
Profit after tax		150
Less Dividends		50
Retained profit for the period		100

Balance sheet as at 31 March 20XX

	£m	£m
Fixed assets		
Premises		1,500
Plant/Equipment	750	
Less Accumulated depreciation	250	500
Total fixed assets		2,000
Current assets		
Stock	50	
Debtors	50	
Cash in bank	50	
	150	
Less Current liabilities		
Creditors	70	
Provision for tax	30	
Overdraft	30	
	130	
Working capital		20
Assets less Current liabilities		2,020

Financed by:
Share capital

Shares issued	1,000
Reserves	500
Share premium	100
Long-term liabilities	
Loans debentures	420
Total capital employed	2,020

3 Using appropriate ratios, analyse the following accounts to evaluate performance in the two years.

Trading and profit and loss accounts for the year ended 31 December

	Year 1 £000	£000	Year 2 £000	£000
Turnover		9,000		12,000
Less Cost of sales		6,300		9,120
Gross profit		2,700		2,880
Less Expenses		1,700		1,820
Net profit		1,000		1,060
Less Corporation tax	540		580	
dividends	420	960	460	1,040
		40		20
Retained earnings b/f		240		280
Retained earnings c/f		280		300

Balance sheet as at 31 December

	Year 1 £000	£000	Year 2 £000	£000
Fixed assets (at cost				
less Depreciation)		9,300		10,200
Current assets				
Stock	1,560		3,020	
Debtors	1,520		2,940	
Balance at bank	640		–	
	3,720		5,960	
Less Current liabilities				
Creditors	1,540		2,780	
Tax and dividends	960		1,040	
Bank overdraft	–		1,800	
	2,500		5,620	
Working capital		1,220		340
		10,520		10,540

Financed by:

Share capital (fully issued and paid up)		6,000		6,000
General reserve	1,440		1,440	
Profit and loss A/C	280	1,720	300	1,740
10% debentures		2,800		2,800
		10,520		10,540

4 The table below shows the financial structure of three companies.

	X Ltd	Y Ltd	Z Ltd
Ordinary shares of £1 each	35	30	10
Reserves	35	20	10
12% loan capital	0	20	50
	70	70	70

(All figures in £m)

Profit before interest and tax is £10 million for each company. The rate of corporation tax is 33 per cent. For each company, calculate the:
(a) interest payments;
(b) tax liability;
(c) earnings available for dividend payments;
(d) earnings per share.

5 The following figures relate to two similar businesses.

	Business A	Business B
Average stock carried at selling price	£40,000	£50,000
Rate of stock turnover	12	6
Gross profit as a % of sales revenue	20	10
Net profit as a % of sales revenue	5	5
Capital employed	£400,000	£150,000

(a) For each business, calculate the:
   (i) sales revenue;
   (ii) net profit;
   (iii) return on capital employed;
   (iv) total expenses as a percentage of sales.
(b) Comment on the expenses involved in running the two businesses.
(c) Assuming that 10 per cent is the general level of interest rates, what can we conclude about the profitability of the two businesses?

28

Cash statements

This chapter looks at two aspects of cash accounting: cash flow forecasts drawn up at the beginning of the time period to which they relate, and cash flow statements drawn up at the end of the period. Although one statement is a plan and a forecast, and the other is a final account (mandatory for larger companies), they share one distinctive feature – the emphasis on the flow of cash in to and out of a business. As a result, these statements omit some items included in the profit and loss account, but, at the same time, include others that are absent from the profit and loss account. As noted earlier, the cash position of a business is of great importance: business failure is caused more by problems over cash flow than by any underlying unprofitability.

Chapter objectives

1 To explain the nature, structure and purpose of a cash flow forecast (cash budget).

2 To develop your skills in producing cash budgets.

3 To explain the structure of cash flow statements.

4 To analyse the role of cash accounting.

Cash in accounts

From the review of profit and loss accounts in Chapter 24 you will be aware that this accounting statement includes all sales during the time period, whether or not payment has been received. Part of the sales will be credit sales, which involve a delay in the receipt of cash. In most cases, the cash will eventually be received, but, for the moment, it should be seen as promised money rather than cash in the bank. At the same time, the cost side of a profit and loss account records all the costs associated with generating the sales for the time period under consideration. Again, some of those costs will be deferred until a later date, with the result that there is no immediate outflow of cash.

Cash statements attempt to redress these deficiencies. They concern only the flow of cash in to and out of the business, not money promised in the future or the provision for future payments. It should be appreciated that 'cash' is not confined to bank notes and coins in the hands of the business, it also includes money deposited in the firm's bank account.

This chapter is concerned with two types of cash flow statement:

● cash flow forecasts (or cash budgets);
● cash flow statements.

The former statement relates to the *expected* future inflow and outflow of cash. The latter statement relates to the *actual flow* (in and out) of cash during the past time period. The **cash budget** is an internal document drawn up for decision making and planning purposes (although it is also used in connection with applications for external finance). The cash flow statement is prepared for external users (shareholders, creditors, employees) as part of the stewardship function of management.

The structure of a cash budget

Let us look at the basic format of cash budgets before we look in greater detail at particular aspects. Figure 28.1 is an example of a cash budget (or cash flow forecast). The column headings show the relevant time periods. The rows across show details of forecast cash movements in each time period. Moving vertically down, we can see

	Jan	Feb	March	April
	£	£	£	£
Cash sales	1,000	1,000	1,200	1,300
Cash from credit sales	0	1,000	1,000	1,200
Total cash inflow	1,000	2,000	2,200	2,500
Stock purchases	1,000	500	600	650
Pay/drawings	800	800	800	800
Electricity	0	0	100	0
Advertising	200	200	100	100
Rent	1,000	0	0	0
Purchase of capital equipment	2,000	0	0	0
Total cash outflow	5,000	1,500	1,600	1,550
Net cash flow	(4,000)	500	600	950
Opening balance	2,000	(2,000)	(1,500)	(900)
Closing balance	(2,000)	(1,500)	(900)	50

Explanatory notes:
1 This is a forecast of cash flows drawn up at the start of the year.
2 Positive and negative items only appear in the budget when a flow of cash in to and out of the business is expected. The timing of sales and purchases is irrelevant – only the timing of *cash* payments is important in this budget.
3 Some items occur each month, whereas others are less frequent. Some of the costs are fixed in advance, whereas others can be altered if overambitious plans are likely to cause cash flow problems.
4 The assumption in this forecast was that half the sales would be cash sales and that half would be credit sales, for which payment would be received in the following month.
5 For an existing business, sales forecasts (such as time series) should be used to estimate the volume of sales.
6 This firm will purchase a large amount of stock at the start of the year, but, in subsequent months, stock purchases are related to expected sales.
7 The final section of the budget is a forecast of the state of the firm's cash or bank account at the end of each month. This budget shows a typical position for a start-up business of an initial overdraft followed by improvement as the cash receipts are expected to flow in.
8 Seasonal fluctuations in sales (not apparent in the example) will result in alternating periods of net inflow and net outflow.

Figure 28.1 An example of a cash flow forecast or cash budget for a start-up business

that the detailed headings are divided into three groups:

- cash inflows;
- cash outflows;
- a summary of net movements of cash

Cash inflows

Receipts from cash sales are credited in the month in question. Receipts from debtors are credited in the month that payment is received, which is likely to be one, two or more months later. When constructing a cash budget from given figures, this is a fairly easy task to accomplish, as the example in Figure 28.2 shows.

Notice that the cash from credit sales is received in the following month, thus producing a lagged effect. For most examination purposes, all you will be asked to do is construct the cash budget on information given to you. However, if you produce a cash budget as part of a project and, more importantly, as part of a real business exercise, you have the problem of making the forecast. There are three aspects to the forecast:

- value of sales;
- proportion of credit sales to total sales;
- time delay before receipt of cash (and the extent of bad debt).

For an established business, the forecast will be based on past experience, taking into account changes in the internal environment of the business, changes in the external environment of the business, changes in productive capacity and the seasonality of business. For a new business, the task is more difficult as there is no past data to go on. However, the forecast must be realistic if it is to be worth while. It should take into account the productive capacity of the business, the experiences of similar businesses, forecast customer demand and trends in the environment. The proportion of credit sales can be forecast by taking into account the nature of the business and the behaviour of targeted customers. For instance, newsagents rely on cash sales, whereas builders have to accept that customers will tend to delay payments.

Cash outflows

The outflows of cash will be itemized under various headings. Some outflows are of fixed amounts and are known in advance (such as interest payments on loans, rent). These and others items are likely to be quarterly or half-yearly payments and will not appear each month. Pay will generate cash outflows in each time period and, unless additional staff are taken on to meet a seasonal peak, will be fairly constant throughout the year.

The most difficult element of cash outflow to forecast is the purchase of stocks. This should be related to customer demand for the final product but should take into account the need to purchase stocks in advance of the peak of sales. As a result, purchases of stock will reflect expected sales in the next time period rather than the present one. In a business with a distinct seasonal pattern, this will add to the problem of cash flow as the

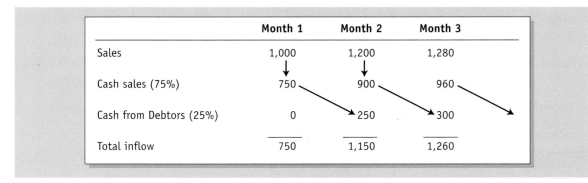

Figure 28.2 Forecast cast inflow

peak in spending occurs before the peak in sales. However, the purchase of sales on credit will mitigate this problem because payment for stock can be delayed to coincide with the peak in sales.

Summary of cash movements

In the first two sections of the cash budget we arrive at totals for net cash flows during the time period. At some times there will be a net cash inflow while at others there will be a net cash outflow. As well as showing a figure for each month, the budget also shows a cumulative figure. To calculate this, we need the opening balance (the state of the account at the start of the time period), to which we add the net cash flow. The resulting figure is the closing balance, which in turn becomes the opening balance for the next time period. For example, see Figure 28.3. Notice that, in the first column, the net flow is outward, causing a surplus to become a deficit by the end of the month. The next time period starts with a deficit, but this is eliminated by a net inflow during the month.

The purpose of cash budgets

The basic purpose of a cash budget is to ascertain the effect that the planned level of output, and its associated costs, will have on the cash resources of the firm. We are not talking about profit but, instead, the amount of cash that the firm has in reserve.

This is especially important in identifying periods of cash shortage, which might require additional external financing in the form of an overdraft. The cash budget will play a major role in securing overdraft facilities, but, if these are not available, the firm might have to overcome the problem in other ways. For instance, one way to reduce cash outflow is to buy less stock, although this might also harm sales. Alternatively, the firm might seek to delay payment to creditors by means of extended trade credit. Another method of overcoming the problem is to reduce debtors by tighter credit control, debt factoring or incentives for prompt payment, or by reducing the period of credit.

It is also useful to identify periods of expected cash surplus. Although this is not a 'problem' in the sense that a cash shortage is, it is useful to forecast periods of surplus (and their duration) in order to put the surplus to good use. This might take the form of:

- early payments to claim discounts;
- interest bearing deposits in banks;
- the purchase of marketable securities (such as shares);
- loans to other businesses;
- forward purchase of materials at times when prices are expected to rise.

Cash shortage is especially common in the case of new start-up businesses. The alternation of shortage and surplus is a feature of businesses in which there is a distinct seasonal pattern to sales. To some extent, all businesses are affected by seasonality, but some are especially prone to

	Month 1	Month 2	Month 3
	£000	£000	£000
Opening balance	10	(2)	1
Net cash flow	(12)	3	4
Closing balance	(2)	1	5

Figure 28.3 Net cash flow

seasonal variations in either demand (as with fireworks) or supply (say, fruit farming). A cash budget does not solve the problem of seasonality, but it does assist in deciding how to cope with the problem.

The cash budget will also assist in identifying problems within the business. Overambitious expansion plans can result in overtrading. This occurs when the expanding business achieves increased sales and profits but a deteriorating cash position because the sales are not translated into cash inflows. An overambitious expansion plan might be detected by a carefully constructed cash budget. This will cause managers to produce a more realistic plan that does not strain cash resources to the same extent.

In addition to helping revision at the planning stage, the cash budget is invaluable in monitoring performance against the forecast. For each month, we can contrast the actual figure against the budgeted one. The difference between the two is known as the **variance**. Cash inflows will be down on the budgeted figure if:

- sales are depressed;
- prices are reduced;
- bad debts exceed expectations;
- more customers than expected buy on credit.

Cash outflows will be higher than the budget if:

- labour is more expensive than expected;
- materials rise in price;
- scrap and waste exceed expectations;
- there are unforeseen events;
- the marketing campaign has to be intensified.

If the net cash flow figure records a negative variance, it might be necessary to take corrective action in order to avoid the problem of cash shortage. It should always be remembered that most business failure occurs as a result of cash flow problems rather than the unprofitability of the venture.

Cash flow statements

The previous section dealt with cash flow forecasts (cash budgets) prepared in advance. We now turn to cash flow statements prepared after the event in order to record the flow of cash in to and out of a firm. These statements are now required of all companies other than those defined as small, and, under FRS 1, they have to be published in a prescribed format.

Before looking in detail at the cash flow statement, it is useful to explain the difference between a cash flow statement and profit and loss account (or income statement). Cash flow statements are confined to flows of cash in to and out of the business and do not take account of provisions and transactions for which there is no movement of cash. By focusing on the cash position of the business it is hoped to avoid the situation in which healthy profits on the profit and loss account disguise severe financial problems resulting from a shortage of cash. The advantages of cash flow accounting can be listed as follows:

- it directs attention to cash flow, on which a business' survival depends;
- creditors are more interested in a company's ability to repay loans than in its declared profit;
- profit is a subjective idea as it is dependent on the accounting conventions and practices used in constructing the accounts, while the flow of cash in to and out of a business is far more objective;
- the cash position of a business is important for management decision making and is also meaningful to shareholders.

These points should not be interpreted as suggesting that a cash flow statement is in any way superior to a profit and loss account, but merely that it provides an alternative perspective on the position of the business.

The statement in Figure 28.4 illustrates the format specified for the cash flow statement in FRS 1. Section A tells us that this business experienced a net cash inflow from its normal trading operation of £1 million. The reconciliation of operating profit to net cash flow will be explained below.

Section B deals with income from investments in other enterprises, less dividends paid. In this particular case, there was a net outflow of £0.1

	£000	£000
A Net cash inflow from operations		1,000
B Returns on investments less payment of dividends		(100)
C Taxation paid		(100)
D Investing activities		
Payments to acquire fixed assets	(1,800)	
Receipts from sales of fixed assets	100	
Net cash outflow from investing activities		(1,700)
E Net cash flow before financing		(900)
F Financing		
Share issue	800	
Repayment of loan	(50)	
Net cash inflow from financing		750
G Change in cash		(150)

Figure 28.4 Example of a cash flow statement

million. The same figure is recorded for taxation paid (Section C). This is not provision for taxation, but the amount actually paid.

Section D records the acquisition and disposal of assets. This company bought £1.8 million of assets but sold others for £0.1 million, thus producing a net cash outflow from investing of £1.7 million.

If we add the totals for each of the four sections, we obtain a figure for net cash flow (E) before the firm resorts to financing by means of share issues and loans. The £0.9 million outflow has to be financed in some way. From section F we learn that a share issue brought in £0.8 million

although £50,000 flowed out as a result of a loan repayment. The net inflow from financing (£0.75 million) was insufficient to match the outflow shown in section E and so the difference was made good by a change in the company's cash position. At the end of the year the company had £150,000 less in its bank account than at the beginning of the year. This fact will not be lost on shareholders and creditors and could act as a constraint on future management decision making.

Table 28.1 shows the main headings in a cash flow statement. Figure 28.5 comments on certain features of these statements.

The format of the statement is easily understood,

Table 28.1 The main headings in a cash flow statement

A Operating activities	Profit adjusted for non-cash items and changes in working capital items
B Returns on investments	Interest/dividend received less interest/dividend paid
C Taxation	Taxes paid – not provisions made
D Investing activities	Payments for, less receipts from, fixed assets
E Net cash flow before financing	A + B + D – C
F Financing	Cash flow resulting from share issues/loan
G Change in cash	E + F

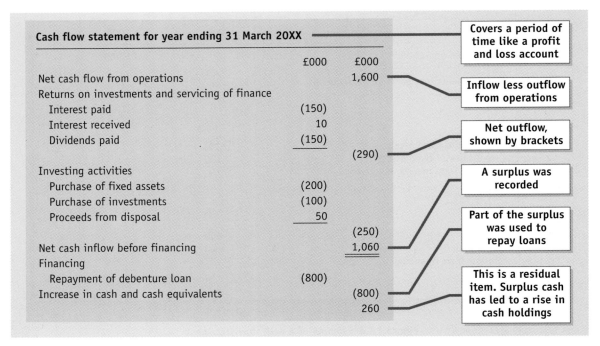

Figure 28.5 A cash flow statement

but what is more difficult to understand is the computation of the £1 million net cash inflow from operations. Where does this figure come from and how does it relate to the operating profit shown in the profit and loss account? To calculate this figure we have to work backwards from operating profits. The reconciliation of operating profit to net cash flow from operating activities can be shown as follows:

	£000
Operating profit	1,300
Depreciation	200
Increase in stocks	(400)
Increase in debtors	(200)
Increase in creditors	100
Net cash inflow from operating activities	1,000

Operating profit, taken from the profit and loss account, is the starting point in the reconciliation. To this is added depreciation. This is a charge against the year's sales revenue, but, as we saw in Chapter 25 it does not involve an outflow of cash. The £400,000 increase in stocks is not a charge against this year's sales revenue as, under the matching principle, it will be charged against the sales revenue in the year in which it is sold. Nevertheless, it has to be paid for and is therefore deducted from the cash flow. Similarly, the increase in debtors represents sales for which cash has not been received. Consequently, although these sales are credited towards the profit and loss account, there was no inflow of cash. This increase in debtors is deducted in the cash flow statement. Conversely, the increase in creditors represents stock purchases for which no cash outflow occurred. This is therefore added back in. By means of this reconciliation (which is always included as a note to the cash flow statement), the operating profit figure is converted into net cash inflow from operations. The reconciliation appears difficult, but, by going through the exercises at the end of the chapter, you will improve your understanding of the topic.

Key concepts

A budget A plan expressed in financial terms.

Cash flow The flow of cash in to and out of a business.

Cash equivalents Short-term investments that can be turned into cash without notice.

Cash flow forecast/cash budget A plan that expresses in detail the cash flow expected over a specified period.

Cash flow statement A statement explaining how cash and cash equivalents have changed over a specified period.

FRS 1 The financial reporting standard that makes the production of a cash flow statement mandatory for larger companies.

Matching The accounting rule that, in calculating profits, all costs are matched against the revenues to which they relate. The use of the matching principle for profit and loss accounts is one reason for the discrepancy between a profit and loss account and a cash flow statement for the same company over the same period.

Provisions Amounts set aside, by charging in the profit and loss account for depreciation or a known liability in the future. As it does not involve a flow of cash out of the business, it will not appear in a cash flow statement even though it appears in a profit and loss account.

Essay questions

1 Evaluate the role of a cash flow forecast in:
   (a) an application for external finance; and
   (b) the internal management of a business.

2 (a) Why was the law changed to require the publication of cash flow statements?
   (b) Analyse ways in which a cash flow statement differs from a profit and loss account.

3 (a) Analyse possible reasons for a cash flow problem.
   (b) Evaluate possible solutions.

4 Analyse the consequences for cash flow of each of the following:
   (a) sale and leaseback of fixed assets;
   (b) hire purchase rather than cash purchase;
   (c) an increase in the debtor day ratio;
   (d) a just-in-time approach to stock purchase.

5 (a) Without a reliable forecast of sales revenue, a cash flow forecast is of little use. Discuss.
   (b) Evaluate techniques of forecasting sales revenue.

Exercises

1 The data below is extracted from the cash budget of a company.

Month	1 £000	2 £000	3 £000	4 £000	5 £000	6 £000
Sales	200	250	300	400	450	500
Purchases of stock	100	100	100	100	100	100
Pay	100	100	100	100	100	100
Electricity			50			50
Advertising	20	10	10	10	10	10
Rates			30			
Miscellaneous payments	10	10	10	10	10	10

(a) Complete the cash budget assuming:
  (i)   an opening cash balance of –£45,000;
  (ii) an equal division between cash sales and credit sales – in the case of credit sales, cash is received in the month following the sale.
(b) Prepare a second cash budget based on the above assumptions and on a one-month delay in the payment for stock (no payment was made in month 1).
(c) Calculate working capital at the end of month 6 based on data from your previous answer.

2 Construct a cash flow forecast from the data below.
At the start of the financial year a firm has a balance of £30,000 in its bank account. The owners expect sales to be as follows:

	£000		£000
January	14	July	70
February	18	August	50
March	18	September	35
April	26	October	30
May	50	November	25
June	62	December	20

One half of sales are likely to be cash sales, with the remaining credit sales expected to be paid in the following month.

Regular monthly expenses will amount to £24,000 and, in addition, there will be £1,500 instalments of the rate bill payable in April and October. Electricity bills of £250 are payable in January, April, July and October. In the same months, it is expected that there will be telephone bills of £200 payable.

3 Dave has decided to open a café in a tourist area. He will spend the first two months of the year setting up his business and plans to open on 1 March. Dave, who has supplied the following information, asks you to produce a cash flow forecast on a month-by-month basis.

	Sales revenue £000	Stock purchases (cash) £000
January	Nil	Nil
February	Nil	0.5
March	1	0.5
April	2	0.5
May	3	0.5
June	4	1.0
July	5	1.5
August	5	1.5
September	3	1.0
October	2	0.5
November	1	0.5
December	1	0.5

● Ten per cent of customers will pay by credit card, which will entail a one-month delay in payment.

- Dave plans to employ part-time staff at a cost of £200 per month from March, rising to £400 per month from June to September.
- Rent on the premises is £4000 per year, payable in two equal instalments in January and July.
- Equipment will cost £5000 to purchase and install. Payment will be in equal instalments in the first five months of the year.
- Dave anticipates that electricity charges will be £100 in March, £150 in June, £200 in September and £150 in December.
- He intends to place a regular advertisement in a local newspaper at a cost of £50 per month from 1 February.
- For personal expenses, Dave will draw £1000 per month out of the business.
- To establish his business Dave has savings of £7000.
  - (a) Produce a cash flow forecast.
  - (b) Advise Dave on the extent of the overdraft limit he should negotiate with his bank manager.
  - (c) Comment on the performance of the business during its first year of operation.

4 John and Sophie have established a small business in a tourist area.
The following information is known:
- on 31 December 2000 they have a credit balance of £500 in their business account;
- the business is owed £200 from credit sales in late 2000;
- in turn, the business has an outstanding debt of £300 for materials purchased in 2000;
- rent on the premises amounts to £1000 per year, payable in equal instalments in January, April, July and October;
- they forecast a quarterly electricity bill of £150 to be paid in February, May, August and November;
- John plans to purchase £200 of materials each month, although payment will be deferred by one month;
- to cope with the retail trade in the summer, John intends to employ part-time labour in June, July and August at a cost of £500 per month;
- they will draw out £700 per month for personal needs;
- Sophie forecasts that the pattern of sales in 2001 will be as follows.

	Sales revenue £
January	1,000
February	1,000
March	1,000
April	1,000
May	1,000
June	2,000
July	2,000
August	2,000
September	2,000
October	1,000
November	1,000
December	1,000

Only 50 per cent will be cash sales. The remainder will be credit sales involving a one-month delay in the receipt of payment.

(a) Produce a cash flow forecast for the business in 2001.

(b) Early in 2001, their suppliers inform John and Sophie that the price of materials will rise by 10 per cent from April. Produce an amended forecast, taking into account the rise in the cost of materials.

(c) In addition to the rise in raw material costs, they are told that they owe £700 in unpaid tax. This must be paid by the end of September 2001. Produce an amended forecast for the remaining months of 2001.

5 The forecast profit and loss accounts for the first three years of a company are:

	Year 1 £000	Year 2 £000	Year 3 £000
Sales	876	1,238	1,890
Less Cost of sales	682	812	1,176
Gross profit	194	426	714
Pay	106	119	137
Bank interest	20	30	10
Telephone	15	18	22
Electricity	15	17	18
Laundry	26	27	28
Advertising	10	20	20
Depreciation	61	71	71
	253	302	306
Net profit/(loss)	(59)	124	408

(a) Explain the distinction between:
   (i) a cash statement and a profit and loss account;
   (ii) gross profit and net profit.

(b) Prepare a cash statement on the basis that all sales are cash sales and that expenses are incurred in the year in question.

(c) Adjust your prepared cash statement to take into account the fact that 10 per cent of sales revenue comes in during the year following the year in which the sale was made.

6 Calculate net cash inflow/outflow from operating activities in each of the following situations.

	£m
(a) Operating profit	2
Depreciation	0.3
Increase in stocks	0.2
Increase in debtors	0.3
Increase in creditors	0.1

(b) Operating profit 10
    Depreciation 2
    Reduction in stock 1
    Reduction in debtors 2
    Reduction in creditors 3
(c) Operating profit 15
    Depreciation 3
    Reduction in stock 2
    Increase in debtors 2
    Reduction in creditors 1

7 From the information below, construct cash flow statements for each of the three companies.

	Company A	Company B	Company C
	£000	£000	£000
Share issue	250	200	Nil
Debenture issue/repayment	200	−100	−200
Receipts from the sale of fixed assets	48	50	20
Tax paid	80	300	200
Payments for fixed assets	400	1,700	600
Dividend paid	75	200	300
Interest paid	105	50	40
Interest received	25	30	Nil
Net cash flow from operations	155	950	1,020
New loan	100	200	500

Financing the business

In this chapter we will look at the sources of finance for private-sector business enterprises and the implications for the business of its choice of finance. A survey of major sources of finance is followed by a detailed look at both debt finance and equity finance.

Chapter objectives

1 To analyse the reasons for firms to seek finance.

2 To distinguish between debt and equity finance.

3 To outline the main sources of finance.

4 To emphasize the importance of the matching principle in finance.

5 To explain the methods of share issue.

6 To analyse the return on shareholdings by reference to key ratios.

The need for finance

Anyone starting a business will have to use some of his or her own savings to buy equipment and materials, and acquire suitable premises. As we saw in the last chapter about cash flow forecasts, expenditure is necessary in advance of the receipt of sales revenue. In some instances, there is a considerable time lag involved and it will be necessary to obtain substantial amounts of finance in advance. Where savings are insufficient, it will be necessary to seek external funds. This might be in the form of borrowing money from a bank. Alternatively, the entrepreneur might choose to combine with another person in either a partnership or a company. Whatever the source, finance will be required at the start-up stage of a business.

Once the business is established, it might also be necessary to obtain further funds for either expansion or the continuation of existing operations. Investment capital is finance to acquire new fixed assets (such as machinery). These assets will either replace existing assets or be added to the stock of assets of an expanding firm. Continuation finance for the day-to-day running of the enterprise and to pay costs as they become due is known as working capital. In an ideal world, this will be financed out of the proceeds of the sale of goods and services, but because the purchase of inputs will precede the sale of outputs, often by months or even years, there is a need

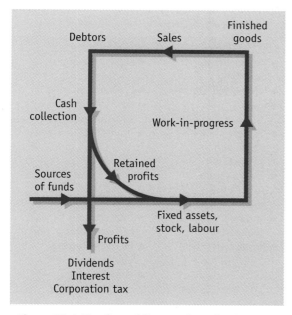

Debtors · Sales · Finished goods

Cash collection

Work-in-progress

Sources of funds

Retained profits

Profits

Fixed assets, stock, labour

Dividends
Interest
Corporation tax

Figure 29.1 The flow of finance through a business

for finance to fill the gap. Figure 29.1 illustrates the flow of finance through a business.

The need for external finance will vary over the life of a firm. It will be greatest when the business progresses to a further stage in its lifecycle. This cycle (which should be distinguished from the product lifecycle) consists of the following stages:

1 **start-up** the establishment of a business;
2 **expansion** a movement beyond 'base camp' as new, higher targets are set;
3 **consolidation** the owners take stock before proceeding to the next stage;
4 **development** a movement into new products and/or a new market;
5 **maturity** the business is established as a secure and diversified business;
6 **decline** this is not inevitable but depends on the ability of management to respond to changing conditions.

Clearly, as the business moves to the expansion and development stages, additional finance is essential. This will be either from internal or external sources.

In addition to financing the acquisition of fixed

assets (such as plant and machinery), funds will be sought in order to:

● develop new products;
● develop new markets;
● deal with an extraordinary situation, such as a large order from clients;
● finance export trade;
● provide working capital (such as stocks of materials).

We need to bear in mind the purpose of the finance as this will affect the choice of source (as we will see later).

Classification of sources

It is possible to classify sources of finance in three ways. First, we should distinguish between **debt finance** (which must be repaid with interest) and **equity finance** (provided by the risk-taking owners of the business). A second distinction that overlaps this one is between **external finance** (provided by outsiders) and **internally generated finance**. Internally generated finance consists of:

● retained profits (profits less dividends paid); and
● accumulated depreciation funds.

Internally generated finance has the advantage that no repayment or interest payment is necessary. However, it is only available as a source of finance to businesses that are already established and generating a positive cash flow.

Third, we can classify finance by its duration. **Permanent finance** takes the form of shares that will not be paid back (redeemed). **Long-term finance** is loans in excess of ten years. **Medium-term finance** covers a period of between three and ten years whereas **short-term finance** is for periods of up to three years. Table 29.1 lists the major forms of finance categorized in three ways.

Debt v. equity

The sale of an equity stake in a business involves surrender of a share of both future profits and decision making. Consequently, the promoter of a business needs to clarify his or her business aim

Table 29.1 Sources of finance

Internally generated	Depreciation Retained profits	Owners' equity (permanent)
Externally generated		
Long-term liabilities (10+ years)	Share issue Debentures Mortgage	
Medium term (3–10 years)	Hire purchase Bank loan Lease Sale and lease back	Loan capital
Short term (up to 3 years)	Overdraft Trade credit Factoring Bill discounting	

Table 29.2 Share capital v. loan capital

Share capital	Loan capital
• Represents ownership	• Represents debts
• Confers membership	• Creditor, not member
• Voting rights	• No rights of participation
• Dividends are part of the earnings of the firm	• Interest is an expense
• Dividends are paid at the board's discretion	• Priority over dividends
• No power to force liquidation	• Interest must be paid to avoid legal action
• No maturity date	• Power to force liquidation
	• Must be repaid

Table 29.3 Factors affecting choice of finance

- Availability of different sources of finance
- Relative costs of different methods
- Consequences for control of the business
- The implications for shareholders' dividends
- Tax implications
- The risk element involved: risky ventures should be financed by equity capital
- Terms and repayment period for loans

before choosing a particular source of finance. We can distinguish between **proprietorial** and **entrepreneurial** businesses. The owners of the former type of business seek to provide self-employment and wish to retain control. This desire to retain control will exceed any desire to expand. In general, they will be satisfied with the existing size of business enterprise, which they can manage effectively. Owners of proprietorial businesses will be reluctant to seek external equity finance and will rely on internally generated funds and loan finance.

Owners of entrepreneurial businesses are keen to expand their business. Not only will they have a greater need for external finance, but their commitment to expansion overcomes any reluctance to share the business with others. Entrepreneurial businesses seek finance from all sources.

In choosing between debt and equity finance, promoters should consider:

- whether or not they wish to share profits;
- whether or not they wish to share decision making;
- the implications of dividends on shares and interest on loans (see Tables 29.2 and 29.3).

Dividends are paid out of post-tax profits. There is no legal obligation to pay a dividend, although there is always a need to keep shareholders satisfied. There is, however, a legal commitment to pay interest on debt as well as to repay the capital sum when it is due. Consequently, debt finance increases the risk of insolvency. This is especially great when a high proportion of a business' permanent finance is in the form of loans. Such businesses are said to be **highly geared**.

The advantages of high gearing can be summarized as follows:

- increased opportunities for equity shareholders;
- the company has increased capital without diluting equity;
- interest on loans is an expense for tax purposes whereas dividend is declared *after* tax has been calculated.

Conversely, there are the following disadvantages:

- increased risk of company failure;
- increased risks for shareholders;
- assets will be pledged, thus reducing control over them;
- dividends fluctuate dramatically;
- reduces prospective creditors' willingness to grant further loans.

Banks will look very carefully at the gearing ratio of a business before granting further loans. If the business is highly geared, there will be a reluctance to grant further loans because of the increased risk of default.

The problems associated with high gearing suggest that the promoters and managers of a business should carefully consider the balance between debt and equity finance.

Long-term debt finance

Irrespective of its form, debt finance differs from equity finance in that:

- as debt, it takes preference in liquidation;
- interest is an expense and must be paid before dividends;
- the rate of interest is either fixed or tied to the current base rate;
- interest payments are tax deductible;
- it may be secured against specific assets.

Debentures (bonds or loan stock) are marketable securities, but, unlike shares, they confer no rights of ownership and are usually redeemed after a fixed period. Like shares, they can be issued at a different price to the nominal value on which the interest rate (known as the **coupon rate**) is fixed. Debentures are secured against specific assets or float as a charge on all assets.

Mortgages are available from banks and building societies, and are used to purchase property. A mortgage can be defined as a loan secured against land and buildings. Commercial mortgages (as distinct from mortgages to house buyers) are available for sums in excess of £50,000 for a period of up to 30 years. Normally the mortgage will cover up to 70 per cent of the value of the property.

Long-term bank loans (up to 20 years) will also be available for sums up to £500,000. Banks will normally want the loan secured against assets and will insist that the business retains an adequate level of liquidity to cover interest payments.

Medium-term finance

Medium-term finance covers a period of between three and ten years. Its major purposes are to purchase machinery with a corresponding life, provide the working capital requirements of a business and convert a persistent overdraft into a bank loan. Medium-term finance usually takes the form of a loan, hire purchase or leasing.

Medium-term loans have the advantage of flexibility, with the possibility of early redemption, but, against this, the business organization must make provision for repayment in a comparatively short time span.

Hire purchase is a method of paying for assets by instalment. The financier remains the legal owner of the asset until the hirer exercises his or her option to purchase at the end of the repayment period. The major advantage of hire purchase is that payment is phased over a period. **Lease purchase** is similar to hire purchase but does not involve the payment of a deposit.

Leasing involves the acquisition of an asset, but ownership does not pass to the user. Hence a lease is a means of financing the *use* of an asset rather than its *purchase*. The advantages of leasing are that:

- it mimimizes initial outlay;
- maintenance is provided with the package;
- the equipment can be updated to avoid obsolescence;
- the user can claim tax relief against lease payments;
- it is a form of 'pay as you use'.

However, there are also disadvantages to consider:

- all payments are outgoings;
- payment is greater in the long run;
- the lease might place limitations on use or compel the use of specified complementary goods;

● the user does not benefit from residual value when the equipment is upgraded.

Sale and leaseback involves the sale by the business of an asset (such as a building) to a finance company that then makes the asset available for the use of the business on a leased basis. It releases capital for use in the business and it is a useful way of raising finance for other purposes. However, it means that the business no longer owns the asset and rent must be paid.

Short-term finance

Short-term finance to provide working capital is necessary because of the time gap between purchase of inputs and sale of assets. Ideally, once a business is established, the flow of cash will finance purchases of inputs and will, therefore, act like a water fountain. Where the flow of cash is delayed or inadequate, a further injection may be needed. The process is depicted in Figure 29.2.

A major form of short-term finance is an **overdraft** from a bank. This is a flexible form of finance, it is unsecured, renewable, and interest is charged only on the negative balance outstanding each day. In the case of a business account that fluctuates considerably, this works out cheaper than interest on other loans. Against these advantages it should be remembered that overdrafts are technically repayable on demand and that interest rates reflect current market rates rather than being fixed in advance.

Delayed payment for materials is known as **trade credit**. Unlike most other forms of finance,

it is provided by suppliers rather than financial institutions. Ostensibly an interest-free loan, the supplier encourages prompt payment by means of a discount. In effect, the loss of discount constitutes the interest payment.

Businesses experiencing problems as a result of their own customers delaying payments may use the services of a **debt factor.** The factor is prepared to purchase debts at a discount. Even though the business seeking repayment does not receive all the money owned to it, there are advantages in early receipt of the money.

Share capital
Authorized and issued capital

Companies issue shares primarily to raise finance for expansion. The amount of money that can be raised in this way is limited to the authorized capital of the company. This will be stated in the capital clause of the Memorandum of Association and in the statement of authorized capital. For example, it might be stated that the nominal capital is £100,000 divided into 100,000 shares at £1 each. Shares can be issued up to this amount, although the company may also choose to issue fewer shares than the authorized amount. Where the issue capital is less than that authorized, a further issue is possible without further authorization. Once the issue capital is equal to the authorized capital, however, no further issues are permitted unless the Memorandum of Association is amended – after approval by existing shareholders.

We should also distinguish between the amount of capital that has been issued and the amount that has been 'paid up'. If a company does not require the whole of the finance from a share issue immediately, it will allow purchasers of shares to pay in instalments. When additional capital is required, further calls will be made on shareholders, up to the point where shares are fully paid. If the company is forced into liquidation, shareholders who have not fully paid for shares will be required to make a contribution up to the full nominal value of shares. When shares are fully paid up, no further claim can be made on the shareholder.

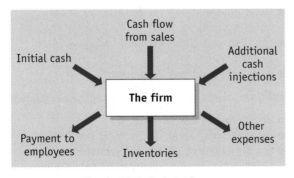

Figure 29.2 Cash to firms

Ordinary and preference shares

We can make a broad distinction between **ordinary (or equity)** and **preference shares**. Both form the share capital of the company but they differ in a number of important respects.

- Dividends are paid to preference shareholders before any are received by ordinary shareholders.
- The dividend on preference shares is a fixed percentage of the nominal value of the shares. Ordinary shareholders receive a dividend that is determined by directors in the light of the profits of the company.
- In most cases, preference shares are cumulative. This means that any arrears on the payment of dividends are made good in subsequent years.

Preference shares clearly involve a lower degree of risk, but the impact of unfavourable tax treatment (compared with debt capital) and inflation has made them less popular.

Ordinary shares (equity capital) are true 'risk' capital. As owners, equity shareholders possess voting rights and, therefore, the opportunity to participate in decision making. However, equity shareholders have the last claim not only on profits but also any sharing out of the proceeds of an assets sale in the event of liquidation.

The return on a shareholder's investment takes the form of:

- an annual dividend paid out of profits;
- a capital gain when shares are sold for a price higher than that at which they were purchased.

Both returns are uncertain. The dividend is dependent on the profitability of the company and capital gains are dependent on the market value of shares at the time the shareholder chooses to dispose of them.

Issuing shares

In the case of private companies, share issues are made privately and no appeal to the public is permitted. Public companies can issue shares in a number of different ways.

- **Offer of sale** This is the most commonly used method of issuing shares. The company sells shares to an issuing house or merchant bank that, in turn, offers them to the public at a higher price.
- **Public issue** Under this method, the offer is made direct by the company rather than through an issuing house.

  Public companies can appeal to the public to purchase shares, usually by means of issuing a prospectus. This is a lengthy account of the company, its structure, voting rights, performance and expectations for the future. The detailed work involved in the share issue is undertaken by a merchant bank or issuing house. To avoid the risk of undersubscription, it is necessary to have the issue **underwritten** by a financial institution. This means that, for a commission, the institution guarantees to buy up any unsold shares. This cost, together with advertising costs and the commission paid to the issue house, makes a public share issue very expensive and so feasible only when very large sums are required.
- **Placing** With this method, the shares are sold privately to clients of the issuing houses that handle the issue. As the cost of such an issue is substantially lower than that of the two previous methods, it is the most commonly used method for smaller issues (especially by companies selling their shares on the Alternative Investment Market (AIM) rather than the full Stock Exchange).
- **Tender** The investing public is invited to submit bids, with the shares being sold to the highest bidder. Market prices will ensure that all shares will be sold, although the price is uncertain. In favourable market conditions, the shares will be sold at a premium, thus bringing additional funds to the company (recorded as share premium in the balance sheet).
- **Rights issue** In a rights issue, existing shareholders are given the option to buy additional shares at favourable prices (or to sell the option to a third party). This is seen

as an inexpensive way of raising finance, but the company is forgoing the higher premiums that would have been available in the open market.

- **Bonus issue** Bonus shares are issued free to shareholders. Obviously this does not raise additional finance for the company, but is a capitalization of accumulated reserves. A problem for public companies is that when the value of real assets is substantially in excess of the share value of the company, it is vulnerable to takeover. A new share issue wards off the danger of takeover and also rewards shareholders with marketable securities that might be preferable to an increased dividend.

Value of shares

Shares have a **nominal** (or face) **value** that does not alter. However, their value in the market will fluctuate with changes in the supply of, and demand for, shares. Market values will also be affected by:

- the profitability of the company and its declared dividends;
- market expectations;
- interest rates (high rates will reduce the attractiveness of a shareholding);
- economic and political factors (such as political uncertainty);
- a takeover bid;
- market activities of a significant shareholder;
- factors that are expected to alter the profitability of the company (say, a large order).

Venture capital

A common problem for small enterprises has been the securing of funds (especially in the £50,000 to £250,000 range) for both start-up and expansion. The problem of the 'equity gap' is that sums in this range have been difficult to obtain and involve a disproportionately high cost. One development of recent decades has improved this situation. The development of a 'venture capital

industry' has increased the range of finance available to small and medium-sized firms.

What is venture capital?

Venture capital involves the sale of equity or a share in a business to a venture capital fund, another business organization or a wealthy individual. The venture capitalist buys an equity share in an unquoted company with high growth potential. This involves risk in that, as an equity shareholder, the venture capitalist is the part-owner of the company.

Venture capitalists are not looking for permanent involvement in the company. Instead, they seek to invest in a growing business that is expected to provide a substantial capital gain over a period of between two and seven years. Institutional investors are typically looking for compound annual capital growth of 35 per cent plus. Private investors may have other reasons for investing, but will still expect a high internal rate of return (see Chapter 30).

Venture capital is often associated with two other developments of recent decades – management buyouts and management buyins. In a **management buy-out**, the management of a company purchases the business with funds provided by a venture capitalist. In a **management buy-in**, a team of outside managers purchase a business, again with funds provided by a venture capitalist. In both cases, managers will provide a relatively small proportion of funds, but will eventually acquire a larger equity share as the business grows and prospers. A significant advantage in such arrangements is the greater motivation and enthusiasm of managers who have a substantial stake in the company. This will facilitate the capital growth sought by the venture capitalist.

As stated earlier, venture capitalists seek profitable investment in a fast-growing business for a period of between two and seven years. At the end of this period, they will seek an **exit** by selling their equity share. The exit is only available from a successful business. Consequently, venture capitalists are not interested in either slow-growing businesses or those with a low profit potential.

Venture capital from the perspective of the company

Venture capital is a possible source of funds for an entrepreneurial business, but not for a proprietorial business.

The entrepreneurial business will seek venture capital at various stages in its development – as:

- seed capital in the start-up stage;
- second-round finance to expand the range of products;
- development capital in the mature stage;
- recovery financing if it is in temporary difficulties – in this situation, venture capital will be available if the venture capitalist is confident about the chances of turning the business around.

The sale of an equity stake has certain advantages:

- the business is not committed to meeting regular interest payments;
- the equity will reduce the gearing of the firm;
- lower gearing will, in turn, make it easier to raise debt finance;
- the venture capitalist will provide management advice to strengthen the business.

The sale of an equity stake means giving up a share of control (and profit). Moreover, as the venture capitalist is looking for a high return, this might be a costly way of raising finance, especially if it is necessary to issue a prospectus.

Key concepts

Authorized share capital The total number and value of shares that a company can issue, as laid down in its memorandum of association.

Borrowed capital/debt capital Finance that has to be repaid.

Capital employed Funds used by a business to acquire assets.

Capital structure The way in which a company has raised its long-term finance by borrowing or equity. The balance between the two.

Corporate venturing Investment by a larger company in a smaller business.

Debenture A long-term loan to a company that takes the form of a marketable security. As a loan, it does not give rights of ownership in the business.

Debt The total amount owed by a business.

Development capital Venture capital to finance the expansion of an established company.

Dividends A proportion of profits paid out to shareholders. Dividends are expressed as a percentage of the nominal value of a share.

Equity Capital belonging to ordinary shareholders. It is share capital plus reserves.

Exit Sale of equity share by a venture capitalist.

Gearing The proportion of a company's capital that has been borrowed – ratio of debt to equity.

Issued share capital The number and amount of shares issued. This is not necessarily the same as authorized share capital and neither is it necessarily the same as paid-up share capital.

Lease An asset hired rather than bought.

Ordinary (equity) shares Shareholders are members and therefore owners of a company. They have rights of participation and in return receive a share of profits. The dividend on ordinary shares is not fixed. Ordinary shareholders come last in terms of both dividends and shares in the proceeds of liquidations. As such, they are the real risk takers in a company.

Preference shares Shares on which a fixed rate of dividends is paid and which have priority over ordinary shares.

Recovery financing Venture capital for companies in difficulty.

Seed capital Finance for the development of ideas or new start-up businesses.

Venture capital Equity investment in an unquoted company.

Essay questions

1 (a) Explain the main sources of long-term finance available to a large public limited company.
  (b) Analyse the implications of financing expansion by long-term borrowing.

2 (a) Explain the sources of long-term finance available to a small, family-owned private limited company.
  (b) Analyse the implications of financing expansion by a share issue.

3 (a) Explain the difference between authorized, issued and paid-up shares.
  (b) Evaluate the proposition that equity finance involves no cost to the business.

4 (a) With reference to the notion of matching sources to purposes explain the differing purposes of short-, medium- and long-term finance.
  (b) Evaluate leasing as a method of acquiring assets.

5 (a) Explain the main sources of short-term finance.
  (b) Evaluate the overdraft as a method of short-term finance.

6 Analyse the implications for a company's balance sheet of each of the methods of financing expansion.

Exercises

1 Read the extract below and answer the questions that follow.

Offer
of 136,974,973 ordinary shares of 10p each

and Placing
of 410,177,800 ordinary shares of 10p each
at a price of 115p per ordinary share
sponsored by
County NatWest
and underwritten by

County NatWest Limited   Charterhouse Bank Limited

The company's growth will be founded on:
- development of the superstore network by means of refurbishment and opening of relocated and new superstores;
- an enhanced and expanded product range that will assist market penetration;
- further vertical integration where there is the prospect of a high volume of sales and a rapid return on investment;
- continuing efficiency resulting from the Group's policy of restraining costs and controlling working capital.

The outlook for the current financial year depends largely on the scale and pace of economic recovery.

Flotation statistics

Flotation price per ordinary share	115 pence
Market capitalization at flotation price	£669 million
Proceeds receivable by the company after expenses	£545 million

(a) Explain the difference between a share offer and a placing.
(b) This share issue was underwritten by County NatWest Limited and Charterhouse Bank Limited. Explain their role in the issue.
(c) Explain the meaning of the price of 115p for a 10p share.
(d) What is meant by market capitalization?
(e) Explain the meaning of the points made relating to the firm's prospects.

2 The following information is adapted from a share prospectus published in the *Daily Business News* in February 1993.

THE WEALD INVESTMENT TRUST PLC
(Incorporated in England and Wales under the Companies Act 1985)

Offer for Subscription
by
Boyds Merchant Bank Limited

of up to 40 million ordinary shares of 10p each with warrants attached at 100p per share payable in full on application.

1 The offer has been partially underwritten by Boyds Merchant Bank to the extent of 28 million ordinary shares. The remaining 12 million ordinary shares have not been underwritten.
2 The authorized share capital will be £5 million in ordinary shares of 10 pence.
3 Shareholders will receive a warrant giving them the right to subscribe to further shares at 100p on the basis of one additional share for four existing shares.
4 The company has no loan capital outstanding or created but unissued.
5 Assuming that the share issue is fully subscribed the estimated net proceeds of the offer will be £38.4 million and estimated net asset value per ordinary share will be 96.05p.

(a) What is the value of the shares being offered?

(b) Why is it important for a share issue to be underwritten? Why would Boyds Merchant Bank be willing to underwrite an issue?

(c) Distinguish between authorized and issued share capital.

(d) Why would prospective shareholders be interested in the extent of the Trust's loan capital?

(e) What conclusions do you draw about the cost of a share issue?

(f) Calculate the net asset value of the Trust.

3 In the table below, you will find a statement of share capital taken from the annual accounts of a public company.

Share capital

	Ordinary shares of 25p each £000	4.2% Cumulative preference shares of £1 each £000	Total £000
Authorized at 31 March 20XX	12,200	200	12,400
Authorized at 1 April 20XX	12,200	200	12,400
Allotted, called-up and fully paid at 31 March 20XX			
36,143,408 ordinary shares	9,036	–	9,036
140,200 preference shares	–	140	140
	9,036	140	9,176
Allotted, called-up and fully paid at 1 April 20XX			
36,032,476 ordinary shares	9,008	–	9,008
140,200 preference shares	–	140	140
	9,008	140	9,148

(a) What is the significance of the fact that the allotted, called-up and fully paid share capital is less than the authorized capital?

(b) Distinguish between an ordinary share and a preference share.

(c) If the dividend on cumulative preference shares is not paid in one year, then it is held over to a later year. This being the case, explain the significance of the existence of 4.2% cumulative preference shares for the dividend payable to ordinary shareholders.

(d) Some ordinary shares were issued during the year in question.

  (i) Calculate how many shares were issued and how much was raised.

  (ii) Suggest reasons for ordinary rather than preference shares being issued.

(e) What procedures are required to increase the authorized capital?

4 Over the past five years, the profits of a company have been as follows:

Year	1	2	3	4	5
Profit (£000)	500	400	300	250	210

Out of the profit there has to be paid, in order of priority:
(i) interest on £200,000 of debenture stock at 10 per cent;
(ii) corporation tax at 35 per cent on profits after interest;
(iii) 10 per cent dividend on £100,000 of cumulative preference shares.

The remainder will be divided equally as:
(i) retained profits;
(ii) dividend on £1 million of ordinary (equity) shares.

(a) For each year, calculate the profits available for distribution to ordinary shareholders.
(b) Comment on the risk involved for each class of investor.
(c) Calculate the retained profits in each year and comment on retained earnings as a source of finance.

5 The data below comes from the annual accounts of a major international company. Study the data and answer the questions that follow.

	Year 2 £m	Year 1 £m
Turnover	2,684	2,541
Operating profit	468	464
Net finance charges	30	21
Net operating profit	438	443
Share of profits from associated companies	22	18
Profit before taxation	460	461
Taxation	79	75
Profit after taxation	381	386
Minority interests	3	2
Profit attributable to shareholders	378	384
Dividends	154	154
Retained profit for the year transferred to reserves	224	230
	£	£
Earnings per share	13.2	13.4
Dividend per share		
interim	1.34	1.34
final, recommended	4.04	4.04
	5.38	5.38
Shareholders' fund per share:	0.52	0.44

(a) Explain the items:
  (i)   share of profits from associated companies;
  (ii) minority interests;
  (iii) profit attributable to shareholders.
(b) The final dividend figure is shown as being recommended. By whom and to whom is the dividend recommended?
(c) What determines the size of the dividend? Explain why there is no change in the dividend.
(d) What is meant by shareholders' fund per share and how is it calculated?
(e) Assuming that the face value of each share is £1, calculate the share capital of this company

6 Study the table below and answer the questions that follow.

Distribution of shareholding between category of beneficial owner 1974 to 2000

Sector of beneficial holder	Percentage 1963	1969	1975	1981	1989
People	54.0	47.4	37.5	28.2	21.3
Charities	2.1	2.1	2.3	2.2	2.0
Public	1.5	2.6	3.6	3.0	2.0
Banks	1.3	1.7	0.7	0.3	0.9
Insurance	10.0	12.2	15.9	20.5	18.4
Pension funds	6.4	9.1	16.8	26.7	30.4
Unit trusts	1.3	2.9	4.1	3.6	5.9
Investment trusts/other financial institutions	11.3	10.1	10.5	6.8	3.2
Industrial and commercial companies	5.1	5.4	3.0	5.1	3.6
Overseas	7.0	6.6	5.6	3.6	12.4
Total	100.0	100.0	100.0	100.0	100.0

(*Source:* Share Register Survey Report, 1989)

(a) Explain the categories of beneficial holder listed in the data.
(b) Describe the trends that are revealed.
(c) Suggest reasons for the long-term decline in the proportion of shares held by individuals. Why was this not reversed in the 1980s when it was declared government policy to create popular capitalism?
(d) Account for the rise in overseas ownership of shares in UK listed companies. Discuss the implications of this trend.

7 Two companies (High Gee and Lo Gee) are identical in most respects. They are charged the same rate of interest, the capital employed is the same and they achieve the same level of operating profits. The only significant difference is their gearing ratio. High Gee has borrowed £7 million at 10 per cent per year and has issued 3 million £1 equity shares. Lo Gee, on the other hand, has financed the bulk of its capital by a share issue. Hence, its debts are only £2.5 million at 10 per cent and it has issued 7.5 million equity shares at £1.

(a) Calculate the gearing ratios for High Gee and Lo Gee using the formula:

$$\frac{\text{Preference shares + Long-term loans}}{\text{Shareholders' fund + Long-term loans}} \times 100$$

(b) Complete the tables below to calculate the percentage dividend on the assumption that all profits are distributed and none are retained.

		Years			
High Gee Company		*1*	*2*	*3*	*4*
Operating profit	(£m)	1.2	1.0	0.8	0.7
− Interest paid	(£m)	0.7			
= Dividend	(£m)	0.5			
% Dividend		16.7%			
$\dfrac{\text{Dividend}}{\text{Equity shares}} \times 100$					

		Years			
Lo Gee Company		*1*	*2*	*3*	*4*
Operating profit	(£m)	1.2	1.0	0.8	0.7
− Interest paid	(£m)	0.25			
= Dividend	(£m)	0.95			
% Dividend		12.6%			

8 Two companies each employed £10 million of fixed capital, although the methods of financing the capital was radically different. Company A obtained 80 per cent of its capital by a debenture loan at 10 per cent, with the remainder being raised by the issue of 2 million shares at £1 each. Company B obtained 20 per cent of its capital by a debenture loan at 10 per cent, with the remainder in the form of 8 million shares at £1.

Over a six-year period, the earnings (net of operating costs) available to service the debt and distribute as dividend were identical for the two companies.

	£000
Year 1	800
Year 2	1,000
Year 3	1,200
Year 4	1,400
Year 5	1,600
Year 6	1,800

(a) Calculate the gearing ratio for each of the two companies.
(b) Calculate the earnings per share, for each of the years, for both companies.
(c) What conclusions can be drawn about the effect of gearing on earnings available for distribution to shareholders?
(d) Identify other ways in which gearing affects the company and its shareholders.

9 The following data have been extracted from the consolidated profit and loss account of a large financial services company.

Profit attributable to shareholders	£100m
Retained profit	£40m
Dividend per £1 share	30p

(a) Calculate:
    (i)   the total amount paid in dividends;
    (ii) the number of shares issued;
    (iii) earnings per share.
(b) Explain the distinction between earnings per share and dividend per share.
(c) The current market value of shares is £1.50. Calculate the price–earnings ratio and explain its significance.

10 The following information relates to a public company for the year ending 30 April 20XX.
    (i)   The company has issued and fully paid share capital of 1 million ordinary shares at £1 each. There are no preference shares and no long-term capital.
    (ii) The market price of shares at 30 April 20XX was £2.50.
    (iii) Net profit, after tax payments of £120,000, was £150,000.
    (iv) The directors propose a dividend of 12p per share for the year ending 30th April 20XX.

Calculate the following ratios:
(a) return on capital employed;
(b) dividend yield;
(c) dividend cover;
(d) earnings per share;
(e) price–earnings ratio.

11 Study the following accounts and answer the questions.

Profit and loss account for the year ended 30 September 20XX

	£000	£000
Sales		65,000
Cost of sales		34,000
Gross profit		31,000
Expenses		42,000
Net loss		(11,000)
Dividends proposed		5,000
Net loss transferred to reserves		(16,000)

Balance sheet as at 30 September 20XX

	£000	£000	£000
Fixed assets (net of depreciation)			33,000
Current assets			
Stock	7,000		
Debtors	9,000		
		16,000	
Creditors due for repayment within one year			
Creditors	14,000		
Dividend	5,000		
Bank overdraft	16,000		
		35,000	
			(19,000)
			14,000
Share capital (£1 ordinary shares)			50,000
Reserves			(36,000)

(a) Explain what is meant by:
- (i) net loss transferred to reserves;
- (ii) reserves of minus £36m.

(b) How will the dividends be financed?

(c) Apart from the obvious point that it is a loss-making business, explain why shareholders should be alarmed by the situation revealed in the accounts.

12 Read the following statement and answer the questions below.

Chairman's statement

PROFITS UP 15% – GROWTH RESUMES

Results

I am delighted to be able to report an improved percentage increase in our pre-tax profits, compared with last year. On turnover of £59.449m, an increase of 12%, we made pre-tax profits of £8.525m, up 15%. After accounting for book profits from property sales as an extraordinary item, profit attributable to ordinary shareholders has improved by 22% to £6.024m. Your directors are recommending a final dividend of 3.64%, making a total of 5.6%, an increase of 23.6%.

Expenditure on fixed assets, mainly property, exceeded £7m for the second year running. Over the last four years, we have invested some £23.5m in new assets, the cash for which has been generated internally. A revaluation of all the company's properties, except the brewery buildings, has been carried out as at 30th March 20XX. This values the properties at £87.863m, resulting in a surplus of £26.329m since the last revaluation in 19XX, a 43% increase over book values. Property assets alone are now equivalent to £3.66 per £1 of ordinary share capital.

(a) Explain the following terms:
- (i) extraordinary item;
- (ii) generated internally;

    (iii) revaluation;

    (iv) book value.

(b) In your own words, explain the final sentence.

(c) Estimate the number of £1 ordinary shares.

(d) Why is revaluation of property necessary from time to time? Explain the implications of revaluation on the company's balance sheet.

(e) Explain the three adjustments that were made to move from pre-tax profits to dividends payable.

(f) What criteria would you use to evaluate the dividend?

Investment appraisal

Investment appraisal involves a series of analytical techniques designed to provide an answer to a basic question: is it worth while proceeding with a planned project?

Chapter objectives

1 To develop an understanding of the major techniques of investment appraisal.

2 To enable you to use the main techniques in appropriate situations.

3 To develop an understanding of the limitations of investment appraisal techniques.

Investment and other projects

The techniques of analysis dealt with in this chapter are usually called investment appraisal techniques. **Investment** is the acquisition of capital equipment, such as machinery, premises and vehicles. It is undertaken for the following reasons:

- to replace equipment;
- to expand productive capacity to meet demand;
- to reduce production costs;
- to provide new facilities in order to produce new products.

We could also use the wider term **project appraisal** as the techniques can be applied to numerous other situations that do not involve the acquisition of capital equipment. For instance, the profitability of a planned advertising campaign can be analysed by means of the same techniques. Readers who are planning to produce a written project (or research assignment) might find the techniques useful in analysing their chosen business issue.

The distinctive feature of investment (and other projects) is that it involves expenditure today (or at least in the near future) to produce some benefit in the longer-term future. The benefit can occur in one of two ways.

In the case of an expansion project, the benefit takes the form of increased production and, hopefully, sales revenue and profits. There are, however, problems with the concepts of profits and sales revenue. In the case of profit, much depends on how it is defined and calculated. In the case of sales revenue, new machinery does not benefit the firm if additional revenue is achieved at the expense of increased costs of complementary inputs. The way to avoid these problems is by analysing additional cash flow net of operating costs incurred in working the new equipment. Expansion projects are analysed by comparing expected additional net cash flow of the asset with its initial cost.

The other type of project does not add output or sales but reduces costs (for example, the acquisition of labour-saving equipment). Hence, the benefit takes the form of lower costs, but the principle is the same. The expected annual reduction in costs is compared with the initial cost of the equipment. The difference between the expansion and cost-reduction projects is illustrated in Figure 30.1.

There is a major problem that should be mentioned at this stage. All business projects involve an element of uncertainty. Expenditure is incurred today, but the benefit is enjoyed some time in the future – and by its very nature the future is uncertain. There is uncertainty about:

● future sales of the product;
● operating costs in the future;
● the life of the equipment.

Past experience might give an accurate forecast about the technical life of an asset in terms of how long it will last. However, the commercial life of an asset (how long it will be profitable) is more difficult to predict. For the moment, we will assume that the future can be predicted with total certainty. By analysing the future benefit and comparing it with the initial cost, we can decide whether or not it is worth while.

The payback method

Payback is the simplest method of project appraisal and is usually preferred by a small business because of its very simplicity. Large businesses use it as a screening method before embarking on one of the more complicated techniques. The **payback period** is the time taken for the in-

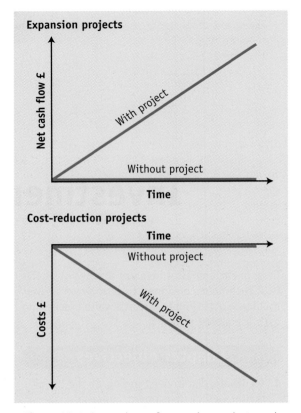

Figure 30.1 Comparison of expansion projects and cost-reduction projects

vestment to generate sufficient cash inflow to pay for itself. Assume a company was considering whether or not to invest in £500,000 of new equipment. The equipment is expected to last seven years and increase the firm's cash flow (net of operating costs) by £150,000, per year over its life. The payback period is £500,000, divided by £150,000 = 3.3 years.

Exercise
Each of the projects involves a cost of £1m, but produces a net cash flow as shown:

Project	Year	1	2	3	4	5
A		0	0.5	0.5	0.5	0.5
B		0.5	0.5	0.5	0	0
C		0	0	0.5	1	1

(All figures in £m)

1 Using a payback rule of:
  (a) two years
  (b) three years
  which projects are worth while?
2 Rank the projects in terms of payback period.

Firms can use this technique in one of two ways. First, a firm could set an upper limit on the time allowed for payback – any project that is not expected to pay back within the period is rejected. Second, when faced with a choice of projects, the payback method can be used to rank projects according to the speed with which they pay back.

The advantages and disadvantages of the payback method are set out in Table 30.1.

Accounting rate of return (ARR)

Unlike payback, **ARR** does take into account the return over the whole life of the asset. It expresses the annual increase in profits resulting from the investment as a percentage of the capital cost. It should be noted that this method uses figures for profits rather than cash flow (a major difference between profit and cash flow is that, in the former, depreciation is deducted).

Table 30.1 Advantages and disadvantages of the payback method

Advantages	Disadvantages
● Simplicity	● It ignores the timing of the return prior to payback
● Quick screening device	● It ignores the earnings after payback
● It places stress on early return, forecasts of which are likely to be more accurate than something long term	● It discriminates against projects that involve a long payback period
● An early return is especially important when liquidity is more critical than profitability	

Example
A capital item costs £1m, is expected to last for five years and produce an annual net cash inflow of £0.5m. The total profit net of both operating costs and initial capital cost (expressed as annual depreciation over five years) is $(5 \times £0.5m) - £1m = £1.5m$. This works out at annual return of £0.3m. As a percentage of the initial investment it is:

$$\frac{£0.3m}{£1.0m} \times 100 = 30\%$$

To recap, the steps to be taken are:

● aggregate the forecast net cash flow;
● deduct the capital cost;
● divide the resulting figure (known as the surplus) by the expected life of the equipment;
● express this annual figure as a percentage of the capital cost.

As with payback, we can use the ARR in two ways. First, the firm might set a predetermined level (say, 25 per cent) and reject any project the expected ARR of which was less than this percentage. Second, when faced with a choice of competing alternatives, projects can be ranked by ARR.

Exercise
A firm is considering four projects. The maximum life of each asset is three years and the capital cost is £100,000 in each case. The table below depicts net cash flow (in £000) in each of the three years.

Project	Year 1	Year 2	Year 3
A	50	50	50
B	100	20	–
C	0	50	140
D	90	60	–

1 Calculate the ARR for each project, but bear in mind that projects B and D have lives of two years, not three.
2 Rank the projects by ARR.

The advantages and disadvantages of this method of investment appraisal are shown in Table 30.2.

Table 30.2 Advantages and disadvantages of accounting rate of return

Advantages	Disadvantages
• Simple to understand	• The timing of the return is ignored
• Relatively easy to calculate	
• Uses yield in all years	

The discounting methods

The two discounting methods that we will look at in this section are:

• net present value;
• internal rate of return.

The payback and ARR methods suffer the major defects of either failing to take account of the total return and/or failing to take account of the timing of the return. The two discounting methods of project appraisal take timing as well as the size of the return into account.

Suppose your grandmother offered you a choice of a £100 money gift today in anticipation of your success in the A level examination or £100 after the results were announced. Which would you prefer? Quite sensibly you will prefer the money today, but let us analyse why. First, you will prefer the money today because of the greater certainty involved. Your grandmother might make the gift conditional on success in your exam. Second, aware of inflation in post-war Britain, you prefer to have the money today because its purchasing power will be greater today than it will be in the future. Both these points are valid, but must not obscure the essential point. Even when the money is guaranteed in the future and when inflation is non-existent, it is still preferable to have the money today. After all, with £100 today you can buy, say, a number of CDs and enjoy them in the immediate future. Alternatively, if you are prudent, you will deposit the money in a building society account and gain interest. The essential point to remember is that it is *always* better to have the money today rather than wait for it. This is the basis of a concept known as the **time value of money**. As £100 today is more valuable than £100 guaranteed in a year's time, we can rewrite the statement as £100 in a year's time is worth *less* than £100 today. It has a lower present value because of the inconvenience of having to wait.

The return on an investment comes in the form of a stream of earnings in the future. The discounting methods of investment appraisal take into account the size of the return over the life of the investment, but make adjustments for the timing. A greater weighting is given to the return in the early years and a lower weighting is given to the return in later years.

The weighting can be calculated from a formula that is derived from the formula for compound interest:

$$PV = \frac{A}{(1 + r)^n}$$

where PV is the present value of a net return in the future
A is the sum concerned
r is the rate of discount
n is the rule of years.

This enables us to calculate the present value of money **net of operating costs** to be received in n years. Hence, £100 in two years at a 10 per cent rate of discount has a present value of:

$$\frac{£100}{(1 + {}^1/{}_{10})^2} = \frac{£100}{(1.1)^2} = \frac{£100}{1.21} = £82$$

The stream over the years is:

$$\frac{A}{(1 + r)} + \frac{A}{(1 + r)^2} + \frac{A}{(1 + r)^3} \quad \cdots$$

If the mathematics look rather daunting, do not worry. Accountants use present value tables to obtain the weighting, or discount, factor. In examinations, you will be given the discount factor and so do not have to work it out (see Table 30.3).

Table 30.3 Discount table

Years					Discount rates					
	[2%]	[4%]	[6%]	[8%]	[10%]	[12%]	[14%]	[16%]	[18%]	[20%]
1	0.9804	0.9615	0.9434	0.9259	0.9091	0.8929	0.8772	0.8621	0.8475	0.8333
2	0.9612	0.9246	0.8900	0.8573	0.8264	0.7972	0.7695	0.7432	0.7182	0.6944
3	0.9423	0.8890	0.8396	0.7938	0.7513	0.7118	0.6750	0.6407	0.6086	0.5787
4	0.9238	0.8548	0.7921	0.7350	0.6830	0.6355	0.5921	0.5523	0.5158	0.4823
5	0.9057	0.8219	0.7473	0.6806	0.6209	0.5674	0.5194	0.4761	0.4371	0.4019
6	0.8830	0.7903	0.7050	0.6302	0.5645	0.5066	0.4556	0.4104	0.3704	0.3349
7	0.8706	0.7599	0.6651	0.5835	0.5132	0.4523	0.39968	0.3558	0.3139	0.2791
8	0.8535	0.7307	0.6274	0.5403	0.4665	0.4039	0.3505	0.3050	0.2660	0.2326
9	0.8368	0.7026	0.5919	0.5002	0.4241	0.3606	0.3075	0.2630	0.2255	0.1938
10	0.8203	0.6756	0.5584	0.4632	0.3855	0.3220	0.2697	0.2267	0.1911	0.1615

Net present value (NPV)

In the **NPV** method, the initial cost of the project is shown as negative (an outflow) and, as the cost is incurred today, it is not subject to discounting. The inward cash flow is shown as positive and is subject to discounting.

In the exercise, after calculating the PV for each year, you should add up the final column, not forgetting to deduct the initial £300,000. The residual value (scrap or trade-in value) is positive as it is a cash inflow that is expected in the future. However, as it is received after five years, the £10,000 is subject to considerable discounting.

The net present value (NPV) is the sum of the discounted cash inflows minus the cash outflow. If the sum of present values of inflows exceeds the capital cost, then the NPV is positive. This means that the project is worth proceeding with. If the NPV is negative, the project should not be undertaken. Where there is a choice of project, the one with the highest (positive) NPV will be chosen.

Exercise

In appraising a £300,000 investment project, a firm uses a discount rate of 10 per cent. The equipment will produce a return (net of operating costs) of £100,000 per year over a five-year period. At the end of the five years, the firm expects to sell the equipment for £10,000.

Calculate the net present value by completing the table:

Year	Cash flow (£000)	× Discount factor	= Present value (£000)
0	−300	× 1	−300
1	100	× 0.909	90.9
2	100	× 0.826	
3	100	× 0.751	
4	100	× 0.683	
5	100	× 0.621	
Residual value	10	× 0.621	
Net present value			

Exercise

After completing the above project appraisal at the 10 per cent rate, recalculate the net present values using a discount rate of
(a) 20 per cent; and
(b) 8 per cent

The relevant discount factors are:

Year	@20%	@8%
1	0.83	0.93
2	0.69	0.86
3	0.58	0.79
4	0.48	0.74
5	0.40	0.68

What conclusions can you draw?

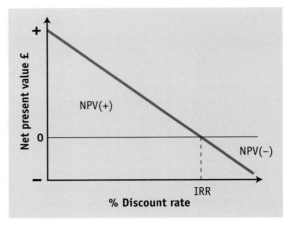

Figure 30.2 NPV of returns from a project at various discount rates to illustrate internal rate of return

An important question to ask is why a specific rate of discount is chosen. This is significant as the profitability of the proposed project depends on the chosen rate of discount. The discount rate selected should reflect interest rates in the market. This is important if the firm has to borrow money to finance the investment. It is also important if the investment is to be financed out of retained profits. The firm should consider what else it could do with the money – in other words, the opportunity cost of the investment in capital equipment is the sacrifice of interest in a financial investment the firm might otherwise have undertaken.

Internal rate of return (IRR)

This is a variation on the discounting method described above. So far, we have used a pre-determined discount rate to assess whether or not the sum of present values minus the initial cost was positive or negative. An alternative method involves the determination, by trial and error, of the discount rate that produces a NPV of zero. This is where the sum of the present values is exactly equal to the capital cost of the project. The discount rate that equates the two is known as the **internal rate of return (IRR)**. If the IRR exceeds the market rate of interest (which has to be paid to secure the funds) then the project

is worth while. If the IRR is less than the interest rate charged, then the project should be rejected. This is shown in Figure 30.2.

Exercise

The cost of an item of capital equipment is £330,000 and the net cash flow is expected to be £100,000 per year for four years.

Using the three discount rates, estimate the IRR.

Year	8%	10%	12%
1	0.93	0.91	0.89
2	0.86	0.83	0.80
3	0.79	0.75	0.71
4	0.74	0.68	0.64

There are two points to mention in relation to this exercise. First, as the annual return is the same in each year, you can use a shortcut in your calculation. Instead of multiplying £100,000 by each discount factor, you can add up the discount factors (3.17 in the case of 10 per cent) and multiply this figure by £100,000. This shortcut *only* applies when the annual return is the same in all years. Second, you should have discovered that none of the rates produces a net present value of zero. However, the 10 per cent rate produces the result closest to zero. The IRR is, therefore, slightly above 10 per cent.

In examinations, it is likely that you will be asked to estimate the IRR or read it off a graph similar to that in Figure 30.2.

You will now realize that NPV and IRR have similarities, but the fundamental difference is that the NPV uses a chosen rate of discount whereas the IRR is an attempt to identity a particular rate. The advantages and disadvantages of the two discounting methods are shown in Table 30.4. Table 30.5 summarizes the four project appraisal techniques.

Conclusion

Project appraisal techniques are important tools in business decision making. They all suffer the fundamental problem of trying to compare the known with the expected. To master the techniques, you should work through the exercises at the end of the chapter.

Table 30.4 The discounting methods

Advantages	Disadvantages
● All cash flows are included ● Takes timing into account	● More complicated than other methods ● The cost of capital is often difficult to ascertain ● Complicated mathematically, but it is based on expectations

Table 30.5 Project appraisal techniques

Method	Description	Single project Proceed if:	Choice of projects Choose the project:
Payback	The time taken to recoup the cost of the investment	the payback period satisfies the test	that pays back in the shortest period
Accounting (or average) rate of return (ARR)	Annual profits as a percentage of the cost of the project	the project's ARR exceeds the test rate	with the highest ARR
Net present value (NPV)	Net cash flow discounted to take account of the time value of money	NPV is positive	with the highest positive NPV
Internal rate of return (IRR)	Identifies the rate of discount at which the discounted cash inflow equals cost – that is, where NPV equals zero.	the IRR exceeds the firm's test rate	with the highest IRR

Key concepts

Accounting rate of return (ARR) The average return from an investment project expressed as a percentage of the cost of the project.

Cash flow The flow of cash in to and out of a business.

Discounted cash flow The discounting of expected future cash flows to take into account the time value of money.

Internal rate of return (IRR) The discount rate that equates the cost of an investment with the present value of expected inflows.

Investment (project) appraisal Techniques for evaluating a proposed investment project.

Net present value (NPV) The discounted value of expected future cash receipts net of the costs.

Payback A method of project appraisal based on the time taken to recoup the cost of the investment.

Essay questions

1 A firm intends to invest in a computer system in order to reduce costs.
   (a) Explain how it should set about calculating the (net) annual return on the investment.
   (b) Propose and evaluate one technique of investment appraisal that it should use.

2 (a) Explain each of the non-discounting techniques of investment appraisal.
   (b) Evaluate the proposition that the discounting methods are superior to the non-discounting ones.

3 (a) Explain the difference between the net present value and the internal rate of return.
   (b) Evaluate each of these two methods of investment appraisal.

4 (a) With reference to each of the techniques of investment appraisal, analyse how the rate of interest on loans affects investment decision making.
   (b) When financing investment from internal sources, firms can ignore interest rates. Discuss.

5 (a) Explain how a computer program can aid investment decision making.
   (b) Analyse non-quantifiable factors that should be taken into account in investment decisions.

6 (a) Analyse ways in which expected inflation affects the process of investment decision making.
   (b) Analyse how uncertainly affects the process of decision making.

Exercises

1 A small firm of accountants is considering the purchase of a computer, which, together with software, staff training and installation costs, will involve an initial outlay of £20,000. The computer will enable the firm to reduce its staff by one clerical worker, whose annual pay is £8000. However, another clerical worker employed by the firm is to be regraded and given a £1500 a year pay rise to operate the equipment. In addition, insurance and maintenance will add £500 to the firm's annual costs. At the end of five years, the firm expects to sell the computer for £5000. Using the discount factors below, calculate the net present value of the return on this investment.

Year 1 - 0.91
Year 2 - 0.82
Year 3 - 0.74
Year 4 - 0.67
Year 5 - 0.61

2 Three projects are currently under consideration by Kirby Air Filters Ltd. Only one project can be undertaken and the expected cash flows associated with each are as follows.

Time (years)	A	B	C
0	−100	−100	−100
1	+100	+10	0
2	+100	+10	+10
3	0	+100	+100
4	0	+100	+100
5	0	0	+150

(All figures in £000)

Calculate the net present value of the cash flows based on an 8 per cent discount rate. (The discount factors are 0.92, 0.86, 0.79, 0.73, 0.68.)

3 It is estimated that the net return on a £750,000 investment will be:

	£000
Year 1	200
Year 2	250
Year 3	250
Year 4	200
Year 5	150
Residual value after 5 years	50

(a) Calculate:
   (i) the payback period;
   (ii) the accounting rate of return.

(b) Calculate the net present value using Table 30. 3 and the following three discount rates:
    (i) 8 per cent;
    (ii) 10 per cent;
    (iii) 12 per cent.
(c) Estimate the internal rate of return.

4 Davidson Pet Foods Ltd is investigating three alternative investment projects, each involving an initial cost of £10 million. The pattern of net returns on the investment is shown in the table below.

Project	A	B	C
Year 1	4	0	8
Year 2	4	1	6
Year 3	8	8	4
Year 4	8	20	4
Year 5	8	20	4
Residual value after 5 years	2	3	0.5

(All figures in £million)

The managing director insists on a three-year payback rule as an initial screening device. Thereafter, the net present value method is used in project appraisal.

Which project would be chosen by Davidson? (The discount factors are: Year 1 – 0.91; Year 2 – 0.83; Year 3 – 0.75; Year 4 – 0.68; Year 5 – 0.62.)

5 Jones and Jones Ltd is considering two investment projects, but only has funds to proceed with one of them. The cash flows associated with each project are shown below.

	Project A £000	Project B £000
Initial cash outlay	200	250
Cash flow		
(net of operating costs)		
Year 1	50	40
Year 2	50	40
Year 3	50	60
Year 4	50	60
Year 5	50	100
Residual (scrap)		
value at the end of 5 years	50	50

(a) For each project, calculate the:
  (i) payback period;
  (ii) accounting rate of return;
  (iii) net present value, using the discount factors shown below.
      Year 1 0.91
      Year 2 0.83
      Year 3 0.75
      Year 4 0.68
      Year 5 0.62
(b) Advise the company on the choice of projects, evaluating the three analytical techniques.

6 The table that follows is derived from a table of discount factors. It shows the present value of £1 at various rates of discount.

Years	8%	10%	12%
1	0.93	0.91	0.89
2	0.86	0.83	0.80
3	0.79	0.75	0.71
4	0.74	0.68	0.64
5	0.68	0.62	0.57

The net cash inflow from a capital investment project is £500,000 p.a. for five years.

(a) Calculate the present value of £500,000 per annum over five years using *each* of the above rates of discount.
(b) The cost of the equipment is £1,890,000. Which of the three rates of discount produces a present value of receipts that is closest to the cost of the equipment?
(c) Estimate the internal rate of return.
(d) Evaluate the profitability of the investment project if the rate of interest is 12 per cent.

7 A company is considering whether to invest in Project X, Project Y or Project Z. It will be unable to invest in more than one of these projects and each will entail an initial outlay of £300,000. The relevant information is shown below.

Forecast profits	Project X [£]	Project Y [£]	Project Z [£]
Year 1	40,000	20,000	20,000
2	40,000	30,000	40,000
3	40,000	50,000	60,000
4	40,000	60,000	80,000

The company is presently earning a return of 12 per cent on capital.

Calculate the accounting rate of return for each project and comment on which project you think the company should adopt.

8 To undertake an order from a large customer, a company would have to invest in new machinery at a cost of £370,000. Cash flow returns are expected to be £90,000 per year for six years, at the end of which the residual value of the asset is expected to be £20,000.
   (a) Calculate the:
      (i)   payback period;
      (ii) net present value of the cash flow at a 14 per cent rate of discount;
      (iii) internal rate of return.
   (b) What other factors should be taken into consideration in deciding whether or not to proceed with the investment?
   (c) Explain the advantages and disadvantages of the above three techniques of project appraisal.

9 For each of the following projects, estimate the internal rate of return:
   (i)   a net cash inflow of £100,000 per year for five years on a £375,000 project;
   (ii)   a net cash inflow of £50,000 per year for six years on a £190,000 project;
   (iii) a net cash inflow of £40,000 per year for eight years on a £250,000 project;
   (iv)   a net cash inflow of £100,000 per year for five years on a £410,000 project.

10 Calculate the net present value of each of the following investments:
   (i)   Project A, for which the initial cost is £600,000, net cash inflow is expected to be £250,000 per year for 4 years and a 10 per cent rate of discount is used;
   (ii) Project B, for which the initial cost is £1.5 million, net cash inflow is expected to be £0.4 million per year for 6 years and an 8 per cent rate of discount is used.

11 Estimate the internal rate of return for each of the following projects:
   (i)   Project A, which has an initial cost of £600,000 and a return of £200,000 per year for 5 years;
   (ii) Project B, which has an initial cost of £500,000 and a return of £100,000 per year for 7 years.

12 Calculate the net present value of each of the following investments:
   (i)   Project A, for which the initial cost is £700,000, net cash inflow is expected to be £200,000 per year for 5 years and a 10 per cent rate of discount is used;
   (ii) Project B, for which the initial cost is £1.5 million, net cash inflow is expected to be £0.5 million per year for 4 years and an 8 per cent rate of discount is used.

13 Estimate the internal rate of return for each of the following projects:
   (i)   Project A, which has an initial cost of £400,000 and a return of £100,000 per year for 5 years;
   (ii) Project B, which has an initial cost of £600,000 and a return of £150,000 per year for 7 years.

14 A firm is considering two projects that produce the following pattern of cash flows.

	Project A £000	Project B £000
Year 0	−250	−200
Year 1	−	60
Year 2	−	50
Year 3	150	90
Year 4	150	90
Year 5	160	90
Year 6	100	90

For each project, calculate the:
(i) payback period;
(ii) accounting rate of return;
(iii) net present value, using a 10 per cent rate of discount.

Decision trees

Decision making takes place against a background of uncertainty about the future course of events. Consequently, in making decisions, known costs are compared with expected pay-offs in the future. By building on the principles of probability that we considered in Chapter 5, we can represent alternative courses of action in a decision tree in which account is taken not only of expected pay-offs but also the probability of achieving different levels of pay-off.

Chapter objectives

1 To explain the principles behind the construction of decision trees.

2 To explain the use of decision trees in decision making.

3 To develop your skills in constructing decision trees and using them to solve problems.

Use of decision trees

A decision tree is an aid to decision making in conditions of uncertainty. Faced with a number of possible actions, the decision maker:

- sets out the alternative courses of action in the form of a tree diagram;
- estimates the possible outcomes of the various actions;
- determines the (subjective) probability for each outcome;
- uses the latter to moderate each outcome and, in so doing, calculates the expected value from each outcome;
- selects the course of action with the highest expected value.

Note that the decision is based not on outcome alone, but on outcome moderated by the likelihood of achieving that outcome.

The advantage of using the decision tree technique is that it clarifies the decision-making process, thus leading to more rational decision making. The types of decision that lend themselves to the decision tree technique include:

- whether or not to introduce a new product or continue with existing products;
- whether or not to launch a new advertising campaign or continue with the existing campaign;
- whether or not to sell off assets for a known

price or continue to use them in conditions of uncertainty;

- whether or not to expand in one location or another.

In all such cases, there is a sequence of inter-related questions to be answered and different estimates of outcomes and the likelihood of achieving those outcomes, to be made.

The structure of decision trees

Figure 31.1 shows a decision tree without numerical data. The decision is whether or not to open a factory.

In decision trees, **squares** represent points at which management decisions have to be made. They are known as **decision nodes**.

The **black dot** at the end of a branch represent the finishing point of a sequence of decisions. **Circles** represent points at which one of a number of outcomes may occur. In this case, we have

different outcomes depending on the state of the economy. A boom will give rise to an outcome different to that in a recession. Unlike the decision nodes, there is no decision to be made at the outcome node as the state of the economy is not under the control of the business organization.

The diagram itself is useful for clarifying issues, but it does not provide an answer to the question of whether or not to open the factory unless we include numerical data. The numerical data is shown in Figure 31.2.

A decision not to open the factory produces a zero return. If a decision is made to open the factory, the net return depends on the state of the economy. If there is a boom, the outcome will be a profit of £5 million. However, there is only a 0.3 probability of a boom. If there is a slump, opening the factory will lead to a loss of £1 million. It is estimated there is a 0.7 probability of a recession. Remember that probability varies from zero (impossible) to one (a certainty). A cautious person would not open the factory as

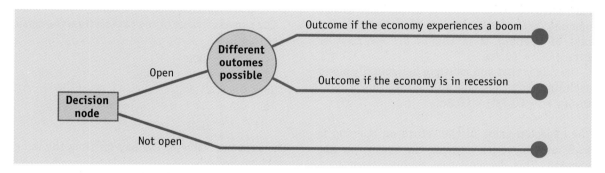

Figure 31.1 The structure of a decision tree

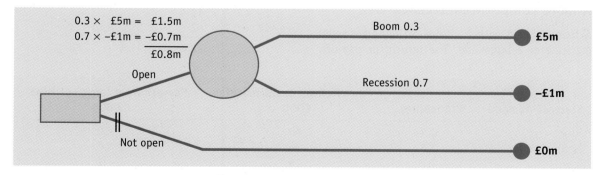

Figure 31.2 A single decision tree

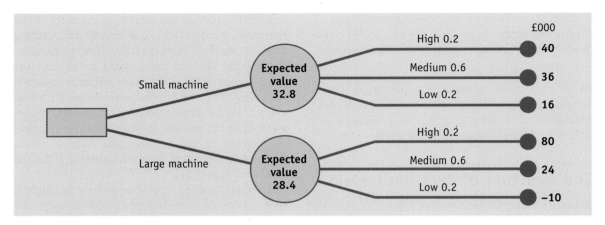

Figure 31.3 A more complicated decision tree

to do so provides the prospect of enjoying high profits, but also the even greater danger of suffering a loss. If a decision is made to open, there is a possibility of enjoying high profits, but there is a greater possibility of suffering a loss.

To solve the problem, we calculate the expected value at each node. This is equal to the outcome multiplied by its probability. In the case of not opening, this is £0 multiplied by 1, or £0. In the case of opening, it is £5m × 0.3 = £1.5m or £1m × 0.7 = £0.7m.

The rule is that you multiply horizontally along each line. You then add up the resulting values: £1.5m + (− £0.7m) = £0.8m.

The expected value of the return on opening is £0.8 million, which exceeds the return on not opening. This decision tree analysis leads to a recommendation to open the factory.

A more complicated decision tree

A firm is faced with a choice of buying a small machine or a large one. The return, or pay-off, will vary depending on the choice of machine and the state of demand. The relevant data is shown below:

Figure 31.3 represents the situation. There is one decision to be made and, therefore, only one decision node. Each main branch has an outcome node from which there are three lines representing the three states of demand.

The expected value of the pay-off from the small machine is:

$$\begin{array}{r} £000 \\ 40 \times 0.2 = 8 \\ 36 \times 0.6 = 21.6 \\ 16 \times 0.2 = \underline{3.2} \\ 32.8 \end{array}$$

The expected value of the pay-off from the large machine is:

$$\begin{array}{r} £000 \\ 80 \times 0.2 = 16 \\ 24 \times 0.6 = 14.4 \\ -10 \times 0.2 = \underline{-2} \\ 28.4 \end{array}$$

State of demand	Probability	Pay-off from small machine £000	Pay-off from large machine £000
High	0.2	40	80
Medium	0.6	36	24
Low	0.2	16	−10

Even though there is a possibility of a much higher pay-off from the large machine, when this is weighed against the probability of success and failure, the small machine represents a better investment.

A decision tree with two decision nodes

Figure 31.4 represents a more complicated example in that the choice of one course of action necessitates a second decision. The decision concerns the sale of land. The owner has the choice of selling it immediately for £1.2 million or developing the land for subsequent sale at a higher price.

The development might take the form of spending £2 million on infrastructure alone or £2 million plus a further £4 million if factory units are built. The various outcomes or pay-offs depend on the state of the economy. The relevant data is shown below.

We have two branches from the left-hand decision node. The first branch is an immediate sell, producing a certain £1.2 million pay-off. On the other branch, there is a second decision node: to develop the infrastructure alone or build the factory. The two branches from this decision node are followed by outcome nodes relating to the state of the economy.

A rule in decision tree analysis is that we work from right to left – that is, we have to resolve the infrastructure or factory decision before dealing with the sale or develop decision.

If the factory is built, the expected value of the pay-off is:

$$£12m \times 0.2 = £2.4m$$
$$£4m \times 0.5 = £2m$$
$$£2m \times 0.3 = \underline{£0.6m}$$
$$\overline{£5m}$$

State of the economy	Probability	Pay-off From infrastructure alone	Factory development
Recovery	0.2	£6m	£12m
No change	0.5	£3m	£4m
Recession	0.3	£1m	£2m

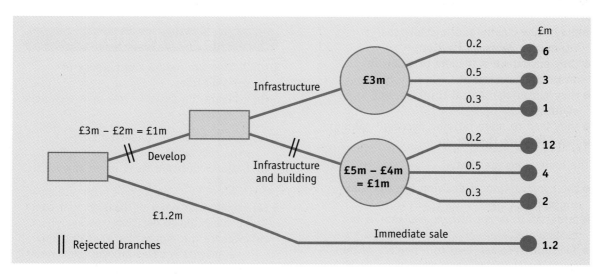

Figure 31.4 A decision tree with two decision nodes

However, we should deduct the £4 million of additional building costs, giving a net expected value of £1 million. The expected value of the pay-off from infrastructure development is:

£6m × 0.2 = £1.2m
£3m × 0.5 = £1.5m
£1m × 0.3 = £0.3m
                  £3m

At this stage we do not deduct the infrastructure development costs as they are common to both courses of action. The analysis so far therefore supports the decision to develop infrastructure only rather than build a factory.

Having made a decision at this node, we block off the rejected line by putting a pair of lines across the rejected path. We now have to choose between an immediate sale raising £1.2 million and infrastructure development. Infrastructure development will produce an expected value pay-off of £3 million, but we now have to deduct the infrastructure development costs of £2 million. This leaves an expected net pay-off of £1.0 million. The decision will therefore be to sell the land without developing it.

Advantages and disadvantages of decision trees

The advantages of decision trees are as follows:

- they show clearly and logically the alternative courses of action;
- they encourage managers to quantify alternative outcomes;
- they encourage logical thinking and planning;
- they lead to more rational decision making;
- new ideas are thrown up.

The limitations are that:

- the construction of decision trees is time-consuming;
- information is not always available or is incomplete;
- decision trees can lead to a neglect of non-quantifiable factors;
- the estimate of probability is subjective, yet it encourages the belief that it is based on hard data.

Key concepts

Decision tree A graphical representation of alternatives in a decision-making problem. The distinctive feature of decision trees is that both outcomes and their probability of occurrence are taken into account.

Expected value The average return attached to a project when the project has a number of uncertain outcomes, each with a monetary value. It is equal to the sum of the alternative and mutually exclusive outcomes multiplied by their respective probability of occurrence.

Mutually exclusive events Events where the occurrence of one event excludes the possibility of the other event(s) occurring.

Probability A numerical assessment of the likelihood of an event occurring. In decision tree analysis, this is a subjective estimate of probability.

Risk Uncertainty quantified with subjective probability.

Uncertainty Unquantified risk.

Essay questions

1 (a) Outline the nature and purpose of decision trees.
  (b) Evaluate the decision tree as a technique of analysis.

2 (a) Explain what you understand by expected value.
  (b) Evaluate decision trees as an analytical tool.

3 (a) Explain four types of decision that could be subjected to decision tree analysis.
  (b) Evaluate the proposition that decision tree analysis is based on sure foundations.

Exercises

1 A double glazing firm has calculated that the average revenue from each sale is £6000. Calculate the firm's expected annual revenue when the probability distribution of yearly sales is as follows.

No. of sales	Probability
800	0.1
810	0.4
820	0.3
830	0.2

2 A double glazing firm has calculated that the average revenue from each sale is £5000. Calculate the firm's expected annual revenue when the probability distribution of yearly sales is as follows.

No. of sales	Probability
1,100	0.2
1,110	0.3
1,120	0.4
1,130	0.1

3 Calculate the expected values of the options given below. Which should be accepted?

Option A		Option B		Option C		Option D	
Probability	Profits £000	Probability	Profits £000	Probability	Profits £000	Probability	Profits £000
0.4	50	0.3	−30	0.4	30	0.3	50
0.6	80	0.5	50	0.5	60	0.3	60
		0.2	80	0.1	100	0.4	90

4 A restaurant owner is faced with a choice of:
 (i) a large scale investment to improve her premises. This could produce a substantial pay-off in terms of increased revenue net of costs but it will involve a cost of £400,000;
 (ii) a smaller-scale investment to refurbish the premises – at £50,000 this is less costly, but it will also produce a lower pay-off;
 (iii) continuing the present operation without change – this last option will not cost anything, but neither will it produce a pay-off in terms of increased net revenue.

   Using the data on the decision tree below, advise the owner on the most appropriate course of action.

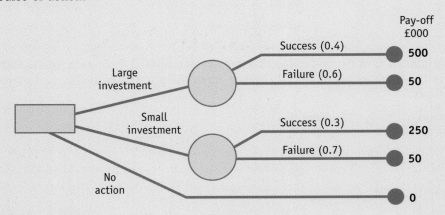

5 A firm is considering whether or not to test market a new product or abandon it. If it takes the latter course of action, it will raise £50,000 by the sale of equipment bought to manufacture the product.

   The test market is expected to cost £100,000 with a 0.7 probability of success and a 0.3 probability of failure. If the test market is a failure, the £50,000 from the sale of equipment will still be enjoyed. If the test market is a success, the expected pay-offs (at varifying levels of demand) are as follows.

Demand	Probability	Pay-off
High	0.25	£600,000
Medium	0.5	£200,000
Low	0.25	–£100,000

(a) Depict the scenario in a decision tree.
(b) Calculate the expected value of the outcome of the test market.
(c) Advise the firm on what it should do.

Cost accounting

In earlier chapters in this part of the book, we investigated financial accounting – that is, accounting for external reporting purposes. This chapter is the first of three dealing with various aspects of cost accounting. Cost accounting is important for internal decision making.

Chapter objectives

1 To explain the purpose of cost accounting.

2 To explain the ways in which costs are classified.

3 To investigate different approaches to costing.

4 To explore the use of costing in the decision-making process.

5 To introduce you to the analysis of variance.

6 To lay the foundation for the subsequent chapters on cost accounting.

Management accounting

Management accounting is concerned mainly with internal reporting to the managers of an enterprise. It emphasizes the control and decision-making rather than the stewardship aspects of accounting. Management accountants seek to support management decision making by the provision of information and the analysis of financial performance. Consequently, the focus of management accounting is the present and future as well as the past (for control purposes). As the data is required for internal purposes, the management accountant is not constrained by the need to comply with regulations on the format for presentation. The main functions of this form of accounting are:

● to classify and calculate costs of production – this is known as **cost accounting**;
● to provide estimates of future expenses and revenues – this is known as **budgeting**;
● to identify inefficiencies within the organization;
● to control costs and manage the flow of cash;
● to seek opportunities – for example, to identify tax breaks, possible cost savings and movements in foreign exchange rates that could be exploited by the firm.

Costs

It is important to state that in this chapter we are concerned with the cost of producing goods (or of providing services) and not the price at which they are sold. These costs are incurred by business organizations when they hire resources (labour, materials, machinery, buildings and so on). A cost is, in effect, a payment for a sacrifice of resources. We should include in the cost of production the notional pay that a sole trader should give him or herself for engaging in producing. This allies with the economist's concept of **opportunity cost** – cost in terms of alternatives that have been sacrificed.

One form of cost that is excluded from this chapter is external costs (often erroneously referred to as social costs). Profit-motivated business organizations will only consider private costs to themselves rather than those inflicted on society at large (pollution, noise and so on).

Classification of costs

As shown in Table 32.1, costs can be classified in a number of ways. First, we can classify by reference to the resources that were hired. Second, we can classify by functional area of management.

Third, by product, job or contract. However, the most important classifications are by type and by behaviour. The distinction in **classification by type** is whether or not the cost is directly or indirectly associated with the production of the goods (or service). Direct costs are wholly and exclusively identified with a particular cost unit (such as a unit of output). Hence, labour and materials used to produce jam tarts in a bakery are direct costs of jam tart production. However, there are other costs that are not directly linked to jam tart production, such as the cost of employing administrative staff or the heating and lighting bill for the bakery. These indirect costs are known as **overheads** and cover administrative and marketing activities. The production overheads include tools used in the production department as well as indirect labour (say, cleaners) and depreciation of plant.

Figure 32.1 illustrates the way in which different categories of costs are added together to give the total cost of production and distribution. An element of profit is added to the total costs to form the selling price.

Table 32.1 Classification of costs

By nature of resource	Materials
	Labour
	Other expenses
By function	Production
	Selling
	Administration
	Distribution
By product, job, contract	
By behaviour	Fixed
	Variable
	Semi-variable
By type	Direct
	Indirect
By type, subdivided by nature of the resources:	
direct	Materials
	Labour
	Other expenses
indirect	Materials
	Labour
	Other expenses

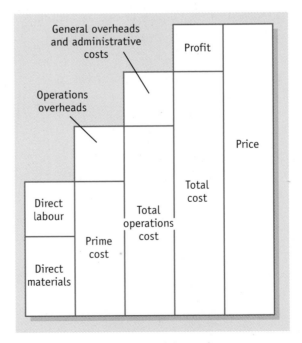

Figure 32.1 A breakdown of costs

Classification by behaviour considers the impact of a change in output on the cost of production. We can distinguish between **fixed costs** (rent, interest payments and so on) and **variable costs** (cost of energy, materials, labour). The former remain the same in the short run, irrespective of the level of production. Clearly, no costs are fixed in the long run, but, in the short run, interest on debts has to be paid whether production is high, low or even zero. Variable costs are those that vary with the level of output. Hence, the greater the output, the greater the quantity of materials used.

In addition to fixed and variable costs, we can also identify **semi-variable costs**. As the name suggests, these costs contain both fixed and variable elements. For example, the rental on a vehicle will include a fixed sum plus an additional variable payment linked to use.

Economists are mainly interested in classification by behaviour, whereas accountants are mainly interested in classification by type.

A common error is to equate fixed costs with indirect costs and variable costs with direct costs. It is true that many indirect costs are fixed while many direct costs are variable, but the matrix in Table 32.2 is intended to demonstrate that fixed and indirect costs, and variable and direct costs are not synonymous.

Depreciation and rent are both fixed costs, yet the former can be identified with a particular product whereas this is not the case with factory rent. Similarly, although raw material costs are variable and can be directly related to specific types of production, the same cannot be said of energy costs. These are obviously variable but are not easily related to particular products.

Table 32.2 Matrix of direct and indirect costs

	Direct	Indirect
Fixed	Depreciation on dedicated machinery	Factory rent
Variable	Raw materials	Energy

The purpose of costing

The basic purpose of costing is to discover the cost of an activity. This might be the cost of undertaking a large civil engineering project or that of producing each unit of a product. Alternatively, we might be interested in the cost of maintaining a particular department of the organization. The investigation of cost is undertaken for four basic reasons:

- to calculate the profitability of a particular venture;
- to provide information of pricing decisions;
- to control expenditure;
- to appraise alternative courses of action.

In essence, cost accounting is part of the control and decision-making function of the organization.

Although the subject of costing is large and complicated, students of Business Studies require just a basic knowledge of three techniques.

- **Full and absorption costing,** which attempts to identify all the costs associated with a particular activity.
- **Marginal costing,** which focuses only on the variable costs and ignores the fixed costs.
- **Standard costing,** which is an attempt to calculate what the costs should be in advance of the activity. Apart from guiding price and other decisions, standard costing is invaluable in discovering what went wrong – that is, comparing the expected with the actual result.

Full and absorption costing

There is a technical difference between full and absorption costing to which we will return, but, for the moment, the essential point is that these methods attempt to identify all the costs associated with a particular activity. It is relatively easy to calculate the direct labour and direct materials costs. It is more difficult to decide how much of the indirect or overhead costs should be identified with a particular activity. This can be illustrated by a simple example. A plumber will charge what appears (to the customer) to be a high price for a simple job, such as replacing a tap. The 'high' charge will cover not just the cost of the tap and the plumber's time but also that particular job's share of overheads. These overheads include the cost of a van, the plumber's telephone bill and the tools that the plumber needs to carry on his or her trade. Every customer will be required to carry a share of these overheads. The problem is *how* to share out these costs.

Full costing is a simplified version of absorption costing. Under the **full costing** method, the total overheads are allocated to each activity in a simple blanket manner. This can be seen in the example given in Figure 32.2.

The full costing method is to devise some formula by which the overhead costs can be divided up. One such method is by reference to material costs. In the example in Figure 32.2, overhead costs are double the total cost of materials. Consequently, the share of overheads should be twice the cost of materials for each product. Hence, the cost of producing A is:

£50,000 + £60,000 + (2 × £60,000)
= £230,000.

The cost of producing B is:

£30,000 + £30,000 + (2 × £30,000)
= £120,000.

The mathematically minded reader will realize that we would have reached the same answer if we had used a 2:1 ratio to divide up the £180,000 of overhead costs. However, accountants express the absorption of overheads as a percentage of an easily calculated cost. This method is relatively simple, although it is somewhat arbitrary. If we divided up the £180,000 in some other way, the answer would have been different.

Absorption costing does not use this blanket approach. Instead, the various types of overheads are apportioned in a distinct way. The most common methods are shown Table 32.3. After overheads are apportioned to particular products, we can then calculate the share of these apportioned overheads that should be absorbed by each unit. This is known as the **overhead absorption rate**. For instance, on the basis of an apportionment formula, an overhead cost of £180,000 might be divided between products in a ratio of 2:1. Therefore, the first product would bear £120,000 of the overheads. If the budgeted (planned) output of the product was 40,000 units, then each unit would be required to absorb £120,000 divided by 40,000 = £3. In the absorption process, different rates would be calculated for each element of the total overheads.

Absorption costing is clearly more complicated than full costing, but both have the advantage of the recovery of all costs. The great weakness is that, whatever method is used, it is arbitrary. Moreover, the absorption rate is only valid if *actual* output is in line with *budgeted* output.

Direct labour cost of product A	£ 50,000
Direct material cost of product A	£ 60,000
Direct cost of product A	£110,000
Direct labour cost of product B	£ 30,000
Direct material cost of product B	£ 30,000
Direct cost of product B	£ 60,000
Total overhead costs	£180,000

Figure 32.2 Example of allocation of overheads in full costing method

Table 32.3 Apportioning overhead costs in absorption costing

Overheads	Basis of apportionment
Rent, rates	Area taken up by the activity
Heating costs	Volume occupied
Cost of personnel administration	No. of employees involved
Indirect labour used	In proportion to direct labour
Fire insurance, depreciation	In proportion to value of capital

For instance, if, in the above example, output was only 30,000, then fixed costs would not have been fully recovered.

Marginal costing

Marginal cost can be defined as the addition to total cost resulting from the production of a further unit of the product or service. In calculating marginal cost we should include the variable costs of producing the extra unit, but we can ignore fixed costs as they are unaffected by the level of activity.

Marginal costing is, therefore, an approach to costing that focuses on variable costs and ignores the fixed costs. Instead of identifying profit, the marginal costing approach identifies the **contribution** from a particular activity. Contribution is defined as sales revenue minus variable costs (contribution per unit is, therefore, price minus variable costs per unit). Although it might appear foolhardy to concentrate on variable costs alone, there are a number of circumstances where marginal costing provides the key to sound decision making. The circumstances are as follows.

Accepting business on a marginal cost basis

This is accepting business on an apparently loss-making basis and can be illustrated by an example. A firm produces 10 million units of a product each year, but has the capacity to produce 12 million units. On a full cost basis, direct costs amount to 55 pence per unit and fixed overheads amount to 35 pence per unit. The product is sold at a price of 130 pence, providing a profit of 40 pence per unit. A major new customer (a supermarket chain seeking a producer of 'own brand' goods) is willing to pay 65 pence per unit for 1 million units in the coming year. Should the manufacturer accept the order?

One's first instinct is to reject the work on the basis that, instead of producing a 40 pence per unit profit, it produces a 25 pence per unit loss. However, this view is shortsighted. The supermarket contract would not result in any rise in fixed costs, which have to be met whether or not

this work is undertaken. The work for the supermarket will generate a 10 pence per unit contribution (£100,000 in total) towards the fixed costs. Analysing the 'special contract' in this way, it becomes more attractive to the manufacturer. However, before the contract is signed, it is worth emphasizing that it is only worth while provided:

- the selling price exceeds marginal cost and, therefore, it produces a contribution;
- spare capacity exists so that the work can be undertaken in addition to regular work;
- no other business is available;
- it does not set a precedent whereby other customers seek to buy at the low price.

Make or buy-in

This has similarities to the 'special contract' analysed above, except that now we are dealing with a firm that faces a choice between continuing to manufacture the product or buying in from an outside supplier. Again, it is explained by means of an example. A firm produces 1 million units of a product for which marginal costs amount to £11 per unit and apportioned fixed overheads amount to £10 million. Costs per unit are, therefore, £21 (£11 + £10). The product is sold at a price of £31.

An outside firm is willing to produce the goods and sell them to the original firm at a price of £19 per unit. The original firm would save, say, £9 million of fixed overheads and could concentrate on marketing the product. Should the work be contracted out?

We should analyse the situation by comparing the 'lost' contribution with the savings. By contracting out the work, the firm experiences a reduction in unit contribution from £20 to £12. The contribution that is sacrificed is, therefore, £8 × 1 million units = £8 million. Against that, the firm saves £9 million in overheads. This produces a net gain from contracting out of £1 million. Provided the quality can be maintained and the supplier does not exploit its powerful position in subsequent years, it is worth while contracting the work out.

A dramatic switch from production to merely marketing the product might appear unlikely, but this technique of analysis can be adapted to situations where a firm is considering contracting out some of its output or buying in components.

Analysis of the performance of a department (or product)

Marginal costing provides a new perspective on the apparently loss-making product or department of an organization. To understand this perspective, it is necessary to contrast a full costing statement with a marginal costing statement (see Tables 32.4(a) and 32.4(b)).

In the full costing statement, each product is apportioned its share of the fixed overheads. The method of apportionment is not relevant to this analysis, but the reader should remember from the account of full costing that there are various ways to share out the overhead costs between products and departments. However, all the methods are arbitrary and this is the main weakness of full costing. In Table 32.4(a), the two types of costs are deducted from sales revenue to give a profit (loss) figure. Notice that product D is making a loss and should be considered for elimination. However, it is only making a loss because of the arbitrary apportionment of overheads. If they had been shared out in some other way, we might find that product D is profitable.

There is a second reason for being cautious about eliminating D. The overheads amount to £24 million in total (one-third of which is apportioned to D). If product D is eliminated, there is no guarantee that (in the short run at least) the total overheads of the company will fall by £8 million. The elimination of D would deprive the company of £26 million of sales revenue and £7 million of contribution. When D's £8 million share of the overheads is reapportioned, the other products become less profitable or even unprofitable. To understand this point, prepare a new full costing statement with D eliminated and its share of overheads reapportioned to A, B and C in the same (3:6:7) ratio as at present.

The marginal costing statement presents the same data but in a different way (see Table 32.4(b)). First, the contribution of each product is identified. Second, there is no attempt to share out the overheads between the four products. Each product is making a positive contribution to the fixed costs of £24 million and the profits of £6 million. Seen in this light, the question of discontinuation of product D does not arise (in the short run at least).

Table 32.4(a) A full costing statement

| | Product | | | | |
	A	B	C	D	Total
Sales revenue	10	20	25	26	81
Variable costs	5	12	15	19	51
Apportioned fixed costs	3	6	7	8	24
Profit (loss)	2	2	3	(1)	6

(All values in £m)

Table 32.4(b) A marginal costing statement

| | Product | | | | |
	A	B	C	D	Total
Sales revenue	10	20	25	26	81
Less variable costs	5	12	15	19	51
Contribution	5	8	10	7	30
Less fixed costs					24
= Profit					6

Standard costing

Standard costs are predetermined costs – in other words, they are a prediction of what costs ought to be if reasonably efficient methods of production are used and if performance matches expectations. One purpose of preparing a statement of standard cost is to make a comparison between actual costs and expected costs. The difference between the two is known as a **variance** and the analysis of the causes of deviations of actual from expected costs is known as **variance analysis**. We will come across something similar in Chapter 34, Budgets, but there is one essential difference between a budget and a standard cost: a budget relates to an entire activity or operation, whereas a standard cost presents the same information on a per unit basis.

We should distinguish between an **ideal**

standard and a **currently attainable standard**. The former is a statement of minimum cost under ideal or most efficient conditions. The latter is that which can be attained by very efficient operations. To calculate standard costs, it is necessary to set 'standards' for each of the elements. The standard for labour will be the expected rate of pay per hour, multiplied by the expected number of hours required to produce each unit. The time element is based on work study, assuming that the workers have adequate levels of skills and motivation and will use agreed working methods.

The standard cost of materials will, similarly, be based on the expected price of materials multiplied by the expected amount of material usage per unit of output. Hence, if a product requires two units of material at £2 per unit, the standard cost of direct materials will be £2 × 2 = £4 per unit of output. Because many, if not most, products require more than one type of material in their manufacture, it will be necessary to produce a composite figure for all materials.

After calculating standards for materials and labour, it is necessary to calculate the expected overhead cost per unit of output. This will be based on an assumption about the level of activity as the overhead costs per unit will vary with the level of activity. Once these standards are established, management can calculate the expected cost of producing each unit of output.

The benefits of undertaking this exercise are that it:

● is an important part of the control process;
● encourages cost-consciousness;
● increases motivation as clear targets are set;
● provides a guide to pricing (including transfer pricing between different sections of the same organization).

Obviously the value of standard costing is dependent on accurate estimates of:

● future prices of labour, materials and overheads;
● the quantity of inputs required to produce each unit of output;
● the level of activity.

There are, however, additional problems. Standard cost data needs to be updated as working methods change. It can also create behavioural problems, such as resentment or fear of being blamed for any variance.

Variance

Variance, as we saw above, can be defined as the difference between the standard costs and the actual costs (between expected revenue and actual revenue). Some variances are unavoidable and cannot be foreseen. Other variances are within the margin of acceptability. What variance analysis is designed to highlight is the unavoidable and unacceptable variance. These variances need to be analysed and explained (see Table 32.5).

As standard costs involve a price element and a quantity element, any variance can be attributed to an unexpected deviation in the price of the input and/or the quantity of the input. Variance analysis is concerned with disentangling the price and quantity elements from the overall variance.

Consider the following example. The standard amount of labour required to produce each unit

---

Table 32.5 Variances

Material usage variance The use of excess quantities of materials reflects inefficiency, incorrect machine setting, theft or defective materials.

Material price variance This reflects unanticipated price changes or errors in purchasing.

Labour efficiency variance Actual labour hours will exceed standard labour hours if untrained workers are used or if employee morale is low.

Labour rate variance This is caused by a rise in rates of pay above standard, the use of higher-grade labour than that specified or the use of labour on overtime rates.

Overhead capacity (volume) variance This arises from a difference between budgeted overhead and the overhead absorbed. Where absorption is related to production time, any unexpected increase in production time will result in variance.

Overhead budget variance This arises from a difference between actual overheads and budgeted overheads. If, for any reason, overheads are different from those expected, variance will result.

Table 32.6 Possible causes of adverse variance

Price	Quantity
Materials	
Price	*Usage*
Inflation	Excessive usage
More expensive supplier	Theft
Poor buying decisions	Reworking
Purchasing in small batches	Defective materials
Use of higher grade materials	Errors
Errors	
Labour	
Labour rate	*Labour efficiency*
Rise in rate of pay	Use of lower-grade or untrained
Use of overtime labour	labour
Use of higher-grade labour	Use of wrong methods
	Poor morale, bad conditions
	Use of defective materials
	Short production runs
Overheads	
Overheads expenditure	*Overhead volume*
Increase in price of services	Fall in the level of activity
Errors in budgeting	

of a product is three hours and the standard price of labour is £6.00 per hour. The firm planned to produce 1000 units at a total labour cost of $1000 \times 3 \times £6 = £18,000$. Actual production was only 900 units. This required 3000 hours of labour for which the total labour cost amounted to £21,000. The overall labour variance is £3000 and this can be attributed to three factors.

First, output was less than that planned. This should have meant labour costs below the £18,000 that was expected and budgeted for. Second, the quantity of labour per unit of output was 3000 divided by 900 = 3.3 hours. The hourly rate of pay was £21,000 divided by 3000 hours = £7. This was also greater than expected.

As mentioned above, the objective of variance analysis is to separate out the various elements causing the deviation of actual from expected performance. After separating the price and quantity elements, the reasons for the variance should then be investigated to reduce the danger of recurrence. Table 32.6 lists possible causes of variance.

Key concepts

Absorption Absorption costing is a system in which all costs are allocated.

Contribution Excess of sales revenue over variable costs. Contribution to fixed costs and profits.

Cost accounting The branch of accounting concerned with the determination and analysis of costs.

Costing Ascertaining the costs of producing goods or providing a service.

Direct costs Costs that are wholly and exclusively identifiable with whatever is being costed. They are directly associated with output.

Fixed costs Costs that do not change as output changes in the short run.

Full cost An approach to costing to recover all costs, direct and indirect.

Indirect costs Costs that cannot be traced to a finished good.

Management accounting The branch of

accounting concerned with the production of data for decision making.

Marginal cost The additional cost of an extra unit of product. Marginal cost is, therefore, dependent on variable costs, not fixed costs.

Mark-up Percentage addition to costs to make up selling price.

Semi-variable cost A cost that has both fixed and variable elements (such as services paid for by a minimum charge, plus a variable cost based on use).

Standard costs Predetermined costs.

Variable cost A cost that varies with output.

Variance Deviation of actual results from expected, budgeted or standard results.

Essay questions

1 Analyse the role of cost accounting within a business organization.

2 Analyse the relationship between the level of output and unit cost.

3 Comment on each of the follwing statement.
  (a) In the long run, there is no such thing as a fixed cost.
  (b) Direct cost is just another name for variable cost.
  (c) Indirect cost is just another name for fixed cost.
  (d) In practice, most so-called fixed costs are semi-variable costs.

4 Analyse the problems confronting a plumber when costing a job.

5 (a) Explain the difference between full and absorption costing.
  (b) Evaluate these methods over marginal or contribution costing.

6 (a) Explain what you understand by contribution.
  (b) Analyse the role of contribution in decision making.

7 Analyse the circumstances in which a firm might be willing to accept an order in which average revenue (price) does not cover average costs.

8 Explain how contribution can be used to answer the following types of business decision:
  (a) whether or not to drop a loss-making product;
  (b) whether or not to accept a loss-making special order;
  (c) whether or not to make or buy in a component.

Exercises

1 Identify:
  (a) fixed costs; and
  (b) variable costs
  incurred in:
  (i)   running a cafe;
  (ii) operating a motorcycle courier service;
  (iii) running a hotel.

2 From the following data, calculate:
  (a) total costs; and
  (b) cost per unit.

Output	500,000 units
Direct labour	£2.5 per unit
Direct materials	£5 per unit
Production overheads	£100,000
Administrative overheads	£30,000
Distribution overheads	£40,000

3 Using the data from question 2, calculate unit costs if output rose to:
  (a) 600,000;
  (b) 700,000.

4 A firm produces three products for which the following results are obtained.

	Total £000	Product A £000	Product B £000	Product C £000
Sales	1,300	300	400	600
Direct labour	450	100	150	200
Direct materials	410	90	140	180
Variable overheads	240	40	100	100
Fixed overheads	90	20	30	40
Total cost	1,190	250	420	520
Profit	110	50	(20)	80

Fixed overheads were allocated in proportion to the cost of direct labour.

  (a) Prepare:
    (i) a full cost statement similar to the above, but with fixed overheads allocated on an equal basis;
    (ii) a marginal costing statement identifying contribution from each product.
  (b) Evaluate the proposal to eliminate product B.

5 A company operating in the engineering industry has divided its production department into three cost centres: pressing, plating and assembly. The direct costs of each centre are recorded below.

	Pressing £000	Plating £000	Assembly £000	Total £000
Direct labour	100	40	200	340
Direct materials	600	100	50	750

Indirect (or overhead) costs come to £1,050,000 or 140 per cent of direct material cost. It has been decided to allocate overheads in proportion to the cost of materials used in each cost centre.

(a) Calculate the:
  (i) share of overheads borne by each centre;
  (ii) total cost of each centre.
(b) Show how the resulting figures would be different if the overheads were divided on the basis of relative shares of direct labour costs.
(c) Explain the distinction between full costing and absorption costing. Which was used by this company?

6 The Essex Bicycle Company produces three models of bicycle. Expected sales and wholesale selling price are as follows:

Model	Quantity	Price
A	500	£300
B	500	£200
C	1,000	£80

The budgeted variable costs of production are:

Model	Parts and materials per bicycle	Labour costs per bicycle
A	£150	£50
B	£100	£40
C	£40	£20

In addition, the company will incur fixed costs of £70,000.

(a) Calculate the:
  (i)   contribution per bicycle for each model;
  (ii) total contribution from each model;
  (iii) budgeted profit.
(b) Prepare a marginal costing statement for the firm.

7 A firm has four departments, one of which shows a loss as shown in the statement below.

	Dept A £000	Dept B £000	Dept C £000	Dept D £000	Total £000
Sales	300	400	150	100	950
Total costs	250	450	110	80	890
Profit (loss)	50	(50)	40	20	60

Fixed costs amounted to £300,000 and these were divided equally between the four departments.

(a) Explain the difference between profit and contribution.
(b) Calculate the contribution from each department.
(c) Present the data in the form of a marginal costing statement.
(d) Present the case for and against the closure of Dept B.

8 Stanley Bennett Ltd produces a range of leisurewear, including a well-known brand of sports shirt. Data relating to the product is as follows:

Selling price:	£12 per shirt
Current output:	100,000 shirts
Fixed costs:	£200,000
Variable costs:	£7 per shirt

The company is considering subcontracting production of this shirt. This would mean that Bennett would merely market the product and, in turn, save £150,000 of fixed costs. The subcontractor would charge Bennett £8 per shirt for undertaking this work.

(a) Calculate the contribution per shirt:
    (i) when Bennett produces the shirts;
    (ii) when the work is subcontracted.
(b) Calculate the 'lost' contribution when the work is subcontracted.
(c) In terms of both financial and other factors, evaluate the proposal to subcontract the work.

9 The TCT Soft Toy Company produces three types of soft toy: a teddy bear, a rabbit and a penguin. The profit and loss account for the year just ended shows that the penguins made a loss and it has been suggested that they be discontinued.

(£000)	Bears	Rabbits	Penguins
Sales	500	350	650
Direct materials	150	80	250
Direct labour	100	100	250
Variable overheads	50	40	60
Fixed overheads	100	80	110
Total cost	400	300	670
Profit/loss	100	50	(20)

Should the penguin be discontinued?
(a) To answer this question, it is necessary to calculate the following:
    (i) the variable cost of producing each of the three types of toy;
    (ii) the contribution from each;
    (iii) the overall level of profits;
    (iv) total fixed costs.
(b) If the penguin is discontinued and we assume that it does not affect sales of the other products, what is the impact on the company's overall profit?

10 Cost accountants at the firm of Sycamore Engineering calculated that the production of each unit of one of their components would require 12 hours of direct labour at a cost of £8.50 per hour. It was planned to produce 3000 units in March of a particular year, but output only reached 2800 units. This was despite the employment of 35,000 hours of direct labour at a cost of £308,000.

(a) Calculate the:
    (i) standard labour cost per unit;
    (ii) actual labour cost per unit;
    (iii) labour variance per unit.

(b) What proportion of the variance can be attributed to an unexpected rise in the:
  (i) hourly rate of pay;
  (ii) quantity of direct labour required in the production of each unit?
(c) Suggest explanations for the variance.

11 The following data relates to two products manufactured by Tunbridge Engineers Ltd.

	Product X	Product Y
Sales budget (units)	300,000	200,000
Hours of labour required per unit	3	2
Selling price	£12	£10
Variable cost	£8	£7

The manpower budget only allows a total of 1,200,000 hours of skilled labour for the manufacture of these two products.

(a) Calculate the maximum output of Products X and Y if:
  (i) maximum labour resources are devoted to Product X with any remainder (from the 1,200,000) available for Product Y;
  (ii) maximum labour resources are devoted to Product Y with any remainder available for Product X;
  (iii) labour resources are equally shared between X and Y.
(b) Calculate the:
  (i) contribution per unit from each product;
  (ii) total contribution from each product for each of the product mixes in (a);
  (iii) unit contribution per hour of labour for each product.
(c) Advise management on the most appropriate product mix by reference to your answers to (b).

12 Jon Simon Ltd has the capacity to produce 150,000 pairs of trousers per year, although it is currently producing at 80 per cent capacity. The cost structure is recorded below.

	Cost per unit	
	Nil–100,000 units	100,001–150,000 units
	(£)	(£)
Materials	3.4	3.8
Labour	3.3	3.7
Maintenance	0.3	0.5

Fixed costs amount to £2.00 per pair at full capacity output and the selling price is £10.

(a) Explain why unit costs rise if output exceeds 100,000.
(b) Calculate the:
  (i) contribution per pair on the first 100,000 pairs;
  (ii) break-even output.
(c) Calculate the:
  (i) total contribution from the first 100,000 pairs;
  (ii) total contribution on the remaining 20,000;
  (iii) total profits.

13 United Engineering Ltd produces three products, for which next month's budget is reproduced below.

	Product A £000	Product B £000	Product C £000	Total £000
Variable costs				
Raw materials	60	40	100	200
Direct labour	40	30	50	120
Variable overheads	10	10	20	40
Fixed cost apportionment	50	30	80	160
Total cost	160	110	250	520
Profit	40	20	80	140
Sales	200	130	330	660

It is known that each product requires equal amounts of the raw materials per unit of output. Unfortunately, only £150,000 worth of the raw materials are available in the month concerned.

(a) Calculate the total contribution for each product.

(b) Advise on the product mix that should be adopted in the changed circumstances.

(c) Assuming that fixed costs remain unchanged and variable costs change proportionately with output, calculate the actual profits during the month.

14 A manufacturer of a wide range of sports goods is investigating the possibility of using a subcontractor to produce one product in its product range. The following data is known:

Current output: 100,000 units
Selling price: £25
Direct costs: £14 per unit
Price to be charged by the subcontractor: £18
Overheads saved when using a subcontractor: £500,000

(a) Calculate the:
   (i) contribution when the manufacturer produces the goods itself;
   (ii) contribution when the subcontractor is used;
   (iii) 'lost' contribution.

(b) On financial grounds alone, should the subcontractor be used? Explain your reasoning.

(c) At what level of output would the manufacturer be indifferent between the two options?

15 A manufacturer is considering using a supply firm to manufacture a component that it is currently making for itself. The following data is known:

Current output: 200,000 units
Direct costs: £15 million
Price charged by the subcontractor: £18 million.
Savings on fixed costs when a contractor is used: £650,000

(a) Calculate the contribution 'lost' when the subcontractor is used.

(b) Basing your decision on financial grounds alone, should the subcontractor be used? Explain your reasoning.

(c) What non-financial factors should also be taken into consideration?

16 From the data below calculate the:
(a) unit costs;
(b) price charged.

    (i) Direct costs per unit: £2.50
          Fixed overhead costs: £200,000
          Output: 40,000 units
          Mark-up on unit costs: 50 per cent
   (ii) Direct costs per unit: £8
          Fixed overhead costs: £700,000
          Output: 160,000 units
          Mark-up on unit costs: 75 per cent

17 The manufacturer of 100 units of a standard product requires two different materials and 15 hours of labour. Full cost details are as follows:

Materials
X: 200 kilos at £1.40 per kilo
Y: 50 litres at £5.20 per litre

Labour
10 hours at £8.00 per hour
5 hours at £6.00 per hour

Overheads
15 hours at £200 per hour

Calculate the:
(a) standard cost of producing 100 units;
(b) selling price of each unit, assuming a 25 per cent mark-up on unit costs.

18 A company makes four products (A, B, C and D). The forecast sales, costs and selling prices are as follows.

Product	Sales (units)	Direct costs per unit £	Selling price £
A	300	250	400
B	400	190	300
C	500	140	250
D	800	80	120

Fixed costs are £160,000 per year and all units produced will be sold immediately.

(a) Prepare a full cost statement for the four products on the basis of the equal allocation of overheads.
(b) Prepare a marginal cost statement.
(c) On financial grounds alone, argue the case for and against eliminating product D from the product range.

Break-even analysis

Break-even analysis (or, to be more correct, cost–volume–profit analysis) is a simple but very useful aid to decision making within business. It can be employed to discover the level of output that is required before profits are made, as well as the level of output required to produce a certain level of profits.

Chapter objectives

1 To develop an understanding of break-even analysis.

2 To enable readers to calculate break-even output, margin of safety and profits by graphical and numerical means.

3 To develop an understanding of the limitations of this technique.

The break-even graph

As we discovered in Chapter 32, costs can be divided into variable costs (such as materials, fuel and labour costs) and fixed costs (such as rent and interest charges). Variable costs rise and fall with output whereas fixed costs remain the same irrespective of output. For the purpose of analysis, we will assume that there is a linear or straight line relationship between costs and output and, separately, revenue output. Suppose fixed costs amount to £200,000 and variable costs are £1 per unit. At zero output, total costs will be £200,000. At an output of 100,000, total costs will rise to £200,000, plus £1 × 100,000 equals £300,000. This can be shown graphically (see Figure 33.1). Fixed costs are represented by a horizontal line (as they are the same irrespective of output) whereas variable costs are superimposed on top. As output rises, variable costs (and, therefore, total costs) also rise. The vertical distance between total costs and fixed costs is the variable cost at each level of output.

Total revenue (TR) can be calculated by multiplying price by the quantity sold. Hence, if the price is £4 per unit and 100,000 units are sold, total revenue is £400,000. The total revenue line rises from the point of origin. As we are assuming a linear relationship, it is only necessary to plot two points that can then be connected with a straight line.

Where the total cost and total revenue curves

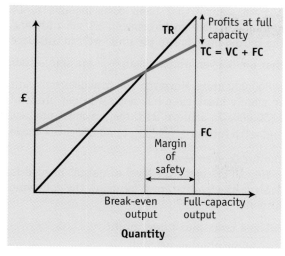

Figure 33.1 Break-even chart

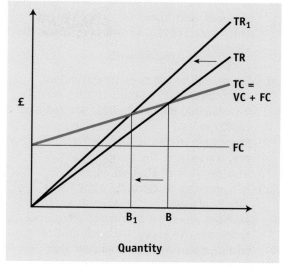

Figure 33.2 A break-even chart depicting a rise in price and a lower break-even point. At the higher price, beak even occurs at B_1 quantity.

cross, the product is neither making a profit nor a loss. It is in fact at the **break-even level of output**. If, for any reason, the firm is unable to reach this level of output, it will suffer a loss from this product. Any output in excess of break even generates profit for the company. The profits can be shown as the vertical distance between the TR and TC lines. As both are straight lines, the greater the level of output, the greater will be the profits. The maximum available profit occurs at the full capacity level of output.

It is unlikely, however, that the firm will be producing at full capacity. There will be a variety of reasons for output being less than full capacity output (such as shortages of resources or inadequate demand). The horizontal distance between the break-even level of output and the current level of output is known as the **margin of safety**. Where break-even output is a high percentage of actual output, the margin of safety and, therefore, the scope for profit is small.

We can see from Figure 33.2 that a rise in price will lower the break-even level of output. Similarly, a reduction in fixed or variable costs per unit will have the same impact.

Calculating break-even output

It is possible to calculate break-even output without the use of graphs. This involves the con-

cept of **contribution**, which can be defined as the excess of price over variable costs. Any money received over the variable costs makes a contribution towards the fixed costs. If we know the contribution per unit, we can easily calculate the number of 'contributions per unit' we require to fully cover the fixed costs. This can be shown in the following example.

Exercise

Assume:
(i)   fixed costs are £500,000;
(ii) the variable cost per unit amounts to £1;
(iii) the selling price is £5 per unit;
(iv) planned output is 200,000 units per year.

Calculate the:
(a) break-even output;
(b) margin of safety;
(c) profits at planned output.

Answer

(a) To calculate break-even output, divide fixed costs by the contribution per unit. Each unit is sold for £5 but variable costs amount to £1 per unit. Consequently, each unit sold contributes £4 to fixed costs, which are £500,000. Break-even occurs at

$$\frac{£500,000}{£4} = 125,000 \text{ units}$$

(b) The margin of safety is current output minus break-even output. In this example, it is 200,000 minus 125,000, which equals 75,000 units.

Break even occurs at 62.5 per cent of planned output. The margin of safety is 37.5 per cent of planned output.

(c) It is possible to calculate profits in a variety of ways, but break-even analysis provides us with a distinctive and simple technique. We know that each unit of output makes a £4 contribution after deducting variable costs. Up to break-even output, the contribution was towards fixed costs; beyond break even, the contribution is towards profits. In this example, profits will be £4 multiplied by the margin of safety of 75,000 units. Hence, profits amount to £300,000.

Break even in terms of sales revenue

The basic technique can be modified to calculate the level of sales revenue required to break even.

Suppose a product involving variable costs of £2 was sold for £6. Fixed costs amounted to £200,000. The formula for break even in revenue terms is:

$$\frac{\text{Fixed costs}}{\text{Contribution per unit}} \times \text{Price per unit}$$

In the example, break even occurs when sales revenue is:

$$\frac{£200,000}{£4} \times £6 = £300,000$$

A target rate of profit

With another slight modification of the basic formula, we can calculate the level of output (or, separately, the level of price) necessary to achieve a certain level of profit.

If we assume that fixed costs amount to £1 million, variable costs come to £5 per unit and the selling price is £10 per unit, we can calculate that break even occurs when $\frac{£1m}{£5}$ are sold – that is 200,000 units. However, the firm does not want to merely break even but seeks a target profit of £200,000. To achieve its target, it must produce and sell a further $\frac{£200,000}{£5}$, or 40,000 units above the break even level.

We can calculate the level of output needed to achieve the profit target by using the following formula:

$$\frac{\text{Fixed costs plus target profit}}{\text{Contribution per unit}}$$

$$= \frac{£1 \text{ m} + £200 \ 000}{£5} = 240,000$$

A variation on this concerns what price a business would have to charge to achieve a target profit at a given level of output. Let us use data from the previous example.

Fixed costs: £1 million
Variable costs: £5 per unit
Chosen level of output: 240,000
The target profit is now £300,000.
What price should the organization charge?

The firm requires a total contribution of £1 million plus £300,000 from 240,000 units of output. This comes to £5.42 per unit. It would have to charge a price of £5 + £5.42 = £10.42 to achieve the profit target from its chosen level of output.

The use of break-even analysis to achieve a profit target can be shown graphically, as in Figure 33.3. To achieve the profit target it is necessary to produce the total revenue equal to total costs plus the target profit. This requires an increase in price to raise the TR line to TR_1.

Criticisms of break-even analysis

Break-even charts may provide a useful way of looking at cost, output and revenue relationships. However, they suffer from a number of limitations:

● Fixed costs are likely to change at different

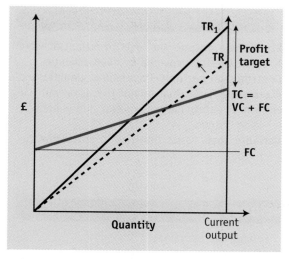

Figure 33.3 A beak-even analysis involving a profit target

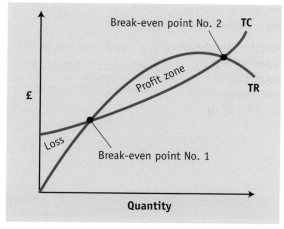

Figure 33.4 Non-linear break even

Note: (a) As output rises beyond a certain point, costs rise disproportionately

(b) To increase sales volume, it is necessary to reduce prices, leading eventually to a TR curve that dips downwards

(c) Profits are maximized at the output where the vertical distance between TR and TC is greatest

levels of activity. Perhaps it would be more accurate to represent fixed costs as a stepped line.

- Neither variable costs nor sales revenue are likely to be linear. Discounts, overtime payments and special delivery charges all contribute to non-linearity. Economists would depict the break-even chart as shown in Figure 33.4.

Accountants would defend the use of linear TC and TR curves by arguing that, over the range of output depicted in the data (this is known as the relevant range), the relationship between volume and both costs and revenue is a linear one. Over the relevant range, certain costs are fixed and the variable costs per unit are constant. Only if the firm goes outside the relevant range will both fixed costs and variable costs per unit change. Similarly, over the relevant range, price per unit is constant, thus giving a straight line TR curve. Again, if the firm moves outside the range, it will have to adjust the price, thus destroying the linearity of the TR curve. This concept of the linearity of the curves being confined to the relevant range means that the difference between the economists' and the accountants' perceptions of break even is not as fundamental as might be assumed.

Conclusion

In this chapter we have investigated break-even analysis as a method of decision making in business. It can be used to discover whether or not profits can be made at the planned level of output. It can also be used in decision making regarding the price to be charged and/or quantity to be sold to achieve a target level of profits. As with other aspects of quantitative analysis, a true understanding of the techniques comes with frequent practice. You are, therefore, advised to work through the exercises at the end of the chapter.

Key formulae

$$\text{Break-even point (in units)} = \frac{\text{Fixed costs}}{\text{Contribution per unit}}$$

Break-even point (in sales revenue)

$$= \frac{\text{Fixed costs}}{\text{Contribution per unit}} \times \text{Price per unit}$$

Margin of safety = Current output minus break-even output.

Profit = Margin of safety × contribution per unit

Level of sales required to achieve target profit (in units) $= \dfrac{\text{Fixed costs} + \text{target profit}}{\text{Contribution per unit}}$

Essay questions

1 Evaluate break-even analysis for business decision making.

2 Analyse the complications for break-even analysis that result from each of the following features of life for real business:
   (a) the non-standard product;
   (b) the multi-product firm;
   (c) the stepped rise in fixed costs;
   (d) the non-linear cost and revenue curves.

3 Using sketch graphs, analyse the consequences for the break-even point of each of the following:
   (a) a rise in fixed costs;
   (b) a rise in variable costs per unit;
   (c) a price reduction;
   (d) fixed costs being a high percentage of total costs.

4 The margin of safety for a product produced by a firm is currently 5 per cent.
   (a) Explain what this means and what are its implications.
   (b) Evaluate strategies to improve the situation.

5 The standard linear break-even chart suggests that profits will always be increased by raising the level of output. Analyse why this is not true in the real world.

Exercises

1 The variable cost of the electric kettle manufactured by Fair Oak Domestic Appliances Ltd is £4. The company, which sells its kettles direct to retailers for £10, expects its net profit for the year just ending to be £270,000 after allowing for fixed costs of £90,000. The productive capacity of the company is underutilized and the marketing manager suggests that a 10 per cent reduction in selling price will bring about a 25 per cent increase in sales.

   (a) Define the term 'contribution'. What is the contribution per unit in the above case?
   (b) What level of sales is necessary to break even?
   (c) If profits are £270,000 after allowing for fixed costs of £90,000, what is the current volume of output and sales?
   (d) Calculate the:
       (i) sales revenue at this volume of sales;
       (ii) sales revenue resulting from the implementation of the marketing manager's proposal.

(e) As a result of the increased volume, by how much has the:
(i) revenue changed;
(ii) costs changed?
(f) Should Fair Oak Domestic Appliances reduce its selling price by 10 per cent?

2 A firm is considering which of the following four prices to charge customers:
A £2.20
B £2.00
C £1.80
D £1.70

The relevant data for decision making is:

Fixed costs:	£1.2 million
Variable costs:	125p per unit
Full capacity output:	2.7m units
Current output:	2.6m units

For each price, calculate the:
(a) break-even output;
(b) margin of safety at both full capacity and current;
(c) profit/loss at both full capacity and current output;
(d) break-even output as a percentage of:
(i) full capacity output;
(ii) current output.

3 Thorn and Hill Ltd has sufficient capacity to produce 120,000 drinking mugs per year. The variable cost of producing each mug is 20p and fixed costs total £20,000 per year. The mugs are sold to wholesalers for 60p each.

(a) Calculate the:
(i) contribution per mug;
(ii) break-even output;
(iii) the margin of safety if current output is 90,000 mugs;
(iv) profits at full capacity.
(b) Assuming that unit variable costs, fixed costs and capacity remain unchanged, calculate the price that Thorn and Hill would have to charge wholesalers to obtain the target profit of £40,000 per year at full capacity output.

4 Smith Limited produces a single product for which the following data is known.

Full capacity output:	200,000 units
Current output and sales:	150,000 units
Selling price:	£10 per unit
Fixed costs:	£1 million
Variable costs:	£2 per unit

The marketing manager suggests that a price reduction to £9 per unit would result in an increase in sales to enable the firm to produce at full capacity.

(a) Construct a break-even graph based on the original price and output level.

(b) Use the graph to determine:
  (i)   break-even output;
  (ii) the margin of safety;
  (iii) profits at current output.
  Verify this data by arithmetical means.
(c) Construct a second break-even graph to depict the situation after the price reduction. Use the graph to determine the level of profit at full capacity output.
(d) Evaluate the marketing manager's proposal.

5 Grey and Fox Ltd has the capacity to produce 150,000 units of their standard product per month. Fixed costs amount to £800,000 per month, while variable costs are £14 per unit. The product is sold at a price of £21 per unit.

(a) Calculate the:
  (i)   monthly profits at full capacity;
  (ii) the break-even level of output.
(b) The company has a profit target of £200,000 per month. Calculate the:
  (i)   level of output needed to reach the target profit;
  (ii) price that would have to be charged to achieve the profit target at two-thirds capacity.

6 The Richardson Pen Company produces a range of products, including a popular brand of steel-tipped pen. It has the capacity to produce six million such pens per year, although at present it is operating at less than full capacity. The pens are sold to wholesalers at 50 pence each. The production of each pen involves variable costs of 30 pence. Fixed costs at the current output level of five million pens are 10 pence per pen.

(a) Using the above information, construct a break-even chart.
(b) Calculate the contribution per pen.
(c) Using arithmetical rather than graphical means, calculate the:
  (i)   break-even output;
  (ii) margin of safety;
  (iii) profit at full capacity.
(d) A hotel chain wishes to place a bulk order for 500,000 pens and is willing to pay 35 pence per pen. The Richardson Pen Company calculates that this special order will involve an additional £10,000 of fixed costs to stamp the hotel logo on the pens. Should the pen company take the order? Explain your reasoning.

7 Davidson Pet Foods Ltd sells 'Georgie Cat' meat products to wholesalers at the price of 15 pence per unit. The variable cost of producing 'Georgie Cat' is 10 pence per unit and fixed costs total £1 million per year.
   There is capacity to produce 40 million units, but low demand has resulted in sales (and output) of 32 million units per year. The Smartprice Supermarket chain is willing to buy five million units at 11 pence per unit. They will be sold under Smartprice's 'own brand'. Meanwhile, the rival Goodprice chain offers to buy six million units at 14 pence each. However, they insist on an option in the contract to allow them to purchase a similar quantity at 14 pence next year.
(a) Define the following terms:
  (i)   contribution;
  (ii) break even;
  (iii) margin of safety.

(b) In the case of the 'Georgie Cat' brand, calculate the:
   (i)   contribution per unit;
   (ii) break-even output;
   (iii) margin of safety;
   (iv) profits at current level of output.
(c) In the absence of the Goodprice offer, should Davidson accept the Smartprice contract? Explain your reasoning and the assumptions you have made in answering the question.
(d) Comment on the Goodprice offer.

8 A manufacturer of dining tables incurs the following expenses:

	£
Annual rent and rates	100,000
Interest payments	10,000
Materials per item	100
Wages per item	200

The tables are sold at a price of £500 and current output is 2000 tables per year.

(a) Calculate the:
   (i)   contribution per table;
   (ii) break-even output;
   (iii) current level of profits.
(b) Calculate the price that would have to be charged to achieve a target profit of £150,000 at current levels of output.

9 The graph below shows profit and loss from the sales of a standardized product that is sold at a price of £2.50 per unit.

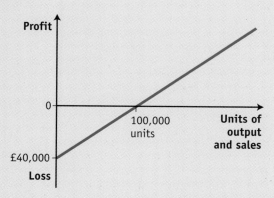

(a) Calculate the:
   (i)   sales revenue at break-even output;
   (ii) variable costs at break-even output;
   (iii) contribution per unit.
(b) At what level of output will profits rise to £66,000?
(c) Calculate the loss when output is 90,000.
(d) Calculate break-even output if fixed costs rise by 25 per cent with price and variable costs unchanged.

10 A company manufactures a product for which the following data is known:

Direct costs per unit: 70 pence
Overheads: £5 million
Current output: 12 million units
Full capacity output: 15 million units
Price: £1.40 per unit

(a) Calculate the:
    (i)   capacity utilization;
    (ii) break-even output;
    (iii) margin of safety;
    (iv) profit at current output;
    (v)   unit costs at current output.

(b) A large supermarket chain is willing to purchase one million units at 80 pence per unit. Should this contract be accepted? Explain your answer.

34

Budgets

The Institute of Cost and Management Accountants defines a **budget** as 'A financial and/or quantitative statement, prepared and approved prior to a defined period of time, of the policy to be pursued during that period for the purpose of attaining a given objective'. In essence, it is a financial plan setting out expected income and expenditure over a future period. For students of business, the budgeting process provides an invaluable insight into the interrelated nature of business activities.

Chapter objectives

1 To develop an understanding of the role and function of budgets.

2 To develop an understanding of the integration of functional budgets into a master budget.

3 To introduce the different types of budget.

4 To introduce budget control.

The purpose of budgets

Budgets are plans of action expressed in quantitative terms. Their essential characteristics are that they:

- are prepared and agreed in advance;
- cover a specific time period;
- are expressed in either financial terms or in real terms (that is, physical quantities);
- relate either to the firm as a whole or to a part of it (such as the marketing department).

Business organizations will produce budgets for the major functional areas: marketing, production, purchasing, administration, research and development, capital expenditure and finance. In addition, a **cash budget** will be prepared. This is a schedule of cash inflows and outflows expected as a result of activities itemized in the functional budgets. The **master budget** is a statement of the future profit/loss account and balance sheet resulting from the operation of the plans.

This initial introduction to the budgeting process demonstrates the role of budgeting in planning (see also Table 34.1). By translating plans into financial terms, clarity and focus is imposed on business planning. The planners are better able to see the financial implications of their plans and ensure that activities are coordinated. Budgeting, therefore, gives unity and direction to business operations.

Table 34.1 Functions of budgets

- To assist the planning process
- To communicate plans
- To coordinate activities and ensure harmony between different parts of an organization
- To motivate staff
- To control and evaluate performance

The people responsible for spending under the organization's budget arrangements are known as the **budget holders**. They are required to make effective use of the financial resources made available to them, and have powers to spend up to, but not beyond, the budget limit. The budget holder can be given considerable discretion within the budget and this can be beneficial in motivating staff. The budget also provides a means of control in that actual performance can be evaluated in relation to expected performance. This aspect is known as **budgetary control**.

Cost, revenue and profit centres

Budgeting is an aspect of what is known as **responsibility accounting**. As the term suggests, it consists of techniques concerned with the responsibility (duty) of middle managers for achieving targets set. They are accountable to top management for the performance of their section, department, division or team. A production manager is responsible for achieving production targets and keeping production costs within defined limits. The production department is, therefore, an example of a **cost centre**. The cost of the department's operations can be calculated and its manager can be asked to account for any serious deviation (known as a variance) from the expected costs. The sales department can be seen as a **revenue centre**. Revenue targets can be set and variances can be studied.

In a large divisionalized organization we can identify **profit centres**. These are sections of the

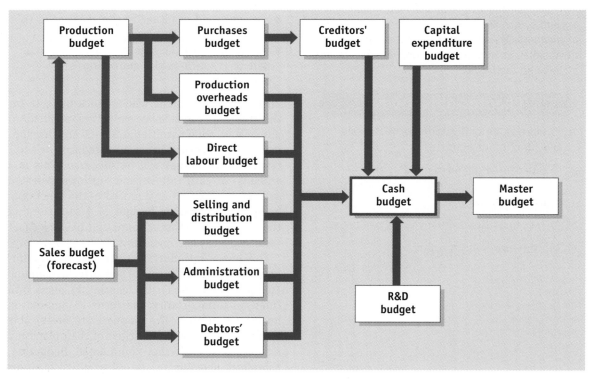

Figure 34.1 The budgeting process

organization for which both costs and revenues can be and are calculated. The profit centre is responsible for its contribution to the overall profitability of the organization. In many respects, it can be seen and treated as a separate business within the organization. We can also identify an **investment centre**, the manager of which is responsible for controlling costs, revenue, profits and investment decisions. The various types of responsibility centres can be seen as sections of the organization for which results are calculated and then assessed. For our purposes, the key distinction is between a cost and a profit centre.

The budgeting process

The process starts with the aims and objectives of the organization, which are likely to be expressed in terms of sales revenues, market share and, ultimately, profits. The ability of any business to achieve high levels of profits will be constrained by the availability of resources and ability/inability to sell the products. The first task in budgeting is to identify the limiting factor(s) and calculate the level of turnover and profit that remains possible within the constraints. With knowledge of the output and sales that are possible, we can then proceed to look at various costs. (See Figure 34.1 for a diagrammatical representation of the budgeting process.)

The sales budget provides estimates of sales broken down by area, unit of the organization and by time period (see Table 34.2). From this sales forecast, it is possible to plan production targets, which are expressed in a **production budget**. This budget is concerned not with costs

Table 34.2 Sales budget

	Jan.	Feb.	Mar.	Apr.	May	June	July	Aug.	Sept.	Oct.	Nov.	Dec.	Total
Product A													
Units 000	50	50	60	60	60	50							700
Value £000	75	75	90	90	90	75							1,050
By channel													
Wholesale £000	25	25	30	30	30	25							350
Retail £000	50	50	60	60	60	50							700
													1,050
By area													
South £000	15	15	18	18	18	15							210
Midlands £000	18.75	18.75	22.5	22.5	22.5	18.75							262.5
North £000	18.75	18.75	22.5	22.5	22.5	18.75							262.5
Scotland £000	15	15	18	18	18	15							210
Wales £000	7.5	7.5	9	9	9	7.5							105
													1,050
Product B													
Units 000	20	20	20	20	22	22							264
Value £000	40	40	40	40	44	44							528
By channel													
Wholesale £000	30	30	30	30	33	33							396
Retail £000	10	10	10	10	11	11							132
By area													
South £000	10	10	10	10	11	11							132
Midlands £000	10	10	10	10	11	11							132
North £000	8	8	8	8	8.8	8.8							105.6
Scotland £000	8	8	8	8	8.8	8.8							105.6
Wales £000	4	4	4	4	4.4	4.4							52.8
													528

Table 34.3 Types of functional budget

Administration	Cost of administration
Capital	Expenditure on capital items
Direct labour	Quantity and cost of direct labour
Marketing	Expenses involved in marketing and the revenue from sales. This can be subdivided into specialist areas such as promotion, selling, distribution
Production costs	Production budget translated into monetary costs
Production overheads	Overhead costs of the production department
Purchases (or direct materials costs)	Quantity and cost of direct materials
Research and development	Expenditure on R & D
Sales	Volume of, and revenue from, sales

but with physical output. It can be translated into a financial budget dealing with costs. This is known as the **production cost budget.** A **selling and distribution cost budget** projects the cost involved in selling the projected level of output.

Of the budgets listed in Table 34.3, most are expenditure budgets as they deal only with the amount of spending. If they impose a limit on spending, they are a type of **appropriation budget.** The exceptions in Table 34.3 are the sales budget (which is a revenue-only budget) and the marketing budget (which covers both revenue and costs).

Having drawn up these budgets covering functional areas, we can proceed to financial budgets that forecast the outcome of the firm's activities. The **creditors' budget** provides a forecast of the firm's credit purchases over time and the corresponding creditor figure in the balance sheets of the future. Similarly, the **debtors' budget** is a forecast of the amount of money customers will owe at some specified time in the future. The

cash budget is better known as the cash flow forecast and this tells us the cash position of the firm at some specific future time.

The final stage involves the drawing up of forecast profit and loss accounts and balance sheets. This is a forecast of what the accounts will look like if the plans are implemented and the expected results are, in fact, achieved. The various strands are drawn together in what is, in effect, a **master budget** covering all operations.

Fixed and flexible budgets

A **fixed budget** concerns a single level of activity. The budget in Table 34.4 shows that, at 100 per cent activity level, costs will total £116,000. The major deficiency of this approach is discovered when we compare actual results with the budget forecasts. Actual activity was only 85 per cent of the maximum possible and costs were only £106,000. This was £10,000 less than that budgeted for. The lower than expected costs reflect not the

Table 34.4 Fixed budget report

	Fixed budget for April	Actual results for April	Variance	Favourable variance (F) or adverse variance (A)
Actual level	100%	85%	15%	A
	£000	£000	£000	
Direct labour	53	47	6	F
Direct materials	37	33	4	F
Fixed overheads	26	26	0	–
Total	116	106	10	F

Table 34.5 Flexible budget report

	Flexible budget for April		Actual results	Variance	F or A
Activity level	100%	85%	85%	85%	
	£000	£000	£000	£000	£000
Direct labour	53	45	47	2	A
Direct materials	37	31	33	2	A
Fixed overheads	26	26	26	0	
Total	116	102	106	4	A

Table 34.6 A flexible budget

	Fixed budget	Price variable costs per unit	Flexible budget for sales of 12,000 units	14,000 units
Sales: in units	10,000		12,000	14,000
	£000	£	£000	£000
Sales revenue	100	10	120	140
Variable costs				
Raw materials	20	2	24	28
Direct labour	20	2	24	28
Factory supplies	10	1	12	14
Sales commission	10	1	12	14
Total	60	6	72	84
Contribution	40	4	48	56
Fixed costs	30		30	30
Profit	10		18	26

efficiency of the organization, but the failure to produce at the forecast level of activity.

More useful than a fixed budget is a **flexible budget**. This shows costs at various levels of activity (see Tables 34.5 and 34.6). Therefore, it is possible to calculate what costs will be if, instead of operating at a target output of 10,000 units per year, the firm produced a different level of output. As Table 34.6 shows, costs do not rise in strict proportion to output. This is because fixed costs remain unchanged at the different levels of output. Only the variable costs rise in proportion with output. A flexible budget makes it easier to produce valid data on variance as it highlights changes in costs caused by changes in efficiency (rather than changes caused by an altered level of production).

Incremental and zero-based budgets

One danger in the budgeting process is that previous data is used as the basis. The status quo tends to be accepted, with a percentage added on for the inevitable cost rises resulting from inflation. This approach is known as **incremental budgeting**.

The alternative is known as **zero-based budgeting** (**ZBB**). Under ZBB, there is a critical review of all activities before they are budgeted for. This is designed to create a questioning attitude and instil discipline in those who formulate and hold the budgets. It is designed to produce better decisions, although, as it is very time-consuming, some compromise is necessary. Organizations

Table 34.7 Advantages and disadvantages of budgets

Advantages	Disadvantages
● Facilitates coordination ● Responsibilities are clarified ● Translates strategic plans into departmental action ● Improves communication ● Control of expenditure ● Scarce resources are used in the most efficient and profitable way ● Performance can be measured against a quantitative target ● Facilitates management by exception, with deviations reported and investigated ● By giving 'freedom within the budget', middle management can be motivated	● Uses resources ● Value depends on the quality of the information ● Can be used mechanically and inflexibly ● Demotivating if participation is not part of the process ● Management becomes overly dependent on the budget and neglects the process of management

adopting this approach will devise a 'rolling programme' of activities that will be subjected to ZBB in a particular year. In the intervening years, before the activities are subject to ZBB again, the incremental approach will be used.

Budgetary control

Budgetary control involves a comparison of actual financial performance against that contained in the budget for the particular activity. The difference between the forecast and the actual figure is known as a variance. If actual costs are less than budgeted costs, it is a **positive** or **favourable variance**. If they exceed budgeted costs, it is called a **negative** or **adverse variance**. An acceptable level of variance will be agreed in advance, but any excessive variance (either positive or negative) will be investigated. In some cases, the variance is unavoidable and relates to matters outside the organization's control. Where the variance is avoidable, however, it needs to be investigated and those responsible held accountable (see Table 34.7).

Conclusion

This chapter has shown that budgeting is more than an accounting process – it is an essential part of planning, controlling and coordinating the activities of functional areas within a business organization. As Business Studies students, we should see it as an *integrating* technique within business. Hence, an understanding of the budgetary process is essential for an integrated approach to Business Studies.

Key concepts

Budget A plan of action expressed in quantitative terms.

Budgetary control A comparison of actual performance with the budget so that, if necessary, corrective action can be taken.

Cost centre A segment of the organization for which costs are calculated.

Fixed budget A budget based on a single level of activity.

Flexible budget A budget that is adjusted for different levels of activity.

Forecast A prediction of future events outside the control of management.

Incremental budget A budget in which the data for the previous year is used as the starting point.

Plan A detailed account of future action to be taken.

Profit centre A segment of the organization for which both costs and revenue are calculated.

Variance Deviation of actual results from budgeted or standard results.

Zero-based budgeting An approach to budgeting in which activities are analysed as if they were being started for the first time.

Essay questions

1 Explain and evaluate the role of budgeting in business.

2 (a) Analyse the difference between a fixed and a flexible budget.
  (b) Which of the two provides the better basis for variance analysis.

3 Explain what is meant by each of the following:
  (a) a sales budget;
  (b) a production cost budget;
  (c) a cash budget;
  (d) a budget profit and loss account;
  (e) a capital budget;
  (f) a marketing budget.

4 Analyse possible explanations for the following:
  (a) costs being greater than expected;
  (b) profits being lower than expected;
  (c) an adverse variance in labour costs;
  (d) a favourable variance in sales revenue;
  (e) the quantity of materials used being greater than expected.

5 (a) Explain the terms cost centre, revenue centre and profit centre.
  (b) Evaluate the benefits of organizing a business in terms of profit centres.

Further reading

Atrill, P., and McLaney, E. (1997) *Accounting and Finance for Non-specialialists*, 2nd ed., Prentice Hall.

Dodge, R. (1994) *Foundations of Cost and Management Accounting*, Chapman Hall.

Hussey, J., and Hussey, R. (1999) *Cost and Management Accounting*, Macmillan.

Fardon, M., and Cox, D. (1995) *Advanced Finance*, Osborne.

Kind, J. (1999) *Accounting and Finance for managers*, Kogan Page.

Knott, G. (1998) *Financial Management*, 3rd ed., Macmillan.

McKenzie, W. (1998) *Unlocking Company Reports and Accounts*, Financial Times Pitman.

Walsh, C. (1996) *Key Management Ratios*, Financial Times Pitman.

Wright, D. (1996) *Management Accounting*, Longman.

Short answer questions

Using specific examples, explain the following accounting terms.

1 Fixed assets.
2 Depreciation.
3 Stock valuation.
4 Debtors.
5 Long-term liabilities.
6 Authorized capital.
7 Reserves.
8 Provision.
9 Creditors.
10 Overdraft.
11 Lease.
12 Goodwill.
13 Management accounting
14 Flexible budget.
15 Overheads.
16 Semi-variable cost.
17 Contribution.
18 Budget profit and loss account.
19 Standard cost.
20 Variance.
21 Gearing.
22 Stock turnover.
23 Window dressing.
24 Intangible asset.
25 Medium-term finance.
26 Shareholders' equity.
27 Debtor days ratio.
28 Liquidity.
29 Retained profits.
30 Operating profits.

Exercises

1 The production department of a manufacturing firm will commence manufacturing a new product on 1 April. The sales forecast for the first seven months is recorded below.

Sales forecast (units)

April	1,000
May	1,200
June	1,400
July	1,400
August	1,400
September	1,200
October	1,200

At the end of each month, it is planned to hold stocks of finished goods equal to half the sales forecast in the coming month (but no work-in-progress is held at the end of any month).

The unit cost of direct materials is £15, while that of direct labour is £10. Overheads of £20,000 will be apportioned to the product each month. Prepare a:

(a) production budget for the first six months;
(b) production cost budget for the period.

2 Peters Engineering Ltd consists of four departments. A, B and C are production departments, while D is the administrative department. As D does not earn revenue, its costs are aggregated and allocated to A, B and C in the ratio of 50:25:25. Each department will be charged interest on its capital employed at the rate of 12 per cent per annum.

	A	B	C	D
No. of employees	200	100	100	20
Average weekly pay	£200	£175	£160	£150
Fixed costs per week	£2,500	£2,000	£2,000	£1,500
Capital employed £000	£100	£100	£80	£40
Other variable costs per unit	£1	£2	£2	£1
Output (units)	1,000	400	500	–

(a) Prepare a weekly budget of the total cost of each production department (including apportioned overheads).
(b) Calculate costs per unit of output in each of the three departments.

3 Complete the budget statement below, not forgetting to include positive and minus signs where appropriate.

	Actual results £000	Budgeted results £000	Budget variance £000
Direct materials	851	862	?
Direct labour	516	610	?
Variable production overheads	80	88	?
Variable administration overheads	70	65	?
Fixed overheads	50	55	?
Total costs	?	?	3
Sales value of production	3100	2995	
Profit	?	?	

4 A company's actual and budgeted sales for one year are as follows:

	Budgeted	Actual
Sales price	£5.20	£5.30
Number sold	25,000	23,000
Direct costs per unit	£2.50	£2.60
Total fixed costs	£31,500	£30,500

(a) For both the budgeted and actual data, calculate the:
   (i)   total contribution;
   (ii) sales revenue;
   (iii) profits.
(b) Produce a statement, using variances, analysing the shortfall in profits.
(c) Explain how it may have occurred.

5 In the table below, the sales and production costs of a single product produced by a large conglomerate are given.

	Budgeted data	Actual data
Sales price	£5.4	£5.5
Quantity	350,000	335,000
Direct costs per unit	£2.9	£3.1
Total fixed costs	£451,560	£442,958

(a) For both *budgeted* and *actual sales*, calculate the:
   (i)   contribution per unit;
   (ii) total contribution;
   (iii) total revenue;
   (iv) total costs.
(b) Produce a statement, using variances, analysing the shortfall in profits.

6 The following cost budget was prepared for a production level of 20,000 units of a component for a washing machine.

	Budget £
Direct variable cost (20,000 × £2)	40,000
Production overheads (semi-variable) (£10,000 + £0.5 per unit)	20,000
General overheads (fixed)	30,000
	90,000

(a) Explain what is meant by a semi-variable cost.
(b) Prepare budgets for the production of 18,000 units; then for 22,000 units.
(c) Actual production of the component was 21,000 units and costs were as follows:

Direct variable costs	£44,100
Production overheads	£20,710
General overheads	£30,000

Calculate the variance per unit on direct variable costs; then on production overheads

7 The budgeted profit and loss account for a company is as follows:

	£000	£000
Sales		22,000
Direct materials	5,000	
Direct labour	8,000	
Variable overheads	2,000	
Fixed overheads	4,000	19,000
Profit		3,000

(a) Redraft the profit and loss account to take into account a 10 per cent rise in the cost of materials, an 8 per cent rise in the cost of direct labour and a £1m rise in overhead costs.
(b) Assuming that there is no change in the quantity sold, by what percentage would prices have to rise to retain the same level of profits as were enjoyed before the cost rise?

8 The following budget relates to the production of 250 units of a product.

	£
Sales revenue	500,000
Labour costs	200,000
Cost of materials	100,000
Overheads	150,000
Profit	50,000

(a) Flex the budget for the following levels of output:
    (i)   240 units;
    (ii) 260 units;
    (iii) 300 units.

(b) Actual output was 300 units, with sales revenue of £550,000, labour costs of £250,000, cost of materials £130,000 and overheads £160,000. Calculate the variances against the flexed budget and suggest reasons for the variances.

9 Complete the budget statement below.

Costs and revenue at different levels of output (£000)

		Budgeted costs and revenue			Actual	Variance
	Per unit	20,000	22,000	24,000	24,000	0
Sales revenue	£15				376	
Variable costs						
Materials	£6				154	
Labour	£4				100	
Variable overheads	£2				50	
Contribution	£3				72	
Fixed costs	£1				28	
Profit					44	

10 Complete the budget statement below.

Costs and revenue at different levels of output (£000)

		Budgeted costs and revenue			Actual	Variance
	Per unit	20,000	22,000	24,000	24,000	0
Sales revenue	£12				276	
Variable costs						
Materials	£3				75	
Labour	£3				100	
Variable overheads	£1				30	
Contribution	£5				71	
Fixed costs	£3				80	
Profit					(9)	

Key skills development

(a) From the Internet, download and then print off the balance sheet of a UK-based public limited company (one way to access the relevant web site is via the Biz/Ed site – see page 90)

(b) Using the data, you have collected for (a), calculate the following for both the immediate past year and for the year prior to that:
  (i)   long-term borrowing as a percentage of capital employed;
  (ii) net book value of fixed assets as a percentage of their historic costs;
  (iii) the liquidity ratios;
  (iv) share capital as a proportion of shareholders' equity.

(c) Give a ten-minute presentation to your class in which you explain and analyse significant features of the balance sheet. Your presentation should include a word processed sheet simplifying the balance sheet and at least one overhead transparency for use as a visual aid. In your presentation, you should make reference to some of the following:

- method of depreciation used;
- the nature of the firm's current assets;
- long-term liabilities;
- issued shares and authorized shared capital;
- the nature of reverses;
- relevant ratios;
- differences between the balance sheet and the simplified balance sheet used in textbook examples.

Part 5

Production and operations

35

Production and operations management

If the marketing manager makes decisions relating to what is produced, the production manager has responsibilities in relation to how it is made. We use the term 'production management' for firms engaged in primary production (mining, oil drilling, forestry) and secondary production (manufacturing). However, for a firm in the tertiary or service sector, production management seems inappropriate and so 'operations management' is the preferred term. Whether the firm produces goods or provides services, the principles of production and operations management (POM) are equally applicable. In essence, the aim of POM is to ensure that goods (or services) are made in the required quantity, to the required standard, at the right time and in the most economically efficient manner.

Chapter objectives

1 To introduce the concept of production as a transformational process.

2 To develop an understanding of the different types of production process.

3 To explain and analyse the functions of production/operations managers.

4 To explore key areas for decisions to be made in production/operations management.

5 To introduce the concepts and techniques involved in production planning and control.

Production as a transformational process

For production to occur, it is necessary to acquire certain inputs. These take the form of capital equipment, materials and human resources, although we should not neglect to mention energy (to power the process) and information (to plan and control the process). These inputs are transformed (or converted) in the productive process. The process will take one of four forms:

● extraction (such as mining);
● analytical techniques (breaking down substances);
● fabrication (joining together, such as welding);
● synthesis ('creating' new substances or assembling components into a whole product).

As Figure 35.1 shows, the transformation of the inputs produces an output, which will take the form of goods, services or information. It should be noted that, although the process is easier to visualize in relation to the production of goods, the concept of transformation of inputs into an

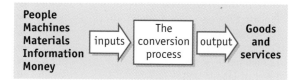

Figure 35.1 The production function

417

output can also be applied to the service sector (where the term **operations** might be considered more appropriate than the word production).

In fact, the distinction between production of goods and provision of services is not as absolute as we might assume. We should see the distinction as a spectrum running from primarily production to primarily the provision of a service. This can be illustrated by considering meals consumed in a restaurant and the servicing of a car. In both cases, the customer is buying a combination of a product (food or oil and parts) and a service (provided by a waiter or car mechanic). Similarly, when people buy expensive, complicated items, they buy both a product *and* a service (advice, after-sales service, credit).

Classification of production processes

This particular classification will assist in the understanding and analysis of production. Five types of process can be identified:

● project production;
● jobbing production;
● batch production;
● line production;
● continuous flow production.

The choice of process will be determined by the financial resources of the firm and the extent to which it seeks to produce a differentiated (as opposed to a homogeneous) product (see Table 35.1).

● **Project production** is used in large-scale projects made to customers' requirements (such as an oil tanker or a civil engineering project). The product is unique and assembled on site using skilled labour and flexible resources. Because of the size and complexity of the task, considerable planning is necessary. Quantitative techniques, such as network analysis, are essential to successful management of the project. It is usually necessary to beak down the overall project into manageable sub-tasks, many of which are subcontracted.

● **Jobbing production** is also concerned with the production of unique, non-standard goods that are made to order. Unlike project production, the items are small-scale ones and made in a workshop (such as made-to-measure suits or sailing boats). The jobbing workshop is arranged by process. Hence, machines carrying out the same or similar operations are clustered together and the product moves from one workstation to another. Multipurpose machinery is combined with skilled, versatile labour. Job producers economize on stockholding as they do not carry stocks of finished goods, but they do

Table 35.1 Production processes

	Jobbing	Batch	Line	Flow
Size of order	Small ←		→	High
Volume of output	Low ←		→	High
Product range	High ←		→	Low
Product variation	High ←		→	Low
Flexibility of process	High ←		→	Low
Dedication of machinery	Low ←		→	High
Capital investment	Low ←		→	High
Make to order/for stock	Order ←		→	Stock
Process time	Long ←		→	Short
No. of set-ups	High ←		→	Low
Cost of set-ups	Low ←		→	High
Economies of scale	Low ←		→	High
Level of labour skill	High ←		→ Low	Monitoring

face other problems. Short production runs invariably raise unit production costs. Specialist equipment is likely to be underutilized and delays between operating sequences will mean that total production time will be greater than processing time.

- **Batch production** As the name suggests, this is the manufacture of different versions of the same basic product in batches (such as in different colours or using different types of paint, different varieties of jam tart and so on). Unlike the previous processes, there is some repetition of production, which is for stock (rather than to order). However, production is not continuous. The relatively short production runs result in higher unit costs than would be the case if production was continuous. Changeover (and clean down) between batches means that resources are idle at times. Consequently, production managers have to plan production schedules to minimize changeovers. The machinery employed will be more specialist than in the earlier processes, but must retain some versatility for different batches.

- **Line production** is best understood by the example of assembly line manufacture of motor vehicles or electrical goods. Specialist (or dedicated) machinery will be used in the process and, because of the high capital investment required, it is essential to achieve a high level of utilization. This necessitates a high level of sales of a fairly standardized product made for stock (rather than to order). Line production links up with a strategy of undifferentiated marketing (whereas job and batch production suggest that the product is tailored to suit the needs of particular customers or market segments). The manpower required is specialist, but low in skills and performing repetitive work. The layout of the factory will be by process in a logical sequence in order to minimize the time and cost of movement. Line producers must invest heavily in stocks of raw materials to prevent stockout, but will keep stocks of work-in-progress to a low level. The great advantage of line production is that, with

long production runs, unit costs will be very low.

- **Continuous flow production** takes line production to its ultimate limit. Dedicated plant is used to manufacture a single product on a continuous (24-hour) basis. It is best understood in terms of chemical manufacture or oil refining. Hence, whereas line production involves the manufacture of discrete objects, continuous or flow production is used for the production of fluids. Most of the characteristics of line production are equally applicable, but there is one vital difference. The main labour task in continuous production is that of *monitoring* the process and, therefore, mainly skilled labour is required.

The production function

The task of the production manager is to plan, resource and control the process of converting raw materials and components into finished products that meet the requirements of customers. In a large organization, the tasks involved will be divided up in some way. For instance, the organization chart shown in Figure 35.2 might be considered fairly typical for a large manufacturing company. We can identify the main functional managers within a production department as:

- the **production manager** (or managers) have responsibility for day-to-day operations;
- the **production engineer** has responsibilities in terms of design and choice of methods;
- The **maintenance engineer** is required to ensure that the equipment is reliable and works efficiently;
- the **production planning and control manager** will have responsibilities in relation to the planning of capacity, the scheduling of production and control of the process;
- the **purchasing and stock control manager** has responsibilities for the purchase of materials and the maintenance of adequate stock levels;
- **quality controller** (see Chapter 37);
- **research and development manager.**

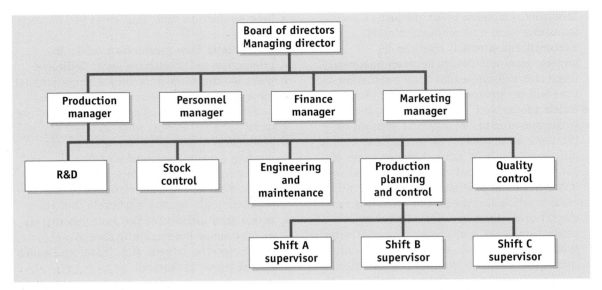

Figure 35.2 An organization chart focusing on the production function

The product

Decisions about product design are of crucial importance to the success of the organization. This is clearly an area where POM and marketing management meet. The marketing department seeks to identify and then satisfy customer needs. However, to accomplish the second task, it has to rely on other departments, most notably the production department. As the short-term interests and objectives of these departments are at times in conflict, there is inevitably some tension. This is seen in cases involving the following issues.

● **New products** The marketing department, conscious of the product lifecycle, will see new products as essential for the long-term success of the business. The production department will look critically at the costs of development, design and retooling (see Chapter 18).

● **Quality** Customers want high quality at a reasonable price and complain to the marketing department if this is not available. The production manager will point out the cost associated with improving the quality of the product.

● **Prices** Marketing people want costs to be low enough for them to set competitive prices in the marketplace. However, satisfying customers in terms of flexible response, high quality and variety raises production costs.

● **After-sales service** An after-sales service is part of the package bought by the customer in the case of complicated products (moreover, the supplier has a legal obligation in the immediate period after the goods are sold). To reduce the cost of the service, it is necessary to ensure high quality and/or use components that are easily changeable. Both solutions add to R&D and production costs.

● **Product variation** The marketing people are aware of the need to tailor products to suit the needs of different market segments. The production manager will point out the inevitable consequences in terms of short, high-cost production runs. Variety reduction or, better still, variety control is a way of reducing costs by minimizing the variety of products, parts, materials, processes and skills used. This can be undertaken in three ways:

– **simplification** elimination of unnecessary variety;

– **standardization** the control of necessary variety;

– **specialization** concentration of effort on those activities where special knowledge is available.

The benefits of variety control can be seen in terms of:
- intensification of selling effort;
- larger production runs with a corresponding reduction in unit costs;
- greater capacity utilization;
- reduction in stockholding;
- simplification of production control.

The plant and processes

This aspect of POM relates to choice of equipment and processes. A number of issues deserve particular attention.

Layout

The layout of a factory or other workplace should be carefully designed to secure maximum:

- flexibility;
- coordination;
- security;
- safety;
- accessibility;
- visibility;
- efficiency;
- minimum handling;
- minimum movement.

Analytical methods can be employed to plan the most efficient layout. It must be stressed that there is no universally applicable ideal layout and much will depend on the nature of the product and production process. We can, however, identify a number of commonly used types.

- **Layout by process** This layout is characterized by the clustering of machinery performing similar tasks. This layout, which is associated with batch production, has advantages in terms of flexibility. Process layout will accommodate many different product routes, it ensures high utilization of machinery in a batch set-up and provides for back-up machinery in the case of breakdown. However, as Figure 35.3

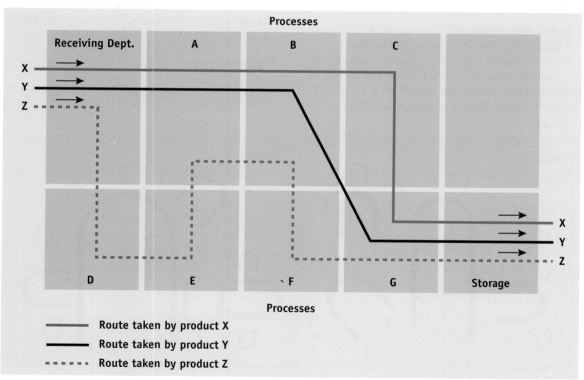

Figure 35.3 Process layout: machines that perform the same function are grouped together

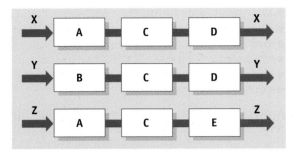

Figure 35.4 Product layout: machines and tasks are arranged according to the sequence of steps in the production of a single product

shows, it does involve greater movement of goods than occurs in layout by product.

● **Layout by product** This is a system in which machines and tasks are arranged according to the sequence of steps in the production of a single product. This layout is associated with line and flow production. It has the advantage that handling is reduced, work is simplified and broken down into smaller tasks, and control of the process is facilitated. However, the prerequisite for product layout is a high volume of output of a limited range of goods (see Figure 35.4).

● **Cell layout** This is associated with a method of organizing known as **group technology**

(GT). GT involves the formation of tasks, jobs and products into 'families', with the resources required being formed into 'cells'. Machines dedicated to the sequences of production are grouped into these cells (see Figure 35.5). The group contains a team of 6–15 workers who work solely in the group. They produce a specified 'family' of products (or carry out a specified family of tasks). The equipment is used solely by the group and is housed in an area (cell) reserved for the group. The group is given considerable autonomy in achieving the targets. The benefits of GT include:

– reduced preparation time;
– improved efficiency as a result of standardization and simplification;
– lower handling time;
– reduction in stocks;
– improved social relations.

● **Fixed position layout** In this system, the resources are taken to the site at which production occurs. This will be the case in a large construction project or where the fragile nature of the service requires assembly on site.

Maintenance

Maintenance work is undertaken to maintain or restore production facilities (machinery, plant,

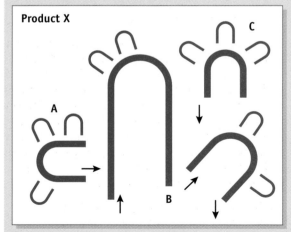
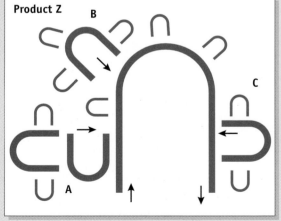

Figure 35.5 Cell layout: machines dedicated to sequences of production are grouped into cells

vehicles and so on). Just as car maintenance is necessary from time to time, so it is necessary to maintain the firm's production facilities to:

- enable the firm to satisfy customer demand;
- maximize the useful life of equipment;
- maintain safety standards;
- minimize production costs;
- minimize the disruption to operating processes.

The production manager is faced with a decision that is not dissimilar to that which confronts the ordinary motorist. Maintenance costs will rise the more frequently the machinery is overhauled. However, breakdown costs *fall* the greater the frequency of overhaul. These breakdown costs include:

- lost production;
- lost sales;
- subcontracting;
- underutilization of other resources;
- rushed maintenance at high cost;
- rushed production at high costs.

Figure 35.6 shows that breakdown maintenance carried out after a failure can prove very costly. Conversely, if maintenance is carried out too frequently, it can also prove very costly. The optimum amount of maintenance is shown at the crossover point, where total maintenance costs are minimized.

Maintenance directed at preventing a breakdown

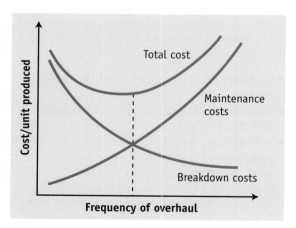

Figure 35.6 The trade-off in maintenance

is known as **preventive maintenance.** Slightly different is what we can call **planned maintenance.** This is maintenance that is organized and carried out with forethought, control and records. The difference between the two is that preventive maintenance aims to prevent breakdown at all costs. Planned maintenance is a rational approach in which it is accepted that allowing *some* breakdowns might prove less costly than preventing them. The **maintenance plan** will specify when maintenance will occur in terms of:

- time (say, every month);
- quantity of work (such as every 10,000 units);
- condition of the equipment; or
- opportunity for maintenance (for example, holiday closure).

Capacity planning

Capacity is the ability to produce. Hence, it is not a measure of what quantity was produced but how much the productive unit is *capable* of producing in a certain time period. **Immediate capacity** – a measure of the amount that can be produced within the current budget – will be determined by:

- the size of plant;
- availability of equipment;
- availability of manpower;
- financial policies;
- availability of materials.

Quite separate is what we can call **effective capacity**, which is limited by the skills and abilities of the manpower involved. Effective capacity is often considerably less than immediate capacity – Muhlemann, et al. quote of figure of 50 per cent and less as being common: 'While it is unlikely that the capacities will ever coincide, it is clear that significant increases in capacity are possible, often by improved production/operations control'. Two conclusions should be drawn.

- the theoretical capacity of the productive unit is not very meaningful when local circumstances conspire to produce a situation below the theoretical maximum;

● increased output is possible if better use is made of existing resources rather than by increasing the quantity of resources available.

The planned capacity of the firm or productive unit will be determined by:

● the firm's marketing and overall objectives;
● forecasts of future demand;
● the constraint of available finance.

Make or buy in?

An alternative to increasing production capacity is to subcontract production to another firm. This might be undertaken either as a temporary measure (for example, to resolve a temporary shortage of capacity) or as a long-term policy. The decision to buy in will be determined by the availability of suppliers and the relative costs involved. The temporary inability to satisfy customer demand from the firm's own capacity will necessitate subcontracting arrangements with other firms. On the other hand, a lack of faith in the supplier's ability to produce goods of a satisfactory quality will discourage the firm from subcontracting production out to others.

Production planning and control (PPC)

Production, like other aspects of business operations, should be planned. As with all plans, we start with objectives before deciding on strategies, tactics and control mechanisms. The basic purpose of **PPC** is to plan the acquisition, utilization and scheduling of resources that will be needed to transform customer requirements into acceptable goods. Harding defines the objective of PPC as satisfying 'customer delivery dates at a minimum overall cost by planning the sequence of production activities'. This will involve planning the supply of inputs so that they are brought together at the right time, in the right location and in the right quantities.

A vital ingredient in planning production levels will be the sales forecasts that emerge from the sales and marketing department. The point of contact between the departments can be called the **interface**. The production–sales interface is concerned with scheduling to satisfy customer demand. Problems over forecasts will affect the production department's ability to satisfy customer demand economically. For instance, an under-estimation of future sales will lead to inadequate stocks and, therefore, rush orders to rectify the mistake. Rush production almost always raises production costs (overtime premium rates, purchase of materials on unfavourable terms).

Another problem at the production–sales interface relates to seasonality of demand. A seasonal pattern of sales is not restricted to the obvious examples (Easter eggs, say). Most products display some seasonality in sales – slipper sales are seasonal despite their use throughout the year. The simple choice for the production department is between the following.

● **A level production plan**, whereby the firm produces in excess for most of the year to build up stocks in time for the seasonal rush. This is costly in terms of investment in stocks and storage space.
● **Chase demand**, whereby the firm increases production immediately prior to the seasonal rush. This assumes that there is the capacity to step up output (in which case, capacity is excessive at other times). The other problem that results is the high costs associated with rush production.
● **A mixed plan**, involving some stockbuilding but also some adjustments to the production level (see Figure 35.7).

After deciding on output levels, the plan has to be implemented. This will necessitate:

● **loading** the assigning of a job to a work centre;
● **sequencing** determining the order in which jobs will be completed;
● **scheduling** stating the times for starting and completing the job (in the scheduling of work, account will be taken of the availability of materials, and the need to minimize downtime – such as cleaning down between batches – and maximize the use of both equipment and labour, which is an area

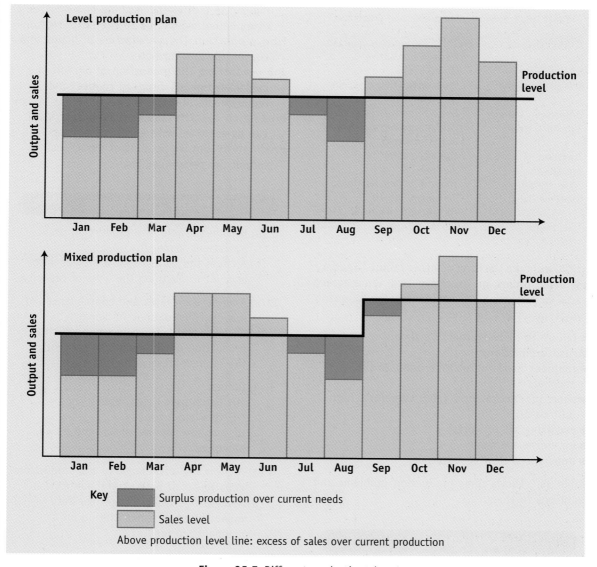

Figure 35.7 Different production plans

of business operations that lends itself to
quantitative techniques);
• **dispatching** or issuing instructions for the
work to be done;
• **progressing** this involves three activities:
the determination of progress on previous
orders; the identification and elimination of
bottlenecks; and the chasing of badly needed
orders (the latter activity, known as

expediting, will not be necessary if other
progressing activities are effective).

Progressing is one of the aspects of the control
function within PPC. Controlling involves obtaining feedback to ensure adherence to the plan,
and to update the plan in the light of changes.
As the objective is to satisfy customers in the
most economical and efficient manner, a failure

Table 35.2 Solving some production problems

Problem	Remedy
Machine breakdowns	Planned preventive maintenance
Low productivity	Productivity bonus scheme incentives
Unforeseen changes	Use alternative materials
Supplier's strike	Use alternative suppliers Buffer stocks
Transport breakdown	Use alternative freight methods
Absenteeism	Improve labour relations
Overtime bans	Temporary labour recruitment, improved labour relations

of PPC will take the form of either failure to satisfy customer orders or excessive and unnecessary costs. In particular, we can identify the following symptoms of PPC failure:

- failure to deliver orders on time;
- rush production;
- frequent need to 'rob' one order to fill another;
- short production runs (and, therefore, high unit costs);
- excessive set-up costs;
- excessive overtime;
- unbalanced flow of materials.

Table 35.2 shows some production problems and solutions to them.

Key concepts

Batch production A mode of producing goods in groups or batches rather than continuously. Batch production is used when the production process is interrupted, such as

moving to a different machine or a necessary delay before moving on to the next stage.

Flow production The manufacture of goods in a continually moving flow.

Job production The production of one-off customized goods designed to meet the requirements of a specific customer.

Production capacity The limit on output that can be achieved with existing resources.

Productivity Output per unit of input, such as output per person per hour.

Essay questions

1 (a) Explain the role of a production or operations manager.
  (b) Analyse the factors that are taken into account in planning the level of capacity.

2 (a) Analyse the causes and consequences of seasonal fluctuations in demand.
  (b) Suggest and evaluate ways in which a production department can cope with the problem of seasonality.

3 (a) Define:
    (i) batch production; and
    (ii) flow production.
  (b) Discuss the implications of these two processes.

4 (a) Analyse the advantages to the production department of product standardization.
  (b) Analyse the disadvantages for the organization of concentrating on a standardized product.

5 (a) What do you understand by batch production.
  (b) Discuss the importance of scheduling for batch production.

36

Stock control

Stock represents an investment by the organization. Money is tied up in goods, the eventual payment for which may be delayed months and even years. However, firms are willing to incur the expense of stockholding in order to ensure continuity of operations. The aim of stock control is thus to maintain continuity while minimizing the cost of stockholding. This chapter will introduce the reader to a simple quantitative technique relating to stock levels.

Chapter objectives

1 To investigate the reasons for holding stock.

2 To analyse the functions of stock control.

3 To develop a quantitative model of stockholding.

4 To contrast traditional stock control with just-in-time methods.

Purchasing

Because production involves a conversion of inputs into outputs, it will be necessary to acquire supplies of raw materials and/or components. Acquisition can take the form of either making the inputs or buying them in from a supply firm. The 'make or buy' decision will be influenced by the availability and reliability of suppliers, delivery times, relative costs and the amount of specialist expertise and dedicated machinery required in the production of components. If the decision is made to buy the inputs from supply firms, the purchasing department has to decide how, and from whom, to acquire the goods.

The basic objective in purchasing is to obtain the right quality, at the right time, in the right quantity, from the right source and at the right price. The purchasing department aims to:

- supply the business with a flow of inputs to meet its requirements;
- maintain continuity of supply by means of good relations with existing suppliers while exploring alternative sources of supply;
- obtain the best value for money, taking into account reliability and quality as well as price.

One policy decision to be made is whether large quantities should be ordered and received infrequently or small quantities should be ordered and received frequently. The case for each is summa-

Table 36.1 Large, infrequent orders or small, frequent orders

Benefits of frequent small orders	Benefits of infrequent larger orders
• Less risk of obsolescence and deterioration • Economizes on insurance • Lower capital requirement • Economizes on space	• Economies of purchasing and delivery • Profits from rise in price of stocks • Security of supply

rized in Table 36.1. This decision is integrally linked with stock control.

We can identify three purchasing policies that can be pursued.

● **Purchase on contract** This is important where continuity of production is essential. Continuity is guaranteed by a contract that commits each side to specific terms. The contract will include an agreement relating to the price to be paid for future deliveries. This can take one of four forms:

  – **fixed-price contract**, in which the price is agreed at the time the contract is signed;
  – **fixed price, subject to adjustment** means that the fixed price can be adjusted on an agreed basis to cover changes in specified costs;
  – **cost plus contract,** which involves the purchaser agreeing to pay suppliers' costs, plus a percentage.
  – a **renegotiable contract**, which allows either side to renegotiate price in the light of subsequent events.

Fluctuations in commodity prices make it especially advantageous to sign a **futures contract**. This is contract to purchase commodities in the future at an agreed price today rather than at the spot price at the time. In addition, an **option to purchase** is not only a useful insurance against future supply problems, it can also be profitably traded in its own right.

● **Speculative buying** This involves purchases in excess of immediate requirements to benefit from anticipated future price movements. Again, the volatility of commodity prices encourages this type of purchasing policy.
● **Hand to mouth buying** Buying only when goods are required means less capital is tied

up and there is less need for storage capacity. On the other hand, the purchase of small quantities raises unit costs and the purchaser may be forced to buy at high spot prices. There are additional problems if inputs are purchased from abroad. Movements in exchange rates will change the sterling prices of foreign inputs. The uncertainty can be reduced by holding bank accounts in different currencies or by buying **currencies forward**. This means agreeing to buy currencies in the future at a price (exchange rate) determined today. This type of action to reduce uncertainty is called **hedging**.

Whatever the purchasing policy, the buyer can expect some discount for either prompt payment (a **cash discount**) or a large-scale order (a **quantity discount**).

A large organization also has to make a policy decision about the degree of centralization there is to be for purchasing. **Centralized purchasing** means that orders are placed, and decisions are made, in a single, centralized purchasing department. Centralized purchasing has the advantage of standardized procedures, utilization of expertise in buying, reduced administrative costs and increased control over expenditure. On the other hand, it can lead to inflexibility, long lead times (delays in obtaining supplies) and a lack of awareness of needs at the local or plant level. The alternative system is decentralized purchasing in which considerable discretion is given to departments.

A final area of purchasing decision making concerns the choice of which (and how many) suppliers. Single sourcing is advantageous in terms of scale of orders, additional leverage on the supplier and the forging of a relationship of trust and goodwill. On the other hand, single sourcing adds to the vulnerability of the firm.

Consequently, there might be a preference for dual or even multiple sourcing. To a large extent, the decision will be influenced by the size of the firm and its orders.

The criteria for choosing a supplier are likely to include:

● available capability and capacity;
● price;
● delivery speed;
● delivery reliability;
● flexibility;
● quality;
● past performance.

An objective method of evaluating suppliers is by means of **vendor rating**. This assesses the performance of suppliers in terms of:

● **Quality** the monitoring of reject batches;
● **Delivery** speed of delivery;
● **Service:**
  – technical know-how;
  – availability and level of technical support;
  – level of field service;
  – degree of cooperation displayed;
  – R&D capacity;
  – level of new product development;
  – readiness to accept responsibility;
  – advice on potential problems;
  – kind and form of warranty offered;
  – speed with which replacement items are delivered.

Values will be attached to suppliers' performance in each of these categories and an objective choice can then be made.

Why stocks are held

To understand the model of stock control, it is first necessary to investigate why firms are willing to invest in stocks. Stocks take three forms:

● **raw materials** waiting to be processed;
● **work-in-progress** or goods that have already been partially processed;
● **finished goods** awaiting sale and/or despatch.

Stocks of raw materials are held to allow for variations in supply and to take advantage of bulk-

---

Table 36.2 The role of stock control

Basic objective: to minimize costs of stock while maintaining adequate levels of stock:

● to ensure adequate supplies of raw materials for production purposes;
● to ensure that finished goods are available for despatch;
● for valuation purposes;
● to control cash tied up in stock;
● to control wastage and pilferage.

---

buying discounts and anticipated price rises. The main reason for holding stocks of work-in-progress is to 'uncouple' the productive process, allowing greater flexibility and improved machine utilization. Finished goods are held in stock so that the firm can cope with variations in demand (such as for seasonal goods) or an expected rise in demand. To cope with high demand, it may be necessary to build up stocks beforehand.

In addition to these stocks, which are the result of careful decisions, firms might also hold unplanned stocks or stocks of unwanted goods. These arise from an inability to sell goods, mistakes in planning, lack of satisfactory stock control procedures and poor communication between the various departments of a firm. Our study of stock control will concentrate on stocks that are planned (see Table 36.2).

Stock control charts

A stock control graph is depicted in Figure 36.1. Each vertical line represents a new delivery (either from an external source or produced internally within the organization). Depletion of stocks as a result of usage or sales is represented by the sloping lines. The rate of depletion can be gauged from the gradient of the lines: the steeper the gradient, the faster the depletion. When stocks fall to the reorder level, a new batch is ordered, but as there is a time gap between the order being made and the delivery of supplies, stocks continue to dwindle. This time gap is known as the **lead time**. In conditions of certainty, there is no need to hold stocks in reserve. Hence, stock levels can fall to zero in the knowledge that a new

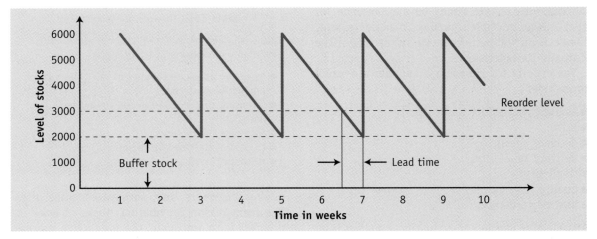

Figure 36.1 A stock control chart

delivery will arrive in time to prevent **stockout** (total depletion of stock). Where depletion rates and lead times vary, it is important to carry a reserve, which is known as the **buffer stock**.

This account suggests that there are several interrelated decisions to be made about stock held:

- the size of the buffer or reserve stock;
- the maximum level of stock to be held;
- the size of the batch to be ordered (the reorder quantity);
- the reorder level (the level that will trigger off the reordering of stock).

The buffer stock

The lower the buffer stock level, the greater will be the likelihood of stockout. Stockout involves costs in terms of:

- lost production;
- lost contribution resulting from lost sales;
- loss of customer goodwill and, therefore, of future sales;
- high unit costs associated with urgent, small batch replacement purchases;
- loss of bulk-buying discounts.

Where stockout costs are high, firms will be especially concerned to hold generous buffer stock levels. We can call a number of mathematical techniques into service to assist in the formulation of a buffer stock policy.

First, an understanding of statistical analysis will enable the firm to identify the minimum level of stock necessary to reduce and even eliminate the possibility of running out of stocks (stockout). A second technique, known as the **Pareto Rule**, enables planners to identify the stock items that deserve special attention.

The probability of stockout can be understood by considering the following example, which is based on the characteristics of a curve of normal distribution. Suppose a shop stocks an item for which demand is, on average, 30 per month, but which fluctuates around this mean. We are told that demand is normally distributed with a standard deviation of five and that deliveries are at the start of each month. What is a safe level of stocks to avoid stockout?

If the firm had 30 in stock at the start of each month, there is a 50 per cent probability of stockout before the end of the month. We know that 34 per cent of the area under a normal curve is within one standard deviation of the mean. Hence, an opening stock of 35 would be sufficient in 50 per cent plus 34 per cent of months. This still leaves 16 per cent of months where stockout will occur. If opening stocks were raised to 40, then stocks would be sufficient in 50 per cent plus 47.7 per cent of months. A firm might be prepared to work on the basis that stockout will only occur in 2 per cent of months (that is, once every four years).

One problem for producers of complicated, assembled goods, such as cars, is that thousands of separate items have to be kept in stock. Should the firm adopt the same elaborate stock control procedures for all items? A low-value, component will not incur high stockholding costs, but the consequences of stockout could be substantial. The Pareto Rule divides stock items into three classes:

- Class A items form 20 per cent of all items, but 80 per cent of value;
- Class B items form 30 per cent of items, but 15 per cent of value;
- Class C items form 50 per cent of all items, but 5 per cent of value.

The logic of the Pareto Rule is that Class A items deserve closest attention as large amounts of finance will be tied up in them. Class C items, such as nuts and bolts, are inexpensive and can be kept at a high level in view of the low cost involved.

Maximum stock levels

High stock levels mean that excess capital is tied up in an unproductive manner. Moreover, storage is costly, especially if:

- temperature or moisture has to be controlled;
- the goods are bulky and take up substantial storage space;
- the goods are of high value and need to be guarded.

Stockholders face risks associated with deterioration, pilferage or a change in the demand for goods. In view of these costs, there will be a desire to hold stock levels down by imposing a maximum limit.

A simple way of calculating maximum stock levels is to calculate the optimum reorder quantity and then add on the chosen levels of buffer stock.

Reorder quantity

Management will seek to discover the reorder quantity that minimizes the total stock (or inventory) cost. If the stocks are purchased from an

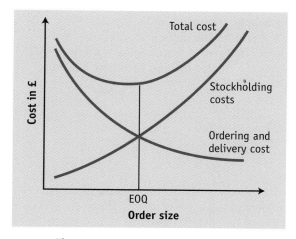

Figure 36.2 Economic order quantity

outside supplier, the optimum level is known as the **economic order quantity (EOQ)**. If the stocks are obtained from internal supplies, the equivalent is known as the **economic batch quantity**.

The EOQ is defined as the order quantity that minimizes the balance of costs between inventory (stock) holding costs and reorder costs. This is shown in Figure 36.2: EOQ is where the total cost is minimized. The cost of holding stocks can be itemized as:

- interest on capital;
- storage charges;
- handling costs;
- insurance costs;
- cost in terms of wastage.

The cost of raising an order can be itemized as:

- clerical costs;
- transport costs.

In the case of the economic batch size of an internal production run, we can substitute the set-up and tooling costs associated with the run for the clerical and transport costs associated with the external purchase.

The EOQ can be calculated from the formula:

$$\sqrt{\frac{2\,pd}{c}}$$

Where p is the procurement cost per batch;
d is the annual use of the material;
c is the carrying or holding cost per annum.

Example

A firm uses 500 units of a substance each year. The cost of procuring each batch is £600 and the cost of holding each unit is £300. The EOQ is:

$$= \sqrt{\frac{2 \times 500 \times £600}{£300}}$$

$$= \sqrt{2000}$$

$$= 44.7 \text{ units.}$$

This shows us that the materials should be ordered in quantities of 44.7 units. As annual use of the material amounts to 500 units, we can conclude that each year the firm will reorder:

$$\frac{500}{44.7} = 11.2 \text{ times per year.}$$

The reorder level that triggers off the order will be determined by the rate of depletion and lead time.

Just-in-time (JIT)

JIT is an inventory (stock) control system associated with Japanese management practices. Under JIT, materials are scheduled to arrive exactly when they are needed on a production line. Suppliers deliver materials only at the exact moment required, hence reducing raw material inventories to zero. Work-in-progress is kept to a minimum as goods are produced only as they are needed for the next stage of production. Finally, finished goods inventories are minimized by matching production to sales demand. The advantages of JIT are that investment in working capital is reduced and the shop floor is less cluttered with work-in-progress.

However, for JIT to be successful, it is necessary to develop a well coordinated production system. We can contrast a JIT demand-pull system with the traditional batch-push system. In the latter, goods are produced in efficient batches only to wait at the next work station for processing. Under the demand-pull system, each work station only produces goods when they are needed by the next station. The traditional method builds 'buffers' into the system. The JIT system necessitates precise scheduling with total coordination to avoid stockout.

In the case of external supplies it is essential to develop close relations with them to ensure fast, flexible and reliable service. Another precondition for successful JIT operations is employee motivation and cooperation. Without wholehearted employee support, a zero-inventory system could result in costly stockouts.

JIT methods are explained further in Chapter 39.

Conclusion

This chapter contrasts the traditional method of stock control, based on quantitative techniques designed to minimize overall stock costs, with the Japanese just-in-time method, which minimizes inventory levels.

The costs of stock ordering and carrying are an important aspect of a firm's overall costs and anything that reduces stock costs will increase profitability. The differing philosophies approach the same issue – that of reducing stock costs – in different ways.

Key concepts

Buffer stock Minimum level of stocks considered desirable.

Economic batch quantity The optimum size for a production batch.

Economic order quantity The order quantity that minimizes total costs in stock control.

Just-in-time An approach to stock management emphasizing low stock levels, frequent deliveries, operator involvement and quality awareness.

Reorder level Reorder level is the stock level at which further supplies must be reordered.

Reorder quantity The quantity that is reordered.

Stock control The control of stocks to ensure that they are adequate for immediate needs without tying up excessive financial resources.

Essay questions

1 (a) With the use of an illustration, outline the features of a stock control graph.

(b) Analyse the costs and benefits of a buffer stock.

2 Analyse the factors to be considered by a firm in deciding on its purchasing policy.

3 (a) What is meant by the economic order quantity?

(b) Analyse the consequences for stock policy of the concept of an economic order quantity.

4 (a) Analyse the implications of a just-in-time stock policy on relations with suppliers.

(b) Analyse the preconditions for a successful policy of just-in-time.

5 Analyse the role of information technology in stock control.

37

Quality management

This chapter will look at two very different approaches to quality. The first involves the use of inspectors to sort out the defective products from the acceptable ones. It is based on the assumption that some defective production is inevitable, but should be contained. The second approach is based on the premise that quality must be built into the product at source and that the aim should be to achieve zero defects.

Chapter objectives

1 To develop an understanding of the different approaches to quality.

2 To introduce the statistical approach to quality control.

3 To introduce the reader to new approaches to quality.

4 To survey modern quality concepts.

What is meant by quality?

It has to be established that quality does not necessarily mean excellence in the sense of a 'Rolls-Royce product'. Essentially, quality is about fitness for purpose: it is 'the totality of features and characteristics of a product or service that bear on its ability to satisfy stated or implied needs' (BS 4778). British Standard 5750 defines quality in terms of fitness for purpose and safety in use.

Quality is a crucial issue at the interface between marketing and production. 'To prosper in today's economic climate, any organization and its suppliers must be dedicated to never-ending improvement, and more efficient ways to obtain products or services that consistently meet customers' needs must constantly be sought. The consumer is no longer required to make a choice between price and quality, and competitiveness in quality is not only central to profitability, but crucial to business survival' (Muhlemann, *et al.*).

Quality has two separate aspects.

● **Quality of design,** meaning that the products are suitable for the purpose to which they will be put. After establishing customers requirements (or their perceptions of quality), these should be met fully in the design and specifications of the products.
● **Quality of conformance,** meaning the extent to which the goods that are produced conform to the specifications laid down. This

aspect of quality concerns the consistency with which the products meet high standards.

Quality procedures are, therefore, designed to ensure that the design of products satisfies customers' requirements and that there are consistently of a high standard as they come off the production line. The importance of quality is undeniable, but the real question is how to achieve and sustain it, and who should be responsible for it.

How to ensure quality

The nature of the quality control process is related to the type of productive process chosen (see Table 37.1).

- In project and jobbing production, tasks and quality are integrated in the sense that employees and supervisors control the process and they control the quality of output.
- At the opposite end of the spectrum, quality is determined by the process in continuous flow production. Employees are engaged in monitoring and, therefore, quality and task are naturally integrated.
- However, batch and line production lead to a de-skilling of the labour force and a tendency to separate quality control from production. Hence, employees and their line managers are responsible for quantitative aspects of output but a separate quality control team has responsibility for ensuring quality. This has

unfortunate consequences, especially in terms of the emphasis on detection of defects rather than ensuring that producers 'get it right first time'.

Proactive or reactive?

Control processes occur before, during or after the event (see Figure 37.1)

- **Preventive or feedforward control** This is a proactive approach to quality in which the control is focused on the inputs – the human resources, machinery and materials. By inspecting and controlling the variables that go into the production process, there will be greater consistency of the quality of the finished product with fewer defective goods produced at the other end.
- **Concurrent control** involves the monitoring of ongoing activities to ensure the consistency of the quality of the product as it is progressing. Both feedforward and

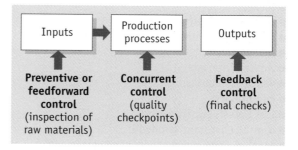

Figure 37.1 Control processes

Table 37.1 Process type and quality control

Type of process	Task	Responsibility for quality
Jobbing	The task and quality are normally integrated and depend on the skills of the people doing and supervising the work	The person performing the task and supervisors
Batch and line	Work has been deskilled	Separate quality control and inspection
Continuous process	Quality determined by the process – quality reintegrated into the task	Built into the process. Monitoring becomes the responsibility of those performing other aspects of the task

concurrent controls can be seen as proactive in that the ideal is to prevent defective products being produced rather than merely scrapping those that are produced.

- **Feedback control (or post-action control)** focuses on the output. It is reactive rather than proactive and is designed to detect defective goods rather than prevent them being manufactured in the first place. It is to this aspect of quality control that we will now turn.

Statistical quality control

Statistical quality control is based on the assumption that perfect quality is unattainable and/or too expensive. As with all business decisions, there is a trade-off between the costs associated with the maintenance of quality and the costs resulting from failures. The costs of failure (the cost of inadequate quality control) include the cost of:

- scrap;
- reworking faulty goods;
- downgrading goods (seconds);
- inspection;
- waste materials;
- warranty claims;
- complaints;
- lost sales opportunities;
- loss of customer goodwill;
- legal claims and costs in connection with product liability.

Against these costs we should consider the cost of maintaining quality. This is consists of the costs of appraisal:

- verification costs;
- inspection costs;
- quality audit;
- appraisal equipment;

and the costs of prevention:

- additional maintenance;
- training;
- special investigations;
- quality planning.

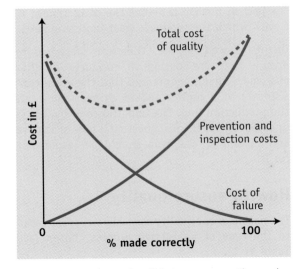

Figure 37.2 The trade-off between prevention and inspection

These three types of costs are traded-off, as shown in Figure 37.2. It should be appreciated that the optimum level of quality control occurs when the rising prevention and appraisal costs intersect with the falling cost of failure. The optimum does not mean zero defects, but the amount of quality control that minimizes the total cost of achieving consistent quality.

In some situations (such as job or project production), it is possible to inspect or test every item, but it is more common to use sampling methods because:

- sampling is quicker;
- sampling is cheaper;
- some tests damage or destroy the product;
- sampling smoothes out random variations;
- deterioration from excessive handling would result from 100 per cent inspection.

Statistical quality control can be divided into acceptance sampling and process control. **Acceptance sampling** involves testing a random sample of existing goods and deciding whether or not to accept an entire lot based on the quality of the random sample. **Statistical process control** involves testing a random sample of output from a process to determine whether or not the process is producing items within a pre-selected range. When the tested output exceeds that range, it is a signal to adjust the process to force output back into the acceptable range. This is achieved by adjusting the process.

Quality control for both acceptance sampling and process control measures either attributes or variables.

Control by attributes is used in situations where the product is either acceptable or unacceptable. Yes/no situations can be analysed in terms of binomial distribution. **Control by variables** refers to measurable features (size, weight and so on) where normal distribution applies.

Control by attributes

To understand the process, it is necessary to be familiar with a number of terms.

Acceptable quality level (AQL) is defined as the maximum number of defective goods per 100 that, for the purposes of acceptance sampling, can be considered satisfactory. This means that, provided the number of defective goods does not exceed the AQL, the batch is passed as acceptable. If the number exceeds the AQL the whole batch is rejected.

Lots are defined as low quality if the percentage of defective goods is greater than a specified amount known as the **lot tolerance percentage defective (LTPD)**.

There is always a danger in statistical quality control that some bad work is passed – the probability of accepting a low-quality lot is termed the **consumers' risk**. Conversely, there is also a danger that goods of satisfactory quality will be rejected in the sampling process. This is known as the **producer's risk** (see Figure 37.3). The stages in this form of quality control are:

- calculate the average number of defectives expected in each batch, together with the standard deviation of the distribution;
- assess the probability of different numbers of defective goods in a single sample;
- fix the risk levels – AQL, LTPD, producer's risk and consumers' risk;
- set the control limits in the form of a control chart (see Figure 37.4);
- implement.

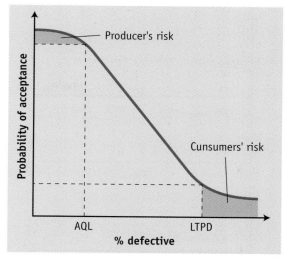

Figure 37.3 Operating characteristics curve (the probability of accepting lots with varying percentages for defective goods)

Action must be taken if the number of defective goods reaches either control limit. Investigation must take place if plot points are moving closer to the limit or are consistently above or below the central line or there is erratic behaviour.

One way to lessen the risks mentioned above is to introduce double or multiple sampling. In **double sampling**, the batch will be accepted if defects are less than a statistically chosen number (says, 2 in 100), rejected if more than a second number (say, 8 in 100) and subject to a second sampling if defects are some number between the two. In **multiple sampling**, the process continues until, on the basis of the cumulative number of defects, it is decided whether to accept or reject the batch.

Control by variables

Normal distribution applies in this type of situation. The procedure to be followed is:

- take a succession of random samples (20 is a typical number) to measure the range of values of the variable, which will be a particular aspect of the product that has to meet a defined level of quality or performance;

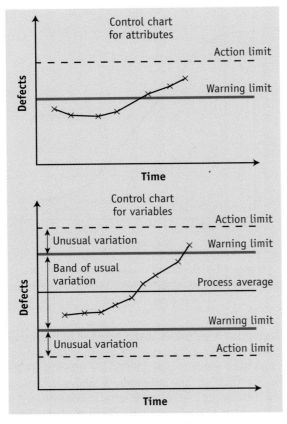

Figure 37.4 Control charts

- calculate the mean values of the samples – these means will form a normal distribution;
- calculate the standard deviation or standard error of the sample means;
- calculate the average range of the samples, which is the average over a number of

samples of the differences between their extreme values;
- determine the levels of risk that are acceptable – risk levels may be described in such terms as no more than two items in 1000 should be defective in the sense of falling outside an acceptable range of values;
- use the calculated mean values, standard error and average range to establish the warning and action limits applicable to a particular risk level;
- draw up a control chart for the variables on the basis of the warning and action lines.

An example of the control chart used for this type of quality control is shown in Figure 37.4. You will notice that there are upper *and* lower limits. Any measurement within the warning limit is acceptable but, as these are passed, there is evidence of a problem – this must be investigated and as the measurement approaches the outer limit, action must be taken.

The quality revolution

Under the influence of a number of 'quality gurus' and following the success of Japanese manufacturing industry, there was a revolution in attitudes to quality in the late twentieth century. Instead of inspecting out faults at the end of the process, the emphasis was placed on building in quality from the outset. The contrast between the two approaches to quality can be shown in Table 37.2.

The change in philosophy was brought about

Table 37.2 Quality control

Old philosophy	New philosophy
• Quality is secondary to profit	• Quality is the best way to ensure profit
• Higher quality means higher cost	• Higher quality means lower costs
• Minimize quality defects	• Zero quality defects
• Quality control is a problem for quality controllers	• Everyone is a quality controller
• Most quality problems are a result of poor workmanship	• Most quality problems are a result of poor management systems
• Quality control problems should be caught and remedied	• Quality control problems should be eliminated

by the influence of W. Edwards Deming, an American who worked extensively in Japan. His 'Fourteen Points for Total Quality Control' are:

1 create and publish, for all employees, a statement of the company's mission (aims and objectives) and ensure that managers constantly demonstrate their commitment to it;
2 everyone, from top management down, must learn the new philosophy (of continuously improving customer satisfaction);
3 employ inspection primarily for improving production processes rather than for detecting and correcting errors;
4 award business to suppliers on the basis of consistent quality and reliability of their products as well as on price (which is secondary to quality);
5 continuously aim to improve the production system;
6 ensure adequate training, both of employees and suppliers (so that all parties know what is expected of them);
7 introduce participatory leadership style in order to achieve employee cooperation;
8 develop a climate of trust between management and employees, and between groups;
9 develop an across-the-board approach to cooperation and teamwork;
10 cease all exhortations and slogans – instead, provide the means to improve customer satisfaction;
11 eliminate numerical quotas for production in favour of instituting methods for improvement;
12 remove barriers to workmanship by providing adequate training and equipment and encouraging pride in each worker's own work;
13 encourage education and self-improvement at every level (including training in statistical control techniques);
14 create a climate where quality improvement is embedded in the organization's culture, from top to bottom.

Joseph M. Juran is another American whose ideas were enthusiastically taken up by the Japanese. Juran has ten steps to quality improvement:

1 build awareness of the need and opportunity for improvement;
2 set goals for improvement;
3 organize to reach the goals (establish a quality council, identify problems, select projects, appoint teams, designate facilitators);
4 provide training;
5 carry out projects to solve problems;
6 report progress;
7 give recognition;
8 communicate results;
9 keep score;
10 maintain momentum by making annual improvement part of the regular systems and processes of the company.

Philip B. Crosby, also American, established the 'Four Absolutes of Quality Management':

1 quality is defined as conformance to requirements, not as 'goodness' nor 'elegance';
2 the system for bringing about quality is prevention, not appraisal;
3 the performance standard must be zero defects, not 'that's close enough';
4 the measurement of quality is the price of non-conformance, not indices.

Note the stress on zero defects or getting it right first time and, once achieved, 'do it over again'. In other words, the quality improvement programme never ends.

Kaoru Ishikawa pioneered quality circles, the fishbone diagram and the concept of company-wide quality control. Ishikawa's philosophy is that quality should not just be restricted to the quality of the product, but also include quality after-sales service, management and human resources. This has the following positive effects:

- product quality is improved and becomes uniform, defects are reduced;
- reliability of goods is improved;
- costs are reduced;
- quantity of production is increased as defective products are eliminated early on

and it becomes possible to make rational production schedules;

- wasteful work and rework are reduced;
- good techniques are established and improved;
- expenses on inspection and testing are reduced;
- contracts between vendors and vendees are rationalized;
- the sales market is enlarged;
- better relationships are established between departments;
- false data and reports are reduced;
- discussions are carried out more freely and democratically;
- meetings are operated more smoothly;
- repairs and installation of equipment and facilities are done more rationally;
- human relations are improved.

All the 'quality gurus' stress that quality should not be seen as a nuisance or a cost, but, rather, emphasis should be placed on the benefits of quality and the true costs of failure to implement quality principles. The benefits include:

- lower costs due to the reduction in waste and scrap;
- fewer delays;
- efficient use of resources;
- higher productivity;
- greater market share as a result of lower prices and superior quality;
- improved business prospects;
- increased employment.

The cost of failure to implement quality is not confined to the cost of scrapping or reworking goods, but, like an iceberg, 90 per cent of costs are hidden as:

- lost orders;
- increased stock levels;
- inefficiency in the use of human resources;
- poor lead time;
- taking up of management time;
- inability to operate just-in-time procedures.

Total Quality Management (TQM)

TQM stands for total (meaning the wholehearted commitment of everyone in the organization), quality (continuously meeting and exceeding customer requirements and expectations) and management (an active process, led from the top). Hence, **TQM** is a process involving everyone in an organization in continuously improving products and processes to achieve, on every occasion, quality that satisfies and exceeds customers' needs. TQM means managing the organization so that it excels in all dimensions of products and services that are important to its customers. TQM is a style of managing that gives everyone in the organization responsibility for delivering quality to the final customer, quality being described as 'fitness for purpose' or as 'delighting the customer'. TQM views each task in the organization as fundamentally a process that is in a customer/supplier relationship with the next process. The aim at each stage is to define and meet the customers' requirements in order to maximize the satisfaction of the final consumer at the lowest possible cost.

This means that, in addition to statistical quality control, it is necessary to bring about a cultural

Table 37.3 TQM

The benefits of TQM	Requirements for success
• Improved quality	• Leadership from the top
• Increased productivity	• Patience to carry through a long-term strategy
• Increased market share	• Communication skills
• Competitive advantage	• A change in culture
• A release of employee potential	• A recognition of quality in all aspects of management
• A motivated workforce	• Recognition and reward
• Increased profits	
• Reduced waste as a result of zero defects	

change in the organization. The new quality philosophy stresses:

- the customer is the driver of changes;
- continuous improvement;
- employee participation;
- partnership with employees;
- commitment from top management;
- trust in workers' abilities;
- flexibility;
- training for the workforce;
- acceptance of responsibility;
- willingness to contribute.

Table 37.3 summarizes the benefits of TQM and how to make it work.

Key concepts

Quality control The process of checking the accuracy of work bought in or completed.

Total Quality Management The attempt to establish a culture of quality throughout the organization. Building in quality rather than inspecting out defective goods.

Essay questions

1 (a) Analyse the importance of quality control to organizations operating in a competitive market.
 (b) Discuss the problems associated with end-of-the-line quality control.

2 Should quality be left to a specialist quality control department? Justify your answer.

3 (a) Analyse the principle of statistical quality control.
 (b) Evaluate statistical quality control as a way of ensuring quality.

4 Total Quality Management (TQM) requires a change in the culture of the organization. Discuss.

5 'Quality is free' (P. Crosby). Discuss.

Efficiency

In the final analysis, production management is concerned with the efficient use of resources to achieve production targets.

Chapter objectives

1 To define effectiveness, efficiency and productivity.

2 To identify ways of improving productivity.

3 To explain and analyse work study techniques.

4 To explain the techniques of benchmarking and business process re-engineering.

Effectiveness and efficiency

These two words are not synonymous. It is possible to be effective in getting the task done and yet at the same time be inefficient by making unnecessary use of resources. We therefore need to be clear about the meanings of the two words.

Effectiveness is concerned with the achievement of objectives – achieving what you set out to do. It can be measured by using this formula:

$$\frac{\text{Actual output}}{\text{Expected output}} \times 100$$

The closer the resulting figure is to 100 per cent, the greater the effectiveness of the organization. In addition to effectiveness in terms of the quantity produced, we can also measure it in terms of timeliness or quality. In each case, we are concerned with what has been achieved rather than the amount of resources used to achieve it.

Efficiency is concerned with the input of resources and can be expressed numerically as:

$$\frac{\text{Resources actually used}}{\text{Resources planned to be used}} \times 100$$

Production efficiency could be expressed in terms of the percentage of scrap produced by a process. However, it is possible to be efficient and yet not be effective – resources could be used sparingly and yet the objective was not achieved. If effectiveness focuses on output and efficiency focuses on inputs we need a measure that links the two. This becomes a measure of productivity.

Productivity

Productivity is a measure of the efficiency with which a firm turns inputs (labour, capital, materials, land) into output. In essence, it is output per unit of input, with an increase in productivity taking the form of:

- producing more with the same quantity of inputs;
- producing the same quantity with fewer inputs;
- output rising faster than inputs or output falling more slowly than inputs.

Labour productivity is a crucial measure of efficiency, given the high share staff pay takes of the total cost of production. It can be measured in two ways:

$$\text{Output per employee} = \frac{\text{Total output}}{\text{Total number employees}}$$

$$\text{Output per person per hour} = \frac{\text{Total output}}{\text{Total hours worked}}$$

The second measure overcomes the problem of increased production and productivity via an increase in the working week disguising the real trend in productivity.

If labour is employed to produce non-standard products, then productivity could be expressed in monetary terms.

$$\text{Value of output per person} = \frac{\text{Value of output}}{\text{Total number employed}}$$

$$\text{Value added per employee} = \frac{\text{Value added by the firm}}{\text{Total number employed}}$$

These value measures reflect the revenue contribution of the average employee, but are distorted by price changes. To measure physical productivity, it is necessary to focus on physical output.

The productivity of the workforce reflects:

- the education, training and skills of the workforce (what economists call human capital);
- the stock of capital at the disposal of workers;
- health and age structure of the workforce;
- the efficiency of the organization (that is the extent to which management is making best use of human resources);
- working conditions, industrial relations and employee motivation.

The productivity of capital can also be measured, but, as the term 'capital' covers a wide range of equipment, it is only meaningful if we use a monetary value for fixed assets. The physical productivity of capital is calculated by dividing output by the stock of capital (for example, output per £1000 of capital equipment). Alternatively, the productivity of capital can be expressed as value of output divided by value of the capital stock. The productivity of capital will reflect:

- the technology incorporated in the capital;
- the age of the capital stock;
- the skills of the workforce;
- production planning;
- inventory management (for example, running out of stock results in enforced shut down);
- product diversity (and, therefore, the amount of 'downtime');
- process and layout.

Some organizations are capital-intensive while others are labour-intensive. In the former, a high proportion of costs are capital costs, whereas in the latter, a high proportion of costs are labour costs. An automated factory making extensive use of robots and an oil refinery are capital-intensive, whereas a textile or clothing factory, using simple technology but an army of labour, is labour-intensive. Comparisons of different organizations is meaningless if we concentrate on single-factor productivity. To overcome this problem, we can use a measure of total factor productivity that is calculated as:

$$\frac{\text{Total output}}{\text{Inputs of all factors of production}}$$

The purpose of collecting productivity data is to detect trends in the level of productivity over-time, compare actual productivity with expected productivity and make comparisons between productivity of different plants. In each case, there is an attempt to identify any problem. Low productivity suggests unsatisfactory performance in terms of:

● planning
● management
● employee motivation
● training
● waste
● processes or systems of work.

What can be done to increase efficiency and productivity?

As is always the case, the first thing to do is analyse the existing situation. This chapter closes with an outline of different techniques of analysis, but, before looking at the methods of analysis, we can identify generic solutions that are likely to emerge from any such study.

● **Work simplification** the elimination of unnecessary operations, movements and paperwork.
● **Rationalization** reviewing and reducing the size and scope of the organization.
● **Capital investment** the injection of capital to purchase new equipment and modernize old equipment.
● **Material utilization** improved control of materials.
● **Improved planning** to increase the utilization of plant and equipment.
● **Changes in the human resource mix** for

example, employing fewer, but more skilled, workers.
● **Facilities improvement** such as making the working environment better by more effective layouts.
● **Organizational change** flattening the structure or downsizing, for example.
● **Simplification and standardization of design** say, reducing variety or simplifying the design to reduce wastage.
● **Outsourcing** that is, buying components in from an outside source rather than making them internally within the firm. The criteria for making and buying in are set out in Table 38.1.

Work study

Work study is a generic term for a series of analytical techniques used to determine the most efficient use of labour in relation to the other inputs into the productive process. It developed from the work of Taylor and Gilbreth in the school of thought that has come to be known as **scientific management** (see Chapter 42). Taylor argued that a systematic study of work operations would result in the identification of the 'best', most efficient and most productive methods of carrying out tasks. The resulting rise in productivity could be shared with the workforce.

Work study aims to:

● improve the flow of work to avoid bottlenecks in production processes;
● improve employee performance;

Table 38.1 Make or buy

Circumstances favouring making	Circumstances favouring buying in
● Cheaper to make ● Low confidence in suppliers in terms of delivery times and quality ● Excess capacity in-house ● The component is strategic to the company – fear that design secrets will be disclosed, for example ● Concern about collusion between suppliers to force up prices ● Where purchasing the component would eliminate specialist knowledge and undermine long-term competitiveness	● Cheaper to buy in ● Confidence in supplier ● Lack of capacity in-house ● Making would require additional investment ● Purchasing might improve cash flow ● The component is simple and producing it in-house would add very little value to the operation

- improve utilization of space, equipment and materials;
- increase efficiency, productivity and, ultimately, profitability;
- provide the basis for incentive pay schemes, such as piece rates, which reward workers for the amount they produce rather than the time spent on the premises;
- improve planning by the provision of standard times and procedures;
- plan a more even spread of work among employees;
- provide a basis for costing of jobs in the future.

Work study has two aspects: method study and work measurement (also known as time study). The distinction between them is illustrated in Figure 38.1.

Method study is the systematic recording and evaluation of ways of doing work (both existing and proposed) as a means of developing easier, more effective methods and thereby reducing costs. The implication is that there is a best method of performing a task and that this can be dis-covered by means of a scientific or methodological approach. The basic steps in **method study** are:

- select the job to be studied;
- observe and record information about the job and methods used, recording devices taking the form of:
  - process or flow charts;
  - motion charts;
  - layout models and templates;
  - string diagrams;
  - film/video;
- examine and analyse the information;
- identify ways of improving the method, which might take the form of:
  - eliminating operations;
  - combining operations;
  - devising different physical movements;
  - altering machines or tools;
  - altering the sequence of operations;
  - eliminating any duplicated effort;
- develop revised/improved methods;
- implement the new method;
- record and evaluate the new method, making adjustments where necessary.

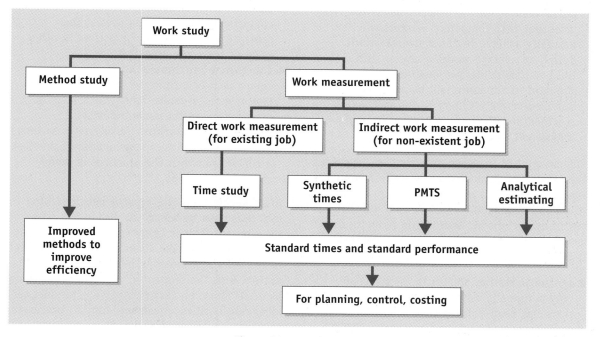

Figure 38.1 Works study

Work measurement is the application of techniques to establish the time for a qualified worker to carry out a particular job. The purpose of measuring the time required to complete a job is to provide information for production schedules, manpower requirements, costing, incentive payments and the monitoring of performance. The basic steps involved are as follows.

● Select the work to be measured.
● Define the basis for measurement.
● Undertake the measurement.
● Obtain details of the work, making allowances for variable factors (such as interruptions) and personal needs.
● Rate the performance of the individual in relation to the average or norm.
● Establish a standard time and a standard performance. **Standard time** is the total time in which a job should be completed at standard performance by a trained and competent individual in normal circumstances. This definition accepts that there are variations in both individual performance and the circumstances in which the work takes place. **Standard performance**, on the other hand, is the rate of output that competent workers will naturally achieve (without overexertion) during an average working day or shift. However, there are two qualifications: standard performance will be achieved provided workers adhere to the methods specified and they are motivated to apply themselves to their work.

This account of work measurement assumes that the job or task is already being performed and is repetitive. How can work measurement be applied to a non-existent job – that is, to a job that has yet to be performed? There is no basis for direct time study, so one of the three techniques of indirect time study can be used:

● **synthetic timing** applies to a job that is only marginally different from one for which there has been a direct time study;
● **predetermined motion time study (PMTS)** requires the identification of basic human motions to which times are attached to build a composite time;
● **analytical estimating**, which is more subjective, is used for one-off jobs and involves an estimate of time based on experience.

Benchmarking

A benchmark is a standard or reference point. The management process of 'benchmarking' came to prominence in the 1980s as a technique of analysing best practice in order to facilitate improvement within the organization. David Kearns (CEO of Xerox) defined it as 'the continuous process of measuring products, services and practices against the toughest competitors or those regarded as industry leaders.' The purpose of the exercise is to help an organization improve its performance and achieve and sustain competitive advantage.

Four types of benchmarking can be identified:

● **competitive benchmarking** involves comparing the performance of an organization's products and processes with those of a key competitor;
● **internal benchmarking** involves comparisons between one part of the organization with similar practices in other parts of the same organization;
● **functional benchmarking** is the direct comparison of a function (say, invoicing) in two or more organizations, which may, or may not be, in the same industry;
● **Generic benchmarking** (also known as best practice or worldclass benchmarking) involves a comparison with the practices of world-class organizations.

After deciding on the type of benchmarking to use, it is then necessary to decide the scope of the exercise. This is likely to comprise those activities that will make a significant improvement in customer relationships and, ultimately, on the bottom line. Consequently, many benchmarking exercises focus on customer service, product service, core business processes, support processes, employee performance, supplier performance, technology and new product development. The benchmarking planning also includes decisions about methods of collecting data. The data will then be analysed to identify 'performance gaps' between the organization and recognized leaders. Action plans are then produced in order to raise performance to a new standard set. After implementation, the results will be monitored in what is a continuous rather than static process. As the industry's best standard improves, a further round of benchmarking and improvement will follow.

The benefits of benchmarking are that it:

- identifies 'best practice';
- facilitates the setting of performance goals;
- identifies ways of improving performance;
- is a proactive improvement process involving learning from others;
- forces companies to look outwards rather than complacently looking inwards;
- motivates staff by showing them what is possible;
- provides early warning of competitive disadvantage;
- can result in a continuous updating of performance.

Benchmarking requires resources and will fail unless there is commitment from top management to implement change arising from the exercise. The only serious disadvantage of the process is that it can result in copying others rather than being innovative.

Business process re-engineering (BPR)

BPR is a philosophy that came to the fore in the 1990s, following the publication of *Re-engineering the Corporation* by Michael Hammer and James Champy (Nicholas Brealey, 1993). It involves the redesigning of core business processes with the aim of streamlining operations and eliminating wasteful non-value-added steps. It requires a radical rethinking of processes from a holistic view, taking into account technologies, strategy, processes and human resources within the whole organization. BPR focuses not on individual functions, but on processes (defined as a set of activities that, in total, produce a result of value to the customer).

BPR has some similarities to TQM as it:

- requires the support of top management;
- emphasizes the importance of teams and empowerment;
- seeks to reduce costs, improve quality and change culture.

It also differs significantly from TQM in that it:

- seeks radical or dramatic change rather than continuous improvement (see Chapter 39);
- takes a zero-based approach in which the first question is whether or not the activity should be eliminated.

Advantages claimed for BPR are that it:

- revolves around customer needs and helps give an appropriate focus to the business;
- brings about cost-reduction, which increases the organization's competitiveness;
- encourages a strategic view of operational processes;
- overcomes the problem of short-sightedness arising from concentration on functional boundaries;
- can result in the elimination of unnecessary activities;
- encourages creativity and innovation in teams.

Criticisms of BPR include that it:

- requires considerable commitment;
- is incorrectly seen as a once-and-for-all cost-cutting exercise, thus producing hostility;
- high costs can damage companies already in trouble;
- requires a high level of expertise and good teamwork.

Key concepts

Benchmarking Setting competitive performance standards against which progress can be measured.
Business process re-engineering Reinvention of how work is carried out within an organization.
Effectiveness Achievement of objectiveness.

Efficiency Producing output without the excessive use of resources.

Productivity Output per unit of input.

Work study The systematic analysis and measurement with the intention of identifying the best available method.

Essay questions

1 (a) Explain each of these terms:
- (i) effectiveness;
- (ii) efficiency;
- (iii) productivity.

(b) Analyse ways of improving the productivity of labour.

2 (a) Outline the methods of work study?

(b) Analyse the problems involved in undertaking work study.

3 (a) What do you understand by work study?

(b) Analyse the role of:
- (i) work measurement; and
- (ii) method study.

4 Explain what is meant by business process re-engineering and analyse its role in operations management.

5 Discuss ways of improving the productivity of capital equipment.

Lean production

Lean production is a collective term for a series of Japanese-inspired measures designed to avoid waste in operations.

Chapter objectives

1 To explore the concept of waste.

2 To develop an understanding of lean production methods.

3 To contrast lean production with traditional production methods.

Waste and techniques that aim to eliminate it

Lean production is an integrated approach to design, technology, components and materials and requires a new culture for the firm. Elements of lean production include well-known techniques, such as just-in-time approaches to stock control, and less well-known techniques, such as time-based management and cell production. Before looking at these techniques in detail, it is worth exploring what is meant by a waste. Seven types of waste are identified by the Japanese proponents of lean production.

- **Waste from overproduction** Producing in excess of demand is clearly a waste of resources.
- **Waste of a waiting time** Work-in-progress that sits waiting for the next stage of the operation involves a waste in that, during the waiting time, value is not being added to the output. Lean production methods concentrate on maximizing the proportion of time used in value-adding activities.
- **Waste of transportation** Transporting goods from one part of the factory to another involves costs in terms of handling, and, again it is not adding value to the output.
- **Processing waste** Processing methods inevitably produce some waste, but lean production requires that this be kept to a minimum.

- **Inventory waste** Excessive stockholdings increase the cost of the product in terms of requiring extra handling, extra space, extra paperwork and extra interest charges.
- **Waste of motion** Movement does not necessarily mean that work is taking place. Movement that does *not* add value to the product should be kept to a minimum.
- **Waste from product defects** Product defects necessitate reworking or the scrapping of defective goods. This involves a waste of time and resources. Moreover, it increases the cost of warrantees and places future business at risk.

Using traditional European or American methods (large-scale production, 'just-in-case' approach to stocks, long lead times and so on), these problems were disguised. However the adoption of lean production principles revealed them again. This can be seen in Figure 39.1, where the sources of waste are shown as boulders in water. At the high water level, the boulders are not visible, but are still present. A lowering of the water (stock level) reveals the problem and forces managers and employees to eliminate the problems. The emphasis is placed on:

- identification of problems;
- problem solving;
- improved utilization of people, space, capital and inventory.

This is done by the adoption of lean production techniques of:

- just-in-time production and stock-holding;
- time-based competition;
- cell working;
- flexibility in working methods;
- teamworking (see Chapter 43);
- continuous improvement, or Kaizen;
- quality circles;
- Total Quality Management (TQM) (see Chapter 37).

Before investigating each in detail, consider Table 39.1, which illustrates the differences between traditional and lean production methods.

Just-in-time (JIT)

JIT involves both production and stock control systems in which work flows are scheduled so precisely that only the smallest amount of work-in-progress is held. This is made possible by

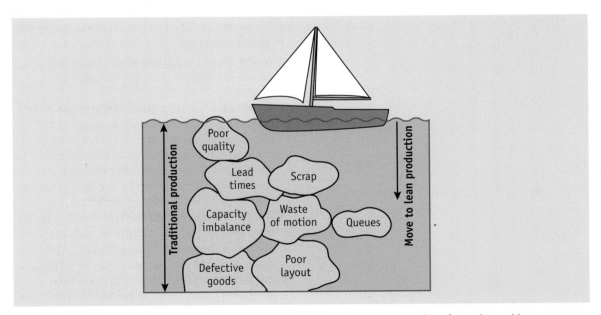

Figure 39.1 Boulders in the river – lower the water level to expose and confront the problems

Table 39.1 Comparison of traditional and lean production methods

Traditional production	Lean production
• Detailed division of labour	• Team production
• High barriers to mobility between jobs	• Flexible workforce
• Just-in-case stockholding – to avoid stockout	• Just-in-time stockholding
• Large batch size	• Small batch size
• Distant relations with subcontractors and suppliers	• Partnership with subcontractors and suppliers
• A few, large deliveries	• Many, small deliveries
• Inspect out defective goods	• Build in quality
• Large, frequent improvement	• Continuous improvement
• Standardized product	• Growing product variety
• Buffers everywhere	• No safety net
• Downward communication	• Multiple communications
• Limited consultation	• Extensive consultation

inputs from the previous stage in the production process arriving 'just in time'. These inputs from the previous stage might be from external sources or internal ones (in which case, the receiving department should be seen as the internal customer of the supplying department).

JIT production reverses conventional approaches to manufacturing.

- 'First sell, then make it'. Production only takes place when there is actual customer demand for the output.
- Production is planned backwards instead of forwards.
- It is a pull rather than push system of production. Each process 'pulls' more parts from the preceding process(es) using a card or signal (known in Japanese as *Kanban*). The *Kanban* (card) is the means by which a customer (or succeeding operation) instructs a supplier (or preceding operation) to send more parts. Using two bins for a component, the empty one is wheeled out to the component production section with its *Kanban* order card. This triggers production of the component that must be completed just-in-time before the other bin runs out.

The requirements of successful JIT production are:

- employee flexibility;
- employee commitment;
- total quality or zero defects;

- preventive maintenance;
- cell production;
- continuous improvement to eliminate bottlenecks.

JIT purchasing from external suppliers involves the use of small, frequent deliveries rather than bulk contracts. This requires the close integration of suppliers with the company's manufacturing process. Features of the two purchasing systems are shown in Table 39.2.

The advantages claimed for JIT production and stockholdings are:

- the right quantities are purchased or produced at the right time;
- higher quality;
- improved customer service;
- minimization of inventory, work-in-progress and waste;
- reduced space requirements;
- reduction in manufacturing lead time;
- increased equipment utilization;
- simpler planning systems;
- increased workforce participation;
- continuous emphasis on improvement and problem solving;
- reduced costs.

There are also disadvantages or at least problems that have to be overcome for successful JIT working:

- it requires a high degree of delegation;

Table 39.2 Conventional and JIT purchasing

Conventional purchasing	Just-in-time purchasing
● Large delivery lot sizes. Deliveries are infrequent	● Small lot sizes, based on the immediate needs for production usage ● Frequent delivery of stock
● Deliveries are timed according to the buyer's request date	● Deliveries are synchronized with the buyer's production schedule
● Multiple sourcing is used to maintain adequate quality and competitive pricing	● Few suppliers are used for each part
● Inventories are maintained for parts	● Little inventory is required because deliveries are expected to be made frequently, on time, and with high-quality parts
● Purchasing agreements are set for the short term. Pressure suppliers by threatening to withdraw business	● Purchasing agreements are long-term. Pressure suppliers, ensuring they feel obligated to perform
● Products are designed with few constraints on the number of different purchased components used	● Products are designed with great effort to use only currently purchased parts
● Minimal exchange of information between supplier and buyer	● There is extensive exchange of information with regard to production schedules, production processes, etc.,
● Prices are established by suppliers	● Buyer works with supplier to reduce supplier's costs and, thereby, reduce prices
● Geographic proximity of the supplier is not important for the supplier selection decision	● Geographic proximity is considered very important

(Adapted from 'A Survey of JIT Purchasing Practices in the US', *Production and Inventory Management,* James R. Freeland 1991)

● it requires a change in the philosophy and culture of the business;
● the advantages of bulk buying are lost;
● the business is vulnerable to a break in supply, including a breakdown in machinery;
● it does not work in the case of irregularly used parts or specially ordered materials;
● JIT purchasing requires reliable and flexible suppliers;
● it requires an atmosphere of close cooperation and mutual trust between the workforce and managers.

Cell working

A cell layout groups together a number of dissimilar machines or processes according to the design of the product being made or the operations required for its production. In this respect it has similarities with product layout but:

● the operation sequence can be varied;
● the flow direction can be varied;
● the workers in the cell are multiskilled;
● the workers are in a team (cell) of 6–15;
● each group enjoys considerable autonomy.

In these respects, cell working combines some of the features of product layout with those of fixed position layout.

Cell working makes for simpler production control and is well suited to the demands of just-in-time production using the *Kanban* system. Benefits claimed for this method of working are:

● reduced material handling;

- reduced set-up time;
- reduces work-in-progress;
- reduced tooling costs;
- great flexibility;
- benefits of teamworking;
- it facilitates quality circles.

Kaizen (continuous improvement)

Kaizen is the Japanese name for a continuous improvement and, as such, is a vital part of Total Quality Management. *Kaizen* is customer-focused in that quality begins with customers – as customer views are continually changing and standards rising, so continuous improvement is required. Significantly, unlike improvements in the Western model, *Kaizen* involves small, gradual, but continuous, changes (see Figure 39.2). The gains are small in the short run, but are substantial over the longer period. Moreover, the emphasis is not just on consolidating but on building on them.

The structured approach to *Kaizen*, which starts with defining the area for improvement, is followed by analysis of the causes of problems. The question 'Why?' is asked at least five times (the five whys), in order to get to the root causes of a problem. This avoids solving the problem at a superficial level. The 5M checklist is designed to ensure that five essential factors are taken into consideration in process improvement or problem solving. The five factors are manpower, machinery,

materials, methods and money. As we will see in the next section, these factors feature in the **fishbone diagrams**, which are also known as **cause and effect diagrams**.

In addition to the 5 Ms, *Kaizen* requires order and discipline in the workplace. The 5Ss refer to the following, all of which begin with the letter S in Japanese:

- cleanliness, with employees being responsible for keeping their own equipment clean;
- orderliness, in terms of putting equipment away in the right place;
- tidiness, with everything in its right place;
- organization of the workplace;
- discipline, by doing this every day and not just periodically.

As with other aspects of lean production, *Kaizen* has implications for the management of human resources. It requires the involvement of everyone, not just a select few champions of change. Employees need to be motivated and empowered to solve problems. It requires a team approach to work and, unlike in the Western model, it does not require a large investment, but it does require a continuing effort to maintain it. Table 39.3 summarizes the main features of *Kaizen* when compared with a western approach to innovation.

Fishbone diagrams

Figure 39.3 shows a fishbone diagram (also known as a cause and effect diagram or an Ishikawa diagram). The fishbone diagram is used in quality circles (see below) as a focal point for discussion. The problem is identified and stated where 'effect' appears on the right. Causes of the problem can be classified as one or other of the 5Ms: machinery, manpower (human resources), materials, methods, and money. Group discussion is used to generate possible causes under these five headings. Anything that may result in the effect being considered should be put down as a potential cause. Once potential causes have been identified, solutions can be suggested.

Fishbone diagrams are especially useful in:

- focusing on causes, not symptoms;

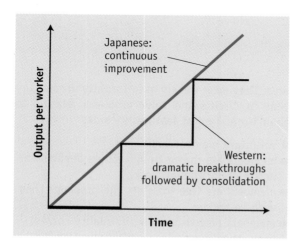

Figure 39.2 *Kaizen* v. innovation

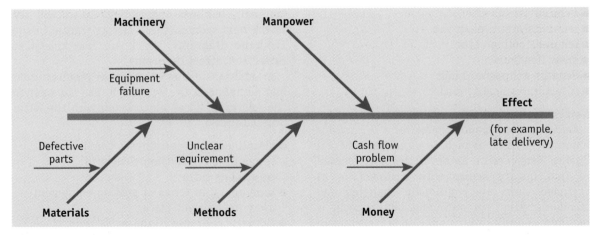

Figure 39.3 Fishbone, or cause and effect, diagram

Table 39.3 A comparison of *Kaizen* and Western approach to innovation

Features	Kaizen	Innovation
Effect	Long-term and long-lasting effect but undramatic	Short-term but dramatic effects
Pace	Small steps	Big steps
Timeframe	Continuous and incremental	Intermittent and non-incremental
Involvement	Everybody	Select a few 'champions'
Approach	Group efforts	Individual ideas and efforts
Mode	Maintenance and improvement	Scrap and rebuild
Practical requirements	Requires little investment, but great effort to maintain it	Requires large investment, but little effort to maintain it
Effort orientation	People	Technology

(Adapted from M. Imai, *Kaizen*, McGraw-Hill, 1980)

- capturing the collective knowledge and experience of a group;
- providing a picture of why an effect is happening;
- establishing a basis for further data gathering and action.

Quality circles (QC)

A quality circle is a voluntary group of between six and eight employees from the same work area. They meet weekly or fortnightly in company time to discuss and solve problems relating to their work. Typical features include:

- voluntary membership;
- members are drawn from a single department or are doing similar work;
- members are free to select the problems they wish to tackle;
- members receive training in quality control tools, meeting skills, teambuilding, project management and presentation techniques;

- meetings are short but frequent;
- a facilitator is available to assist the QC;
- solutions are evaluated in terms of cost-effectiveness;
- findings are presented to management;
- the QC will implement and monitor solutions that have been agreed.

To succeed, a QC requires:

- the commitment and support of top management;
- full consultation with staff;
- a participative approach by management and appropriate systems and style of managerial behaviour;
- delegation of decision making;
- trust and goodwill on all sides;
- an effective support structure of consultation and negotiation;
- support of trade unions and/or staff representatives;
- an effective training programme, including the development of quantitative skills;
- continuous monitoring and review of results.

If successful, the QC will produce benefits in terms of

- increased productivity;
- increased quality;
- improved motivation and morale;
- job enrichment;
- greater awareness of shop floor problems.

Time-based competition (TBC)

It is said that time is money, but, in fact, it is more than that. It is the manager's main resource and a competitive weapon in its own right. TBC is based on the proposition that the time it takes to get a product from conception to the customer and provide goods and services to market can be the key to competitive advantage.

The total time taken to get the product through the supply chain (through a chain of internal and external customers) is known as throughput time. Unfortunately, time will be wasted in the chain. TBC seeks to eliminate the waste involved in unproductive time, the origins of which can be found in:

- preparation
- waiting time
- unnecessary movement
- overproduction
- rejects
- set-up time
- process waste
- administration
- untidiness
- bottlenecks.

These 'problems' add to cost, but not to value. By eliminating unproductive time, it reduces costs and improves the firm's responsiveness to customers, thus increasing the firm's competitive advantage. The classic example of TBC was Honda's ability to produce new models of motorcycles at a rate that far exceed that of its main rival – Yamaha. We can also understand the concept in relation to 'made to order' spectacles. Traditional opticians provide spectacles within a week to two weeks, but we all know that the glasses were not being worked on continuously during the week – the order was waiting in a queue for most of that time. The new 'within one hour' opticians (such as Vision Express) operate by eliminating the unproductive time in the manufacture of spectacles.

In *Competing Against Time: How time based competition is reshaping global markets*, George Stalk and Thomas M. Hout proposed a number of rules of response.

- **the 0.05 to 5 rule**, which highlights the fact that, on average, the proportion of time that value is being added to a product or service is between 0.05 and 5 per cent of the total time spent in the system.
- **The 3/3 rule**, which states that the 95 to 99.95 per cent of time that a product or service is idle is split into three components, each accounting for a third of the time. The three components are completion of the batch that the product or service is part of; physical and intellectual rework; and management decision time. As a result,

working harder has little impact, but working smarter and on the right activities can have a dramatic impact on time and cost.

- **The ¼ to 2 to 20 rule**, which states that, for every quartering of the time required to produce a product or service, productivity will double, and there could be a 20 per cent cost reduction.
- **The 3 × 2 rule**, which expresses the advantage of time-based competitors: a growth rate of three times the average with twice the profit margin.

It is also argued that TBC using lead production principles enables firms to increase variety and quality at lower costs. This reverses traditional thinking, which saw product variety and high quality as factors that would *raise* costs. To achieve variety, it is necessary to use just-in-time methods, cell working and flexible capital.

To sum up, the benefits of TBC are that:

- by speeding new product development, firms can achieve a competitive advantage;
- speeding up the production process leads to savings in stocks and working capital;
- firms can behave opportunistically as new product ideas emerge and as new market segments appear;
- it can increase customer satisfaction;
- it leads to greater flexibility.

Key concepts

Cell production production in self-contained units in which machines and workers are grouped together in cells.

Just-in-time a manufacturing system designed to minimize holdings of stock.

Kaizen Japanese for continuous improvement.

Kanban system of cards that pull component supplies through a factory.

Lean production collective term for Japanese waste-saving measures.

Quality circles discussion groups that meet regularly to discuss issues relating to production and quality.

Time-based competition strategies to eliminate unproductive time in operations.

Essay questions

1 Waste is defined as an activity that does not add value. Discuss the implications of this statement.

2 (a) What do you understand by lean production?
(b) Evaluate two aspects of lean production.

3 (a) Explain the following Japanese terms:
(i) *Kaizen*;
(ii) *Kanban*.
(b) Analyse their importance within the lean production philosophy.

4 Discuss the benefits of, and the preconditions for, successful quality circles.

5 Time is an important weapon in securing competitive advantage. Analyse the principles and benefits of time-based competition.

Critical path analysis

Critical path analysis is a technique mainly associated with the planning of large-scale projects, although the principles are equally applicable to any project made up of discrete parts. By analysing activities and identifying the critical path, it is possible to make more rational decisions on the allocation of resources.

Chapter objectives

1 To explain the purpose of critical path analysis.

2 To explain the principles involved in constructing network diagrams.

3 To assist the reader in developing skills in relation to critical path analysis.

4 To analyse various types of float.

5 To explain the role of critical path analysis in resource allocation.

Network analysis

Network analysis is a generic term that covers a group of related analytical techniques, one of which is known as critical path analysis (CPA). These techniques are used to aid the planning and control of complicated projects, such as the construction of a building or bridge, installation of a computer system, launching of a new product or developing a new missile system.

The common feature of such projects is that they are made up of a number of smaller tasks, which have to be carried out in sequence. A network diagram is constructed to show sequential relationships between the various components. This enables planners to calculate the minimum time needed to complete the project and identify critical activities where delay would prevent completion of the overall project within the minimum time specified. By identifying these critical activities, managers can pursue a more rational approach to the planning of resources.

The aims of network analysis are to:

● facilitate the planning and coordination of large projects;
● identify critical activities that determine the total duration of the project;
● identify activities that cause, or are likely to cause, bottlenecks and delays;
● determine when resources and components are needed;
● plan the use of resources;

- reduce and eliminate idleness;
- identify important linkages and sequential, dependent relationships;
- reduce costs by reducing waste;
- facilitate the taking of corrective action when performance falls below that specified in the plan.

A simple network

Before looking at the 'rules' of network analysis, let us consider a simple example.

Activity	Order
A	–
B	has to follow A
C	has to follow A
D	has to follow B
E	has to follow C
F	has to follow E
G	has to follow D and F.

If we plot this on a network diagram, the result is as shown in Figure 40.1. The lines represent activities; the circles (known as **nodes**) show where one activity ends and another begins. Notice that B and C follow A, but B and C can occur concurrently. D and E are not dependent on each other, but G cannot start until both D and F have been completed. To complete the overall project, all seven activities have to be completed.

If we know the time taken to complete each activity, it is possible to calculate the overall time needed for the project and to identify the critical activities.

Activity	Time (hours)
A	1
B	2
C	1
D	3
E	1
F	1
G	2

The minimum time needed to complete the project is eight hours (1 + 2 + 3 + 2). Assuming resources are available, activities C, E and F can be completed in three hours concurrently with activities B and D, which together take up five hours. The latter two activities, together with A and G, are the critical ones – if any of these activities are delayed, then the project will not be completed in eight hours. C, E and F are non-critical activities in that there is scope for delay (known as float) without delaying overall completion. By identifying the critical path, management can ensure that sufficient resources are devoted to these activities.

We are now in a position to list a set of rules for drawing a network.

Rules of drawing networks

As networks are concerned with logical sequences of activities, it is necessary to construct them according to a set of rules and conventions.

- There is one entry and one exit point in a network. In other words, there is a starting and a finishing point.

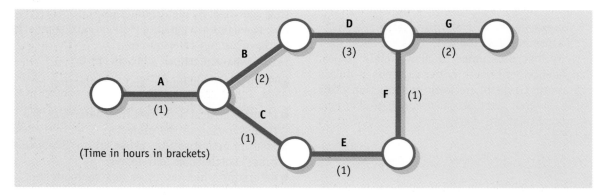

Figure 40.1 A simple network

- Networks are drawn from left to right, but not necessarily to scale. Thus, the duration of an activity is not reflected in the length of the line.
- **Activities** (parts of a project that consume time and resources) are shown by a straight line.
- **Events** (transitions between activities) are shown by **circles.**
- Events are identified by letters or numbers from left to right.
- Every activity must have a preceding event (known as a **tail**) and a succeeding one (known as a **head**).
- No activity can start until its tail event has been reached.
- An event is not complete until all activities leading to it have been completed.
- All activities must be tied into the network – either they contribute to the progression or they must be discarded as a 'dangler'.
- There must be no loops – the essence of a network is a progression of activities, moving onwards in time.

The main relationships between activities are depicted in Figure 40.2, where there are two activities coming out of a tail, they can occur concurrently, but neither can start until the preceding one has been completed. Where two activities go into a head event, the succeeding one cannot start until both the preceding activities have been completed.

Dummy activities

Included in some network diagrams there will be a dotted line. This is known as a **dummy activity**, defined as one that consumes neither time nor resources. In other words, it is an imaginary activity, but is designed to show a clear, logical dependency between activities so as not to violate yet another rule of network construction. This is the rule that activities must not share the same tail event and the head event with any other activity.

Non-critical activities and float

In Figure 40.3 the time duration (in days) has been inserted on a simple network diagram. What we are looking for is the sequence of activities that determines the minimum time required to complete the project – that is, to reach node 11. The critical path is highlighted as activities A, G, H, K, M and N. To move from node 2 to node 10 takes $1 + 4 + 7 + 1 = 13$ days on the lower sequence of activities. This is considerably longer than the $1 + 1 + 1 + 2 = 5$ days on the upper sequence of activities. The path incorporating activity K is also longer than the detour via J and L as the latter only takes two days compared with seven for activity K. The critical path is clearly A, G, H, K, M and N. The project cannot be completed in under 16 days. If any of the critical activities is delayed in starting or takes longer than expected, the project will not be completed in this time.

Delays can occur with non-critical activities without delaying the overall completion time. For instance, K takes seven days, whereas J and L combined take only two days. Consequently, it is possible to delay either J or K by up to five days (combined) and still have enough time to complete activity L at the same time as K is completed. The possibility of putting back the starting time without delaying overall completion is known as **float**. There is no float with critical activities, but there is float with non-critical ones. Before exploring this further, it is necessary to define a number of concepts. We will refer to the more detailed node diagram shown in Figure 40.4.

Figure 40.4 shows the same activity B as in Figure 40.3. The numbers on the left-hand side of the two nodes are the node numbers from the previous figure, but additional information is shown to the right-hand side. In the upper quadrant, we have the earliest starting time (EST) of the activity following the node. Activity B cannot start until after the first day for the simple reason that it follows activity A, which takes one day to complete. Activity C has an EST of two days, and it cannot start until after two days as activities A and B have to be completed. In the lower quadrant, we have the latest finishing time (LFT) of the preceding activity. This is defined as the latest time an activity can finish without delaying the completion of the project as a whole. The activity preceding B has to be completed in one day as it is on the critical path. Hence, the

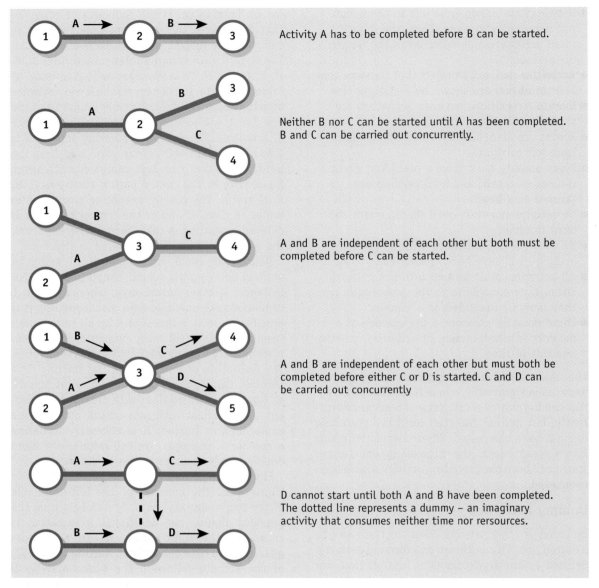

Activity A has to be completed before B can be started.

Neither B nor C can be started until A has been completed. B and C can be carried out concurrently.

A and B are independent of each other but both must be completed before C can be started.

A and B are independent of each other but must both be completed before either C or D is started. C and D can be carried out concurrently

D cannot start until both A and B have been completed. The dotted line represents a dummy – an imaginary activity that consumes neither time nor rersources.

Figure 40.2 Basic features of a network

LFT at node 2 is one. The LFT at node 3 is nine. To understand this, refer back to the original diagram and explanation. The critical path from node 2 to node 10 takes 13 days. The non-critical path takes five days, although one was used up on activity B. Consequently, provided activity B is completed by the ninth day; there is sufficient time to complete the non-critical upper sequence of activities.

You calculate the EST by cumulatively adding up activity times, starting from the left of the diagram and moving to the right. Always remember that where two activities enter the node, then the EST will be the later of the two times

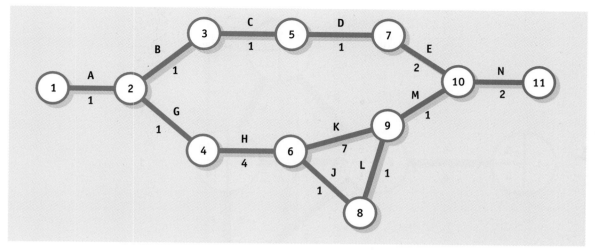

Figure 40.3 Identifying the critical path

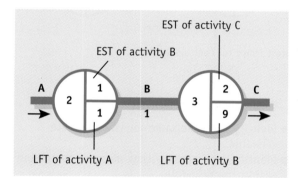

Figure 40.4 Earliest starting (EST) and latest finishing times (LFT)

as the succeeding activity cannot start until both preceding activities have been completed.

In addition, we can identify the earliest finishing time – that is, the earliest time an activity can be completed. This will be equal to the cumulative total of duration time for all activities to date.

You calculate the LST by moving from the right (the final completion time) and then subtracting the duration of preceding activities. The latest starting time is the latest time an activity can be started without delaying the project as a whole. The earliest/latest times are illustrated in Figure 40.5.

With starting and finishing times calculated at

each node, we can now identify and calculate three types of float.

Three types of float

We have seen that float is the amount of slack that exists for non-critical activities. It is the time an activity can be delayed and/or allowed to overrun without delaying the completion time for the project as a whole. In fact, there are three types of float:

- **total float** is the amount of time a path of activities can be delayed without affecting overall project completion;
- **free float** is the amount of time an activity can be delayed without affecting the commencement of the next activity at its EST;
- **independent float** is defined as the amount of time an activity can be delayed when all preceding activities have been completed as late as possible and all succeeding activities are started as early as possible (it is called independent float because it does not affect the float on preceding or subsequent activities).

The formulae for calculating each of the floats are:

Total float = Latest finishing time for the activity (LFT) – Earliest starting time (EST) for the activity – Duration of the activity

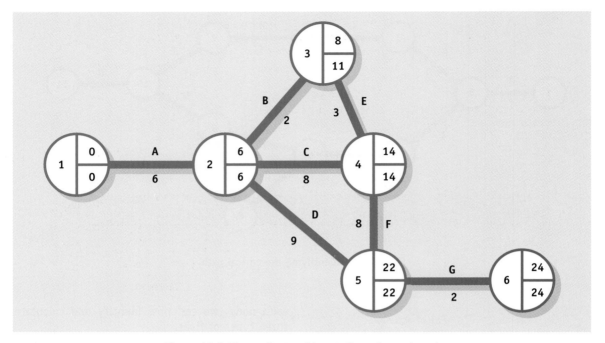

Figure 40.5 The earliest and latest times for each node

Free float = EFT – EST – Duration.

Independent float = EFT – LST – Duration.

To understand the method, study Figure 40.6 and try the exercises at the end of this chapter.

Resource constraints and Gantt charts

So far, we have assured that the organization has sufficient resources to commence each activity whenever it wants. However, suppose the organization was constrained by limited resources of labour and equipment, the network can be used to plan the use of resources. Obviously, resources must be diverted to critical activities if the project is not to be delayed. This can be shown in a **Gantt chart** (see Figure 40.7). This kind of chart provides a simple visual representation of a schedule. It is an especially useful format for managers to use because it makes it easy to communicate stages and timeframes to other members of the team.

To produce a Gantt chart:

● identify the timeframe for the complete schedule;
● identify each activity that must be completed within the schedule;
● for each activity estimate:
   – the time it will take;
   – when it must be completed;
   – when it can/should commence.

Each activity is shown by a horizontal bar on the chart. Notice that critical and non-activities are distinguished and float periods for non-critical activities are identified. The non-critical activity can be shifted to any time shown in the bar.

Applications of network analysis

Network analysis can be used when planning and controlling large projects in fields such as construction, research and development and computerization. By planning in this way:

● completion times can be calculated;

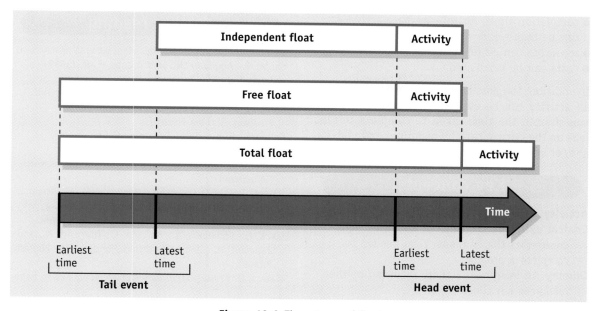

Figure 40.6 Three types of float

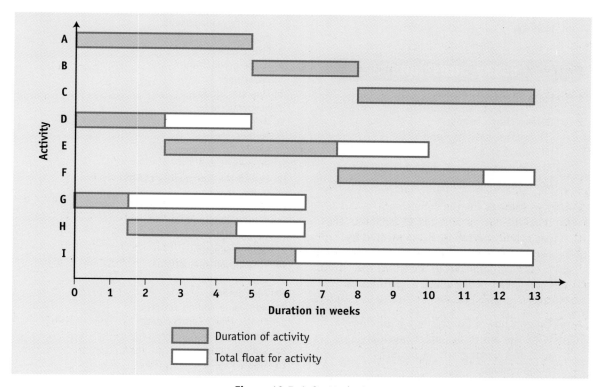

Figure 40.7 A Gantt chart

- completion times for intermediate activities can be monitored;
- resources can be prioritized;
- costs can be calculated.

In addition, the possibilities and costs of crashing an activity can be evaluated. **Crashing** is when you shorten the time taken to complete certain jobs on the critical path by assigning extra labour and/or equipment.

Key concepts

Activity A task that consumes time and resources.

Critical path The sequence of activities that determines the minimum time needed to complete a project.

Dummy An imaginary activity requiring neither resources nor time.

Float The amount of time an activity can be delayed without delaying the overall project.

Network diagram An illustration of the sequence of activities.

Node Representation of the start and finish of an activity.

Essay questions

1 Evaluate the role of critical path analysis.

2 (a) Define these terms:
   (i) critical activity; and
   (ii) total float.
   (b) Analyse ways in which identification of float can play a part in project planning.

3 Analyse reasons for the following.
   (a) It might not be possible to complete the project in the timescale suggested by network analysis.
   (b) A crash programme to speed up the completion of a project might add to costs.

4 (a) Explain how a Gantt chart is produced.
   (b) With the aid of examples, evaluate the role of a Gantt chart in project management.

Further reading

Barnett, H. (1996) *Operations Management,* Macmillan.

Chase, R., Aquilano, N., and Jacobs, F. R. (1998) *Production and Operations Management: Manufacturing and services,* 8th ed. Macgraw-Hill.

Greasley, A. (1999) *Operations Management in Business,* Stanley Thornes.

Galloway, R. L. (1993) *Principles of Operations Management,* Routledge.

Johnson, B. (1998) *Managing Operations,* Butterworth Heinemann.

Naylor, J. (1996) *Operations Management,* FT Pitman.

Slack, N. (ed.) (1997) *The Blackwell Encyclopedic Dictionary of Operations Management,* Blackwell.

Slack, N., Chambers, S., Harland, C., Harrison, A., and Johnson, R. (1998) *Operations Management,* 2nd ed. Pitman.

Waters, D. (1999) *Operations Management,* Kogan Page.

Short answer questions

Using an example from a specific business, explain the following terms.

1 Capacity management.
2 Productivity.
3 Effectiveness.
4 Batch production.
5 Downtime.
6 Flow production.
7 Economic order size.
8 Work-in-progress.
9 Method study.
10 Scientific management.
11 Producer's risk.
12 End-of-the-line quality control.
13 Buffer stock.
14 Lead time.
15 Control chart.
16 Layout by product.
17 Lean production.
18 Time-based competition.
19 Quality circle.
20 Zero defects.
21 Non-value-adding activities.
22 Continuous improvement.
23 *Kanban.*
24 Critical path.
25 Float.
26 Gantt chart.

27 Resource constraint.
28 Multisourcing.
29 Just-in-time.
30 Capacity utilization.

Exercises

1 Draw a network diagram to illustrate the sequence of activities below.

Activity	Preceding activity
A	–
B	A
C	A
D	C
E	B
F	E
G	D, F

2 Draw a network diagram to illustrate the sequence of activities below.

Activity	Preceding activity
A	–
B	–
C	A
D	A
E	A
F	C
G	C
H	C
I	B, D
J	F, I
K	E, H, G, J
L	I
M	K, L

Note: There is one dummy in this network.

3 The completion of a project involves a number of different operations, some of which occur concurrently and others sequentially. The various operations, their sequence, time duration and labour requirements are set out below.

Operation	Sequence of activities – the activity is only possible after:	Time (days)	Labour required
A		5	10
B	A has been completed	1	5
C	A has been completed	1	5
D	C has been completed	2	5
E	Both B and D have been completed	20	12
F	E has been completed	1	5
G	C has been completed	3	3
H	F has been completed	6	2
I	A has been completed	5	3
J	G, H and I have been completed	6	10

(a) Draw a network diagram to illustrate the above sequence of events.

(b) Identify the critical path. Assuming the absence of labour constraints, calculate the minimum time needed to complete the project.

(c) A hold-up in supplies results in a delay in the commencement of:
    (i)   activity B by 4 days;
    (ii) activity I by 5 days;
    (iii) activity G by 10 days.
    In each case state, with reasons, whether or not the delay leads to a failure to complete the project in the minimum time.

(d) Ignore the delays in (c) above. Unfortunately only 12 workers are available at any one time. Is it possible to complete the project in the minimum time period? Explain your answer, making clear the assumptions you have made.

4 The network diagram below shows the relationship between activities necessary to complete a project.

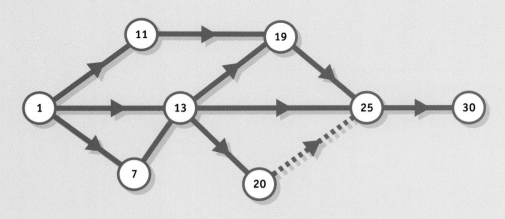

The estimated times (in days) and the estimated labour requirements for the performance of each activity are:

Activity	Time (days)	Labour required (no. of workers)
1–7	4	3
1–11	5	7
1–13	8	4
7–13	12	2
11–19	10	2
13–19	7	6
13–20	10	3
19–25	15	3
20–25	0	0
25–30	19	5

(a) Identify the critical path and calculate the earliest finishing time.
(b) Calculate
    (i)   the EST;
    (ii) the LFT;
    (iii) the float for each activity.
(c) If only 12 workers are available at any one time, is it possible to complete the project in the time identified in (a)?

5 Fill in the data on each of the nodes below and calculate the float for each activity.

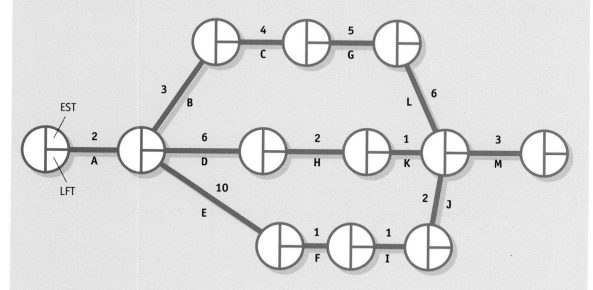

The numbers are the time required in days.

6 The pattern of sales and production during a calendar year is shown in the graph below.

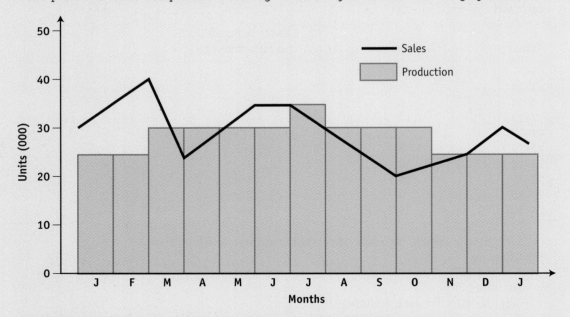

(a) Suggest reasons for the changing level of sales during the year.

(b) Suggest reasons for the changing level of production.

(c) Assuming that 30,000 units represents the normal monthly output, offer explanations for the higher output during June. What are the implications for the firm's costs?

(d) Suggest problems that arise within the production department from the changing level of sales.

7 The Cosy Slipper Company concentrates on producing a range of slippers. Fifty per cent of its output is sold under its own 'Cosy' brand. The remainder is produced under contract for a large retail chain for sale under the store's own brand.

The graph depicts the volume of sales and output over the year.

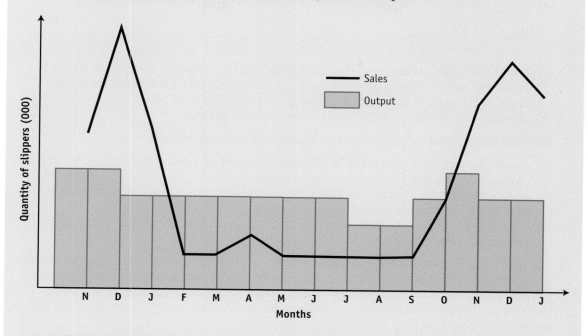

(a) Why do retail chains market 'own brand' goods? What are the advantages and disadvantages to manufacturers of producing retailers' own brands under contract?
(b) Suggest reasons for fluctuations in the volume of:
   (i) sales; and
   (ii) output.
(c) Analyse the production, personnel and financial problems associated with such fluctuations.
(d) Suggest marketing techniques to reduce the seasonal fluctuations in sales.
(e) Analyse the implications for the production department of diversifying into new products, such as trainers.

8 A chemical manufacturer uses two essential substances in its processes. Both substances are expensive to store, but the firm cannot afford to run of supplies.

	Substance X	Substance Y
Annual use (N)	1000 litres	500 litres
Annual holding cost (C)	£2 per litre	£4 per litre
Buying cost (B)	£10 per order	£20 per order
Delivery time (D)	2 weeks	1 week

(a) Explain the terms:
  (i) economic order quantity;
  (ii) buffer stock;
  (iii) reorder level.
(b) For each substance, calculate the economic order quantity using the formula:

$$EOQ = \sqrt{\frac{2\,BN}{C}}$$

(c) The firm will reorder supplies when stocks fall to a level equal to an amount required during the deliver or lead time. For each substance, calculate the level of stocks that result in the placing of a new order (assume a working year of 50 weeks).
(d) Calculate the number of deliveries of each substance per year.

9 Calculate the economic order quantity in each of the following situations.

(a) Annual demand for a product is 80,000 units, the cost of holding each unit is £0.50 per year and it costs £20 to have an order delivered.
(b) Annual demand for a product is 150,000 units, the cost of holding each unit is £3 per year and it costs £50 to have an order delivered.
(c) Annual demand for a product is 250,000 units, the cost of holding each unit is £10 per year and it costs £70 to have an order delivered.

10 The Davidson Pet Food Company produces a range of pet foods including 'Georgie Cat' biscuits and meat products. It sells the latter in sealed plastic containers purchased from Plastic Containers Ltd. The Davidson Company carries a stock of plastic containers, which are essential for the continued production of 'Georgie Cat'. Diagram A depicts the stocks of plastic containers during 1994.

In 1994, Davidson launched a new product in the 'Georgie Cat' family brand. Although it had undertaken extensive market research, it soon discovered that customer orders were substantially greater than expected. Diagram B depicts actual and projected orders for the new product. Unfortunately, Davidson has little spare capacity and, consequently, cannot step up output of the new product without switching resources from established products.

Diagram A

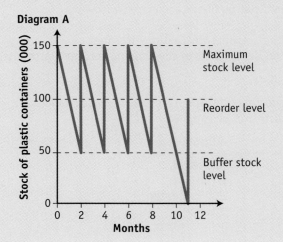

Diagram B

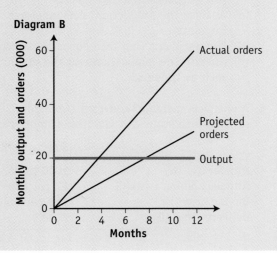

(a) Calculate the lead time for plastic containers.

(b) How many containers are delivered each time?

(c) Why do you think the buffer stock level was set at 50,000 and the maximum stock level at 150,000?

(d) Suggest explanations for what happened in the eleventh month.

(e) Why does the Davidson Pet Food Company buy in its plastic containers?

(f) What is meant by a family brand? Give real-life examples.

(g) At the end of which month did the shortage of the new product become real?

(h) What factors should Davidson consider when switching resources from one product to another?

(i) One solution for Davidson is to subcontract production of some of its products to the rival Jones and Green Pet Food Company. Under what circumstances might Jones and Green be willing to produce 'Georgie Cat'?

(j) Why did Davidson's market research prove to be inaccurate?

Part
6

People in organizations

An introduction to human resource management

In the past, the 'people' part of an A level course went under the title people in organizations. Now, the modern term 'human resource management' – HRM for short – is used. This is the term that has virtually replaced 'personnel management', but a question to consider is whether or not it is merely a new name for an old concept.

Chapter objectives

1 To define the term human resource management.

2 To contrast HRM with personnel management.

3 To identify the major areas of HRM.

What is HRM?

Some people object to the term human resource management. This tends to be for one of two reasons.

● They object to what they see as the dehumanizing of employees, seeing them as 'human resources', but the fact is that employees are human resources that are combined with the organization's other resources. HRM does not rule out fair treatment of employees, who are the organization's most important resource.

● They regard HRM as personnel management under a new name. This criticism is also unjustified. First, HRM is based on a philosophy that is different from personnel management. Second, HRM is not the preserve of the personnel department. Marketing managers, production managers and production supervisors are not personnel managers, but they do manage human resources and are, therefore, 'human resource managers'.

We will explore the differences between personnel management and HRM in the next section, but, first, we need a definition for HRM. M. Armstrong (in *A Handbook of Human Resource Management Practice*, Kogan Page, 1999) defines HRM as 'a strategic, coherent and comprehensive approach to the management and development of the organization's human resources in which every aspect of that approach is wholly integrated with the overall management of the organization. HRM is essentially an ideology.' Storey defines HRM as 'a distinctive approach to employment management that seeks to achieve competitive advantage through the strategic development of a highly committed and capable workforce, using an integrated array of cultural, structural and personnel techniques.' In essence, HRM has moved away from the 'hiring and firing and welfare approach' of personnel management and towards a focus on the use of human resources to achieve strategic objectives. It is the emphasis on strategic issues and integration with other functions that singles HRM out from personnel management.

HRM is based on four principles.

- Employees must be seen as valued assets in which to invest. Sustainable competitive advantage is achieved by people – it is 'human capability and commitment which, in the final analysis, distinguishes successful organizations from the rest' (Storey).
- HRM is of strategic importance and, therefore, needs to be considered by top management in the formulation of the corporate plan.
- Commitment not compliance. 'The key levers (the deployment of human resources; evaluation of performance and the rewarding of it) are to be used to seek not merely compliance but commitment.' In other words, employees should not be forced to work grudgingly, but by obtaining their wholehearted commitment.
- Strategic implications of HRM. HRM is, therefore, seen to have long-term implications and be integral to the core performance of the business. It must be the intimate concern of line managers. Line managers have the responsibility of managing their staff. The role of the personnel function is to enable line managers to fulfil their HRM responsibilities effectively.

HRM and traditional personnel management are contrasted in Table 41.1

Hard and soft HRM

Two distinct approaches to HRM can be discerned. The **soft approach** is closer to the traditional personnel approach. Soft HRM is an integrated strategic function that is concerned with nurturing people because they are human beings whose feelings should be considered and, moreover, developing this valuable resource is the best way to achieve results.

The **hard approach** to HRM is also based on the belief that human resources are the key assets, but the emphasis is placed on:

- getting the most out of people;
- using them in the most productive way.

Table 41.1 How personnel management and HRM differ

Personnel management	HRM
• Advisory and administrative	• Strategic
• Not central to the organisation	• Seen as essential
• Mediating role between management and workforce	• A central management role
• The preserve of specialists	• All managers and supervisors are human resource managers
• Emphasis on written rules and procedures	• Stress on flexibility
• Collective bargaining and negotiations	• Consultation and participation
• Management hierarchy	• Team-based structure
• Collective rewards and benefits	• Individual rewards and benefits
• Tightly defined jobs	• Loosely defined jobs
• Employees must be monitored	• Employees are to be nurtured
• Controlled access to training	• The learning organization

Whether soft or hard, the aims of HRM are to:

- enable management to achieve organizational objectives via its workforce;
- enable people to utilize their full potential;
- foster commitment;
- integrate human resources policies with business plans;
- establish an environment to unleash the creativity and energy of the workforce;
- encourage flexibility in the interests of an organization that is able to adapt to the environment and achieve excellence.

HRM activities

Subsequent chapters deal with HRM issues in greater detail, but the following list identifies the main areas of management activity associated with the HRM philosphy:

- **organization design and effectiveness** especially in relation to teamwork, communications, customer service and change management;
- **resources** providing human resources required by means of recruitment, retention and training programmes;
- **performance management** improving performance by means of appraisal;
- **reward management** for example, linking pay to performance;
- **motivation** redesigning jobs and devising rewards to motivate employees;
- **commitment** the integration of the needs of the individual with those of the organization;
- **employee relations** policies and procedures to encourage cooperation to the mutual benefit of all;
- **flexibility** by means of multiskilling, redesigning jobs and new patterns of work;

- **quality** as a way of life;
- **culture management** influencing behaviour and thereby attitudes by means of resourcing, performance management and reward strategies.

Key concepts

Competition advantage Aspects of the organization that give it an 'edge' or advantage over its rivals.

Human resource management A strategic, coherent and comprehensive approach to the management and development of the organization's human resources.

Personnel management Management or administration of the recruitment, welfare and training of employees in an organization.

Essay questions

1 (a) Explain the role of a personnel manager in a large company.
  (b) Analyse the ways in which personnel work interrelates with other functional areas of management.

2 Is human resource management merely a new name for personnel management? Justify your answer.

3 Analyse the differences between hard and soft HRM.

4 HRM places personnel work at the centre of strategic management. Discuss.

5 Employees are the firm's most important resource in modern business. Discuss.

Leadership and motivation

Getting high-level performance out of the human resource is crucial in the achievement of organizational goals. This chapter looks at theoretical and practical issues relating to motivation and leadership.

Chapter objectives

1 To introduce the reader to major issues relevant to the study of people in organizations.

2 To outline the major schools of thought on management.

3 To review the development of theories relating to leadership.

4 To review the development of theories relating to motivation.

5 To analyse management strategies to motivate the workforce.

Why are leadership and motivation so important?

Management is concerned with the effective and efficient deployment of resources. Human resources are clearly the most important resource available to business organizations. However, human resources are different from all others – they have feelings and do not respond in a mechanistic and entirely predictable way. These resources have not so much to be managed or directed, but led. Hence, the role of a manager is to be a leader and achieve organizational objectives by developing a partnership with people.

Motivation is defined as an influence that causes people (in this case employees) to want to behave in a certain way. Motivation combined with ability results in performance. The motivated worker is:

● keen to be at work;
● takes pride in their work;
● does not display negative attitudes towards the organization;
● displays a high level of commitment and gets satisfaction out of work.

The benefits to the organization can be seen in:

● higher productivity levels:
● lower labour turnover;
● lower absenteeism,
● improved quality with less waste,
● greater willingness to accept rather than resist change,

- greater willingness to contribute ideas and take on responsibility.

A major factor in employee motivation is how the individual is managed or led. It is to this that we first turn.

Leadership

Leadership is the art or process of influencing people so that they perform assigned tasks willingly and in an efficient and effective manner. Leadership is, therefore, crucial in motivating and inspiring the workforce, so it is not surprising that writers on management have addressed the following questions.

- What is the essence of leadership?
- What makes for an effective leader?

It is useful to distinguish between managers and leaders. **Managers** have legitimate or positional power as a result of an appointment to a particular position. **Leaders** may be appointed or 'emerge'. The source of their ability to influence others comes from their expertise or from their personality. Ideally, those appointed to the position of manager should have leadership qualities. However, it is not uncommon for those appointed to be bereft of leadership qualities. This distinction between managing and leading is shown in Table 42.1.

Traits and skills

Early studies of leadership attempted to identify traits common to leaders. Some studies concentrated on physical traits (such as energy, appearance) while others concentrated on intelligence or personality (such as aggressiveness, enthusiasm, self-confidence) or social characteristics (such as interpersonal skills).

Gary Yuki (*Leadership in Organizations,* Prentice Hall, 1997) lists the following traits as being the characteristics most successful leaders have:

- adaptable to situations;
- alert to the social environment;
- ambitious and achievement-oriented;
- assertive;
- cooperative;
- decisive;
- dependable;
- dominant, (having a desire to influence others);
- energetic;
- persistent;

Table 42.1 Managers v. leaders	
Managers	**Leaders**
- Functionaries	- Innovators
- Protect their operations	- Advance their operations
- Accept responsibility	- Seek responsibility
- Control employees	- Trust employees
- Competent	- Creative
- Specialist	- Flexible
- Minimize risk	- Take calculated risks
- Accept speaking opportunities	- Generate speaking opportunities
- Set reasonable goals	- Set challenging goals
- Pacify	- Challenge
- Strive for a comfortable working environment	- Strive for an exciting working environment
- Use power cautiously	- Use power forcefully
- Delegate cautiously	- Delegate enthusiastically
- View workers as employees	- View workers as potential followers

(Adapted from Elwood N. Chapman, *Leadership: What every manager needs to know,* Chicago Science Research Associate, 1989)

- self-confident;
- tolerant of stress;
- willing to assume responsibility.

You should make an honest self-evaluation to gauge the extent of your leadership abilities and/or potential. As well as traits (which are qualities or characteristics), we can also identify the skills that leaders need to acquire. The difference between these concepts is that a **trait** is something we are either born with or develops early in life (depending on which stance you take on the 'nature versus nurture' debate) whereas **skills** are acquired. They relate to what we can *do* rather than what we *are*. Over the years, various writers have identified the following skills as being required of a leader:

- intelligence
- creativity
- tact and diplomacy
- communication skills
- knowledge
- persuasiveness
- social skills
- self-discipline
- organizational abilities.

The main weakness of the traits–skills approach

to the study of leadership was the imperfect correlation between these attributes and the leaders who were studied. For instance, research shows the most leaders possess many but not all of the attributes that have been identified. Consequently, many management theorists have preferred to analyse behavioural patterns or 'styles of leadership'.

Styles of leadership

This approach to the study of leadership focuses on the behaviour of the leader. It is first necessary to identify the main styles before looking at specific theories related to these styles of leadership behaviour (see Figure 42.1).

The autocratic style

The **autocratic leader** is authoritarian and assumes responsibility for all aspects of the operation. Communication is one-way, with little or no scope for feedback. Within the autocratic style, we can identify the 'tough' autocrat, who demands total compliance from the workforce, and the 'kindly' autocrat (or paternalist), who demands compliance on the basis that 'the boss knows best'.

The autocratic style is seen as efficient and, indeed, it is essential in some circumstances.

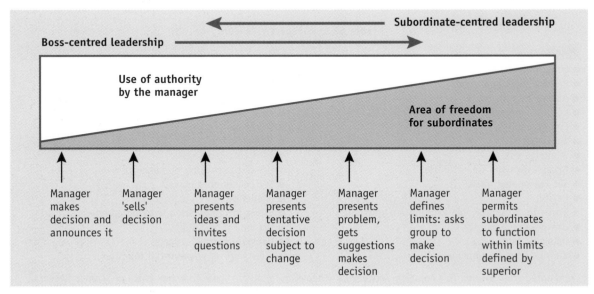

Figure 42.1 Continuum of leadership behaviour

For instance, uniformed services (such as the fire service) have to be run on autocratic lines; similarly, a symphony orchestra is conducted by an autocrat.

There is a clear chain of command with no ambiguity and so autocratic leadership produces quick decisions. However, the autocratic style creates frustrations and resentment. The work group becomes very dependent on the leader and will be unable to act independently. An autocratic style can and does work, but much depends on the qualities of the leader and the compliance of the group. In most organizations today, employees demand greater participation in decision making.

The democratic style

The **democratic or participative leader** seeks the opinions of subordinates and strives for mutual understanding. 'Democratic' implies acceptance of group decisions, but most democratic managers consult yet retain the ultimate responsibility for decision making. Perhaps 'consultative' is a more apt description for this style of leadership. It is especially appropriate where experienced workers need to be fully involved in their work.

Participation results in improved decision making, higher morale and greater commitment. However, consultation is time-consuming and there is always the danger of loss of management control and an attempt to evade responsibility.

The laissez-faire or free rein style

The free rein-style leader sets goals for subordinates and clear parameters within which they should work. Once the objectives have been established, the reins of control are dropped and the subordinate is left alone to achieve their objectives. This style works well when subordinates are willing and able to accept responsibility. The freedom of manoeuvre motivates the enthusiastic worker. However, there are risks associated with this style as success is dependent on the competence and integrity of subordinates.

In Table 42.2 the three styles of leadership described above are compared, while Figure 42.1 is a classic model of the spectrum of styles.

We now turn to theories associated with motivating employees.

Scientific management

The principles of scientific management were developed in America in the early decades of the twentieth century by Frank and Lillian Gilbreth, Henry Gantt and, most important of all, Frederick Taylor.

Taylor was critical of contemporary management and work practices. Management had abdicated control over the workplace and left manual workers to control the methods of operations. The piecerate system in use at the time did not provide an incentive for increased effort; instead, workers

Table 42.2 Leadership styles

Aspects	Authoritarian	Democratic	Laissez-faire
Nature	Leader retains all authority and responsibility	Leader delegates a great deal of authority while retaining ultimate responsibility	Leader grants responsibility and authority to group
Assignment of tasks	Leaders assign people to clearly defined tasks	Work is divided and assigned on the basis of participatory decision making	Group members are told to work things out themselves and do the best they can
Communication	Primarily a downward flow of communication	Active two-way flow of upward and downward communication	Primarily horizontal communication among peers
Primary strength	Prompt, orderly and predictable performance	Enhances personal commitment	Permits self-starters to do things as they see fit without interference
Primary weakness	Stifles individual initiative	Time-consuming	Group may drift aimlessly in the absence of direction

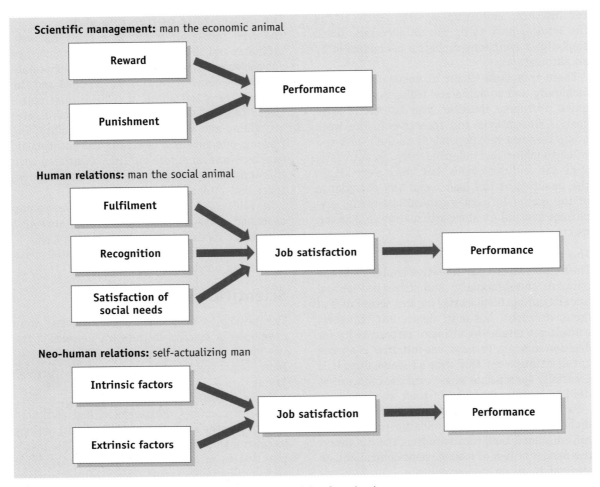

Figure 42.2 Models of motivation

restricted output because they feared working themselves out of a job. Taylor's solution was the application of scientific principles to improve methods of operation in order to secure an increase in productivity. Taylor's ideas are contained in his book *The Principles of Scientific Management* (Harper & Bros, 1914). His famous four principles of scientific management were as follows.

● **The development of a true science of work** All knowledge that has hitherto been kept in the heads of workers should be gathered and recorded by management. 'Every single subject, large and small, becomes the question for scientific investigation, for

reduction to law'. Very simply, he argued that management should apply techniques to the solution of problems and should not rely on experience and 'seat-of-the-pants' judgements.

● **The scientific selection and progressive development of workers** Workers should be carefully trained and given jobs to which they are best suited. Although 'training' is an important element in his principles of management, 'nurturing' might be a more apt description of his ideas of worker development.

● **The bringing together of the science and the scientifically selected and trained workers** The application of techniques to

Table 42.3 Benefits and drawbacks of scientific management

Benefits	Drawbacks
<ul><li>Improved working methods resulted in enormous gains in productivity</li><li>The measurement and analysis of tasks provided factual information on which to base improvements in methods and equipment</li><li>It provided a rational basis for piece-work and incentive schemes that became more widely used</li><li>There were considerable improvements in working conditions</li><li>Management became more involved with production activities and were thus encouraged to show positive leadership</li></ul>	<ul><li>Jobs became more boring and repetitive</li><li>Planning, design and control became divorced from performance</li><li>Workers become virtual adjuncts to machines, with management having a monopoly on knowledge and control</li><li>Deskilling, excessive specialization, repetition and so on cause workers to become alienated and frustrated</li></ul>

decide what should be done, using workers who are both properly trained and willing to maximize output, should result in maximum productivity.

● **The constant and intimate cooperation between management and workers** 'The relations between employers and men form without question the most important part of this art.'

From these principles emerged a stress on:

● division of labour;
● application of logic to the management process;
● full managerial control over the workshop;
● measurement of work;
● piece-rate systems of payment;
● standardization.

Taylor can be criticized for concentrating on the instrumental aspects of human behaviour to the neglect of psychological and social variables; he saw the worker as a machine fuelled by money. However, this should not be interpreted as Taylor being opposed to the welfare of workers. In fact, Taylor believed in harmony between workers and management, and thought this would emerge in their common interest in increased productivity. If scientific methods are adopted and work is accurately measured, there must be no artificial limit on the earnings of the efficient worker. Thus, both workers and management could benefit from the application of the principles of scientific management (see Table 42.3).

The human relations school

The human relations school reflects the influence of sociologists and psychologists on the development of management theory. Business organizations were seen not as impersonal formal structures, but as social systems in which psychological and emotional factors have a significant influence on productivity. As in all major schools of thought, there are considerable differences between the various writers included under the umbrella, but the following strands of thought are present in the works of the human relations school:

● performance can be improved by good human relations;
● managers should consult employees on matters that affect them;
● leadership should be democratic rather than authoritarian;
● employees are motivated by social and psychological rewards and are not just 'economic animals';
● the work group plays an important part in influencing performance.

The first significant research undertaken by a member of the human relations school was Elton

Mayo's experiments at the Hawthorne works of the Western Electric Company in Chicago (1923 to early 1930s). Mayo altered the working environment (for example, by adjusting the lighting) to study the impact on the productivity of workers. He discovered that whatever he did was followed by a rise in productivity. From these experiments, he concluded that employees worked harder if they believed that management was concerned about their welfare. If work appears to have meaning and if people feel valued, they will be more content in their work and more productive. This relationship between attention paid to workers and the subsequent rise in productivity has become known as the 'Hawthorne effect'.

Mayo continued with his Hawthorne experiments and identified the importance of the working group to performance. Classical theory had focused exclusively on the formal organizational structure (defined as that structure rationally and deliberately decided on to achieve the organization's goals). Mayo, however, focused on the informal organization that developed out of the interactions between *people* within the organization. Strong group cohesion will enhance the performance of the organization if group objectives are compatible with organizational aims. However, group pressures (such as on the quantity of work to be undertaken in a day) might conflict with organizational aims. Managers should be sensitive to social groupings and strive to harness the efforts of such groups to achieve the firm's objectives. The main conclusions of the Hawthorne experience were that:

- an individual's identity is strongly associated with his or her group, so workers should be considered less as individuals and more as members of the group;
- an individual's affiliation and sense of belonging to the group can be more important to him or her than monetary rewards and other working conditions;
- groups can be formal (set up by the organization) or informal (chance social groupings) – both can exercise a strong influence over the behaviour of individuals at work;

- managers and supervisors would do well to take group behaviour into account when seeking to extract the maximum amount of work from their subordinates;
- non-monetary rewards play a central role in determining the motivation of the employee;
- a high degree of specialization is not necessarily the most efficient system of working.

After the Second World War, there developed a **new** or **neo-human relations school.** This brought deeper psychological insight into the motivation of workers. We can distinguish between content theories and process theories. **Content theories** try to analyse the needs that motivate people. In a list of content theories we should include:

- Maslow's hierarchy of needs;
- Herzberg's two factor theory;
- McGregor's Theory X and Theory Y;
- McClelland's Theory.

The **process theories** concern the thought processes that influence behaviour. Expectancy and equity theories are the most well known of the process theories.

Content theories

The distinctive feature of this group of theories is that they focus on what motivates people, namely a need that must be satisfied. The need is satisfied by a reward that is either extrinsic to the task (such as money) or intrinsic (job satisfaction). As we saw, early writers on management belong to the classical and scientific management schools in which man was seen as a rational, economic animal. As workers were motivated by desire for extrinsic reward, the appropriate strategy to motivate them was to link pay to output. Although this somewhat simplistic view of human motivation has been challenged and amended, we would be foolish to ignore the importance of pay as a motivating factor.

Abraham Maslow's hierarchy of needs
People are motivated to act by the desire to satisfy the basic requirements of continued biological existence. Once these needs have been satisfied, we seek to satisfy higher-level needs.

Figure 42.3 Maslow's hierarchy of needs

The concept of a hierarchy of needs (see Figure 42.3) has two important consequences. First, unless and until a lower-order need has been satisfied, higher-order needs do not motivate. It is, therefore, of little use to attempt to motivate by emphasizing creativity unless people possess the requirements for continued existence.

Second, once a need is satisfied, it no longer motivates. Only *unmet* needs motivate. Hence, once the lower-order needs have been satisfied, further motivation can only come by giving employees greater scope for autonomy and creativity.

Frederic Herzberg's two factor theory

Herzberg distinguished between **motivators** (which give positive satisfaction) and what he called **hygiene, or maintenance, factors**. The latter do not give positive satisfaction, but their absence will cause dissatisfaction.

The use of the word 'hygiene' can be explained by considering it in its normal usage. If you neglect to clean the kitchen, you will eventually suffer the consequences. However, if the kitchen is thoroughly cleaned and therefore hygienic, it does not *guarantee* good health. Herzberg's hygiene factors (which equate to the lower levels of Maslow's hierarchy) include pay, conditions, supervision and pensions. These have to be satisfactory to secure effort from the workforce, but

they alone are not enough. In other words, they are a necessary but not sufficient condition for motivation.

Herzberg's motivational factors equate with social needs, self-esteem and self-actualization in the Maslow hierarchy. The motivators are intrinsic to the work and include a sense of achievement, autonomy, responsibility and recognition. Translated into practical management, Herzberg's theory led to the notion of **job enrichment**. This involves giving the individual employee greater autonomy by removing some of the hierarchical controls. By enriching the job, management seeks to increase employee motivation.

Table 42.4 identifies hygiene factors and motivators.

McGregor's Theory X and Theory Y

In *The Human Side of Enterprise* (McGraw-Hill, 1960), Douglas McGregor contrasted two sets of assumptions about workers' attitudes to work and responsibility (see Table 42.5). **Theory X** depicts the 'economic man' characteristic of Taylor's scientific management. The Theory X employee is, therefore, a reluctant worker who has to be coerced and given extrinsic rewards. The **Theory Y** worker prefers autonomy, responsibility and gains a sense of achievement from work.

It is important to realize that McGregor was not saying that there are two types of worker. Instead he argued that managers have these two contrasting sets of assumptions about workers and this conditions their treatment of the workforce.

Acceptance of the negative Theory X view of workers results in:

● autocratic leadership;
● traditional organizational structures;
● centralization of decision making;
● scientific management;
● a stress on extrinsic factors (pay and punishment).

Acceptance of the more positive Theory Y results in:

● a democratic or even free rein style of leadership;

Table 42.4 Herzberg's two factor theory

Hygiene factors		Motivators	
Pay and benefits	These include basic income, fringe benefits, bonuses, holidays, company car and similar items	Achievement	Reaching or exceeding task objectives is particularly important because the 'onwards and upwards' urge to achieve is a basic human drive. It is one of the most powerful motivators and a great source of satisfaction
Working conditions	These conditions include working hours, workplace layout, facilities and equipment provided for the job	Recognition	The acknowledgement of achievements by senior staff members is motivational because it helps to enhance self-esteem. For many staff members, recognition may be viewed as a reward in itself
Company policy	The company policy is the rules and regulations that govern employers and employees		
Status	A person's status is determined by their rank, authority and relationship to others, reflecting a level of acceptance	Job interest	A job that provides positive, satisfying pleasure to individuals and groups will be a greater motivational force than a job that does not sustain interest. As far as possible, responsibilities should be matched to individuals' interests
Job security	This is the degree of confidence that the employee has regarding continued employment in an organization		
Supervision and autonomy	This factor concerns the extent of control that an individual has over the content and execution of a job	Responsibility	The opportunity to exercise authority and power may demand leadership skills, risk-taking, decision making and self-direction, all of which raise self-esteem and are strong motivators
Office life	This is the level and type of interpersonal relations within the individual's working environment	Advancement	Promotion, progress, and rising rewards for achievement are important here. Possibly the main motivator, however, is the feeling that advancement is possible.
Personal life	An individual's personal life is the time spent on family, friends and interests – restricted by time spent at work		

Table 42.5 McGregor's Theory X and Theory Y

Theory X	Theory Y
● People dislike work and will seek to avoid it ● Workers are unambitious, irresponsible, lazy, and not to be trusted ● Workers have to be controlled ● Such people have security as their greatest need	● People enjoy work ● People seek responsibility ● They do not wish to be controlled ● Workers' desire to satisfy social and self-actualizing needs

● more flexible structures:
● decentralization of decision making;
● a search for appropriate ways of motivating the workforce;
● a stress on factors intrinsic to the work itself.

David McClelland's needs theory

McClelland was concerned more with differences between individuals than understanding common factors in motivation. He was concerned with three needs:

- **n-Ach** the need for achievement;
- **n-Pow** the need for power;
- **n-Aff** the needs for affiliation or belonging.

The dominance or otherwise of these needs influences the behaviour of the individual. An Olympic gold medallist has a strong need to achieve (n-Ach), whereas other people have a greater desire to be 'one of the boys' (n-Aff).

N-Ach is a key factor in human motivation and is developed by environmental factors (parental influence, education, values of society). People with high n-Ach:

- seek tasks over which they can exercise personal responsibility;
- seek tasks that are challenging but within their mastery;
- want feedback on performance;
- have a low n-Aff.

McClelland's theory contains both 'good' and 'bad' news for managers. The fact that n-Ach is developed by cultural or environmental factors suggests that, with appropriate training schemes, it can be fostered within the workforce. On the other hand, people with high n-Ach are not good team players. A high n-Ach is invaluable for those undertaking individual pursuits, but can cause frustration for those working in a bureaucratic organization.

McClelland's research led him to the conclusion that n-Ach is not hereditary but results from environmental influences. McClelland outlined

four steps people take in attempting to develop achievement drive:

- strive to attain feedback on performance – reinforcement of success serves to strengthen the desire to attain higher performance;
- develop models of achievement by seeking to emulate people who have performed well;
- attempt to modify their self-image and see themselves as needing challenges and success;
- control day-dreaming and think about themselves in more positive terms.

Table 42.6 contrasts the motivational theories of Maslow, Herzberg and McClelland.

Process theories

Process theories concern not the needs that have to be satisfied, but the thought processes that influence behaviour. Two such theories can be identified:

- expectancy theory, and
- equity theory.

Expectancy theory

To understand expectancy theory (associated with Broom and Porter and Lawler) consider why athletes train so hard. First, they perceive that there is a link between the amount and type of training and their performance – training will improve performance. Second, there is a link between performance and reward – there is a gold medal for the first across the line, but only a

Table 42.6 A comparison of needs theories

Maslow's needs hierarchy	Herzberg's two factor theory	McClelland's needs theory
Physiological	Dissatisfiers	
	● company policy	
	● supervision	
Safety	● pay	
	● working conditions	
Social	Satisfiers	Affiliation
	● recognition	
Esteem	● responsibility	Power
	● advancement	
Self-fulfilment (self-actualization)	● achievement	Achievement

silver for the second-placed runner. Third, athletes perceive that the rewards (whether of money, fame, status) are desirable and attractive. However, there is a further factor to consider – the likelihood of achieving the goal. Athletes will only train hard if they believe there is a reasonable chance of achieving success.

In **expectancy theory,** effort is linked not just to the desire for a particular outcome, but moderated by an evaluation (expectancy) that, if a particular course is followed, a particular outcome will be attained. The theory can be illustrated in diagrammatical form (see Figure 42.4) or an equation:

Motivation = f (Σ ExV)

where f (   ) is a function of
Σ is the sum of
E = expectancy or a subjective measure of the probability of success
V = valence or a measure of how much a particular outcome is desired.
The conclusions that can be drawn are:

- individuals will only act when they have a reasonable expectation that their behaviour will lead to the desired outcome;

- effort alone is insufficient – it has to be accompanied by ability and skill;
- job satisfaction results from effective job performance (a sense of achievement) rather than the other way round;
- job design is, therefore, of crucial importance.

Lawler identified the implications of expectancy theory as being the following:

- find out what rewards employees value;
- specify the exact behaviours that reflect good levels of performance;
- ensure the desired levels of performance are within employees' capabilities;
- ensure that the links between effort, performance and rewards are clear to all employees;
- ensure that the rewards on offer do not conflict with other rewards from different organizational sources;
- ensure that the rewards are not seen as trivial;
- ensure that the level of rewards actually matches levels of performance;
- ensure the reward system is fair and equitable;
- design pay and reward systems so that

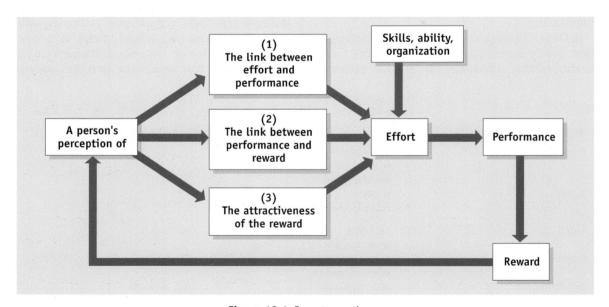

Figure 42.4 Expectancy theory

LEADERSHIP AND MOTIVATION

performance is rewarded, not other factors, such as length of service;

- design jobs in such a way as to provide opportunities for people to satisfy their own needs in their work;
- allow employees to be involved in decisions affecting the types of rewards on offer.

Equity theory

Equity theory focuses on the way that people are inclined to adjust their behaviour according to their perception of the fairness of their own inputs and receipts from performing a task compared to the inputs and receipts of other people performing comparable tasks. In return for an input (effort, skill, training), the worker receives a reward (pay, status, fringe benefits). Equity exists when the ratio of one person's outcome to his or her input equals other workers' ratios. Inequity exists whenever the input–outcome ratios are not in balance. In simple language, workers will feel a sense of injustice if their efforts are not rewarded in a way commensurate with the rewards of others (relative to their efforts). Perceived inequity results in tensions within the individual and efforts to bring his or her input–reward ratio in line with those of others. This might mean reducing effort to restore the (subjective) balance between the input–outcome ratios – (see Figure 42.5).

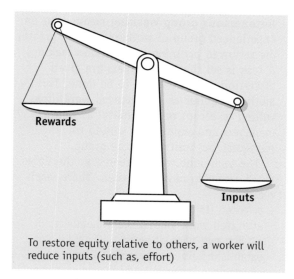

To restore equity relative to others, a worker will reduce inputs (such as, effort)

Figure 42.5 A state of inequity

Practical motivational measures

What motivates in one situation is not guaranteed to motivate at other times and in other places. However, we can identify the major factors affecting motivation as being:

- pay rates, if only as a hygiene factor;
- security of livelihood;
- prospects of promotion, advancement and improvement in living standards;
- social grouping (the informal organization);
- style and quality of leadership;
- the nature of the work;
- sense of challenge in relation to the worker's ability;
- desire for autonomy and responsibility;
- opportunities to participate in decision making;
- working conditions (if only as a hygiene factor).

Pay will be dealt with in Chapter 45 and so the following survey deals with the intrinsic factors. Modern industrial processes often involve extreme division of labour. Although this has been the route to increased output and efficiency, repetition results in boredom and alienation, the symptoms of which are high labour turnover, low productivity and a general disinterest in work. To increase job satisfaction for the benefit of both, the organization and its workers, management should consider **job design.** This can be defined as the application of motivational theories to the structure of work so as to improve productivity and the sense of satisfaction. A well-designed job will:

- use the skills and abilities of the individual to their full potential;
- be reasonably challenging;
- provide some variety;
- be considered worth while and meaningful by employees;
- provide some degree of autonomy;
- provide opportunities for working as a team.

In designing, or redesigning, jobs, one or more of the following strategies should be developed:

- **Job rotation** This involves the systematic and planned movement of employees from one job to another to provide them with variety and stimulation. It increases the experience of employees and provides for individual development. In itself, job rotation provides some enrichment to work.

- **Job enlargement** This involves a redesign of the job so that a series of tasks is combined into a new, broader job that gives variety and challenge to employees. By increasing the scope of the job, the sense of wholeness of the job will increase, thereby motivating the worker doing that job. However, job enlargement should not result in over-burdening of the worker.

- **Job enrichment** This is defined as a job design that incorporates achievement, recognition and other high-level motivators. In essence, it means increased job satisfaction as a result of greater autonomy and participation in the process of decision making. Herzberg suggested seven principles of job design:
  - a limited removal of controls but the retention of accountability;
  - greater emphasis on accountability;
  - development of greater expertise by specialization;
  - a unit of work that is complete in itself;
  - increased authority and responsibility;
  - feedback on issues that had previously only been available to supervisors;
  - increased complexity within tasks to make them more demanding and rewarding.

Another writer on job design, Richard Hackman, identified five key dimensions to any job:

- **skill variety** the job utilizes different skills and abilities;
- **task identity** the job is meaningful and whole;
- **task significance** the job affects the work of others;
- **autonomy** the job gives freedom and discretion to act;
- **feedback** the job feeds back information about performance.

It follows that there are five main ways to enrich jobs:

- **combine tasks** give more than one part of the work to do;
- **form work units** give a meaningful sequence of work to do;
- **establish client relationships** give responsibility for personal contacts;
- **vertical loading** give responsibilities normally given to superiors;
- **open feedback channels** give direct performance summaries.

Recommended practices include:

- increasing the responsibility of individual workers;
- giving people a complete unit of work and thereby reducing specialization;
- providing workers with more information;
- encouraging participation;
- giving workers scope to vary the methods, sequence and pace of work;
- providing greater autonomy and responsibility;
- allowing workers to increase their expertise.

By these methods, the employee is able to satisfy the social, self-esteem and self-actualizing needs that are the essence of the neo-human relations theory.

- **Autonomous group working** Autonomy means self-determination or independence. **Autonomous group working** means that an experienced group of workers is given greater discretion in planning and decision making. A task is set, but the workers are given discretion as to how it is to be done. This method requires an experienced workforce willing to accept responsibility, as well as managers and supervisors willing to relinquish authority over the group.

  The technique was pioneered at the Volvo truck assembly unit in Sweden. There, each team:
  - selected its own leader;
  - allocated work among team members;
  - set its own pace of work;
  - established its own targets (subject to constraints imposed by higher management);
  - assumed full responsibility for quality control.

Volvo reported the following results:
- productivity increased;
- management/employee communications were enhanced;
- quality improved;
- labour turnover reduced dramatically.

● **Changing work schedules** Job satisfaction can be increased by adopting the alternative strategy of changing work schedules. This might mean a compression of the working week, hence motivating the worker with the prospect of increased leisure time. Alternatively, a flexitime system of working allows the worker, within certain constraints, to choose their starting and finishing times. By giving people greater control over their lives, it is hoped that motivation will be increased.

The demotivated worker

Signs that indicate a worker is demotivated include absenteeism, low productivity, low-quality work and obstructiveness. Although ultimately the problem can be dealt with by disciplinary procedures and dismissal, it is preferrable to deal with the problem in a more positive way, as shown in Table 42.7.

Dealing with absenteeism

Absenteeism is a sign of low morale. We are not concerned here with absence caused by genuine illness, but deliberate non-attendance at the workplace by employees. The rate of absenteeism can be calculated as follows:

$$\frac{\text{No. of working days lost in a period}}{\text{Total potential working days in a period}} \times 100$$

It is quite possible that a high percentage of absences can be attributed to a small percentage of employees under the 80:20 rule. Nevertheless, it causes considerable problems in terms of:

● lost production;
● missed targets;
● high sick pay and cover costs;
● higher administrative costs.

An effective set of measures for controlling absenteeism could include:

● careful job design to make work more satisfying;
● job rotation to make work more interesting;
● increased employee participation in decision making;
● smaller working groups;
● allowing employees to work flexitime;

Table 42.7 Motivating the poor performer

Examples of poor performance	Causes of poor performance	Solutions
● Absenteeism	● Lack of job knowledge	● Preventing the problem:
● Time-wasting	● Lack of skills	– recruitment and selection
● Missing deadlines	● Stress	– probationary period
● Resisting change	● Health problems	– advice, support, guidance and training
● Bad timekeeping	● Inadequate training	– review meetings
● Upsetting customers	● Poor working conditions	– realistic targets
● Lack of commitment	● Family problems	● Managing the problem:
● Output low in quantity and/or quality	● Poor management	– early identification
● Withholding information	● Cultural differences	– meetings
	● Group pressure	– targets
		– regular reviews
		– monitoring and support
		– disciplinary procedures as a last resort
		– formal warnings and, if not heeded, dismissal

- allowing job sharing;
- accurate recording of rates of absenteeism and communication of records to department/individuals;
- employee counselling arrangements for persistent non-attenders.

Disciplinary action

Disciplinary action is likely to be initiated by management in one of the following situations:

- **poor performance** such as failure to work to an accepted standard or negligence;
- **misconduct** for example, failure to obey reasonable orders; unacceptable behaviour; poor attendance; bad time-keeping; or infringement or non-observance of rules.
- **gross misconduct** falsifying claims sheets; or malicious damage to the employer's property, for example.

Gross misconduct can result in instant dismissal (although the employer will have to prove gross misconduct if the dismissed employee seeks legal redress). Poor performance and misconduct can lead to dismissal, but both employment law and good personnel practice demand that the matter be dealt with fairly, constructively and in accordance with agreed procedures.

The ACAS Code of Practice lays down that the disciplinary procedure should:

- be in a written form;
- indicate the various forms of disciplinary action that may be taken;
- specify who has the authority to exercise disciplinary action;
- ensure that individuals are informed of the disciplinary charges against them;
- permit individuals to state their case and be accompanied by a 'friend' (usually a union representative);
- provide for a right of appeal.

Dismissal for a disciplinary offence (other than gross misconduct) is usually the final act of a process which that includes:

- an oral warning given to the employee by an immediate supervisor;
- a first written warning given by a line manager, but with a copy sent to the personnel department;
- a second written warning issued in conjunction with the personnel department;
- suspension (with or without pay) pending a formal disciplinary hearing;
- a disciplinary hearing with the right to be accompanied by a 'friend';
- right of appeal;
- dismissal.

After dismissal, the employee has the right to pursue the matter in an employment tribunal. The procedure outlined above is not enshrined in law, but it is recommended good practice. For the sake of harmonious relations, it is important to ensure that justice is not only done, but is *seen* to be done. See Table 42.8, adapted from *Employment Resourcing* by M. Corbridge and S. Pilbeam (Financial Times Pitman, 1998).

Grievance procedures

Employees might have a grievance relating to:

- terms or conditions of employment
- supervision
- discrimination
- bullying
- sexual harassment
- health and safety
- excessive workload.

It is important for employers to deal with such grievances. Failure to do so will result in loss of staff, wider disputes or claims for constructive dismissal (defined as the legal right of an employee to resign owing to the improper behaviour by the employer and still claim payment for wrongful dismissal).

The Employment Protection Act 1978 requires the employer to establish and notify staff of grievance procedures. Typically, the grievance procedure will specify various tiers of management to which the issue can be taken and include the right to be accompanied and/or represented. Employers are required to specify whom an employee can refer a grievance to and inform all

Table 42.8 The principal incremental stages of a disciplinary procedure

Nature of the disciplinary matter and the procedural stage	Management response and action	Level of management administering procedure
• Misconduct that is not serious • More serious misconduct or repeated misconduct for which an oral warning has already been given	• Oral warning • Written warning	• Team leader or supervisor • Supervisor or line manager
• Serious misconduct or repeated misconduct for which a written warning has been given	• Final written warning and/or action short of dismissal	• Line manager and/or senior manager
• Gross misconduct or further misconduct for which a final written warning has been given	• Dismissal or action short of dismissal, such as transfer, demotion or suspension	• Senior manager

new employees of the procedure. It is good practice to handle all grievances within seven days.

Performance appraisal

Performance appraisal is a process whereby an individual's performance is reviewed against previously agreed goals, and where new goals are agreed that will develop the individual and improve performance over the forthcoming review period.

The reasons for developing an appraisal scheme are to:

- improve current performance;
- provide feedback on performance;
- increase motivation;
- identify potential;
- identify training needs;
- aid career development;
- award salary increases;
- solve job problems;
- let individuals know what is expected of them;
- clarify job objectives;
- provide information about the effectiveness of the selection process;
- provide information for human resource planning.

A typical appraisal scheme would involve:

- identification of criteria for assessment, perhaps based on job analysis, performance standards, job and person specifications and so on;

- the preparation by the subordinate's manager of an appraisal report;
- an appraisal interview, for an exchange of views about the results of the assessment, targets for improvement, solutions to problems and so on;
- review of the assessment by the assessor's own superior, so that the appraisee does not feel subject to one person's prejudices (formal appeals may be allowed, if necessary, to establish the fairness of the procedure);
- the preparation and implementation of action plans to achieve improvements and changes agreed;
- follow-up, monitoring the progress of the action plan.

Key concepts

Autocratic/authoritarian leader A leader who makes all the decisions and then informs others.

Autonomy/independence Employee autonomy is having the freedom and authority to make decisions.

Democratic leader One who accepts the decision of the majority. In business organizations it is rare that decisions are left to a majority of the workforce. In practice, leaders might consult and allow limited scope for majority decisions, but retain ultimate control over key decisions.

Equity/fairness Equity theory of motivation concerns subjective assessments of fairness of rewards in relation to input of effort.

Expectancy theory A theory of motivation that focuses on the employee's expectations of the outcome of effort.

Free rein/*laissez-faire* leader One who sets targets but leaves subordinates to determine how they are to be achieved.

Hierarchy of needs A list of needs drawn up by Abraham Maslow that are satisfied in order of priority. Once a need is satisfied, it no longer motivates.

Job enrichment Motivation by means of making work more challenging and interesting so as to make full use of each individual's abilities.

Leadership The ability to influence the thoughts and behaviour of others.

Leadership traits The (assumed) characteristics necessary in a leader. This approach to the study of leadership failed because of the numerous exceptions to any rule that can be identified.

Motivation Incentives to exert effort. All forces and influences that cause employees to want to behave in a certain way.

Theories X and Y Douglas McGregor's contrasting sets of assumptions about the attitudes of employees and the ways in which they are treated as a result.

Two factor theory Frederick Herzberg's division of motivating factors into hygiene factors (those that are necessary but not sufficient conditions) and motivators (which act positively to motivate).

Essay questions

1 (a) Outline the principles of scientific management.
(b) Does scientific management have any relevance to the modern world? Justify your answer.

2 Evaluate the contribution of Elton Mayo to our understanding of people at work.

3 (a) Compare and contrast the theories associated with Maslow and Herzberg.
(b) Suggest and evaluate strategies that apply Herzberg's theory in the workplace.

4 (a) Outline both equity and expectancy theories.
(b) Discuss how these theories can be applied to the work situation.

5 Discuss the principles of job enrichment.

6 (a) Outline McGregor's Theory X and Theory Y.
(b) Did McGregor produce a theory about different types of workers or different types of management? Justify your answer.

7 (a) Outline two approaches to the study of leadership.
(b) Is there a single best style of leadership. Justify your answer.

43

Teams

Teamwork is now established as an essential aspect of an efficient, high-performance organization. This chapter looks at why teamwork is so highly valued and what makes for an effective team.

Chapter objectives

1 To understand the nature of a team.

2 To analyse the benefits of teamworking.

3 To understand the evolution of teams.

4 To analyse the features of an effective team.

5 To explore empowerment within teams.

Definitions

A **group** is a collection of people working together for their common benefit and in pursuit of a common goal. Edgar G. Schein (*Organizational Psychology*, Prentice Hall, 1980) defines a group in psychological terms as 'any number of people who:

● interact with one another;
● are psychologically aware of one another;
● perceive themselves to be a group.'

This definition indicates that the collection of people in a group share most, if not all, of the following characteristics:

● definable membership
● group consciousness
● a shared sense of purpose
● interaction
● the ability to act in a unitary manner.

A **team** is also a group in that it conforms to the characteristics outlined above. However, not all groups are teams. Some groups in the workplace are informal and not deliberately created to achieve organizational goals. Informal groups will be explored below, but, first, we need a definition of a team (or work group). 'A team is a small collection of people with complementary skills who are committed to a common purpose, performance goals and approach for which they hold themselves mutually accountable' (J. Katzenbach and

D. Smith, *The Wisdom of Teams* Harvard Business School Press, 1993).

The team is the basic unit of performance for most organizations. It is created and energized by performance challenges set by superiors. It brings together a complementary set of skills, experience and insights and is consciously created to achieve organizational goals.

In essence, the difference between a team and a group is that a group is a number of people with shared interests whereas a team is a small group of people who work together to achieve the same organizational goals.

The ways in which people in teams work together has changed over the years, and Table 43.1 delineates those changes.

As part of the Hawthorne investigations (see Chapter 42), Elton Mayo observed a group of 14 men working in the bank wiring room of the Western Electric Company in America. The men formed their own subgroups or cliques, within which there arose natural leaders. The group worked to a norm of 6000 units of output per day despite a financial incentive scheme that rewarded workers for higher levels of production. The group pressures on individual workers were stronger than the financial incentives offered by management.

The **informal groups** had their own codes of behaviour. These included:

● not being a 'rate buster' – not exceeding the production norm set by the group;
● not being 'squealer' – not saying anything to management that harms group members;
● not being a 'chiseller' – not producing at too low a rate;

● not being officious – not taking advantage of seniority or attempting to maintain social distance.

Continued membership of the group was dependent on conforming to these rules. There were sanctions for those who broke the group rules. These were likely to involve cold shouldering the offender to force him or her to come into line. Alternatively, it might have taken the form of making jokes at the expense of the non-conformist or excessive criticism or ridicule. The positive benefits of group membership included:

● friendship;
● support;
● self-respect;
● satisfaction from being with people with similar ideas and attitudes;
● psychological security;
● an opportunity for members to establish their own identities;
● access to an informal communication network (the grapevine).

Management must not ignore the existence of informal groups. The ideal for the organization is to ensure that these groups work towards organizational goals and, in effect, convert them into teams.

Why are teams so important?

The simple answer to this question is that teams outperform individuals acting alone and they also outperform large organizational groups. The relatively small team is flexible so it can respond

Table 43.1 Teamworking: old and new	
Traditional workplace	**New workplace**
● One person, one job	● Teams and teamwork
● Tall organizational structure	● Flat organizational structure
● Top-down decisions	● Shared decision making
● Lifetime job	● Uncertainty over employment
● Watchdog supervisor	● The supervisor as coordinator
● Conflict	● Collaboration
● Training is unplanned	● Training is related to core business
● Regular (cost of living) pay rises	● Performance-related pay

to changing needs and events. It recognizes the fact that people feel a need to belong to a working group, take pride in contributing to the group and want it to achieve a high performance level.

Charles Handy recognized that formal work groups or teams are established to:

- solve problems;
- improve decision making;
- manage and control work (work that is best carried out as a group task, for example);
- distribute work (in autonomous work groups members allocate tasks);
- process tasks and thereby increase efficiency and effectiveness;
- increase commitment and involvement;
- resolve conflict;
- test and ratify decisions;
- develop new ideas.

Among the benefits of teams are:

- improved performance in terms of quality, productivity, flexibility, speed and customer service;
- better job design;
- increased motivation and commitment;
- lower costs;
- increased learning;
- increased ability to attract and retain the best people;
- reduced duplication of effort;
- increased cooperation;
- improvement in the quality of decisions;
- greater flexibility;
- easier adaptation to change;
- improved relationships;
- reduction in destructive conflict;
- an opportunity for employees to perform to the best of their abilities.

Stages in the evolution of teams

In an important article published in 1965 ('Development Sequence in Small Groups', *Psychological Bulletin*) B. W. Tuckman identified stages in the evolution of teams (see also Figure 43.1).

- **Forming** In this stage, the group members get to know one another. They discuss objectives and the composition of the group and begin to establish roles within the group. Relationships are characterized as polite but guarded and watchful.
- **Storming** This is an uncomfortable stage in which there is conflict, resistance to the demands of the task and possibly challenges to the leadership of the group. Conflict resolution will result in a redefinition of aims and roles within the group.
- **Norming** This is the stage at which members begin to fully cooperate with each other. Norms are established and individuals are more open with each other. Constructive criticism built on trust leads to enhanced performance.
- **Performing** The group is now mature, with a strong sense of shared objectives. Despite any remaining differences, group members work in a cooperative manner with a resulting improvement in performance. This is the stage at which the group becomes self-managing. Tasks are allocated, leadership is established, everyone understands their role and is prepared to contribute.
- **Adjourning or mourning** This presupposes that the group only needs to exist for a limited time period and can be disbanded after achievement of the objectives. This stage should be characterized by an evaluation and review of the group's performance. Disbanding should be marked by a ceremony, such as a farewell party.

Tuckman's work teaches us lessons about:

- selection of group/team members;
- the development of group norms;
- leadership styles in relation to the stage of development;
- the need to give space for groups to go through the stages and not to bypass any of them;
- the problems associated with change within the organization – with the breaking up of work teams we have to go through the procedure again to establish new teams.

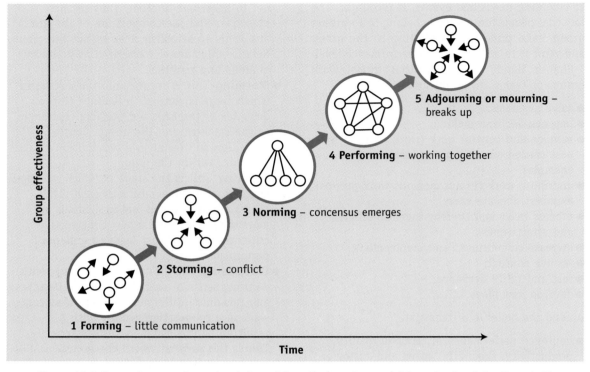

Figure 43.1 Stages in group formation (adapted From Tucker: *Group and Organizational Studies*, 1977)

Effective teams

Evidence of effective teams can be found in:

- high output;
- high productivity;
- low rate of labour turnover;
- low absenteeism;
- low accident rate;
- quality of output;
- minimization of stoppages;
- achievement of group and individual targets.

The way to achieve effectiveness is by:

- ensuring a high commitment to the achievement of targets;
- clear understanding of the group's work;
- clear understanding of each member's role;
- ensuring trust between members;
- open communications using all channel networks (see Chapter 4);
- sharing ideas;
- group problem solving;
- members working to develop their abilities;
- leadership;
- motivation;
- encouragement of creativity;
- constructive resolution of any conflicts;
- encouraging mutual support.

Team roles

In *Management Teams: Why they succeed or fail* (Butterworth Heinemann, 1996), R. Meredith Belbin identified eight[*] (later increased to nine) roles that interact to form a fully effective team. It is possible for an individual to fulfil more than one role, but it is essential that each role is covered. The roles, contributions and allowable weaknesses are shown in Table 43.2, which summarizes Belbin's conclusions. Notice that as well as defining the role, Belbin also identifies weaknesses that are allowable in each of the

Table 43.2 Belbin's team roles

Role	Contribution	Allowable weaknesses
Plant	Creative, imaginative, unorthodox, problem solving	Dislikes detail, resents criticisms, weak in communication
Resource investigator	Develops new contacts and ideas, extrovert, popular, good communicator	Not an original thinker, quickly loses interest
Coordinator	Chairperson, mature, confident, clarifies goals, promotes decision making, delegates well, good listener	Can be seen as manipulative, not necessarily the cleverest
Shaper	The catalyst who turns plans or ideas into action, challenging, dynamic, has drive and courage	Prone to bursts of temper
Monitor/ evaluator	The analytical thinker who provides a quality check, dependable, discerning, sober	Lacks drive and ability to inspire others, overly critical
Teamworker	Supports others by listening and helping, cooperative, mild, perceptive, diplomatic, calms the waters	Indecisive in crunch decision, can be easily influenced
Implementer	A good organizer and administrator, disciplined, reliable, turns ideas into practical action, conservative	Inflexible, slow to respond to new ideas
Completer	Ensures the group meets its targets, painstaking, conscientious, anxious, searches out errors	Inclined to worry, nit-picker, reluctant to delegate
Specialist	Has specialist knowledge and skills, single-minded, dedicated, self-starter	Narrow contribution, dwells on technicalities, overlooking the big picture.

people undertaking the roles. These weaknesses are to be expected and allowed for.

Belbin's work is invaluable for the lessons it provides in terms of:

- selecting team members to cover all nine roles;
- assignment of tasks to individuals;
- predicting team conflict – clashes between the role-holders.

Team briefings

The **team briefing** is a key feature of team-working. It provides an opportunity for managers and supervisors to talk to their teams about what is happening in the workplace. Unlike a general meeting, the briefing is focused and deliberately limited in time and scope. The Industrial Society's guidelines on team briefing recommend that:

- they be held on a regular basis;
- they take place in small teams;
- they should last no longer than 30 minutes;
- the central message should come from senior management;
- the message should cascade down through no more than *four* levels of people;
- the message should reach all employees within 48 hours;
- they should provide an opportunity for questions;
- the central message should contribute no more than 30 per cent of the total message;
- the team should be based on a common production or service area, rather than an occupation;
- general discussions should be discouraged.

The advantages and disadvantages of team briefings are set out in Table 43.3.

Table 43.3 Team briefings

Advantages	Disadvantages
• Improve communications • Ensure regular communication • Keep managers in touch • Develop trust, cooperation and commitment • Help people deal with change • Prevent misunderstanding • Reinforce the role of the team leader	• Can become too rigid and cast in stone • Tend to involve downward communication • Information may not be relevant to the audience • Shift, part-time and dispersed workers may find it difficult to attend • Team leaders might not have the skills or personality to run meetings effectively • Without important new information to give, the briefings can degenerate into trivia and become moaning sessions

Empowerment and teams

Empowerment is the process of giving people more scope or power to exercise control over their work. Empowerment provides opportunities for people to use their abilities and make decisions close to the point of impact. It is, however, more than delegation – it is an opening up of the creative power of employees and is based on the beliefs that:

- staff abilities are underused;
- it is necessary to have faith in people's competence and trust them to get on with the job;
- problems can rarely be solved by one person acting alone, but can by people acting in a team.

American management expert Rosabeth Moss Kanter argues that people must be given the appropriate authority, time and resources to carry out tasks. This implies that management:

- involve people, trusting them, tolerating failure and guaranteeing (where possible) proper employment and career paths;
- encourage personal initiative and facilitate opportunities to try out new ideas, take risks and so on;
- establish ways in which people can actually get started, even if the innovations are initially small in scale and associated with workplace tasks or routines rather than large issues, such as products, processes or systems – Kanter describes this process as 'energizing the grass roots';

- provide the appropriate organizational power tools, which Kanter describes as consisting 'of supplies of three "basic commodities" that can be invested in action: information (data, technical knowledge, political intelligence; expertise); resources (funds, materials, space, time); and support (endorsement, backing, approval, legitimacy)';
- use self-managing teams, project groups, quality circles and so on endowed with the appropriate degree of operational autonomy and encouraged them to develop an innovative culture;
- recruit, socialize and train enterprising staff (as well as suppliers, subcontractors and distributors as partners within the supply chain) in the values and practices of technology assessment, innovation and maintain the knowledge base;
- provide proper praise, incentives and rewards for innovatory achievements, 'brave attempts' and the updating of the knowledge base.

It is argued that empowerment within teams:

- improves commitment and motivation as employees take ownership of the problem and solution;
- generates ideas for improving products and service;
- unearths talent;
- reduces time taken by managers to sort out other people's problems;
- improves customer service;
- improves performance;

- provides a greater sense of achievement than is the case otherwise;
- reduces operational costs by eliminating unnecessary layers of management;
- speeds up decision making and reaction times.

If badly handled, the empowerment process can:

- cause resentment among junior managers;
- cause anxiety;
- cause a breakdown in control of staff;
- lead to frustration if expectations are not fulfilled;

- cause resentment if extra responsibility is not accompanied by extra pay.

Key concepts

Empowerment The practice of giving employees the right to control their activities.

Group A number of people who interact with one another.

Team A working group, the members of which cooperate and coordinate their activities and enthusiastically work to achieve the group's aims.

Essay questions

1 (a) Distinguish between a team and a group of people.
(b) Analyse the benefits of working in teams.

2 (a) What do you understand by an autonomous work team?
(b) Analyse the benefits of organizing work in this way.

3 What makes for effective teamworking? In your answer, make reference to appropriate theories.

4 (a) Outline the phases in the development of a group or team.
(b) Discuss the relevance of this line of enquiry.

5 Evaluate the relevance of Belbin's theory of group roles.

Human resource planning

This chapter looks at strategies that can be used to secure human resources in the quantity and quality required to achieve organizational objectives.

Chapter objectives

1 To analyse the process of human resources planning.

2 To explain methods of recruitment and selection.

3 To analyse methods of introducing flexibility to the organization's human resources.

4 To analyse labour turnover.

5 To explain methods of downsizing.

6 To explore issues relating to training.

Human resource planning

Human resource planning (see Figure 44.1) involves strategies for (or rational approaches to) the:

- acquisition;
- retention;
- utilization;
- improvement;
- disposal;

of the human resources of an organization. As the plan involves many of the resourcing activities of personnel management, we can see it as an 'umbrella' under which other activities occur.

The process of human resource planning should be seen within the context of the overall plan and objectives of the organization. For instance, to achieve a 10 per cent increase in sales volume, it might be necessary to increase the workforce by 6 per cent. The human resource plan is concerned with the acquisition of sufficient human resources to achieve the organization's objectives.

The main reasons for undertaking human resource planning are to ensure that the organization:

- is able to attract and retain staff in sufficient numbers and with the appropriate skills to be able to operate effectively and achieve its objectives;
- fully utilizes the staff employed;
- is able to ensure that employees receive all the training and development necessary for

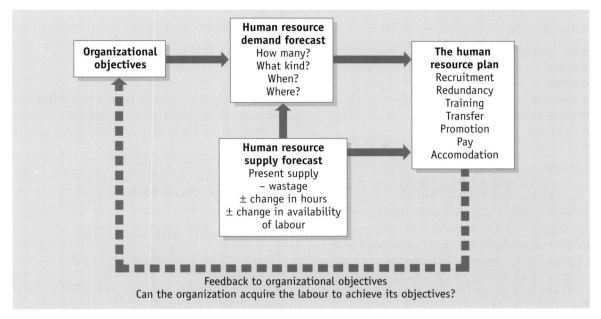

Figure 44.1 Human resource planning

effective performance in their current roles and develop the flexibility to be able to undertake other roles as the need arises;

- is able to anticipate and meet changes in the demand for its services or in the labour supply;
- is able to meet future human resource requirements from its own internal resources;
- ensures that equal opportunities for promotion and development are available to staff;
- keeps control of human resource costs and effectively anticipates the staffing costs of new initiatives.

Human resource demand

The first task for human resource planners is to assess current and future requirements in relation to the organization's marketing, production and capital investment plans.

The requirements should be identified both in terms of *quantity* of labour (that is, the number of man hours) and *quality* of labour. It is possible for an increase in overall human resource needs to be consistent with a decline in the need for a particular type or grade of worker. The skills mix of the workforce will be subject to change in the same way that quantity of labour is subject to change.

The planners will be aware of the financial constraints on their plans. Irrespective of the merits of the case, if finance is not available, the increase in staff will not occur. The planners will also take into account the current and expected levels of productivity. From the study of production, you will remember that productivity is output per unit of input (in this case, it is output per man hour). An anticipated 10 per cent rise in productivity will mean that existing output can be produced with fewer workers (not 10 per cent fewer, as you might think, but 9 per cent). Alternatively, with the same workforce, it is possible to produce 10 per cent more goods. It is, therefore, essential to include productivity in the calculation of human resource needs.

Supply of labour

Having calculated the human resource requirements, it is necessary to analyse the supply of labour. In a human resources audit the present workforce of the organization will be analysed in terms of:

- age structure
- skills
- grade
- turnover
- absenteeism
- overtime
- work practices.

The statistics gathered regarding age structure and turnover enable planners to project the likely shape of the workforce in the future. The data on absenteeism and overtime is important in that by 'supply of labour' we do not mean just the number of workers, but also the number of man hours supplied. Hence, a reduction in the average working week from 40 to 35 hours is the equivalent of a 12.5 per cent reduction in the workforce. The audit should also involve an investigation of manpower utilization to identify situations in which the organization is not making full or best use of its employees.

The external supply of labour is also analysed in the human resource plan. Data will be collected on:

- local and national demographic trends;
- local housing and transport;
- migration;
- the employment activities of other firms;
- changes in the local economy;
- national agreements on conditions of employment

After conducting an audit of existing supply, the planners will forecast future supply to compare it with future demand.

Human resource programmes

The data gathering and analysis is a prelude to the production of programmes and policies designed to acquire the human resources necessary to achieve the overall objectives of the organization.

Programmes and policies are produced for:

- recruitment
- training and development
- promotion

- pay
- productivity
- transfer
- retirement
- redundancy.

In relation to the latter, it should be appreciated that a result of the planning exercise might be a reduction in the human resource needs of the organization.

As with all plans, a control and evaluation mechanism should be built in to provide the basis of planning in the next cycle.

Recruitment and selection

The appointment of 'the right person to the right job at the right time' is crucial to the success of any organization and is a major activity of the human resources department. The process can be divided into three main stages:

1 defining the requirements of the organization;
2 recruitment – attracting a field of suitable applicants;
3 selection – choosing the best candidate for the job.

Figure 44.2 illustrates the stages of the recruitment and selection process.

Defining the requirements

Before advertising a vacancy, it is necessary to clarify what qualities, competences and qualifications are sought in the ideal candidate. Without a clear and agreed profile of the type of skills and so on that the firm is seeking, the selection process is likely to be unsatisfactory and will contribute to later problems (such as high staff turnover, dissatisfaction and a failure to make optimum use of resources).

The process of defining the requirements should start with an analysis of the job. **Job analysis** is the process of collecting, analysing and setting out information about a job under the following headings:

- overall purpose
- content (tasks to be performed)

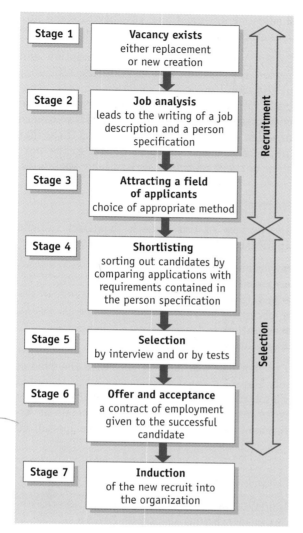

Stage 1	**Vacancy exists** either replacement or new creation
Stage 2	**Job analysis** leads to the writing of a job description and a person specification
Stage 3	**Attracting a field of applicants** choice of appropriate method
Stage 4	**Shortlisting** sorting out candidates by comparing applications with requirements contained in the person specification
Stage 5	**Selection** by interview and or by tests
Stage 6	**Offer and acceptance** a contract of employment given to the successful candidate
Stage 7	**Induction** of the new recruit into the organization

Recruitment

Selection

Figure 44.2 Recruitment and selection

- accountability
- performance criteria (on which assessment will be made)
- competences (such as knowledge, skills)
- responsibilities
- organisational factors (structure of the organization)
- environmental factors
- factors likely to motivate (or demotivate) employees
- training needs.

Job analysis is for internal purposes and it is important in terms of job evaluation for pay purposes, for planning training programmes and for efficient and effective recruitment. The analysis will be used in the drawing up of a **job description**. This document – which is a broad statement of the purpose, duties and responsibilities of a job – will be composed of the following elements:

- job title;
- purpose of the job;
- main tasks to be performed;
- basic organizational structure, in particular a statement of to whom the postholder is accountable and for whom he or she is responsible;
- limits of authority;
- resources available to the postholder;
- targets to be achieved and criteria for assessing performance;
- special circumstances (such as shift work).

Job descriptions are essential for those charged with making the appointment and also for applicants who will make their case for appointment on the basis of the job outlined in the description. Once the appointment has been made, the job description continues to perform a useful role. Both management and the employee have a clear statement of what is expected of the successful applicant. This enables management to insist on full compliance with the terms of the job description. At the same time, the employee has a strong case for declining to do tasks that were not included in the description. The job description can also be used in job evaluation to establish pay structures and help in identifying training needs.

However, detailed job descriptions can cause problems. Especially in a rapidly changing environment, rigid adherence to a job description could stifle innovation and much-needed change. At the same time, employees might choose to confine their efforts to the minimum required in the description.

In addition to a job description, the recruiting organization should draw up a **person specification.** The difference between this and a job description is simple: the job description deals with the job, whereas the person specification deals with what would make the ideal person for the job. Hence, the person specification will cover:

- knowledge
- intelligence
- general and specific skills
- experience
- qualifications
- age
- physical characteristics
- personality.

Many organizations base their person specifications on the Rodgers seven-point plan, as shown in Table 44.1.

Alternatively, Munro Fraser's five-fold grading system can be used:

1 impact on others, such as whether or not the job bring the postholder into contact with others;
2 qualifications and experience – the minimum qualifications needed for a particular job;
3 innate abilities, that is, aptitude for learning;
4 motivation – some jobs present opportunities for creativity and self-development and are, therefore, more appropriate for people with drive and enthusiasm;

5 adjustment – emotional stability to stand up to stress and ability to get on with people.

Careful preparation of the job description and person specification will increase the efficiency of the recruitment and selection process, especially if there is a clear distinction between those characteristics that are essential (and the absence of which would debar a candidate) and those that are merely considered to be desirable. The next stage of the process is to seek suitable applicants.

Recruitment

The purpose of this stage is to attract suitable applicants. The main sources of candidates are:

- internal;
- external advertisements;
- private employment agencies;
- jobcentres;
- education and training establishments;
- unsolicited letters and calls.

The choice of method will vary with the type of job. Hence, manual workers are often recruited via job and training centres whereas management posts are usually filled after publishing an advertisement. As a general rule, the more specialized

Table 44.1 The Rodgers seven-point plan

Quality	Description
1 Physical	This covers health, physique, age, appearance, hearing and speech. Physical attributes may be added or removed as necessary
2 Attainments	Including academic attainments, training received, knowledge, skills and experience already developed
3 Intelligence	The general intelligence, specific abilities and methods for the assessment of these
4 Special aptitudes	Any special aptitudes, such as mechanical, manual, verbal, numerical, creativity and so on
5 Interests	Personal interests as possible indicators of aptitudes, abilities of personality traits (such as intellectual, practical/constructional, physically active, social, artistic)
6 Disposition	Personality characteristics needed (such as equability, dependability, self-reliance, assertiveness, drive, energy, perseverance, initiative, motivation)
7 Circumstances	Personal and domestic circumstances (such as mobility, commitments, family circumstances and occupations)

or more senior the post, the more it is likely to be nationally advertised.

In the recruitment and selection process, it is important to take account of various pieces of legislation referred to in Chapter 8. The Equal Pay Act 1970 obliges employers to offer equal pay to men and women undertaking the same work. The Sex Discrimination Act 1976 and the Race Relations Act 1976 prohibit discrimination on grounds of gender or ethnic origin. The Data Protection Act 1984 compels the registration of computer-based records. In addition, the Employment Protection Acts 1975 and 1978 give employees various statutory rights.

Selection

Having attracted a number of applicants, it is now necessary to select the most appropriate candidate. Rarely is selection based purely on written evidence (that is, letter, application form, reference and testimonial). More often, the written evidence provides the basis for short-listing suitable candidates. Actual selection is based on interviews, possibly combined with some of the following activities:

- ability test of achievement to test what the candidate knows and can do;
- ability test of aptitude to predict latent potential to meet job requirements;
- tests of personality;
- group situational tests in which candidates are observed performing a variety of tasks as a team.

The term **assessment centre** is used to describe a collection of assessment methods applied to a cohort entry where specifically designed tests and exercises are worked through by all applicants. The activities span several days and include a series of tests, group activities and interviews. At the end of the process, assessors meet for a final discussion to determine an overall weighting of candidates.

Whatever selection test or method is used, it is important that it should:

- be inexpensive relative to the importance of the job;
- measure what it is intended to measure (an intelligence test should measure intelligence and not learned responses, for example);
- should give a consistent result;
- should discriminate between candidates in terms of intelligence, ability, aptitude and personality;
- rank candidates;
- be relevant to the job.

Contract of employment

When the successful candidate is selected, he or she is offered a contract of employment. All contracts of employment contain implied (or unwritten but, none the less, binding) terms. It is implied that the employer should act reasonably and pay for work carried out. It is also implied that the employee will obey reasonable instructions and be loyal and cooperative. In addition, there will be specific terms (known as the terms and conditions of employment). These will relate to the:

- date of commencement
- pay
- hours of work
- holiday entitlement
- sickness pay
- pension
- period of notice
- title of job
- disciplinary procedures
- grievance procedures.

Included in the contract should be a clear statement of the identity of both sides to the agreement. To avoid future legal complications, it is essential for both sides to agree to specific terms and conditions and for the employee to know exactly who is their employer.

Induction

This is the process of introducing the new employee to the organization and the organization to the new employee. It is very important to devise an induction programme to ensure that employees:

- are integrated as quickly as possible;
- understand their responsibilities;

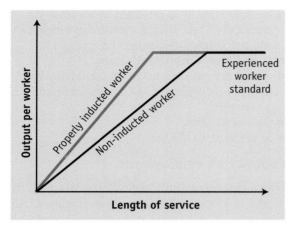

Figure 44.3 The benefits of induction

- learn relevant aspects of the mission, culture, policies, procedures and methods of working;
- feel comfortable, motivated and productive as soon as possible.

The absence of an induction programme is likely to reflect in a delay in new employees reaching level of productivity of the experienced worker (see Figure 44.3). It is also the case that the badly inducted worker is more likely to leave in the early weeks of employment than one who has been part of a good programme, thus raising labour turnover. This is because of what is known as the induction crisis – the critical phase when new starters are most likely to leave.

A well-planned induction programme can help to decrease labour turnover by ensuring that newcomers settle quickly into their jobs and reach an efficient standard of performance as quickly as possible. Such an induction programme should cover the following:

- conditions of employment;
- procedures for absence and holidays;
- timing of meal breaks;
- discipline and grievance procedures;
- welfare issues;
- the organization, its history and culture;
- the geography of the workplace;
- key personnel – who's who in the organization;
- safety;
- training arrangements;

- the pay system;
- trade unions and staff associations.

The flexible firm

There are ways of overcoming labour shortages other than recruiting full-time employees from external sources. Internal recruitment could take the form of promotion or transfers from the existing labour force. To aid the process, it is important to undertake and maintain a skills inventory – a database on the skills that employees possess. Overtime working by existing employees could be used, although the payment of an overtime premium will mean a rise in unit costs. Consequently, many modern organizations are moving to greater flexibility by means of greater use of non-standard labour (see Figure 44.4).

The nucleus of full-time permanent employees (the 'core') perform key tasks and use skills specific to the organization. This core is then surrounded by one or more groups of peripheral workers:

- part-time employees;
- temporary employees;
- agency staff;
- self-employed people.

The peripheral workers have lower job security (although the EU Part-time Workers Directive now gives equal rights to part-timers), and normally undertake routine and, to some extent, ancillary tasks. This combination of core and periphery workers provides employers with the flexibility they require in the rapidly changing business world. The size of the 'periphery' can be expanded or contracted in response to changes in the planned level of production. At the same time, the existence of the periphery generates a greater sense of job security in the core, leading to greater functional flexibility.

The creation of a periphery distinct from the core is frequently criticized as it is viewed as:

- exploiting low-paid labour;
- failing to create what are sometimes called 'proper jobs'.

However, irrespective of our personal view, we

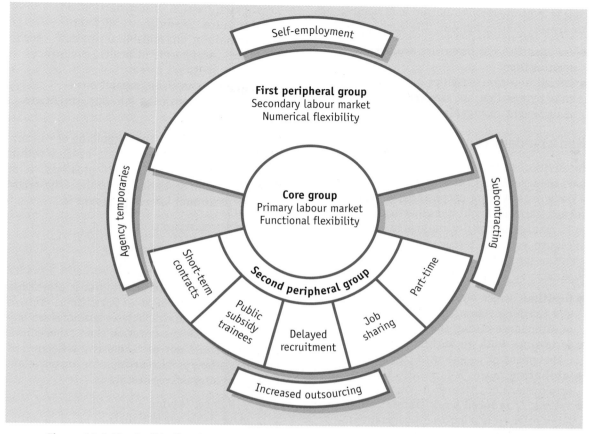

Figure 44.4 The flexible firm (Atkinson Institute of Manpower Studies, University of Sussex, 1984)

should try to understand the reasons for employing non-standard labour from the perspective of the employer.

Part-time workers are employed:

- to perform tasks for which there is insufficient need for full-time employees;
- to match staffing levels to demand;
- because of employees' preference for part-time work;
- to retain valued staff;
- to reduce pay and non-pay costs;
- because such workers are less likely to be unionized;
- because such workers have fewer statutory rights (although this is changing with EU directives);

- because their higher turnover results in greater flexibility.

Temporary (including agency) workers are employed:

- to provide short-term cover;
- to match staff to demand;
- because some employees prefer temporary work;
- to reduce pay and non-pay costs;
- because of lower unionization;
- to provide cover in a period of changing staff levels.

Subcontracting or outsourcing is the transfer of internal activities to a third party. Examples include HRM activities (such as training, payroll management), information systems, security,

509

college refectory services and grounds maintenance are usually contracted out. The aims are to:

- use expertise not otherwise available in the organization;
- offload non-core activities and concentrate on activities that are seen as central to the achievement of organizational objectives.

Non-standard contracts

In addition to standard full-time and standard part-time contracts, employers have developed a range of new work patterns designed either to recruit staff who might not otherwise be available or to manage seasonal variations in work without excessive costs in terms of temporary staff or overtime payments. These non-standard contracts include:

- **flexitime,** which allows staff to decide starting and finishing times (subject to the constraint of attendance during the core period);
- **term-time work** to facilitate the employment of people with children;
- **jobsharing** again, it facilitates the employment of those with young children;
- **voluntary reduced work time** as an alternative to leaving the organization;
- **employment breaks** to facilitate the return to work of mothers;
- **sabbaticals** or unpaid leave of absence;
- **annual hours** where workers are required to work a specified number of hours per year at the management's discretion – this avoids the problem of overtime payments during the peak with insufficient work at off-peak times;
- **zero hours contract** a contract of employment where the worker is not guaranteed any work, but must wait on standby until required, and is only paid for hours actually worked.

Retaining staff

There are various reasons for employees to leave an organization, but they can usually be grouped as follows:

- separation due to management action –

disciplinary action, dissatisfaction with performance, redundancy and so on;
- involuntary or unavoidable separation – such as death, retirement, ill health, pregnancy, marriage, partner's career;
- voluntary or avoidable separations – dissatisfaction with the job, pay, conditions and so on.

It is this last category that should be of concern to management as it suggests a malaise within the organization. To highlight problems, it is useful to devise statistical measures. The crude measure of **annual labour turnover** is:

$$\frac{\text{Number of separations}}{\text{Average number employed}} \times 100$$

Here, 'separation' means employees who leave for whatever reason. More meaningful is a measure that excludes unavoidable separations. This is not to say that unavoidable separations are any less costly to the organization than other kinds, but they should not be taken as a reflection of human relations problems within the organization. Hence, an alternative measure is:

$$\frac{\text{Number leaving} - \text{unavoidable separations}}{\text{Average number employed}} \times 100$$

This can be used as an indicator of staff morale, although, like all statistics, it should be handled with caution. We should not extrapolate from a 25 per cent annual turnover that there would be a 100 per cent turnover over four years. It could be the same few posts involved time and again. Another revealing statistic is the **stability index**, which records the stability of the core of the workforce:

$$\frac{\text{Number with over one year's service}}{\text{Total number employed one year ago}} \times 100$$

Obviously, a certain amount of labour turnover is essential for the health of any organization. A stagnant workforce is likely to become complacent and set in its ways. For the organization to respond to the changing environment, the injection of new blood is essential. Moreover, labour turnover is the only way to avoid the problems that accompany an ageing workforce (declining productivity, declining flexibility and so on). However, there are costs associated with labour turnover. These can be identified as:

- lost production while the post is not filled;
- lost production during training periods;
- cost of recruitment and training;
- break-up of work groups and undermining of morale;
- cost of mistakes made by trainee;
- payment of bonuses to other workers until a replacement is found.

It is the responsibility of the human resource manager to devise strategies to reduce an excessively high turnover. Suitable strategies might include:

- improving the process of employee selection, induction and training;
- ensuring that employees are being fully utilized;
- improving working conditions;
- promoting group morale and cohesiveness;
- job enrichment, rotation and enlarging;
- demonstrate that promotion prospects exist;
- overhaul the pay structure.

Clearly, there are constraints on the human resource manager's ability to effect a reduction in turnover. The most obvious constraint is that an increase in pay would have to be sanctioned by a higher authority within the organization.

Downsizing

Downsizing is reducing the size of an organization, especially in terms of reducing the number of people in order to make it more profitable.

An organization might have surplus labour for a number of reasons:

- new technology reduces the labour required or changes the type of labour required;
- falling demand for the product;
- poor human resource planning;
- insolvency of the business.

The least painful way of shedding labour is to allow **natural wastage** to occur. This means not replacing staff as they leave. Unfortunately, natural wastage may be insufficient to produce the reduction in workforce sought by the organization.

Shedding staff by **voluntary redundancy** is often the first resort of the employer. It is less painful and disruptive than compulsory redundancy. However, in the case of large-scale shedding of labour, it is unlikely to be sufficient and might result in the loss of the more enterprising and valuable workers. The offer or enforcement of early retirement has similarities with voluntary redundancy, except that it is targeted at the worker who is already close to retirement. Clearly, it has advantages to both the individual and the organization, but may result in the loss of experienced people. Moreover, early retirement poses financial problems for pension funds and it has been curtailed in some occupations.

When voluntary solutions to the problem of excess staff are inadequate, the organization may be forced to resort to compulsory redundancy. As we saw in Chapter 8, under the Employment Protection Act, redundancy is a 'fair' reason for dismissal provided there is adequate warning, consultation and compensation, and provided it is carried out fairly and on agreed lines.

The most common method of selecting people for redundancy is **last in, first out (LIFO)**, in which newcomers are dismissed before long-serving employees. This is seen as fair, it reduces compensation payments, it enables the organization to retain experienced individuals and, as younger people are likely to go, it is less disruptive to individuals. However, LIFO has drawbacks in terms of an ageing workforce and that there is then an absence of fresh blood. It does (indirectly) discriminate against women and suffers the basic defect that length of service does not necessarily coincide with particular skill, aptitude, enthusiasm or merit in the individual.

Retention by merit (value to the organization) means that those who perform well are kept, while the less effective workers are made redundant. For an organization, this has clear benefits, but problems arise in appraising performance and justifying the selection of those to be made redundant. For the employee, dismissal on this basis will be seen as a personal failure, thus adding to the problem of being made redundant.

There is no painless way of effecting redundancy, but the agreed method should attempt to balance the interests of the organization with the effects on individuals.

Training

The emphasis on quality, competitiveness and employee participation, coupled with the rapid pace of technological and other change, has raised the importance of training, both for the organization and the nation as a whole. No longer confined to initial training at the start of a working life, training is seen as a continuous process occurring throughout a working life. The benefit to the organization of training its staff will be seen in terms of:

- increased efficiency and productivity;
- reduction in costs;
- reduction in supervisory problems and grievances;
- reduction in accidents;
- improved quality;
- improved motivation and morale among employees;
- encouraging a culture of flexibility;
- developing a culture of learning;
- easing skills shortages;
- planning for succession.

The individual will also benefit in terms of:

- the acquisition of new skills;
- increase in employment prospects;
- improved promotion prospects;
- increased ability to cope with the pressures of work resulting in less stress at work;
- increased job satisfaction.

A planned approach to training starts with a **training needs analysis.** This seeks to identify the gap between:

- the knowledge and skills *possessed* and the knowledge and skills *required*;
- *actual* performance and *target/standard* performance.

The analysis is not confined to individuals, but to teams, departments and the corporation as a whole. The training need is any shortcoming, gap or problem that prevents the individual or organization achieving its objective and can be overcome or reduced by training. The advantage of a systematic approach to training is that it:

- ensures resources are targeted at identified priorities;
- links with the appraisal system;
- is a base for improving performance;
- plays a vital part in gaining the Investors in People award.

With training needs identified, the next stage is to:

- define training objectives;
- prepare programmes – this will involve making decisions about the method of delivering training;
- implement the plans;
- evaluate the training programme.

Training can be provided internally or externally. Internally provided training (as shown in Table 44.2) can be **on-the-job** (instruction at the workstation) or **off-the-job** (lectures, demonstrations provided by the employer, but away from the workstation). Internal training is seen as directly relevant, up-to-date and based on an understanding of the real problems facing the employee.

External training is provided by colleges (both long courses leading to a recognized qualification or short courses) and by private training

Table 44.2 Training methods

On-the-job	Off-the-job
• Demonstration	• Lectures
• Coaching	• Case studies
• Do-it-yourself training	• Role playing
• Job rotation and planned experience	• Discussion groups
• Technology-based training (TBT)	• Development centres
	• Group dynamics
	• Action learning
	• Projects
	• Business games
	• Outdoor training

organizations. External trainers will have advantages in terms of breadth of experience, provision of an outside perspective and credibility based on experience and knowledge. Conversely, such training might be insufficiently tailored to the requirements of the organization. The way to overcome the latter problem is for the training provider and the organization purchasing training services to reach a clear agreement on the training programme.

As training is a costly investment in people, it should be subject to evaluation in which the following questions should be asked.

- What are the objectives of the training programme?
- At what level are the objectives set?
- Against what criteria is training to be evaluated?
- When should evaluation take place?
- Who should do the evaluation?
- To what extent are changes in the firm the effect of training?
- Is it possible to compare the costs of training with financial gains in performance? (cost–benefit analysis).

The final question is crucial – did the training provide value for money?

It is relatively easy to identify the costs involved in training in terms of the:

- cost of accommodation;
- hire of trainers and equipment;
- pay to trainers;
- lost production as a result of absent trainees;
- travel costs;
- the additional pay to trained workers.

The benefits are less easy to measure, although we could think of benefits in terms of the costs of *not* training employees, which would result in the:

- need for additional recruitment to buy skills not available within the organization and replace staff who leave because of a lack of training opportunities;
- reduced productivity arising from less efficient working methods or less developed skills;

- longer time taken for individuals to become fully proficient;
- reduced ability to adapt to changing conditions or to innovate;
- increased likelihood of accidents;
- less motivated workforce with consequent lower productivity;
- less awareness of, and commitment to, organizational objectives.

Investors in People (IiP)

IiP is a national standard aimed at helping organizations develop their staff. The aim is to improve business performance and competitiveness by means of a planned approach to setting and communicating objectives and developing people to meet the objectives. The IiP award is a recognition of the organization's commitment to training. The practical benefits of working towards and achieving the IiP standard are:

- **improved earnings, productivity and profitability** skilled and motivated people work harder and better, productivity will improve, extra effort will be made to close sales and a positive impact will be seen on the bottom line;
- **reduced costs and wastage** skilled and motivated people constantly examine their work to contribute to reducing costs and wastage;
- **enhanced quality** investing in people significantly improves the results of quality programmes – indeed, Investors in People adds considerable value to BS 5750, ISO 9000 and other total quality initiatives;
- **improved motivation** as a result of greater involvement, personal development and recognition of achievement, motivation is improved, which leads to higher morale, improved retention rates, reduced absenteeism, readier acceptance of change and identification with the organization beyond the confines of the job;
- **customer satisfaction** Investors in People is central to helping employees become customer-focused, thus enabling the

organization to effectively meet customer needs at a profit;

- **public recognition** Investors in People status brings public recognition for real achievements measured against a rigorous national standard, it helps to attract the best-quality job applicants and may also provide a reason for customers to choose specific goods and services;

- **competitive advantage due to improved performance** Investors in People organizations develop a competitive edge.

Key concepts

Core worker Employees regarded as being of central importance. The term is usually taken to mean full-time permanent employees, although, within this group, it is possible to distinguish between key workers and others.

Human resource management (HRM) Those aspects of management that deal with the human side of business enterprise. HRM is more than a modern term for personnel management – it represents a shift in philosophy.

Labour turnover A measure of the extent to which employees enter and leave an organization. A high turnover can be seen as a reflection of low morale.

Human resource planning A comparison of the organization's existing human resources against its forecast needs, with a statement of planned strategies to eliminate any discrepancy.

Peripheral workers Part-time, temporary and subcontracted workers who are not part of the core. A modern trend is to achieve flexibility by means of a small core workforce and a large peripheral workforce.

Recruitment and selection Attracting a field of applicants to fill a vacancy (recruitment) and selecting an appropriate person (selection).

Redundancy Termination of employment caused by an inadequate level of work. Redundancy

is a 'fair' reason for dismissal, but only if it is carried out according to procedures laid down in law.

Training Investment in human resources to improve effectiveness and/or efficiency.

Unfair dismissal The sacking of a protected employee for any reason other than incapacity, misconduct, redundancy or some other substantial reason.

Essay questions

1 Evaluate the role of job descriptions and person specifications in recruitment and selection.

2 Critically analyse the modern trend towards a slimmed down core and large group of periphery workers.

3 Evaluate the interview as a method of selection. Suggest ways in which the interview can be supplemented by alternative methods of selection.

4 (a) Outline the principles of human resource planning.
  (b) Assess the value of human resource planning.

5 (a) Analyse the likely causes of high labour turnover.
  (b) Suggest and evaluate solutions to the problem of high labour turnover.

6 (a) What factors should be considered before making workers redundant?
  (b) Evaluate the alternatives to redundancy.

7 (a) What should be included in a programme of induction?
  (b) Evaluate the benefits of a formal programme of induction.

8 (a) Explain how you would set about evaluating a programme of training.
  (b) Discuss the benefits to an organization of recognition as an Investor in People.

Reward management

The philosophical change from personnel management to HRM is reflected in new approaches to rewarding employees. This chapter looks at employee rewards from the perspective of the organization. It should be studied in conjunction with Chapter 46, in which trade unions enter the picture.

Chapter objectives

1 To understand the role of employee rewards in securing organizational objectives.

2 To distinguish between old and new approaches to pay.

3 To explore various types of pay system.

Employee rewards

Reward is a wider concept than *pay*. It includes pay, remuneration and compensation and 'represents a portfolio of managerial practices where financial and non-financial elements are flexibly directed at enabling and rewarding employees who add value in the interests of competitive advantage' (M. Corbridge and S. Pilbeam, *Employment Resourcing*, Financial Times Pitman, 1998). Note that the definition places employee rewards in the context of strategies to achieve organizational objectives.

The components of employee rewards are:

- **base pay**, which can be expressed as an annual (salary), weekly or hourly rate;
- **additions to base pay**, which take the form of:
  - individual performance-related pay;
  - bonuses for successful individual, organizational or team performance;
  - incentive payments for reaching target levels of performance;
  - commission related to sales generated;
  - service-related pay or increments for each year of service;
  - skills (or knowledge-based) pay;
  - competence-related pay, linked to the level of competence;
  - allowances for shift working, call-outs, living in London.

The sum of base pay and additions

represents the total earnings of the employee;

- **employee benefits (indirect pay)**, which include:
  - pension
  - sick pay
  - insurance cover
  - company car.

So, if we aggregate these three, we get total remuneration – the value of all payments and benefits received by employees.

- **non financial rewards** include any rewards that focus on peoples' needs for achievement, recognition, responsibility, influence and personal growth.

Objectives of a pay system

The objectives of an organizations' pay system are devised to help it:

- **compete in the job market** if pay levels are set too low, the organization will find it difficult to attract and retain human resources;
- **achieve value for money** that is, to ensure that spending on pay is cost-effective in that it encourages value-added performance without excessive expense;
- **motivate people to achieve superior levels of performance.**

The major theories on motivation all stress the need for a satisfactory reward system. The scientific management school views money, in the form of piece-rate payments, as the major motivator. For Herzberg, pay was a hygiene factor, which means that if pay is too low employees will be demotivated, but if they receive a fair or higher rate, other issues will become motivators. Equity theory emphasizes the importance of fairness in terms of relative pay. If employees consider themselves unfairly treated, they will respond by reducing their effort. Expectancy theory also sees pay as an element in effort–outcome expectancies. For McClellan, pay is important to high achievers because it serves as performance feedback and as a measure of the accomplishment of goals.

To ensure that the pay system motivates, it is essential that it is seen as equitable, consistent and transparent. Equity requires that people are paid in accordance with their contribution to the organization. It should be equitable to both sides and between different employees. Consistency requires that people are paid according to the level of their job and performance. A person's reward should be related to factors that they control (such as quantity and quality). Transparency requires that the pay system is disclosed to people so that they know the basis on which they are paid. Notification of bonus earnings should be prompt, to provide quick feedback. Obviously, the incentive should be substantial as a weak incentive is of little use. Ideally, it should be based on individual performance, but, where this is not possible, it should be based on team performance.

Graded structures

A **graded pay structure** consists of a hierarchy of pay grades into which jobs of broadly equivalent value are slotted. Attached to each grade is a pay range that provides for variations linked to individual performance competence or skill. The range is expressed in percentage terms so that an 80–120 per cent range means that pay will range from 20 per cent below to 20 per cent above the mid-point chosen for the pay range. Similarly, the differentials between grades are fixed in percentage terms – a 20 per cent differential means that the mid-point of one grade is 20 per cent above the mid-point of the grade below. This could result in some overlapping of pay in different grades. The advantages and disadvantages of a graded structure are shown in Table 45.1.

Job evaluation

This is defined as a method of analysing a job to assess, in non-financial terms, its standing relative to other jobs. It is important to realize that it is the job and the demands that it places on the jobholder that are analysed – not the performance of the individual currently in the post. The purposes of the exercise is to determine pay rates, especially in terms of differentials

Table 45.1 Graded structures – advantages and disadvantages

Advantages	Disadvantages
● Clear indication of pay relativity	● Grade boundaries are a matter for judgement
● Easy to explain	● Grade drift possible as a result of pressure for upgrading
● Provides a framework for pay relativity	● Leads to rigidy
● Provides for control	● Expectation that all reach top of grade irrespective of performance

between grades. The techniques of job evaluation are as follows.

- **Job ranking** Each job is assessed as a whole and its relative importance to the organization is established. Jobs are ranked in order of importance.
- **Job classification** This is similar to ranking except in terms of the order of events. Grades and pay are identified first and then jobs are compared with these outlines and slotted into the appropriate grade.
- **Points rating system** Jobs are broken down into a number of factors (training, skills, supervision required). Each factor is given a weighting and then the value of a job is assessed by totalling the points awarded to its component factors.
- **Factor comparisons** Jobs are broken down as in the points rating system, but each factor is given a monetary value. Where large numbers of jobs are involved, benchmark jobs may be selected at various intervals in the organization and placed in order. These jobs provide a framework for placing other jobs.

The advantages of job evaluation are that it:

- provides a rational basis for pay differentials;
- in based on job content, not personal merit;
- should result in equity between grades;
- plays a major part in ensuring that there is no discrimination in pay between the sexes.

However, job evaluation does also have some major drawbacks:

- although it attempts to be scientific, in practice, there is a large element of subjective judgement;
- it results in pay that is unrelated to performance;

- it establishes pay differentials but not absolute levels of pay;
- it supports rigid hierarchical organizations and concepts of status, which operate against flexibility, and assumes that people are commodities that can be fitted into defined roles;
- it has to be updated as job requirements change.

Time rates

Under a **time rate system**, earnings are calculated by multiplying the hourly time rate by the number of hours at work. The obvious defect of this system is that pay is not related to effort or output, but merely to the time spent at work. Not only does this not provide an incentive to work hard, it can actually *encourage* time-wasting. By prolonging the work, the employees can obtain overtime pay. Typically, these are premium rates, 25 or 50 per cent greater than the basic hourly rate. Despite these defects, time rate systems are widely used, especially where:

- employees have no control over how fast they do their work;
- output cannot be measured or attributed to individuals or groups;
- output is of a non-standard type;
- quality, accuracy or care would be jeopardized by a system that relates pay to output;
- periods of enforced but temporary idleness occur.

Piece rates

Under a **piece rate system**, the earnings of an individual worker (or group of workers) are related to the quantity of items produced. It is only appropriate when:

- the output is standardized;
- the output is measurable;
- there is a link between effort and output;
- output can be attributed to an individual worker (or a group) so that each receives a reward commensurate with effort.

Price-work systems are designed to provide workers with an incentive to increase output. Needless to say, they will only succeed in this aim if workers are motivated by the prospect of increased pay. One problem faced by management is that informal groups of employees might set a pay effort norm, separate from management's intention. Consequently, there are a number of variations on piece-work systems, shown in Figure 45.1. Figure 45.1(a) shows a strictly linear relationship with no guarantee of basic pay, while (b) shows a piece rate as a supplement to a basic minimum rate of pay. To discourage excessive effort and output, there is a variation on this combination of rates, shown in (c). Output beyond the standard performance is discouraged by a lower piece rate above this level of output.

All piece-work systems require a programme of work study to set piece rates that are sufficiently challenging to the workforce and yet capable of achievement. If the rate is too low, it will demotivate; if it is too high it will lead to excessive costs and/or provide an inadequate challenge. See Table 45.2 for a summary of the advantages and disadvantages of piece and time rates.

Measured day work

Measured day work (MDW) is a payment system in which pay is fixed on the clear understanding that employees maintain a performance level specified in the agreement. It has the advantage of greater stability in earnings, but the trade-off is less flexibility in output. Employees will work to achieve the agreed level of performance.

We can identify the situations in which it is appropriate as:

- those in which piece rates are inappropriate;

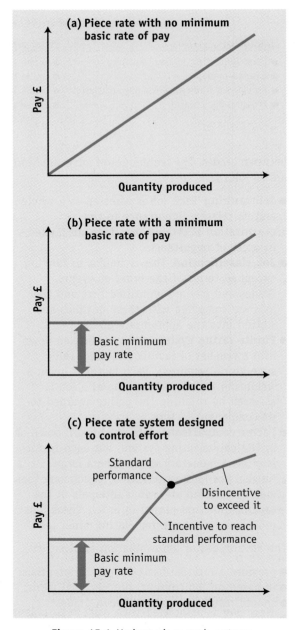

Figure 45.1 Various piece-work systems

- process-type operations (such as in chemical plants);
- those where the job cycle is long;
- those where accurate measurement of operations is possible;

Table 45.2 Time rates v. piece rates

Time rates Advantages	Piece rates Advantages
● Less harmful to quality ● Less harmful to health of employees ● Simple, easy to understand ● Appropriate in most circumstances	● Stimulates effort ● Encourages workers to devise improved methods ● Simplifies costing
Disadvantages	**Disadvantages**
● Does not provide incentive for increased effort ● Requires supervision of workforce ● Employers vulnerable to work-to-rule sanctions by unions	● Must be adjusted for local circumstances ● Only appropriate in particular circumstances ● Encourages workers to 'cut corners', endangering safety and quality

● those where work study staff are available to determine standards;
● those where supervision is possible;
● those where unions are responsive.

Despite the inherent problems of MDW, it has been successfully introduced to provide a premium level of pay for a sustained level of performance.

New pay and old pay

The distinction between new and old approaches to pay was developed in 1990 by E. E. Lawler (*Strategic Pay* Jossey-Bass, 1990). **Old pay** is characterized by:

● bureaucratic salary administration;
● organizational hierarchy;
● rigid job evaluation and grading;
● incremental progression;
● detachment of pay from the strategic objectives of the organization;
● concern for fairness, consistency and equity.

It is argued that old pay will inhibit organizational responsiveness in the changing environment.

New pay is associated with a more turbulent environment, increasingly competitive pressure and leaner, flatter and more flexible organizations. Essential characteristics of new pay include:

● the integration of pay with organizational strategy;
● the use of pay and reward as a lever on employee performance;
● integration of pay and reward strategies with

other aspects of human resource management;
● rewarding contribution made rather than seniority or status;
● 'broadbanding' to encourage flexible working;
● flexible benefit, which aims to provide individual choice with a diverse workforce;
● a market approach, in which pay reflects the commercial worth of employees.

The transition from old to new pay is reflected in the trends shown in Table 45.3. Three aspects of new pay are explored in the remainder of this chapter.

Performance-related pay (PRP)

PRP links financial rewards to individual, group or corporate objectives. The main aims of PRP are to:

● motivate employees;
● increase commitment to organizational objectives;
● develop a performance culture;
● reward contributions made to organizational success (as distinct from rewarding effort);
● recruit and retain high-quality employees;
● deliver a message about performance expectations.

These are the arguments for introducing a system of PRP, but it must also be appreciated that there are major problems associated with PRP:

● money is not the only motivator;
● PRP might encourage short-termism;

Table 45.3 Trends in pay systems

Declining trends in pay	Emerging trends in pay
• Inflation-linked rises	• New pay – integration with corporate strategy
• Annual pay rises	• Market driven
• Collective pay bargaining	• Broadbanding
• Incremental pay (linked to length of service)	• Flexible benefits
• Traditional job evaluation	• Competence-based pay
• Allowances and add-ons	• Performance-based pay
• Inflexibility	• Longer-term pay deals
	• Flexibility

(Adapted from M. Corbridge and S. Pilbeam, *Employment Resourcing,* Financial Times Pitman 1998)

- attention is focused on volume and speed – not quality;
- intrinsic interest in a task declines when someone is given only external reasons for doing it;
- PRP is costly to introduce;
- PRP can cause 'pay drift' (pay rising without a commensurate increase in performance);
- a PRP scheme will be demotivating if people feel that they are unable to achieve the performance standard or that assessment/appraisal is not objective and not fair.

Broadbanding

Broadbanding is defined as the compression of a hierarchy of pay grades or ranges into a small number of wide bands, each of which spans the pay opportunities previously covered by several pay ranges. This approach to pay has become popular because of delayering and the need for greater flexibility. Broadbanding helps to eliminate the obsession with grades and encourages employees to move laterally to jobs where they can develop their careers and add value to the organization.

In a broad-based pay structure, there will be four or five wide pay bands. Each band will have a target rate of pay (determined by the market rate of a key benchmark role within the band). Around the target will be a pay zone so that, as employees take on wide responsibilities or increase their competence, they will receive extra pay

within the band. This removes pay rises from promotion to a new post.

Advantages claimed for broadbanding are that it:

- promotes lateral (sideways) career development;
- increases flexibility;
- provides a flexible system of rewards for those whose role is widened or skills/knowledge is increased;
- is consistent with a flatter organizational structure;
- not constrained by narrow grades and the bureaucracy of traditional job evaluation;
- focuses on paying people for what they contribute, rather than what their job title is.

Against this, there are the following disadvantages:

- it restricts promotion opportunities;
- employees in formerly high grades may feel that broadbanding has devalued their job when they are placed in the same band as employees previously in a lower grade;
- it is difficult to ensure that there is equal pay for equal value work.

Profit-related pay

A distinction has to be made between profit-sharing (a scheme that allocates some bonus according to profitability, without putting at risk basic pay) and profit-related pay (which does involve basic pay). In the former scheme, the only element at risk is the bonus on the basic pay, whereas in the latter scheme low profits will reduce or even eliminate the basic pay.

The advantages of linking pay (or at least pay bonuses) to profit are that it:

- encourages employees to identify with the company;
- provides an incentive to work harder;
- makes staff profit-conscious;
- fosters commitment to the future of the organization.

However, it is difficult to design a workable system that is fair (to shareholders as well as employees) and provides an incentive. One aspect of the equity problem is definition of profit as the profit figure depends on accounting practices and can be manipulated by accountants. The incentive problem of profit-related pay is that reward is not linked to individual effort and performances.

The elements combined in new pay

The shift towards new pay has resulted in pay to the individual being the aggregate of:

- **base pay** market-driven, to reflect the commercial worth of the individual, but including increments within broad bands;
- **flexible benefits** a benefits package that allows for choice (the 'cafeteria' approach);

- **individual profit-related pay** bonuses based on a subjective judgement about individual performance; and/or
- **team profit-related pay** a variable pay element to reflect the contribution of the team;
- **a share in organizational success** this takes the form of profitsharing in the private sector or gainsharing in the public sector.

Table 45.4 summarizes the different type of pay.

Table 45.4 Compensation – a summary

Type	Description
Hourly wage	Fixed amount per hour
Salary	Amount per year
Piece rate	Fixed amount per unit of output
Sales commission	Fixed percentage of sales revenue
Profitsharing	Distribution of specified percentage of profits
Performance-related pay	Bonuses related to performance
Gainsharing	Distribution of specified percentage of cost savings

Key concepts

Bonus scheme Employee incentive applied either individually or to a group.

Broadbanding The compression of a hierarchy of pay grades into a small number of wide bands.

Job evaluation The placing of jobs in order of rank so that employees can be rated fairly.

Measured day work Pre-specified daily output in return for a fixed daily rate of pay.

Performance-related pay Payment of a bonus linked to a subjective measure of individual performance.

Piece rate Pay related to number of units of output.

Profit-related pay An element of pay is linked to company profits.

Salary A fixed annual amount, payable in 12 or 13 equal instalments.

Wage Weekly cash payments that are subject to fluctuation depending on overtime, piece rates, bonuses and so on.

Essay questions

1 Discuss the principles of reward management.

2 Evaluate piece rates in comparison with time rates.

3 (a) Explain what is meant by new (as opposed to old) pay.
  (b) Evaluate two of the features of new pay.

4 (a) Explain the differences between piece rates, commission and performance-rated pay.

(b) Discuss the problems associated with performance-related pay.

5 Evaluate profit-related pay as a way of motivating the workforce. In your answer, make reference to appropriate theory.

6 (a) Explain what you understand by:
     (i) delayering; and
     (ii) broadbanding of pay.
  (b) Evaluate broadbanding in the light of the trend towards delayering.

46

Industrial relations

After reviewing pay from the perspective of the organization, we now bring trade unions into the analysis.

Chapter objectives

1 To describe the roles of unions.

2 To explore different approaches to industrial relations.

3 To investigate the collective bargaining process.

4 To explore new-style agreements.

5 To explain techniques of employee participation.

Trade unions

Trade unions can be defined as all organizations of employees, which include, among their functions, that of negotiating with employers with the object of regulating conditions of employment. Unions negotiate with employers on pay and condition in the process known as collective (as distinct from individual) bargaining. Other functions include acting as a channel of communications between employers and employees, providing assistance to individual members (for example, with grievances or in disciplinary matters) and helping employees participate in the process of decision making, both in the workplace and nationally. The main categories of trade unions are shown in Table 46.1.

Management attitudes to unions

Management's attitudes to trade unions range from:

- outright hostility and opposition to organizations seen as stirring up trouble; to
- reluctant acceptance of organizations that are seen as a necessary evil; to
- enthusiastic acceptance of organizations that are a legitimate expression of employee opinion and an essential channel of communication.

These differences in opinion result from differing

Table 46.1 Categories of trade unions

Categories	Description
Craft unions	Recruit members from distinct trades or occupations, historically linked to an apprenticeship system. Originally, such unions aimed to preserve jobs within the craft exclusively for their members. Technological change has blurred and sometimes eliminated the craft skills, and unions have survived by changing their membership boundaries to incorporate other areas.
Industrial unions	These are dominant in Germany, but have been slow to develop in the UK. They aim to represent all employees in a particular industry, regardless of the type of work they do
General unions	Broad-ranging unions, representing a variety of industries and job types, with little restriction on potential membership. Some are so extensive that they have been termed 'super-unions'
Occupational unions	Recruit members within a particular occupation or group, such as teachers, police or firefighters
White-collar unions	Concentrate on non-manual occupations, such as banking

perceptions of the balance between the challenge posed by the existence of unions and the benefits to management derived from unions.

Because unions exist, management policies and decisions are subject to more effective challenge. The existence of unions has also forced management to disclose more information, and such information has been subject to more rigorous analysis than would have been the case in the absence of unions. Unionization of the workforce has contributed to the trend towards a more democratic or participative style of leadership.

These comments might be seen in a negative light by some elements within management, although it can be argued that the challenge posed by the unions can improve the quality of decision making.

It is likely that unionization of the workforce has increased the cost of the firm's operation in terms of higher rates of pay, improvement in conditions of work and the development of more formal personnel procedures. Higher costs are usually seen in a negative light, but it should always be remembered that higher rates of pay do not necessarily mean higher unit costs of production. If the pay rise contributes to a corresponding rise in productivity, it can be seen as self-financing, with no rise in unit costs.

A final management perspective on unions relates to ideas on conflict. Does the existence of trade unions contribute to, or even cause, conflict within the organization? Alternatively, do trade unions provide a channel for the expression of discontent with the result that conflict is minimized?

Two opposing perspectives can be identified – unitary and pluralist. The **unitary** view is that management and labour have identical interests and, hence, may be expected to pull together towards the same objective. Management expects workers to act as a team and assist the firm in achieving its objectives. Dissent, conflict and industrial action are seen as the result of malevolent interests, troublemakers and bad communications.

In the opposing **pluralist** view, conflict of interest and, therefore, disagreements are the normal and inescapable state of affairs. Management should accept that conflict occurs and should seek to resolve conflict by establishing sound procedures for settling disputes. The major differences in the two perspectives are summarized in Table 46.2.

Collective bargaining

The **Advisory, Conciliation and Arbitration Service (ACAS)** defines **collective bargaining** as

Table 46.2 Perspectives on industrial relations

Unitary	Pluralist
● Rejects role of trade unions	● Fully accepts role of trade unions
● They undermine loyalty and authority	● Incorporates them into the system
● They introduce conflict	● Normal for employees to have their own leaders
● They cause workers to make unreasonable demands	● Need to harness the union structure
	● They bring order into collective bargaining, disputes, discipline and grievances
● They block change	● Encourages union membership
● Resists trade union recognition	● Provides facilities for unions – training, clerical support and time off
● Employees should trust management to be objective and impartial	● Managers should have to justify their decisions, particularly on major changes
● Certain issues, such as investment policy, are technical. They are not suited to consultation	● The act of consultation is often as important as the decision itself – the actual decisions are often the same as if management had not been consulted
● Conflict should not arise. If it does, it is caused by troublemakers, rumour, incompatible personalities or misguided employees. The solutions are to get rid of agitators, improve communication, educate employees	● Conflict is an indicator of morale, but absence can indicate stagnation
	● A degree of conflict is normal and inevitable
	● Unions do not cause conflict, they express conflict that is already latent
	● Procedures are needed to handle conflict constructively – it need not destroy relationships

'the process whereby procedures are jointly agreed and wages and conditions of employment are settled by negotiations between employers, or associations of employers and workers' organisations'. As stated earlier, the rationale for trade union negotiation on behalf of employees is that, individually, workers are in a weak position and are unable to negotiate on a basis of equality. In collective bargaining, employers will be represented by those executives who have the responsibility and authority to conduct negotiations. In some sectors of the economy (such as engineering), unions negotiate with associations of employers who, again, seek strength in collective action.

The ACAS definition highlights the fact that negotiation deals with both procedural and substantive matters. **Procedural** agreements establish a framework of rules by which **substantive** issues can be negotiated. Procedural agreements are usually open-ended (subject to a period of notice if either side wishes to renegotiate procedural arrangements) and deal with:

● recognition (such as which unions should be included in bargaining);
● arrangements for representation;
● procedures for handling disputes;
● grievance procedures;
● redundancy procedures;
● definition of matters to be covered in substantive bargaining.

Substantive agreements usually run for a limited period of time and deal with the terms under which workers are employed. Typically, they relate to pay, incentive schemes, working hours, holiday entitlement, pensions, manning levels and sickness pay.

Traditionally, collective bargaining in the UK has taken place at three levels – national, company and plant or local. National bargaining involves unions (individually or collectively) and employers' associations. A national agreement usually lays down minimum standards of pay and conditions and is designed to protect individual employers from competitors who might otherwise take advantage of the situation. The national agreement will be supplemented by company- and local- (plant-) level agreements. A company may choose to be more generous over pay and/or conditions than is allowed for in the national agreement. The local agreement is designed to take account of local circumstances (such as local shortages of labour). For instance, a piece rate system of pay must always include a locally negotiated element to take account of particular local circumstances.

This three-tier system is being subjected to considerable change. Employers, encouraged by the free market governments of Thatcher and Major, favoured company-based (and preferably locally based) bargaining rather than bargaining between monopoly suppliers and monopsony demanders of labour.

The pay bargaining process

The first stage in the bargaining process is for each side to decide on its objectives, taking into account the relative bargaining strengths of the two sides (see Figure 46.1). As well as deciding on the global amount in a pay claim, unions will also have objectives in terms of how the pay rise will be distributed (equally or weighted in favour of certain groups). At the same time, management will decide on the size and distribution of the offer.

The second stage is for each side to present its case. Union pay claims are usually based on one or more of the following points.

● **Rise in the cost of living** Pay rises below the rate of inflation are seen as pay cuts in real terms. Unions will always bargain to maintain pay in line of inflation.

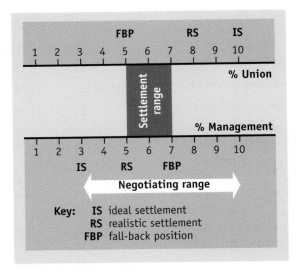

Figure 46.1 Collective bargaining

● **The need for attractive rates of pay** in order to recruit and retain adequate numbers of employees of the right calibre.
● **The need to maintain pay differentials** Pay claims are often based on the desire to secure pay rises in line with comparable groups of workers and the need to maintain pay differentials in relation to less skilled workers. Although bargaining to preserve the relative position in the pay league is an understandable tactic, it should not be allowed to fossilize the pay structure. Pay differentials should change as the nature of the job changes.
● **Productivity rises** Productivity is defined as output per unit of input (in this case output per man hour). Productivity bargaining involves a trade-off – in return for pay rises, unions agree to changes in working practices to increase productivity.
● **The need to compensate employees** for some recent change in conditions, technology or working practices.

Management pay offers are usually based on the need to recruit sufficient labour of the right kind, while at the same time maintaining the firm's competitiveness. Successful negotiation usually involves a compromise that is satisfactory to both sides, but short of their original objectives. However, before the agreement is reached, one of the sides may seek to test the resolve of the other side.

Industrial disputes

Failure in negotiation leads to the declaration of a dispute that might result in one of the following forms of industrial action:

- withdrawal of cooperation;
- work-to-rule;
- overtime ban;
- token strike;
- indefinite strike.

Just as war is a failure of diplomacy, so industrial action can be seen as a failure of the bargaining process. Negotiation gives way (temporarily at least) to action that is bound to cause harm. Although strikes are designed to hit the employer, the workers themselves, customers, the public, government and economy will also suffer to a greater or lesser extent (see Table 46.3). In a prolonged dispute, it often becomes a war of attrition, with victory going to the side that can hold out the longest.

The resort to industrial action depends on:

- the availability and likely effectiveness of sanctions – for example, a union that threatens to take action must be sure that members will act, as a union will be weakened if its bluff is called;
- the rules of behaviour laid down in procedural agreements;
- the ability and astuteness of negotiators;
- the degree of trust in the relationship – where trust is substantial, there is less likelihood of a resort to sanctions;
- the degree of power and dependence – if there is little likelihood of alternative employment, *management* is in a powerful bargaining position; where the employer relies heavily on key workers whose skills are not present in the immediate external environment, the *union* is in a strong bargaining position.

Table 46.3 The harmful consequences of strikes

For employers	● Loss of output ● Reduction in sales revenue/ profits ● Loss of custom ● Cash flow problems ● Harm to reputation ● Disruption
For customers	● Inconvenience ● Shortages
For the economy	● Loss of exports ● Import penetration ● Decline in tax yield ● Additional claims on social services ● Loss of foreign confidence in sterling ● Reduction in income
For strikers	● Threat to jobs of closure or reduction in capital investment ● Reduction in local income reduces trade
For other firms	● Problems in acquiring inputs

Mediation, conciliation and arbitration

To resolve a dispute, one or other side may seek the assistance of the Advisory, Conciliation and Arbitration Service (ACAS), which was established in 1975 to be independent of the government. The role of ACAS is apparent from its name – it offers advice on industrial relations matters, such as grievance procedures and communications within an organization. When engaged in **conciliation**, ACAS helps the two sides to reach a mutually acceptable settlement. ACAS brings the two sides together, but, when conciliating, it does not impose a settlement.

The **arbitration** process is semi-judicial, with a neutral third party making an award based on the justice of the case. Traditionally, this has usually been a compromise between the claim and the offer, but, with single-union, no-strike agreements, there has been a movement to compulsory **pendulum arbitration**. The arbitrator will choose between the union's claim and the management's offer, rather than compromise between the two. Supporters of pendulum arbitration argue that it encourages both sides to act reasonably. Detractors, however, point out that the outcome is victory for one side and defeat for the other, leaving a sense of grievance.

Mediation, which is another service offered by ACAS, lies some way between conciliation (bringing the two sides together) and arbitration (making an award). The mediator will seek to guide the two sides towards a compromise agreement.

Table 46.4 sets out how ACAS works.

New-style agreements

Industrial changes in the late twentieth century included the decline of old industries and their replacement by new, high-tech, often foreign-owned, industrial enterprises. Japanese multi-nationals, in particular, insisted on a new-style of industrial relations based on a new-style agreement that includes some or more of the following:

- a shift from multi-employer to single-employer bargaining;
- decentralized (or plant-level) bargaining;
- single-union agreements, in which only one

union covering the whole workforce is recognized;
- single-table bargaining, in which unions representing both manual and non-manual workers bargain at the same time and place;
- harmonization – the same conditions of employment for all workers;
- no-strike agreements – a commitment to settle by means of arbitration;
- pendulum arbitration;
- pay review bodies;
- insistence on flexible arrangements as a means of achieving efficient use of human resources.

Trade unions and the law

There were numerous changes to the law relating to trade unions enacted under the Conservative Government of 1979 to 1997. This was the culmination of a long period of criticism of unions for abusing their monopoly power. Particular criticisms were as follows:

- restrictive labour practices led to overmanning and the blocking of new technology;
- unions were insufficiently democratic in their procedures;

Table 46.4 Third party dispute resolution			
	Role	**Approach to dispute resolution**	**How settlement is reached**
Conciliator	a catalyst seeking to narrow disagreements	Supports negotiating process, helping parties clarify objective extent of differences, identify possible solutions and find formulae to settle dispute	Responsibility for settlement rests jointly with the parties to the dispute
Mediator	a proposer of recommendations	More proactive approach than conciliation. From assessment of parties' written cases, the mediator makes proposals that may resolve the dispute or provide a basis for further negotiation	Responsibility lies with the parties, but the mediator's views may be influential
Arbitrator	An award-maker to end a dispute	Arbitrator agrees terms of reference from parties, takes written and oral evidence and makes an award based on the issues	The arbitrator decides on the resolution of the dispute and the award is usually binding on both parties.

(Adapted from M. Corbridge and S. Pilbeam, *Employment Resourcing*, Financial Times Pitman, 1998)

Table 46.5 The law before and after the Conservative Government of 1979–97

Area	1979 position	1997 position
Dismissal of strikers	No selective dismissal	Selective dismissal permitted in the case of unofficial action. Selective re-employment of sacked strikers is permitted
Definition of trade disputes	Any dispute over terms and conditions of employment of any person	Dispute between workers and employers over terms and conditions
Legal immunity for unions	Wide immunity for trade unions in strikes where workers break their contracts	Secondary, sympathetic and political strikes are unlawful and do not confer immunity from civil action
Ballots	No legal requirement	Secret postal ballot before any industrial action
Damages for unlawful action	Unions could not be sued for damages as a result of losses incurred by industrial action	Industrial action that falls outside legal requirements makes the union liable for damages
Closed shop	Could be enforced – dismissal for non-union workers was 'fair'	Dismissal for non-membership of a union Is automatically unfair

- interunion conflicts, in the form of demarcation disputes, inflicted harm on employers;
- many strikes were **unofficial** (called by shop stewards without union sanction) and called without notice (known as **wildcat strikes**);
- unions undermined the competitiveness of British industry, thus contributing to cost-push inflation and/or unemployment;
- the **closed shop** – which compelled employees to join a company-recognized union – interfered with the civil rights of both non-union workers and employers;
- UK industrial relations practices contributed to what was perceived as a bad strike record and, thus, further undermined the competitiveness of British industry – trade unions were seen as both a symptom and, perhaps, the cause of the so-called 'British disease', which was producing the perceived de-industrialization of the UK economy;
- unions were blamed for cost-push inflation;
- unions were blamed for pricing labour out of jobs;
- powerful public-sector unions distorted the purpose of public-sector services from consumers to employees.

Conservative reforms had the effect of weakening trade unions in ways shown in Table 46.5.

Worker participation

By **worker participation** we mean the inclusion of employees in the decision-making process. This can be contrasted with the situation that applies in classical capitalism where the right to make decisions rests solely with the risk-taking owners of the business. It is true that, in the largest organizations, the shareholders delegate authority to directors and managers. The legitimacy of managers is enhanced by their expertise, but, nevertheless, it rests ultimately on the delegation of authority from the owners. Employees are seen as hired hands who sell their labour in return for pay.

Worker participation (and even worker control) was a major aim of the nineteenth-century socialist movement. This can be seen in the work of people such as Robert Owen and Karl Marx, as well as in the French syndicalist movement of the early twentieth century. When British miners pressed for the nationalization of the mining industry, they envisaged that State ownership of the mines would be accompanied by workers' control. The form of nationalization that was eventually adopted in the 1940s fell short of the miners' demand.

Except in the form of workers' cooperatives (often established to save an ailing firm), workers' control has not been on the agenda in recent decades. However, participation in decision making has been advocated by diverse groups of people, not just labour supporters and trade unionists. For a summary of the case for and against worker participation, see Table 46.6.

Forms of participation include:

- **worker directors** employee representatives on the board of directors;

- **work council** employee representatives on a council to discuss issues relating directly to employees;
- **consultative committees** employee representatives consulted on issues such as health and safety;
- **quality circles**;
- **team briefings.**

For participation to be successful, the objectives of participation must be defined, discussed and agreed. The representatives must be trained and properly briefed, and trust must exist between the two sides. Without these preconditions, it is likely that the scheme will prove counter-productive.

Table 46.6 Worker participation

The case for	The case against
• Extension of democracy into the workplace	• Time-consuming
• Increased satisfaction and personal development	• Workers lack technical knowledge
• Improved motivation, increased commitment	• Employees take a short-term view
• Improved industrial relations	• Conflict of interests
• Utilizes the knowledge and experience of workers	• Decisions should be made by risk-takers and the experts to whom the authority is delegated, otherwise
• Development of consensus	interferes with managers' right and duty to manage
• Improved information flow	• If representation is via unions, workers who are not members will lose out

Key concepts

Advisory, Conciliation and Arbitration Service (ACAS) A UK body, established in 1975, to assist in the settlement of industrial disputes.

Arbitration Settlement of a dispute by the intervention of a neutral third party.

Closed shop An arrangement whereby all employees in an organization have to belong to a specified union. This is now virtually outlawed in the UK.

Collective bargaining Bargaining between employers and trade unions acting collectively on behalf of members.

Employee relations Various aspects of the relationship between employers and employees.

Employers' federation An association of employers within a sector of the economy of country.

Incomes policy Government intervention in the pay negotiation process used to keep pay increases under control.

Industrial action Generic name for sanctions imposed by unions in support of a pay claim or some other dispute.

Industrial democracy Attempts to increase employee participation in decision making.

Industrial dispute Dispute between employees and employers.

Industrial relations Issues raised by the relationship between employers and employees, via union representation.

Negotiation The process of reaching an agreement by discussion.

Participation Involvement of employees in decision making.

Restrictive labour practice A policy of organized labour to control the way work is organized to preserve the interests of workers.

Staff association A recognized association of employees that fulfils some, but not all, trade union functions.

Trade dispute A dispute between an employer and employees.

Trade union An organization of employees established to further their interests.

Essay questions

1 (a) Explain what you understand by a claim and an offer in collective bargaining.

(b) Analyse the factors that each side takes into account in collective bergaining.

2 Analyse the cases for and aganinst:
(a) individual rather than collective bargaining;
(b) local rather than national bargaining.

3 Trade union protection for workers leads to job losses. Discuss.

4 Analyse the causes for and against trade unions in the twenty-frst century

5 (a) Evaluate the benefits of different schemes of employee participation.

(b) Discuss the preconditions for a successful scheme of participation.

Organizational culture and change

The term **organizational culture** covers the values and norms of behaviour in an organization. These have a profound impact on the way people work and, therefore, on the success, or otherwise, of an organization. It is only by understanding organizational culture that performance can be improved and change be effected.

Chapter objectives

1 To define and explain organizational culture.

2 To identify different cultures within organizations.

3 To analyse the process of managing change.

What is organizational culture?

Each organization is unique. Even if two organizations are identical in size, formal structure and product range, they will each have unique features. These intangible, but, none the less, pervasive features of the organization are known as the culture (or climate or personality) of the organization.

The most straightforward definition of the organizational culture is simply 'the way we do things around here'. More detailed definitions include the following:

- 'The ideologies, beliefs and deep-set values which occur in all firms ... and are the prescription for the ways in which people should work in those organizations'. (Harrison, *Harvard Business Review*, 1972);
- '(the organization's) customary and traditional way of thinking and doing things, which is shared to a greater or lesser degree by all members and which the new member must learn and at least partially accept, in order to be accepted into the services of the firm' (E. Jaques, *The Changing Culture of a Factory*, Garland, 1987);
- 'The basic values, ideologies and assumptions which guide and fashion individual and business behaviour. These values are evident in more tangible factors such as stories, rituals, language and jargon, office decoration and layout, and prevailing modes

of dress among staff' (D. C. Wilson, *Managing Organizations*, McGraw-Hill, 1990);

- 'The pattern of shared beliefs, attitudes, assumptions and values which, although they may not have been articulated, shape the way people act and interact, and strongly influence the way that things get done' (M. Armstrong, *A Handbook of Human Resource Management Practice*, Kogan Page, 1999);
- The values and beliefs that are central to the organization and fashion the behaviour of individuals within that organization.

Organizational *culture* should be distinguished from the organizational *climate*. The latter is defined as the general atmosphere or ethos in the workplace. Culture should also be distinguished from *management style*, which is the habitual way in which managers run the organization.

Organizational culture is a powerful force that moulds and shapes the behaviour of individuals within the organization. For Wilson, it is a control mechanism (demarcating acceptable and unacceptable behaviour), organizational history, a means of achieving commitment and a recipe for success. It will be embedded deep within the organization and can exist independently of management. Consequently, although procedures and structures can be altered in a relatively short period, the culture of an organization can only be changed (if at all) over a long period of time.

The manifestations of organizational culture

Organizational culture manifests itself in organizational behaviour – that is, how managers and employees behave in the context of the organization. Organizational culture has an impact on five aspects of the organization:

- **corporate values** strongly held beliefs about what is right and wrong and that lead people to take certain forms of action, which, in turn, are reflected in:
  - the language used;
  - stories and myths about the past;
  - norms of behaviour;
  - rituals and rites of the organization;
  - heroes and role models.
- **organizational climate** the working atmosphere as perceived and experienced by people involved in the organization, which will include how people feel about and react to the culture of the organization;
- **management style** the way in which managers exercise authority;
- **organizational behaviour** meaning the ways in which people interact within the organization;
- **structure** for example, the degree of flexibility in the organization.

The culture of an organization can be compared with the submerged part of an iceberg. It makes up the bulk of the structure, but is not immediately apparent (see Figure 47.1).

Influences on organizational culture

Organizational culture arises from many sources, including:

- the philosophy of the founders;
- its history and traditions;
- the nature and activities of the business;
- size;
- ownership;
- technology;
- external factors;
- goals and objectives;
- location
- managers and employees;
- the customers.

Analysing organizational culture

Some organizations (such as IBM) have a paternalistic culture, in which employees are well-rewarded and looked after for their hard work. Others have a customer-oriented culture (such as Marks & Spencer). Some organizations tend to be bureaucratic or conservative while others are optimistic and innovative. The analysis of the culture of the organization starts with a **culture audit**, which is a systematic recording of all the

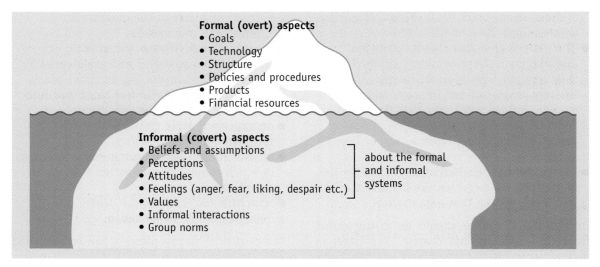

Formal (overt) aspects
- Goals
- Technology
- Structure
- Policies and procedures
- Products
- Financial resources

Informal (covert) aspects
- Beliefs and assumptions
- Perceptions
- Attitudes
- Feelings (anger, fear, liking, despair etc.)
- Values
- Informal interactions
- Group norms

about the formal and informal systems

Figure 47.1 The organizational iceberg
(Adapted from W. L. French and C. H. Bell, *Organizational Development*, Prentice Hall, 1984)

factors that go into making up an organization's culture. This will involve an extensive questionnaire concerning the following.

● **Norms**
- How managers treat subordinates.
- How subordinates react.
- The prevailing work ethic.
- Status and the attitude to status.
- Attitude towards ambition, performance, power, internal politics, loyalty.
- Approachability of top management.
- Degree of formality.

● **Core values (especially if not defined in a mission statement)**
- Care and consideration for people.
- Care for customers.
- Competitiveness.
- Enterprise.
- Equity in the treatment of employees.
- Excellence.
- Growth.
- Innovation.
- Market/customer orientation.
- Focus on organizational needs rather than people's needs.
- Performance orientation.
- Productivity.

- Provision of equal opportunities for employees.
- Quality.
- Social responsibility.
- Teamwork.

● **Organizational climate**
- Flexible or bureaucratic.
- Formal or informal.
- Hierarchical or loosely structured.
- Friendly or distant.
- Cooperative or individualistic.
- Status-conscious or free and easy.
- Relaxed or stressful.
- Reactive or proactive.
- Innovative or stick-in-the-mud.
- Political or apolitical.
- Profit-conscious or cost-conscious.
- Action-oriented or *laissez-faire*.

● **Management style**
- Autocratic or democratic.

By asking the following questions (adapted from those in M. Armstrong, *How to be an Even Better Manager*, Kogan Page, 1994), the organizational culture of a firm can be ascertained.

● Do people feel they are given enough responsibility?
● Do people know what is expected of them, in

terms of objectives and standards of performance?

● Is there adequate feedback to people on their performance?

● Is there sufficient challenge in the jobs given to people and sufficient emphasis on doing a good job?

● Are people given enough support by their managers or supervisors in the form of guidance or help?

● Is the emphasis in the organization on hard, dedicated work or is it fairly relaxed?

● Do people feel fairly rewarded for the work they do?

● Do people feel promotion policies are fair?

● Is there an emphasis on positive rewards rather than punishments?

● Is there a lot of bureaucracy and red tape around the organization or is the approach to work reasonably flexible and informal?

● Is there an emphasis on taking calculated risks in the organization or is playing it safe the general rule?

● Is management open about what the company is doing?

● Is there a general atmosphere of warmth and good fellowship?

● Do managers and other employees want to hear different opinions?

● Is the emphasis on getting problems out in the open rather than smoothing them over or ignoring them?

● Do people feel that they belong to a worthwhile company and are valued as members of work teams?

From the data collected organizational culture can be analyzed and classified.

Types of culture

Organizational or adventurous

A simple distinction can be made between a bureaucratic (or risk-averse) culture and an adventurous (or entrepreneurial) culture. In a **bureaucratic culture**:

● there is an emphasis on role and procedures;
● new ideas are often dismissed;

● roles are precisely defined;
● structures are hierarchical;
● there is an emphasis on dealing with problems;
● stability and experience are highly valid attributes;
● making the right decisions is less important than making the decision in the right way;
● it is almost impossible to change the corporate mindset;
● Command and control appear to be the dominant processes.

An **adventurous culture** is characterized by:

● an emphasis on taking advantage of new opportunities;
● a welcome given to new ideas;
● motivation and innovation are valued characteristics;
● staff are allowed autonomy and able to show initiative;
● flat, flexible structure;
● minds and policies are frequently changed, according to circumstances.

Charles Handy (in *Understanding Organizations*, Penguin, 1993) identified four types of culture, and these are now described.

Power culture

'The employee does what he or she is told.' This type of organization is characterized by an all-powerful head. Power is centralized, with the structure of the organization taking the form of a web spreading out from the centre. There are few rules and systems in such an organization. Consequently, employees need to be able to anticipate correctly what is required of them by the power-holder. Getting it right contributes to a happy, satisfied organization. Getting it wrong leads to low morale and a high turnover of staff.

Power cultures have advantages in terms of flexibility, with the possibility of moving quickly to secure competitive advantage over rivals. However, success depends on the quality of the central figure. Unless succession is prepared for, the organization will lose direction and stagnate (or even decline) following the retirement or death of the central figure. It will also be difficult to maintain control as the organization grows in size.

Role culture

'The employee acts within the parameters of his or her job description.'This type of culture can be seen in large bureaucracies. Structures and procedures are planned in a rational and logical way. The name for this type of culture is derived from the fact that emphasis is placed not on the individual, but on the role, post or position within the firm. In this way, the organization's existence can be sustained beyond the present incumbents. Other features include an abundance of rules, the hierarchical nature of power and clear definitions of authority.

Role culture is clearly comparable with Weber's ideal-type bureaucracy, possessing the same advantages but also the same disadvantages. Its great merit is predictability and stability, but, weighed against this, there is a built-in inertia. Hence, role culture organizations can succeed in a stable environment, where products are standardized and product lifecycles long. They find it more difficult to adapt to changing circumstances and tend to be conservative rather than innovatory.

Task culture

'The employee acts in the way he or she considers suitable for the task.'This type of culture is characterized not by a single source of power or a hierarchy, but by autonomous project teams. Stress is placed on teamwork (rather than individual effort and reward) and accomplishing the task.

The great advantage of this type of culture is flexibility and the benefits that come from greater autonomy and cross-functional teamwork. However, it works best in connection with short-term projects. Consequently, it is difficult to produce economies of scale or any great depth of expertise. Moreover, task groups are difficult to control once they are underway.

Person culture

'The individual does his or her own thing.' Here the individual is the central point. The firm, its organization and systems exist to serve the individuals who form it. Not only is this type of culture rare in business organizations, it is only appropriate for small partnerships in the professions. As an organization grows, it will take on a life of its own, independent of the interests of its members. Consequently, it will develop into a role or power culture.

It is important to remember that neither this nor the previous cultures described above is right or wrong. Any one of them could be right or appropriate in the particular circumstances of the organization.

Mechanistic v. organic organizations

In *The Management of Innovation* (Tavistock, 1961), T. Burns and G. M. Stalker classified organizations as being either mechanistic or organic. The former has a bureaucratic approach, based on clear structures, procedures, formal communications and controls. The latter is more fluid, with greater flexibility, broad job descriptions and informal procedures. The distinction is illustrated in Table 47.1.

The conclusion drawn from Burns and Stalker's analysis is that:

● organizations are generally moving from the mechanistic to organic style as the pace of change necessitates greater flexibility and rapid response;
● there is no single best style as particular circumstances will dictate which is the most appropriate – small organizations dependent on new technology benefit from an organic style, whereas a large organization in a stable environment can benefit from a mechanistic approach;
● the two styles should be seen as part of a spectrum, with no organization entirely one or the other;
● to be most effective, the management style should match that of the unit or organization.

This approach to management is known as **contingency theory** – instead of believing that there is one single best way, strategies should be seen as appropriate for the circumstances.

Table 47.1 The characteristics of mechanistic and organic organizations

Mechanistic	Organic
● Specialized differentiation and definition of tasks in the organization	● Contributive nature of special knowledge to the total concerns of the organization
● Hierarchical supervision and reconciliation of problems	● Redefinition of tasks and responsibilities in terms of interaction with others
● Precise definition of job responsibilities, methods, rights and obligations	● Commitment to the organization beyond any technical/ precise definition – such commitment more valued than loyalty
● Perceived location of superior knowledge at the top of the hierarchy	● Network structure of control, authority and communication
● Vertical interaction of individuals, between subordinate and superiors	● Omniscience not imputed to senior executives; knowledge located anywhere in the organization, and this location may become centre of authority for a given issue
● Insistence on loyalty to organization and obedience to superiors	● Lateral, rather than vertical, direction of communication
● More prestige attached to job than to more general knowledge, experience and skills	● Communication consists of information and advice rather than instructions and decisions

(T. Burns and G. M. Stalker, *The Management of Innovation*, Tavistock, 1961)

Why is culture important?

The real questions are do people love their work and are they proud to be associated with the employer or do they dread the thought of work, find every day stressful and long for Friday? How people answer these questions will, in great part, depend on the culture of the organization they work for. Culture is important because it:

● affects the degree of employee motivation;
● will affect labour turnover (the rate at which individuals join and leave the organization);
● affects the morale and goodwill of employees (and, therefore, absenteeism);
● is reflected in the reputation of the organization;
● can affect productivity and efficiency;
● can affect the quality of work;
● influences the degree to which change is accepted.

It is to change that we now turn.

Change

Responding to change is essential in business and so is a central theme in Business Studies. Managers have to, first, identify the external and internal pressures for change. These include:

● competition;
● changing technology;
● changes in customers' needs;
● changes in customers expectations;
● demand for increased quality;
● stakeholder expectations;
● employees' expectations;
● the financial environment.

Second, managers have to develop strategies in response to the changes in the environment. These strategies are likely to involve change within the organization. It could take the form of a change in location, product range, working practices, work teams or technology. 'Change will result as a consequence of the interaction between equipment (technology), processes (working procedures), organizational structures and people. A change to any one of these four elements will inevitably lead to changes to the others, because the organization is a living, evolving system' (Institute of Management Business Checklist, *Marketing and Strategy*, Hodder & Stoughton, 1999).

Reactions to change

Any change is likely to cause discomfort to the people most affected and, as a result, they are likely to react in some way. We can portray the reaction of people to change in a spectrum running from acceptance to active resistance (see also Figure 47.2):

- **acceptance**
  - enthusiasm;
  - cooperation;
  - passive resignation;
- **Indifference**
  - apathy;
  - minimal contribution;
- **passive resistance**
  - regressive behaviour;
  - non-learning behaviour;
  - protests;
  - working to rule;
- **active resistance**
  - minimal work;
  - slowing down;
  - personal withdrawal;
  - intentional errors;
  - sabotage.

In addition to overt forms of resistance (strikes and so on), there are many more cases of frustration being demonstrated in terms of absenteeism, low morale, low productivity and high labour turnover. This type of resistance is less dramatic, but more insidious than strikes.

Why change is resisted

It is essential to analyse *why* change is resisted if management is to devise strategies to overcome it. The barriers can be either at the group (or organizational) or individual level.

Organizational barriers include:

- **structural inertia** change threatens the logic of the way things are currently done;
- **the existing power structure** change obviously threatens those whose power is most threatened;
- **resistance from work groups** as change will threaten the group;
- **the failure of a previous initiative** this will make people hostile to other proposed changes.

Individual resistance is caused by a combination of economic, social and psychological factors, as follows:

- **economic**
  - fear of job loss;
  - fear of loss of earnings;
  - reduced promotion prospects;
  - increased workload;

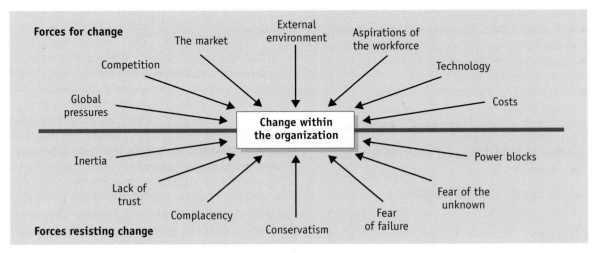

Figure 47.2 Forces causing and resisting change within an organization

- **social**
  - break-up of work groups;
  - change in relationships;
  - fear of increased supervision and control;
- **psychological**
  - insecurity;
  - fear of inability to cope;
  - inability to adjust;
  - loss of previous freedom;
  - loss of self-esteem (if change involves a lowering of status);
  - fear of the unknown;
  - loss of control;
  - change means implied criticism;
  - misunderstanding of the nature of the change;
  - lack of trust in the proponents of change;
  - loss of power and influence;
  - resentment at not being consulted.

Strategies to overcome resistance to change

After analysing what the causes of resistance are, then strategies can be devised to overcome them. Before we look at these strategies, it is useful to identify features of those organizations that are more receptive to change. In such organizations:

- people are informed and consulted as early as possible;
- the advantages of change are identified;
- trust is built up;
- retraining and other support is available;
- feedback is encouraged;
- clear objectives are set;

- responsibility is allocated;
- employees are involved in both planning and implementing change;
- change is incremental rather than dramatic;
- management is willing to compromise;
- employees do not feel that their autonomy or security is threatened.

The six strategies to overcome resistance to change that were famously identified by Kotter and Schlesinger (in 'Choosing Strategies for Change', *Harvard Business Review*, 1979) are as follows:

- **education and communication** to help people understand the need for change – this can be effective if there is mutual trust, but it is very time-consuming;
- **participation and involvement** of people in planning and implementing change – again, this is potentially effective, but it is time-consuming and can result in a compromise that is less than ideal;
- **facilitation and support**, which means retraining and counselling – this is expensive, time-consuming and there is no guarantee of success;
- **negotiation and agreement**, which means incentives to accept change;
- **manipulation and cooptation** this involves buying off leaders of resistance and selective use of information (leaks) – not only does this raise ethical questions, it can also store up trouble for the future;
- **explicit and implicit threats** these might work, but are likely to cause resentment and can lead to strike action.

Table 47.2 Matching strategies to causes of resistance

Source of resistance	Suggested strategy
● Fear of unknown	● Offer information and support
● Poor timing	● Delay change – wait for a more appropriate time
● Contrasting interpretations	● Information – group discussions
● Insecurity	● Clarify intentions
● Need for change not recognized	● Demonstrate the problem/opportunity
● Threat to vested interests	● Enlist key people in planning change
● Different personal ambitions	● Extra incentives

Force field analysis

In his seminal work *Field Theory in Social Sciences*, K. Lewin analysed the pressures for change in terms of their equilibrium with pressures resisting change.

Table 47.3 Force field analysis – pressures for change v. resistance to change

Pressures for change	Resistance to change
● Changing nature of workforce	● Economic reasons
● Changing technology	● Fear of the unknown
● Knowledge explosion	● Habit
● Quality of work life	● Security
● Product obsolescence	● Organizational structure
	● Resource limitation
	● Threats to power
	● Organization culture

In order to bring about a change in the state of equilibrium, the organization can:

● increase those forces pushing for change;
● decrease those forces maintaining the status quo;
● use a combination of these two strategies.

Lewin argued that modifying those forces maintaining the status quo might produce less tension and resistance than increasing forces for change. Consequently, focusing on these forces is likely to produce a more effective strategy for change. His model comprised three sequential steps:

1 **unfreezing** reducing those forces maintaining an organization's behaviour in its current state;
2 **moving** shifting the behaviour of the organization to a new condition, which involves developing and implementing new values, attitudes and behaviour by means of changes in organizational structures and processes;
3 **re-freezing** the organization stabilizes in the new state of equilibrium, reinforced by new structures, cultures and processes.

A champion for change

Change programmes benefit from having a champion to galvanize the plan for change. The champion must possess the following attributes:

● a vision with passion and commitment;
● clear values;
● energy and stamina;
● charisma;
● communication skills;
● innovative ideas and approaches;
● be an achiever;
● a delegator;
● a persuader;
● teambuilding skills.

Change champions are able to push through the required changes.

Developing a change culture

Change will be easy to introduce if acceptance of it is part of the culture of the organization. The Institute of Management identifies the following as essential to the process of building a change culture.

● Build commitment by:
  – sharing information as widely as possible;
  – allowing for suggestions, input and differences from widespread participation;
  – breaking changes into manageable chunks and minimizing surprises;
  – making standards and requirements clear;
  – being honest about the downside of change.
● Develop a culture that supports change by:
  – recognizing prevalent value systems;
  – creating a blame-free culture of empowerment and pushing down decision making;
  – breaking down departmental barriers;
  – designing challenging jobs;
  – freeing time for risk and innovation;
  – focusing on the interests of all stakeholders (including employees).
● Get the people right by:
  – recognizing staff needs and dealing with conflict positively;
  – being directional without being directive;
  – involving everyone;
  – earning commitment and trust;
  – developing relationships;

- understanding how teams work;
- recognizing your limits and others' strengths.

Key concepts

Norms Rules or standards. Accepted behaviour within a group.

Managing change The process of planning and implementing changes in strategy or working methods.

Organizational climate/corporate climate The working atmosphere within the organization.

Organizational culture/corporate culture The personality or character of the organization. It evolves over a long period and leads people inside the organization to behave in characteristic ways without necessarily thinking about it.

Values A set of ethical principles and beliefs that guide actions. They can be seen as what owners and executives believe to be right and, therefore, what conditions their behaviour.

Essay questions

1 (a) What do you understand by organizational culture.

(b) Analyse the factors that influence the culture of an organization.

2 Analyse ways in which the culture of an organization influences the behaviour of people within the organization.

3 (a) Account for the accelerating pace of change in business.

(b) Analyse the causes of resistance to change.

4 Suggest and evaluate ways of getting employees to accept change within the organization.

5 Using appropriate examples, analyse the relationship between:

(a) organizational culture and organizational objectives;

(b) organizational culture and organizational ethics/social responsibility;

(c) organizational culture and the history of the organization.

6 Japanization is defined as the integration of Japanese management techniques into UK firms. Analyse the problems of introducing Japanese management styles into:

(a) an existing UK firm;

(b) a newly established business operating on a green field site.

Further reading

Armstrong, M. (1999) *A Handbook of Human Resource Management Practice*, 7th ed. Kogan Page

Armstrong, M. (1998) *Managing People*, Kogan Page.

Attwod, M. and Dimmock, S. (1996) *Personnel Management*, 3rd ed., Macmillan.

Bratton, J., and Gold, J. (1999) *Human Resource Management: Theory and practice*, 2nd ed. Macmillan.

Corbridge, M., and Pilbeam, S. (1998) *Employment Resourcing*, Financial Times Pitman.

Currie, D. (1997) *Personnel in Practice*, Blackwell.

Foot, M., and Hock, C. (1996) *Introducing Human Resource Management*, Longman.

Graham, H., and Bennet, R. (1998) *Human Resource Management*, 9th ed., Financial Times Pitman.

Maund, L. (1999) *Understanding People and Organisations*, Stanley Thornes.

Pettinger, R. (1999) *Effective Employee Relations*, Kogan Page.

Tyson, S., and York, A. (1996) *Human Resource Management*, 3rd ed, Made Simple Books.

Short answer questions

Critically explain each of the following terms using examples from specific business organizations.

1 Induction procedures.
2 Equal opportunities policies.

3 The role of the personnel officer.
4 Non-financial methods of motivating staff.
5 The measurement, and monitoring, of absenteeism.
6 Recruitment procedures.
7 The extent of trade union membership.
8 The use of part-time employees.
9 Grievance procedures.
10 Consultation with employees.
11 Leadership styles.

12 Performance appraisal.
13 Investers in People.
14 Selection methods.
15 Flexitime.
16 Performance-related pay.
17 Profit-related pay.
18 Job enrichment.
19 Teamworking.
20 Labour turnover.

Exercises

1 Produce:
(a) a job description:
(b) a person specification for each of the following jobs:
    (i)   the driver–conductor of a one-man operated bus;
    (ii) a sales assistant in a clothes shop;
    (ii) a receptionist at a veterinary surgery;
    (iv) a delivery van driver.

2 As personnel manager in a large food processing plant, you are asked to produce a report on labour turnover at the plant. Your report should cover:
(a) The nature and extent of the problem;
(b) reference to the cost of labour turnover;
(c) recommendations to reduce the problem.

The following background information will be of assistance.
● The plant is female-intensive by a proportion of 4 to 1.
● The turnover rate is 20 per cent per year, but as high as 40 per cent in some departments.
● Despite the high turnover, there is a high proportion of staff with five or more years; service.
● A large new shopping centre has been built near by.

3 You are the personnel manager at a large factory. The board of directors agrees to a major reorganization involving the introduction of new technology and the redundancy of 500 employees. You have been asked to prepare a report on the implementation of the plan. The report should include reference to:
(a) the law relating to redundancy;
(b) principles and procedures to be adopted to preserve good labour relations;
(c) recommendations on ways to obtain acceptance of new technology;
(d) the training implications of new technology.

4 As the staff development and training officer of a large manufacturing company, you are required to prepare a report in response to the memorandum below. The company employs 10,000 manual workers and 1500 non-manual workers. The company has access to a staff college and is faced with intense competition from domestic and foreign rivals. Consequently, training to equip staff to compete with the competition is given a high priority within the company.

Memorandum

From:　　　Managing Director
To:　　　　Training Officer

Subject:　*Training of junior management*

I would like you to make proposals for a staff development programme that includes the following headings:

(a) induction
(b) training within the company
(c) staff college
(d) external training and educational facilities.

I should also like you to outline the benefits that the development programme would provide.

---

5 As the regional official for the National Union of Garden Furniture Makers, you have been asked to advise the workforce of Smith and Jones Ltd on how to present its annual pay claim.

Smith and Jones Ltd employs 200 manual workers at its factory. Of these, 150 workers belong to your union, with the remainder belonging to either the Transport and General Workers Union or no union at all. Following a £2 million investment programme at the factory, the productivity of workers rose by 10 per cent. Smith and Jones are anxious to expand output further, but the firm is constrained by problems in recruiting labour. Moreover, the factory suffers from an annual 30 per cent labour turnover ratio. Last year, profits were £1.5 million and inflation is currently running at 8 per cent per year.

As a professional union officer, you will attempt to predict and counter the arguments that Smith and Jones will use to keep the pay rise as low as possible. The industry is very competitive and this reduces the ability of Smith and Jones to pass on cost increases. The current high interest rates reduce disposable income and, therefore, the demand for garden furniture.

Finally, the NUGFM is a moderate union, the members of which have never been on strike, either at Smith and Jones or elsewhere. All the evidence suggests that they would be reluctant to take strike action over this year's pay claim.
(a) In report form, prepare a submission for an appropriate pay claim, supporting your case with information from the above account as well as suitable outside material.
(b) In a separate report, advise the union committee at Smith and Jones of an appropriate strategy in the event of the claim not being accepted.

Key skills development

1 Produce a wordprocessed report on human resource management in a locally based firm. It should cover the following:
- recruitment and selection;
- induction programmes;
- appraisal;
- motivational techniques;
- grievance and disciplinary procedures;
- communications;
- employee representation;
- hierarchical structures, such as flat/tall, span of control.

Your report should include terms of reference, an explanation of data sources, data collection, data analysis and clear conclusions. Where appropriate, include quantitative data and illustrations.

2 Choose one of the following as a topic for a short presentation:
(a) broadbanding pay;
(b) labour turnover;
(c) absenteeism;
(d) equal opportunities policies;
(e) delayering;
(f) job enrichment;
(g) empowerment;
(h) numerical flexibity.

For your presentation, you should prepare appropriate handouts and overhead transparencies. Include real-life illustrations of your chosen topic.

3 You are going to interview candidates for the post of marketing assistant in a medium-sized company manufacturing toys.
(a) Prepare and type up a list of ten questions that you are going to ask each of the candidates.
(b) Prepare a rating sheet that could be used in the interview.
(c) Conduct a mock interview using your chosen questions (with follow-up questions where appropriate) and your rating sheet.

Strategy

Strategic issues

The distinctive feature of A2 compared with AS Business Studies is the former's emphasis on strategic as distinct from operational matters. Not only do strategic considerations add an extra dimension of analysis, they are the ultimate factors in integrating the subject.

Chapter objectives

1 To develop an understanding of strategy.

2 To understand the nature of strategic decisions.

3 To outline the strategic process.

4 To explore selected strategic issue.

5 To explore the concept of competitive advantage.

What is strategy?

The word strategy comes from the ancient Greek word for generalship. Strategies are general programmes of action involving the deployment of resources to achieve organizational objectives. Kenneth Andrews defines **strategy** as 'the pattern of decisions in a company that determines and reveals its objectives, purposes, or goals, produces the principle policies and plans for a achieving these goals.' In other words, it concerns the 'big issues' of where the organization is going, which markets it seeks to operate in, the range of its products and its intentions for the medium to long term.

Strategy is essential in terms of:

- defining objectives;
- providing a coherent framework for decision making;
- facilitating consistency in decision making;
- defining the organization's markets (or competitive domain);
- the achievement of competitive advantage over rivals;
- differentiating managerial roles.

As the formulation of strategy goes to the heart of the organization's purpose, it is natural that strategic decision making remains the preserve of the highest tiers of management. **Strategic management** is the process by which an organization establishes its objectives, formulates strategies to achieve these objectives, implements the strategies and monitors progress towards achievement of the objectives.

Mintzberg suggests various definitions of strategy. His 5 Ps of strategy are based on the notion that the term is used in different ways according to its context. The 5 Ps are:

- **plan** a consciously defined course of action showing how leaders try to establish direction for the organization;
- **ploy** a specific manoeuvre intended to directly outwit a competitor;
- **pattern** a consistent, intentional or unintentional pattern of behaviour within a stream of actions;
- **position** a means of defining an organization in relation to its competitive environment;
- **perspective** the concept or character of an organization – its collective mind, intention or behaviour.

Strategic decisions

The following are all examples of strategic (as distinct from operational or tactical – see Table 48.1 for examples of both) decisions, and are those relating to:

- diversification, acquisitions and divestments;
- choice of markets;
- product range;
- positioning within the market;
- long-term financing;
- choice of technology;
- the organizational structure.

What unites the above list is that all concern the scope of an organization's activities – that is, where it is going in the future. They all have major resource implications for the organization and they all condition the lower-level (tactical and operational) decisions that will have to be made in order to 'fill in the details' of the overall strategy.

The development of a corporate strategy

The steps involved in creating and implementing a corporate strategy are the following.

- **Definition of mission and corporate objectives** The mission sets out the purpose of the organization and what it hopes to achieve. Without a clear mission statement, it may be difficult to decide on the most suitable option. The objectives clarify the mission by providing more detail about the things that the organization hopes to achieve.
- **Analysis of internal and external situations (SWOT and PEST analysis)** An assessment of the organization's resources, marketing standing and current capabilities provides a better understanding of what the organization can achieve. Assessing the external environment involves a consideration of changes that will impact the firm.
- **Strategic choice** this involves identifying the options that have emerged from the analysis, comparing and evaluating the options and

Table 48.1 Strategic v. operational decisions

Strategic decisions	Operational decisions
• Made by senior management	• Made by middle and junior management
• Crucially important	• Of medium to low importance
• Have substantial resource implications	• Some resource implications
• Long-term impact	• Short- to medium-term impact
• High risks involved	• Medium- to low-risk
• General principles	• Very detailed statements
• Major consequences for the firm	• Minor consequences for the firm
• Made against a background of uncertain data	• Made against a background of substantial data

selecting the best one, the one most likely to achieve the objective set. Commonly used criteria for evaluating strategic options include:
- return on investment;
- risk;
- impacts on ownership and control;
- potential for growth;
- stability of earnings;
- prestige to the organization;
- social responsibility.

Influences on corporate strategy are shown in Figure 48.1.

● **Implementation of the strategy** This will involve strategies for the whole organization and its different parts. Resources will be required to implement strategies and, therefore, targets must be set and budgets must be drawn up.

● **Monitoring and control** Strategies must be evaluated in terms of the extent to which objectives are achieved as a result of implementing them.

Table 48.2 demonstrates the importance of strategy to firms.

It is not possible here, or, indeed, appropriate for A level purposes, to cover the vast range of

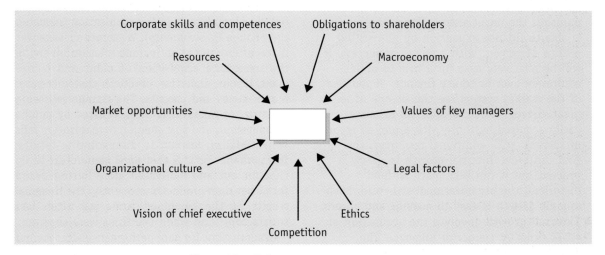

Figure 48.1 Influences on corporate strategy

Table 48.2 Short- and far-sightedness

Symptoms of short-sightedness	Symptoms of far-sightedness
● No formally documented strategies	● A written statement of mission communicated to the workforce
● No attention devoted to long-term competitive advantage	● Emphasis on sustainable competitive advantage
● Rigid structure	● Flexible structure
● Emphasis on the status quo	● Emphasis on change
● Downward communication dominates	● Communication in all directions
● Borrowed ideas	● Heavy investment in R&D
● Concern for short-term profit	● Emphasis on increased market share, growth and future profit potential
● Labour is seen as the hired hand	● Labour is viewed as a valuable human resource
● Stopgap training	● Long-term development of employees
● Firefighting – in the short-term	● Managers concerned with long-term implications of their action

strategic decisions that occur in organizations. Hence, in the remainder of this chapter we will concentrate on a limited number of strategic options related to:

- size and growth;
- direction of growth;
- the acquisition of competitive advantage.

How businesses change size

Firms can grow in a number of ways.

- **Internal (organic) growth** involves the expansion of the existing firm. It can be seen as a natural outcome of business success in a system that rewards the successful but punishes the unsuccessful. The profitable firm is able to finance expansion by reinvesting profits. Moreover, with a record of success, it will be relatively easy for a firm to obtain additional loan or equity finance. Supporters of the market system see this as one of its great virtues. Financial and real resources are easily acquired by those with a proven record of success. With additional resources, the firm can grow. Internal growth is a slow process, but it can take place without disturbing the organizational structure. Such organic growth is easy to manage and absorb.
- **External growth** involves the acquisition of other firms by merger or takeover. The distinction between the two is frequently blurred, but merger implies a measure of voluntary agreement and a fusing of the organizations rather than just a change in ownership. A merger would normally involve a share exchange, so that shareholders acquire shares in the new, merged company.
- **Takeover (or acquisition)** implies that a predator firm swallows up another firm by buying its shares. Usually, the company that is taken over remains distinct, but now a controlling interest is enjoyed by the predator firm. In a **friendly takeover,** the company being taken over actually encourages it. In a **hostile takeover,** the company being taken over fights to prevent the predator from obtaining a controlling

interest. It should be realized that public limited companies are always open to takeover as there are no restrictions on the transfer of shares in the company. This vulnerability is increased if shareholders are dissatisfied with the performance of the company or if it is undercapitalized.

Problems with mergers and takeovers

The underlying motive for any takeover (or merger) is the belief that it will prove profitable, yet the results can often be disappointing. In part, this is because merger or takeover is merely a change in ownership and ultimate control. To gain the full benefits, a merger or takeover has to be followed by integration (reorganization following the change in ownership). A merger or takeover is too often seen as an instant solution involving the immediate acquisition of plant and equipment, labour, expertise, products, customer base, brand names and patents. The change following a merger or takeover is often resisted by middle management, and post-merger reorganization fails to materialize, leading to disappointing results. It is perhaps also true that some mergers are badly thought out and motivated more by the desire for power than profit. Consequently, the financial results of the combined firms are often less satisfactory than when the firms were separate.

Other reasons for poor performance after merger are:

- increased size, leading to diseconomies of scale;
- loss of key employees in the upheaval of merger;
- shortage of funds after financing a takeover;
- share issues to finance merger, leading to the dilution of shares and therefore a reduction in earnings per share (to the annoyance of shareholders);
- inadequacies of senior management in a new, large organization.

Given the disappointment with the large merged organization, it is not surprising that there has been a trend in the opposite direction, towards the smaller organization concentrating on its core activities.

De-integration

De-integration is the opposite of acquisition, in that the firm or group *reduces* the scope of its activities, rather than expands them. De-integration is usually prompted by a desire to raise finance, save management time, increase efficiency, prevent takeover or concentrate on the business' core competences. The latter are defined as the skills that are at the heart of the company's business. Food and clothes retailing are the core competences of Marks & Spencer, even though the company is involved in other activities.

De-integration can take the following forms.

- **De-merger** This involves the creation of two quoted companies out of one existing one. Shareholders receive shares in the new company in proportion to their shares in the old company. Examples include the splitting of Courtaulds into Courtaulds PLC and Courtaulds Textiles, and the division of ICI into ICI (chemicals) and Zeneca (pharmaceuticals).
- **Divestment** This involves the selling of subsidiary companies, such as Asda selling MFI and British Aerospace selling Rover to BMW. Often, such divestments are prompted by a desire to get rid of parts of the group that no longer 'fit' the corporate strategy. A hastily acquired subsidiary or one that came as part of a 'job lot' will be a likely candidate for divestment, especially if there is a shortage of cash (see Table 48.3 for reasons behind divestment.)
- **Contracting out** Both in the private and public sectors, there is a trend towards the contracting out of non-core services, such as catering, cleaning, transport. This is part of a trend towards a concentration on core competences.
- **Management buyouts (MBOs)** If the rise of the professional manager led to the divorce of ownership from control, the management buyout phenomenon represents the remarriage of ownership and control. As the term implies, it involves management (or employees in an employee buyout) buying an equity stake in the company. The Americans use the more accurate term **leverage buyout** as the bulk of finance comes from financial institutions rather than from employees and management. Typically, the members of the management team:
  - invest their own money, often secured against their own homes;
  - obtain an equity stake in the company;
  - increase their equity stake over the years;
  - control the business, although the financial institution will usually appoint a non-executive director to represent its interests.

Separate from a management buyout is a **management buyin**. This involves an outside management team buying into a business on a similar basis to a buyout.

Buyouts and buyins arise from a number of circumstances. For instance, the National Freight Corporation was privatized by means of a management and employee buyout. The management of a company in receivership might be willing to buyout a company rather than allow it to fold or, alternatively, be acquired by an outside company. Another situation giving rise to a management buyout would be the approaching retirement of

Table 48.3 Reasons for divestment

Offensive reasons	Defensive reasons
• To refocus the business on core activities • To raise finance for core activities • To improve the return on capital	• To raise finance to prevent it from collapsing • To avoid acquisition by a predator company • To improve return by selling off underperforming parts of the business • Risk aversion • Difficulties of managing a diverse range of businesses

a substantial shareholder-director in a medium-sized listed company. Again, a management buyout might be prompted by a reluctance to allow the business to be acquired by outsiders.

The advantages of an MBO to the vendor are that it:

- raises cash;
- reduces borrowings;
- enhances the corporate image;
- facilitates a concentration on core competences.

The new owner-managers benefit from acquiring a business in which:
- there is continuity of employment;
- there is commitment from staff with a personal financial interest;
- owner-managers have expertise;
- there are strong incentives for efficiency;
- they are free to pursue their own strategies;
- they might benefit from outside expertise in the form of non-executive directors nominated by lenders.

Direction of growth

Mergers and acquisitions can be classified in terms of the direction of the movement.

Horizontal

Horizontal growth occurs when two firms combine and they are at the same stage in the production of a good or service (such as would happen with two supermarkets or two oil refineries).

The reasons for this type of merger or takeover are to:

- reduce competition and secure market domination;
- secure the advantage of being a larger buyer of inputs;
- reduce risks;
- increase financial strength;
- prevent price wars and/or duplication;
- compete in world markets;
- protect themselves from a hostile takeover;
- rationalize production;
- link processes;
- achieve economies of scale;

- acquire the intangible assets of other companies, such as goodwill, trade names, patents and so on.

Vertical

Vertical growth happens when there is a merger or takeover of firms at different stages in the chain of production. The acquisition of a firm at an *earlier* stage is known as **backward integration** (identified by (B) in the list below); if it takes place at a *later* stage, it is known as **forward integration** (shown by (F) below).

The aim of a vertical acquisition is to:

- secure supplies and control the quality of inputs (B);
- safeguard outlets for the product (F);
- establish a distribution network (F);
- link successive stages in production (B and F);
- eliminate middlemen and absorb their share of profit (B and F);
- gain economies of scale (B and F);
- crowd out competitors from suppliers (B) or outlets (F).

Lateral

Lateral growth occurs in instances of a merger or takeover of two firms that produce related goods using similar techniques of production, but which do not compete directly with one another. An example of this would be a merger of a supermarket and a furniture store chain, while another would be a merger of a watchmaker and a manufacturer of scientific instruments. Such a merger is prompted by the desire to:

- diversify;
- increase financial strength;
- increase utilization of capacity;
- achieve economies of scale;
- acquire intangible assets.

Conglomerate

A **conglomerate** is the result of a merger or takeover of firms in totally unrelated markets. This type of merger is prompted by the desire to:

- diversify and thereby spread risks;
- increase financial strength;
- overcome the problem of slow growth by

developing new markets and new areas of business;

● overcome problems of seasonality in sales;
● achieve further economies of scale;
● control the development of rival industries;
● acquire intangible assets;
● engage in asset stripping or the sale of assets, such as property.

This last point is a less acceptable reason for a takeover, prompted as it is not by the desire to run the business, but, instead, to destroy it and profit from its assets.

F. T. Haner (in *Business Policy Planning and Strategy*, Winthrop, 1976) analyses what motivates companies to merge and acquire in terms of a spectrum running from offensive to defensive action. Offensive acquisitions are motivated primarily by a desire to achieve gains in market share, technology, financial strength and managerial talent. Secondary reasons are to achieve diversification of a countercyclical and counterseasonal nature.

At the defensive end of the spectrum, firms might seek protection by combining. They try to protect themselves against loss of market share, new low-cost producers, product innovations by others and hostile takeovers. At the extreme of defensiveness, we have mergers for survival purposes, prompted by the threatened loss of markets (to other products), raw material supplies and capital (due to technological obsolescence).

Directional matrices

A **directional matrix** enables a firm to analyse its strategic objectives. It sets out options for the future direction of the organization. One of the earliest examples of a matrix was that developed by Igor Ansoff in 1957 (see Figure 48.2). Known as the Ansoff Matrix, it analyses the options in terms of markets and products.

● **Market penetration** takes the form of increasing sales of existing products in existing markets (the same goods to the same people). As there is no change in either product or type of customer, the additional sales are only possible by changes in market

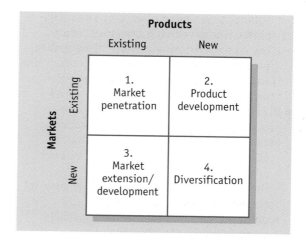

Figure 48.2 The Ansoff Matrix

strategy (price, promotion, channels of distribution). The aim is to increase usage among existing customers or to encourage people to switch from other brands. This strategy will be pursued when:

– the overall market is growing;
– the company is in a strong market position;
– the company is unable or unwilling to invest in new products or markets.

● **Product development** means selling new products to existing markets. It is a strategy that will be adopted if:

– there is growth potential in the market;
– the company holds a high share of the market and enjoys a distinctive competitive advantage;
– the changing needs of customers demand new products;
– the company is strong in R&D.

● **Market extension/development** involves selling existing products to new markets, such as a new segment or new markets in a geographical sense (new regions, new countries). This strategy will be adopted for the following reasons:

– the company's distinctive advantage lies with the products and it also has strong marketing competence;
– the company has identified new

opportunities, such as repositioning the product or developing new uses for it;
- the company's resources are structured to produce a particular product or product line and it would be very costly to switch technologies.

- **Diversification** means developing new products for new markets. The reasons for pursuing such a policy are as follows:
  - objectives can no longer be met without diversification;
  - the company has large amounts of cash in reserve;
  - diversification promises to be especially profitable;
  - to avoid dependence on a single product;
  - to strengthen existing products by synergy;
  - to compete on all points with a rival firm;
  - to take advantage of 'downstream opportunities', such as byproducts.

This strategy is particularly risky: 'Here the company has given up all hope of building on the known and introduces new products to new markets ... a desperate move. History is littered with epitaphs to companies who failed to make diversification work' (M. McDonald and Leppard, *Marketing by Matrix* Butterworth Heinemann, 1992).

A similar matrix is that associated with America's General Electric Company. It was developed not to analyse particular products, but, instead, to analyse profit centres within a large organization. The two dimensions are the strength of the business in the area concerned and the attractiveness of the particular market in which it is competing. The criteria for assessing the business, strength and the market attractiveness are shown in the Table 48.4.

As Figure 48.3 shows, the GEC screen has three gradations on each axis.

The matrix can be conveniently divided into three regions: invest, investigate and ignore. The top left section (labelled A) consists of activities in which the firm has competence and the market is very attractive. This is where a company wants to be and is worth further investment of resources and marketing effort. The middle section (labelled B) should be carefully monitored. Investigations will centre on whether or not there is scope for improvement in either the business' strength or market attractiveness. The bottom right of the matrix (labelled C) is where the company does *not* want to be. If a market is not attractive and, moreover, the company is not good at serving this market, then to carry on or to start marketing products in these areas will be a waste of resources.

Table 48.4 Criteria for assessing business strength and market attractiveness

Business strength	Market attractiveness
● Relative quality	● Growth rate
● Production capacity	● Accessible market size
● Production flexibility	● Competitive intensity
● Product adaptability	● Profit margins (historically)
● Unit cost of production	● Differences between competitive offerings
● Price position	● Existence of technical standards
● R&D capabilities	● Compatible infrastructure
● Brands owned	● Ease of obtaining payment
● Company image	● Sensitivity to interest rates
● Market share	● General volatility
● Range of commercial contacts	● Degree of regulation
● Influence on regulatory bodies	● Barriers to entry
● Delivery performance	● Rate of technological change
● Service facilities	● Likelihood of political stability
● Channel access of distribution network	● Potential for supply 'partnerships'
● Size/quality of salesforce	● Availability of market intelligence

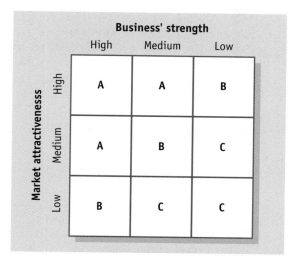

Figure 48.3 The GEC screen

A similar matrix is that developed by Kenichi Ohmae in *The Mind of the Strategist* (McGraw-Hill, 1982). Again, it pits market attractiveness against corporate strength and recommends the following courses of action:

● **serious entry into the market** a favourable market is entered, and quickly withdrawn from if it is not viable;
● **selective growth** investments are concentrated where advantage can be maintained;
● **all-out struggle** effort is concentrated on maintaining strength and profit structure;
● **limited expansion or withdrawal** attractive, low-risk, expansion opportunities are sought, withdrawing if they prove unsuccessful in practice;
● **selective expansion** the organization expands in profitable, low-risk segments;
● **maintenance of superiority** productivity is improved while avoiding large-scale investment;
● **loss minimization** fixed costs are minimized and investment avoided, rapidly withdrawing when loss is unavoidable;
● **overall harvesting** profitability is emphasized by switching from fixed to variable costs;
● **limited harvesting** profitability is protected even if loss of market position is involved.

Competitive advantage

Competitive advantage is the ability of the organization to outperform its competitors in terms of profitability, market share or growth. The higher return means that it will be able to commit more retained profit to reinvestment in its strategy, thus maintaining its lead over its competitors in the industry. When this superiority is maintained successfully over time, this is **sustainable competitive advantage**. Conversely, competitive advantage can be lost when management fails to reinvest the superior profit so that, in the longer run, the advantage is not maintained.

The bases of sustainable competitive advantage are:

● economies of scale and greater efficiency;
● an organization's flexibility;
● speed of response;
● financial strength;
● reputation or corporate image;
● superiority of the company's products;
● customer base;
● customer knowledge;
● distribution channels;
● salesforce;
● promotion;
● service support;
● research and developments;
● patents;
● technology;
● experience;
● manufacturing flexibility;
● process efficiency;
● product quality;
● employee relations;
● workforce flexibility;
● human resources;
● customer loyalty;
● access to low-cost labour.

Core competences

Core competences are a set of differential skills, complementary assets and routines that provide the basis for a firm's competitive capabilities and sustainable advantages in a particular business. They are:

- possessed by companies the performance of which outstrips the industry average;
- unique to the company;
- difficult to copy;
- relate to fulfilling customers' needs;
- based on distinctive relationships with customers, distributors and suppliers;
- based on superior skills and knowledge.

The Economist Intelligence Unit identifies the following uses for the concept:

- to guide diversification by enabling the identification of basic strengths;
- to drive revitalization by an identification of core business areas;
- to guard competitiveness by making it possible to recognize key skills earlier (many firms realize what they have lost by outsourcing or divestment only when it is too late);
- to provide a focus and justification for R&D in the development and maintenance of core competences;
- to inform the selection of strategic alliances that build on complementary core competences.

Porter's generic strategies

Harvard academic Michael Porter identified three routes to competitive advantage, as shown in Figure 48.4.

A cost leadership strategy

Competitive advantage is sought by minimizing costs as a result of implementing efficiencies and economies of scale. This enables the company to pursue a competitive pricing policy. By producing at the lowest cost, the manufacturer can compete on price with every other producer in the industry and enjoy high unit profits. Logically, only one company can achieve the position of cost leadership in a particular market.

A differentiation strategy

This involves developing unique product advantages, improving branding and benefiting from increased customer loyalty. The product must be (or must be perceived to be) distinctive in terms of:

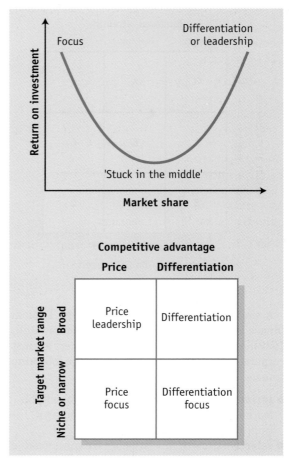

Figure 48.4 Porter's generic strategies

- colour differences;
- size differences;
- different wrappings or containers;
- variants of the product for different market segments – children, adults and so on;
- small changes in the products' formulations to maintain their novelty value;
- different technical specifications.

For the strategy to succeed, the unique features must be valued in some way by customers.

A focus strategy

This strategy is based on segmenting the market and focusing on particular market segments. The firm will not sell its products industrywide (in contrast to a differentiation strategy), but will instead focus on a particular type of buyer or geographical area.

The two main types are:

- a **cost-focus strategy**, which involves selecting a segment of the market and specializing in a product (or products) for that segment, or by concentrating on a small geographical area, and thus the firm can keep costs to a minimum;
- a **differentiation-focus strategy**, which involves selecting a segment of the market and competing on the basis of product differentiation for that segment.

Porter's final conclusion was that too many firms fail to make a choice between these three strategies. As a result, they are 'stuck in the middle', unable to achieve competitive advantage. Such firms earn lower than average profits.

Marketing strategies

Market leader

This is where a firm is generally recognized as the leader. Typically, it will have the largest market share. By 'virtue of its pricing, advertising intensity, distribution coverage, technological advance and rate of new product introductions, it determines the nature, pace and bases of competition. It is this dominance which typically provides the benchmark for other companies in the industry' (R M. S. Wilson, C. Gilligan and D. J. Pearson, *Strategic Marketing Management*, Chartered Institute of Marketing, Butterworth and Heinemann, 1992).

The market leader will pursue strategies designed to expand the total market and, at the very least, defend its market share. In this, it will use its competitive advantage, which is most likely to be one of the following:

- superior product;
- perceived advantage;
- low-cost operations;
- legal position (such as a patent);

- superior knowledge and contacts;
- offensive attitudes (aggressive marketing).

Market challenger

As the name suggests, the firm adopts an aggressive stance to gain market share at the expense of the leader. The long-term aim of such a firm is to displace the market leader. This will be achieved by one or more of the following strategies:

- price discounting;
- product innovation;
- improved quality;
- intensive advertising;
- innovation in distribution;
- product proliferation;
- development of new markets.

Market follower

A market follower is distinct from a market challenger in that the former will pursue a less aggressive policy to maintain market share rather than gain share at the expense of rivals, which is what a market challenger aims to do. Market followers will follow closely, or at a distance, or will follow the leader selectively.

Market niches

A firm following this strategy succeeds by concentrating on a small, specialist part of the market to avoid a head-on clash with larger companies in the market. Niche marketing is not the same as concentrated marketing. The latter refers to the targeting of a narrow group of customers, while niche marketing is about concentrating on a narrow product range.

A niche is attractive to a small firm if it:

- is of sufficient size to be profitable;
- has growth potential;
- is of negligible interest to major competitors;
- is an area for which the firm has the required skills and resources;
- is possible for the firm to build up customer goodwill to defend its position.

Key concepts

Business strategy The manner in which organizations intend to compete in order to achieve their goals.

Competitive advantage The edge organizations have over others in their market or industry.

Mission The overall aim or goal of the organization, frequently detailed in a mission statement.

Strategic management The process by which an organization establishes its objectives, formulates actions designed to meet objectives in the desired timescale, implements actions and assesses progress and results.

Strategic issues Issues requiring urgent action if the organization is to survive and prosper.

Strategy A programme of initiatives to define and achieve objectives.

Essay questions

1 With the use of examples taken from the functional areas of management, analyse the differences between strategic and tactical decisions.

2 (a) Explain the generic strategies identified by Professor Michael Porter.
  (b) Analyse the factors that should be taken into account when selecting each of the generic strategies.

3 Evaluate the case for both internal (organic) growth and external growth.

4 (a) What do you understand by:
    (i) de-merger; and
    (ii) core activities.
  (b) Analyse the reasons for de-merger being a strategy favoured by some business organizations.

5 Account for the disappointing results that often follow a merger or takeover.

6 Adapting the concept of the product lifecycle, analyse the ways in which an organization is likely to evolve as it moves through history. Your answer should include reference to organizational structure, organizational culture, product range and human resource management.

7 Analyse the intensity of competition in the:
  (a) motor industry;
  (b) perfume industry; and
  (c) retailing of records (CDs) with reference to the:
   ● bargaining power of suppliers;
   ● bargaining power of buyers;
   ● threat of substitition of rival products;
   ● ease of entry of newcomers;
   ● market shares of existing players.

Further reading

Institute of Management Business Checklists, all published by Hodder & Stoughton, 1999
  Informational and Financial Management
  Marketing and Strategy
  Operations and Quality Management
  Personnel Policies,Training and Development
  People Management
  Small Business Management
Bennett, R. (1997) *Management*, 3rd ed. Financial Times Pitman.
Bennett, R. (1999) *Corporate Strategy*, 2nd ed., Financial Times Pitman.
Dawson, T. (1998) *Introduction to Management*, Tudor.
Campbell, D., Stonehouse, G., and Houston, B. (1999) *Business Strategy*, Butterworth Heineman.
Naylor, J. (1999) *Management*, Financial Times Pitman.
Pettinger, R. (1994) *Introduction to Management*, Macmillan.
Stutely, R. (1999) *The Definitive Business Plan*, FT Prentice Hall.

Webb, P., and Webb, S. (1999) *Small Business Handbook,* Financial Times Pitman.

Short answer questions

Using examples taken from specific businesses, explain the following terms,
1 A strategic decision.
2 The Ansoff Matrix.
3 Diversification.
4 Acquisition.
5 Synergy.
6 Horizontal integration.
7 Strategic planning.
8 Strategic marketing.
9 Strategic HRM.
10 Generic strategies.

Study skills

Assessment in Business Studies – preparing for the examination

This the final chapter of this book, is intended to provide advice to you as you prepare for examination and project work.

Chapter objectives

1 To provide advice on notetaking and time management with reference to examination revision.

2 To describe the forms of assessment used for Business Studies.

3 To provide advice on the main forms of assessment used at A level.

4 To provide insight into dealing with the case studies that are a distinctive feature of examinations in Business Studies.

5 To explore synoptic assessment.

6 To offer advice on the nature and format of coursework.

7 To offer some guidance on the suitability of particular topics and the way to assess project titles.

Changes in terminology

Teachers and students have to get used to the new terminology – examination boards are now awarding bodies, modules are now units, syllabuses (or syllabi) are now subject specifications and subject cores are now subject criteria. Cynics might point out that the changes are merely cosmetic ('a rose by any other name ...'), but there was a definite purpose behind the changes in terminology. In part, this was to establish greater consistency with the phrasing used in GNVQ documents – 'awarding bodies', 'specifications' and 'units' are all GNVQ terms. Lining A levels up with GNVQs is designed to facilitate the combining of academic and applied or vocational studies. The single award GNVQ is based on six units and so is a GCE A level. The change to criteria and specifications emphasizes the importance at A level of testing what students can *do* rather than merely what they *know*. The word 'syllabus' suggests factual content whereas 'specification' suggests what candidates will be required to do in relation to the factual content. It will take time for the new terms to be adopted naturally (especially by teachers used to the old terms), but it is important to appreciate that the name-changing process had a definite purpose.

Revising for the examinations

Your first task in preparing for the examinations is to be clear about what you are required to do in them. This means looking again at the specification and studying a part of the document that is much neglected by candidates – namely, the assessment objectives. These state what the examinations seek to test. The assessment objectives indicate the importance of knowledge, analysis and evaluation. For example, one of them is that 'candidates will be expected to interpret data by distinguishing fact from opinion'. This is something that you can expect to be asked to do in the examination.

You should also have access to past examination papers, not to attempt to predict the questions, but, instead, to understand the nature of the examination and the style of questions you will be asked. Recent past papers can be purchased from the awarding bodies. Also available are the examiners' reports on past examinations and the mark schemes used by examiners in previous years. These are useful documents to read, but they should not be seen as a substitute for thorough and detailed revision using notes made over the course of your A level studies.

Note taking

Most examination schemes in Business Studies include a substantial proportion of compulsory questions. This means that you cannot pick and choose between topics within the syllabus, but must cover all aspects of the subject. This requires you to have made a comprehensive set of notes in class and from your own reading of textbooks, specialist books from the library and articles in quality newspapers and magazines. A gap in your notes could cost you dearly in the examination, so you should rectify any deficiency by checking topics off against the statement of syllabus content.

The style of your notes is very much a matter of personal choice. Some people prefer a linear style, while others construct spider diagrams to try to summarize the main issues relating to a particular topic. It is likely that notes acquired over the course will be extensive and so require some editing in the run up to the examinations. It is better to do this yourself than to buy a set of revision notes or cards. The fact is that, no matter how good the revision notes are, by buying them you are depriving yourself of the valuable exercise of using your own notes and shaping them to your own requirements. The effort of editing the notes will help you to learn and memorize their content. Also, at the end of the process, you will have a compact, intelligible set of notes (perhaps in the form of a card index or with the main points emphasized with the aid of a highlighter pen). Table 49.1 points out some common mistakes students can make with their notes.

Forms of assessment

The awarding bodies use a variety of methods to assess candidates' knowledge, understanding and ability in A and AS level Business Studies. Each scheme of assessment has unique features, although most share the following common features:

● a project or research assignment;
● data response questions;
● case study examinations.

The traditional essay question (more correctly called a 'free response question') has disappeared from many Business Studies schemes of assess-

Table 49.1 Pitfalls to avoid in making notes

General layout	Note structure	Content
● Unsuitable paper	● Absence of labels	● Patchy coverage
● Variations in paper size	● Insufficient headings and	● Omission of major points
● Cramped notes	indentations	● Too much unnecessary detail
● Topics jumbled together	● Disorganized material	● Ambiguity
● Poor handwriting		● Insufficient use of your own words
● Absence of page numbering		● Photocopied material

ment, but, given the importance of formal essay writing in most forms of examination, it is worth developing essay-writing skills. Another type of question used by some boards is the short answer question. Before dealing with each form of assessment, let us look at the skills that examination candidates are required to demonstrate:

- **knowledge** what the candidate knows;
- **comprehension** what the candidate understands;
- **application** the use of an idea or technique in a given situation;
- **analysis** the ability to break down an idea or concept into its essential components;
- **evaluation** the ability to determine the significance of something.

In addition, awarding bodies are required to include assessment of quality of language. This is defined in terms of clarity of expression, the structure and presentation of ideas, and grammar, punctuation and spelling.

Data response questions

The term 'data response' covers two types of question. First, there is the quantitative type of question, which requires candidates to analyse figures in order to produce a solution. Second, there are questions based on a passage of writing.

Quantitative questions

For the less mathematically minded students it should provide some comfort to realize that A level Business Studies tests comprehension and application of business concepts and techniques of analysis. The quantitative aspects of the syllabus are present not for their own sake, but for their usefulness in analysing business problems and in the search for a solution. Usually, the concept involved in the quantitative method is intellectually demanding, but the actual mechanics of calculation are relatively easy. For example, discounted cash flow is a challenging concept, but the questions on it are often straightforward in terms of the calculations involved. The same principle applies to questions based on statistical theory or operations research (such as network analysis).

When approaching quantitative questions, you should set down all your workings. Calculators are usually permitted and are very useful, but do not neglect to set out the calculation stage by stage. Students who tap a few numbers into their calculator and simply write down their answer do themselves a great disservice. First, it is easy to make a mistake – even with a calculator. Second, the incorrect answer with no workings set out will result in a zero mark as there is no evidence of the method used. Third, examiners are looking for the process used to reach the answer. In Business Studies, this is more important than the answer itself.

'Comprehension' questions

Some papers include questions based on a passage of writing – for example, a newspaper article). These are designed to 'test comprehension and application with some analysis and synthesis'. If the answers are contained in the passages, they are properly called data response questions. As an examination candidate, you are being asked to demonstrate understanding by extracting and then explaining relevant points from the passage. If the question instructs you to answer 'from the information in the passage', you are confined to the material printed on your question paper. In such situations, there are no marks for bringing in additional material.

In some data response questions, the answer is not in the passage. The purpose of these questions is to generate interest or stimulate the candidate. These questions are more properly called 'stimulus response questions'. As the answer is not in the passage, you are required to call on the knowledge and skills you have acquired during the course. Typical data response questions are subdivided, with a range of data response and stimulus response sub-questions.

When approaching a data response or stimulus response question, you should:

- take account of the marks available for each part of the question – this reveals the relative importance of each part of the question and this should be reflected in the length of your answer and the time devoted to it;
- answer the question fully and in the manner

required – failure to answer the question as set is one of the major causes of disappointing examination results;

● answer the question in your words – you must avoid the temptation to copy out phrases or sentences from the question as repetition or even paraphrasing of the wording does not demonstrate understanding and so it is not sufficient to answer the question;

● extract 'evidence' from the passage – these questions should not be seen as stand alone questions as the passage is included to provide evidence and stimulate interest so it should be used as such.

The last two points above suggest that there is an optimum degree of detachment from the passage when answering this type of question. You should extract relevant points from the passages, but express them in your own words.

Free response (essay) questions

When approaching essays (and other forms of question), it is important to analyse the question in order to identify what it is getting at. Key words in the question should be identified and thought about very carefully. You should work on the basis that examiners choose their words with great care and that each word has significance in the question. For instance, a 'why' question ('Why advertise?') is very different from a 'how' question ('How would you advertise?'). You should always answer the question as set and not attempt to provide an answer that is to a question that you were *hoping* for. Examiners only give credit for relevant points, so, irrespective of the quality of an idea or the way in which it is expressed, if it does not answer the question *as set*, you will not gain any marks.

It is always a good idea to open with definitions of key concepts in the question, even if they are not expressly requested. The first paragraph should set the scene, explaining the overall direction of your answer. However, be careful not to give away too many ideas in the opening paragraph as repetition does not make for a good answer. The scene-setting opening paragraph should be kept brief and to the point.

The subsequent paragraphs should deal with the main points of the question in detail. Many students have difficulty constructing paragraphs well, choosing either the one-sentence paragraph, reminiscent of a tabloid newspaper, or the continuous stream, which becomes difficult to read. The key point about a paragraph is that there is an essential unity within it. Paragraphs should deal with one idea or a combination of related ideas on a single theme. That theme should be exhausted before you move on to the next theme by starting a new paragraph.

Ensure that you have tackled all aspects and parts of the question. A common fault is excessive concentration on the first part of the question with only a brief reference (if any) to the second part. When you remember that questions are typically based on an incline of difficulty, with marks weighted towards the later components, you can appreciate the folly of this approach.

The final paragraph should be a conclusion. It should not attempt to sum up everything that has been written in previous paragraphs, but, instead, directly address the question as set. Examiners will be looking for a direct answer to the question in this concluding paragraph.

Table 49.2 sums up the dos and don'ts of writing an essay.

Case studies

Case studies are a distinctive feature of Business Studies courses. All schemes of assessment use case studies either as a whole examination (such as OCR and Edexcel) or as a substantial part of an examination in which there are other elements. In addition, case studies are an important tool of learning. Tony Newby (in *Cost-effective Training*, Kogan Page, 1992) says that 'Case studies are a useful training tool to assist people to learn about the process of problem solving; whether or not people get the 'right' answer is neither here nor there.

The strengths of the case study as a training technique are that it enables people to identify hidden elements of the problem-solving process and to practise problem-solving skills, in particular:

● to recognize (and challenge) unquestioned

Table 49.2 The dos and don'ts of essay writing

Do	Don't
● Answer the question as set	
● Analyse the question	● Ignore the instructional words
● Plan your answer	● Jump straight into your answer
● Include an introduction	● Give too many ideas away in your first paragraph
● Define all key terms	● Write a list
● Divide your answer into logically arranged paragraphs	● Ignore the later parts of questions
● Develop points in full	● Use colloquialisms
● Include a conclusion that directly addresses the question	● Try to summarize everything in your conclusion
● Provide examples and illustrations where appropriate	
● Answer all parts of the question	
● Write legibly	
● Ensure that each 'sentence' really is a sentence	
● Discriminate between relevant and irrelevant points	

assumptions, values and attitudes in the parties to the process;

● to analyse the available information and draw out conclusions and implications from the facts;

● to arrive – by one means or another – at decisions.

Geoff Easton writes (in *Learning from Case Studies*, Prentice Hall, 1982) that a case study or case history ('case' for short) 'is a description of a situation. The typical case consists of a few pages of written description of an actual situation facing an organization. It will usually describe how the current position developed and what problem a key personality in the case is currently facing.'

As an aid to learning, Easton identifies six skills developed by the case study method.

● **The analytical skills of handling information** 'You learn to classify, organize and evaluate information. You learn to recognize when vital information is missing and how it might be obtained. Using this information, you attempt to understand the situation as described. In doing so you practise thinking clearly and logically.'

● **Application skills** Case studies provide you 'with practice at applying concepts, techniques and principles' and the opportunity to judge when various techniques of analysis are appropriate.

● **Creativity skills** 'Creativity is particularly important in generating alternative solutions to the problems uncovered by logical analysis.' A and AS level students must adopt a creative, imaginative approach to solving the problem highlighted in the case study. Although rational and quantitative analysis are essential, it is important not to ignore imaginative insight.

● **Communication skills** Students are required to communicate their solutions to the problem that has been identified. In an examination, this takes the form of written, numerical and graphical forms of communication. When case studies are used as a learning aid, communication can be by other means (such as oral presentations).

● **Social skills** 'Case discussions are essentially social processes. You can learn to communicate, listen, support, argue, guide and control yourself.' These comments are relevant for case studies used in the learning process and for the pre-issued case study examination used by Edexcel and OCR.

● **Self-analysis** Easton writes that 'cases provide a useful forum for analysing your values.' He is mainly referring to ethical and moral issues raised by case studies. Such issues are less present in case studies at A and AS level, but are by no means absent from the scene,

The skills referred to by Easton are required in A level case study examinations. The underlying question is always 'What action would you take to solve the problem?' However, the question is never asked in such a bold and open-ended manner.

The practice of awarding bodies in relation to the release of case study material varies. The purpose of the advance issue of the material (but not the questions) is to provide students with sufficient time to read, digest and discuss the material, and to conduct further investigation. In the case of a lengthy case study, it is difficult to absorb and comprehend the material in a short time in the tense atmosphere of the examination room. Prior issue enables candidates to study the material calmly, but there are particular problems associated with the pre-issued case study. There is a great temptation to believe that:

- knowledge of the case study is, of itself, sufficient;
- 'question spotting' is the key to examination success.

Obviously, a case study will provide clues about the areas of the subject that are likely to feature in the questions. Where students go wrong is, first, in ignoring the theoretical studies under-taken during the course and, second, in ignoring the interrelationship between case study material and other areas of the syllabus. In addition, A level examiners are quite capable of setting a great variety of questions based on, or inspired by, the case study material (some of which might be 'distracters' to test powers of evaluation).

Handling a case study

This section deals specifically with the pre-issued case study, but it is also relevant when case studies are used as a learning tool. On receipt of a case study, you should do the following.

- **Read and comprehend the material** Early readings will be concerned with familiarization with the content of the material. Later readings will help you to fully appreciate the subtle nuances in a well-written case study. It is a good idea to use a highlighter pen to mark all significant words and check their definitions in a good dictionary (for general words) or a specialist dictionary, for words such as those referred to in this book. The key concept sections at the end of each chapter of this book are also an important source of reference.

- **Analyse the situation in the case** For this you should conduct a SWOT analysis (in so far as this is possible) on the firm in the case study. Make notes on the situation described in terms of finance, production, personnel and the relationship with the external environment. By careful analysis, you should identify the problems facing the firm (take care to distinguish between problems and symptoms) and the main opportunities presented to them.

- **Collect relevant information** At this stage, you are advised to link the case study with general revision. The pre-issued case study indicates those syllabus areas that are likely to feature in the questions. You should undertake intensive revision of these topics, remedying any deficiencies in your notes. You should not, however, neglect general revision of other topics.

It is also advisable to investigate general features of the relevant industry. For instance, if the case study deals with production and personnel issues in a bakery, it is advisable to have some general background knowledge of this industry. If the case study deals with the marketing of double-glazing, find out about how these products are marketed. This is not to say that you will be required to demonstrate specialist knowledge of industries, but the knowledge you acquire will give you an advantage in tackling questions in which you are asked to make appropriate sug-gestions to solve a problem in the firm featured in the case study.

- **Identify the analytical techniques that may be of use** These techniques will include decision trees, investment appraisal, break-even analysis, SWOT analysis, statistical techniques and ratio analysis. For instance, a set of accounts will possibly generate a question on ratio analysis. It is foolish not to investigate ratios in advance, but it is equally foolish to use them inappropriately in your answer.

● **Generate and select alternative courses of action** Implicitly or explicitly, the questions will revolve around solutions to problems mentioned in the case study material. As an examination candidate you are being asked to generate alternative solutions, evaluate the alternatives and communicate your recommendations. The generation of alternative solutions requires knowledge and imagination. The evaluation of alternatives requires analytical skills.

A particular feature of case study examinations is that they involve alternative solutions about which people can legitimately disagree. There is, therefore, no 'right' answer. Examination candidates are required to argue and defend their proposed solution and assessment is based on the quality of the argument advanced. The emphasis is on the process by which the candidate formulates a proposed solution rather than the solution itself. As mentioned earlier, in relation to quantitative questions, this underlines the importance of communicating your thought processes as well as the final answer. It is, therefore, essential to argue the case in full, explaining all points in detail, stating both sides of the argument where appropriate and identifying the assumptions on which the answer is based. Examiners are looking for a demonstration of the various intellectual skills identified in the assessment objectives and you should seek to show your understanding and ability to the fullest extent.

● **Communicate your answer** Your answers (to the questions that the examiners have set) should combine some theory with evidence from the case study. It is equally a mistake to answer the question as a free response, essay question, believing that theory is sufficient. Use the case study like a coal mine from which you extract the evidence you need to back up your argument.

For candidates facing unseen case studies there are similar processes to go through, but they occur in the examination room itself.

Table 49.3 sums up how to tackle pre-issued case studies and 49.4 lists the topics that relate to particular areas of business.

Synoptic assessment

Synoptic assessment is a compulsory part of GCE A level. The Qualifications and Assessment Authority (QCA) has imposed a minimum for synoptic assessment of 15 per cant of overall assessment, although it is probable that awarding bodies will raise the synoptic element beyond 15 per cent. Before exploring this further, let us consider the meaning of the word 'synoptic'. A

Table 49.3 The dos and don'ts of pre-issued case studies

Do	Don't
● Read and comprehend the case study	● Neglect general revision
● Identify the main issues	● Ignore the theoretical background
● Be ready to define all relevant terms	● Rely on question spotting
● Collect relevant background information and theory	● Overlook apparently inconsequential evidence
● Decide on appropriate techniques of analysis	● Assume that there is a single answer to the question
● Combine theory with case study evidence	● Answer the (non-existent) question that you hoped
● Answer the questions in full	to see
● Answer the question set	
● Remember that the process of analysing the material is as important as the 'solution'	

Table 49.4 A framework for approaching case studies

External Environment	Accounting	Marketing	Production	HRM
● SWOT	● Accounting	● Marketing	● Location	● Personnel
● PEST	system	organization	● Production methods	organization
● Demand	● Finance	● Products	● Production	● Human resource
● Competition	● Gearing	● Product lifecycle	planning/control	planning
● Legislation	● Profitability	● New product	● Maintenance	● Recruitment
● Government policies	● Liquidity	development	● Purchasing	● Pay policy
● External costs	● Budgeting	● Buyer behaviour	● Stock control	● Training/
	● Investment	● Market structure	● Quality control	development
	appraisal	● Pricing policy	● Work study	● Welfare, health
	● Asset control	● Promotion	● Employee motivation	and safety
	● Employee	● Distribution		● Industrial relations
	motivation	● Market and		● Worker democracy
		marketing research		● Employee
		● Employee		motivation
		motivation		

dictionary definition of synoptic is 'taking or affording a comprehensive mental view' (Oxford English Dictionary). In other words, it is holistic rather than fragmented. The QCA subject criteria states that:

● synoptic assessment should address the requirement that A level Business Studies specifications should encourage students to see the relationship between different aspects of the subject;
● synoptic assessment involves the explicit integration of knowledge; understanding and skills learned in different parts of the A level course;
● synoptic assessment relates to all the assessment objectives, but a single examination paper would not necessarily examine candidates' understanding of the connections between all parts of the course – rather, it would sample candidates' understanding of connections between some parts of the course;
● where a specification contains options, synoptic assessment should focus on the elements contained within the compulsory content.

The synoptic element in subject specifications focuses on business strategies. In AQA's scheme,

the objectives and strategies unit draws together all the subject content areas in terms of 'integrating themes which emphasize the interactive nature of the business world.' 'Candidates are required to recognize the interrelationships between objectives and an uncertain business environmental, and to devise and evaluate strategies which aim to anticipate, respond and manage change.' The business strategy unit is the synoptic element of the OCR specification. The emphasis is placed on 'strategy, its nature, development, implementation and critical evaluation in the context of specific organizational and business situations.' The unit builds on material from previous units, raising understanding from AS to A2 level, but candidates are required to use concepts, conventions, theories and techniques across the functional areas of business – namely, marketing, production, accounting and human resource management. The other English awarding body, Edexcel, also uses corporate strategy as the unifying element as it brings in interaction with the external environment, top management decisions, change, organizational culture, objectives and the interaction of the four functional areas referred to above.

Synoptic assessment (which must, of necessity, be at the end of a course of study), is more than a case study examination containing a series of self-contained questions on discrete areas of the syllabus. The questions themselves must be synoptic and invite candidates to explore inter-relationships. It will be easy to spot a synoptic question if it is written in terms of 'Analyse the impact of X on the:

(a) marketing department;
(b) human resources department;
(c) production department; and
(d) finance department of a manufacturing firm.'

However, at A level, it is unlikely that there will be an explicit statement of the synoptic nature of a question. Instead, candidates will have to interpret the question and explore the possible linkages. The following are intended as examples of synoptic questions where there is no explicit mention of their synoptic nature.

- 'Analyse the possible impact of a rise in interest rates on a manufacturing company.'
- 'Analyse the possible sources of competitive advantage for a company.'
- 'Analyse the problems associated with, and the solutions to, seasonal variations in the pattern of sales.'
- 'Suggest and evaluate strategies to improve cash flow.'
- 'Evaluate the appropriateness of a company's marketing strategies.'

In each of the above cases, a good candidate will take the answer into areas beyond the ostensible topic of the question.

Let us explore examples of topics that can be answered in this way. A question on just-in-time methods, for example, is located in the production part of the specification. The answer is likely to include reference to 'production' topics, such as inventory/stock levels, plant layout, quality and production runs. A good answer will also take the topic into the other functional areas of:

- HRM – motivation, empowerment, organizational structure;
- marketing – quality, customer satisfaction, product variety and responding to customers' needs;

- accounting – investment in working capital, cash flow, impact on final accounts;
- external environment – relationship with suppliers.

Consider a synoptic question inviting candidates to analyse the consequences of changing the price of a product. Ostensibly, this is a marketing question and requires candidates to set pricing policy within the context of the marketing mix.

Strong students will link price changes with quantity demanded using the concept of price elasticity of demand. According to this rule, when demand is inelastic, price and sales revenue changes move in the same direction. On the other hand, when demand is elastic, they move in opposite directions.

This opens up other areas of the syllabus. A change in revenue is likely to mean a change in profitability and cash flow. The price change will be reflected in a company's profit and loss account and in its balance sheet. The price change could be analysed using break-even charts, thus linking a change in marketing strategy with both financial and cost accounting.

However, there are other links. Any change in demand for a product will have implications for the production or operations department. Changes may need to be made to the size of production runs and to the scheduling of production. This will have a knock-on effect on the production of other goods. In the long run, the company may need to look at making changes to its capacity, bringing in issues related to new investment, such as sources of finance and methods of investment appraisal.

Any change in output levels will have implications for the human resource function. The company may need to change the number of people it employs, its balance of skills or the way in which labour is organized.

The company operates in a competitive environment, not in a vacuum. Competitors can be relied on to react to any changes in a rival company's pricing policy. This, in turn, leads to an analysis of market structure and the behaviour of companies. There will also be implications for suppliers.

Levels of response

In the past, examiners awarded marks on the basis of one mark for a valid point plus a further mark or two for a development of the point. There were clear merits in this approach to marking, but it tended to reward knowledge and encourage a simple listing of points. Logically, the point by point approach could result in full marks for mere lists of facts, none of which were explained or developed. To prevent this situation, a ceiling was placed on marks for 'list-type answers', but this could still result in exam success where there was little or no evidence of the higher-order skills of application, analysis and evaluation.

Modern marking schemes (which can be purchased from awarding bodies) are based on the 'levels of response' approach. When using this method, examiners are required to make a judgement as to the quality of an answer in terms of levels. Typically these are as follows.

- **Level 1 (L1) Knowledge** In this answer, the candidate demonstrates that he or she knows the material, but is unable to go beyond the mere facts. The marks available for such an answer will place it below E grade. In other words, it is not possible to gain an A level by a series of answers at Level 1. This does not mean that knowledge is unimportant. In fact, it must be realized that it is impossible to proceed to higher levels without a sound foundation of knowledge.
- **Level 2 (L2) Application** This is the ability to apply basic terms, concepts, theories and methods to the problem being addressed. An example to illustrate the difference between L1 and L2 relates to Herzberg's theory of motivation. A clear statement of the theory would attract a high mark in L1, but does not constitute application. To get into L2, it is necessary to apply Herzberg to issues such as job design in a work situation.
- **Level (L3) Analysis** Analysis is defined as breaking down information into component parts and identifying the assumptions on which a particular line of reasoning depends.

Analysis will include presenting the advantages and disadvantages of a particular issue, suggesting causes and consequences and commenting on decisions or situations. To demonstrate analysis, an examination candidate has to be able to select, organize and interpret the information. A series of good analytical answers will ensure success at AS and A level, but, to secure the highest marks, it is necessary to produce answers of L4 standard.

- **Level 4 (L4) Evaluation** To demonstrate this skill, the candidate has to demonstrate their ability to make reasoned judgements. This is not just a conclusion, but a conclusion based on the material presented. Evaluation includes the following:
  - presenting a balanced argument resulting in a conclusion;
  - assessing and appraising the value or worth of information;
  - prioritizing from a range of strategies;
  - recognizing the limitations of information given;
  - judgement after comparing and contrasting.

To illustrate how the examiners use the levels approach, consider a 20-mark question, where mark bands are 0–5, 6–10, 11–15, 16–20 for each of the levels. Examiners will first make a judgement as whether or not the answer exhibits evaluation. If it does, then a mark between 16 and 20 will be awarded (and this will be sufficient to secure a grade A if replicated over the whole assessment). If there is no evaluation, the examiner will look to see if analysis has been demonstrated. If this is absent, then is there evidence of applying theory to the situation in the question? If not, the answer is, at best, based on knowledge, for which a maximum of 5 is possible (5 out of 20 replicated over the whole assessment means failure in the examination).

The advice offered to candidates is to know and apply the material, but also to make sure your answer contains analysis and a judgement. Knowledge is a necessary, but not sufficient, condition for exam success.

Command words

Command words are the instructions contained in an examination question. They state what the candidate is required to do in relation to the topic. To secure good marks, it is important to understand what is meant by the command words.

Account for To give reasons for or explain.

Analyse To break a topic down into its component parts.

Assess Weigh up and evaluate options or arguments. Determine the importance of something.

Comment Draw conclusions from the evidence in the form of a stated opinion.

Compare Identify similarities and differences.

Consider Weigh up the options.

Critically analyse Look in depth at an issue from the perspective of a critic.

Define Give the exact meaning of a term.

Describe Give an account of.

Discuss Put forward both sides of a case before coming to a conclusion.

Discuss critically Discuss, but there is a hint that there may be a reason to be sceptical of the theory being discussed.

Distinguish between Demonstrate an understanding of the differences between two concepts.

Evaluate Make a reasoned judgement about the validity of a particular argument or statement.

Examine Inspect closely, investigate.

Explain Make clear and give reasons.

How Show details of how something is achieved and so on.

Justify Give evidence for a particular point of view.

Outline Describe without detail. Give the main feature of.

State your assumptions State the factors you assume before reaching your conclusion.

Suggest Put forward an idea.

To what extent Requires candidates to make a judgement about the degree to which a statement, theory, evidence is true.

Project/coursework in Business Studies

The starting point

You should begin by obtaining a clear statement of what is required for the particular specification. The definitive statement of what is required is contained in the specifications and any accompanying 'Notes for Guidance' published by the relevant awarding bodies. These will:

- explain the nature of the task;
- offer some examples of project titles;
- state the length of the work;
- state the format in which it should be written.

The marking scheme for projects is usually available as a public document and you should study it very carefully. It will tell you the skills (explanation, analysis, evaluation and so on) that you will be required to demonstrate and their relative importance. Irrespective of the examination scheme, you will find that, at A level, a high proportion of the marks are awarded for the higher-level skills of analysis and evaluation. Description and explanation should not be neglected, but, by themselves, will not produce a high mark.

The title

The next step on the road to a successful project is the choice of a suitable title. This must emerge after extensive preliminary research.

In evaluating titles, the following questions should be asked.

- Is it valid – does it conform to the course requirements?
- Will it satisfy the requirements of examiners?
- Will it lead to a genuine Business Studies project?
- Is it feasible for an A level student with limited time and other resources?
- Is sufficient material available to the candidate?
- Does it provide scope for investigation, analysis and evaluation?
- Does it accurately convey the topic to be investigated?
- Will it produce a clear conclusion?

A title based on a question to be addressed is always better than one that starts:

- 'A study of ...';
- 'An evaluation of ...';
- 'A comparison of ...';

Do not choose a title that:

- leads to a project devoid of Business Studies content;
- leads to a descriptive and inconclusive project;
- requires commercially sensitive information, which will not be forthcoming;
- is large and unwieldy (an A level student is unlikely to produce anything worth while on 'the quality of British management' or 'the role of information technology in the workplace').

Hypothesis testing and projects

One thing that irritates examiners when marking projects is misuse of the term 'hypothesis'. A hypothesis is a theory to be proved or disproved by reference to the facts or a provisional explanation of anything. This indicates that it is a tentative theory awaiting proof.

The following are examples of hypotheses:

- 'An £x million rise in government expenditure will reduce unemployment by £y';
- 'A rise in real income will lead to increased spending on foreign holidays';
- 'An increase in advertising expenditure will lead to a rise in sales'.

These statements are all capable of being tested by reference to the facts.

The following are not hypotheses as they can be neither proved nor disproved:

- 'The government should reduce the level of VAT';
- 'Marks & Spencer should spend money on advertising';
- 'Firms should use quantitative techniques of analysis'.

These are all opinions or value judgements; they cannot be tested as true or false.

When you come to write your project, do not use the term hypothesis unless it is, genuinely, a hypothesis. If your project title is about a true hypothesis by all means use the term, but be modest in your claims about proving it. First, because we are dealing with human behaviour, it is not possible to claim the same degree of certainty as natural scientists would claim for their theories. In other words, just because an event happened on 100 occasions out of 100, this is no proof that it will happen on the 101st. Second, it is extremely unlikely that you will be able to collect sufficient data to enable you to prove a hypothesis. Third, hypothesis testing requires considerable knowledge and ability in statistics. All you will be able to legitimately claim is that the evidence you have collected supports the hypothesis – that is, it lends weight to it but does not prove it. Modesty in your claims will impress your examiner more than wildly exaggerated claims.

Length and presentation

Project length has proved to be a controversial area in examining. The typical A level project is 5000 words long, but you should refer to the awarding body for an exact statement of length. If the body requires you to produce a project in the 'region of 5000 words', you should seek to achieve the target plus or minus 300/400 words. No one will mind (and they probably will not know) if the project is 5350 words long, but 7000 or 3000 words is clearly not in the 'region of 5000 words'. If the board states a minimum and maximum number of words, you must keep it within the stated limits. If the project is excessively short, you will not be demonstrating the skills that earn the marks. If it is too long, you will have failed to produce a concise report in the form required. This might cost you marks. Because you are unlikely to produce a high-quality report within the word limit at the first attempt, you should work on successive drafts.

Presentation is also of vital importance in project writing. Check the examination requirements relating to the form it should take (manuscript or word processed). Invest in a simple folder or binder to ensure that it is pleasing to the eye without being unnecessarily cumbersome. Do not forget to make a photocopy of your project in case the original is lost. In the case of projects involving a debriefing interview, there is an extra reason for retaining a copy – to use in preparation for the interview. If you produce a piece of work in which you can take pride, it can also be useful in higher education or job interviews and as part of your Record of Achievement.

Data presentation

Any worthwhile project will include some numerical data from either a secondary or primary source. Obviously, such data should only be included if it is relevant, appropriate and referred to in the text. Choose the most appropriate way of presenting the data. This might be in the form of tables – in which case, do not forget to provide a title, a reference to the source of the data and a clear statement of the units in which you are working. You might feel that some form of graphical presentation of the data is appropriate and is visually more attractive. Once again, ensure that a title and sources are provided, that axes and graphs are labelled and that the scale is clearly stated. Do not contrive situations to (unnecessarily) use as many forms of graph as possible. In the same way, do not make excessive use of pie charts when the data could be more efficiently covered in table form. The key word here is 'appropriate' forms of presentation.

The structure of the project

A project should be structured in the following way:

- **The title page,** containing the:
  - title of the project;
  - name of the author;
  - name of the institution;
  - candidate and centre number;
  - date of completion of the project.

It is helpful if the title page is visible from the outside.

- **The abstract** This is a summary of the report. It should be 100–200 words in length and should provide a framework for the project.

- **Acknowledgements** to people and institutions who have been helpful.
- **Contents page**.
- **A concise statement** of the problem, question or issue.
- **The background** This is likely to be a descriptive section setting the scene, explaining the current situation and providing background information (including an input of theory). It is a mistake to allow this section to be too lengthy.
- **The evidence** This section will contain data collected in the investigation, such as market research findings, costings and so on. Be selective with the information you present. Only include it if it is relevant to your topic and helps to answer your question.
- **Analysis** After the evidence has been presented, it has to be analysed and evaluated. This means drawing conclusions from the data and noting limitations in the data and techniques of analysis.
- **Conclusion** The project should have started with a question to be addressed. The concluding section of the project should contain a clear answer to the question that was asked. Examiners expect to see a clear and definite conclusion, for which marks are available in the marking scheme. The conclusion should be the culmination of the investigation, be well founded in the data and directly answer the question. For instance, if the project is in the form of an investment appraisal, the conclusion will be either 'yes, the firm should proceed with the proposed investment' or 'no, it should not proceed'. If the title promised recommendations for action, the conclusion should take the form of recommendations. One thing that should *not* be included is new information.
- **Appendices** These should be limited to data that the writer considers important, but which do not fit easily in the text (such as photocopies of relevant statistics). Do not include material in an appendix unless you directly refer to it in the text. Do not pad out a project with printed material that, because it is clearly not your own work, will not attract marks.

Synoptic essay questions

A good answer to each of the following questions requires material from at least two major areas of the subject. The questions are deliberately designed to be open-ended, so answers can develop the material in a variety of ways.

1 Suggest and evaluate strategies to cope with the problems of a rise in the value of the country's currency against other major foreign currencies.

2 Suggest and evaluate strategies to cope with the problem of seasonality in sales.

3 Analyse the implications of, and problems associated with, the introduction of new labour-saving equipment.

4 Analyse the impact of telephone banking on retail banking in the UK.

5 Analyse possible causes of a decline in profitability.

6 Suggest and evaluate both short- and long-term strategies to cope with the problem of shortage of skilled labour.

7 Analyse the likely consequences of a diversification of a firm's product range.

8 Suggest and evaluate strategies to cope with the problems resulting from a rise in interest rates.

9 Suggest and evaluate strategies to cope with a rise in labour costs.

10 Analyse the likely impact of a new competitor on the financial performance of a company. Suggest and evaluate strategies to maintain market share.

11 Analyse the impact of the accelerating pace of technological change on each of the functional areas of business management.

12 Analyse the consequences for UK business of each of the following:
   (a) EU enlargement to include Eastern Europe;
   (b) acceptance of the Social Charter.

13 A single market with a single currency. Analyse the impact of these developments in the EU on each of the four functional areas of management.

14 Analyse the consequences of the adoption of total quality for the management of a firm's resources.

15 Analyse the implications of flow line production techniques on the other functional areas of management.

16 Analyse the consequences for the marketing and other departments of a move away from premium pricing.

17 (a) What do you understand by a divisionalized business organization?
   (b) Analyse the implications of divisionalization for the way in which the firm is managed.

18 Shorter production runs and shorter product development times. Discuss the implications of these trends on the management of resources.

19 Discuss the implications of a strategy of de-merger to concentrate on core competences.

20 Analyse the implications of, and the constraints imposed on business by, the Data Protection Act.

21 Analyse the implications of the development of the Internet for business organizations.

22 Analyse the factors that will have been taken into account in the formulation of a strategic objective of a 5 per cent increase in the volume of sales in the coming year.

23 Analyse the internal and external constraints on a business organization.

24 Analyse the consequences of the adoption of a policy of differentiated marketing in which a number of market segments are targeted.

25 Suggest and evaluate strategies to cope with the problem of recession.

26 Suggest and evaluate strategies to cope with a shortage in an important raw material.

27 Analyse the implications of just-in-time approaches to manufacturing.

28 Analyse the consequences of a move to 24-hour working.

29 Discuss the implications of changing from selling exclusively own brand products to selling a range of branded products.

30 Analyse possible explanations for an adverse variance from a cash budget (cash flow forecast).

Appendix: Coursework diary

Date started:

....

Centre name/number:

....

Student name/number:

....

Title of coursework:

....

....

Title approved by:

....

Sources

Primary data	Details
	....
	....
	....
	....
Secondary data	....
	....
	....
	....

	Target date	Actual date
Stage 1 Submit coursework checklist		
Stage 2 Submit draft introduction (including research intentions)		
Stage 3 Evidence of research (primary and secondary)		
Stage 4 Collection/recording of data (in draft format)		
Stage 5 Analysis and interpretation of date (methodology and reasons)		
Stage 6 Development of conclusions/ recommendations/evaluations Bibliography List of references		
Stage 7 First draft		
Stage 8 Second draft		

Deadline for final submission: ....

Index

Absenteeism 491–2
Absorption costing 381–3, 386
Accelerator principle 138–9
Acceptable quality level (AQL) 437
Accountability 38–40, 44
Accounting 21, 171, 289–414
Accounting rate of return (ARR) 361–2, 366
Acid test ratio 313–14, 316, 322, 323
ACORN classification 229, 230
Act of incorporation 8
Adaptation 273
Administration 17–18, 324
Administrative theory *see* classical organization theory
Advertising 199, 203, 228, 241, 242, 244–8, 250, 272
Advisory, Conciliation and Arbitration Service (ACAS) 524–5, 527–8, 530
After-sales service 420, 439–40
Agents 108–9, 261–2, 263–4
Aggregate demand 144–5, 149
Alternative Investment Market (AIM) 11, 347
Annual general meetings (AGMs) 11
Annual reports 13–14
Ansoff Matrix 553–4
Appropriation account 292, 295
Appropriation budget 406
Articles of association 9, 18
Asset-led marketing 274
Assets 300–7, 359–71
Auditor's report 13–14
Authority 36, 38–40, 44
Authorized share capital 346, 349
Autonomous group working 490–1
Averages 61–2, 216–18

Balance of payments 144, 149, 166–7, 168, 173
Balance sheet 292, 300–910
Balance sheet equation 301
Bankruptcy 17
Bar charts 58
Base year 62–3
Batch production 419, 421, 426, 435
Behavioural theory of the firm 128–9

Benchmarking 446–7
Binomial distribution 71–3
Boom phase 139
Boston Matrix 239, 240
Brands 199, 230, 237–8, 240, 271–2
Break-even analysis 394–402
Break-even level of output 395–8
Broadbanding 520, 521
Budget holder 404
Budgets 337, 379, 403–14
Buffer stock 430–1, 432
Bureaucracy, theory of 35, 36–7
Business Environment Risk Index (BERI) 268
Business lifecycle 343
Business Names Act 1985 6–7
Business plans 30–1
Business process re-engineering (BPR) 447
Business rate 157

CAD *see* Computer-aided design
Cadbury Report on Corporate Governance (1992) 12
CAM *see* Computer-aided manufacturing
Capacity planning 423–4
Capital 300–7, 349
Cartogram 60
Cash 302, 311, 315–16
Cash budgets 315, 330–4, 337, 403, 406
Cash equivalents 337
Cash flow forecasts *see* cash budgets
Cash flow statements 330–1, 334–6, 337
Cash statements 330–41
Caveat emptor 116
Cell working 452–4, 456
Census 209
Central tendency 61–2
Centralization 41–4
Certificate of incorporation 9
Certificate of trading 10
Chairman's report 13
Change 537–41
Channels of distribution 199, 261–6
Chisnall, P. M. 207

CIM *see* computer-integrated manufacturing
Civil law 106–7, 116–17, 118
Class interval 73
Classical management theory 35
Classical organization theory 35, 36
Collective bargaining 524–7, 530
Commanding 22
Common market 169
Communication nets 50–1, 54
Communications 46–55
Company law 9, 10, 13, 97, 173
Company secretary 13
Competition 130
  export opportunities 165
  government policy 158–60, 162, 173
  marketing plan 277–8
  technology 99
Competitive advantage 88, 455–6, 555–7
Competitor analysis 29–30
Competitor-oriented pricing 258, 259, 260
Complementary goods 120, 123
Computer systems 83–4
Computer-aided design (CAD) 84, 86, 89
Computer-aided manufacturing (CAM) 86–7, 89
Computer-integrated manufacturing (CIM) 86–7
Concentrated marketing 230, 231
Conditional events 69–70
Conformance 434–5
Conservative Party 152, 153, 155, 157–8, 161, 172, 526, 528–9
Constraints 25, 34, 105, 253–5
Consumers
  behaviour 225–32, 243–4
  boycotts 180
  definition 225, 232
  protection law 116–17, 118, 154, 159, 173
  utility 119
Contingency theory 40, 536
Continuous flow production 419
Continuous improvement 453, 454, 456
Contracting out 551
Contracts 97, 107–8, 110–11, 118, 507, 510
Contractualization 158
Contribution 383, 386, 395, 398
Control 22, 32–4, 39–41, 44
Coordination 22, 34
Core competences 555–7
Corporate objectives, marketing plan 276
Corporate strategy 27–8, 548–50
Correlation 66–8, 73
Cost accounting 379–93
Cost centre 404, 408
Cost of sales 292–5
Cost-based pricing 255–7, 259, 260
Costs
  break-even analysis 394–7
  cost accounting 379–93
  economies of scale 125–7
  inflation 141, 142, 143
  promotional mix 243
  subnormal profit 129
Coupon rate 345
CPU *see* central processing units
Credit 116–17, 314–15, 346

Creditors
  average payment period 312, 322, 324
  balance sheet 302, 307, 311–12
  insolvent companies 17–18
  limited liability companies 8–9
Creditors' budget 406
Criminal law 106–7, 116, 118
Critical path analysis 457–71
Cross-elasticity of demand 123, 130
Cross-subsidization 199
Culture 103–5, 227, 532–7
Current asset ratio 313, 316, 322, 323
Current assets 302, 307, 311, 316
Current liabilities 302, 307, 311, 316
Customer-oriented pricing 257–8, 259, 260
Customers
  definition 225–6
  marketing 274
  motivation 203
  pricing 254–5, 257–8, 259, 260
Customs union 169, 173

Dagmar model 243–4
Damages 108, 109
Data 25, 56, 57–61, 88, 203–12
Data Protection Act 1984 83, 88–9, 507
Databases 83, 85–6, 88–9
Davidson, Hugh 275
De-integration 551–2
De-merger 551
Debentures 345, 349
Debt capital 349
Debt factor 346
Debt finance 343–5
Debtors 314–15
  average collection period 314, 322, 324
  balance sheet 302, 307
  cash budgets 332
  working capital 311
Debtors' budget 406
Debts 7, 8–9, 315, 334
Decentralization 41–4
Decision making 23–6, 38–9, 56, 228, 232, 372–8
Decree of specific performance 106, 108
Defendant 106
Deflation 143, 145, 149, 167
Delegation 38–9, 44
Delphi method 215
Demand 119–23, 130
  aggregate 144–5, 149
  consumer behaviour 226
  elasticity of 121–3, 130, 226, 253–4, 257, 272
  investment 138–9
  Keynesianism 144–5, 147
  pricing 252–4
Demand curve 119–21
Demography 100–3, 105
Depreciation 302, 304–5, 307
Deregulation 158, 162
Design 234–6, 420, 434
Desk research 204–5, 206–7, 212
Desktop publishing (DTP) 84–5, 89
Destroyer pricing 258

Differential pricing 129, 257
Differentiated marketing 230–1
Diffusion process 231–2
Direct costs 386
Direct mailing 241
Direct marketing 263, 265–6
Direction of communication 47, 48, 54
Directors 11–13, 128, 177
Disciplinary action 492, 493
Discounted cash flow 366
Discounting 362–5
Discretionary income 226, 232
Dismissal 113–14, 492
Dispersion 64–6, 73
Disposable income 226, 232
Distribution 70–3, 197, 201, 261–6, 269–71
Divestment 551
Dividends 292, 302, 322, 324, 325, 344, 347
Double entry bookkeeping 290, 300, 307
Downsizing 511–12
DTP see desktop publishing (DTP)
Duty of care 12, 109, 115–16

E-mail 88, 89
Earnings per share 322, 324–5
Economic batch quantity 431, 432
Economic environment 97, 98, 104, 105, 119–63
Economic growth 135, 139–41, 144, 149
Economic and monetary union (EMU) 169–71, 173
Economic order quantity (EOQ) 431, 432
Economic policy 151–63
Economies of scale 125–7, 130, 158
EDI see electronic data interchange
Effectiveness 442–3, 447
Efficiency 442–8
Efficiency ratios 321, 322, 323–4, 325
EFTA see European Free Trade Association
EGMs see extraordinary general meetings
Elasticity of demand 121–3, 130, 226, 253–4, 257, 272
Elasticity of supply 124, 130
Electronic data interchange (EDI) 171
Employees
    see also human resource management
    absenteeism 491–2
    disciplinary action 492
    dismissal 113–14
    efficiency ratios 324
    health and safety 83, 114–15, 172
    part-time 110, 508–9
    retaining 510–11
    rewards 515–21
    rights 110–16
    vicarious liability 109–10
Employment law 110–16, 118, 172, 492–3, 507, 511
Empowerment 500–1
EMU see economic and monetary union
Enterprise Zones (EZ) 161
Entrepreneurial businesses 344
Entrepreneurial structure 41, 42, 43
Environment 29, 95–105, 164–74
Environmental audits 181–3
Environmental protection 173, 175–91, 179–83
Equal Pay Act 1970 113, 507

Equilibrium price 124, 130
Equipment 359–71, 422–3
Equity 307, 348
Equity finance 343–5
Equity shares 347
Equity theory 489, 494, 516
Ethical investment 180–1
Ethics 176, 177–9, 183
European Free Trade Association (EFTA) 168
European Social Fund 173
European Union 167–73
    competition law 159–60
    employment law 110, 111, 115, 172
    environmental laws 180
    law 107
    regional aid 161
Evaluation 25, 26
Exchange rate 136, 143, 149, 174
    appreciation/revaluation 173
    balance of payments 166–7
    depreciation/devaluation 173
    EMU 169, 170, 171
    export opportunities 165
Expectancy theory 487–9
Expected value 376
Expenses see overheads
Experiments 205, 207
Exporting 164–5, 269, 273
Extension strategy 199
Extraordinary general meetings (EGMs) 11
Extrapolation 218–20, 221

Factors of production 130
Fair Trading Act 1973 117, 159
Family decision-making 232
Family lifecycle 228–9
Fayol, Henri 22, 36, 44
Feedback 54
Fiduciary duty 12
Field research 207–9, 212
Finance 21, 28, 125–6, 303, 342–58
Financial accounting 289–90
First in, first out (FIFO) 292–3, 294, 295
Fiscal policy 145, 149
Fishbone diagrams 453–4
Fixed asset turnover 322, 324
Fixed assets 304–5, 307
Fixed budget 406–7, 408
Fixed costs 381, 383, 386, 394–8
Flat organizations 40–1
Flexible budget 406–7, 408
Flow production 426, 435
Fluctuations 215–21
Focus groups 204, 207
Food and Drugs Act 1955 116
Force field analysis 540
Forecasts 28, 31–2, 214–24
Formal communication 47, 48–9, 54
Formal organization 37
Foss v. Harbottle (1843) 11
Four Ps 199, 279–80
Four Ss 181
Franchises 14–16, 18

Free market system 152–4, 160
Free trade 168, 169, 174
Free Zone 161
Frequency 61–2
Frequency curves 59
Frequency polygon 58–9
Friedman, Milton 146, 177
FRS 1 334–5, 337
Full costing 381–3, 386
Functional structure 27–8, 37–8, 41, 42, 43
Futures contract 428

Gantt charts 462, 463
Gap analysis 31–2
GATT see General Agreement on Tariffs and Trade
Gearing 321, 322, 324, 325, 344–5
GEC screen 554–5
General Agreement on Tariffs and Trade (GATT) 165,
  167, 174
Gilbreth, F. 444
Global product 271–2, 273
Going concern 290
Goodwill 306
Government 98, 140–1, 151–63
Green business 181, 183
Green movement 180
Grievance procedures 492–3
Gross profit 291, 295, 321–2
GROUP 19
Group technology 422
Groups 495–6

Hardware 83
Health and safety at work 83, 114–15, 172
Hedging 428
Herzberg, F. 485, 486
Hierarchy of needs 227–8, 484–5, 494
Hire purchase 345
Histograms 58
Historical comparison 215, 325
Human relations school 483–9
Human resource management 21–2, 171, 439–40, 453,
  475–7, 502–14
Hygiene factors 485, 516
Hypothesis 67

ICT see information and communications technology
Imports 165, 167, 168, 174
Income 226, 232
Income elasticity of demand 123, 130, 226
Income policy 143
Incremental budgeting 407, 408
Independent events 69
Index numbers 62–4, 73
Indirect costs 386
Induction 507–8
Industrial disputes 527–8, 530
Industrial market 225–6, 229, 232, 242, 263, 264
Industrial policy 158–62
Industrial relations 523–31
Inferior goods 123

Inflation 141–3, 144, 149
  boom phase 139
  Keynesianism 144–5
  monetarism 146
  moving average 216
  national income accounts 136
  pay 526
Inflation indexes 63–4
Informal communication 54
Informal organization 37
Information 56, 87, 88
Information and communications technology (ICT)
  82–91, 171
Infrastructure 157
Injections 135, 137
Injunction 106
Innovation 99
Insolvency 17–18
Intangible assets 301
Interest rates 139, 143, 145, 147, 166, 171, 324
Interfirm comparison 325
Internal rate of return (IRR) 364–5, 366
International environment 164–74
International marketing 267–73
International Stock Exchange (ISE) 11
Internet 87–8, 90
Interquartile range 64–5
Interventionism 144–5, 153–4, 155, 158–62, 163
Invention 99
Investment 138–9, 143, 149, 180–1, 348–9
  see also gearing
Investment appraisal 359–71
ISE see International Stock Exchange
Issued share capital 346, 349

Jargon 49–50
Job analysis 504–5
Job description 505–6
Job design 489
Job enlargement 490
Job enrichment 485, 490, 494
Job evaluation 516–17, 521
Job rotation 489–90
Jobbing production 418–19, 426, 435
Just-in-time (JIT) 432, 450–2, 456

Kaizen 453, 454, 456
Kanban system 451, 452
Keynesianism 141, 143–7, 149
Kotler, Philip 99–100, 237, 255, 274, 275

Labour
  see also employees; human resource management;
    unemployment
  demographic trend 100, 103
  economies of scale 125
  EU Social Charter 172
  non-standard 508–10
  productivity 443
  supply side policy 148
  turnover 510–11, 514

Labour Party 155, 172
Laissez-faire 149, 152–3, 155, 158, 163
Laspeyres approach 64
Last in, first out (LIFO) 293, 294, 295
Lead time 429–30
Leadership 34, 478–94
Lean production 449–56
Learning curve 278
Lease purchase 345–6
Legal environment 97–8, 104, 105, 106–18
Liabilities 300–7, 311, 316
Lien 108
Lifestyles 104
Limited liability 8–9, 10, 18
Line graphs 59, 60
Line management 39, 40, 44
Line production 419, 435
Liquid assets 316
Liquidation 17, 18
Liquidity ratios 313–14, 321, 322, 323, 325
Loan Guarantee Scheme 162
Loans 324, 343–5
Lorenz curve 60–1
Loss leader prices 259

Macroeconomics 134–50
Maintenance 422–3
Management 19–34
    economies of scale 126
    leadership 478, 479–81
    social responsibility 177
    style 533
Management accounting 379, 386–7
Management buy-ins 348, 551–2
Management buy-outs 348, 551
Management by exception 57
Management information systems (MIS) 33, 88
Managerial theories of the firm 128
Margin of safety 395, 398
Marginal costing 127, 130, 238, 381, 383–4, 387
Marginal efficiency of capital (MEC) 139
Marginal pricing 256–7
Marginal rate of withdrawal (MRW) 137
Marginal revenue 127, 130
Mark-up 322, 387
Market failure 153–4, 163
Market forces 152–3
Market price 124
Market research 197, 201, 202, 203, 212
Market segmentation 228–31, 244, 257, 272
Market share 252–3
Market surveys 215
Market testing 148
Market-oriented pricing 259
Marketing 20
    channels of distribution 261–6
    consumer behaviour 225–32
    definitions 195–7
    economies of scale 126
    green 181
    international 267–73
    objectives 279, 281
    planning 199–201, 274–85

production planning and control 424
products 233–40
    strategy 28, 197, 279–80, 281, 557
    tactics 197, 275, 279, 280, 281
Marketing audit 276, 277, 281
Marketing mix 199, 230–1, 279
Marketing orientation 199
Marketing research 202–13
Marketing-oriented firm 196–7
Marketization 158
Maslow, A. 227–8, 484–5
Master budget 406
Matching 290, 337
Maternity rights 111–12
Matrix organization 41, 42, 43
Mean 61–2, 73
Mean deviation 65
Measure of dispersion 73
Measured day work (MDW) 518–19, 521
MEC *see* marginal efficiency of capital
Media 47, 48, 50, 245–7, 250
Median 61–2, 73
Memorandum of association 9, 18, 346
Memory 228, 238
Mergers 550, 552–3
Microeconomics 119–33
Minimum wage 113
Mintzberg, Henry 22, 23
MIS *see* management information systems
Mission statement 26
Mixed economy 5–6, 98, 130, 152
Mode 61–2, 73
Monetarism 141, 143–7, 149, 153
Money supply 141, 143, 145, 146–7, 149
Monitoring 26
Monopoly 127–8, 129, 130, 154, 158–60, 254
Mortgages 345
MOST 27
Motivation 478–94, 516
Moving averages 73, 216–21
MRW *see* marginal rate of withdrawal
Multinational corporation 270, 273
Multiplant specialization 126
Multipliers 137–8, 149, 165–6
Mutually exclusive events 69, 376

National income accounts 134–6
National minimum wage 113
Need theory 486–7
Needs, hierarchy of 227–8, 484–5, 494
Negligence 109, 118
Net present value (NPV) 363–4, 366
Net profit 291–2, 295, 322
Network analysis 457–62
New pay 519, 521
New product development (NPD) 233–6, 240
New products 231–2, 420
Niche marketing 240, 557
Noise 50, 54
Normal distribution 70–1, 73
Northern Ireland 152
Not-for-profit sector 6
NPD *see* new product development

Nuisance 106, 109, 118, 180
Numerical information 56–81

Objectives 24–5, 26–34, 279, 281
Objects clause 9, 18
Occupiers' liability 115–16
Old pay 519
Oligopoly 128, 130, 154, 158, 254
One-way communication 47–8, 54
Operating systems 83
Operational decisions 24
Operational objectives 27
Operational planning 29
Opinion leaders 231
Opportunity 105, 276
Opportunity cost 380
Ordinary shares 347, 349
Organizational culture 532–7
Organizations 5–18
    centralization v. decentralization 41–4
    change 537–41
    flat 40–1
    functional structure 19–22, 27–8, 37–8, 41, 42, 43
    governance of 11–13
    growth 550–3
    objectives 26–34
    structures 35–45
    tall 40–1
    types 8–18
Organizing 22, 34, 37
Overdrafts 302–3, 315, 346
Overhead absorption rate 382
Overheads 256, 295, 380, 381–3
Overtrading 16–17, 313, 334

P/E ratio see price-earnings ratio
Paasche approach 64
Packaging 238, 241
Panel consensus 215
Parent Leave Directive (PLD) 111
Pareto Rule 430–1
Partnerships 7–8, 9, 17, 18
Pay 112–13, 515–21
Payback method 360–1, 366
PDI see personal disposable income
Peak pricing 129, 256
Penetration pricing 252–3, 257–8, 260, 272
Perceived value pricing 257
Perfect competition 127, 130
Performance appraisal 493
Performance-related pay (PRP) 519–20, 521
Person specification 505–6
Personal disposable income (PDI) 136–7
Personal selling 201, 225, 241–2, 244, 248–50
Personnel management 28, 475, 477
    see also human resources
PEST analysis 29, 277
Phillips Curve 145
Pictograms 60
Pie charts 59
Piece rate system 517–18, 519, 521
Pioneer pricing 257–8

Plaintiff 106
Planning 22, 28–32, 214, 403–8, 502–514
Planning laws 97, 152, 180
Plant 421–3
PLD see Parent Leave Directive
POISE 275
Political environment 97, 98–9, 104, 105
Pollution 179–83
Population 57, 73, 100–3
Porter, Michael 277–8, 556
Positioning 201, 236–7, 240, 244, 257
Positive action 112
PPC see production planning and control
Preference shares 347, 349
Presentations 53–4
Pressure groups 180, 183
Price 252–60
    consumer protection law 116
    demand 119–23, 124–5, 253–4
    EMU 171
    equilibrium 124
    Keynesianism 144
    marketing strategy 197, 272–3
    national income accounts 135–6
    production and operations management 420
    regulation 124–5
    supply 123–5
    traditional theory of the firm 127–8
Price discrimination 129–30, 257, 260
Price elasticity of demand 130, 226, 253–4, 257, 272
Price elasticity of supply 124, 130
Price lining 259
Price makers 127–8, 130, 254
Price takers 127, 130, 254
Price-earnings ratio (P/E ratio) 322, 325
Primary data 57, 73, 204–5, 212
Private companies 10, 18, 347
Private sector 5–6
Privatization 157–8, 163
Probability 68–73, 372–8
Procedures 24
Producer Price Index 64
Product
    design 234–6, 420
    international marketing 271
    marginal costing 384
    marketing 233–40
    positioning 201, 236–7, 244, 257
    production 420–1
    promotional mix 242–3
    variation 420–1
Product development 197, 198, 201, 553
Product failure 236
Product lifecycle 197–9, 200, 201, 242–3, 247–8
Product line 238–9
Product mix 201, 233–40
Product planning and development 197
Production 21, 417–26
    abroad 269–71
    budget 405–6
    effiency 442–8
    just-in-time 432, 450–2
    quality 435
    strategy 28

Production planning and control (PPC) 424–6
Productivity 443–7, 448, 503, 524, 526
Profit centres 404–5, 408
Profit and loss account 289–99, 330, 334
Profit maximization 127, 252
Profit-related pay 520–1
Profitability ratios 321–3, 326
Profits 127, 129, 252, 395–8
Project appraisal 359
Project production 418, 435
Promotion 197, 201, 241–51, 272, 278, 280
Promotional mix 201, 242–3, 250
Proprietorial businesses 344
Provisions 315, 337
Prudence principle 290, 292
PSBR see public-sector borrowing requirement
Psychology 227–8
Public companies 9, 10, 10–11, 18, 347–8, 550
Public expenditure 157
Public sector 6, 98, 148
Public-sector borrowing requirement (PSBR) 143
Publicity 241, 242
Pull strategies 265, 266
Purchasing 125, 427–9
Push strategies 265, 266

Qualitative research 203–4
Quality 234–41, 254–5, 257, 420
Quality circles (QC) 454–5, 456
Quantitive methods 56–81
Quantitive research 203–4
Quantum meruit 108
Questionnaires 208–9

Racial discrimination 112, 507
Range 64–5, 73
Ratio analysis 321–9
Reasonable care 114
Receivership 17–18
Recession 139, 149, 166
Recruitment 504–10, 514
Redistribution of wealth 153–4, 156, 157
Redundancy 113–14, 511–12, 514
Reference groups 104, 227
Reflation 141, 145, 146, 149
Regional policy 160–2, 163, 173
Registrar of Companies 9, 10
Reorder level 432
Reorder quantity 431–2
Reports 52–3
Resale Price Acts 1964 and 1976 116, 159
Resale price maintenance (RPM) 116, 159
Research and development (R&D) 126, 234, 258
Reserves 303–4, 307
Responsibility 36, 38–40, 44
Responsibility accounting 404–5
Restrictive trade practices (RP) 159–60
Retail Price Index (RPI) 63–4, 141, 149
Retailers 261, 262, 263–5, 266
Return on capital employed (ROCE) 322, 323
Revenue centre 404
Reward management 515–22
Risk 68, 203

Risk bearing 126
RPI see Retail Price Index
RPM see resale price maintenance
Rules 24

Safety at work 83, 114–15, 172
Sale of Goods Act 1979 116, 117
Sale and leaseback 346
Sale and Supply of Goods Act 1994 117
Sales 280, 292–5, 424
Sales promotion 201, 241, 242, 243, 248–50
Sales revenue 315, 395
Sales-oriented firm 196
Sampling 209–12
Scalar chain 36, 38
Scatter diagrams 67–8
Scientific management 35, 36, 444, 481–3, 516
Scotland 152
SDA see Sex Discrimination Act
Seasonality 215, 216–20, 424
Secondary data 57, 212
Secondary research 204–5, 206–7
Segmentation 201, 228–31, 232
Selling 196, 324, 406
Semi-log graphs 59–60
Semi-variable costs 381, 387
Sex discrimination 111, 113
Share capital 344, 346–8
Shareholders 8–9, 11, 18, 128, 177, 292, 344
Shareholders' funds 303
Shareholders' ratios 321, 322, 324–5, 326
Shares 10–11, 344, 346–8
Single currency 169–71, 174
Single market 172, 174
Situational audit 29
Skewness 66, 73
Skills 22–3, 479–80
Skim pricing 257–8, 260, 272
Small and medium-sized enterprises 13, 162
SMART criteria 26–7
Smith, Adam 152, 177
Social environment 97, 100–105
Social responsibility 175–7, 178, 183
Socialization 227
Socio-economic classifications 229
Sociocultural factors 103–5
Software 83–6
Sole traders 6–7, 17, 18
Span of control 39–41, 44
Spreadsheets 84, 85, 89, 90
Staff personnel 39, 40
Staff relations 44
Staffing 34
Stakeholders 129, 175, 176, 183
Standard costing 256, 381, 384–6, 387
Standard deviation 65–6, 70–1, 211–12
Standards 33
Start up 333, 342, 343, 348
Statistical quality control 436–8
Stock 84, 302, 307, 311, 312–13, 427–33, 450–2
Stock turnover 314, 322, 323–4
Stock valuation 292–5
Stockout 312, 430–1

'Stop-go cycle' 145, 146
Strata charts 59
Strategic decisions 24
Strategic objectives 27
Strategic planning 29
Strategy 22, 27–8, 197, 275, 279–80, 281, 547–59
Study skills and examinations 1–2, 563–77
Substitute goods 120, 123
Supply 123–4, 130
Supply curve 123–4
Supply-side policy 141, 147–8, 149, 172
Surveys 205, 207–9, 212, 215
SWOT analysis 30, 182, 277

Tabulation 57–8
Tactical decisions 24
Tactical objectives 27
Tactical planning 29
Takeovers 550, 552–3
Tall organizations 40–1
Tangible fixed assets 301–2
Target pricing 256
Targeting 201, 230–1, 232, 279
Taxation 155–7
    direct/indirect 155, 156, 162
    environmental laws 180
    inflation 64, 142
    profit and loss account 292
    progressive 153–4
    supply side policy 148
Taylor, Frederick 444, 481–3
Team briefing 499, 500
Teams 495–501
Technology 97, 99–100, 104, 105, 125
Termination of business enterprises 16–18
Test marketing 207, 235
Theory of the firm 127–9, 254
Theory X and Theory Y 485–6, 494
Third-country markets 165
Threats 276
Time rate system 517, 519
Time series analysis 215–16, 221
Time value of money 362
Time-based competition (TBC) 455–6
Tort 106, 109, 115, 118
Total Quality Managament (TQM) 440–1, 447
Trade unions 148, 523–9
Trades Description Act 1968 116, 117
Trading account 291
Traditional theory of the firm 127–8
Training 512–13, 514
Traits 479–80, 494
Trends 95–6, 215–21, 277
Two factor theory 485, 486, 494

Ultra vires 9, 11
Uncertainty 68
Underwriting 347
Undifferentiated marketing 230, 231
Unemployment 141, 142, 149
    balance of payments deficit 167
    boom phase 139
    Keynesianism 144, 145, 146
    market failure 154
    monetarism 146–7
    recession 139
Unfair dismissal 113–14, 514
Unique selling points (USPs) 31
Unsolicited Goods Act 1971 116, 117
USPs see unique selling points
Utility 119, 225

Value analysis 235
Value-added tax (VAT) 7, 156, 161
Variable costs 381, 387, 394–7
Variance 65, 384, 385–6, 387, 408
VAT see value-added tax
VDUs see visual display units
Vendor rating 429
Venture capital 348–9
Vicarious liability 109–10, 118
Visual display units (VDUs) 83
Voluntary sector 6

Wales 152
Waste 181, 182, 183, 449–50
Web sites 90
Weber, Max 36–7, 38
Weighted average 63–4
Weighted average cost (AVCO) 293, 294, 295
Weights and Measure Act 1985 116
Wholesalers 261, 262, 263–5, 266
Window dressing 295, 306
Women 103, 111–12
Word processing 83, 84, 90
Work study 444–6, 448
Work-in-progress 307
Worker participation 529–30
Working capital 301, 303, 311–20, 323, 342–3
Working Time Directive (WTD) 1998 113, 114, 172
World Wide Web 87, 90
Wrongful dismissal 114
WTD see Working Time Directive

'Z' charts 60
Z scores 70–1
Zero-based budgeting (ZBB) 407–8, 409